EARTHKIND
A Teachers' Handbook on Humane Education

Photograph: EarthKind works through humane education — a powerful weapon against cruelty — to lay the foundations for a kinder tomorrow.

Members of EarthKind's youth group 'Earthlings' *from top clockwise*: Casper Palmano, Rukshana Khan, Carla Tiramani, Keri Flynn.
Dogs *from left*: Rory (owned by Theresa Ramirez), Forest (owned by Rebecca Coe).

Photograph by James Keary

EARTHKIND
A Teachers' Handbook on Humane Education

David Selby

tb

Trentham Books

First published in 1995 by Trentham Books Limited

Trentham Books Limited
Westview House
734 London Road
Oakhill
Stoke-on-Trent
Staffordshire
England ST4 5NP

© EarthKind1995

British Cataloguing in Publication Data
A catalogue record for this book is available from the
British Library.

ISBN: 0 948080 88 4

Designed and typeset by Trentham Print Design
Limited, Chester and printed in Great Britain by
Bemrose Shafron (Printers) Limited, Chester

To Mum and Dad
who
took me down Green Lane
and
across the Three Fields

ACKNOWLEDGEMENTS

This book has arisen out of an Animal Welfare in Education Project undertaken by the author at the Centre for Global Education, University of York. The Project, which ran from September 1989 until April 1992, was funded, in its initial stage, by the St. Andrew Animal Fund and the Universities Federation for Animal Welfare, and, in its second and principal stage, by EarthKind UK.

I would like to thank Cindy Milburn, formerly Chief Executive of EarthKind, for recognising the importance of, and helping initiate, the Project. I would also like to place on record my considerable debt of gratitude to Margaret Cooper and Claire Weeks, respectively Chair and Publications Officer of EarthKind, for their enthusiastic commitment and support.

Heartfelt thanks are due to Pam Ko, Secretary to the International Institute for Global Education (IIGE), University of Toronto, for word processing the manuscript often under tremendous pressure; also, to Janet Munro, IIGE Secretary, for undertaking a range of research assignments connected with final manuscript preparation, and to Gail Slavin and Chris Flanagan, formerly of the Centre for Global Education, for their work as Project secretaries.

My wife, Bärbel, gave me unfailing support as I laboured with the task of completing the manuscript whilst accommodating to a new cultural and work environment. My thanks to her also for the photograph on page 106.

Special thanks are also owed to all the teachers who participated in the Project through involvement in in-service workshops, developing and field testing activities, and implementing humane education programmes in their schools. Fiona Heads, presently Acting Deputy Head at Parnwell Primary School, Peterborough, and Jackie Harvey, Deputy Head at Thorpe Primary School, Peterborough, deserve to be singled out for their work in devising programmes of activities for Key Stages 1 and 2. Signal contributions were also made by Carol Adamthwaite, Phil Brooke, Sandra Bush, Diane Chadwick, Amber Carol, Sherri Gilbert, Pam Gill, Margaret Jardine, Marie Lardino, Valerie Lisckai, Keith Robinson and Stuart Twiss.

I am indebted to Kay Kinder and John Harland of the Northern Office of the National Foundation for Education Research (NFER) for the many insights arising out of their evaluation of the impact of the Project's in-service workshops and classroom activities and materials. The NFER evaluation was commissioned by EarthKind.

I am extremely grateful to Kazi Ahmed for permission to reproduce his magical picture, Dolphin Kingdom, on the back cover. For me, it encapsulates, in a profound way, the spirit of EarthKind. Readers interested in Kazi's work can contact him at #1801 - 1644 Nelson Street, Vancouver, B. C., V6G 2Y9. Warm thanks are also owed to Patricia Brown for her excellent line drawings accompanying several of the activities. Readers interested in Patricia's work can contact her c/o EarthKind, Humane Education Centre, Bounds Green Road, London N22 4EU.

I would also like to thank the following for their help and support: Celia Bennett, Secretary, British Veterinary Association Animal Welfare Foundation; Patty Finch, Executive Director, and Willow Soltow, U. S. National Association for Humane and Environmental Education; Kevin Flack, Information Officer, League Against Cruel Sports; Ann Harriman, Education Officer, Animal Aid; Tricia Holford and Will Travers, The Born Free Foundation; Daphne Kasriel, Public Relations Officer, National Anti-Vivisection Society; Carol McKenna, Campaign Director, Respect for Animals; Frances Miller, Executive Director, Beauty Without Cruelty Charity; Liz Ormerod, The Mount Veterinary Surgery, Fleetwood; Rick Shepherd, North York Board of Education, Toronto; Robin Smith, Northern Regional Organiser, British Union for the Abolition of Vivisection; Jacqueline Southee, Scientific Executive, Fund for the Replacement of Animals in Medical Experiments; David Spratt, Life Support.

The author and publishers would also like to thank all the organisations and individuals who kindly gave us permission to reproduce photographs, text and illustrations for free or at a special rate in view of EarthKind's charity status.

Contents

SECTION THREE: The EarthKind Curriculum

SECTION FOUR: The EarthKind Teacher

SECTION FIVE: The EarthKind School

Sources, Resources and Bibliography

USING THIS BOOK

Section One explores the theory, practice, aims and objectives of humane education.

Section Two offers a wide range of activities for the primary and secondary classroom. The Activities section of each chapter is preceded by an Introduction outlining the key concepts, terms and issues falling under the chapter topic, and a Documents section. Teachers are encouraged to draw upon the information provided in introducing topics, debriefing activities and leading discussions. Resource requirements for activities are based on a class size of thirty unless otherwise indicated. The timings given are approximate and refer only to the activity as described under Procedure. Teachers should bear in mind that debriefing and discussion are essential features of the learning process and sufficient time should be allowed for these to take place. An appropriate age range is given for each activity but teachers should exercise their discretion. With due amendment, the activities can be made suitable for age groups older or younger than those specified. The Activities Index (pp. 0-00) enables the reader quickly to locate a particular activity. Teachers should note that the symbol P means that the material on that page can be photocopied without restriction. The activities, save where separately acknowledged in the Source section, were developed entirely by the author.

Section Three looks at subject-based opportunities for humane education and explores the potential for humane education within National Curriculum cross-curricular dimensions and themes. Primary and secondary teachers describe topics and courses they have developed and implemented.

Section Four presents a profile of the humane teacher. The profile can provide a useful stimulus or framework for staff development work. Activities for teacher education are offered; also sample staff development programmes. With due amendment, a number of the activities included in this section can also be used in the primary and/or secondary classroom.

Section Five offers a checklist for the humane school and can, similarly, be used for staff development purposes.

The listing of animal rights and welfare organisations offering services to schools (pp. 401-406) should prove helpful to teachers in their programme and topic planning and resourcing.

EARTHKIND EDUCATION

Animals are in our power in every sense. They cannot speak. Whatever their size or strength, they can be reduced to nothing by our destructive capability. And yet without animals, we ourselves would be nothing. We cannot exist without the other living creatures on Earth. Such a sterile world would be death to man in mind and spirit as well as body.
— Michael Fryer, Founder, EarthKind

Never have the animals been in greater need of human compassion. .... The time will soon be here when my grandchild will long for the cry of the loon, the flash of a salmon, the whisper of spruce needles, or the screech of an eagle. But he will not make friends with any of these creatures and when his heart aches with longing he will curse me. Have I done all to keep the air fresh? Have I cared enough about the water? Have I left the eagle to soar in freedom? Have I done everything I could to earn my grandchild's fondness?
— Chief Dan George

Let us rise to the challenge, fight to save the Ark of Life, and leave a legacy of love. Let your lifestyle be your life statement. We have sacred work before us. Be Earthkind
— Jan Hartke, President, EarthKind USA

Sources: Michael Fryer and Jan Hartke, *The Living World*, September 1992, vol. 3, no. 11, 9; Chief Dan George, *My Spirit Soars*, Surrey, British Columbia, Hancock House, 1989, 8-9.

Chapter 1

The Humane Education Family

Humane Education

Humane education is a field with a long pedigree and ambitious project that goes far beyond classroom consideration of humanity's relationship to non-human animals. 'The humane education movement is a broad one,' wrote Sarah Eddy in *Friends and Helpers* (1897), 'reaching from humane treatment of animals on the one hand to peace with all nations on the other. It implies a step beyond animal rights. It implies character building. Society first said that needless suffering should be prevented: Society now says that children must not be permitted to cause pain because of the effect on the children themselves.'[1] Witness, too, the claims made for humane education by the US National Parent-Teacher Association Congress in 1933:

> Children trained to extend justice, kindness, and mercy to animals become more just, kind and considerate in their relations with one another. Character training along these lines in youths will result in men and women of broader sympathies; more humane, more

law-abiding — in every respect more valuable — citizens. Humane education is the teaching in the schools and colleges of the nations the principles of justice, goodwill, and humanity toward all life. The cultivation of the spirit of kindness to animals is but the starting point toward that larger humanity that includes one's fellow of every race and clime. A generation of people trained in these principles will solve their international difficulties as neighbours and not as enemies.[2]

The practice and reinforcement of kindness, of care and compassion towards animals, through formal and non-formal educational processes is, thus, viewed as having a range of positive spin-offs in terms of pro-social attitudes towards people of a different gender, ethnic group, race, culture or nation.

In the 1980s, a decade when global environmental issues soared into prominence, humane educators began to more readily recognise and explore their common interests with the environmental educator, a courtship in which the latter, more often than not, displayed a marked degree of reluctance. The new-found interest in wider environmental concerns was clearly signalled in 1988 when the Humane Society of the United States (HSUS), one of the most influential humane organisations globally, renamed its educational arm the National Association for Humane and Environmental Education (NAHEE). The current working definition of humane education offered by NAHEE reaffirms the broad focus of concerns and broad scatter of goals embraced by humane educators over the last hundred years:

> Humane education involves far more than the teaching of simple animal-related content. It is a process through which we: (1) assist children in developing compassion, a sense of justice, and a respect for the value of all living creatures; (2) provide the knowledge and understanding necessary for children to behave according to these principles; and (3) foster a sense of responsibility on the part of children to affirm and to act upon their personal beliefs.[4]

A similar melding of environmental, animal- and human-related concerns is evident in the pronouncements of UK humane educators in recent years. 'Humane education is a vast subject area covering our treatment of animals, each other and the Earth we live on,' writes Cindy Milburn. 'Its objective is to achieve compassionate change which challenges the selfish and anthropocentric attitudes that have encouraged exploitation of each other, animals and the world to the point where we are now threatening our very survival on this planet. Humane education aims to provide the basis for responsible planetary citizenship.'[5]

The altogether commendable rhetoric notwithstanding, a perusal of current humane education curricula and learning materials from Canada, the United Kingdom and the United States suggests that humane education in practice narrows its focus to animal-related issues and that, with the exception of environmental themes,

little studied effort is being made to relate the learning taking place to the broader goals laid down for the field. Equity, justice, development and peace form part and parcel of the constellation of hoped-for outcomes but such concerns are rarely built into learning programmes in a conscious, consistent and structured way. *The Humane Education Resource Guide* for New York City Board of Education, which mandates the teaching of humane education in its elementary schools, specifies seven learning objectives for courses of instruction in the field. These are:

- ❑ a reverence for life
- ❑ respect for animals as living creatures
- ❑ proper behaviour towards wildlife
- ❑ action-oriented concern regarding care of caged animals (zoos, shelters, pet shops, classrooms)
- ❑ an understanding of laws regarding animal treatment
- ❑ an understanding of and concern for keeping the environment safe and natural for all life
- ❑ a responsible attitude to pet ownership.[6]

The lesson plans in the *Guide* focus on pets and pet ownership, wild animals in the locality, animal behaviour, similarities between animal and human needs, animal protection legislation, interdependencies within nature, environmental protection and endangered species. *People and Animals*, the excellent but now discontinued four-volume curriculum guide developed by the then US National Association for the Advancement of Humane Education (now NAHEE), covering pre-school years to grade 6, offers a similar spectrum of topics. Each volume has sections on: 'Human/Animal Relationships' (similarities and differences between humans and animals, human attitudes to

> *Why is compassion not part of our established curriculum, an inherent part of our education? Compassion, awe, wonder, curiosity, exaltation, humility — these are the very foundation of any real civilisation, no longer the prerogatives of any one church, but belonging to everyone, every child in every home, in every school.*
> — Yehudi Menuhin[3]

animals, animal welfare, animal-related careers); 'Pet Animals' (human needs met by pets, pet choice, responsible pet ownership); 'Wild Animals' (natural interdependencies, human responsibility to natural environments and wildlife, effects of human encroachment on the natural world); 'Farm Animals' (reasons for farming, human responsibilities to farm animals, consequences of food production practices).[7] Similarly, although the Toronto Humane Society regards the ultimate aim of humane education as 'developing respect for all animals and people',[8] its publications for schools tend to focus on animal-related topics and only rarely draw the parallels and establish the links that would help achieve that aim. Within such materials, admirable as they very often are, the realisation of an unfractured compassion and seamless sense of justice extending to all of humankind, to individual animals, and to all species and ecosystems, remains largely a matter of faith, not strategy. There is less than complete conjunction between the broad goals laid down for humane education over the years and the (relatively) confined focus of the teaching/learning programmes and resources available. The principal areas presently covered by humane curricula and materials are summarised below:

1. **Human/animal relationships, similarities, differences**
   — including human/animal needs; animal rights (limited treatment); human/animal characteristics: animal welfare: animal welfare legislation.

2. **Responsible pet care**
   — especially in primary school materials (this heading includes the care and treatment of captive animals in schools).

3. **Farm animals**
   — needs, human responsibilities to, humane treatment of, vegetarianism, veganism.

4. **Wild animals in the wild**
   — ecology; endangered species; biodiversity; humanity's impact on the natural environment; pros and cons of fishing, hunting, trapping.

5. **Wild animals in captivity**
   — pros and cons of aquaria, circuses, dolphinaria, menageries, zoos.

6. **Animal experimentation/school dissection**
   — necessity for, ethics of, alternatives to.

Humane Education: The 'Ultima Thule' of the Progressive 'Educations'

Having conquered most of Britain, the Romans looked northwards to places such as the Hebrides and the Shetland Islands and referred to them as 'Ultima Thule'; the far-away, unknown, region. Within the constellation of progressive 'educations' which have come to prominence in the last thirty years — human rights, environmental, peace and development education and education for gender and race equity to recite some of the principal ones (see *Fig. 1*) — humane education enjoys such a position. It is noticeable by its absence from the theoretical literature, curricula and programmes of each education. It is below the horizon. Beyond the pale. In the sections that follow, it will be suggested that the interface — the degree of 'family likeness' but also the tensions and conflicts — between humane education and each of the fields should be openly, honestly and thoroughly explored. For the humane educator, dialogue with overlapping 'educations' may well provide the stimulus and direction for closing the observed gap between goal rhetoric and curriculum reality. For proponents of the other educations dialogue may, at the very least, sharpen understanding of the basis upon which they lay claim to a place in the school curriculum. At best, it will reveal, and cause

Fig. 1

AREA	FOCUSES
Development Education	● Third World (geographical expression)
	● North-South interdependencies and inequalities
	● Third World (as an expression of powerlessness covering all peripheralised, disadvantaged and downtrodden peoples and groups)
	● Sustainability
Environmental Education	● Local ecology
	● Spaceship earth
	● Sustainability
Human Rights Education	● Moral and legal rights
	● Liberty-oriented human rights (individual liberties)
	● Security-oriented human rights (rights to physical/psychological well-being)
	● Duties/responsibilities
Peace Education	● Interpersonal/intercommunity/international
	● Negative peace (absence of personal violence and war)
	● Positive peace (presence of equitable and just structures and relationships within and between societies)
Gender Equity Education	● Equal opportunities
	● Dealing with attitudinal sexism
	● Dealing with structural (systemic) sexism
Race Equity Education	● Cultural diversity
	● Dealing with attitudinal racism
	● Dealing with structural (systemic) racism

attention to be directed towards, conceptual, contentual and pedagogical blindspots that have, perhaps, long gone unnoticed. In the process all sides may discover new friends. A 1991 survey of Canadian animal advocates by Canadians for Health Research found that 'they were likely to be involved with other movements: the environment (98%); civil rights (88%); anti-apartheid (86%); feminist (83%); anti-war (83%); students rights (70%); and gay rights (58%)'.[9]

Human, Animal and Environmental Rights

Human rights theorists claim that human beings are entitled to special consideration. In the first place, the argument goes, we are sentient creatures and, so, must be protected from pain. Second, and more important, we are rational, self-aware, and capable of sophisticated understanding and communication. We also possess moral autonomy, a conscience, and a sense of history, progress and purpose. These attributes mark us out and entitle us to be the only proper focus of human moral concern. Whilst we may object to cruelty to animals, our objection arises primarily, if not entirely, out of the negative impact that cruelty may have on both perpetrators and observers. It is its consequences for human beings that matters. 'Apartheid between man and 'beast' ', is, thus, upheld.[10]

The exclusivity of human rights doctrines is increasingly under challenge from two interrelated but less than entirely compatible schools of thought, both of which have contributed richly to humane education in recent years. Animal liberationists, critiquing the claim to specifically human rights as speciesist (or human chauvinist), taking the intrinsic value of each sentient being as their point of departure, and condemning society as we know it as predicated upon the abuse and exploitation of animals have not only given a sharper and status quo critical dimension to humane education but have also exposed the rifts between those espousing rights and welfare positions (see *Fig.* 2). The human-centred conception of morality implicit in human rights doctrines has also been challenged by environmental or 'green' thinkers in their call for a new ethical system embracing not only our relationships with other human beings and society, but also with the natural environment in all its organic and inorganic manifestations. Biocentric egalitarianism, a central tenet of green thinking, has found a ready acceptance within humane education given its emphasis on the intrinsic value of the non-human world.

Animal liberationists (or 'humane moralists', as they have been called[11]) argue that the tests proposed as qualifying human beings as exclusively worthy of moral regard are failed in part or whole by some humans; for instance, the brain damaged, the retarded, the senile, the insane. Yet we extend our rights protection to them. The argument here is not that we should act outrageously and counterintuitively by withdrawing such protection (for there are strong reasons connected with the love and inherent value we vest in nonparadigm humans, and with their ever-present but latent potential, that deter us from any withdrawal of rights) but that we should recognise and rectify the hypocrisy and double standards inherent in not extending protection to animals. The problem comes through applying objective criteria for moral standing selectively and in such a way as 'to make the class of morally considerable beings coextensive with the class of human beings'.[12] 'This,' declares Peter Singer, 'is speciesism, pure and simple, and is as indefensible as the most blatant racism. There is no ethical basis for elevating membership of one particular species into a morally crucial characteristic. From an ethical point of view, we all stand on an equal footing — whether we stand on two feet, or four, or none at all.'[13]

One strand within animal rights theories, developed particularly by Tom Regan, argues that non-rational but nonetheless intelligent non-human animals, possessing complex awareness and consciousness, are

Fig. 2

The Animal Rights Perspective	The Animal Welfare Perspective
Animals have intrinsic value; they are not there to serve human ends; they should not be used as such.	It is morally defensible to use animals for human ends but only if their welfare and well-being is, as much as possible, ensured at all stages of their lives
Animals possess rights, including the right to life and freedom from cruelty; they should be freed from the systematic oppression meted out to them by human beings.	The treatment of animals matters in that animals merit respect; ill-treatment also undermines the basis of our own claim to rights (i.e. by undermining our dignity and essential humanity)

entitled to be treated as moral ends in themselves just as are infants, the severely retarded and other non-reasoning humans. 'Moral patients' (aware, but incapable of making rational decisions), whether human or non-human, thus, possess rights as much as 'moral agents' (humans capable of rational decisions). The yardstick for possession of rights is subjective consciousness and complex awareness.[14]

A second strand, represented principally by Peter Singer, builds its case upon grounds of sentience, i.e. the capacity to have conscious experiences such as pain and pleasure. Sentience, argues Singer, 'is the only defensible boundary of concern for the interest of others'.[15] Or, as Jeremy Bentham put it: 'A full-grown horse or dog is beyond comparison a more rational, as well as a more conversable animal, than an infant of a day or a week or even a month, old. But suppose they were otherwise, what would it avail? The question is not, Can they *reason*? nor Can they *talk*? but, *Can they suffer*?'[16] 'The capacity for suffering and enjoyment,' Singer asserts, '*is a prerequisite for having interests at all,* a condition that must be satisfied before we can speak of interests in a meaningful way. It would be nonsense to say that it was not in the interests of a stone to be kicked along the road by a schoolboy. A stone does not have interests because it cannot suffer. Nothing that we can do to it could possibly make any difference to its welfare. A mouse, on the other hand, does have an interest in not being kicked along the road, because it will suffer if it is.'[17] That animals do feel pain, it should be added, seems a relatively uncontroversial proposition, as evidenced by the fact that laws against cruelty to animals go unquestioned by the vast majority of people. 'Everything that we know about the behaviour, biology and neurophysiology of .... nonhuman mammals, indicates that they are capable of experiencing the same basic types of physical suffering and discomfort as we are... Doubts about the sentience of other animals are no more plausible than doubts about that of other human beings.'[18]

The animal rights school has, however, some serious and daunting questions to answer. Do all non-human animals have rights and, if so, do they all possess them to the same extent? If complex consciousness is the criterion for possession of inherent value and, hence, rights, how do we determine which animals pass and fail the test? Should animals and humans failing the consciousness test be accorded no rights? If sentience is a key determinant in the possession of rights, are the rights of species to be graded according to degree of sentience? If so, is it morally worse to kill and eat a rabbit (highly sentient) than to boil and eat a dozen oysters (minimally sentient)? Where do the tsetse fly, the malarial mosquito, the locust, the tapeworm and the myriad organisms that invade our

---

All invitations must proceed from heaven perhaps; perhaps it is futile for men to initiate their own unity, they do but widen the gulfs between them by the attempt. So at all events thought old Mr. Graysford and young Mr. Sorley, the devoted missionaries who lived out beyond the slaughterhouses, always travelled third on railways, and never came up to the Club. In our Father's house are many mansions, they taught, and there alone will the incompatible multitudes of mankind be welcomed and soothed. No one shall be turned away by the servants on that veranda, be he black or white, not one shall be kept standing who approaches with a loving heart. And why should the divine hospitality cease here? Consider, with all reverence, the monkeys. May there not be a mansion for the monkeys also? Old Mr. Graysford said No, but young Mr. Sorley, who was advanced, said Yes; he saw no reason why monkeys should not have their collateral share of bliss, and he had sympathetic discussions about them with his Hindu friends. And the jackals? Jackals were indeed less to Mr. Sorley's mind, but he admitted that the mercy of God, being infinite, may well embrace all mammals. And the wasps? He became uneasy during the descent to wasps, and was apt to change the conversation. And oranges, cactuses, crystals and mud? And the bacteria inside Mr. Sorley? No, no, this is going too far. We must exclude something from our gathering, or we shall be left with nothing.

Edward Morgan Forster. *A Passage to India*

bloodstream and make us ill stand in the animal rights landscape? What of plant rights? Also, how do animal liberationists square their belief in an animal's right to life with the realities of nature in which many animals survive only by killing others? Does not such a philosophical position place on us the moral obligation, impossible to fulfil as it may be, of protecting the mouse from the cat?[19] Then there are questions surrounding exactly what rights are being claimed for non-human animals. Clearly, animal rights proponents are not claiming that animals should enjoy an array of rights similar to that claimed for human beings in the Universal Declaration of Human Rights of 1948 (e.g. the right to a fair trial, the right to political asylum, the right to form and join trade unions). But do they agree with Richard Stanford who writes: 'when I speak of rights for animals, I refer to two very specific concepts: the right to life and the right not to be tortured'?[20] If they do, how helpful is such a statement anyway? One view would be that it is too vague to be helpful in resolving particular and practical conflicts between the rights of humans and the rights of other species or in offering guidance to humans on how to behave towards the wider animal world. Another would be that its very strength as a statement lies in its vagueness in that, once acknowledged as a general standard to guide our conduct, it will prompt moral reflection and debate as day-to-day situations arise.[21]

Animal liberationists do not, for the most part, claim that the moral status of animals is identical to that of humans. Singer argues for equal *consideration* which, he is at pains to point out, does not imply equal or identical *treatment*.[22] Tom Regan, like Richard Stanford, holds only that animals should enjoy *some* but not *all* of the moral rights claimed by human beings.[23] Elaborating and refining these basic positions, Mary Anne Warren identifies two important differences between the rights of humans and animals; the first involves the

content of those rights, the second concerns their strength, i.e. the *strength* of reasons required to override them. For most animals, she argues, the right to physical freedom need not be as broad as we claim for ourselves. With notable exceptions, such as the great whales and migratory birds which need as much (if not more) space than humans, animals can live in relatively confined areas corresponding to their natural habitat with no obvious physical or psychological suffering. Also, as touched upon above, there are aspects of human freedom that do not apply to animals. Second, given that so far as we can tell, animals lack the sort of long-range hopes, plans and ambitions that 'give human beings such a powerful interest in continued life', their right to life 'is generally somewhat weaker than that of human beings'. 'It is, perhaps, weak enough to enable us to justify killing animals when we have no other ways of achieving such vital goals as feeding or clothing ourselves, or obtaining knowledge which is necessary to save human lives. Weakening their right to life in this way does not render meaningless the assertion that they have such a right. For the point remains that *some* serious justification for the killing of sentient non-human animals is always necessary; they may not be killed merely to provide amusement or minor gains in convenience.'[24]

Whilst arguing that an animal's right to freedom from pain may, in some respects, be stronger than that of a human being (in that the latter has the intellectual ability and imagination to rise above the immediacy of the pain and to recognise that it is likely to stop), Warren also concludes that the other moral rights of animals 'are somewhat less stringent than corresponding human rights'. Her conclusion is based upon the (apparent) lack of moral autonomy in animals. Humans exercise moral autonomy (by, for instance, evaluating, choosing, taking responsibility for their actions and being critically self-aware) in ways which, to the best of our knowledge, animals do not. Whilst lack of autonomy does not negate the claim to rights, especially basic rights such as the right to life and freedom from suffering, it provides, Warren suggests, good grounds for according relatively stronger rights to (most) human beings.[25] The capacity for moral autonomy also lies behind the contractual nature of rights in human societies. 'I will respect your rights, and exercise responsibility towards you, and I expect you to behave towards me in similar fashion.' Animals cannot be part of any such spoken or unspoken contractual reciprocity. They cannot demand their rights. Nor can they be called to task for not exercising their responsibilities. 'Consequently,' writes Warren, 'it is neither pragmatically feasible nor morally obligatory to extend to them the same *full and equal* rights which we extend to human beings... On the other hand, this argument implies that if we *do* discover that certain non-human animals are capable of moral autonomy (which is certainly not impossible), then we ought to extend full and equal moral rights to those animals.'[26] Warren's conclusion steers the argument closer to a variation of the welfarist position: that, recognising the (relatively weak) rights of non-human animals, it is morally defensible to rear, use and kill animals if no alternative presents itself; if, at all stages of their life, the animals are humanely treated; and if their death is accomplished painlessly.[27] In the final analysis, if we do not view the needless infliction of pain as inherently wrong, then our moral objection to cruelty to human beings stands philosophically on fairly thin ice.

The input of environmental or 'green' thinkers has made the debate over human-animal relationships very much a 'triangular affair'.[28] In contrast to the individualistic focus of animal liberationists, concerned as they are with the needs and interests of each sentient creature, environmental moralists, influenced by the thinking of Aldo Leopold, have propagated

the idea that 'the good of the biotic *community*' should be the yardstick for measuring 'the value of individual organisms or species' and 'the rightness or wrongness of human actions'.[29] Hence, whilst the liberationist would denounce the death of individual members of a species caused by hunting; those espousing what Leopold refers to as the 'land ethic' would not necessarily denounce hunting if the species *per se* was not endangered or the environment damaged. Leopold, in his highly influential, *A Sand County Almanac* (1949), is unabashed in his references to fishing and hunting.[30] The good of the biotic community might, indeed, require nothing less. 'To hunt and kill a white-tailed deer in certain districts may not only be ethically permissible, it might actually be a moral requirement, necessary to protect the local environment, taken as a whole, from the disintegrating effects of a cervid population explosion.'[31] Given that the effect upon ecological systems is the decisive factor in determining the ethical quality of human actions, other conclusions follow. First, certain animals, such as predators at the top of the food chain and those grimly holding on to a significant ecological niche, may well matter more than others. Second, certain plants will be more important than animals in terms of the 'stability, integrity and beauty' of the biotic community and, as such, it would be defensible to kill animals threatening those plant communities.[32] Third, it is conceivable that inorganic elements within the landscape might deserve greater protection than particular animals. In the case of the schoolboy kicking the stone and then kicking the mouse, cited earlier, an advocate of the land ethic might, in certain special circumstances, wish to afford most protection to the stone. Fourth, the situation of domestic and farm animals, save as it

Trapping — no necessary consensus between environmentalists and liberationists.

impacts on the natural environment, is of little consequence (Leopold, it appears, never gave serious consideration to the ethics of factory farming). For some proponents of the land ethic, domestic animals count as less than alive. 'Domestic animals,' writes Baird Callicott, 'are creations of man. They are living artefacts, but artefacts nevertheless... There is something profoundly incoherent (and insensitive as well) in the complaint of some animal liberationists that the 'natural behaviour' of chickens and bobby calves is cruelly frustrated on factory farms. It would make almost as much sense to speak of the natural behaviour of tables and chairs... It is literally meaningless to suggest that they be liberated. It is, to speak in hyperbole, a logical impossibility. Certainly it is a practical impossibility.'[33]

Thinkers such as Baird Callicott have tended to see a virtually unbridgeable gulf between the liberationist and land ethic positions; the one atomistic and individualistic, the other holistic and predicated upon the integrity of ecosystems. Others see the two positions as complementary, especially if the rights of animals are conceived of as being less strong than those accorded to human beings. 'On this view, it is wrong to kill animals for trivial reasons, but not wrong to do so when there is no other way of achieving a vital goal, such as the preservation of threatened species.'[34] A second, apparent, inconsistency is also felt by some to be more illusory than real; i.e. the attribution of rights by the animal liberationist on the basis of sentience and the (seemingly contradictory) ascription by some leading-edge environmentalists of moral rights to nonsentient elements of the biosphere, such as mountains, rocks, rivers and ecosystems *per se*.[36] Recognising the weakness of the liberationist position as a basis for protecting the environment (in its exclusion of the non-sentient) and the weakness of the land ethic as a basis for the protection of animals (in its downgrading or denial of the rights of the sentient individual), a synthesising position would be to speak at one and the same time of the rights of individual animals and the intrinsic value of those elements of the natural world which are not themselves sentient. 'Respecting the interests of creatures who, like ourselves, are subject to pleasure and pain,' writes Warren, ' is not inconsistent with valuing and protecting the richness, diversity and stability of natural ecosystems.'[37] It is beyond question the case that both the liberationist and environmentalist would join hands in rejecting William Baxter's now fairly notorious assertion that 'damage to penguins, or to sugar pines, or geological marvels is, without more, simply irrelevant... Penguins are important because people enjoy seeing them walk about rocks... I have no interest in preserving penguins for their own sake'.[38]

This compromise position brings us close to the view of humanity's relationship with animals and the environment that has traditionally obtained in aboriginal cultures. Speaking in broad terms, the aboriginal view of the natural world, is one of deep respect and reverence bred of both altruism and self-interest. Simon Lucas, a chief of the Nuu Cha Nulth people of the west coast of Vancouver Island and noted opponent of the clear-cut logging of the island's temperate rainforests, puts it this way: 'Those animals have a right to those forests too. They belong there — it is as much theirs as it is ours. If the water can no longer

If we see 'the Earth' as the web of life that sustains us, then there is no question that the web is weakened, that the Earth is sick. But if we look at it from another side, from the view of the living Earth itself, then the sickness is not that of the planet, the sickness is embodied in human beings, and, if carried to its illogical conclusion, the sickness will not kill the Earth, it will kill us. Human self-importance is a big part of the problem. It is because we human beings have one power that no other creatures have — the power to upset the natural balance — that we are so dangerous to ourselves... We are not the strongest of all the beings in Creation. In many ways, we are the weakest. We were given original instructions by the Creator. Those instructions, to put them as simply as possible, were to be kind to each other and to respect the Earth.
— Joseph Bruchac[35]

support the salmon, if the land can't support the deer and bear, then why do we think it will support us?'[39] Embedded in the environment, and dependent upon the plants, animals and other features of the natural landscape for our sense of identity and our very survival, we should take from the natural world only according to our real needs and only after deep reflection on the meaning of what we are doing. To cut a plank from a tall cedar, to cull a whale, to take a bear for food is an act calling for humility and contrition. 'If we take the lives of any other being in (the) circle of Creation,' writes Joseph Bruchac of the Abenaki nation of Vermont, 'it must be for the right reason — to help the survival of our own people, not to threaten the survival of the insect people or the whale people. If we gather medicinal herbs, we must never take all that we find, only a few. We should give thanks and offer something in exchange, ... and we should always loosen the earth and plant seeds so that more will grow.'[41] A similar way of seeing the world lies behind the traditional prayer of propitiation recited by the Mayan farmer preparing to inflict a wound on the land (see box below). We should, thus, walk lightly on the Earth. We should recognise the kinship and interconnectedness of all life-forms and realise that unremitting destruction of nature, of the animals and plants that are our 'brothers' and 'sisters' (the 'insect people', the 'whale people', the 'tree people') ultimately lays waste to ourselves... Our imagination, our sensitivities, our intelligence, our sense of the divine, derive from the beauty and grandeur of the Earth (they would have developed far less spectacularly in a plain, barren planetary environment). As we destroy that outer world, we destroy our inner world and the very potential we possess to become more than we presently are... We may need to kill animals but should do so only with the most compelling justification... We should never make animals suffer... We should always be compassionate. Statements from aboriginal

---

'What will you leave me Grandfather?'

'All of my territory with everything you find on it.
All kinds of animals, fish, trees, all the rivers,
that is the heritage I leave you.
Down through the generations
this is what you will need for survival.

Don't ever forget what I am going to tell you.
During your lifetime do as I do — respect all the animals, don't ever make them suffer before you kill them,
don't ever waste anything by killing more than you need,
and don't ever try to keep an animal in captivity
because the animals are necessary for the survival of
future generations. '

— A dying Innu man to his grandson[40]

---

sources offered prefatory to and within this chapter are testimony to the priceless contribution indigenous groups are making to the development (rediscovery?) of a humane and life-loving ethic.

The unfolding of the argument would tend to suggest that the concerns of the environmental and human rights educator are, indeed, inseparable from those of the humane educator. In actuality, proponents of the two fields have fought shy of discourse.

Within the United Kingdom 'one of the key traditions that fed into what became environmental education was rural studies'

Oh God, my father, my mother,
lord of the hills and the valleys,
spirit of the forest, look after me.
I will do as I have always done.
I will make you my offering.
I want you to know I will hurt your heart,
but please allow me.
I am going to stain you,
destroy your beauty,
farm you so that I can live.

— Pop Wuj, sacred book of the Quiche-Mayas[42]

If you see things in terms of circles and cycles, and if you care about the survival of your children, then you begin to engage in commonsense practices. By trial and error, over thousands of years, perhaps, you learn how to do things right. You learn to live in a way that keeps in mind, as native elders put it, seven generations. You ask yourself — as an individual and as a nation — how will the actions I take affect the seven generations to come? You do not think in terms of a four-year presidency or a yearly national budget, artificial creations that mean nothing positive in terms of the health of the Earth and the people. You say to yourself, what will happen if I cut these trees and the birds can no longer nest there? What will happen if I kill the female deer who has a fawn so that no animals survive to bring a new generation into the world? What will happen if I divert the course of this river or build a dam so that the fish and animals and plants downstream are deprived of water? What will happen if I put all the animals in my game bag?

— Joseph Bruchac[43]

which, until the early 1970s, 'did much good work in introducing children to basic concepts of animal welfare, growing plants, food production and ecology'. With increasing pressure on the curriculum and within a context of rising environmental concern, rural studies proponents and practitioners sought to coalesce their interests with those of environmental education as 'something of a survival strategy'. The net result was that rural studies was submerged within the larger field. 'With the demise of rural studies — and the move away from direct contact with animals and plants — animal welfare has pretty much dropped out of the concerns of environmental education.'[44] Another potential animal rights/welfarist thrust within environmental education was lost in the 1980s when environmental organisations steered away from the 'endangered species' approach that they had earlier promoted in favour of a more thoroughgoing 'ecological' approach.[45] The renaming of the World Wildlife Fund as the World Wide Fund for Nature is indicative of this trend. Two fields which have a 'family likeness' of the nuclear rather than extended kind have, thus, drifted apart.

There are a number of worries here. First, there is the danger that in their altogether commendable pursuit of holistic, ecological goals, environmental educators lose sight of the needs and rights of particular species and of particular members of each species. 'To regard animals primarily as parts of the environment,' writes David Cooper, 'is to reduce them, and not see them in terms of their possessing rights which impose obligations on us. In fact, animals are no more bits of the environment than residents of a village are. Both, rather, have an environment, in which they pursue their lives.'[46] Or, as Patty Finch puts it: 'We need to remind environmental educators, who are often predisposed to the humane ethic, that without humane education, environmental education reaches the mountains, but not the trapped coyote; the oceans, but not the aquarium-bound whale; the Arctic, but not the clubbed seal; the cities, but not the stray dog; the open ranges but not the cinched rodeo horse; the farm-lands, but not the crated veal calf; the endangered species, but not the abused animals'.[47] Second, it is unmistakably the case that many topics addressed by the humane educator have environmental impact. Trapping and the international trade in animals threatens ecosystems; slurry from intensive farming is held to be the major pollutant of rivers and underground water; hundreds of miles of hedgerows have been ripped out to grow feed for factory-farmed animals; escapees from fur farms have had a significant, often adverse, effect on local environments; methane from cattle herds is a significant contributor to global warming. Extending the same point, there is the risk that the contribution an animal rights/welfare perspective can make to achieving the environmentally sustainable society, principally through proposing vegetarianism and veganism as alternatives to current patterns of food consumption[48] will be overlooked within environmental education programmes and materials (for further discussion, see pp. 26-8). Fourth, lack of dialogue may mean that potential areas of *tension* between humane and environmental interests will be left unaddressed. For instance, growing environmental awareness in the late 1980s

A Humane Education
Poster, USA, 1988

TOGETHER
*environmental education
and
humane education
can reach...*

the mountains <u>and</u> the trapped coyote...

the oceans <u>and</u> the aquarium-bound whale...

the arctic <u>and</u> the clubbed seal...

the cities <u>and</u> the stray dog...

the farmlands <u>and</u> the crated veal calf...

the open ranges <u>and</u> the cinched rodeo horse

Expand your environmental education focus...

Discover Humane Education!

Contact: The National Association for the Advancement of Humane Education (NAAHE), Box 362, East Haddam, CT 06423. Free catalog upon request.

NAAHE is a division of The Humane Society of the United States and a charter member of The Alliance for Environmental Education.

led to demands for eco-friendly products and more stringent food safety standards. This, in turn, led to a tenfold increase in the number of animals being used in toxicity testing between 1987 and 1990. As Michael Balls, Director of the Fund for the Replacement of Animals in Medical Experiments, declared: 'It is not particularly easy to be 'green' and anti-vivisectionist'.[49] Fifth, there is mounting evidence that school students feel very strongly about animal cruelty and abuse. On the basis of 'starting where the shoe hurts', an exploration of animal welfare and rights issues may be the entry point to a wider environmental consciousness for many young people. Sixth, there is the internal contradiction inherent in embracing an holistic or 'broad focus'[50] approach to environmental education which, by definition, includes built and social environments as much as natural environments, and then excluding consideration of the treatment of animals in intensive farms, homes, laboratories, circuses and zoos as though they were 'outside the environment'.

Whilst recognising that environmental educators might eschew animal rights and welfare issues for pragmatic reasons (e.g. fear of the 'crank' or extremist image, fear of handling issues that come very close to, indeed enter, the home), any educational, expression of a biocentric ethic will necessarily involve a welding of humane and environmental education. 'We need to articulate an ethical principle able to embrace and integrate concerns both for animal welfare and the health of the environment,' concludes David Cooper. 'This is not easy. A utilitarian principle of minimising the suffering of sentient creatures has nothing to say directly about the treatment of non-sentient Nature. A 'stewardship of the Earth' principle, on the other hand, cannot furnish arguments against vivisection or the Draize test... The plea is that this particular revolution should embrace the cause of all animals before the momentum is lost.'[51]

Human rights educators also need to be drawn into discussion and debate. The objections raised by animal liberationists concerning the basis of the claim to exclusively human rights have not yet found their way into the deliberations of human rights educators or into the programmes and materials they have devised for schools. A recent compendium on human rights education, published under the auspices of the Council of Europe, makes no reference to the challenge to human rights emanating from the animal rights school.[52] Similarly, a recent seminal work on citizenship education, a field that overlaps considerably with human rights education, contains no reference to the reconceptualisation of citizenship that could be held to follow from a biocentric ethic or consideration of bioregionalism.[53] There is a self-referential tendency here which is not to the benefit of human rights (and citizenship) education. An open dialogue would at the very least, challenge assumptions, sharpen understandings and open up a rich new seam of controversial issues for the classroom agenda. In their evaluation of the project on which this book is based, Kay Kinder and John Harland of the National Foundation for Education Research report the case of one secondary teacher whose human rights programme was considerably enhanced by using 'student-friendly' animal rights issues as an entrée to the area of human rights:

> I came to the conclusion that animal rights/animal issues were something that young people were immediately attracted by. It was something that was of great interest to them, whereas when I tried out or colleagues tried out, courses or activities linked to human rights, we sometimes felt that wasn't very successful ... for a whole range of reasons ... picking out some of the reasons: human rights was difficult for youngsters because ... they just didn't have the background, they don't necessarily look at the news and they have a very sketchy background knowledge of world issues and world

affairs or even things that are going on in their own locality but, at the same time, they do have an interest in things like animal welfare — that is something which is immediately accessible to them and that was worth a try, as a way into something which we had designated as important — the whole area of human rights and citizenship and community issues and rights and responsibilities. We wanted another way into that.[54]

Under scrutiny in any three-way discussion between environmental, humane and human rights educators, would be the very appropriateness of the concept of rights (and other central ideas within present ethical discourse) for an ecological or holistic paradigm and code of ethics.[55] 'Environmentalism,' writes Alastair Gunn, 'seems incompatible with the Western obsession with individualism, which leads us to resolve questions about our treatment of animals by appealing to the essentially atomistic, competitive notion of rights.'[56] On a flower-strewn Greek hillside in the Spring of 1992, environmental educator Stephen Sterling and I debated the relative merits of the concepts of 'rights' and 'needs' from an holistic standpoint. Subsequently, Stephen wrote:

> I would not argue for doing away with the concept of rights. I agree that it is a very useful and necessary defence against violations which of course are sadly many. However, I think one reason we have to insist on rights so much, is that society is relatively blind to needs, which I feel is a much more 'real', 'ecological' and stronger concept. If we had a strong concept of personal, material, spiritual, social etc. needs which was a fundamental part of our social ethos and honoured in our economic and political organisation, there'd be less need to assert rights.[57]

Stephen's comments were accompanied by a list of, as he saw them, tendencies inherent in the two concepts (reproduced, with minor amendments, in *Fig. 3*).

Fig. 3

Rights (tendencies)	Needs (tendencies)
• Often arbitrarily defined or grounded	• More incontrovertible (harder to dispute)
• More capable of corrupt use	• Less capable of corrupt use
• Capable of infinite expansion	• Imply limits
• Can be claimed as absolute	• More likely to be seen as relative. More conducive to consensus on extent
• Demand acceptance	• Invite sympathy/empathy
• Rationalist (logically argued — perhaps on spurious grounds)	• More intuitive, based more on the function of being fully alive and aware
• More exclusive, competitive	• More inclusive and respectful of others

Circles of Compassion: Animals, Race and Gender

Until he extends the circle of his compassion to all living things, man will not find peace.
— Albert Schweitzer[58]

I think about how hard it would be for me to engage in any kind of action now for justice and peace with the remains of murdered flesh in my body. — Alice Walker[59]

Reactionary phases notwithstanding, the history of modern liberation movements is one of wave after wave of excluded and oppressed groups seeking entry into what Albert Schweitzer called the 'circle of compassion'. The perimeter of the circle at any point in history would be arbitrarily determined, resting upon criteria and assumptions that would in course of time be questioned first by those outside of the circle and then by increasing numbers within its bounds. As the inconsistencies and incongruities in the standpoint of those holding to the status quo became glaringly obvious, their position would become untenable, the circle expanded, and consensus reached on new criteria for inclusion. Underpinning each widening of the circle were hierarchical intellectual structures involving 'concepts of 'higher' and 'lower' in which the former inevitably exploits the latter'.[60] Groups newly admitted to the circle would often consciously or unconsciously collude with the hierarchical paradigm embedded in the circle concept, even though it had earlier been employed to justify their own exclusion and oppression and was still responsible for a greater or lesser curtailment of the rights and freedoms they now in theory enjoyed.

A number of feminist and black writers have argued that women's and black groups should eschew such collusion by considering the oppression of animals. In the first place, they argue that the justifications, dynamics, strategies and tools of oppression possess marked similarities and that one form of oppression has readily drawn upon another. In the fairly recent past, women, blacks, the poor, the blind and the deaf, as well as animals, have been subject to moral disqualification on the grounds of inability to reason. In denying blacks and women their rights, white male opinion often likened them to animals; as being insufficiently rational to be included in the category of personhood.[61] Thus deemed inferior, they were more easily treated as such. Blacks, held by some pro-slavery writers to be a different species[62], were subjugated as slaves, saleable units of production whose feelings and interests, like those of the horse and oxen, were of little or no consequence. Oppression of animals, with its markets, auctions, branding, crowded forms of conveyance and treadmill conditions, it has been suggested, provided the prototype for oppression of black people through slavery.[63] 'Because society's opinion of animals was so low, racist authors propagandised against blacks by comparing them to negative stereotypes of non-human animals... The 'Brute Negro'... One of the most blatant ironies of these comparisons is that this stereotyping of blacks rests upon stereotyping of animals which are false in their own right.'[64] Similarly, women have been objectified and stereotyped, the language of patriarchy drawing extensively upon animal nomenclature. Women are described as 'birds', 'bunnies', 'chicks', 'fillies', 'pets', 'bitches' and 'cows' — their vaginas are 'pussies' or 'beavers' — whilst animals themselves become 'pork' (instead of pig), 'veal' (instead of calf) or 'beef' (instead of cow).[65] 'In pornography,' suggests Norma Benney, 'women are treated as meat.'[66] Marjorie Spiegel in her book, *The Dreaded Comparison* (1988), draws a range of startling parallels between human and animal slavery: the removal of children from their parents ('In the eyes of the white slave-holders, black people were 'just animals', who could soon get over separation from a child or other loved one'[67]); transportation

('The horrors of the Middle Passage, with its cramped conditions, pools of excrement and urine, 'acceptable' mortality rates, seemingly interminable length of duration, and finally insanity leading to violence and cannibalism, have been projected into modernity in the form of factory farming'[68]); hunting('runaway slaves were hunted down in much the same manner as animals are today'[70]); vivisection ('At a rally in San Francisco protesting the use of animals in research, Alameda County supervisor John George said 'My people were the first laboratory animals in America.' Indeed, blacks suffered at the hands of scientists just as animals continue to do today'[71]). A full understanding of one manifestation of oppression is, thus, contingent upon some understanding at both a conceptual and descriptive level of oppression in its other manifestations.

At issue, too, is whether those confronting different oppressions can, with any degree of consistency and credibility, and without ultimate harm to their own goals, build walls around their respective causes and concerns. For Marjorie Spiegel, all manifestations of oppression arise out of hierarchical power structures that should be subjected to simultaneous and multilateral

challenge. For blacks or women, for example, to deny that their cause bears any relationship or similarity to that of animals, is to play into the oppressor's hands:

> Any oppression helps to prop up other forms of oppression. This is why it is vital to link oppressions in our minds, to look for the common, shared aspects, and fight against them as one, rather than prioritising victims' suffering (the 'either-or' pitfall). For when we prioritise we are in effect becoming one with the oppressor. We are deciding that one individual or group is more important than another, deciding that one individual's pain is 'less important' than that of the next. This often leads to infighting, if you will, amongst the oppressed or defenders of the oppressed, doing little to upset the very foundations of cruelty. Comparing the suffering of animals to that of blacks (or

It is easy to form a prejudice against a group that is 'different' to your own. Consequently the victim may be chosen because of colour, creed or sex. It is even easier to find a victim that you can rule by virtue of reason. At the bottom of the pile that leaves one group. After blacks, Jews, women and children, we have animals. They are ideal as man-made victims because they are different, identifiable and vulnerable.

— Noel Sweeney[69]

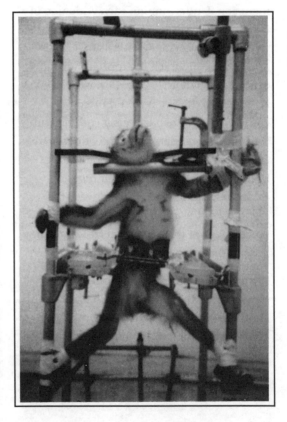

The dreaded comparison: one of the parallels drawn by Marjorie Spiegel.

any other oppressed group) is offensive only to the speciesist; one who has embraced the false notions of what animals are like. Those who are offended by comparison to a fellow sufferer have fallen for the propaganda spewed forth by the oppressors. To deny our similarities to animals is to deny and undermine our own power. It is to continue actively struggling to prove to our oppressors, past and present, that we are *similar to* our oppressors, rather than those whom our oppressors have also victimised. It is to say that we would rather be more like those who have victimised us, rather than like those who have also been victims.[72]

The task of liberating animals from cruelty and exploitation, whilst a commendable goal in its own right, is of central importance for human liberation in that it will 'lessen the oppression of blacks and other groups suffering under the weight of someone else's power'. For the same reason, education for race and gender equity should share a symbiotic relationship with each other and with humane education. 'By eliminating the oppression of animals from the fabric of our culture,' concludes Spiegel, 'we begin to undermine some of the psychological structures inherent in a society which seems to create and foster 'masters'. With a philosophy of universal respect for others' lives, treating anyone — human or non-human — in a cruel manner begins to be unthinkable.'[73] For those struggling against the oppression of human beings, it is particularly appropriate and validating to extend the field of concern to creatures that do not have the capacity to respond to their subjugation; to demand, or organise for, entry into the circle.

A number of leading-edge feminist thinkers have arrived at very much the same conclusion and have voiced strong concerns that women, struggling for their own rights, 'should not participate in the victimisation of those even worse off than ourselves in the patriarchal pecking order'.[74] 'Liberty is a holistic concept,' writes Norma Benney. 'It is neither fair nor just to claim freedom for ourselves, without at the same time claiming freedom for the creatures which share the planet with us, who are cruelly oppressed from birth to death by patriarchal attitudes and systems, and who do not have women's power to organise themselves.'[75] 'Rather than seeing the liberation of women in isolation,' write Leonie Caldecott and Stephanie Leland, 'we conceive of our struggle in the larger context of human liberation and, furthermore, in the context of liberating the earth and all life upon it from the suffocating, annihilating grip of patriarchy.'[76] As an example of the contorted thinking that selective indignation can engender, Benney cites a feminist group on a protest demonstration carrying a placard saying 'A rapist is an animal. Put him behind bars where he belongs', non-human animals being incapable of rape and having no place behind bars. Looking at the same point from different directions, she also cites the cases of Amnesty International having tests performed on pigs so as to accumulate evidence regarding torture of prisoners, of the Vegetarian and Vegan societies refusing to carry advertisements about a publication for lonely lesbians, of marchers on a demonstration for friendship to the Earth settling down afterwards to ham sandwiches.[77] In her essay, 'The feminist traffic in animals' (a title deliberately chosen to invoke the classic feminist phrase, 'the traffic in women'), Carol Adams argues that only vegetarian food should be served at feminist conferences. To embrace pluralism by having a vegetarian option alongside meat options is to go against the central feminist stance that the domestic (or personal), the economic and the political cannot be divorced. The pluralist position, she asserts, endorses the reprivatisation of the domestic, takes an area of personal decision and action out of political debate and, thereby, erodes the very basis upon which women have managed to place domestic issues on the public agenda. The divisions between politics, economic and domestic issues,

Adams writes, 'continue to be accepted even by many feminists when the issue is animals; and the response by dominant groups is to banish the issue back to a zone of discursive privacy'.[78]

Ecofeminist thinking has not only questioned the tendency to divorce women's issues from the subjugation of animals; it has also condemned the essentially male construction of animal rights philosophies. Ecofeminist writers see the devastation of the environment as an inevitable outcome given the value placed within patriarchal society upon the 'male' characteristics of aggression, control, domination and exploitation. The rape of women and the rape of the wild, some argue, issue from the same mindset and psychological source. 'In patriarchy,' writes Andrée Collard, 'nature, animals and women are objectified, hunted, invaded, colonised, owned, consumed and forced to yield and to produce (or not). This violation of the integrity of wild, spontaneous Being is rape. It is motivated by fear and rejection of Life and it allows the oppressor the illusion of control, of power, of being alive.'[79] Abetting the culture of domination has been the paramountcy accorded to scientific rationalism which in its most extreme, Cartesian, manifestation regards animals as unfeeling automata.[80] Scientific rationalism seeks understanding through separation rather than connection and constructs hierarchies of worth based upon empirical (often quantifiable) criteria. For Constantia Salamone, Josephine Donovan and other animal rights feminists, current mainstream animal rights theories fall into the rationalist trap. Tom Regan privileges 'a notion of complex consciousness not far removed from rational thought' whilst Peter Singer's sentience yardstick, as he himself recognises, in practice involves a weighing of interests of one (or more) sentient creatures against one (or more) others ('there could conceivably be circumstances in which an experiment on an animal stands to reduce suffering so much it would be permissible to carry it out').[81] The rationalist orientation of both men's work, Donovan suggests, springs from an attempt to counter charges that animal liberationists are 'emotional' or 'sentimental'.[82] In so reacting they collude with the post-medieval split between reason and emotion that has served patriarchy so well. A feminist animal rights theory, on the other hand, calls for different ways of knowing and understanding that are intuitive, synthesising and life-loving: ways that respect 'the aliveness and spirit (the 'thou') of other creatures', that understand that 'they and we exist in the same unified field continuum', that appreciate that 'what we share — life — is more important than our differences'.[83] Sara Ruddick calls for an attitude of 'attentive love' in which the question ever to be asked is 'What are you going through?'. 'Were vivisectionists to ask such a question,' concludes Donovan, 'we would not have vivisection... We should not kill, eat, torture, and exploit animals because they do not want to be so treated, and we know that. If we listen, we can hear them.'[84] To Stephen Sterling's list of tendencies inherent in the 'rights' and 'needs' concepts (*Fig. 3*), we might wish to add 'masculinist orientation' and 'feminist orientation' respectively. Certainly, a feminist theory of our relationship with animals brings us close to the 'relational sensibility' characteristic of indigenous peoples.[85]

Research into child and adult attitudes towards animals bears out the feminist analysis that males are acculturated into a rationalist and dominance-oriented paradigm. In their extensive survey of adult American knowledge of, and attitudes and behaviours towards, wildlife, Stephen Kellert and Joyce Berry conclude that 'gender is among the most important demographic factors in determining attitudes about animals in our society'.[86] Whilst males scored significantly higher in their knowledge of animals, women expressed far stronger emotional attachment to individual animals (particularly pets), greater concern about a variety of animal cruelty issues and less support for exploitation of and dominance over animals. 'Women voiced significantly greater opposition to laboratory experimentation, rodeos, use of leghold traps, killing of nonendangered animals for fur, and hunting for recreational and meat-gathering purposes.'[87] Men expressed greater concern about species and habitat conservation but also reported far more participation in activities such as hunting, trapping and fishing.[88] Kellert and Berry see their findings as consistent with earlier US research which had identified 'the tendency of males to derive greater satisfaction than females from competition and mastery over animals, as well as from their exploitation'.[89] David Paterson's research into UK children's attitudes towards animals bore similar results. Boys tended to be more knowledgeable about animals than girls, but girls were generally more sensitive than boys (with one exception — a significant proportion of girls attending public schools felt fox-hunting to be justifiable although their male counterparts fell in with the strong rejection of hunting by both boys and girls in state schools).[90]

The insight that different manifestations of exploitation, injustice and oppression have the same source, have similar dynamics and are interlinked, speaks for an alliance of the anti- racist, anti-sexist and humane educator. Each field is concerned with counteracting negative and repressive attitudes that fuel discrimination and injustice (attitudinal racism, sexism, speciesism); each addresses political, economic and social systems that have grown out of, and in turn reinforce, those attitudes (structural/systemic racism, sexism and speciesism).

A helpful way of highlighting the linkages between humane education and education for race and gender equity is through the study of the many individuals who have championed the cause of both human rights and animal rights. William Wilberforce campaigned to abolish the slave trade and against cruelty to animals.[92] Great Victorian social reformers such as Lord Shaftesbury, Sir Samuel Romilly, Jeremy Bentham and John Stuart Mill also spoke out against the abuse of animals.[93] Abraham Lincoln said: 'I am in favour of animal rights as well as human rights. That is the way of the whole human being'.[94] Black leaders and spokespeople, including Toussaint L'Ouverture of Haiti, ex-slave Frederick Douglass, civil rights campaigner Dick Gregory and Alice Walker, have emphasised the importance of defending the rights of animals as part of a multi-pronged assault on people and structures that mete out oppression.[95] Early feminists who also advocated either vegetarianism or animal welfare reform included 'Mary Wollstonecraft, Harriet Beecher Stowe, Lydia Maria Child, Elizabeth Blackwell, Elizabeth Stuart Phelps Ward, Susan B. Anthony, Victoria Woodhull, Elizabeth Cady Stanton, the Grimké sisters, Lucy Stone, Frances Willard, Frances Power Cobbe, Anna Kingford, Caroline Earle White and Agnes Ryan.'[96]

More fundamentally, however, we need to adjust our learning programmes and learning approaches so that students become aware of the commonalities that mark out all forms of oppression and are sensitised to the needs of other human beings and animals. This will not only

---

I became a vegetarian in 1965. I had been a participant in all of the 'major' and most of the 'minor' civil rights demonstrations of the early sixties, including the March on Washington and the Selma to Montgomery March. Under the leadership of Dr. King, I became totally committed to non-violence, and I was convinced that non-violence meant opposition to killing in any form. I felt the commandment 'Thou shalt not kill' applied to human beings not only in their dealings with each other — war, lynching, assassination, murder and the like — but in their practice of killing animals for food and sport. Animals and humans suffer and die alike. Violence causes the same pain, the same spilling of blood, the same stench of death, the same arrogant, cruel and brutal taking of life. One night...I made the decision never to eat meat again. I had become firmly convinced that the killing of animals for food was both immoral and unnatural.

- Dick Gregory[91]

require new topic configurations within the curriculum but also according greater priority to learning techniques that promote empathy, intuition, imagination, co-operation and the ability to synthesise (see *Chapter 2*). To recall Sara Ruddick's phrase, the goal is to have students continually ask 'What are you going through?'

A specific area in which anti-racist, anti-sexist and humane educators might enter dialogue is that of bias in school texts and resources. Whilst much has been done to remove race and gender bias in school materials, distorted images of humanity's actual relationship with animals still abound. There may be picture book women or members of ethnic minorities working on the farm or at the zoo, but the image of the farm or zoo is often of an idyllic, contented community and, as such, far removed from reality. Anthropomorphic depictions of animals are commonplace, especially in primary school texts. The hidden curriculum also subtly reinforces animal abuse. 'Let us expose conservation education,' writes Patti Finch,' as often constituting a deliberately distorted and inaccurate curriculum, designed to support pro-hunting arguments... Let us expose dissection as containing a hidden curriculum of desensitising children.'[97]

The task of bringing the three 'educations' together will not be without anguish or tension. Marjorie Spiegel's profound insights notwithstanding, there will be anti-racist educators who rankle at the comparison of black and animal oppression and who baulk at ever airing her comparison of slavery and animal exploitation in the classroom because of the negative impact it might have on white attitudes and black self-image. Some anti-sexist educators will react similarly to the suggestion that women's and animal liberation are inextricably linked. Recent controversies over halal meat point to the fact that there are specific cultural practices involving animals layered with potential

controversy. A fairly recent and promising development has been the establishment of a Black Environment Network to rectify the relative lack of black participation in environmental and humane causes.[98] Significantly, its founder, Julian Agyeman, contributed an article to the *Humane Education Newsletter,* calling for a broad educational approach that 'takes on board all the issues; global education, development education, human rights education, environmental education, humane education' in an 'exciting synthesis'.[99]

Humane Education and Peace Education

The concept of peace has taken on significant new dimensions in the past forty years. In the early days of peace research, the initial focus was on direct violence, i.e. actual physical violence directed towards one or more people as in assault, torture or warfare. In consequence, peace was construed negatively (absence of personal violence or war). In the late-1960s and 1970s, attention shifted to the concept of indirect or structural violence, i.e. violence, as it were, done to people by social, political and economic systems.[101] The system of

Fig. 4[100]

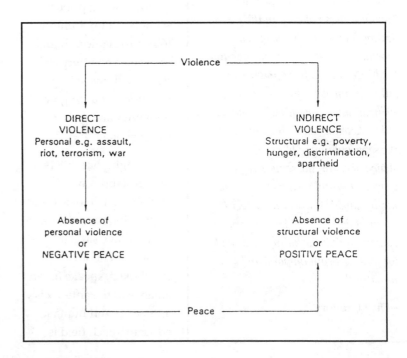

Problems of peace	Values underlying peace
Violence and war	Non-violence
Inequality	Economic welfare
Injustice	Social justice
Environmental damage	Ecological balance
Alienation	Participation

Fig.5[102]

apartheid in South Africa and the built-in inequalities in the world trading system were often cited as clear cut examples of structural violence. The reverse of structural violence was the concept of positive peace, i.e. the presence of equitable and just structures and relationships within and between societies. Johan Galtung, a leading peace researcher, postulated five problems of peace. Turning these around, Hicks identified five values which must underpin any definition of peace (*Fig. 5*). Such promising frameworks notwithstanding, animal-related issues are noticeable by their absence from the theory and practice of peace education.

> *A horse! a horse! my Kingdom for a horse !*
>
> — William Shakespeare, *Richard III, iv. 7*

Key theoretical overviews such as Betty Reardon's *Comprehensive Peace Education. Educating for Global Responsibility*, David Hicks' own *Educating for Peace* and Birgit Brock-Utne's *Educating for Peace. A Feminist Perspective*[103] are at pains to embrace the promotion of environmental responsibility as a key goal of peace education yet there is an essentially anthropocentric quality in what they write (for instance: 'students should have a concern for the environmental welfare of all the world's people and the natural systems on which they depend'[104]). None recognise the rights and needs of animals as such as proper subjects for consideration within peace education curricula, preferring to work within an exclusively holistic conception of environment. All recognise the centrality of issues of power, domination and aggression to the peace educator but all stop short of applying those concepts to the relationship between humans and non-human animals. A similar blindspot is to be found in

collections of peace education classroom activities. William Kreidler's work, for instance, includes activities of a general kind on establishing peaceful and harmonious relationships with the environment but references to animals are restricted to anthropomorphic animals stories used to illustrate issues of human conflict and to stimulate reflection on conflict resolution processes.[105]

Taking a narrow-focus (disarmament-specific) conception of peace, there is an overwhelming case that the role of animals in warfare, military training and weapons development be considered. In the First and Second World Wars, horses, mules and camels were used, as they traditionally had been by the military, as beasts of carriage and burden. In the First World War dogs were also used for mine detection, sending messages, carrying ammunition (especially grenades) and for restoring field communications (laying thin telephone cable across 'no man's land' by unrolling minute reels attached to their backs); in the Second World War, elephants were used for hauling logs in bridge construction and for transporting refugees in Burma.[106] Use by the American army of starving Kamikaze 'tankdogs', conditioned to receiving their food only under tanks and fitted with explosives and triggers to blow up the panzers of the Third Reich, portended future developments.[107] More recently, human invention (but certainly not compassion) has devised ever more sophisticated and horrific roles for animals in pursuit of the military purpose.

First, animals have been extensively used for testing new weaponry. In the post-Second World War period, it became common practice in nuclear tests to tether different domestic animals at various distances from the centre of a blast. Animals 'unfortunate enough to survive would then be studied for the severity of wounds sustained, symptoms of irradiation, and to see how long it took them to die'.[108] With the onset of concepts such as 'limited theatre' nuclear war, primates were used to gauge the effects of radiation on soldiers' work performance in the combat zone.[109] The testing of chemical weapons on animals has gone on unabated since the first use of poison gas in the western trenches in 1915. Usually without anaesthetic, animals have been administered deadly or incapacitating chemicals such as mustard gas, chlorine, riot gas, vomit gas, nerve gas and binary poison gas (i.e. two harmless components that, brought together, become deadly). Typically, too, some would be administered experimental antidotes in anticipation of the enemy developing something similar or 'blowback' on the battlefield.[110] The chemicals used with such deadly effect in Vietnam — Napalm, Agent Orange, 245T — 'will all have been extensively tested on animals'.[111] Between the First and Second World Wars, the development of biological or germ weapons of warfare began to take a huge toll on animal life. One authority estimates that, during World War II, the US biological warfare establishment, Edgewood, in Maryland, consumed more than a quarter of a million mice, rats, guinea pigs, hamsters and rabbits *each month*.[112] In 1942, under the supervision of officers from the UK Chemical Defence Experimental Establishment at Porton Down, Wiltshire, anthrax, a deadly respiratory disease, was dropped in the form of a bomb on the Scottish island of Gruinard to which sheep had been shipped.[113] Scientists observed the effect of the bomb. Gruinard remains uninhabitable up to the present day, a metaphor perhaps for the horror, secrecy and impenetrability of the chemical and biological weapons industry.

Experimentation on animals of a rather different kind has taken place under the heading of wounding research. In military laboratories around the world animals are routinely shot. In 1984, following anger in the House of Commons after it was discovered that monkeys had been shot in the head in experiments on 'high velocity missile heads' at Porton Down, the Ministry of Defence revealed that between 1977 and 1983 wounds involving 194 penetrating injuries and 438 blast-type injuries had been administered to sheep, pigs, rabbits and monkeys.[114] Whilst a public outcry led to a ban on the wounding of cats and dogs in US military laboratories in 1983, the shooting of thousands of goats and pigs each year continues at five Defense Department facilities.[115] In Sweden and Finland, pigs have been shot in 'battlefield conditions' to give military physicians practice in field surgery.[116]

Second, animals have been used as soldiers. In 1989 it was disclosed that the Israeli military in Southern Lebanon were using specially trained dogs to carry bombs and gas canisters to guerrilla-occupied positions where their load would be detonated by remote control.'[117] In 1971 the US navy began using dolphins in its 'Swimmer Nullification' program directed against North Vietnamese frogmen. Dolphins, with high-pressure gas canisters and needles attached to their backs, would seek out and impale the enemy. Over a fifteen-month period, almost sixty North Vietnamese divers — and, accidentally, two US frogmen — were imploded by the dolphins' needles, according to a researcher.'[118] Since then, dolphins, porpoises, sea lions and whales have been trained and employed to recover missiles and military hardware from the sea bed (including a nuclear bomb that had fallen into the sea from a navy plane flying near Puerto Rico).[119] Dolphins have also been trained by the US navy to attach limpet mines to vessels in a program called 'tag-a-ship'.[120] So worried were the two sides in the Cold War about their opponents' advances in 'behavioural technology' surrounding cetaceans that the Soviet Union outlawed the butchering of dolphins for food and the USA intelligence worried about the looming spectre of a 'dolphin gap' between the superpowers.[121]

Animal populations also suffer from the catastrophic consequences of warfare. A recent, horrendous, example was the Gulf War. The discharge of oil into the Gulf triggered a major ecological disaster, decimating populations of turtles, dolphins and sea birds, including the endangered Socotra cormorant. Countless animals were killed or injured by bombs, land mines and artillery whilst pollution from five hundred oil well fires poisoned or choked to death many more. Kuwait's pre-war population of 15,000 cattle was reduced to 2,500 animals. A population of 800,000 sheep was reduced to 10,000; 10,000 camels to 2,000; 3,000 horses to 500. Only after the relief of Kuwait City was the World Society for the

Protection of Animals able to verify rumours that Iraqi soldiers had gone on an orgy of torture and killing at Kuwait Zoo.[122] The phenomenon of military discipline breaking down in the heat and aftermath of battle, manifested in outbreaks of robbery, rape, pillage and 'cleansing' of the conquered, carries within it dire consequences for animal as well as human populations.

The Gulf War provides a powerful illustration of how issues of human and animal rights, peace and conflict, environment and development, ethnicity and gender, can coalesce within a single event.

Taking a broad-focus conception of peace (absence of direct violence, injustice and ecological damage), the case for inclusion of animal-related issues within the research and educational agenda is equally compelling. It is, to say the least, surprising that peace researchers and educators have failed to recognise the structural (as well as physical) violence embedded in the intensive farm, the animal laboratory, the trap line and fur trade industry, the zoo, the circus; also, that they have failed to point up the many connections between animal exploitation and environmental degradation (p. 13). Taking a different, but related, tack, it is interesting to note that whilst peace educators have been concerned to both explore and explode 'enemy' or negative images of other peoples, their attention has fallen short of non-human animals. The failure to establish dialogue with humane educators is all the more surprising given that non-violence is 'a central tenet of the animal movement'.[123]

An area of pivotal significance for both the humane educator and peace educator, and for professional educators and society in general, is the issue of abuse and violence inside and outside the home. Recent path-finding studies have established a strong link between cruelty to animals and acts of violence against people, with animal abuse

Hawksbill Turtle being recovered from oil spilled during Gulf War, 1991. Saudi Arabia. (Photo: RSPCA/ J.Westloke)

often a precursor to child abuse. The studies have found that:

- ❑ in one community in England, 83% of families with a history of animal abuse had been identified as having children at risk from abuse or neglect;

- ❑ of 57 families treated by New Jersey's Division of Youth and Family Services for incidents of child abuse, pets had also been abused in 88% of cases, usually by the parent;

- ❑ a behavioural triad of cruelty to animals, bed wetting and fire setting in childhood is strongly indicative of likely violent behaviour in adulthood;

- ❑ there is a significantly higher incidence of behaviour involving cruelty to animals, usually prior to age 25, in people who go on to commit mass or serial murders (Albert De Salvo, the 'Boston Strangler', for instance, had, as a youth, trapped dogs and cats in orange boxes and shot arrows through the crates).

The research indicates that the abusers (usually male) consider children and animals as chattels, have very low tolerance levels and are replicating behaviours experienced during their own childhood. Motivations for cruelty include a desire to control, retaliation, a need to let out pent-up aggression, a wish to shock, and sadism. Animals are often abused by parents as scapegoats or as a means of punishing children. Delinquent parents often report that they had favourite, consoling, pets that were taken away from them as a punishment. Given such evidence, it is remarkable that many of our schools do not have clearly laid out policies and strategies for dealing with reported or volunteered cases of animal abuse and that humane education programmes enjoy, at best, a marginal place in the school curriculum.[124]

Issues of power, domination, oppression and victimisation are shared concerns of the peace and humane educator. 'When someone is ill-treated or relegated to a demeaning position in society,' writes Margorie Spiegel, 'they will respond by venting their frustrations on someone whose societal position is even lower than their own... By destroying or tormenting the weak, such as a rabbit or a child, the oppressors become the master who has in turn tortured them. Their own victims' helpless writhings echo what they have felt, and temporarily replace them in the role of victim... As long as their anger is directed at an innocent instead of at the perpetrator of their own victimisation, the cycle — once started — will probably not be broken.'[125]

Humane Education and Development Education

There are currently 1.28 billion cattle populating the earth. They take up nearly 24 percent of the land mass of the planet and consume enough grain to feed hundreds of millions of people... The ever-increasing cattle population is wreaking havoc on the earth's ecosystems, destroying habitats on six continents. Cattle raising is a primary factor in the destruction of the world's remaining tropical rain forests. Millions of acres of ancient forest in Central and South America are being felled and cleared to make room for pasture land to graze cattle. Cattle herding is responsible for much of the spreading desertification in the sub-Sahara of Africa and the western rangeland of the United States and Australia. The overgrazing of semi-arid and arid land has left parched and barren deserts on four continents. Organic run-off from feedlots is now a major source of pollution in groundwater. Cattle are also a major cause of global warming. They emit methane, a potent global warming gas, blocking heat from escaping the earth's atmosphere... Today, about one-third of the world's total grain harvest is fed to cattle and other livestock while as many as a billion people suffer from chronic hunger and malnutrition.[126]

This, in powerful summary, is the case made by Jeremy Rifkin in *Beyond beef. The Rise and Fall of the Cattle Culture* (1992). Weaving together animal, environment, development and health issues, Rifkin describes how the global cattle industry has created an inequitable, inhumane and health-costly 'protein ladder' in which the richer nations, especially the USA, consume most of the bounty of the planet 'via an intermediary, the steer'.[127] Whilst millions in the economically rich North indulge themselves unthinkingly on meat, and then anguish over excess fat, high cholesterol levels, heart disease and cancer, many more millions live with chronic malnourishment and starvation.

The ethical case against meat is simply put. It takes a lot of land to feed animals. 'An area the size of five football pitches will produce enough meat to keep two people alive. If maize was grown instead, the same amount of land would keep ten people alive. With wheat it would be 24 people, and with soya beans, 61 people.'[128] It is estimated that on a vegetarian diet the world could support a human population six times greater than its current 5.3 billion. If each Westerner cut their meat intake by fifty per cent, it would save enough food to feed two people who would otherwise starve.[129] Meat eating also involves immense cruelty to animals. They are dehorned, debeaked, castrated, shorn, forcibly impregnated, injected with antibiotics and growth hormones, factory farmed, separated from their offspring, transported and slaughtered often less than humanely because of the financial imperative of piecework. 'Can we,' asks Michael Prowse, 'really justify this behaviour when more people could be fed — and more kept healthy — by growing beans?'[130]

The reality is that the multi-billion pound meat industry continues to flourish and grow. Some sixty per cent of the European Community's imported animal feed comes from developing countries.[131] Whilst fifteen million children perish from malnutrition each year, the world's cattle consume a quantity of food equal to the calorific needs of 8-7 billion people, i.e. nearly double the present human population of the planet.[132] 'I have no doubt,' writes Prowse, 'that red meat will go the same way as tobacco. We must prepare to apologise for this anti-social and unhealthy habit.'[133]

Development education is concerned with interdependencies and inequalities within North-South relationships globally; it seeks to expose and redress the inequities and injustices woven into the economics and politics of those relationships. Like environmental education, it is increasingly, and properly, preoccupied with educating for sustainability. The case for an alliance between humane and development education is simply this: that the massive world-wide exploitation of (particularly) domestic animals feeds from and into the horrendous exploitation and deprivation of people globally. Issues of land reform are inescapably locked into issues of animal abuse; the debate about vegetarianism is, in large part, a debate about global poverty.

Such insights are only rarely given thoroughgoing attention in development education programs and materials. Fairly typical are Heather Jarvis' *We Are What We Eat!*, an activity manual on food, nutrition, wealth and poverty which touches upon, without ever adequately exploring, the politics, economics and ethics of meat-eating and vegetarianism, and George Otero and Gary Smith's *Teaching About Food and Hunger*, which offers one unit, out of some thirty, on 'meatless meals' and asks students to consider the justifiability of meat eating not from the point of view of animal cruelty and exploitation but solely in terms of the energy lost in converting grain into meat and the questionable value of meat for a healthy diet. Both publications omit humane/vegetarian organisations and humane education resources from their resource lists.[134] *The Question of Food*, the World Food Association of Canada's teaching unit on world food issues, addresses the question, 'Can Hunger be

Eliminated?', without any reference to, let alone exploration of, the vegetarian case.[135] A recently-published UK collection of essays on development education conspicuously fails to make any links between development and animal-related issues.[136]

Inevitably, some will have strong reservations about the attention given to animals in the face of so much human suffering. This concern was well expressed by a teacher attending a summer institute on global education in Victoria, British Columbia, in the summer of 1993:

> Two concerns I have: in some of the exercises today about futures I heard people talk a lot about nature and animal protection but I never heard anyone the whole morning talk about human rights — the kids dying on the streets of Bogota, Lima, Rio and Manilla. OR the child sex trade that *Time* wrote about a few weeks ago. OR just the number of kids that die every day because of malnutrition, lack of vaccines, dysentery.[137]

The suggestion here, and throughout this chapter, is that it is not a question of choosing between compassion for animals or compassion for human beings but rather that animal and human concerns should coalesce. 'It has been said that animal-rights activists misdirect their compassion,' writes Richard Stanford, 'and that their concerns should be focused on humans. Fundamentally, I cannot disagree with this sentiment. However, when I help animals I do not believe I am ignoring humans. Quite the contrary, for the two are inextricably linked. When I protest against factory farming, I am not only condemning the treatment of animals; I am also condemning the degradation of the environment and the loss of the small family farm caused by agribusiness. When I protest against vivisection, I also condemn the bad science which suggests that evidence extrapolated from animal research can be applied to humans. We have ample evidence with drugs such as thalidomide ... and many

Times Higher Education Supplement

ELEPHANT EDUCATION (with thanks — and apologies — to Robin Richardson)

'The world we live in,' said the official report, 'contains elephants. The country's education system should therefore reflect our need to know about and to understand elephants. Policies should be developed, and resources provided, for more and better quality elephant education.'

'Elephant education!' exclaimed the people when they heard this recommendation. 'We are not entirely sure what that is.' Six blind people went forth to find out.

The first blind person went to the Ivory Coast in West Africa, since this is a country actually named after elephants, albeit only partially. This first blind person studied the record of the Ivory Coast's trading relations with the countries of North America and Europe, and the record of the *Parti Democratique de la Cote d 'Ivoire*, its use of power, pressure and resources over forty years; and concluded that elephant education is basically another term for development education.

The second blind person went to a film called *The Elephant Man*, and studied elephantiasis, the swelling of limbs, the development of obstructions in the flow of lymph and the overgrowth of subcutaneous tissue; and in looking thus at sickly growth, this second blind person concluded that elephant education is basically another term for health education.

The third blind person studied the diverse ways in which human beings relate to elephants. We corral them in keddahs, hump them with howdahs, train them for traction, process them in parades, zombify them in zoos, strait-jacket them in circuses. This third blind person saw bars and barriers, exploitation, injustice, oppression, constraints on freedom; and concluded that elephant education is basically another term for humane and human rights education.

The fourth blind person studied the escalation in the arms race which took place when Hannibal of Carthage, in 220 BC, resolved to use elephants in his war of liberation against the particular form of imperialism know as *pax romana*. Seeing thus both direct and structural violence, this fourth blind person concluded that elephant education is basically another term for peace education.

The fifth blind person went to a fast-food restaurant, and studied on its menu the array of Jumbo burgers, Jumbo sandwiches and Jumbo pizzas; reading between as well as along the lines of the menu, the fifth blind person had a vision of kitchens and boardrooms, of women working and men managing. And recalling the statistic that women do 70% of the world's work, this fifth blind person concluded that elephant education is another term for gender equity education.

The sixth blind person studied a distinctive literary genre in which the inner and essential nature of elephants is frequently explored and expressed. It consists of a litany of questions and answers. Question: why do elephants paint the soles of their feet yellow? — Answer, so that they can float upside down in the custard without being seen. Question: how can you tell when you are in bed with an elephant? — Answer, because he has an E embroidered on his pyjama jacket. Studying this literary genre, the sixth blind person realised that elephants must suffer from a negative self-image and, very probably, from a lack of adequate assertiveness training, and concluded that elephant education is another term for self-esteem building programs.

The six blind people went their separate ways, and published separately their respective conclusions. They applied separately for money from charitable foundations and from local and central government; set up separate working parties, networks, professional associations, standing conferences, committees of enquiry; published separate journals, magazines, bulletins and newsletters; set up separate resource centres and support services; formulated separate sets of aims, objectives and schemes of work; competed for the attention of headteachers and for space, time, resources and energy in each and every individual school in the land.

They completely failed, however, to realise any of the values which they wished to promote; and also failed to effectively and fully address their main focus of concern. They failed even to prevent the extinction of the elephant population. Thus, in the next official report, the story of elephants was assigned to the history curriculum.[139]

others where extensive research on animals had horrific consequences for humans.'[138]

Calling this chapter 'The Humane Education Family' is not intended to imply that the several 'educations' reviewed should regroup under the umbrella title of 'humane education'. Rather it is to suggest that the relationship between humane education and each of the fields should be conceived of as holographic. A hologram is a three-dimensional 'photograph' created by laser technology. Amongst its most astonishing properties is that *the part contains the code of the whole*. Hence, a hologram of a face, if broken, can be reconstructed from, say, the hologram of the nose. Similarly, a mature and comprehensive understanding of any one of the 'educations' reviewed here will, whatever the source of the educator's initial interest, lead out to all the other 'educations'. Within such a process, humane education will no longer be 'Ultima Thule'.

> *In the heaven of Indra, there is said to be a network of pearls, so arranged that if you look at one you see all the others reflected in it. In the same way each object in the world is not merely itself but involves each other object, and in fact is every other object.*
>
> - The Flower Garden Sutra

References

1. Cited in National Association of Humane and Environmental Education, *KIND workshop leader's guide*, NAHEE (67 Salem Road, East Haddam, CT 06423, USA), 1991, 2.

2. *Ibid.*, 3.

3. Cited in Wynne-Tyson, J., *The extended circle. An anthology of humane thought*, Cardinal, 1990, 300.

4. Savesky, K., & Malcarne, V., eds., *People and animals. A humane curriculum guide, levels a, b, c, d*, National Association for the Advancement of Humane Education, 1981, iii.

5. Editorial in *Humane Education Newsletter*, vol. 3, no. 2, Summer 1992, 2.

6. Mitchell, A., *et al.*, eds., *Humane education resource guide. A guide for elementary school teachers*, New York City Board of Education, 1985, 3.

7. Savesky, K., & Malcarne, V., eds., *op. cit.*, iv.

8. Takagi, C., *Friend for life*, Toronto Humane Society, 1988, 3.

9. Stanford, R., 'A simple test of our morality', *The Globe and Mail* (Toronto), 9 July 1991, A16.

10. Baird Callicott, J., 'Animal liberation: a triangular affair', in Scherer, D., & Attig, T., *Ethics and the environment*, Prentice Hall, 1983, 57.

11. *Ibid.*, 58.

12. *Ibid.*, 59.

13. Singer, P., ed., *In defence of animals*, Basil Blackwell, 1985, 6.

14. Regan, R., *The case for animal rights*, Routledge, 1988, especially 151-6. For a full discussion of animal consciousness, see Dawkins, M.S., *Through our eyes only? The search for animal consciousness*, Freeman, 1993.

15. Singer, P., *Animal liberation*, Thorsons, 1983, 9.

16. *Ibid.*, 8.

17. *Ibid.*, 9.

18. Warren, M.A., 'The rights of the nonhuman world' in Elliot, R., & Gare, A., *Environmental philosophy*, Open University Press, 1983, 113.

19. Ritchie, D.G., 'Why animals do not have rights' in Regan, T., & Singer, P., eds., *Animal rights and human obligations*, Prentice-Hall, 1976, 41 et seq.

20. Stanford, R., *op. cit.*, A16.

21. Midgley, M., 'Duties concerning islands' in Elliot, R., & Gare, A., *op. cit.*, 171-6.

22. Singer, P., *Animal liberation*, Thorsons, 1983, 3.

23. Warren, M.A., *op. cit.*, 112.

24. *Ibid.*, 115-17.

25. *Ibid.*, 117-19.

26. *Ibid.*, 119-20.

27. See, also, Lafollette, H., 'Animal rights and human wrongs' in Dower, N. *Ethics and environmental responsibility*, Aldershot, Avebury, 1989, 88-9.

28. Baird Callicott, J., *op. cit.*, 72.

29. Warren, M.A., *op. cit.*, 110.

30. Leopold, A., *A Sand County almanac*, Ballantine, 1991 (see, for instance, 181-6, 284-5).

31. Baird Callicott, J., *op. cit.*, 61.

32. *Ibid.,.*

33. *Ibid.,* 67-8.

34. Warren, M.A., *op. cit.,* 126.

35. Bruchac, J., 'The circle is the way to see' in *Story Earth. Native voices on the environment,* San Francisco, Mercury House, 1993, 8.

36. See, for instance, Stone, C., 'Should trees have standing — toward legal rights for natural objects' in VanDeVeer, D., & Pierce, C., *People, penguins and plastic trees. Basic issues in environmental ethics,* Belmont, California, Wadsworth, 1986, 83- 96.

37. Warren, M.A., *op. cit.,* 130.

38. Baxter, W.F., 'People or penguins' in VanDeVeer, D., & Pierce, C., *op. cit.,* 215.

39. Cited in Knudtson, P., & Suzuki, D., *Wisdom of the elders,* Toronto, Stoddart, 1992, xxviii. I am indebted to Simon Lucas for the many insights gained as we talked on the fishing wharf at Tofino, Vancouver Island, in August 1993.

40. Cited in Ashini, T., 'We have been pushed to the edge of the cliff' in *Story Earth. Native voices on the environment,* San Francisco, Mercury House, 1993, 14.

41. Bruchac, J., *op. cit.,* 9.

42. Chay, R.Q., 'The corn men have not forgotten their ancient gods' in *Story Earth,* San Francisco, Mercury House, 1993, 21.

43. Bruchac, J., *op. cit.,* 12-13.

44. Stephen Sterling to Selby, 7.3.1991.

45. *Ibid.,.*

46. Cooper, D., 'Grey greens', *The Living World,* vol. 3, no. 7, Spring 1991, 6.

47. Finch, P., 'Learning from the past' in Paterson, D., & Palmer, M., eds., *The status of animals. Ethics, education and welfare,* Humane Education Foundation/CAB International, 1988, 69.

48. Bunyard, P., & Morgan-Grenville, F., eds., *The green alternative,* Methuen, 1987; Singer, P., *Animal liberation,* Thorsons, 1983, 171-201.

49. Wilkie, T., 'Why it's not easy to be green and kind to animals', *The Independent on Sunday,* 5 January 1992, 2.

50. Greig, S., Pike, G., & Selby, D., *Earthrights. Education as if the planet really mattered,* Kogan Page/World Wildlife Fund, 1987, 29.

51. Cooper, D., *op. cit.,* 6.

52. Starkey, H., ed., *The challenge of human rights education,* Cassell, 1991.

53. Heater, D., *Citizenship. The civic ideal in world history, politics and education,* Longman, 1990.

54. Kinder, K., & Harland, J., *Animal welfare in education project: evaluation of the curriculum materials,* York, NFER, 1992, 8.

55. Dobson, A., *Green political thought,* Harper Collins, 1990, 48.

56. Gunn, A.S., 'Why should we care about rare species?', *Environmental Ethics 2,* no. 1, spring 1980, cited in Warren, M.A., *op. cit.,* 126.

57. Sterling to Selby, 21.4.1992.

58. Cited in Wynne-Tyson, J., *op. cit.,* 462.

59. Walker, A., *Living by the word. Selected writings, 1973-1987,* San Diego, Harcourt, Brace, Jovanovich, 1987, 172.

60. Benney, N., 'All of one flesh. The rights of animals' in Caldecott, L., & Leland, S., *Reclaim the Earth. Women speak out for life on Earth,* The Women's Press, 1983, 141.

61. *Ibid.,* 144; Spiegel, M., *The dreaded comparison. Human and animal slavery,* Heretic Books, 1988, 23; Donovan, J., 'Animal rights and feminist theory' in Gaard, G., ed., *Ecofeminism. Women, animals, nature,* Philadelphia, Temple University Press, 1993.

62. Spiegel, M., *op. cit.,* 19.

63. *Ibid.,* 25-6.

64. *Ibid.,* 31.

65. Benney, N., *op. cit.,* 150.

66. *Ibid.,* 148.

67. Spiegel, M., *op. cit.,* 43.

68. *Ibid.,* 50- 1.

69. Sweeney, N., 'Animalkind and human cruelty. Racism, sexism and speciesism revisited', *The Vegan,* Autumn 1990, 22.

70. Spiegel, M., *op. cit.,* 57.

71. *Ibid.,* 61.

72. *Ibid.,* 24-5.

73. *Ibid.,* 27-8.

74. Benney, N., *op. cit.,* 141.

75. *Ibid.,* 142.

76. Caldecott, L., & Leland, S., eds., *op. cit.,* 7.

77. *Ibid.,* 143-4, 148.

78. Adams, C.J., 'The feminist traffic in animals' in Gaard, G., ed., *op. cit.,* 199. See, also, Adams' *The sexual politics of meat,* Polity Press, 1990.

79. Collard, A., *Rape of the wild. Man's violence against animals and the Earth,* Women's Press, 1988, 1.

80. Midgley, M., *Animals and why they matter,* Athens, University of Georgia Press, 1984, 11.

81. Donovan, J., *op. cit.,* 168-73.

82. *Ibid.,* 167-8.

83. *Ibid.,* 183.

84. *Ibid.,* 183, 185.

85. *Ibid.,* 182.

86. Kellert, S., & Berry, J., 'Attitudes, knowledge and behaviours towards wildlife as affected by gender', *Wildlife Society Bulletin,* no. 15, 1987, 370.

87. *Ibid.,* 366.

88. *Ibid.,* 366-7.

89. *Ibid.,* 369.

90. Paterson, D., 'Assessing children's attitudes towards animals' in Paterson, D., & Palmer, M., eds., *op. cit.,* 62.

91. Spiegel, M., *op. cit.,* 96.

92. Ryder, R.D., 'The struggle against speciesism' in Paterson, D., & Ryder, R.D., eds., *Animal rights — a symposium,* Centaur, 1979, 9, 13.

93. *Ibid.,* 8, 222-3.

94. Spiegel, M., *op. cit.,* 95.

95. Paterson, D., & Ryder, R.D., eds., *op. cit.,* 225; Spiegel, M., *op. cit.,* 9-10, 94, 96.

96. Donovan, J., *op. cit.*, 173.

97. Finch, P., in Paterson, D., & Palmer, M., eds., *op. cit.*, 69.

98. For details of the Black Environment Network, write to Judy Ling Wong, National Development Co-ordinator, BEN, Inner Cities Unit, 26 Bedford Square, London WC 1 B 3HU.

99. Agyeman, J., 'Environmental education and global politics', *Humane Education Newsletter*, vol. 3, no. 1, Spring 1992, 5.

100. Hicks, D., *Education for peace. Issues, principles and practice in the classroom*, Routledge, 1988, 4, 6.

101. *Ibid.,*.

102. *Ibid.*, 7.

103. Reardon, B.A., *Comprehensive peace education. Educating for global responsibility*, New York, Teachers College Press, 1988; Hicks, D., *op cit*; Brock-Utne, B., *Educating for peace. A feminist perspective*, Pergamon, 1987.

104. Hicks, D., *op cit.*, 16; see also, Reardon on the concept of humane relationship, *op. cit.*, 59.

105. Kreidler, W.J., *Elementary perspectives 1. Teaching concepts of peace and conflict*, Cambridge MA, Educators for Social Responsibility, 1990.

106. Cooper, J., *Animals in war*, Heinemann, 1983, 54-69, 73-113.

107. Johnson, W., *The rose-tinted menagerie*, Heretic Books, 1990, 297.

108. Fisher, C., *The military abuse of animals*, BUAV, 1987, 4.

109. *Ibid.*, 6. McGreal, S., 'Monkeys go to war', *Mainstream*, Winter 1981, 20-2.

110. Metz, H., 'The Pentagon's secret war on animals', *The Animals' Agenda*, June 1987, 23-5.

111. Fisher, C., *op. cit.*, 12.

112. Metz, H., *op. cit.*, 26.

113. Fisher, C., *op.cit.*,12.

114. Sharpe, R., 'No peace for animals', *Greenscene*, no. 4, April/May 1989, 16-17.

115. Metz, H., *op. cit.*, 24.

116. Fisher, C., *op. cit.*, 14.

117. Greanville, D.P., 'Israel — the dogs of war', *The Animals' Agenda*, March 1989, 28.

118. Metz, H., *op. cit.*, 27.

119. Lubow, R.E., *The war animals*, Doubleday, 1977, 114-26; Cooper, J., *op. cit.*, 163.

120. Metz, H., *op. cit.*, 27.

121. Cooper, J., *op. cit.*, 163; Johnson, W., *op. cit.*, 298.

122. Lorez, J., 'The silent victims of the war', *Animals International*, vol. xi, no. 37, Summer 1991, 5-8.

123. *Humane Education Newsletter*, vol. 1, no. 2, 2.

124. Information on the links between animal and child abuse are taken from Finch, P., *Breaking the cycle of abuse*, National Association for Humane and Environmental Education, 1989, and from the many documents available in the humane education resource centre established by Elizabeth Ormerod, The Mount Veterinary Surgery, 1 Harris Street, Fleetwood, Lancashire, FY7 6QX. Extremely useful were notes on animal and child abuse penned by Phil Arkow, Humane Society, Pikes Peak Region, 633 South 8th Street, Colorado Springs, Colorado 80905, USA; and Elizabeth Ormerod's own article, 'Humane education', *Journal of Society for Companion Animals Studies*, Spring 1990, vol. 2, no. 2, 9-10. On the link between childhood cruelty and future criminality see, for instance, Kellert, S.R., & Felthouse, A.R., 'Childhood cruelty toward animals among criminals and noncriminals', *Human Relations*, vol. 38, no. 12, 1985, 113-29; Felthouse, A.R., & Kellert, S.R., 'Violence against animals and people: is aggression against living creatures generalised?', *Bulletin of the American Academy of Psychiatric Law*, vol. 14, no. 1, 1986, 55-68; Lockwood, R., 'Two-legged animals', *Social Issues and Health Review*, February 1987, 146.

125. Spiegel, M., *op. cit.*, 82-4.

126. Rifkin, J., *Beyond beef. The rise and fall of the cattle culture*, Dutton, 1992, 1-2.

127. *Ibid.*, 164.

128. Gellatley, J., 'Why you should be a vegetarian', *The Vegetarian*, February 1992. 39.

129. *New Internationalist*, January 1991, 11.

130. *The Living World*, September 1992, vol. 3, no. 11, 31.

131. Gold, M., *Living without cruelty*, Green Print, 1988, 58.

132. Gellatley, J., *op. cit.*, 39.

133. *The Living World*, September 1992, vol. 3, no. 11. 31.

134. Jarvis, H., *We are what we eat!* UNICEF-UK, 1992; Otero, G., and Smith, G., *Teaching about food and hunger*, Denver, Colorado, Centre for Teaching International Relations, 1989.

135. World Food Day Association of Canada, *The question of food. A teaching unit on world food issues*, Teachers Press, undated.

136. Osler, A., ed., *Development education. Global perspectives in the curriculum*, Cassell, 1994.

137. I am grateful to Carmen Kuczma for permission to reproduce this quotation.

138. Stanford, R., *op. cit.*, A16.

139. 'Elephant Education' is a revised version of Robin Richardson's well-known fable. See Richardson, R., *Daring to be a teacher*, Trentham, 1990, 91-2.

Chapter 2

Humane Learning

Education

The traditional way of education
was by example and experience
and by storytelling.

The first principle involved was total respect
and acceptance of the one to be taught.
And that learning was a continuous process
from birth to death.
It was a total continuity without interruption.
Its nature was like a fountain
that gives many colours and flavours of water
and that whoever chose could drink as much or
as little
as they wanted to and whenever they wished.
The teaching strictly adhered
to the sacredness of life whether of human
or animals or plants.

But in the course of history there came a
disruption.
And then education became 'compulsory
miseducation'
for another purpose, and the circle
of life was broken
and the continuity ended.

It is that continuity which is now taken
up again in the spiritual rebirth
of the people.

— Arthur Soloman[1]

What to Rescue from the Fire?

'Humane education is important. If we can influence children's attitudes when they are still young, they will grow into responsible adults. Those responsible adults will in turn influence their children and others in society. 'An ounce of prevention is worth a pound of cure.' 'A stitch in time saves nine.' Humane education makes sense.'[2] So write Edward Vockell and Frank Hodal in introducing one of the earliest studies (1980) into the effects of humane education programmes on children's attitudes to animals.

The Vockell-Hodal study, conducted throughout the Hammond (Indiana) public school system, focused on the impact of a typical one-shot humane education programme of the kind often offered to schools by officers of humane societies. Classes were visited by volunteer non-teachers who had received a training programme in animal-related issues (but not in teaching methods). The volunteers gave age-appropriate presentations, with audio-visual support, on a range of topics connected with animal needs and welfare. Posters and printed materials were left with the students. The researchers contrasted the attitudes of students in these so-called 'intensive treatment' classes with those of students in 'light treatment' classes (receiving posters and print-form materials but no presentation) and control classes (receiving neither materials nor presentation).

Student attitudes to animal life were assessed using the 'Fireman Test' devised by Vockell and Hodal. The test scenario is that a boy's house is burning down and beyond saving. The firefighter tells the boy that he can rescue only three items from the fire. The student is required to choose the three items from a list of ten (a dog, cat and canary and seven inanimate objects). The rationale behind the test is that students with a positive concern for animal life will opt for the pets, 'since they cannot be replaced in the same sense that an inanimate object can be replaced and since the animals would actually undergo pain if left in the fire'.[3] The test was administered to students between the ages of eight and twelve.

Vockell and Hodal report that although both 'treatment' groups registered more positive attitudes to animals than the control group, there was no significant difference between students exposed to 'intensive' and 'light' treatment. 'The addition of the speaker (*which was by far the most expensive and time-consuming part of the program*) had no additional impact.' In conclusion, the researchers serve notice that there should be no complacency amongst humane educators with regard to the efficacy of teaching and learning strategies employed. 'We need to find out what methods result in or sustain humane attitudes and incorporate those methods into our programs.'[4]

Subsequent research has illuminated particular characteristics of effective humane teaching and learning programmes. For instance, a study conducted in Boston, USA, in 1983 highlighted the importance of sustained exposure to humane issues, internal coherence within the programmes offered and the thoroughgoing integration of teachers in their planning and execution.[5]

Other studies have reaffirmed the importance of 'intensive instruction' (i.e. regular interventions over a prolonged period of time) in fostering humane attitudes.[6] Research by Vanessa Malcarne confirmed that student role-playing of animals and other children in distress can increase empathy for, and altruism towards, both animals and children. Her study, which used the 'Fireman Test' alongside other research instruments, also found some evidence of transference of empathetic attitudes from animals to other children and vice-versa in the light of the role play.[7]

Generally speaking, the research reflects the paucity of opportunities for implementing, let alone researching, coherent, comprehensive and sustained programmes of humane education and, at root, the peripheral position accorded to humane education in school curricula. Significantly, it fails to draw upon research findings from contiguous or overlapping fields, such as those reviewed in *Chapter 1*. Vanessa Malcarne's work aside, it also reflects the information-led, traditional flavour of most programmes. A rather different pedagogical philosophy, in which forms of interactive and experiential learning are given prominence within a warm, open and democratic classroom climate, is required if we are to realise the goals of humane education. The rest of this chapter seeks to explain why.

The Medium is the Message

Marshall McLuhan's observation, 'the medium is the message', provides some valuable insights when applied to the classroom. If the 'medium' of learning is characterised by individual competition, working in silence, a compartmentalisation of knowledge into subject areas and discrete learning packages, an emphasis on learning through abstract concepts, minimal opportunities to share personal feelings and opinions, what are the subliminal 'messages' the students receive? Do such 'messages' accord with the goals of humane education?

Picture a secondary classroom in which a teacher, concerned to foster peaceful attitudes and allegiance to democratic, peaceful, change processes, lectures to her class on examples of non-violent change movements in contemporary history. The occasion is marked by absence of any information/opinion flow between those present. In such a learning situation, the praiseworthy nature of the topic notwithstanding, the teacher's goal is undermined by a critical disharmony between medium and message. Or, put another way, two contradictory messages, one overt, one covert, are received by the students: the overt (the content of the lecture) saying that peace-oriented values matter very much; the covert (the unidirectional and non-participatory nature of the session) signalling that peace-oriented values matter very little. The intentions of the teacher are likely to be more effectively realised if the medium is constructed so as to synchronise with, and reinforce, the lesson's overt message.

Similarly, the humane classroom necessitates a harmonisation of 'message and 'medium'. If some of the principle 'messages' of humane education concern compassion, kindness, harmony, justice, equity and peacefulness, then these need to be reflected in the climate, ethos and quality of relationships evident in the classroom. In practice this means a range of concrete things such as emphasis on dialogue between the students themselves and between students and teacher, a valuing of the contribution all can make to the learning process, co-operative learning, a decentralisation of sources of power, decision-making and

'Good morning, class!
Today I will prepare you for the future.
Listen carefully,
and don't interrupt!
Are there any questions?...
None?
Good!'

— Albert Cullum[8]

initiative-taking within the learning community, and sustained commitment to esteem-building and group-bonding processes within learning programmes. The concept of 'intrinsic value', central to the humane educator's perception of all living things, likewise calls for an honouring of the insights, experiences, perspectives, skills and qualities which individual learners bring to the classroom. The humane teacher's commitment to ecology also has processive as well as contentual ramifications. Drawing upon ecological principles, the teacher will seek to create a classroom in which the concept of interdependence is enshrined within co-operative learning situations and in which a diversity (ecology) of teaching and learning approaches are offered.

Valuable insights into the question of congruence between medium and message in the humane classroom are offered by the field of political education. Political educators refer to learning *about*, learning *for* and learning *in* (or *through*). Learning *about* is a knowledge-oriented process concerned with the assimilation of facts, concepts, data and evidence. Characteristically, it involves a vertical or top-downwards relationship between teacher and class. As an exclusive approach to realising the goals of humane education, dissonance between topic and process will almost certainly arise in that humane issues will be discussed using teaching techniques and classroom dynamics that fall short of the humane. Learning *for* places the emphasis on skills acquisition. Hence, learning *for* a humane world will involve, for instance, developing skills in communication, co-operation, decision-making, empathy, negotiation and change advocacy/agency. In the process, knowledge goals remain in place but lose their primacy. As skills are only developed by practising them, the classroom inevitably becomes more participatory. In consequence, there will be greater harmony between 'medium' and 'message'. Learning *in* or *through* humaneness takes matters an important stage further. The knowledge and skills elements remain but, in addition, the precepts and values of humane education are reinforced through the climate and environment of the classroom. There are high levels of participation, interaction and dialogue. A premium is placed upon caring, sharing, trusting relationships; on genuineness. The classroom is a kind place; it is 'a friendly classroom for a small planet'.[9] Both the overt and covert curriculum promote and reinforce humaneness.

Classrooms of Affirmation

'Self-esteem,' says Nathaniel Branden, 'is the reputation we acquire with ourselves.'[10] For Dennis Lawrence it is the individual's *evaluation of* the discrepancy between their self-image (what the person is) and their ideal self (what the person would like to be). For a child, that evaluation will depend on how significant adults in her life react to her level of achievement. Support spiked with 'an optimum amount of pressure — just enough to cause the child to care but not too much so that he/she becomes distressed' will help maintain a high self-esteem whilst too much anxiety or zeal on the part of the adult will breed a sense of failure that easily becomes generalised (low self-esteem). Teachers are, thus, in a pivotal position to influence level of esteem positively or negatively.[11] Theirs is a heavy responsibility.

There is a vast body of research evidence demonstrating a positive correlation between self-esteem and achievement. The child enjoying high self-esteem is likely to be socially and academically confident. She will have retained an eagerness for new learning and new challenges. The child with low self-esteem will lack confidence and will tend to shy away from social and learning opportunities in the expectation of failure or humiliation.[13] Jack Canfield and Harold Wells have developed 'the poker chip theory of learning' to explain the 'extensive and overwhelming evidence' that cognitive learning increases when self-esteem increases: learning is a risk-taking business, the more poker chips (the higher the self-esteem) a student has, the more prepared she is to take chances, to risk failure.[14] Michele and Craig Borba cite research which shows that self-concept is a better predictor than intelligence test scores of a child's future academic success.[15]

> I was good at everything
> — honest, everything! —
> until I started being here with you.
> I was good at laughing,
> playing dead,
> being king!
> Yeah, I was good at everything !
> but now I'm only good at everything
> on Saturdays and Sundays...
>
> - Albert Cullum[12]

If the student with high self-esteem is likely to achieve more and be a more confident risk-taker in her learning, she will probably be more altruistic and positive towards others.[16] Negative self-image is likely to be displaced into negative attitudes and behaviours to other people in the near and wider community. Priscilla Prutzman *et al.* argue that 'poor self-image is at the root of many conflicts that exist in school today', on the grounds that it is difficult to feel positive about others if we cannot feel positive about ourselves.[17] Stanley Coppersmith sees low self-esteem as a probable root cause of bullying.[18] A body of research on primary-age children, adolescents and adults indicates that positive self-esteem correlates strongly with indicators of pro-social adjustment such as caring, generosity and sharing.[19] Strong links have also been identified between commitment to democratic values and processes and level of self-esteem. Edward Cell postulates that 'perhaps the dominant factor in sapping our courage to stand against injustice is the erosion of our sense of worth. The more we question our worth the more easily we are controlled'.[20] Barbara Schubert and Marlene Bird write: 'A good self-image and a feeling of self-worth renders one capable of self-determination ... a keystone of a true democratic society'.[21] High self-esteem has also been found to be linked, in older school students, with a preparedness to take action

Creating classrooms of affirmation (Photo: Alexandra Ketteley/EarthKind)

if faced with challenge or crisis, as against an attitude of resignation, despair or expectation that someone else will confront the problem.[22]

In the field of animal companionship studies, there is an abundance of research literature on the therapeutic and esteem-building effects of close contact with animals, especially pets. Children who are shy, isolated or aggressive, who have suffered abuse or neglect, who are disruptive or tend to truant, or who have learning difficulties, can be positively helped through caring, and being responsible, for an animal.[23] The opportunity for non-threatening, non-judgmental, non-verbal, yet highly tactile, companionship can be vital in helping a child regain a sense of self-worth and the ability to relate more easily to others. US programs giving prisoners a companion animal to look after have had startling results in terms of improved prisoner self-esteem, improved personal relationships between prisoners and prisoners and warders ('pets as facilitators'), reduced conflict and violence, fewer

suicides, improved community participation amongst inmates and reduced rates of recidivism.[24] 'Animals provide prisoners with uncritical love and affection and an acceptable opportunity for touch,' comments Liz Ormerod. 'Animals are friends that can be trusted when faith in others is lost. For many prisoners having a pet is the first time they have known the responsibility of caring for another living being. In learning how to care for animals, prisoners are also learning how to care for themselves and other people.'[25] Excellent results have also been achieved by Ormerod and colleagues through opening up a senior citizens' sheltered housing complex to pets. Following their introduction, the community took on new life, purpose and vigour and individuals felt a new sense of self-respect.[26] Similarly, staff at West Humber Collegiate School, a secondary school in Etobicoke, Toronto, testify to the very positive effect of introducing a range of pets into the school: reported cases of conflict and vandalism declined markedly and a greater sense of community became evident across the student body.[27]

Animals in the Classroom

by Valerie Licskai and Sherri Gilbert, Withrow Avenue Public School, Toronto

Pets can live anywhere in the classroom — on land, in ponds, in cages, in aquariums, in terrariums, and in the loving arms of children.

Children in our integrated learning disabilities class, who learn with animals, have experienced many hours of unconditional affection. Education today guarantees that every child's needs will be met. These needs cannot simply be achieved by teaching the three R's. Sometimes a well-meaning and caring teacher is not able to reach certain children. Children in our activity-based, family-centred classroom often fill this void through interactions with our menagerie.

The variety of wildlife (who have become an extremely important and vital part of our learning environment) have been selected with a multitude of specific needs in mind.

Each animal comes with a very personal history. Butterscotch, our New Zealand Red (a rabbit of enormous size) was born and hand-raised in the classroom. Butterscotch actively seeks attention from any person entering our territory. His unconditional love (characterised by tugs on cuffs, licking, circling, and hopping on laps) is welcomed by the children, especially those who lack confidence, self-esteem, and the ability to work in co-operative groups.

Chi Chi Chinchilla and our Guinea Pig draw out the nurturing tendencies of those students whose home life often lacks security and stability. The nervous disposition of these animals encourages the students to develop a calm and gentle manner.

Our iguanas, Aristotle and Plato, joined our family after having been abused and neglected. Frightened and distrusting, it took weeks of gentle perseverance before they learned to trust their new care givers. Now they are often seen accessorising daily wardrobes as the children attend to their daily assignments. Their unusual appearance and past experience encourage children with similar histories.

Our conversationalists, Alex (mynah bird) and Chico (cockatiel), encourage oral communication. Those children who might not otherwise have a friend with whom to share, feel comfortable talking with our birds. Non-threatening responses build confidence in all children.

The tranquillity of the fish and turtle ponds provide a peaceful retreat from the often hectic daily agenda. Many children take advantage of this serene setting to practice their oral reading skills. This nonthreatening atmosphere encourages risk-taking.

The students take full responsibility for providing for all the needs of all our animals. Daily responsibilities include cleaning, feeding, grooming, and loving each animal individually. The children work in cooperative groups to provide for these essential needs. Families volunteer to take the pets over the weekend or during vacation periods. Butterscotch has also vacationed with our families in many beautiful Muskoka summer homes! When a pet becomes ill, the children accompany an adult to the veterinarians. Fund raisers are held to cover the costs of the vet bills. Added expenses which are considerations before adopting pets include suitable housing so that animals run freely for the majority of school time. Butterscotch is litter trained and has the run of the third floor. Feeding our zoo is no small task. Pet food and vitamins are expensive as are the bedding for the guinea pig and iguanas. It is important to take these into account. But, the intrinsic rewards far outweigh the monetary costs.

It is our belief that animals in the classroom play a vital and essential role in the education of today's youth. Academic, social, and emotional needs are fostered through the children's interactions with their animal family.

Right: Iguana embellish the students' daily wardrobe. Below: Chi Chi, the Chinchilla, drawing out the nurturing tendencies in the students.

The animal companionship approach is not without its attendant drawbacks and dangers. First, it may be logistically and physically impossible to provide animal companionship for all those students suffering from low self-esteem. In the final analysis, animal companionship is a self-esteem building strategy for the few rather than the many. Second, it is in essence an anthropocentric and instrumentalist approach with a rationale primarily based

on the practical and emotional benefits for people rather than animals. As such, teachers need to be aware of the messages students might be receiving subliminally. Third, there is the related and ever-present risk of the animals not being treated as well as they should be.

A more generally viable approach is to build 'classrooms of affirmation' in which, in a conscious and sustained way, students are encouraged to identify and acknowledge the strengths and contribution of others. This, it is suggested, will have positive spin-offs not only for students' attitudes to self, each other, and other people, but also towards animals. Characteristics displayed by students with an affirmative sense of self and others would include:

❑ the ability to assess realistically both the strengths and weaknesses of their own work;

❑ the ability to recognise the worth of others, and give affirming feedback to classmates;

❑ the ability to accept constructive criticism and suggestions in an open-minded manner, without becoming overly defensive;

❑ the ability to work co-operatively in a group, accepting the contributions of each member without needing to dominate or impose one's ideas on others;

❑ the ability to react reasonably and assertively in conflict situations, without relying on physical and verbal aggression.[28]

Carolyn Zahn-Waxler *et al.* are critical of theories of child personality that depict young children as egocentric, demanding and hedonistic. Such theories, they maintain, tend to draw on material collected in interview, a situation where young children appear to disadvantage in that they cannot put into words their acts of caring, sense of justice, and understanding of moral issues. Children's early empathetic proclivities, they suggest, can be built upon and reinforced by learning programmes that give active recognition to the universality of basic emotions amongst human beings and other mammalian species and, also, offer clear messages about the importance of care and compassion. Learning designed to foster empathetic and humane attitudes and behaviours would include:

❑ warm and accepting relationships between students and teacher;

❑ learning materials realistically portraying feelings and distress;

❑ opportunities for children to have direct experience of helping;

❑ explicit explanations about the feelings and circumstances of victims;

❑ general codes stating positions on altruism, aggression and morality in simple explicit terms.[29]

Role modelling by significant adults, they stress, is of critical significance in fostering empathy for people and animals. 'The parent (teacher) who conveys his moral values as principles only, but does not translate these into real, caring actions, accomplishes a limited kind of learning in the child. Generalised altruism appears to be best learned from parents (teachers) who inculcate the principles and show real altruism in their everyday interactions[30] (my parentheses). Or, put another way, adults need to walk their talk.

A major problem in building classrooms of affirmation is often teachers' own lack of self-esteem. Self-esteem, it has been suggested, is linked to preparedness to take risks. Teachers with low self-esteem often lack the confidence to experiment with new forms of teaching, learning and classroom relationship; they do not readily accede to the devolution of power implicit in participatory learning processes. Level of self-esteem, it has also been suggested, directly affects whether we view others positively or negatively. Teachers with low self-esteem often tend towards a

conservative, or minimalist, view of students' willingness to learn, intrinsic motivation, capacity for self-direction and self-organisation. As students (whose self-esteem has not been nurtured) revert to forms of guerrilla warfare in an effort to subvert a dehumanised learning situation, that view will seem confirmed. 'Without teachers themselves being confident and having high self-esteem,' writes Lawrence, 'they are not easily going to be able to enhance the self-esteem of the children in their care.'[31]

The humane, esteem-building teacher is accepting, genuine and empathetic. She is non-judgmental and always accepting of the student's personality (whilst not necessarily always approving of her behaviour); she is a 'real person' and does not hide behind a professional 'mask'; she is able to appreciate what it feels like to be the other person and looks and listens for the feelings and meanings behind what the student does and says.[32]

Divide and School

My teacher is like a battle tank
Roaring at the enemy
The enemy is us
And the roaring is the lessons.
He keeps us in a prison camp
Torturing us each day
And he will keep on torturing us
Till our minds are worn away.

— Roderick, UK.

Don't you see my rainbow, teacher?
Don't you see all the colors?
I know that you're mad at me.
I know that you said to color
the cherries red and the leaves green.
I guess I shouldn't have done it backwards.
But, teacher, don't you see my rainbow?
Don't you see all the colors?
Don't you see me?

— Albert Cullum[33]

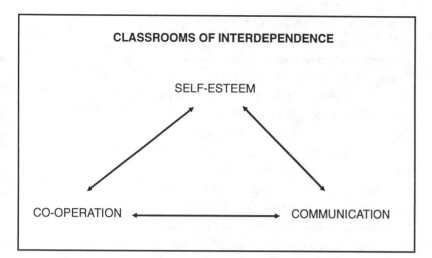

CLASSROOMS OF INTERDEPENDENCE

SELF-ESTEEM

CO-OPERATION ⟷ COMMUNICATION

Fig. 1[34]

Classrooms of Interdependence

If the humane teacher prioritises esteem-building, she also sets great store upon developing co-operative attitudes and skills and honing communication skills.

David and Roger Johnson have identified three basic ways in which students relate to each other and to the teacher in working towards a learning goal:

❑ *individualistic* — when a student's achievement of the goal is unrelated to the achievement of the goal by other students;

❑ *competitive* — when a student perceives that she can obtain her goal if, and only if, all the other students with whom she is linked fail to obtain theirs;

❑ *co-operative* — when students perceive that they can achieve their goal if, and only if, all other students with whom they are linked achieve theirs.[35]

Co-operative learning structures accord most closely with the aims and philosophy of humane education. First, they are built upon a recognition of the intrinsic worth of each learner and a valuing of everybody's contribution to the learning process. Second, they involve a 'winners all' approach to learning and, as such, help to reinforce self-esteem levels, whereas individualistic and, especially, competitive learning can result in a devaluing of students who achieve less (humane organisations running competitions with prizes need to ask some serious questions of themselves here). Third, they provide fruitful contexts for the sharing of feelings, opinions and perspectives and are, thus, effective in promoting empathetic attitudes and sensitivity towards others. Co-operative learning has also been found to be more efficacious the greater the degree

Co-operating to form messages — students at St. Michael's School, Wood Green, North London, work on Petcare Messagematch (see p.156) (Photo: EarthKind/ Alexandra Ketteley)

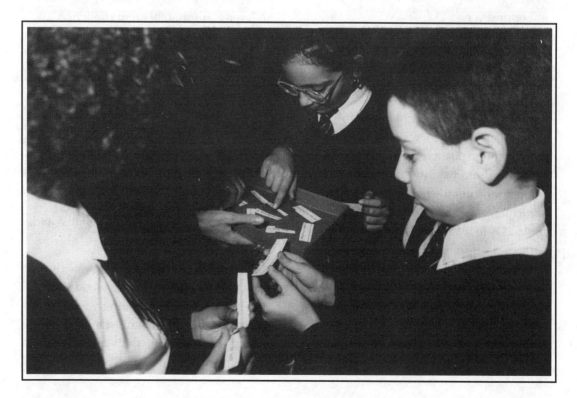

of conceptual learning involved. Additionally, it has been found that higher order skills development will take place in co-operative learning situations in which the task undertaken generates controversy or conflict of ideas, opinions and theories (as compared with individualistic study of controversy, or a group task based on a non-controversial issue).[36] Such conclusions would seem to be of great significance for humane education given the complexity, controversiality and value-laden nature of many of the issues.

Regular immersion in co-operative learning contexts also allows students to experience the class not as a collection of disconnected individuals, but as an interrelated system in which the actions and input of each member affect, and are affected by, the actions and input of others. Through co-operative activities, students can, from an early age, gain concrete experience of the highly complex idea of interdependence, a key concept in humane education. A lived experience of classroom interdependencies can provide the bedrock for an internalised understanding of interdependencies between humans and animals, within ecosystems, and between forms of injustice and oppression.[37]

Sixth, there is a growing body of evidence linking co-operative learning with positive attitudes to others. David and Roger Johnson have found that co-operative learning experiences, compared with individualistic and competitive situations, promote more positive relationships between ethnic majority and ethnic minority students: the interdependence of group participants working towards a common goal tends to result in interpersonal attraction which, in turn, enhances the self-esteem of all participants.[38] The Johnson brothers also claim that differences of all kinds, whether to do with ethnicity, gender, class or handicap, are positively respected and valued in co-operative group structures if they are perceived as resources which can

help the group accomplish a variety of goals.[39] Alfred Davey's research with primary school children in diverse areas of England indicates that ethnicity will significantly drop in importance as a factor in friendship choice if the children are consistently placed in 'contexts of neutral and mutual dependency', i.e. in groups where co-operation is needed to achieve a particular goal.[40] The centrality of effective communication (including listening) skills to co-operative learning also, it appears, has pro-social spin-offs; research suggests that there is a direct linkage between, on the one hand, positive attitudes to self and to others, including those in distress, and on the other hand, the ability to express thoughts and feelings clearly, and to listen carefully and actively.[41] The humancentric nature of the research cited notwithstanding, there is every reason to surmise that the pro-social attitudes nurtured by co-operative learning will also manifest themselves in more humane and compassionate attitudes towards animals.

Agitating the Comfortable

The most productive learning contexts are manifested by a delicate and tensile balance between comfortability and challenge. The well-affirmed learning group is better able to handle a challenge to its individual and collective values and perspectives creatively; members will be more open, honest and forthright about their opinions; and readier to work through conflicts of opinion. Should the level of challenge become over-intense or unsafe, the need will arise for further esteem-building and group-bonding. The role of the teacher combines a comforting of the agitated and an agitating of the comfortable.

A lecture by a teacher can undoubtedly provide the requisite agitation and should be a learning strategy sparingly and judiciously employed amidst a range of other approaches. The challenge to prevailing values, perspectives and

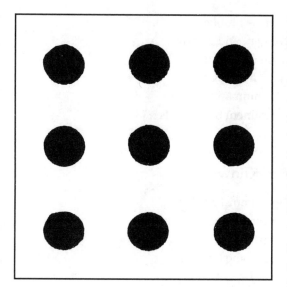

Fig. 2

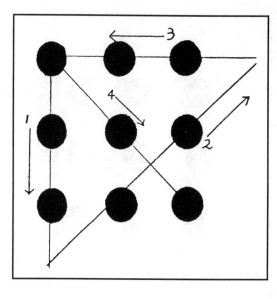

Fig. 4

Fig. 3

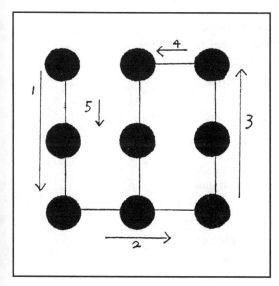

paradigms is, however, most effectively and economically achieved on a regular basis through forms of interactive and experiental learning. The activity chapters of this book offer many examples of students, working individually or in pairs, being asked to determine their personal position on an animal-related issue (perhaps by ranking, clustering or sequencing cards or pictures) before moving into larger groups (say fours, then eights) and, finally, a class debriefing session. Even in a seemingly monocultural group, where one perspective might seem to obtain, students will experience a succession of challenges as they are asked to explain, justify, and, if possible, reach consensus around their respective viewpoints in successively larger arenas. The comfort of individual or small group work gives way to the challenge of large group work, a challenge that is more readily faced in the confidence bred of what has gone before. *Where Do We Draw the Line?* (p.141), *Tackling a Statement* (p.143) and *Zoo Diamond Ranking* (p.241) are representative examples of this process.

Forms of experiential learning include simulation games (mirroring or reconstructing real events or situations on a classroom scale), role play, and so-called experiential units (which seek to provide a group-generated, hence original, experience within an artificially-constructed framework). A fertile context for practising communication, negotiation, decision-making, problem-solving and other skills, they also offer tremendous scope for subsequent mutual exploration of attitudes, perspectives and values. They can provide for students an emotional 'slap on the face'; a sudden awareness of their assumptions and limited worldview that, sensitively debriefed and carefully nurtured, can stimulate the intellect into accommodating new insights and perspectives. Activities such as *Splitting Images* (p.218), *Factory Learning* (p.179) and *At Arms' Length?* (p.238) are good examples of experiential learning activities.

The importance of agitating the comfortable is nicely illustrated by the *Nine Dot Problem*. Pairs are given a sheet of paper containing nine dots (see *Fig. 2*) and are asked to connect all the dots using only straight lines and without removing the pencil from the paper. The facilitator walks around monitoring progress and prompting pairs to strive for ever fewer lines in accomplishing the task. After several minutes, a pair that has used five lines to connect the dots is asked to draw their solution on the board or overhead projection transparency (one five-line solution is given in *Fig. 3*). A pair

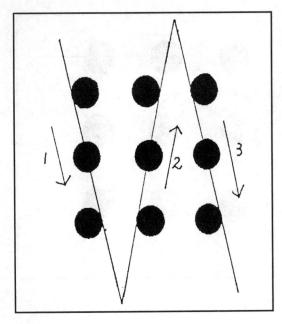

Fig. 5

that used only four lines is then asked to demonstrate their method (*Fig. 4*). Their solution is discussed. The breakthrough to four lines is achieved by setting aside the unconsciously self-imposed limitation of not trespassing outside the square of dots. Some pairs will accomplish the task in three lines (*Fig. 5*); this involves divesting oneself of yet another assumption, i.e. that the lines must pass through the centre of each dot. Some will possibly have linked the dots together with one line; for instance, by drawing a fat line using the length of a stick of chalk or by folding the paper so all the dots are aligned and driving a pencil through them. Mathematicians may demur but the point is that theirs is not the only perspective on what constitutes a line.[42] Activities such as the *Nine Dot Problem* help us realise how many assumptions we carry around with us and how they can inhibit learning and constrict creativity; they demonstrate the need for nimbleness, flexibility and receptivity in responding to challenge.

Learning processes in which interactive and experiential learning figure prominently not only provide students with a constant multi-directional challenge to their attitudes, perspectives, values and mindsets; they also contribute significantly to the development

of higher order skills such as problem solving and lateral, divergent and creative thinking. They are an essential feature of the humane classroom in which students are called upon to reappraise humanity's relationship with, and treatment of, animals and the environment.

Relational Modes of Knowing

The theory of knowledge or epistemology underpinning schooling can be described as compartmentalist. The current curriculum of most classrooms carries some important subliminal messages:

❑ sentences, events, situations, plants, animals, etc., are to be understood by analysing them and reducing them to their separate parts;

❑ the ability to think logically, 'apply' reason and organise what is learnt sequentially is prized whilst the ability to respond intuitively and from the heart is of less consequence;

❑ whatever connections are discerned between different phenomena are of secondary importance;

❑ the learner is separate from what is studied and observed;

❑ outer-directed learning (focusing on externalities) is valued more than inner-directed learning (focusing on self, self-in-the-world; personal growth and transformation);

❑ the ability to control really matters (whether it is control by teacher of her class, 'mastery' by the student of her learning brief, or organisation of knowledge into tidy categories, compartments and hierarchies);

❑ certainty is preferable to hesitancy and uncertainty.

It has become common in educational circles to speak of there being a hegemony of 'left-brain' learning in our schools. Split-brain research has shown that the two hemispheres of the brain process information in different yet complementary ways. The left hemisphere tends to break up information into component parts; to analyse those parts, label, categorise and compartmentalise them, and to control verbal and auditory processes. The right hemisphere synthesises information, sees wholes rather than parts, detects meaning from patterns and tends to control visual and spatial processes. The left hemisphere tends to deal with the abstract and the rational, the right with the emotional and intuitive.[43] Whilst we must avoid what Theodore Roszak calls 'the split-brain follies'[44] and recognise that the two hemispheres of the brain operate as a functioning whole, it is indubitably the case that schooling has traditionally accorded most value to mental processes that have their source primarily in the left side of the brain. The reasons for this are to be found in questions of assessment (the outcomes of left-brain learning are easier to assess and quantify), questions of dominance and control (a synthesising and multi-contextual way of perceiving makes it harder to establish tidy order in what is learnt, and over whoever is learning) and, at root, in the prevailing compartmentalist paradigm within education and society.

Humane education, concerned with fostering dynamic compassion for all life and respect and reverence for the planet, calls for an alternative epistemology, one that accords at least equal prominence to relational and affective modes of knowing. Rosemary Radford Ruether has argued that rationalist and linear modes of knowing are 'ecologically dysfunctional'; that outcomes of the compartmentalist mindset have been our alienation from the actual world, our exploitation of animals, our project of devastating and seeking to dominate nature (because it is not us).[45] She calls for 'a new form of human intelligence' moving beyond 'the linear, dichotomised, alienated consciousness characteristic of the 'left-brain' mode seen in masculinist scientific epistemology'.[46] 'We must respond to a 'thou-ness' in all beings. This is not romanticism or an anthropomorphic animism that sees 'dryads in trees,' although there is truth in the animist view... We respond not just as 'I to it,' but as 'I to thou,' to the spirit, the life energy that lies in every being in its own form of existence.'[47] Josephine Donovan concurs: 'What is needed is a more 'disordered' (if order means hierarchical dominance) relational mode that does not rearrange the context to fit a master paradigm but sees, accepts, and respects the environment'.[48] Douglas Sloan calls for a valuing of insight that 'penetrates beyond the fixities and particulars of the given to an underlying wholeness that is the source of all genuine knowledge'.[49]

The nurturing of relational modes of knowing, of ecological responsiveness, calls for a wide and varied range of learning approaches that foster sensitivity, allow feelings to be aired, shared and valued, that promote, to recall Sara Ruddick (p. 20), an attitude of 'attentive love' to all beings and entities. In practical terms, this will involve

---

Ecological thinking ... requires a kind of vision across boundaries. The epidermis of the skin is ecologically like a pond surface or a forest soil, not a shell so much as delicate interpenetration. It reveals the self ennobled and extended ... as part of the landscape and the ecosystem, because the beauty and complexity of nature are continuous with ourselves ... we must affirm that the world is a being, a part of our own body.

— Paul Shepard[50]

The robins sang and sang and sang,
but teacher you went right on.
The last bell sounded the end of the day,
but teacher you went right on.
The geranium on the window sill just died,
but teacher you went right on.

— Albert Cullum[51]

the use of guided fantasy and visualisation techniques, multisensory learning that calls upon the senses of smell, taste and touch as well as hearing and seeing, movement and dance, drama and role play, meditation and relaxation. A culture of attunement to the voice of self, others and planet, thus nurtured, is a prerequisite of an internalised humane ethic.

Letting the Outside World In, Letting the Inside World Out

This chapter has focused upon the importance of interactive and experiential learning. The additional point needs making that humane education needs to breach the divide that separates the classroom from the outside world. First, students need structured personal involvement with the natural world if they are to be helped to understand how ecosystems work, appreciate the beauty of the natural world and develop positive, caring attitudes to the Earth. Steve van Matre's acclimatisation programmes have sharpened our understanding of the potential of such structured involvement.[52] Second, students' knowledge of animal-related and environmental issues is less likely to remain inert if they can acquire personal experience of those issues in the field. 'Few members of a junior high school class,' says Alan Bowd, 'presented with literature and a lecture on the cruelty of battery hen farming will act to change battery hen farming, although they may express a negative attitude toward the practice. Consider, however, a group which visits such a facility, examines alternative egg-producing arrangements, and in this context is required to stop eating battery eggs for a week as part of a project... Their knowledge is less likely to remain inert, and will be accessed and applied to relevant situations outside the classroom (such as choosing, perhaps, not to eat egg dishes in restaurants).'[53] Third, if a central aim of humane education is to foster compassion

> *The day had become like half a night,*
> *but you put the classroom lights on.*
> *The wind blew the papers off your desk,*
> *but you just closed the window.*
> *The trees waved, like they were calling out*
> *to us ...*
> *'Turn to page 67,' you said.*
>
> — Albert Cullum[54]

for animals, then it is clear that students should have the opportunity to exercise that compassion through action-oriented projects in the community. Experience of, and reflection upon, change agency is also important if students are to develop the skills and confidence for responsible and active citizenship. The question of animal-related school-based action projects is more fully considered in *Chapter 15*.

In *Petals of Blood* by novelist Ngugi wa Thiong'o, a teacher at a village school takes his students out of the classroom for their botany lesson. His aim is to give them a hands-on experience of flowers. He teaches them the names of the flowers and their constituent parts, and feels proud to be imparting hard, factual information. But the dynamic of the lesson changes, and his self-satisfaction falls away, as the children offer vivid poetic metaphors to describe the flowers ('petals of blood') and ask unanswerable questions about why God allows beauty to be destroyed by letting worms eat some of the flowers and about humankind, law, god and nature.

> *Classroom corners — stale and pale!*
> *Classroom corners — cobweb covered!*
> *Classroom corners — spooky and lonely!*
> *Teacher, let me dance in your classroom*
> *corner!*
> *Let the outside world in!*
>
> — Albert Cullum[57]

Man ... law ... God ... nature: he had never thought deeply about these things, and he swore that he would never again take the children to the fields. Enclosed in the four walls he was master, aloof, dispensing knowledge to a concentration of faces looking up at him. There he could avoid being drawn in. But out in the fields, outside the walls, he felt insecure.[55]

For the humane educator, the challenge, both inside and outside the classroom, is to take risks, to celebrate life in all its insecurity and uncertainty. 'Education,' writes Robin Richardson, 'should be helping to change the world, to make it less oppressive and stifling, less unequal, and should be helping to build, on the contrary, greater equality and justice, greater and wider access to life and unfolding. We believe these things, and we believe too that learning should be through firsthand experience, through immersion in living and confusing reality, and through passionate reflection, argument and dialogue: it cannot be, and must not be, limited to places called classrooms, nor to didactic instruction by teachers, and deferential note-taking by learners.'[56]

References

1. Posluns, M., ed., *Songs for the people: teachings on the natural way. Poems and essays of Arthur Solomon*, Toronto, New Canada Publications, 1990, 79.

2. Vockell, E., & Hodal, E.F., 'Developing humane attitudes: what does research tell us?', *Humane education*, June 1980, 19.

3. *Ibid.*, 20.

4. *Ibid.*, 21.

5. Malcarne, V., 'Evaluating humane education; the Boston study', *Humane education*, March 1983, 12-13.

6. See, for instance, Hein, G.E., *Massachusetts Society for the Prevention of Cruelty to Animals Outreach Program evaluation. Final report*, Boston, Massachusetts, MSPCA, 1987.

7. Malcarne, V., *The effects of roleplay and maximisation of perceived similarity on children's empathy with other children and animals*, unpublished honours thesis, Stanford University, 1981.

8. Cullum, A., *The geranium on the window sill just died but teacher you went right on*, Harlin Quist, 1971, 60.

9. The phrase is borrowed from Prutzman, P., Burger, M.L., Bodenhamer, G., and Stern, L., *The friendly classroom for a small planet*, New Jersey, Avery, 1978.

10. Branden, N., *Honouring the self*, J.P. Tarcher, 1983, cited in *Marilyn Ferguson's book of pragmagic*, Pocket Books, 1990, 81.

11. Lawrence, D., *Enhancing self-esteem in the classroom*, Paul Chapman, 1988, 2-6.

12. Cullum, A., *op. cit.*, 40.

13. Lawrence, D., *op. cit.*, ix, 6.

14. Canfield, J., & Wells, A.C., *100 ways to enhance self-concept in the classroom*, Prentice Hall, 1976. 7.

15. Borba, M., & Borba, C., *Self-esteem. A classroom affair*, Minneapolis, Winston Press, 1978, 2.

16. Lawrence, D., *op. cit.*, 24.

17. Prutzman, P., *et al.*, 35.

18. Borba, M., & Borba, C., *Self-esteem. A classroom affair. Volume 2*, Minneapolis, Winston Press, 1982, 3.

19. Mussen, P., & Eisenberg-Berg, N., *Roots of caring, sharing, and helping*, San Francisco, Freeman, 1977.

20. Cell, E., *Learning to learn from experience*, Albany, State University of New York Press, 1984, 24.

21. Schubert, B., & Bird, M., *Self-image*, Reflections & Images (6607 Northridge Drive, San Jose, California, 96120, USA), 1979, ii.

22. Haste, H., 'Everybody's scared — but life goes on: coping, defence and action in the face of nuclear threat', *Journal of adolescence*, cited in Fountain, S., *Learning together. Global education 4-7*, Stanley Thornes/World Wide Fund for Nature/Centre for Global Education, 1990, 5.

23. Ormerod, E., 'Humane education', *Journal of Society for Companion Animal Studies*, Spring 1990, vol. 2, no. 2, 9.

24. Whyman, M., 'Companion animals and offenders', paper presented to the Annual Conference of the Society for Companion Animal Studies, University of York, 24/25 September 1990. Ormerod, L., *Animals in prisons*, mimeo, 1988, 1.

25. Ormerod, E., *Animals in prisons*, mimeo, 1988, 1.

26. Liz Ormerod is a veterinary surgeon. Her humane education resource centre, Companion Animals in Rehabilitation and Education (CARE) is located at The Mount Veterinary Surgery, 1 Harris Street, Fleetwood, Lancashire, FY7 6QX.

27. I am indebted to Heather Goodson, Environmental Coordinator, West Humber Collegiate, 1675 Martin Grove Road, Etobicoke, Ontario M9V 3S3, for giving me the opportunity to tour the school and talk to staff.

28. Fountain, S., *op. cit.*, 6.

29. Zahn-Waxler, C., Hollenbeck, B., & Radke-Yarrow, M., 'Teaching to be kind: learning to be caring — the origins of altruism and empathy', *Humane education newsletter*, vol. 1, no. 2, summer 1990, 9.

30. Zahn-Waxler, C., Hollenbeck, B., & Radke-Yarrow, M., 'The origins of empathy and altruism' in Fox, M.W., & Mickley, L.D., *Animal welfare science 1984*, Nijhoff, 1984, 34.

31. Lawrence, D., *op. cit.*, 44.

32. *Ibid.*, 22.

33. Cullum, A., *op. cit.*, 36.

34. I am indebted to Susan Fountain for introducing me to this model and to many of the insights in the following discussion.

35. Johnson, D.W., & Johnson, R.T., *Learning together and alone: co-operation, competition and individualisation*, Prentice-Hall, 1975, 7.

36. Johnson, D.W., & Johnson, R.T., 'The socialisation and achievement crisis: are co-operative learning experiences the solution?' in Bickman, L., ed., *Applied social psychology annual 4*, Beverley Hills, Sage, 1983, 145-7.

37. Fountain, S., & Selby, D., 'Global education in the primary school', *Aspects of education* (journal of the Institute of Education, University of Hull), no. 38, 1988, 36.

38. Johnson, D.W., Johnson, R., & Marvyama, G., 'Interdependence and interpersonal attraction among heterogeneous and homogeneous individuals', *Review of educational research*, 52. 1983. 5-54.

39. Johnson, D.W., & Johnson, R., *Learning together and alone: co-operation, competition and individualisation*, New Jersey, Prentice-Hall, 1975, 195-6.

40. Davey, A., *Learning to be prejudiced. Growing up in multi-ethnic Britain*, Edward Arnold, 1983.

41. Musson, P., & Eisenberg-Berg, *op. cit.,.*

42. Adams, *Conceptual blockbusting*, New York, W.W. Norton, 1979, 11-13.

43. Williams, L.V., *Teaching for the two-sided mind*, New Jersey, Prentice-Hall, 1983, 13-38.

44. Roszak, T., *Unfinished animal*, Faber & Faber, 1976, 56.

45. Ruether, R.R., *Sexism and god talk. Towards a feminist theology*, Boston, Beacon, 1983, 89-90.

46. Donovan, J., 'Animal rights and feminist theory' in Gaard, G., ed., *Ecofeminism. Women, animals and nature*, Philadelphia, Temple University Press, 1993, 181.

47. Ruether, R.R., *op. cit.*, 87.

48. Sloan, D., ed., *Towards the recovery of wholeness. Knowledge, education and human values*, New York, Teachers' College Press, Columbia University, 1981, 2.

49. Cited in Seed, J., *et. al.*, *Thinking like a mountain*, Heretic Books, 1988, 9.

50. Shepard, P., cited in Greig, S., Pike, G., & Selby, D., *Greenprints for changing schools*, WWF/Kogan Page, 1989, 11.

51. Cullum, A., *op.cit.*, 58.

52. See, for instance, Van Matre, S., *Acclimatisation*, Martinsville, Indiana, American Camping Association, 1972, and *Sunship Earth*, American Camping Association, 1979.

53. Bowd, A., 'The educational dilemma' in Paterson, D., & Palmer, M., *The status of animals. Ethics, education and welfare*, Humane Education Foundation/C.A.B. International, 1989, 56.

54. Cullum, A., *op. cit.*, 30.

55. This description of, and passage from, *Petals of blood* is taken from Richardson, R., *Daring to be a teacher*, Trentham, 1990, 4-5.

56. Richardson, R., *op. cit.*, 5.

57. Cullum, A., *op. cit.*, 12.

Chapter 3

Aims and Objectives

AIMS

What, in summary, are the aims of humane education? Four broad aims can be identified: the development of a biophilic (life-loving and life-affirming) ethic; consciousness of interconnectedness; consciousness of values and perspectives; commitment to democratic principles and processes.

Biophilic Ethic

Under this heading falls the cultivation of kindness and compassion towards human beings and non-human animals, respect for the inherent value of natural environments and all living things, a concern to maintain bio and cultural diversity, a reverence for the beauty of the Earth, its people and other lifeforms, and an outright rejection of all forms of cruelty, exploitation and oppression. Encompassed, too, are: self-esteem building; a commitment to developing individual potential in its complimentary bodily, emotional, intellectual and spiritual dimensions; a readiness to see learning as a journey without fixed or final destination in which challenge, uncertainty and risk are inevitable features of any process of personal growth and transformation.

Interconnectedness

Under this heading the learner acquires an understanding of systems, of how phenomena and events are bound up in complex, dynamic and multi-layered relational webs; how natural and human-made systems interact; how human decisions and actions often adversely affect other animals and the natural environment and then rebound with detrimental, sometimes disastrous, consequences for human communities; of the consequent need for humane, environmentally-friendly and sustainable lifestyles; how the well-being of future generations is also deeply dependent upon the choices we make and the actions we take; how people are part of nature and share much in common with non-human animals. Under this heading, too, the learner comes to understand how her health, well-being and sense of self influence, and are influenced by, the condition of the planet.

Values/Perspectives

Under this heading the learner comes to realise that she, like others, has her own particular perspective that has been shaped by factors such as age, class, creed, culture, ethnicity, gender, ideology, language, location, nationality and race. She recognises that her understanding of animal-related, environmental and other issues will be significantly extended through openness and receptivity to other perspectives; and that such receptivity can be profoundly liberating in its challenge to previously unexamined assumptions. She understands that underpinning any perspective (including her own) is a value system which demands examination and clarification and that the challenge of different perspectives will often also involve a values challenge and, perhaps, a values modification. Also embraced by this heading is the complementary development of critical discernment with regard to values, beliefs, perspectives and the media.

Democratic Principles and Processes

Under this heading the learner commits to democratic values such as respect for reasoning; acceptance of diversity in ideas, opinions, perspectives and practices; concern for the welfare of others; peaceful and creative resolution of conflict; fairness; equity; justice and freedom. She embraces a conception of citizenship that is multi-layered (local to global), that encompasses the notions of intergenerational equity and accountability, that is active and participatory, and no longer leaves animals outside the 'circle of compassion'. In preparing for active citizenship, the learner acquires the confidence, mindset, insights and skills needed for effective and responsible change agency and change advocacy in a democratic society.

OBJECTIVES

Set out below are lists of knowledge, skills and attitudinal objectives for humane education designed to satisfy the broad aims laid out above. The lists are by no means comprehensive but are intended to help teachers in designing, monitoring and evaluating learning programmes.

■ *KNOWLEDGE OBJECTIVES*

1. PERSONAL

(a) **Self-awareness**: students acquire an understanding of their own physical, intellectual, emotional and spiritual capacities and potential; their strengths, weaknesses and principal areas needing development.

(b) **Perspective**: students understand that their own perspective has been shaped by a combination of factors particular to their own circumstances and experience, that it is not universally shared, and that personal growth often arises from challenges to that perspective.

2. DIVERSITY

(a) **Biodiversity**: students understand the importance of preserving the rich diversity of lifeforms on Earth and the threat that human activity presents to many of them.

(b) **Cultural diversity**: students understand that people in different cultures perceive and treat animals in different ways and should appreciate the reasons for those differences.

(c) **Learning diversity**: students understand that there are many ways to learn, that each individual has preferred ways of learning but that there are real benefits to be had from persevering with new and initially uncomfortable learning styles and situations.

3. INTERCONNECTEDNESS

(a) **Systems**: students develop an understanding of how natural and human-made systems function, evolve and change.

(b) **Interdependence**: students understand the concept of interdependence and how people, other lifeforms, places, events and issues are linked together in a complex web of interdependent relationships.

(c) **Sustainability**: students understand the concept of sustainability; that the health and well-being of individuals, communities and the Earth have many interrelated dimensions; that actions and behaviours that degrade the environment will eventually impact adversely upon our quality of life and survival chances.

4. ENVIRONMENT

(a) **Environment as an holistic concept**: students appreciate that environment is an all-embracing concept that includes the natural environment, the built environment, the social (including school) environment, and interpersonal and intrapersonal environments; also that these environments are interacting and interdependent.

(b) **Environmental degradation**: students know about the causes and effects of environmental degradation and the measures that are being or could be taken at all levels, personal to global, to combat it.

(c) **Perspectives**: students become familiar with a range of perspectives on the underlying causes of our current environmental condition and treatment of animals, including indigenous and feminist perspectives and the perspectives of counter-cultural groups, ethnic minorities and the major world religions.

5. ANIMALS

(a) **Commonality**: students recognise that many of the needs, characteristics, emotions, impulses and behaviours common to human beings are also common to many non-human animals.

(b) **Animal rights**: students understand the various arguments made for according rights and moral status to animals and the implications of those arguments.

(c) **Animal welfare**: students have an understanding of the concept of animal welfare and of the behavioural and practical implications of welfarism.

(d) **Exploitation**: students know about the use, abuse and exploitation of animals as sources of food, materials and entertainment and in animal experimentation/school dissection; they also become familiar with principal arguments surrounding, and humane alternatives to, each form of use; they recognise the connections between individual and institutionalised cruelty to animals.

(e) **Images**: students understand the sources and consequences of negative images of animals in language, literature and audio-visual media.

(f) **Legislation**: students develop a critical understanding of current animal protection and welfare legislation.

(g) **Humane movements**: students know about key historical and contemporareous developments in the humane movement nationally and internationally (philosophies, organisations, notable individuals, important initiatives and events).

(h) **Vegetarianism**: students develop an understanding of the arguments surrounding meat-eating so they can make an informed assessment of the economic, development, environmental and health implications of vegetarian and vegan diets.

6. PLANETARY CITIZENSHIP

(a) **Plural and parallel citizenship**: students understand that citizenship in the contemporary world is no longer the monopolistic preserve of the nation state but that the individual also simultaneously draws identity from, and has allegiances and loyalties to, the locality, the province, the regional community (e.g. the EU), the bioregion and the planet.

(b) **Rights and responsibilities**: students become familiar with key international documents such as the Universal Declaration of Human Rights (1948) and the Convention on the Rights of the Child (1989); they learn key human rights concepts, ideas and terms, about violations of human rights and success stories in the defence of rights; they understand the basis of current critiques of the species exclusivity of human rights doctrines.

(c) **Prejudice and discrimination**: students understand the nature and workings of prejudice, in themselves and others, and how prejudice can lead to discrimination on grounds of age, class, creed, ethnicity, gender, ideology, language, nationality, sexuality, race or species; they also learn about means of combating prejudice and discrimination at personal, societal and global levels.

(d) **Oppression**: students learn about the attitudinal and structural aspects of oppression on grounds of age, class, creed, ethnicity, gender, ideology, language, nationality, sexuality, race or species; they understand, too, that all forms of oppression possess marked similarities and that different forms of oppression feed off and sustain each other.

(e) **Negative and positive peace**: students understand the concepts of negative and positive peace; they understand the ways in which animals are used in warfare and weapons refinement; they recognise the treatment of animals as a manifestation of both physical and structural violence.

(f) **Underdevelopment**: students understand the links between the global exploitation of animals, especially through the beef industry, and distorted development/underdevelopment as manifested in malnutrition, starvation, high incidence of disease, and inequalities within and between societies.

(g) **Active citizenship**: students know of the avenues and strategies for active engagement in social, political and environmental issues at all levels, local to global; they appreciate the potential, limitations, pitfalls and ramifications of different types of action.

(h) **Alternative futures**: students become aware of a range of alternative futures at a series of interrelated levels, personal to global, and understand that action (or inaction) in the present will help shape the future.

■ *SKILLS OBJECTIVES*

1. INFORMATION MANAGEMENT

(a) **Receiving and expressing**: students develop competence in receiving, expressing and presenting information, ideas and feelings through observing, reading, writing, listening, talking, questioning and other investigative tools, movement, graphical and other non-verbal communication processes.

(b) **Organising and processing**: students develop competence in classifying, analysing, synthesising and sequencing information, ideas and feelings.

(c) **Evaluating**: students develop competence in determining the quality, appropriateness and/or priority of information, in distinguishing fact from opinion, and in recognising bias and perspective.

2. PERSONAL GROWTH

(a) **Centering**: students are able to utilise a range of skills, such as relaxation, meditation, focusing, deep breathing and imagery, so as to heighten their awareness of the connection between body, mind and spirit.

(b) **Physical and emotional well-being**: students are able to maintain their physical and emotional well-being by means of appropriate dietary and lifestyle decisions.

(c) **Handling change**: students are able to handle changes and challenges effectively and to translate shocks, setbacks and transitions into transformative learning experiences.

3. INTERPERSONAL

(a) **Assertiveness**: students are able to articulate clearly their desires, feelings, preferences, viewpoints and value positions in a firm but respectful manner.

(b) **Nurturing**: students are able to nurture and maintain positive and trusting personal relationships through openness, sharing and constructive, affirmatory feedback.

(c) **Co-operation**: students are able to work and play co-operatively, ensuring the effective participation of all members of a group in the realisation of a common goal.

(d) **Negotiation**: students are able to make contracts, compromise and reach mutually satisfactory agreements or conclusions.

(e) **Handling controversy**: students are able to engage in discussion of controversial issues in ways that are congruent with the values of respect for reasoning and truth, fairness, toleration, concern for the well-being of others, acceptance of diversity and peacefulness.

4. DISCERNMENT

(a) **Values, beliefs and perspectives**: students are able to identify and clarify their own animal-related and environmental values, and to modify their values and beliefs to accommodate new perspectives, ideas and information.

(b) **Decision-making**: students are able to make informed decisions about animal-related issues on the basis of sound information gathering, organising and weighing evidence, and intuition.

(c) **Ethical judgement**: students are able to select and use criteria to determine the moral rightness or wrongness of any behaviour towards, or treatment of, another human being or non-human animal.

(d) **Media discernment**: students are able to decode/deconstruct images of animals in the media and identify the cultural practices, ideas, and ideological and values messages they contain.

(e) **Anthropocentrism and anthropomorphism**: students are able to discern anthropocentric attitudes and anthropomorphic depiction of animals in texts, lectures, films and other media.

(f) **Congruence**: students are able to discern inconsistencies within and between their own (and others') professed attitudes to animals and their actual behaviours and patterns of consumption.

(g) **Aesthetic appreciation**: students are able to judge, appreciate and articulate their feelings about the beauty of animals and natural or built environments.

5. IMAGING

(a) **Creative thinking**: students are able to move outside their established frameworks of thought to generate fresh insights and perspectives.

(b) **Problem-solving**: students are able to solve problems through a combination of effective information management, creative thinking, flexibility and intuition.

(c) **Perception of relationship**: students are able to perceive and identify patterns, relationships, connections and commonalities between phenomena.

(d) **Holistic perception**: students are able to see particular situations, phenomena, ideas and events as parts of a whole.

(e) **Empathy**: students are able to draw upon their experience and imagination to empathise with the predicament and feelings of other human beings and non-human animals.

(f) **Visualising**: students are able to visualise probable, possible, preferred and humane futures at all levels, personal to global; they are able to visualise the probable and possible consequences of proposals, strategies and blueprints for achieving a better future.

6. PARTICIPATION

(a) **Action research**: students are able to involve themselves in an issue to the extent that they understand its personal, ethical and political implications, who the stakeholders are and what is at stake; they are able to formulate strategies for effective change and, if appropriate, implement them.

(b) **Change agency/advocacy**: students develop the social and political action skills necessary for effecting change and influencing social trends and directions, e.g. writing letters, mounting publicity campaigns, lobbying, petitioning.

(c) **Ethically-grounded participation**: students are able to determine where the dividing line is for them between acceptable and unacceptable forms of social and political action.

■ *ATTITUDINAL OBJECTIVES*

1. RESPECT FOR SELF

(a) **Belief in own potential**: students possess a sense of their own worth; a belief in their physical, intellectual, emotional and spiritual potential; and the confidence and conviction that they can contribute to social and environmental improvement.

(b) **Genuineness**: students demonstrate genuineness in identifying, owning and sharing thoughts, feelings and emotions.

(c) **Curiosity**: students are endlessly curious and reflective about themselves, their relationships with others and their interactions with their environment.

2. RESPECT FOR PLANET

(a) **Reverence**: students possess a sense of curiosity, awe and wonder about the Earth, about people and about the myriad lifeforms on the planet.

(b) **Aesthetic appreciation**: students appreciate the beauty of the natural world, of human beings and animals, the built environment and human art and artefacts.

(c) **Sense of place**: students recognise the part environments play in helping form an individual's identity and maintain a sense of self; they recognise the unique character, hence irreplaceability, of particular natural environments.

(d) **Altruism**: students appreciate the need to override selfish, sectional or immediate interests for the overall good of the biotic community, now and in the future.

(e) **Precautionary principle**: students learn to err on the side of caution with regard to any development that could contribute to environmental degradation or unsustainability, placing the burden of proof on its promoters.

(f) **Responsibility**: students develop a sense of personal responsibility for the quality of environments, local to global.

RESPECT FOR OTHER BEINGS

(a) **Recognition of individuality**: students regard each human being and animal as an individual with meaning and purpose, not as an object.

(b) **Value**: students recognise and have respect for the intrinsic value of all living things regardless of their perceived worth to people.

(c) **Kindness:** students cultivate caring, compassionate and altruistic attitudes to other people and to animals; especially the distressed, oppressed, exploited, disadvantaged, downtrodden and marginalised.

(d) **Diversity**: students approach other, especially indigenous, cultural beliefs, practices and worldviews with a respectful, enquiring and valuing mindset, recognising that there is much to learn from them.

(e) **Level of comfort**: students feel comfortable and secure in direct interaction with animals.

(f) **Pet ownership**: students develop a responsible attitude to pet purchase and ownership.

4. RESPECT FOR JUSTICE AND RIGHTS

(a) **Concern for justice**: students are prepared actively to demonstrate solidarity with all victims of injustice, exploitation and oppression.

(b) **Commitment to equity**: students have a commitment to principles of equity as the basis upon which relationships between individuals, groups and societies should be organised.

(c) **Equality of consideration**: students embrace the principle of equality of consideration.

(d) **Intergenerational equity**: students have a commitment to ensuring that present generations leave an environment at least as healthy, diverse and productive as the one they inherited.

5. TOLERANCE OF UNCERTAINTY

(a) **Provisionality**: students are prepared to tolerate provisionality in their lives and learning, recognising that there are no clear cut, easy or final answers to personal, environmental or social problems.

(b) **Risk taking**: students are prepared to risk challenge, discomfort and set backs in seeking to enrich their learning and in pursuit of personal growth.

(c) **Insecurity**: students approach periods of self-doubt, insecurity and seemingly insuperable challenge as carrying within them the potential for transformative learning and personal growth.

6. DISCERNMENT WITHIN RECEPTIVITY

(a) **Receptivity**: students show receptivity to different ideas and perspectives and a readiness to modify their views as and when appropriate.

(b) **Critical discernment**: students demonstrate a critical and discerning attitude towards opinions, perspectives and policies on animal, environmental and social issues.

7. INVOLVEMENT

(a) **Co-operation**: students acquire a readiness to co-operate with others in learning, problem solving, decision making and responding to ethical, environmental and social problems; they recognise the need for co-operation at community, provincial, national, regional and global levels in pursuance of justice and sustainability.

(b) **Active reflection**: students are sensitive to the need to reflect actively upon and, if necessary, change their personal lifestyle to help secure a sustainable, healthy and humane future.

(c) **Active involvement**: students are prepared to involve themselves actively in projects and initiatives to achieve social and political change towards a sustainable, healthy and humane future.

THE EARTHKIND CLASSROOM

Chapter 4

The Convivial Classroom

INTRODUCTION

Conviviality suggests celebration, joyfulness, playfulness, sharing; a sense of individual and collective well-being, of connectedness and togetherness, of feeling warm and secure in each other's company. In *Chapter 2*, these very characteristics were put forward as the hallmarks of the humane learning environment. Such an environment, it was argued, not only promotes altruism, generosity and kindness but also gives students the security to confront the challenge of animal rights and welfare issues in an open, honest and forthright manner. In this chapter a range of activities for promoting a convivial classroom atmosphere is offered.

The chapter is divided into three sections. The first, *Icebreakers and Mood Changers*, includes introductory name games; introductory activities allowing students to exchange personal information in non-threatening circumstances; loosening-up activities designed to raise energy levels, reduce personal anxiety and group tension and to change the pace and mood of the learning process; also random grouping activities. The second, *Valuing Ourselves and Others*, comprises activities designed to build individual self-esteem and

to realise the concomitant goal of affirming the group as a whole. The emphasis is upon developing in each class member a sense of personal worth and belief in their own potential and ability to contribute to the learning process in a unique way, genuineness, appreciation and respect for others. The third, *Working Together*, offers a range of co-operative group activities.

The division of the activities into discrete sections is, in the final analysis, artificial. The introductory activities are esteem building and call for co-operation; the affirmatory activities are, likewise, co-operative in form and will, inevitably, deepen students' knowledge and understanding of each other; the group co-operation activities will take further the process of affirming both individuals and the class as a whole. In the same way, most of the activities described in *Chapters 5 to 15* are co-operative in nature and likely to reinforce both individual and group esteem. The activities in this chapter should not be seen as simply prefatory to the 'real' work on humane issues. It is crucial that esteem building, group bonding and co-operative learning are kept in sight as ongoing features of the humane classroom.

ACTIVITIES
ICEBREAKERS AND MOOD CHANGERS

■ GESTURE NAME GAME

The group forms a circle. The facilitator, encouraging spontaneity and a lively pace, explains that each person in turn will give their forename and surname, accompanying each name with a particular gesture that goes with the rhythm of the word. Hence, Sue Martin might raise her left hand while saying 'Sue' and bend and unbend her knees on the two syllables of 'Martin'. The whole group repeats the name and gestures twice. It is a good idea to go around the circle more than once and return to the game if it becomes clear that names have not been remembered.

■ INITIALS GAME

Standing in a circle, each person thinks about the initials of their name and decides upon two positive qualities, based upon the initials, that describe themselves. Hence, Sue Martin might see herself as 'Sincere, Mature'. She begins the game by introducing herself ('I'm Sue Martin; Sincere and Mature'). The person to her left (e.g. Tony Brown) introduces himself and reintroduces Susan ('I'm Tony Brown, Tidy and Bright; this is Sue Martin, Sincere and Mature'). The next person introduces herself and re-introduces Tony and Susan. The next introduces himself and reintroduces the two students before him (i.e. dropping Susan). A good fun activity that gives students a chance to think about themselves and each other in an affirming way.

■ KATE THE KOALA

With all participants in a circle, the facilitator begins by introducing herself using her first name and the name of an animal with which she feels she can identify and which begins with the same sound as her own name, e.g. 'Hello, I'm Kate the Koala'. Going around the circle all participants likewise introduce themselves. The alliteration employed is an effective aid to memorising names. The activity can be used as a springboard for work on positive and negative perceptions of animals (see activities, pp.120-128, 274-278).

■ SELF PORTRAITS

Suitable for
Primary/secondary

Time needed
15 minutes

Resources
½A4 sheet of plain paper for each participant; crayons *or* felt tip pens *or* paints; a clear classroom space.

Procedure
Students are given five minutes in which to represent on the sheet of paper things they like doing. Drawing is encouraged, but words can be used as well. At the end of this time, each student pins her piece of paper to herself, or simply holds it in front of her, and begins to walk around the classroom, meeting and talking with other participants about the activities depicted on the paper. Students are encouraged to meet and share their interests with a number of participants during the time available.

Potential
A non-threatening introductory activity which allows personal information about hobbies, leisure pursuits and interests to emerge. Security is provided by allowing participants to have a graphic record of their favourite pursuits — and by sharing them on a one-to-one basis — rather than asking each student to tell the rest of the group. Participants can discover commonalities of interest; students who have minority interests have the opportunity to disclose and explain these. An interesting discussion point is the frequency with which animals appear in the illustrations (the activity can be followed up by *Special Animals*, p. 108). *Self Portraits* is an effective icebreaker for use with a group of students who do not know each other, or have only met each other in a 'work' capacity.

■ *MUSICAL MEETINGS*

Participants walk around briskly in a large clear space with music playing. When the music stops, each participant shakes hands with the nearest person and a mutual exchange of personal information takes place until the music restarts (15-20 seconds). The process is repeated but a new partner must be found each time. *Note:* because of the level of noise generated by pairs in lively discussion, a considerable volume of sound is needed to interrupt.

■ *GROUP INTRODUCTIONS*

Students form groups of six and then divide into pairs. Each person has three minutes to introduce herself to her partner; to say something about her background, to describe her personal interests and preoccupations and to identify the most important things classmates should know about her. The listener should prompt with questions, if necessary. Groups of six then reform. Group members have a maximum of two minutes to introduce their partner to the group (alternatively, they speak as though they are actually their partner using the first person form).

■ *PRU-EE*

Participants spread out in a large, clear space and close their eyes. The facilitator touches one person on the shoulder — she is now Pru-ee and remains silent and still. Other participants move gently around, trying to make physical contact with each other. When contact is made, one participant enquires 'Pru-ee?'; if the other also responds with 'Pru-ee?' they both move on. When a participant comes across Pru-ee (who, of course, does not respond to the question), she becomes part of Pru-ee by maintaining physical contact and remaining silent. Pru-ee grows and grows until everyone is joined up. Participants then open their eyes, usually to gasps of surprise!

■ *ANIMAL SYMPHONY*

Suitable for

Primary/lower secondary

Time needed

10 minutes

Resources

An open classroom

Procedure

Students each choose an animal that makes a distinctive sound. Calling out the name of the animal, they move around and form groups of the same animal or of animals of a similar genre (e.g. farm animals, big cats, reptiles). When this has been achieved to everybody's satisfaction, a conductor is chosen and the groups arrange themselves around the conductor as though they are instrumental sections of an orchestra. The conductor then leads the orchestra in an animal noise rendition of one or two popular tunes.

Potential

A quick, humorous activity that can be employed as an icebreaker or as a means of allowing the class to 'let off steam' between activities demanding serious consideration of humane issues. Alternatively, the activity can be used as a lighthearted introduction to work on animal communication.

■ *MENAGERIE*

Suitable for

Primary/secondary

Time needed

5 minutes

Resources

An open classroom space. Thirty slips of paper each carrying the name of a well-known wild, farm or pet animal possessing a distinctive sound. There should be no more than ten sets in all, i.e., the name of each animal should appear on at least three slips. A cardboard box or other container.

Procedure

Students dip into the cardboard box and take a slip of paper. Refraining from talking or showing their slip to others, they think about the sounds that the animal makes. At a given signal, they close their eyes and move about the room making only animal sounds. The object is to find all other animals of one's own kind. Students should keep making their sounds and moving around until they are sure that all the animals of each type are grouped together.

Potential

A noisy and amusing co-operative activity that serves as an icebreaker and as an enjoyable means of organising students into random groups for a further group activity.

Variation

Students with eyes open, undertake the activity by imitating the actions and movements of the animal in question but in silence.

Source

Adapted from an activity in Smith, S., and Tait, J., *Teaching for peace*, Victoria, Australia, Hodja, 1987. Variation: author.

■ *CO-OPERATIVE GURNING*

Participants stand in a circle. The facilitator pulls a funny face, turns to the person to her left who tries to imitate her face. As she, in turn, turns to her left, she alters the face in some particular before passing it on to the next person. Once the face has travelled some way around the circle, the facilitator starts another face travelling to the right and, later, another to the left. Sounds can be added to each face.

This activity generates a great deal of laughter and merriment. It is very useful for achieving a swift change of mood following a period of intense discussion around a controversial issue and for reaffirming group solidarity before proceeding to confront a new challenge.

As a staff development activity, it can also be used to promote reflection on the nature of change. To what extent are the intentions of innovators (e.g. curriculum reformers) refracted as they travel from person to person (e.g. teacher educator to teacher) away from source? How easy is it to cope with wave after wave of change and changes coming from different directions simultaneously? Once participants were attuned to the climate of merriment generated by the activity, did they find it easier to initiate change? What implications does the activity have for those wishing to foment change?

■ *THE SOURCE*

One student goes out of the room while the rest of the class decide who will be the 'source'. The student returns and stands in the middle of circle. Everybody in the circle copies what the 'source' does, e.g. blinks, shuffles, yawns, runs a hand through their hair. The student in the middle tries to identify the 'source' (who will be hard to find if her movements are sufficiently gentle and discrete).

■ *ZOOM*

Participants stand in a circle. The facilitator makes the sound of a sports car, 'Zoom', passing the sound on to the person on her left or right. The sound is passed quickly around the circle by each participant in turn. At an appropriate point, the facilitator introduces a second sound, 'Eeek!', which represents the squealing of brakes as the car stops and spins round — continuing in reverse direction around the circle. Any participant can then apply the brakes and send the car the other way. A third sound can be introduced: 'Whoosh!', which powers the car across a river to land at the opposite point of the circle, to continue travelling in the same direction around the circle.

This activity generates much laughter and enjoyment. Once the facilitator has introduced the sound and what they represent, the activity is controlled by the participants who have to make decisions as individuals which directly affect the direction of the group exercise — a common feature of participatory learning which here underlies a simple, but pleasurable group experience.

■ *RAINSTORM*

Participants stand in a fairly close circle. The facilitator (who could be a student) rubs her hands together and then makes eye contact with each participant in turn, who imitates and continues the action and sound until the facilitator makes renewed eye contact, thus initiating a new motion. The first action (the wind rustling the leaves) is followed by finger snapping (the first drops of rain), hands slapping thighs (steady rainfall) and feet- stamping (the storm's crescendo). The storm then dies down as the stages are followed in reverse order until all participants are still and quiet. Rainstorm is an excellent closing activity for a lesson or workshop session.

Variation

A less teacher-directed version can be achieved if participants stand front-to-back in a circle. Any participant can start the first motion, but should hold her hands up above shoulder level so that the participant behind her can see and copy. The second motion is performed likewise; the third can be done by each student slapping (gently!) the back of the participant in front of them, and the fourth (feet stamping) is accompanied by participants holding the shoulders of the person in front. The motions then continue in reverse order as above.

■ *GOING DOTTY*

Suitable for

Primary/secondary

Time needed

5 minutes

Resources

Small, self-adhesive coloured dots, in at least four colours, one for each participant. An open classroom space so that students can move about freely.

Procedure

Students form a circle, close their eyes and remain silent. Each participant has a coloured dot stuck on their forehead. The different colours should be spread amongst the class so that neighbouring students do not have the same colour, but there should be an approximately equal number of each colour.

Students then open their eyes and try to form groups of the same-coloured dots without speaking or pointing.

Potential

A simple exercise with a variety of possible uses. It establishes very quickly the need for co-operation among individuals in order to solve a group task; there is a degree of affirmation in bringing individuals together through a short, enjoyable problem-solving exercise; it heightens the importance of non-verbal communication. At a conceptual level, the exercise provides an illustration of interdependence; at a practical level, it can be used as an enjoyable way of organising students into random groups for a further group exercise.

■ PAIRED NUMBERS

Suitable for

Upper primary/secondary

Time needed

5 minutes

Resources

None, except a clear space.

Procedure

Participants stand in a circle and number themselves, starting at 1 and going around the circle until everyone has a number. (*Note:* if there is an odd number in the group, the last two participants share one number.) The facilitator mentally adds 1 to the total number in the group and then asks participants find a partner with whom their combined score will equal that number. For example, in a group of thirty students, the combined score for each pair will be 31.

Potential

A fun way to organise participants into pairs for further work, this activity also provides some practice in basic computation skills.

Extension

To create groups of four.
Once in pairs the lower number is subtracted from the higher number giving each pair a positive score; e.g. for participants numbered 1 and 30, their pair score is 29. Pairs then have to seek out other pairs with whom their combined score will equal the total number in the group; i.e. in a group of thirty, the pair with a score of 29 joins up with the pair whose score is 1.
(*Note*: if the total number of participants is not divisible by 4, one pair will be unable to find a matching pair.)

■ OTHER GROUPING ACTIVITIES

Counting Off

Students are counted off, each being given a number between, say, 1 and 4. All the 1s make a group, all the 2s and so on.

Adding

In a class of, say, 30, the students are numbered 1 to 30. Individuals are asked to pair with the number that makes 30.

Alphabetically

Students form into alphabetical groups according to their surname. The groups are to coalesce until the size of group required for the next activity is achieved.

Sources of short description activities:

Gesture Name Game, Initials Game, Musical Meetings, Pru-ee, Zoom and **Rainstorm**: Judson, S., ed., *A manual on non-violence and children.*
Others: author

VALUING OURSELVES AND OTHERS

■ *AFFIRMATION SHEETS*

A sheet carrying the name of a particular student is placed on the classroom bulletin board. It is left there for a few days and other students are encouraged to write positive statements concerning the featured student. When the sheet is taken down it is given to the student. The procedure is repeated until all students have had the chance to be featured.

■ *THIS IS MY LIFE*

Each month space is allocated on the bulletin board or classroom wall for up to four students to present their life story through a brief autobiography or time line, photographs and relevant memorabilia. A blank sheet can be left for other students to pose questions (to be answered at a special class session) or to write affirming statements. This activity can be effectively linked with *Affirmation Sheets* (above).

■ *BEST QUALITIES*

The class is divided into equal sized groups. Each student has a sheet pinned to her back. At the top of the sheet is written: 'Some of my best qualities are ...'. Students are asked to write positive statements about each member of the group on the small slips of paper provided, taking the six words at the top of the sheet as the beginning of their statement. Slips are taped to the appropriate student's sheet. The sheets are unpinned and read silently. If the student wishes, she can write her name at the bottom of the sheet and have it displayed on the classroom wall.

■ *HIDDEN QUALITIES BILLBOARD*

Students form groups of three or four. Working on their own, group members list between four and six qualities they see themselves as possessing but of which others seem unaware. Lists are shared. The group's task is to light upon an effective way of advertising one or more of each person's hidden qualities. Working co-operatively, advertisements for each person are designed and drawn up for display on the class *Hidden Qualities* billboard. Alternative ways to portray the hidden qualities are through dramatic sketches, staged television commercials, puppetry and class interviews.

■ *STRENGTH BOMBARDMENT*

Students break into groups of five of six. Focusing on one person at a time, each group bombards her with all the strengths and qualities they can see in her. Members of the group take it in turns to act as recorder, listing what is said and handing the list to the person when the bombardment is finished. Only positive qualities are to be contributed and 'put-downs' avoided. Nobody's list should be more than, or less than, fifteen items. After everybody's strengths have been bombarded, groups are asked to identify the different types of strengths that emerged from the activity. Groups report back on their findings. Plenary discussion follows. As a potentially powerful reinforcer of this activity, students can be encouraged to ask their parents to similarly bombard the strengths they see in them

■ *ALTERNATIVE NICKNAMES*

Nicknames often do little to bolster (and often undermine) self- esteem. This activity is designed to alert students to the effect of a nickname on the person concerned and to identify a preferred alternative. Working in groups of six, students one by one share their thoughts on their nickname(s). The group then brainstorms (see p.205) the qualities, strengths and talents of each group member. Out of the brainstorming, the group lights upon two or three alternative nicknames based on each person's positive aspects. The person in question embraces one of the names, opts for her old nickname or decides that she is happiest with no nickname at all. Whole group reporting back follows.

■ *AFFIRMATION PAPER CHAINS*

A stock of 20cm x 3cm assorted coloured strips and a pot of paste are kept in a designated place. Each time a student witnesses someone making a positive comment about, or acting in a caring way towards another student, she writes the name of the person and a description of the comment or action on one of the strips of paper. The slip is added to the *Affirmation Paper Chain* hung from the classroom walls. From time to time, all the links in the chain are read out and discussed, and a new chain started. Each section of the chain must be kept at a height that students can reach and read. Chain entries can be used as a basis for special awards and certificates (see p. 70).

■ FRIENDLY BOX

Students are informed that for a whole week they are going to keep track of all friendly actions they do for one another. The week-long activity begins with two sharing circles (see p.67). In the first circle, students say what friendliness means to them; in the second, they describe an occasion when somebody was friendly to them. They are then introduced to the *Friendly Box,* a box with a posting slot on top, at the side of which is a pile of slips of paper. It is explained that whenever a student experiences an act of friendliness, they are to complete a slip giving the person's name and describing the friendly action. At the end of each day, the slips are removed from the box and read aloud. A trickle of slips on Monday may become a deluge by Friday.

■ FRIENDLY TREE

A large paper cut-out of a tree with lots of branches is affixed to the wall. A number of cards are 'hung' from the branches on short pieces of thread; on each card is printed a friendly act, e.g. 'talk to someone who you don't often talk to', 'help someone out with her work', 'write/draw someone a friendly note/picture', 'share something with a classmate', etc. At the beginning of each day, a group of students select a card each and are encouraged to carry out the friendly act at some time during the day. The cards are put back on the tree at the end of the day in readiness for the next.

■ KINDNESS BLOSSOMS

The trunk and branches of a tree are painted on a large sheet of paper by the students. Underneath the trunk the words, *The Kindness Tree*, are printed. The sheet is hung from the classroom wall. Duplicate tree blossoms are made from coloured paper. Each time an act of kindness to another student or to an animal is observed or reported, the teacher writes details of the act on a blossom and

attaches it to the tree (e.g. 'Greg shared his crayons with Jenny'; 'John shampooed and groomed his dog, Jasper'). From time to time, the need for kindness to both other humans and animals is discussed.

■ SILHOUETTES

Working in small groups students take turns to trace each other's silhouette. This can be done either by drawing around the person as she lies on, or stands against, a large piece of paper, or by projecting her silhouette onto a piece of paper as she stands in front of an overhead projector. Silhouettes are then cut out and mounted on a piece of paper of contrasting colour upon which the name of the student is written. One option is for all the silhouettes to be stuck on the classroom walls and for students to go around writing affirming comments on each silhouette save their own. Another is for one silhouette to be featured each day and affirming comments to be written up or attached. Special awards and certificates (see p.70) can be pasted onto silhouettes. A variation on *Silhouettes* is called *On My Mind.* Students pair up and draw profiles of each other's heads. Then, after spending time interviewing each other about things on their minds (anxieties, concerns, hopes, preoccupations), they create a collage of personal thoughts around each profile. When students have had the opportunity to review each others' displayed head profiles and thoughts collage, the class discusses the degree of overlap and commonality that can be discerned.

■ ROUND ROBIN INTERVIEW

Participants roam around the room for 10-15 minutes interviewing each other to find out personal information such as likes and dislikes, pets, best attributes and favourite television programmes. Students can write notes during each interview. When the group comes together one person comes to the front and gives her name. Other students who have met her then venture any information they have, one comment per student, so that a full description of her character and interests is built up. Another student then comes to the front and the process is repeated until everyone has been introduced.

■ CIRCLE TIME

Sharing circles can be a mainstay of the affirmatory classroom. The idea is very simple. Students stand in a circle so that everybody can see each other. The facilitator (or a student) introduces the circle theme. Then everybody has a chance to contribute thoughts or feelings as the right to speak passes from one person to the next. The class can decide to go round the circle more than once. Circle time can be used to affirm the qualities of each class member or the group:

- ❑ I am glad to be me because...
- ❑ A success I had recently is...
- ❑ I feel proud that...
- ❑ I feel happy to be in this group because...
- ❑ (Name of person to left), you remind me of a (name of an animal, flower, tree) because...
- ❑ (Name of person to left), I've appreciated you lately because ...
- ❑ (Name of person to left), I'd like to have your (description of positive quality)

It can also be used to share news, to develop mutual awareness through the expression of feelings ('I feel sad when...'; 'I feel best when people...'), to brainstorm ideas (see p.205), to promote empathy with people and animals using glove puppets (see p. 159), to resolve conflicts and/or grievances. As a conflict/grievance resolution exercise, the students involved can be given two minutes each of uninterrupted time to present their side, then a further minute to clarify any points. After the group has been given two minutes' quiet time for reflection, the sharing circle begins with students giving their opinions on the issue on the first round and their suggestions for resolution on the second. Circle time can also be used after a particularly successful or powerful activity for a sharing of feelings, or reflections on what has been learnt or of appreciation of what others contributed to the activity. In every case the right to 'pass' should be respected by the facilitator although the consequences of not contributing when the object of a sharing circle is to affirm others should be discussed by the group.

■ FEELINGS CARD GAME

Working in pairs or in groups of three of four, students take a set of ten to twenty *Feeling Cards* from an envelope. The cards, each carrying a single feeling word (e.g. angry, excited, shy, hurt, lonely, scared, upset), are shuffled and placed face down on the table. A student picks up the top card and recounts an experience or occasion when they had that feeling. Other group members then briefly recall a time when they experienced similar feelings. Group members take it in turns to pick up, and speak to, a card, the process continuing until the teacher calls a halt. Another approach to this activity is to have an unfinished sentence on each card, e.g. 'I felt very upset when...', 'When I make a mistake, I...', 'If I could develop one aspect of my personality, it would be...'.

■ SHARED FEELINGS

A useful activity for helping students understand that many of their more uncomfortable feelings and experiences are not purely personal but are shared by others. Students form groups of five or six. A statement is written up by the teacher, for example:

- ❑ I never do anything right. What's the use of trying?
- ❑ I feel so alone. Without friends.
- ❑ Oh, what a mess I've made of things. It's too embarrassing.
- ❑ I was really excited about what had happened but nobody wanted to know.
- ❑ I wish I'd thought before I opened my mouth.
- ❑ I felt really stupid. I wish the Earth had swallowed me up.

Individuals are given two minutes to think of occasions when they have experienced the feelings described in the statement. Then, one by one, they recount those occasions to the group (questions can be asked). The group then discusses the common elements in their experiences.

■ *DEVELOPING EMPATHY THROUGH STORY TELLING*

Suitable for

Primary/secondary

Time needed

20 minutes per session following an initial 60-minute symbol production and story preparation session.

Resources

Paper, felt pens, scissors

Procedure

In the first session students devise their own personal logo, symbol or totem. A large version is posted on the classroom wall and a number of smaller versions made. Students also prepare to tell a story about a person or event that changed and/or significantly influenced their life and/or engendered strong emotion in them personally. A random sequence of storytelling is determined for future sessions with the teacher included as one of the storytellers (prior to the first storytelling session, the teacher prepares her own symbol copies and story).

At each subsequent session, the storyteller of the day places a pile of her symbols in the circle as she begins her story. If a listener identifies with an aspect of the story, she quietly retrieves one of the storyteller's symbols (some may want to hear all the story before they can connect with it). When the story is finished, those with symbols describe the connections they made with what has been told. At the end of the session, they stick the symbol they have acquired on their own large version symbol on the classroom wall.

Potential

This ongoing activity creates empathy between members of the class. The tangible acknowledgement of connection helps all the group recognise commonalities of life experiences and emotions. As students stick more and more small symbols to their own large-version symbol, they will realise how much they have in common with other members of the class. The storytelling is, thus, an esteem-building and bonding and, hence, empowering process.

Source

An activity devised by four Ontario teachers: Veronica Church, Maple Grove School, Lanark; Lois Kuebler, Moira Secondary School, Belleville; John Martyn, Peterborough Victoria, Northumberland & Newcastle RCSS Board; Jim Rule, London School Board.

■ *RAINBOW*

Each student receives a sheet with six boxes down the left-hand side. Working on their own, they colour in each box with one of the colours of a rainbow (i.e. red, orange, yellow, green, blue, violet). Against each box they write a statement about themselves beginning 'colour me (name of colour) when ...'; for instance, 'colour me violet when a friend irritates me'. *Circle Time* (see p.67) is then called and students take turns to share their 'red' statements before moving on to their 'orange', 'yellow' and other statements (the right to 'pass' is, of course, respected). A useful sharing activity that helps students realise that events and emotions that may appear unique to them are experienced and felt by many, if not most, people. As such, it can help bond a group together.

■ *INNER WARMTH*

Working on their own, students are asked to write down as many things as they can think of that make them feel warm inside. Their ideas should be spread all over their sheet of paper. They are asked to:

❏ draw a rectangle around every item that requires money in order to experience it;

❏ draw a triangle around every item that does not involve the company of others;

❏ draw a circle around every item that involves the company of, and interaction or sharing with, others.

It is pointed out that some items might require the drawing of more than one shape. Groups of six are formed and students asked to share and discuss their findings. What shape was used most often? By what shape(s) do items that students treasure the most tend to be enclosed? What does this suggest about us individually and us as human beings? Did any items fit neither a rectangle, a triangle or a circle? Why? Has anything been learnt that will make the group rethink and adjust how they relate to others? Plenary discussion follows. A useful activity for promoting self and group esteem, an appreciation of what others value, empathy and sensitivity towards other people.

■ *INEXPERIENCE*

Students in groups are asked to think of real experiences that they have never had which they imagine nearly everyone else has had. They write out these experiences on slips of paper which are collected up and stuck onto a large sheet, with spaces in between each slip. Students then visit each group's sheet and affix sticky dots around the description of any experience which they too have not shared. Discussion that follows might focus on differences and similarities in experience, feelings about inexperience and invited descriptions of relatively uncommon experiences.

■ *KNEE SHAKERS*

The teacher introduces the activity by talking about fear; different kinds of fear and different things that cause fear. She should be self-disclosing about her own fears. Students are then asked to list on a sheet of paper ten things that make their knees shake most and to explain why that is the case. In an open classroom space, students move around and share their list with individual after individual. If somebody shares a fear they have written down, they write the person's forename against that item. In the discussion that follows, students give feedback on fears they found they had in common with other class members; also, they report on fears that others had written down which they share but had forgotten to include in their own list. An excellent activity for promoting identification with the human feelings expressed by others. The acknowledgement of common emotions and experiences can be a crucial element in building a well-affirmed group. Should fears of particular animals surface during the activity, the teacher may judge it appropriate to move on to activities such as *Animal Adjectives* (p.121), *Animal Affirmation* (p.120) and *Big Bad Wolves?* (p.125).

■ *WANTED POSTERS*

Working in pairs, students help each other complete a *Wanted!* sheet (see *Fig. 1*). They weigh and measure each other, sketch each other's face and paste the sketches to the poster; they discuss each other's qualities and talents (seeking the views of other students if necessary). The work complete, the class discusses the different messages that the word 'wanted' can convey. On parents' evening, the name and picture of each student can be masked and each parent asked to identify her or his child's poster!

Fig. 1

WANTED!
Name............................
Height........................
Weight.........................
Hair.............................
Eyes............................
Likes to..
....
Can often be found....................................
....
Special Qualities and Talents
....

■ *CONNECTING RAINBOWS*

The rainbow has international significance as a symbol of harmony and peace. *Connecting Rainbows* memos (see *Fig. 2*) are made available in the classroom for students to thank a classmate who has contributed to their sense of well-being and self-esteem through some act of kindness and consideration or through a few meaningful or well-chosen words. They can also be written to the class as a whole. At the outset, the teacher should model the use of the memos as an encouragement to the students. She can, of course, continue to send (and receive) messages.

■ *SPECIAL AWARDS AND CERTIFICATES*

A variety of blank awards and certificate cards are made available in the classroom; for example, the 'helping hand' award, the 'caring for others', the 'special congratulations' and the 'kindness to animals' (see *Fig. 3*) certificates, covering a variety of occasions and events in home, community and school life. These cards are filled in with appropriate words by the teacher and students and are presented to the deserving class member in recognition of her as a person and of her qualities and achievements. Awards should not be confined to the end-of-year recognition of an élite: *all* students need to receive special congratulations throughout the year.

To:

From:

You connect my
rainbow when

Fig. 2

Fig. 3

KINDNESS TO ANIMAL CERTIFICATE

AWARDED TO: _____

FOR: _____
_____
_____

Signed: _____

Date: _____

P

■ *FAVOURITE ANIMAL*

Suitable for

Secondary

Time needed

30 minutes

Resources

Sheet of paper and pen/pencil for each student

Procedure

Working individually and without discussion, students are asked to jot down the name of their favourite animal and, after only brief reflection, the three qualities that most give it its character. They are then asked to choose a second favourite animal and to note down its three most significant qualities. The process is repeated for a third favourite animal. *It is important the students are given a new instruction each time rather than being told at the outset to choose three animals and their three most significant qualities; also, that they are given only a short time for reflection about the three animals' qualities.* Students are then asked to write a number '1' against the animal with the qualities they would most wish to possess themselves, number '2' against the animal whose qualities best represent how they actually see themselves and number '3' against the animal whose qualities most closely represent how they feel others actually perceive them. At the bottom of the page they write brief notes on why they think other people generally fail to recognise certain of their qualities and on what they, and others around them, might do to help them become the 'animal' they would most like to be.

Students then choose a partner. Prior to discussion, each partner uses the back of her sheet to write down the name of the animal which, in their view, best sums up their partner. They also list its three most significant qualities.

Partners then share their work, particularly exploring the degree to which their wished-for self, perceived self and view of others' perception of self overlap or fail to overlap, why that might be and the degree of consensus/mismatch between how they see themselves and how their partner perceives them. When the facilitator judges the moment to be ripe, whole group discussion can follow.

Potential

A revealing and potentially very emotional activity that should only be attempted when levels of individual self-esteem and group security are reasonably high. It is typically, but not necessarily, the case that the qualities of the first choice of animal represent how individuals feel they would like to be, that the second choice represents how they in fact see themselves and that the third choice represents how they think others see them. A plenary session can begin by exploring whether this was in fact the case and, if the facilitator deems it appropriate, can continue with a sharing of student reactions to the animal/qualities chosen by their partner. To what extent did the choice come as a surprise? With what animal — '1', '2' or '3' — did the partner's choice accord most closely? Is the partner's perception likely to prompt any reappraisal of self-image or reprioritisation of most valued qualities? To what extent do group members feel misunderstood? How might this have come about? What could group members do, individually and collectively, to help each other realise their wished-for self?

Sources of short description activities

Affirmation Sheets, Best Qualities, Hidden Qualities Billboard, Rainbow, Inner Warmth, Knee Shakers and **Connecting Rainbows**: Stanish, B., *Connecting rainbows*; **Strength Bombardment**: Canfield, J., & Wells, H.C., *100 ways to enhance self-concept in the classroom*; **This is My Life** and **Shared Feelings**: Cedoline, A.J., *The effect of affect*; **Friendly Box, Friendly Tree, Kindness Blossoms, Silhouettes** and **Wanted Posters**: Borba, M. & C., *Self-esteem: a classroom affair*; **Affirmation Paper Chains** and **Special Awards and Certificates**: Borba, M., and C., *Self-esteem. A classroom affair. Vol. 2.* Others: author.

WORKING TOGETHER

■ *ANIMAL SOUNDS*

The group sits in a circle in a darkened room with their eyes closed. Going around the circle from the facilitator's left, they select and mimic an animal sound of their choice (a sound cannot be chosen twice). The facilitator, who has a large ball, makes her sound and then the sound of the animal to which she intends to roll the ball. The 'animal' in question replies and the facilitator rolls the ball in her direction. If the roll is accurate and the 'animal' receives the ball, she responds with her sound and the 'animals' applaud the success by making all their sounds in unison (a useful reminder of all the 'animals' present). If another 'animal' receives the ball, she makes her sound but there is no chorus of congratulation. The receiver then makes the sound of another 'animal'; that 'animal' replies and the process continues.

■ *CO-OPERATIVE JIGSAWS*

Suitable for

Lower primary

Time needed

30 minutes

Resources

Two copies each of five identically sized black and white photographs (approx. 25cms x 20cms) on a humane or animal theme; one copy of each photograph is divided into twelve pieces — the same twelve shapes being used to divide each photograph (see *Fig. 4*). The second copies are used as guides. The pieces are divided amongst five envelopes — eight of the pieces belonging to one photograph plus one piece each from the other photographs; thus the contents of each envelope will form the rectangular shape of the photograph but four of these pieces will not belong to the photograph. Five desks or tables; an area to get together for discussion before and after the activity.

Procedure

The five envelopes containing the pieces (mixed as suggested in *Fig. 5*) are placed one per table. The five guide photographs are retained. The

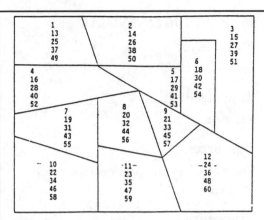

Suggested way of dividing up the photographs.
Numbering system for five photographs: I to 12, 13 to 24, 25 to 36, 37 to 48, 49 to 60.

Fig. 4

students gather together to discuss the five guide photographs (e.g. Who and/or what is in each photograph? What are they doing? What similarities and differences are there between the subjects of the photographs and themselves? What feelings do the photographs stir?). The students are informed that they are going to do some jigsaws in groups. It is emphasised that the object of the activity is for the class to complete five jigsaws and that the activity is not complete until all five are finished.

Fig 5

A	1	2	51	4	41	6	31	8	9	10	11	24
B	13	14	3	16	53	18	43	20	21	22	23	36
C	25	26	15	28	5	30	55	32	33	34	35	48
D	37	38	27	40	17	42	7	44	45	46	47	60
E	49	50	39	52	29	54	19	56	57	58	59	12

Suggested distribution of numbered pieces in the five envelopes.

The students now split into five groups by choosing their own partners or through a random grouping activity (see p.64). Each group takes a guide photograph and goes to one of the desks. The guide photograph may or may not be the one for which they find they have most parts in the envelope. It is up to the class to co-operate and sort things out. They are to find their own solution. The teacher, however, encourages movement between tables and other forms of co-operation. If any group completes a jigsaw, it is again emphasised that the object is to complete five jigsaws.

When all jigsaws are complete, the students are brought together to further discuss the content of photographs and also to discuss any points with respect to co-operation, conflict, communication and negotiation raised by the activity.

Potential

This activity focuses on the skills and attitudes necessary for effective co-operation whilst affording the opportunity to discuss some humane/animal issues. Skills practised include discussion, listening, negotiation, conflict avoidance/resolution and interpreting photographic data. As such this activity can be used prior to some of the activities described in *Chapter 12*.

Variation

With older students the set of photographs can be used without the aid of guide photographs.

> *As the activity progressed, I noticed one child hide a piece in his hand after trying it in the correct position. He held onto this piece until after the completion of two of the other jigsaws before placing it back into the appropriate jigsaw. By then he must have realised that I was giving no acclaim either to individuals or groups for completing jigsaws but simply turning their attention to others still engaged in the task.*
>
> — Newcastle infant teacher

Source

Allan Simpson, West Walker Primary School, Newcastle upon Tyne

■ *CO-OPERATIVE LOOPS*

Suitable for

Lower primary

Time needed

20 minutes

Resources

Drawing paper; pencils or black crayons; coloured pencils or crayons

Procedure

Each student is given a piece of paper and the class is split into two groups, e.g. gooseberries and strawberries. One group starts to draw with a pencil from the top left corner of the paper to the bottom right corner making five loops as they draw. The second group starts at the bottom left corner and ends at the top right, again making five loops.

Each loop has then to be coloured in with a different colour. However, each student can only use two colours. They must, therefore, get help from each other to complete the colouring.

When all have finished their colouring the students are asked to join their lines together into one continuous line, perhaps by standing in a circle holding their pieces of paper if there is an even number in the class.

Potential

A useful activity for promoting co-operative attitudes and skills; also for practising communication and problem-solving skills.

Source

Alan Simpson, West Walker Primary School, Newcastle upon Tyne

> *When it came to joining together children first tried joining up with their friends. This, of course, only worked when friends happened to be in the other group. They quickly understood that in order to join up their lines they needed to alternate 'gooseberries' and 'strawberries'.*
>
> — Newcastle infant teacher

■ *CO-OPERATIVE SQUIGGLES*

Students form pairs. With their eyes firmly closed, they put their pencils in the middle of a large piece of paper then move the pencils around (never taking them off the paper) until they think all areas of the paper have been covered by squiggles. Opening their eyes, pairs must agree upon a picture they can make out of the squiggles. The pictures are drawn and finished products shared.

■ *THREE-PERSON DRAWING*

Seated in threes around tables, students are asked to take turns in drawing a group picture. They are not to decide on a subject beforehand and are to refrain from talking while they work. A maximum length of time is given for each turn (5-10 seconds) but students are at liberty to draw lines of any shape or size. It is emphasised that they should try to transmit their ideas and intentions to each other through what they draw. Somebody in the group acts as timekeeper at all times. Some ten to fifteen minutes should be allowed for the activity. In the debriefing, groups should be asked to say whether the picture was completed to their satisfaction and, if not, why not. Did anybody feel frustrated? Did anybody feel ideas were being forced upon them? Did anybody become angry because their drawn signals were misunderstood or their ideas not followed? What lessons can be drawn from the activity about what makes effective group co-operation?

■ *TEAR-A-DACTYL*

Students form groups of four. Each group is given a large piece of newspaper and asked to tear out the shape of an animal. Before starting, the group is to agree on the choice of animal. Each person has one tear at the newspaper before passing it on. After attempting the activity a second time using non-verbal communication during the tearing stage, groups are asked to repeat the task a third time without first agreeing on an animal and without talking. Groups then report back on their experiences, the emotions engendered by the activity and how they handled those emotions.

■ *RIVER CROSSING*

Suitable for

Lower primary

Time needed

25 minutes

Resources

Large open space; P.E. mats in a long line; a card per student showing either feet or hands crossed out.

Procedure

Students sit in a group and each is given a card. It is explained that the long line of mats is a river that everyone has to cross. Attention is drawn to the cards. If feet are crossed out, students are not permitted to put their feet into the water. If hands are crossed out, they cannot put their hands in the water. The teacher asks for suggestions on how to get everyone across. Students are selected to try them out. When it is established that they need to be helped or to help others if everyone is to cross, the class is given time to work on a solution. They are reminded that success is only achieved when everybody is safely across the river.

Potential

An activity which develops co-operation, self-esteem and problem solving skills. The class is affirmed by success. Questions to be asked include: How did you get across? How did you feel waiting for help? Did you help anyone? How did you feel once over the river?

Source

Jean Winterburn, West Walker Primary School, Newcastle upon Tyne

River Crossing

A most enjoyable activity with high levels of co-operation and problem-solving in evidence. Many solutions were offered such as wheelbarrows, piggybacks and various ways of carrying. We found some children were quite uninhibited about offering help to others and crossed the river many times, whilst some wanted to be independent.

— Newcastle infant teacher

■ *HUMAN JIGSAW*

Suitable for

Lower primary

Time needed

15-20 minutes

Resources

A clear area, preferably carpeted

Procedure

The rules of the activity are first explained. A chain is to be formed by joining one hand to the person before. As students join the chain they can either sit, stand, kneel or lie down but must avoid doing the same as the person with whom they are joining hands. When the chain is formed, students are urged to look and take notice of where they are in the chain or human jigsaw and asked to drop hands, walk around the room and return to make the same formation.

It is probably best to do this activity twice as the first time the students may be too concerned with the rules to obtain the full benefit from the activity.

Potential

An activity that will help to reduce the inhibitions students have about physical contact and that will increase awareness of others. It also emphasises the need for observation and memory as well as co-operation.

Variations

1. The activity can be attempted with small groups.

2. As students become more confident and secure, different types of body contact can be encouraged.

3. The activity can be attempted with blindfolds.

4. The activity can be attempted on a further occasion with the re-forming of the jigsaw not taking place until a few hours have elapsed.

Source

Alan Simpson, West Walter Primary School, Newcastle upon Tyne.

■ *CO-OPERATIVE BALLOONS*

Suitable for

Lower primary

Time needed

20-30 minutes

Resources

Four large baskets or boxes; inflated balloons, one per two children; thin card strips, 3cms x 65cms, one per child; large clear area, preferably a hall; even number of participants needed (the teacher can make up the numbers).

Procedure

A large basket is placed in each corner of the room. Students sit in circle formation with the inflated balloons placed in the centre. Each student is given a card strip and told that they can only hold their strip at one end. They are then told that the problem is to pick up the balloons using the strips and take them to the boxes. The activity commences. With younger children, the teacher can ask for suggestions. Each suggestion is tried. If no solution is forthcoming the teacher can draw attention to the number of balloons, the number of children and the fact that they can hold the end of each other's card strip.

> *The first suggestions were all solutions involving individuals, either of the flicking or wafting variety. After a time the children were directed to think about the number of balloons and people. One child then got the idea that someone could get hold of the other end of the strip. It was agreed that this was alright. They tried scooping the balloon and keeping it in the air but this was not successful. Then two tried making a 'cradle' but the balloon floated off. Another child then suggested using the two strips in a pincer-like grip. This worked. Everyone joined in to place the balloons in the baskets. This was found to be fun.*
>
> — Newcastle infant teacher

Potential

Allows for the solution of a problem by active co-operation. The activity also gives scope for imagination, listening to others, seeing number relationships and practicing co-ordination. Suggested lines of questioning in the debriefing might include: What did you think when first faced with the problem? How did you arrive at a solution? Can you think of any similar problems which might have similar solutions?

Source

Alan Simpson, West Walker Primary School, Newcastle upon Tyne

■ *NAME THE PET*

Students form groups of six and sit in a circle. Each student has paper and a pencil. Six pictures of pets (e.g. a kitten, a puppy, a baby rabbit, a budgerigar, a hamster, a guinea pig) are passed around the circle. Without talking, students write down their first, second and third choice of name for each pet. Then, taking the pets one by one, they share and explain their name choices. The sharing completed, their group's task is to reach consensus on the name of the pet. Having decided upon a name for each pet, they are asked to review their overall choice. If anybody in the group remains dissatisfied, their task is to try to allay that dissatisfaction, if at all possible, by renegotiating their 'package' of choices. This is an activity giving practice in co-operative group decision making. In reporting back and discussion, students should be asked to reflect upon the decision-making process as well as announcing the names chosen.

■ *THE PEANUT GAME*

Students are asked to form pairs and to sit at different sides of a table so they can clasp hands for arm wrestling. The teacher holds up a large bag of peanuts in their shells and tells the class that each time their partner's hand touches the table they will win a peanut until the bag is empty. When the signal to begin is given some pairs will struggle to force each other's arm down. Others will realise that a co-operative approach, in which each in turn allows the other to press their arm to the table, will enable the pair to accumulate quickly a high score. The debriefing should focus on the relative merits of the competitive and co-operative approaches. The dilemma should also be posed of how the peanuts might best be distributed. Are those with the largest totals (gained through co-operation) entirely happy with an uneven distribution of peanuts?

■ *WHAT'S YOUR SMELL?*

Suitable for

Primary/secondary

Time needed

10 minutes

Resources

Five bottles of different aromatherapy oils (e.g. rose, citron, lavender, mango, peppermint); an open space.

Procedure

Students stand silently in a circle with their eyes closed, holding out their hands. A droplet of one of the oils is placed in everyone's palm so that the five oils are distributed randomly yet equally around the circle (it helps the distribution of the

> *Get down on all fours and look around; the view is more limited than when you stand. That's why smell is important to a four-legged animal. An animal on its hind legs can see farther than it can smell. Erect animals with good eyesight can detect approaching danger as well as opportunities farther away. Therefore a more sophisticated long-distance visual system, building on the improved sight acquired earlier in the treetops, probably evolved in human beings along with upright posture.*
>
> — Robert Ornstein & Paul Ehrlich[1]

oils if students grip their hands together as a signal when they have been given some oil). With eyes still closed, students then rub the oil between their hands and take in its smell. Opening their eyes, but still avoiding speaking, they try to form groups according to shared smell.

Potential

This activity, sometimes called *Co-operative Sniffs*, provides a memorable co-operative learning and non-verbal communication experience. A lot of laughter — and some unease — can result from the sole reliance on the sense of smell. These reactions can be used to trigger class discussion. How did it feel having to smell each others' palms? Why the laughter? Why did some students feel uneasy? How important is smell to human beings relative to other senses? To which animals does smell matter most? Why? What would it do to the way we see the world, what benefits and disbenefits would there be, if smell was a human being's most highly developed sense?

> *Excellent. Students love this kind of activity. A must for all 'senses' topics, it will foster class cohesiveness.*
>
> - Kent secondary teacher.

Extension

Having formed groups, students are taken to a large indoor room where particular areas, at some distance from each other, have been scent marked using the five oils. Each group's task is to find its own territory. This offers students an experiential introduction to the concept of animal territoriality.

Source

Extension devised by Merebeth Switzer of Learning Alternatives, Portland, Ontario, Canada.

Sources for short description activities

Co-operative Jigsaws, Co-operative Loops, River Crossing, Human Jigsaw and **Co-operative Balloons**: Baker, T., *et. al.*, *Co-operating for a change*; **Co-operative Squiggles** and **Tear-a-Dactyl**: Church, A., *et. al.*, *Co-operation in the classroom*; **Three-Person Drawing**: Stanish, B., *Connecting rainbows*; **Animal Sounds**: Judson, S., ed., *A manual on non-violence and children*; **Name the Pet**: Borba, M., & C., *Self-esteem. A classroom affair. Vol. 2*. Others: author.

References

1. Ornstein, R., & Ehrlich, P., *New world. New mind*, Methuen, 1989, 34.

NOTE: The full reference for the texts listed on pp.64, 71 and above is given in the *Humane education and related fields* section of the *Select Bibliography* (pp.407-8).

Chapter 5

The Web of Life

1.8 M	30M

INTRODUCTION

Scientists have described and named about 1.8 million species of plant and animal. In the last ten years they have come to realise that there are vast numbers of species as yet unrecorded. Estimates vary, but an oft-quoted guess is 30 million species in all. This is likely to err on the conservative side. An environmental scientist working for the British government recently suggested the figure might be as high as 80 million whilst another expert calculated that there might be another 10 million undiscovered species dwelling in the deep ooze on the world's ocean beds. A recent study estimated that the world's coral reefs teem with some 423,000 species, of which 90 per cent are unknown[1]. None of these estimates of life on Earth include the single-celled micro-organisms — the algae, bacteria and fungi — which would be impossible to count.

Species are now being lost at a frightening rate. It has been estimated that the planet is currently losing about 140 species a day as a result of human activity. Forecasts suggest that 10 per cent of species may have vanished by 2000, a third by 2020 and that, by 2050, half of the species alive today will have been lost forever. They will have gone before we knew they were there.

Biodiversity is the term used to describe the variety of living organisms on Earth and the variety of ecological communities they inhabit. The richest habitat of all is the tropical rainforest. Described by ecologists as 'climax ecosystems', most of the undiscovered plant and animal species live in the forests. There are excellent reasons for their richness and diversity. Rainfall and climate are constant and there are no seasons; the main environmental fluctuation with which organisms have to cope is between night and day. The enormous productivity of the rainforests allows for fine specialisation so that many tree species are unique to tiny geographical areas. Each species has its own particular train of plants and creatures that rely upon it and upon which it relies. Ecological communities within the forests are, thus, very varied and each unimaginably rich in plant, insect and animal life. It is said that there may be as many ant species in a single bush in Peru as

Opposite: pristine rainforest and destroyed rainforest (Friends of the Earth)

in the whole of the British Isles; that 125 acres of rainforest in peninsular Malaysia are home to more species of tree than the whole of North America[2]. An English forest may have no more than a dozen tree species whilst an hectare of tropical forest may have over two hundred[3].

The rainforests are now being cleared at an astonishing rate. Rainforests once covered an area twice the size of the United States — about 4 billion acres. Half of that area is now gone. The planet is currently losing an area of rainforest half the size of Finland each year; the size of a football field each second. At the present rate of destruction, a third of the rainforests now remaining will have gone by 2030. There are four immediate causes of rainforest destruction: logging, agriculture, cattle ranching and mineral extraction. Underpinning these causes is economic poverty. Developing countries, lying in the rainforest zones, find themselves caught in a world trading system that discriminates against the raw materials producer. They are also burdened with debt repayments to international banks for loans negotiated as part of earlier efforts to achieve economic growth. To pay off their debts, the governments of these countries have turned to the rainforests; allowing forests to be cleared for cattle ranching and large-scale agricultural projects growing 'cash' crops such as bananas, coffee and cotton, and permitting poor farmers to move into virgin rainforest to fend off calls for 'land reform' (i.e. changes in land ownership away from rich, and in favour of poor, landowners). Because rainforest soil is of intrinsically poor quality — the forests only exist because of their special survival system (see *document 13*) — agriculture of any form is only possible for five to seven years before the land turns to desert. The farmers and ranchers must then cut down new tracts of virgin forest.

Mineral extraction, to feed the industrial processes of the rich world, is equally damaging. The new machinery employed allows for opencast mining exposing the mineral reserves below the surface. Besides destroying the surface vegetation, vast amounts of silt and mineral pollution are released into rivers by the heavy rains. The polluted silt often causes the flooding and ruination of agricultural land downstream.

Arguments for maintaining biodiversity come from several standpoints. Some are moral and philosophical. Amongst these are the 'deep green' or biocentric argument that ecosystems and their inhabitants have as much inherent right to dwell on the planet as human beings. Another is that the extraordinary beauty and variety of the natural world enriches our lives and is a source of aesthetic and intellectual pleasure and inspiration. A third arises from the metaphysical insight that our very identity and the qualities we prize most in ourselves — our imagination, our sensitivities, our sense of the divine — derive from the beauty and grandeur of the Earth and that, if we devastate the planet, we lay waste to ourselves (*documents 1, 2, 3, 4, 5, 15*).

These arguments are unlikely to stop the chainsaws. They have limited appeal for governments of developing countries confronted with poverty, hunger and huge debts to pay.

Utilitarian and hard cash arguments probably provide the best immediate way forward for protecting biodiversity. The utilitarian position is that the rainforests should be preserved because of the part they play in maintaining the planet's air conditioning and water systems, changing carbon dioxide to oxygen and regulating climatic patterns (*document 10*). The forests, the utilitarian argument continues, are also a vast storehouse of potential foods, medicines and renewable raw materials that will benefit humankind (*documents 7, 8, 16*). To destroy the forests is to put at risk our own future.

At this point, utilitarian considerations merge with the hard cash argument that the rainforests should be preserved for long-term 'sustainable exploitation'. Recognising the genetic riches they contain, the forests should be preserved and their market value recognised (*document 11*). To assist in their preservation, 'debts-for-nature' agreements, where developed countries write off the debts of rainforest countries in exchange for conservation, should be negotiated.

It is such thinking that lies behind the convention on biodiversity signed by world leaders at the Earth Summit in Rio de Janeiro in June 1992. At the Summit the rich countries of the 'North' (excluding the USA) agreed to help the countries of the 'South' to protect plant and animal diversity through additional development aid.

A markedly different perspective on the biodiversity debate is offered by those that remind us that species loss has happened before only for evolution to make good the loss. The loss of many species, they add, would not materially affect the ability of (simplified) ecosystems to function. Those holding such views are, nonetheless, convinced that the current rate of species loss and the encroachment of humankind upon habitats presents an unprecedented and, perhaps, deadly threat to nature's recovery potential (*documents 9 and 14*).

Although this discussion has focused upon the tropical rainforests, species in other habitats are also facing extinction directly or indirectly as a result of the actions of human beings. Rhino populations throughout the world, for example, are being depleted as a result of commercial hunting to supply the illegal trade in horn which is used for decorative daggers in the Middle East and for medicine in parts of Asia. Certain species, such as the prairie dog of North America, are being exterminated as pests that damage crops. The populations of at least half the 250 bird species that breed in North America are in decline as a result of deforestation primarily caused by the logging industry (*document 18*). Sewage discharge and soil erosion threaten the

destruction of tens of thousands of coral reef species (*document 17*). Pollution, arising out of the use of harmful substances in agriculture and industry, can also drive species to the edge. Kemp's Ridley Turtle, for instance, is suffering because of mounting levels of pollution flowing from the Mississippi river into the Gulf of Mexico.

The activities in this chapter are designed to raise awareness of the interlocking nature of living things within an ecosystem. Ecosystems close to home are explored as are those within tropical rainforests. The activities lead on to consideration of the human impact on ecosystems and the question of whether environments *per se* have rights. The documents that follow offer a range of viewpoints on humanity's place in the web of life and the importance of maintaining biodiversity for both human and planetary well-being.

School students explore an ecosystem
(Photo: EarthKind)

DOCUMENTS

1. *What is man without the beasts? If all the beasts were gone, men would die from a great loneliness of spirit. For whatever happens to the beasts soon happens to the man. All things are connected.*

This we know. The earth does not belong to man: man belongs to the earth. This we know. All things are connected like the blood which unites one family. All things are connected.

Whatever befalls the earth befalls the sons of the earth. Man does not weave the web of life, he is merely a strand in it. Whatever he does to the web, he does to himself.

— Chief Seattle's oration to his tribal assembly, Pacific northwest, USA, 1854[4]

2. There is an awe and reverence due to the stars in the heavens, the sun and all heavenly bodies, to the seas and the continents, to all living forms of trees and flowers, to all the forms of life in the sea, the animals of the forests and the birds of the air. To destroy a living species is to silence forever a divine voice.

— Thomas Berry[5]

3. ECOLOGY

Catchwords are crystallisations of desires. 'Ecology' has become the motto of our age because it holds the promise of reuniting what has been sundered and of healing what has been wounded — in short, of nurturing the whole. Indeed, the inability of modern institutions to see beyond the horizon of their specific interests and to answer for the (so-called) side-effects of their actions is now on record. Their high level of efficiency is based on indifference to all consequences that do not enter their own immediate calculations. Even the Third World has not been spared this: intensive agriculture causes the water table to sink; energy policies tolerate the clearing of rainforests; chemical factories sow disease, sometimes even death.
— Wolfang Sachs, 1992[6]

4. *IN THE NAME OF PROGRESS*
We often use the word progress to describe what has taken place over the past few decades. There is no denying that in some areas our roads have improved and that electricity is more readily available. But can we say that there is real progress? Who has benefited most and who has borne the real costs? The poor are as disadvantaged as ever and the natural world has been grievously wounded. We have stripped it bare, silenced its sounds, and banished other creatures from the community of the living.

The destruction of any part of creation, especially the extinction of species, defaces the image of Christ which is etched in creation. The various strands of our Christian vision envisage a profound renewal which must affect our people, our culture and our land. It challenges us to live once again in harmony with God's creation.

— Catholic Bishops of the Philippines, pastoral letter to the faith on ecology, Jan. 1988.[7]

5. WE ARE THE ROCKS DANCING

Every atom in this body existed before organic life emerged 4000 million years ago. Remember our childhood as minerals, as lava, as rocks? Rocks contain the potentiality to weave themselves into such stuff as this. We are the rocks dancing. Why do we look down on them with such a condescending air? It is they that are the immortal part of us.

When humans investigate and see through their layers of anthropocentric self-cherishing, a most profound change in consciousness begins to take place. Alienation subsides. The human is no longer an outsider, apart. Your humanness is then recognised as being merely the most recent stage of your existence.

'I am protecting the rainforest' develops to 'I am part of the rainforest protecting myself. I am that part of the rainforest recently emerged into thinking.' What a relief then! The thousands of years of imagined separation are over and we begin to recall our true nature.

— John Seed, 1988[8]

6.

BAZ '86

9

7. Twenty-five per cent of prescription drugs contain products derived from plants. Nobody knows exactly why the willow tree decided to produce aspirin in its bark, why one family of drugs from the paw-paw has powerful cytotoxic, anti-cancer or antimalaria properties, or why the Pacific yew should produce quantities of taxol, now an important anti-cancer drug.

Not all plant chemicals convert to medicines. One Amazon tree — slower to grow, at a disadvantage in the competition for light, uses the crudest means to protect itself from insect attack.

At the first bite it exudes a sticky substance which simply cements the predator's jaw so that it will never bite again. It is, of course, the plant that makes the world go round: rubber.

— Tim Radford, *The Guardian*, 1992[10]

8. *These forests are the medicine chests and food stores of the future: plant genes yet undiscovered in them may provide drugs to combat cancer or Aids, or broaden the dangerously narrow range of food plants we grow. The Madagascar rosy periwinkle is the source of two powerful drugs used to treat leukaemia and Hodgkin's Disease. The serendipity berry, found in West Africa, is a slimmer's fantasy — 3,000 times sweeter than sugar but with fewer calories..*

— David Nicholson-Lord, 1992[11]

9. EVERY SPECIES DOESN'T MATTER

His own view is that every species doesn't matter. The evidence of fossil records shows that at many points in the earth's history, life was simplified dramatically before diversity rose again.

In an average world, average species will go on doing the job of managing the planet's air-conditioning system perfectly well. But biological diversity would be the globe's saviour under extreme conditions: 'All the rare species that are sitting there adapted to drought and coping with fire. The system keeps working if you spread the risk among several different characters, each of which is better at working under different conditions.'

'I think the answer to the questions of species redundancy will not please the conservationists. I think that is regrettable. It could turn out that the planet could be an awful lot simpler and still work perfectly well. In terms of conservation, the equivalent question is: how many medieval cathedrals do you need?'

'A small number of species are undoubtedly keystone species or critical ecological engineers. Take the Yellow Pages, remove one business at a time, and say: how many businesses would go bust because you removed that business? If you took London Transport away, a huge number of businesses would collapse.'

Thus, elephants maintain the African savannah; sea otters, by eating the sea urchins that eat the kelp, are the conservators of the Pacific fishery and even of the bald eagle; a tiny land snail that can eat through limestone is the only source of nitrogen for the Negev desert. Other keystone species may reveal themselves only as they become extinct, and whole chains of creation then collapse along with them.

'What we are doing to the planet is not sustainable. All the evidence suggests that current rates of extinction are three or four orders of magnitude higher than the fastest periods of extinction in the fossil record,' says Professor Lawton. 'In other words we are now doing things to the planet which have never been experienced in the whole of the past 600 million years.'

Interview with Professor John Lawton, Natural Environment Research Council, *The Guardian*, 1992[12]

10.

Mini-planets on which world depends for air conditioning

Tim Radford explains the vital role of trees in sustaining nature and the needs of man

FORESTS are a key part of the world's air-conditioning system. Trees take carbon dioxide from the air and lock it away for long periods as carbon, returning the oxygen on which all animal life is based.

Trees are also important in the global water system. Their vast networks of roots and the litter of humus under them acts as a sponge to trap rainfall and protect topsoil from erosion by wind or water.

The rainforests, in particular, are the key to the climates of the tropics; a high proportion of the rain that falls each day is simply vapour transpired from the forest itself; that is, every day the forest bathes itself in water condensed from its own steam.

Each species of tree is almost a self-contained "mini-planet" for whole communities of small creatures. They also provide timber, fruit, medicines and building materials for man.

In 1989 three US botanists measured the market value of latex and fruits harvested by Indians and tappers from a hectare of Peruvian forest, and found that the forest yielded a better economic return than the timber that stood upon it, and considerably better than the cattle that might graze upon a clear-felled hectare.

Most of the environmental alarm has centred on the tropical forests. Much of the original forest or wildwood in Europe disappeared long ago; vast parts of North America have been cleared. In the past 10 years, according to the Food and Agriculture Organisation, the temperate and sub-Arctic forests have increased slightly.

But in the tropics, an area roughly the size of Lebanon disappears every year to the international timber companies and the slash-and-burn cultivators. Much of the worry has centred not on selective logging — the taking of valuable trees in a way that leaves the others standing — but on clear-felling.

In a climate that is alternately baking sunlight and heavy rain, this destroys the often fragile soil on which the forest depends, making regeneration difficult or impossible.

This in turn affects climate patterns. In the last century, mean monthly temperatures in Djakarta, Indonesia, where logging has been heavy, have increased by 1.66C. The number of "dry" months each year — in which not enough falls for rice to grow — has grown from four to five.

The problem of the forests cannot be separated from the problem of biodiversity — the rainforests, particularly, are the richest of all the earth's habitats — but it goes wider than that.

The forests matter to the people who live in and by them, but they matter as much to others thousands of miles away. The people of the Bangladesh delta now suffer periodic flooding because the forests of the Himalayan hillsides have been stripped: millions of tons of water that would have been held and slowly released in the dry season now cascade downhill towards the sea, not to water the crops but to wash them away — along with villages and livelihoods.

— The Guardian, 8 June 1992[13]

---

11. The potential wealth that lies in exotic plant biodiversity has already been recognised by many Least Developed Countries

The world can be crudely divided into the gene-rich, technology-poor South and the technology-rich, gene-poor North. The great storehouses of plant genetic diversity lie mostly within the borders of the poor countries, which are now beginning to exploit this capital asset. Plant breeders from Europe and North America no longer have *carte blanche* to plunder the genetic resources in the tropics. The owners of biodiversity are taking the first steps along the road to controlling its exploitation and thereby protecting its future. Costa Rica has already signed a licensing agreement with Merck for the right to exploit chemicals derived from its rainforest. Many more such agreements are sure to follow.

— Phillip Gates, 1992[14]

---

12. *The loss of 1 rainforest plant species can cause the loss of 30 animal and insect species that depend on it.*[15]

---

13. The Amazon Rainforest's Survival System[16]

WATER CYCLE

1. Rain falls in the forest.

2. The forest absorbs half the water... and sweats it back into the atmosphere.

3. The other half runs into the rivers and down to the Atlantic Ocean where clouds form and return to the forest.

NUTRIENTS CYCLE

1. Shallow roots collect nutrients from water and forest litter.

2. Creepers and orchids take nutrients from rain and trap growth-inducing nitrogen on their leaves.

3. Special natural chemicals help leaves cope with difficult conditions and prolong life. Leaves fall as litter to the forest floor.

LIFE CYCLE

1. Forest giants die and fall, clearing the forest around them for new plants.

2. Fast growing, light-loving plants grow first.

3. Animals arrive and excrete seeds new to the area.

4. Longer living trees and future giants dominate again.

14. No Vacant Niches

In the scale of geological time, extinction is a natural process, an inevitable consequence of evolution. Rare global disasters, such as meteorite impacts, have also wiped out vast numbers of species. But there are many differences between these past waves of extinction and today's destruction. They were chance events, whereas current extinctions are unnecessary and preventable. Past mass extinctions were followed by a rebound of species diversity, as organisms evolved again to fill vacant niches over millions of years of geological time. But unless self-control or a cataclysmic disaster puts an end to the excesses of habitat destruction by humanity, there will be no vacant niches. Biodiversity will be subjected to relentless pressure and won't recover. The only way to forestall this is through active conservation.

— Phillip Gates, 1992[17]

---

15. The irreversible loss of species, which by 2100 may reach one-third of all species now living, is especially serious. We are losing the potential they hold for providing medicinal and other benefits, and the contribution that genetic diversity of life forms gives to the robustness of the world's biological systems and to the astonishing beauty of the earth itself.

Much of this damage is irreversible on a scale of centuries, or permanent. Other processes appear to pose additional threats. Increasing levels of gases in the atmosphere from human activities, including carbon dioxide released from fossil fuel burning and from deforestation, may alter climate on a global scale. Predictions of global warming are still uncertain — with projected effects ranging from tolerable to very severe — but the potential risks are very great.

Our massive tampering with the world's interdependent web of life — coupled with the environmental damage inflicted by deforestation, species loss, and climate change — could trigger widespread adverse effects, including unpredictable collapses of critical biological systems whose interactions and dynamics we only imperfectly understand.

Uncertainty over the extent of these effects cannot excuse complacency or delay in facing the threats.

— World Scientists' Warning to Humanity[18]

---

16. *The most fundamental requirement is that we protect the diversity of species. There can be no greater condemnation of our stewardship of the Earth than the fact that around 50 species of animals and plants are becoming extinct every day. Not only is this a crime, it is also very stupid. We can learn a lot from the natural world to benefit us. And any reduction in the genetic base leaves future generations more exposed.*

— Charles Kennedy, M.P. [19]

17. SAN FRANCISCO — The world's coral reefs may be teeming with an estimated 423,000 strange and exotic species, 90 per cent of them unknown to science, according to a study presented yesterday.

Many of the plants, animals and microbes around and inside the reefs may vanish before they are even identified, swept into extinction on a scale rivalling the disappearance of species in the destruction of rain forests, said the study's author, Marjorie Reaka-Kudla.

'The risk of extinction is extremely high in marine environments,' said Ms. Reaka-Kudla of the University of Maryland in College Park.

Researchers don't know precisely how fast the world's coral reefs are disappearing, but it is clear that sewage discharge and soil erosion are destroying coastal reefs in many areas around the world, Ms. Reaka Kudla said.

The consequences could be even greater than for extinctions on land, because of the enormous biological wealth and diversity in the oceans, Ms. Reaka-Kudla said.

'The oceans contain many more major groups of animals that have undergone separate evolution for hundreds of millions of years,' she said at the annual meeting of the American Association for the Advancement of Science.

The vanishing reef dwellers are also a mostly unexploited source of potential medicines, said Rita Colwell, president of the University of Maryland's Biotechnology Institute in Baltimore.

'We are just beginning to realise the human, societal and economic value of the diversity in a real way,' said Ms. Colwell, who was not connected with Ms. Reaka-Kudla's study.

She noted, as an example, that researchers recently identified a substance in a red sea sponge that blocks the activity of a key enzyme in the AIDS virus.

Researchers also worry that the loss of species in the reefs will upset the ocean's food chain, disrupting fisheries upon which many people depend for their survival, Ms Reaka-Kudla said.

In a separate study, Ms Colwell reported that previously unrecognised viruses are present in huge quantities in the ocean, making up a significant portion of all the oceans' 'biomass,' or living stuff:

The viruses are so different from anything else known that researchers have not yet figured out how to grow them in the laboratory for further study, Ms. Colwell said.

The discovery of the viruses is one more indication of the extent of the undiscovered and untapped richness in the oceans, she said.

'We're now just beginning to get a glimpse into this wonderful diversity that is functioning, that we must not destroy,' Ms Colwell said.

— *The Globe and Mail*, 21.2.1994[20]

---

18. Why birds are disappearing

Habitat loss
- **Deforestation.** At least half the 250 bird species that breed in North America and winter to the south have declined in recent years.
- **Forest fragmentation.** In North America, parasitic cowbirds infest more than half of other songbirds' nests in many areas where clearings have been cut into forests.
- **Plowing of grassland.** Once-abundant species such as Eurasia's bustards and North America's prairie chickens have all but disappeared.
- **Desertification.** White-throat warblers that breed in Britain but winter in Africa have declined by 75 per cent in 27 years.
- **Draining of wetlands.** North America's most common ducks have declined by 30 per cent in 27 years.

Pesticides
Widespread use of DDT in Africa has caused birds' egg shells to become too thin, leading to declines in populations of at least six birds of prey. Use of carbofuran on Virginia fields left tens of thousands of dead birds.

Chemicals
- **Acidification of streams.** Disappearance of fish has destroyed food supply for loons on northern lakes.
- **Lead shot and sinkers.** Consumption of lead scattered by hunters and fishermen has caused widespread lead poisoning of swans, geese, ducks and loons.
- **Oil spills.** Oilfield spills during the Persian Gulf war attracted and killed thousands of water birds. Exxon Valdez spill killed 300,000 birds.

Exotic species
Introduction of the brown tree snake on Guam caused extinction of four of the island's five bird species. Roaming house cats in Victoria, Australia, kill 13 million small animals a year, including members of 67 bird species.

Overhunting
In Italy alone, 50 million songbirds end up on dinner plates each year.

— Howard Youth, The Worldwatch Institute[21]

---

19. *Death is one thing. An end to birth is something else.*

— Dr. Soule & Dr. Wilcox[22]

---

20. Extinct is forever.

— Body Shop teeshirt

ACTIVITIES

■ *WOOLLY WEB*

Suitable for

Primary

Time needed

25-40 minutes

Resources

A set of *You Are* cards; 30 badges, several balls of wool; an open space.

Procedure

Students are each given a blank badge and a *You Are* card and are asked to familiarise themselves with what they are and what nourishment they require. They display this information on their badge in words and pictures. A large circle is formed. The teacher explains that they are going to connect each living thing to its food sources using wool. With the teacher's help they do just that. The activity can begin with an animal high up the food chain and follow the connections down to the other end of the food chain. The wool should be wound round each student's waist. This can be done while the students are seated. Eventually all students should be connected in some way in a huge spider's web of wool.

Potential

The web of wool offers a potent symbol of the interlocking nature of all the elements, organic and inorganic, in an ecosystem. It is a tangible and visual representation of interdependence in ecology. The discussion that follows should highlight the web-like nature of the interdependencies. Individual living things can be picked out and their food chains followed to their sources. This will highlight the importance of water, soil and sun and also of microscopic organisms. The students can be asked to stand and the discussion can continue as to the effect on the web should one animal disappear. The web need not be destroyed; those who may be adversely affected can be asked to sit down. Reasons for the disappearance of parts of the web can be discussed: amongst others, pollution, agricultural practices and urban sprawl. If one part disappears, for example, the frogs, what will happen to those living things which the frog eats? And then what happens to the food source of those creatures? The activity gives great scope for exploring balance and imbalance in nature, and humanity's role in jeopardising and maintaining balance.

Variations

1. The activity can be adapted to suit any ecosystem that the students have studied simply by writing new *You Are* cards.

2. Instead of giving each student a *You Are* card, they can be given to pairs of students. One student could form part of the circle, remaining stationary, while the partner moves around making connections with the wool.

3. Students could research different living things in an ecosystem and make their own *You Are* cards. Care must be taken to ensure that interlinking of everyone can occur.

Source

Adapted by Jackie Harvey from *Woolly Thinking* in Pike, G., and Selby, D., *Global teacher, global learner*, Hodder and Stoughton, 1988. 141.

YOU ARE CARDS

YOU ARE A FOX You eat * water shrews * duck	**YOU ARE AN OWL** You eat * water shrews * frogs	**YOU ARE A KINGFISHER** You eat * minnows * sticklebacks
YOU ARE A STICKLEBACK You eat * water fleas	**YOU ARE A GREAT DIVING BEETLE** You eat * baby fish * damsel flies	**YOU ARE A MOTH** You eat * plant leaves (as a caterpillar) * nectar
YOU ARE A DRAGONFLY You eat * moths * butterflies	**YOU ARE A TADPOLE** You eat * pond weed * plant leaves	**YOU ARE POND WEED** You need * food from water * sunlight
YOU ARE DUCK WEED You need * food in water * sunlight	**YOU ARE A DUCK** You eat * water fleas * duck weed	**YOU ARE A WATER BOATMAN** You eat * pond weed * water spiders
YOU ARE A WATER SPIDER You eat * water beetles * dragonfly nymphs	**YOU ARE A POND SKATER** You eat * pond weed sap * plant sap	**YOU ARE A MINNOW** You eat * water boatmen * water fleas
YOU ARE A WATER IRIS You need * food in the soil * sunlight	**YOU ARE A MARSH MARIGOLD** You need * food in the soil * sunlight	**YOU ARE A BUTTERFLY** You eat * plant leaves (as a caterpillar) * nectar
YOU ARE A FROG You eat * dragonflies * butterflies	**YOU ARE A NEWT** You eat * pond skaters * tadpoles	**YOU ARE A TOAD** You eat * water beetles * moths

P

YOU ARE A WATER SHREW	YOU ARE AN OTTER	YOU ARE PLANKTON(MICROSCOPIC PLANTS & ANIMALS)
You eat * water snails * damselflies	You eat * mussels * fish	You need * food from water * sunlight
YOU ARE A DRAGONFLY NYMPH	YOU ARE A DAMSELFLY	YOU ARE A MUSSEL
You eat * water boatmen * pond skaters	You eat * moths * butterflies	You eat * microscopic plants * microscopic animals
YOU ARE A WATER SNAIL	YOU ARE A WATER FLEA (DAPHNIA)	YOU ARE SOIL
You eat * pond weed * duck weed	You eat * microscopic animals * microscopic plants	You contain * minerals dissolved from rocks that help plants grow * particles of decayed plants and animals that living plants feed upon

YOU ARE WATER	YOU ARE THE SUN
You contain * minerals dissolved from rocks that help water plants grow * particles of decayed plants and animals that provide food for pond plants and small pond creatures	You *provide warmth and light so that plants grow. *encourage rain to fall by making water evaporate; the vapour forms clouds and falls as rain.

P

■ *FOOD CHAIN*

Suitable for

Primary

Time needed

20 minutes

Resources

Pile of 27 paper 'lettuce leaves' and a pile of 27 paper 'corns' for each group of three students. An open space in which to act out the food chains.

Procedure

The teacher introduces the idea of food chains to the students. If this activity follows *Woolly Web*, the children will already have some understanding of the concept. Using soil, lettuce, rabbit, fox and vulture, the teacher can explain that green plants, such as lettuce, use the food in the soil for energy as well as making some from sunlight. The rabbit is not able to do either of these because it is an animal, so it eats the lettuce and uses up the energy in the lettuce leaves. The fox eats the rabbit and uses up the rabbit's energy and when the fox dies it may in turn be eaten by a vulture or other scavenger. What is left of the dead fox decays to become part of the soil and the cycle begins again. It is explained that each time something is eaten not all the energy is transferred to the eater. Students are assigned to the roles of rabbit, fox and vulture (or other scavenger) and are told that the lettuce leaves represent the food (energy) created out of soil and sunlight. The 'rabbit' eats the lettuce leaves, i.e. holds them, and then goes on to perform some rabbit-like actions while the teacher explains that some of the food (energy) eaten by animals is burned up in activity. The 'rabbit' drops one third of the leaves. It is explained that some food (energy) is passed on as waste. The 'rabbit' drops another third of the leaves. The rest of the food becomes part of the rabbit's body. The 'rabbit' is eaten by the 'fox' who takes the remaining 9 leaves. The two-part dropping of the leaves is repeated. When the 'fox' dies the vulture (or other scavenger) eats the body and uses the remaining food energy. A short discussion on how energy decreases at each level of the food chain should follow. Where, in the opinion of the class, is the energy of the remaining three leaves spread? The students then recreate the activity in groups of three using soil, corn, cow and human as components.

Potential

A simple and enjoyable activity which helps students to understand a difficult concept, i.e. the relationship between the supply of food energy and the levels of a food chain. The following questions might be asked in debriefing the activity. How do we make available more energy for humans: by eating vegetables directly or by feeding them to an animal and then eating the animal? Which could our world support more of: plant eaters or animal eaters? Could humans eat all of the same plant foods that we now grow for animals? If not, why not? The discussion can consider that in many parts of the world there isn't enough food to feed the human population and can explore reasons for those shortages.

Extension

The students go on to explore other food chains which are headed by humans. Facts and figures can be presented showing how much plant food it takes to produce a kilo of beef; this could lead to some mathematical work on how much land it might take to produce this food. The figures can be compared with the amount of vegetable food for human use that could be produced on the same area of land (see p.27). The students could research alternatives to meat, and perhaps invite members of vegetarian or vegan organisations to visit class and speak.

Source

Jackie Harvey.

■ *FROGS AND FLIES*

Suitable for

Primary

Time needed

20-25 minutes

Resources

Up to thirty paper 'flies' for each student who is not a frog or acting the role of pollution; five frog badges, masks or hats; one pollution badge, mask or cloak; a large chart with six columns to be used for recording estimates, an open space.

Procedure

Students sit in a circle. Five are assigned the role of frog and given appropriate identification. They sit in the centre of the circle. One student is assigned the role of pollution and given the appropriate badge, mask or cloak. She remains seated in the circle. The teacher gives paper flies to each unassigned child, explaining that a fly is to be fed to each of the frogs every time she claps her hands. Following this initial round, the teacher explains that the activity is going to be repeated, but this time with pollution playing an active role. After the first clap and feeding of the frogs, pollution will eliminate one of the frogs by taking it from the centre of the circle and will do the same after each subsequent clap. Students are to 'feed' each of the spaces where the removed frogs were. Before the second round actually begins, the class estimates how many flies there will be on the floor after each of the six claps. The estimates are written in the six columns of the chart. After each clap and feeding session, the flies on the floor are counted, the actual number recorded on the chart and, if deemed necessary, subsequent estimates adjusted. The activity ends with the five frogs replaced by five piles of flies.

Potential

This activity is probably most effective if students have taken part in *Woolly Web* previously, as it builds upon the concept of interdependence explored in that activity. It will, however, stand alone. A simple, enjoyable activity which illustrates the role of frogs in maintaining population levels of flies and other insects. The results on the chart at the end of the activity should be discussed. The following questions might be included in the discussion: What might life be like for humans if there were no more frogs and the fly population grew unchecked? What might life be like for other animals under the same circumstances (e.g. horses, dogs)? Why is it important to ensure the continued survival of all the links in the chain/web? Students should be encouraged to think of other examples of ill-effects following the removal of a species from an ecosystem.

Variation

Animals other than frogs and flies can be chosen.

Source

Jackie Harvey.

■ *RAINFOREST FANTASY*

Suitable for

Upper primary/secondary

Time needed

40 minutes

Resources

A clear space in a classroom, preferably carpeted; paints, brushes, water and a sheet of paper for each student.

Procedure

Students are asked to take up a relaxed position, seated or lying on the floor, and to close their eyes. The facilitator further promotes a relaxed state by slowly reading the following text in a gentle voice, allowing for pauses at regular intervals:

Try to make yourself as relaxed and as comfortable as possible... Listen for a moment to the sounds you can hear outside the room... to sounds inside the room... Be aware of how you're sitting or lying... Just let yourself relax... Let the feeling of relaxation spread through your body... Be aware of your toes... Squeeze them tightly... relax them... squeeze them... relax them. Let the relaxation spread up through your ankles, your calves, your knees, your thighs... Let the relaxation flood through your stomach, your chest, your neck, your shoulders and down your arms... Squeeze your hands tightly... let them relax... squeeze them... relax them... Let the muscles of your face relax.

IN THE RAINFOREST

You find yourself in the middle of a rainforest. You look, cautiously, around you in the gloomy light. Your eyes follow the slender trunk of a tree straight upwards to a dense green canopy through which thin shafts of light appear. Twisted around the trunk, all the way to the top, is a rope-like vine appearing to strangle the tree. You then notice other vines, thick and thin, straight and curly, clinging to every tree and plant, forming a tangled mass in every direction. Following a woody vine down to the ground, you notice that the forest floor is surprisingly bare. Few plants or flowers grow out of the thick, spongy mat of roots beneath your feet though many large tree roots stick up out of the ground like giant wooden snakes. Some trees seem to be propped up by thick buttresses growing out of their trunks, as though they are very old buildings in danger of collapse. Mosses and lichens cover everything in a cloak of soft green velvet from which curious plants with bulbous stems and thick, waxy leaves emerge. Around your feet, weird and wonderful fungi sprout up like mushrooms in a variety of shapes and colours.

As you stand there, feeling very small beneath the towering trees, you become aware of the stillness of the forest. It's a bit eerie, like being in a deserted place. Then, gradually, you pick out some sound: the snuffling of a wild pig rummaging around amongst the roots nearby; the squawking of a pair of blue and yellow macaws flying overhead; the scampering of a troupe of spider monkeys high up in the branches of a fig tree; and in the far distance, the drawn-out groan of a giant tree toppling over and finally crashing onto the forest floor.

You become aware, too of the ceaseless activity of insects, many of which you've never seen before. You recognise some of them — butterflies, beetles, ants — but their size is astonishing. You feel as though you've shrunk in size, a bit like *Alice in Wonderland* when she falls down the rabbit hole. A bright blue butterfly on a nearby fern opens its wings, each as big as the palm of your hand. The millipede inching its way along a twisting vine must be nearly the length of your foot; and the giant snail stuck to the bark of the tree above your head seems in danger of being crushed by the weight of its own enormous shell. Your attention is caught by a thin never-ending line of leaf-cutting ants, each carrying a piece of green leaf or stalk several times larger than its own body size.

Feeling a little bolder, you move forward gingerly, ducking underneath the trailing vines and stepping over ankle-twisting roots. As you move, your clothes stick to your back and legs and your head throbs in the hot, humid air. There is a damp, earthy smell everywhere, occasionally overpowered by the sweet scent of an unknown plant. Suddenly, huge drops of water fall on your head. Looking upwards, you realise that you are caught in a tropical storm; however, the green canopy formed by the tree branches high above you is like a giant umbrella, with just a few holes in it. As you watch the raindrops trickling down the tree trunks, the whole forest seems to burst into life. Insects that you've never seen before scurry out of their tree homes, anteaters scuffle around searching for food with their long sticky tongues. A wonderful array of moths, butterflies and birds display their full colours above your head. Higher still, howler monkeys roar and parakeets cry out.

And then a strange thing happens. You feel yourself being lifted off the ground. You are floating upwards towards the green canopy. You pass nimbly through a tangled knot of vines and, looking down, you catch a fleeting glimpse of a jaguar as it glides through the undergrowth. In a small clearing down to your right a spotted deer and her young are feeding. As you gently rise, more light filters through and you find yourself amongst the lower branches of the trees. Here, a long way from the ground, is a wholly different world. You watch the amazing acrobatics of squirrels, mice and monkeys swinging and leaping from tree to tree; snakes, lizards and frogs seem to slide and slither along the branches, whilst the curious three-toed sloth hangs serenely upside down, camouflaged by the green algae growing on its fur.

Now you are in the thick of the green canopy itself. Huge spreading branches end in sprays of pink and purple flowers; still clinging to the trees, the longest vines fight for available space and sunlight with giant ferns and bright yellow orchids. Brilliant splashes of colour are provided by birds of paradise and the great orange beaks of the toucans. Monkeys chatter away but with an ever watchful eye on the monkey-eating eagle which hovers above the canopy. You feel the heat of the sun on your head as the rain clouds drift away and you are thrust out into the deep blue of the sky. As you drift higher the vast green ocean of rainforest spreads out beneath you. You can spot the glinting lines of rivers winding through the trees; here and there, in a clearing, thin plumes of smoke show where families of nomadic people are living and farming the land. On the distant horizon, the menacing clouds of dark smoke tell a different side of the rainforest story.

After a somewhat longer pause, the facilitator moves into the following introductory script:

Imagine yourself leaving the classroom, floating up into the clear blue sky... you look down and see your school far beneath you... getting smaller... You can now see the outlines of other towns and cities, hills and forests, lakes... and you begin to see the outline of the (name of country), framed by the sea... and now the continents of the world... (longer pause)...You feel yourself starting to descend... you can just pick out the shape of a country that you don't recognise... you can now make out details of rivers, hills, a city, a town... you seem to be descending towards a mass of trees that stretches in every direction to the horizon... you're floating gently down through a space between huge branches... down and down until your feet touch the soft and springy ground...

The facilitator continues by reading *In The Rainforest*, allowing sufficient time after each new image for students to really grasp and 'live' the experience. Relaxing background music can be useful to help set the appropriate tone (New World Cassettes, Paradise Farm, Westhall, Halesworth, Suffolk IP19 8BR, have a selection of music suitable for guided fantasies and visualisations, including Terry Oldfield's *Spirit of the Rainforest*, and will forward a catalogue on request).

At the end of the reading, the facilitator should offer a reverse version of the introductory script above to return the students to the classroom before asking them to open their eyes. Without any discussion, students use the painting materials to portray an aspect or image of the fantasy journey of significance to them. An 'art gallery' can be set up as a means of prompting general discussion about rainforests.

Potential

This fantasy journey is designed to give students a vivid understanding of a tropical rainforest ecosystem as a precursor to work on the complex issues surrounding rainforest destruction. It conveys a lot of factual information about the rainforest and its inhabitants, presented through a medium which is a powerful aid to learning for many students. Follow-up work could take any number of directions, from providing a more

scientific and explicit account of the forest ecosystem to research, discussion and writing about deforestation and its potential ramifications for the planet. Students who are not used to fantasy or visualisation activities may need to practise the necessary skills through some introductory techniques. Guidelines for using fantasy and visualisation techniques can be found in Pike, G. and Selby, D., *Global Teacher, Global Learner*, Hodder and Stoughton, 1988, pp. 184-193. Good sources of introductory activities are Hendricks, G. and P., and Wills, R., *The Centering Book*, Prentice- Hall, 1975 and Hendricks, G. and Roberts, T., *The Second Centering Book*, Prentice-Hall, 1977. Other fantasy journeys using the environment can be found in Seed, J., *et al.*, *Thinking Like a Mountain. Towards a Council of All Beings*, Heretic Books, 1988.

■ *WEB OF LIFE*

Suitable for

Upper primary/secondary

Time needed

30 minutes

Resources

A classroom area marked by tape containing eleven chairs (the rainforest); balls of blue, green, yellow and brown wool; two pairs of scissors; a *Web of Life* card and a badge containing the name and a line drawing of the plant/creature described in the card for each student; a guidance chart (*Fig. 1*). The activity is designed for a group of thirty-five students. If the number is less, the number of *Canopy* cards should first be reduced (but the Canopy group should always be the largest). To shorten the time required for the activity, the number of *Connector/Reporter* cards can be increased.

Procedure

Students are informed that they are going to explore life in a virgin tropical rainforest. Cards are distributed and the guidance chart revealed. The students with *Emergent Layer* cards are first asked to take up position, standing on three chairs that are not in close proximity. Other students representing plants and animals then take up their positions, those with *Canopy* and *Forest Floor* cards ensuring they are evenly spread across the rainforest area. The teacher then explains that the object of the activity is to identify dependencies between the different plants and animals in the rainforest. The cards are to be read carefully. Students representing the matapalo and kapok tree are asked to read their cards aloud as is any other student who feels they do not fully understand the content of their card. The activity continues with dependencies discerned being symbolised by the hand to hand linking of the relevant students with wool. This is done by the two or more students acting as Connectors. A dependency is symbolised using the appropriate coloured wool for the dependent plant or animal. Hence, the dependency of a plant/animal in the canopy on a plant/animal in the emergent layer would be represented in green. If the relationship is, however, of an

Layer	Wool Colour	Position
Emergent Layer	Blue	Stand on Chairs
Canopy	Green	Stand on Floor
Understory	Yellow	Sit on Chairs
Forest Floor	Brown	Sit on Floor

Fig.1

interdependent nature, the two students would end up being linked by both green and blue wool. The activity continues until as many connections as possible have been established. Debriefing begins with the two Connectors taking on their Reporter responsibility and interviewing individuals about the nature and number of their interconnections (an effective approach is for the Reporter to follow linkages through the web by moving always to an individual mentioned by the last interviewee). One of their tasks is to mention any connections that have been overlooked.

Potential

A lively and visually powerful way of demonstrating how the plants and animals of the tropical rainforest are dependent on each other for survival. Students can be asked what they have learnt about the rainforest from the activity and if the exploration of the rainforest environment held any surprises for them. An interesting discussion point, likely to raise issues of central importance, is whether the matapalo (the strangler fig) is a good or bad feature of the rainforest. For older students, questions surrounding the *value* of the rainforest, and of the individual plants, and animals within it, may provoke discussion. Should we protect the rainforest because it is valuable to human beings (e.g. as a source of new medicines from plants, as a focus for leisure and tourism) or does it have *intrinsic* value (i.e. value in its own right)? Does the forest as an entity have rights? Do species within the forest and individual members of those species have rights? If so, what kind of rights are we talking about?

Extensions

1. The student representing the matapalo fig lets go of her strands of wool. Those whose wool goes loose let go of their strands, and so on. Are any connections left?

2. Students prepare a rainforest mural.

3. Students research the life of indigenous peoples in rainforests and write additional cards demonstrating their relationship with the rainforest environment. The activity is undertaken a second time incorporating some of the additional cards. What is the effect on the web? Students then research the impact of loggers, new settlers and tourists on the rainforest environment. What is their impact on the rainforest's web of life?

4. Students investigate a local natural environment in the company of a naturalist or ecologist. They seek details of interdependencies within that environment, prior to developing their own *Web of Life* activity based upon the information gathered. The activity developed is subsequently attempted with younger students.

Source

Adapted from 'An Interdependent System' in Murphy, C.E., *What have you got to lose? New World tropical rainforests*, Stanford Program on International and Cross-Cultural Education, undated, 7-27.

WEB OF LIFE CARDS

CONNECTOR/REPORTER	CONNECTOR/REPORTER
Your role is to link plants and animals in the four forest layers. Ask people to share their card and say who they think they depend upon and who depends upon them. Make hand to hand links using pieces of wool (pairs of scissors are available). A dependent relationship should be represented using the wool colour appropriate to the dependent plant/animal. A two-way dependency should be represented using the two appropriate colours of wool. When asked, interview individuals about their connections.	Your role is to link plants and animals in the four forest layers. Ask people to share their card and say who they think they depend upon and who depends upon them. Make hand to hand links using pieces of wool (pairs of scissors available). A dependent relationship should be represented using the wool colour appropriate to the dependent plant/animal. A two-way dependency should be represented using the two appropriate colours of wool. When asked, interview individuals about their connections.
EMERGENT LAYER	**EMERGENT LAYER**
You are a **matapalo** (strangler fig). Your name means tree killer. You have aerial roots growing down to the ground. You are all wrapped around the kapok tree and at first need it for support but your trunk becomes very thick and slowly squeezes the kapok tree to death. All your twists and turns create places for plants and animals to live. Your leaves are sun seekers and are up in the emergent layer competing with the kapok leaves for sunshine. Once you have developed enough to 'strangle' the kapok, you become a free standing tree.	You are a **tiny green parakeet.** You and your flock are feeding on the tiny seeds of the kapok tree. It is your favourite food. As a breeze comes up, some of the kapok seeds on which you are feeding fly off with the silken kapok thread.

P

CANOPY

You are an **eyelash viper**. You are a beautiful emerald green snake and look just like your home of green moss. You are way up in the canopy in a part of the kapok tree that has rotted away and is hollow. You eat insects, lizards and frogs.

EMERGENT LAYER

You are an old **kapok tree**. You are very tall and stand above the other trees around you. Parrots, macaws and insects fly up from the canopy to sit on your broad branches. Sloths sometimes climb up to sun themselves. Wrapped around your thick trunk is a matapalo (strangler fig). It is eating your food and slowly squeezing you to death. A heavy load of tank bromeliads hang from your branches.

CANOPY

You are a **poison arrow frog** (dendrobate). You are a very good parent. When it is time to lay eggs you crawl up into the canopy and lay your eggs in a tank bromeliad. This way the eggs have lots of moisture and fish cannot eat them. Under your skin is a poison that kills predators when they bite you. The local indigenous people catch you and tip their arrows in a solution of poison made from your skin.

CANOPY

You are a **green Amazon parrot.** You and your whole flock are stuffing yourselves with the ripe figs of the matapalo. You never fly down to the forest floor.

CANOPY

You are a **whip scorpion.** You live in a hollow part of the kapok tree and come out in the evening to roam up and down the matapalo trunk looking for roaches and crickets to eat. Your tail has a very poisonous sting. You range back and forth from the understory to the canopy.

CANOPY

You are a **oio do aqua** (paper wasp). Your name means 'crying eye' and you sting very hard. You are about two inches long and live in a lizard-size hole in the matapalo in the understory.

CANOPY

You are a **nectar-eating bat.** You come out at night and feed on pollen from the blooms of the kapok and other trees in the canopy and the understory. As you fly from flower to flower you provide a valuable service to the trees: pollen sticks to your body and falls off into other tree flowers, pollinating them.

CANOPY

You are a **tank bromeliad**. You catch large amounts of water in your cupped long slender leaves. A poison arrow frog (dondrobate) has crawled up from the forest floor and laid her eggs in your tank. You are an epiphyte, which means you are a plant that is supported by another plant. You can store water and prevent yourself from drying out by closing your cells when it is dry. You live in the canopy on a kapok limb. Seeds of the matapalo fig often fall near you and use your decayed matter to help them grow. Birds and bats pollinate you.

P

CANOPY

You are a **passion flower vine.** Heliconid butterflies lay their eggs on your leaves. When the larvae hatch out they eat your leaves. Other insects cannot do this because your leaves are poisonous. Sometimes you develop a new poison and kill the butterfly caterpillars, but they then develop an immunity to your poison.

CANOPY

You are a **heliconid butterfly.** You can eat the poisonous leaves of the passion flower. Birds cannot eat your caterpillars because the poison stays in their bodies. You warn that you are poisonous by wearing bright colours that tell predators you are dangerous to eat. You fly around the canopy and understory.

CANOPY

You are a **gecko** (a kind of lizard). You have a blue-black body and a rust orange head. You spend your day fighting for territory with other geckos. You live on the trunk of the matapalo fig and hide in some of its many holes when a predator such as a bird turns up. They are particularly fond of eating you.

CANOPY

You are an **orchid plant**. You live in the canopy on a limb of the kapok tree. Like the bromeliad you are an epiphyte and store water. You are a very special orchid. You grow in an ant's nest. As you grow, the ants use your roots to enlarge their nest. You get some food from them. They eat insects that would otherwise eat you.

CANOPY

You are one of a 600,000 swarm of **army ants**. You are crawling along the forest floor eating and tearing apart everything in your path. You are eating cockroaches, scorpions, millipedes, katydids (grasshoppers), wasps, beetles, termites and other ants. You form a column and march up into the canopy. When your group is moving, nothing is safe. You navigate by smell. The people of the forest use your powerful jaws as sutures for bad cuts, instead of sewing up the wound.

CANOPY

You are a **bird-eating spider.** You live high up in the canopy and eat birds and snakes. You jump on your prey and suck the fluid out of them.

CANOPY

You are one of a group of **howler monkeys**. You are greeting the rising sun with a loud roar typical of your group. You feed on fruits in the canopy trees and only come to the forest floor to rescue young who fall out of the trees. As you crash back and forth, many of the fruits from the tree you are in fall to the forest floor.

CANOPY

You are a **sloth.** It is hard to see you. You move so slowly, green algae grows in your hair and you blend in with the trees. Moths lay eggs in this algae and the hatching larvae eat it. You eat the leaves of the tree you hang in. When they are gone, you slowly move to another spot. Once a week you descend from the canopy to defecate. You carefully bury your waste products at the base of the tree and climb back up. By so doing, you nourish the tree.

P

CANOPY	UNDERSTORY
You are a **hummingbird.** You have to eat every ten to fifteen minutes. You fly around the tallest trees in the canopy and emergent layer. You help pollinate these trees by transferring the pollen that has brushed on to you to other flowers.	You are an **emerald tree boa**. You live on branches. You are camouflaged, blend in with the foliage and strike out at the rodents that form a main part of your diet.
CANOPY	UNDERSTORY
You are a **capuchin monkey.** You leap easily from branch to branch in the canopy. You eat figs from the matapalo and many fall to the forest floor. Some fall into tank bromeliads and begin to grow.	You are a **hooded warbler bird.** You migrate in the winter to the tropical rainforest and follow swarms of army ants to get your dinner.
CANOPY	UNDERSTORY
You are a **toucan**. You fly in the canopy and come to the ground in open places in the forest. You use your big beak to help crack the hard seeds and fruits you eat. This helps them germinate.	You are a **jaguar.** Your spots help keep you camouflaged as you lie in wait for small animals to eat. Your favourite place is a low tree limb, where you pretend to be the leaf pattern. You have no predator but humans.
UNDERSTORY	UNDERSTORY
You are a **philodendron**. You twine around anything to get to the light. Your leaves are small lower down but larger at the top where there is light. You can even grow on the matapalo. Insects and birds rest on you and eat parts of you.	You are a **cacao tree.** Your flowers grow straight out of your trunk and hang down. You make a large hard fruit, the seed of which gives us chocolate. You are pollinated by nectar-eating bats. The people that live in the forest eat your fruit and sell your seed to be ground up as raw chocolate. Unless you are planted on a tropical farm you do not grow near other cacaos.

P

UNDERSTORY

You are an insect called a **leaf mimic mantid**. You look just like a leaf and move like a leaf. Your predators have a very difficult time seeing you. You can be found anywhere there are leaves.

UNDERSTORY

You are a **palo santos tree.** Your name means 'holy stick'. Nothing will grow within a two-foot ring of you. Nothing can touch your bark without receiving a paralysing sting. You have worked out a partnership with some ants. You produce a nectar in your hollow trunk that they feed on and they in turn sting everything that gets near.

FOREST FLOOR

You are a **walking stick insect.** You can be very large. You hide in debris on the forest floor and look like a stick. You are related to leaf mimics.

UNDERSTORY

You are a **mosquito.** You carry the encephalitis virus which leads to inflammation of the brain. You got this virus from biting a bird who had it. You will give it to the first human you bite.

FOREST FLOOR

You are a **look-alike beetle**. You live on the back of an ant and even look like one. You calm them by grooming them. When you are hungry, you eat the ant larvae.

FOREST FLOOR

You are a lowly **fungi.** You help the whole tropical rainforest survive. You break down all the matter that falls to the forest floor and return phosphorus and potassium to the forest plants that they need to grow. You are so efficient at this that you return twenty times the amount of these chemicals to the plants that they lose to the rains. If the forest is removed, you die for lack of things to digest. When you die, none of the plants that depend on you can grow back. Without plants the animals die. You are truly the most important element in the rainforest.

FOREST FLOOR

You are a **peccary** (wild pig). You dig up roots to eat. You also like to be near troops of monkey so you can gorge yourself on the fruit they knock down from the canopy.

P

■ *ENVIRONMENTAL AUDIT*

Suitable for

Secondary

Time needed

A block of time out of school and one or two in-class sessions.

Resources

Notepads and pencils (and, possibly, a loaded cassette tape recorder for each pair of students).

Procedure

Working in pairs, students go out of school to question adult members of the community about a favourite place from childhood. What kind of place was it? Why was the place meaningful to them? What do they especially recall about it? Having obtained a picture of the place and its childhood significance, the students ask about the place described, as it is today. Is it the same? If not, how has it changed? Is it cleaner, quieter, less crowded? Is it still recognisable? Does it have the same meaning? How does the person feel about what has happened to the place? When the class convenes, pairs report on their findings and discussion follows.

Potential

This activity is a potentially powerful way of helping students understand a distinctive human experience of the modern age — the experience of loss, most notably of nature. It is this experience, perhaps more than any other, that has given rise to modern environmentalism, and it is rooted in the seemingly inescapable urbanisation of the planet. How many of the adults questioned cited natural environments as their favourite place? What does this say about our needs as human beings? How many registered a sense of loss at the alteration or destruction of that place?

Extension

Students go on guided tours of favourite places that have changed in the company of the adults concerned. The class takes photographs of the places and records the adults' comments. The photographs and transcribed comments are displayed in a public place in the school.

ADDITIONAL RESOURCES

For the teacher ...

- ☐ Caulfield, C., *In the rainforest*, Picador, 1985.
- ☐ Secrett, C., *Rainforests*, Friends of the Earth, 1986.
- ☐ *New Internationalist*, no. 184, June 1988, 'Tree of life: stop the chainsaw massacre'.
- ☐ *New Internationalist*, no. 219, May 1991, 'Thirst for justice: the people of the Amazon'

For the classroom ...

- ☐ *Endangered species animal rummy educational card game*, Safari Ltd., Box 630685, Ojus, Florida 33163, USA.
- ☐ Lyle, S., 'Forest environments' in Hicks, D., & Steiner, M., *Making global connections. A world studies workbook*, Oliver & Boyd, 1989. Activities introducing 8-13 year olds to the sources of wood we use, temperate and tropical rainforest environments and the causes and effects of tropical rainforest destruction.
- ☐ Lyle, S., & Roberts, M., *A rainforest child*, Greenlight Publications, 1986. An activity pack for 8-13 year olds. Available from Greenlight Publications, Ty Bryn, Coomb Gardens, Llangynog, Carmarthen, Dyfed, SA33 5AY.
- ☐ McKisson, M., & MacRae-Campbell, L., *Endangered species: their struggle to survive*, Tucson, Arizona, Zephyr Press, 1990. A versatile program of activities for grades 4 to 12, this is one of the seven units in the Zephyr global problem solving series.
- ☐ Murphey, C.E., *What have you got to lose? New World tropical rainforests*, Stanford Program on International and Cross-Cultural Education (SPICE), undated. Fourteen primary/lower secondary units with materials for photocopying. Available from SPICE, Littlefield Center, Room 14, 300 Lasuen Street, Stanford University, Stanford, CA 94305-5013, USA.
- ☐ 'Timber!' in Pike, G., & Selby, D., *Global teacher, global learner*, Hodder & Stoughton, 1988, 204-211. A simulation game for upper secondary students in which participants take up the role of various groups with an interest in the tropical rainforests.

❑ Sakamoto, E., *The endangered species activity book. A teacher resource*, Toronto, Coursework Solutions Inc., 1991. Collection of learning activities for grades 7 to 9 on endangered species with particular emphasis on Canadian wildlife.

❑ The World Society for the Protection of Animals (Park Place, 10 Lawn Lane, London SW8 lUD) publishes an *Endangered species fact pack* as well as single sheets on endangered species.

❑ *Key humane organisations to contact (see* Organisations *list): Born Free Foundation, Environment Council, World Society for the Protection of Animals.*

❑ *Other organisation to contact: World Wide Fund for Nature, Panda House, Catteshall Lane, Godalming, Surrey GU7 IXR (tel: 0148- 426444; fax: 01483-426409).*

References

1. Radford, T., 'Chronicles of deaths foretold', *The Guardian*, 5.6.1992, 30; *The Globe and Mail* (Toronto), 21.2.1994, A6.
2. Nicholson-Lord, D., 'How long have we got?', *The Independent on Sunday*, 31.5.1992, 4.
3. Radford, T., *op. cit.*, 30.
4. Seed, J., *et. al.*, *Thinking like a mountain. Towards a council of all beings*, Heretic Books, 1988, 71.
5. Berry, T., cited in CAFOD, *Renewing the Earth. Study guide for groups*, Catholic Fund for Overseas Development, 1989, 93.
6. Sachs, W., 'Whose environment?', *New Internationalist*, no. 232, June 1992, 21-2.
7. Citied in CAFOD, *op. cit.*, 69.
8. Seed, J., 'Beyond anthropocentrism' in Seed, J., *et. al.*, *op. cit.*, 35-6.
9. CAFOD, *op. cit.*, 30.
10. Radford, T., 'Healing force of evolution', *The Guardian*, 6.6.1992, 6.
11. Nicholson-Lord, D., *op. cit.*, 4.
12. Radford, T., 'Chronicle of deaths foretold', *The Guardian*, 5.6.1992, 30.
13. Radford, T., 'Mini-planets on which world depends for air conditioning', *The Guardian*, 8.6.1992, 6.
14. Gates, P., 'World in traction. A planet recovery manual', *BBC Wildlife*, vol. 10, no. 6, June 1992, 55.
15. *The Guardian*, 6.6.1992, 6.
16. 'Natural magic', *New Internationalist*, no. 219, May 1991, 10.
17. Gates, P., *op.cit.*, 55.
18. *World scientists' warning to humanity*, Union of Concerned Scientists (26 Church Street, Cambridge, MA 02238, USA), April 1993.
19. Kennedy, C., 'Living in harmony', *The Living World*, vol. 3, no. 7, Spring 1991, 14.
20. *The Globe and Mail* (Toronto), 21.2.1994, A6.
21. Youth, H., *The Globe and Mail*, 21.2.1994, A7.
22. Cited in McKisson, M., & MacRae-Campbell, L., *Endangered species: their struggle to survive*, Tucson, Arizona, Zephyr Press, 1990, 2.

Chapter 6

Animals and Ourselves

INTRODUCTION

All the creatures of the earth are our kin. They sleep in our cosmic home, eat at our table, share our air and water, and play with our children. We are composed of their bodies and they of ours. Each of us represents but a brief manifestation of the flow and cycling of life here. In human families we speak of blood lines, but in reality, each of us is intimately related to all the creatures of the earth. — Steve Van Matre.[1]

The twenty-four activities in this chapter explore human-animal relationships. From our first cuddly toy, through childhood pets to walks in wild places that revive our careworn adult spirits, animals play a significant part in our lives. Some of the relationships we form with them are mutually beneficial but the majority serve our needs and desires at the expense of the animals concerned. A greater sensitivity to the needs and rights of animals follows, in part, from recalling what we are. It is important that young people are made aware that they, as humans, are also animals and share many common characteristics with other members of the animal world. Hence, following two introductory activities designed to demonstrate the significance of animals and animal-related issues in our lives, a section of activities (*Similarities and*

Differences) is devoted to exploring the degree of similarity between humans and animals in terms of bodily parts, emotions, behaviours, social organisation, needs, and responses to physical and psychological pain. The activities also provide a springboard for some early consideration of the question of animal rights. If many animals also possess the capacity for pain and pleasure, upon which our claim to human rights is in part based, then do those animals have rights too? What, then, are our responsibilities to animals? The third section (*Images of Animals*) explores positive and negative images of animals, the sources of those images, and how negative images can translate into cruelty and abuse. The final section (*Use/Treatment of Animals*) includes activities designed to raise awareness of the degree of abuse and oppression of animals embedded in our daily lives. Alternative, animal-friendly, forms of consumption and life-style are raised and their viability considered. The section also contains a number of activities asking students to clarify their value positions concerning the generality and specifics of human treatment of animals. Issues surrounding the degree of congruence in society's attitudes to animals are continually raised. These are especially important for young people to consider. 'We start sending our kids conflicting messages about animals at an early age. With one hand we give them cute and cuddly stuffed animals to sleep with at night; with the other we serve them animals as meals. And while grown-ups use the word 'meat' instead of 'dead animals' to describe their dinner, eventually the day comes when every kid understands that his hot dog was once a living creature. That may be his or her first philosophical dilemma: Why are we eating the animals we love?[2] Towards the close of the section are activities asking students to consider the parallels and connections between abuse and oppression of animals and abuse and oppression of people.

INTRODUCTORY ACTIVITIES

■ *PEOPLE SEARCH*

Suitable for

Upper primary/secondary

Time needed

15 minutes

Resources

A *People Search* hand-out for each student. An open classroom space so that participants can move freely about.

Procedure

Students move around the open area searching for a person who can respond in the affirmative to each of the items in the hand-out. The person's name is written in the space next to the item and must appear on the sheet only once. Participants are encouraged to volunteer additional information during each exchange and, where items refer to feelings, to share the experience at greater length. The activity can continue until everybody's hand-out is as complete as possible or can be halted after a suitable period. Students then gather together to discuss how much they found they had in common and to reflect on what was shared.

Potential

A lively activity enabling students to discover a great deal about each other very quickly. It also provides an excellent opportunity for helping participants see that their personal concerns for animals and the environment — which they may

Mixed messages: sign outside a Camden, Maine, seafood shop'(Photo: Bärbel Selby)

Good as a warm-up activity. Works well with a new group in helping to break down barriers. It is a good idea to leave the possibility of students adding two or three of their own ideas at the bottom of the sheet before mingling.

— Kent secondary teacher.

It raised the question of legal/illegal activities. 'How far would you be prepared to go to defend an animal's rights?' Also, the question of why some animals, such as snakes, get such a bad press.

— Cambridgeshire secondary teacher.

PEOPLE SEARCH

Find someone who:

1. Has felt really happy recently   ————————————————

2. Has been alone in a wilderness area   ————————————————

3. Has helped a stray pet   ————————————————

4. Is scared of spiders   ————————————————

5. Feels worried about the future   ————————————————

6. Is an active member of an animal
   welfare group   ————————————————

7. Has been chased by a bull   ————————————————

8. Uses soaps and cosmetics that
   have not been tested on animals   ————————————————

9. Has heard an environmental/animal
   protection success story recently   ————————————————

10. Has good feelings about the future   ————————————————

11. Has visited a veterinarian recently   ————————————————

12. Has touched or handled a snake   ————————————————

13. Stopped another human being or
    an animal being badly treated recently   ————————————————

14. Would never wear fur   ————————————————

15. Has a special relationship with a
    particular non-human animal   ————————————————

16. Has felt angry recently   ————————————————

17. Does not agree with hunting   ————————————————

18. Has one or more bird feeders in
    her/his garden   ————————————————

19. Has read an upsetting story concerning
    the treatment of animals recently   ————————————————

20. Tries to stick to a healthy diet   ————————————————

P

feel do not enjoy wide currency — are shared by many others. Questions to trigger discussion might include: 'What did you learn about someone in the class that surprised you?'; 'Did you realise before that you had so much in common with other members of the class?'; 'What feelings/experiences did you find others had experienced too?'; 'Did you find that you shared with others similar concerns about animals?'; 'Was it hard or easy to talk about feelings?'; 'Why?'. The hand-out can be simplified, and the number of questions cut down, for younger students.

■ *SPECIAL ANIMALS*

Suitable for

Primary/secondary

Time needed

25 minutes

Resources

A *Special Animals* sheet, such as that offered overleaf, for each student; an open space.

Procedure

Each student moves around the room trying to find someone for whom an animal on the sheet is in some way special or significant (e.g. as a pet, as connected with a memorable moment in their lives, as a cause of delight or fright). Having found someone and having listened to the explanation of the animal's significance, she writes the name of the person against the animal and notes down the reason(s) it is special. Only one answer can be obtained from a particular

individual. She then proceeds to talk to others, writing in further names as she meets individuals for whom an animal has a special meaning.

Potential

A lively activity enabling students to get to know each other better, it points up the important part that animals play in our lives. The activity provides an opportunity to practise listening and questioning skills, students sharing what they have found out in plenary session.

Variations

1. Students can be given blank sheets and asked to fill in the names of animals special to them before the interaction begins.

2. (For infants). A *Special Animals* sheet containing line drawings of animals is used. A student choosing an animal writes her name in the appropriate box of her questioner's sheet.

3. Students' names are written in *red* against animals that, for them, have negative connotations and in *blue* against animals that evoke a positive response. The total number of red and blue responses for each animal are counted and recorded and the results analysed and discussed in a plenary discussion session.

Source

Variations 2, 3: Fiona Heads

> *Very successful. The children greatly enjoyed the activity. It enhanced their ideas about animals and their connections with animals. Quite suitable for this age group.*
>
> — Hertfordshire primary teacher (10-11 year olds).

Fig.1

P

RABBIT	DONKEY	SPIDER	BIRD OF PREY
GOAT	MONKEY	CAT	SQUIRREL
SNAKE	DOG	DEER	HAMSTER
HORSE	SALMON	MOUSE	SWALLOW

SIMILARITIES AND DIFFERENCES

What goes on in the brain of this amazingly human-like creature? — Voice-over from a National Geographic movie about gorillas.[3]

■ *ANIMAL PARTS*

Suitable for

Primary

Time needed

25 minutes

Resources

A copy of the *Animal Parts* sheet.

Procedure

Students are asked to brainstorm the physical parts that animals have in common. The teacher makes a list on the board or overhead projection transparency. Any problems (e.g. are wings arms?) are discussed. Each student is then given a single picture from the *Animal Parts* sheets and asked to circulate around the room to find other members with whom they can form a 'parts' group. This stage of the activity is complete when students have found all those with pictures of similar parts of the body (e.g. all the 'legs' are together). Groups then dissolve and students are asked to form groups of composite parts of a single animal (e.g. the head, eye, mouth, ear and leg/foot of a rabbit). This will require very careful attention and close co-operation as some parts of the different animals will initially seem quite similar (the 'head' pictures will help in identification of eyes, mouths and ears).

Potential

A co-operative activity enabling students to recognise physical similarities and differences between a selected group of animals and underlining the point that human and non-human animals share many physical characteristics. In the debriefing the question of which body parts were easy to sort into animal groups and which not so easy will provide a useful springboard for discussion.

Extensions

1. A collection of posters of animals and humans is put on display. Groups are allocated a set of pieces of paper (each set of a different colour) and strands of wool of the same colour. A colour key is established (e.g. those with green paper write 'How I hear' on each piece, those with blue paper 'How I see' and so on). Groups attach one of their pieces of paper close to each poster with a piece of wool linking the paper and the relevant part of the body as it appears on the poster. Alternatively, or additionally, students use the wool to connect similar body parts on the different posters.

2. Working in pairs, students take turns to lie down on large sheets of paper while their partner draws around their body with a thick felt pen. Each student decorates the outline so as to create a life-size portrait. On other pieces of paper, each draws an image of their pet or favourite animal. The four pictures are stuck to the wall in close proximity and wool used to connect similar body parts. Explanatory labels are added. The task can be extended so that students write in non-physical characteristics shared by the humans and animals. This activity can usefully be linked to *Silhouettes* (p.66).

Source

Fiona Heads.

ANIMAL PARTS

 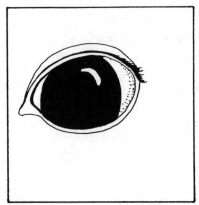 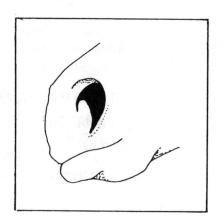

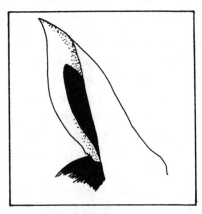 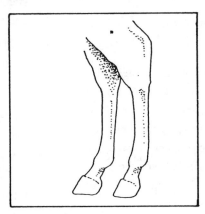

 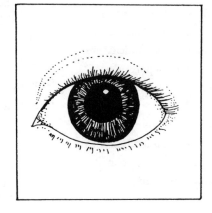 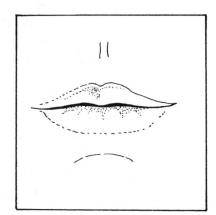

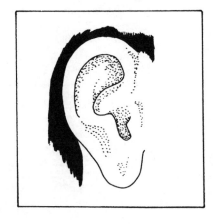 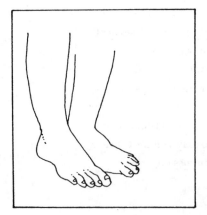

P

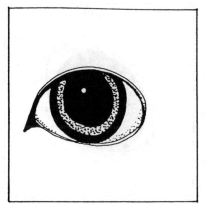
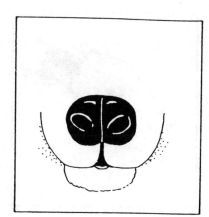

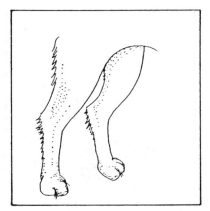

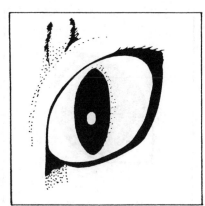
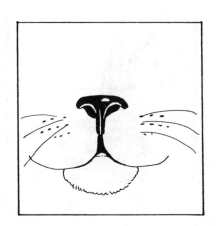

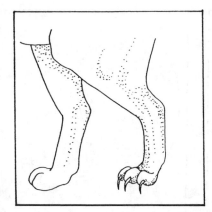

P

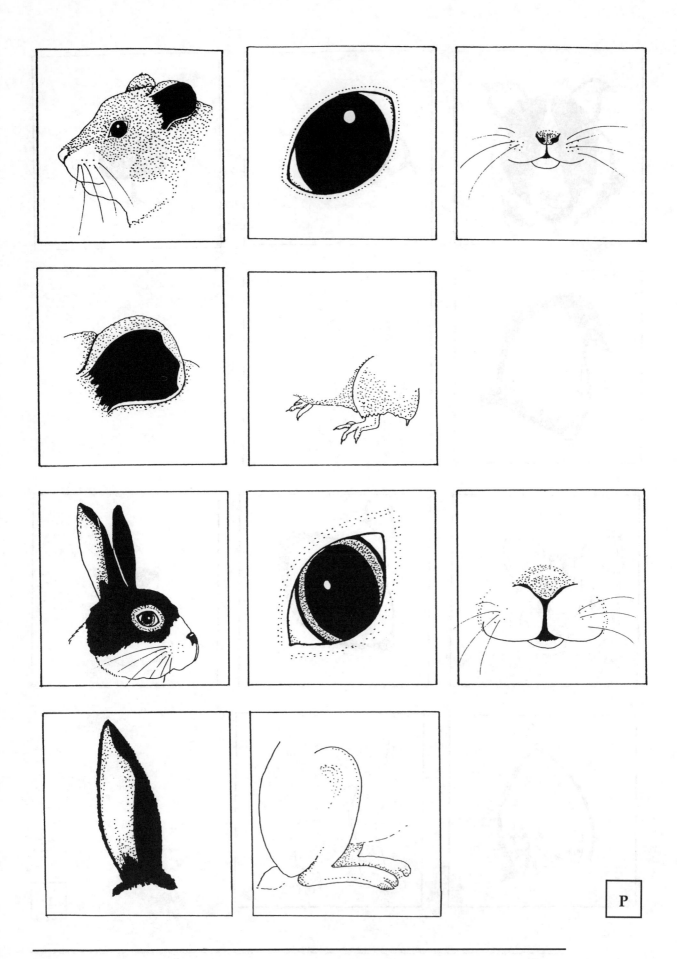

P

■ *ANIMAL AND HUMAN CHARACTERISTICS (1)*

Suitable for

Upper primary/secondary

Time needed

60 minutes.

Resources

Twelve slips (quarter A4 sheets) of paper of one colour for half the class; twelve slips of a second colour for the other half. A pot of paste or paste stick, felt pens and two sheets of sugar paper, sellotaped together, for each four students. Blu-tak.

Procedure

Students form into pairs and the paper is distributed so that partners have twelve slips of paper each, each set of a different colour. A list of twelve characteristics is revealed (a sample list is given in *Fig. 2*). Students with slips of the first colour write brief descriptions/anecdotes (one per slip) drawing preferably, but not necessarily, on their own experience, of how *non-human animals* demonstrate each of the twelve characteristics. Their partners write

Fig. 2

descriptions/anecdotes of how *human beings* manifest those same characteristics. During the writing stage discussion is to be avoided.

The task completed, partners share the examples they have chosen and briefly discuss the degree of difference/similarity in animal and human characteristics pointed up by their work.

Pairs join together to form groups of four. Having shared and discussed their descriptions/anecdotes and provisional conclusions, their task is to devise a *Human and Animal Characteristics* chart using their written slips but also employing drawings, cartoons and comments to convey their thinking regarding the degree of commonality and difference between human and animal characteristics and behaviours. The chart should signal both agreements and disagreements within the group. Charts are stuck on the classroom walls and students move around reading each others' work. Plenary discussion ensues.

Potential

An effective means of beginning to explore the degree of overlap between human and animal characteristics. Plenary discussion can be structured around group and individual reactions to a range of important questions. Did students find it equally easy to think of animal and human examples of each characteristic? Are there other characteristics, not in the list of twelve, that really distinguish humans from animals? Are humans 'superior' to animals, and, if so, in what sense? Did students rate certain characteristics above others (e.g. reason above instinct)? Is it anthropocentric to do so? Are the differences between humans and animals sufficient to allow for the acceptance of specifically human rights and the rejection of animal rights? What does the activity suggest about how we should regard and treat animals?

Variation

(For younger students). The class forms into small groups (twos or threes). Half the groups work on examples of animals demonstrating the listed characteristics; half on human examples. Groups then join to conduct an animal-human comparison.

CHARACTERISTICS

1. the ability to feel and express pleasure

2. the ability to suffer and show pain

3. the ability to think things out and solve problems

4. the ability to learn

5. the capacity to act and respond instinctively

6. the ability to show affection

7. the ability to play

8. the ability to care for the young

9. the ability to build things

10. the ability to know right from wrong

11. the ability to communicate

12. the ability to remember things

Extension

Students undertake research into animal behaviours to test the validity of views expressed in the plenary discussion.

Source

Variation: Fiona Heads.

■ ANIMAL AND HUMAN CHARACTERISTICS (2)

Suitable for

Primary/secondary

Time needed

60 minutes

Resources

Up to twenty-five sugar paper charts stuck around the classroom walls, each having one of the following as a heading: Feels/Expresses Pleasure; Experiences Pain; Learns; Experiences Fear; Has a Sense of Purpose; Raises/Cares For Young; Communicates Feelings; Communicates Thoughts; Feels Guilt; Sociable; Mourns Death of Loved Ones; Is Compassionate; Shows Affection/Love; Builds Things; Uses Tools; Laughs; Thinks Things Out; Is Self-Conscious; Behaves Instinctively; Shows Loyalty; Shows Gratefulness; Has a Memory; Has a Sense of the Past; Has a Sense of the Future; Can Plan; Can Weigh Arguments; Can Understand Complex Ideas; Shows Contentment; Can Be Ambitious; Can Function Within a Complex Social Organisation; Intuitive; Co-operative. An equivalent number of slips of paper of another colour for each student. Pots of paste. Six coloured sticky dots per student. An *Only Humans* sheet (see sample, *Fig. 3*) per group of four students.

Procedure

Students are invited to write brief examples of how animals manifest each of the characteristics shown on the charts. They are asked to limit themselves to one example per slip and one slip per characteristic. Having written examples for as many characteristics as they can, they paste their slips on the appropriate chart. They are then given six sticky dots and, avoiding discussion, are asked to place them in the top right-hand corner of the charts for the six characteristics that, in their view, most reveal the essence of what it means to be human. Groups of four to six are then formed to explore and discuss outcomes. To generate discussion, each group is given a list of *Only Humans* statements to accept, reject or qualify. Plenary reporting back and discussion follows.

> *Highly successful. Many words needed explaining (e.g. compassionate, complex, instinctive) but the children greatly enjoyed this and all felt it had strengthened their positive attitudes towards other living beings. Although far more thought people mourn (more than) animals, many had moving accounts of how their pets had mourned and sometimes died when they had lost a partner. They also thought it important for animals to show guilt ... which somewhat surprised me. We discussed this and they said that animals cause far less destruction, murder and suffering than do humans and therefore humans should feel more guilt than animals.*
>
> — Hertfordshire primary teacher (10-11 year olds)

Potential

This activity can raise some problematic and fundamental issues surrounding human and animal characteristics and, by extension, human and animal rights. Were there characteristics for which students could not think of animal examples? Are these the characteristics that really distinguish humankind from other creatures? Do they make humans 'superior'? Do the characteristics common to both humans and animals manifest themselves in qualitatively different ways?

Are the qualities regarded by the class as essential to our very humanity (i.e. the characteristics attracting most dots) the ones for which animal examples were hardest to find? If so, what are the implications? Or, do animals possess some — or all — of them too? In that case, what are the implications? Are the differences between humans and animals qualitatively and quantitatively sufficient to support a claim for specifically human rights (as against rights for both human and non-human animals)? Which characteristics in particular do students feel provide a sound basis for a firm claim to rights for both humans and animals?

ONLY HUMANS

Only humans can communicate in a sophisticated way

Only humans get together to enjoy themselves

Only humans show real emotions

Only humans have a sense of right and wrong

Only humans have an understanding of progress

Only humans use reason and logic

Only humans live in well-organised societies

Only humans can love

Only humans can rise above instinctive behaviour

Only humans are capable of self-reflection

Fig. 3

Given the issues thrown up by the activity, would the concept of needs provide a sounder basis for the protection of both human and animal interests than rights (see p.16).

Variations

1. Students are given a second set of sticky dots of a different colour. They are asked to place the dots in the top left-hand corner of the charts for the six characteristics most strongly representing the essence of animals. The degree of overlap and difference in the spread of the two sets of dots, and the implications that can be drawn, then becomes a major focus of the debriefing session.

2. For younger students the number and conceptual difficulty of characteristics addressed should be reduced.

Source

Variation 1: Amber Carroll.

■ *MY NEEDS ARE YOUR NEEDS*

Suitable for

Primary

Time needed

35 minutes

Resources

A set of *Needs* cards for each pair of students

Procedure

The teacher discusses with the class the activities they have been engaged in since leaving school the evening before. Activities put forward by students are listed (e.g. playing, eating, washing, sleeping). The class proceeds to discuss whether pets and other animals have the same needs (for play, food, cleanliness/health, sleep, etc.). Students are encouraged to offer examples of animals fulfilling those needs. Students form into pairs. Each pair is given a set of *Needs* cards. They are asked to place the cards upside down on a table surface and jumble them up. One of the pair, and then the other, picks up a card. If the pictures match (e.g. the bowl of breakfast cereal and the bowl of dog food are picked up) the pictures are left face up. If not, the pictures are replaced face down. Only one card can be picked up at a time. Students are encouraged to help each other by remembering, and pointing out, the location of specific pictures.

Potential

A co-operative learning activity, that also practices memory skills, designed to raise awareness that humans and animals share many of the same basic needs.

Variation

Pairs of students are each given a sheet of sugar paper. The ends of the paper are folded into the centre and the paper opened to reveal three sections. The class is provided with old magazines and colour supplements, scissors and paste. Pairs cut out a picture of a child and paste it in the left section. Next they cut out a picture of a cat, dog or other pet and paste it in the right section, leaving the large middle section blank. The pair then browse through the magazines, cutting out pictures of items that both the child and the pet need each day. These are pasted in the middle section and labelled. Reporting back and discussion follows.

Extension

Students draw two-part picture of themselves a) helping to meet the needs of another human being and b) helping to meet the needs of their real (or imagined) pets. *A Meeting Needs* art collection is displayed on the classroom walls.

Source

Fiona Heads.

■ *EXPLORING NEEDS*

Suitable for

Top primary/secondary.

Time needed

40 minutes.

Resources

Three pictures of individual people (the pictures should show different types of people, e.g. a child, an adult, an elderly person, a disabled person, and should include both genders and reflect the multi-racial nature of society); three pictures of animals (a pet, a farm animal, a wild animal); two pictures of plants (a potted house plant, a wild plant). Ten sheets of sugar paper; ten felt pens; a pot of paste.

Procedure

Students form into groups of four. Each group is given a picture and sticks it at the top of their sheet of sugar paper. Groups are asked to list all the things they can think of that the subject of their picture needs so as to ensure its well-being and survival. Their task complete, they are asked to pair up with another group that has considered a different type of subject and to explore the degree of commonality in the lists produced. Items can be added to the original lists as discussion unfolds. The combined groups report back, identifying the needs they found to be common and those they felt to be particular to the subjects of the two photographs. The results can be collated on a class chart (see *Fig. 4*)

P

NEEDS CARDS

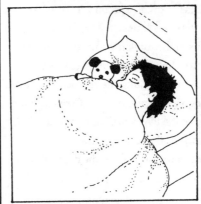

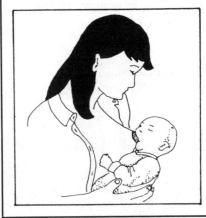

NEEDS CARDS

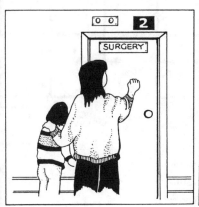

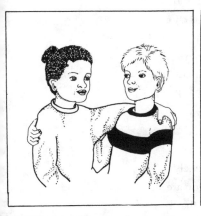

Potential

A simple yet effective means of helping students identify the basic human needs essential for physical and emotional well-being (e.g. adequate food, water, shelter, clean air and living conditions, companionship, love and affection, freedom from pain/fear/stress, freedom of movement) and of demonstrating that most of those needs are shared by animals and some by plants. Plenary discussion can begin by asking the class to reflect on the collated results and, depending on age and ability, upon some or all of the following questions. What needs mark humans out from animals and plants? Is the 'needs gap' between humans and animals larger than between animals and plants or vice-versa? On reflection, are there further needs that should be added to the chart? What happens if the needs listed are not met? Do the needs of humans, animals and plants matter equally? If so, why? If not, why not? Are there particular groups of human beings whose needs are ignored or overlooked? What changes would have to take place to satisfy the needs of all humans? Would those changes impact positively or negatively on the needs of other life forms? What would be the impact on human society if we sought to meet the needs of animals? Would any such attempt be feasible or desirable? Would we be prepared to accept the costs, economic and otherwise, involved?

It can be explained to the class that, today, human needs are often expressed in terms of *rights* (i.e. things which in all fairness and justice we are entitled to have or do). If animals' needs are in many ways similar to human needs does this mean they also possess rights? Do plants have rights too? Or, do we possess characteristics and qualities which mark us out as special and superior and, as such, the sole or principal possessors of rights?

Extensions

Students compile a list of questions raised by the activity and put the questions to an invited panel (panel members could include a psychologist, a social worker, a veterinarian, a dog trainer, a member of a humane society, a botanist and a wildlife conservation officer).

NEEDS PHOTO SUBJECTS											
HUMAN 1											
HUMAN 2											
HUMAN 3											
ANIMAL 1											
ANIMAL 2											
ANIMAL 3											
PLANT 1											
PLANT 2											

Fig 4

■ *SUFFERING*

Suitable for

Primary

Time needed

60-90 minutes

Resources

A large piece of paper for each group; an *Animal Suffering Card* per pair; felt pens for each group.

Procedure

Students form groups of four and are asked to brainstorm what they understand by suffering (their brainstorm should also include examples of situations involving suffering). Ideas are written in felt pen on the large piece of paper provided. After 15-20 minutes the class collects together. Each group presents their brainstorm results to the class, and the teacher summarises feedback and builds up a class collection of ideas and examples on the board or overhead projection transparency. The discussion that follows should focus on the causes of suffering as shown in the examples. Are many examples related to physical suffering? Why do you think this is so? Is that the only form of suffering? What other forms are represented? Can you suffer because your feelings are hurt? Because you are bored and have nothing to do? Because you are lonely? Because you miss someone? Because you are frightened? Examples can be added to the class collection as the discussion progresses. Students should come to realise that suffering can involve more than physical pain or injury. At an appropriate point, they can be asked if they think that animals can suffer for a similar range of reasons. This point is discussed. The children then return to their original groups. Each group splits into pairs and each pair is given an animal suffering card. Pairs discuss the situation described in their card and decide how each situation might cause the animal involved to suffer. Groups of four then reconvene. Each pair takes it in turns to read their card to their partners and to explain how they feel the situation causes suffering and what kind of suffering is involved. The partners then try to suggest ways in which the suffering might be alleviated. The students can summarise their discussions by drawing a picture of the situation and writing both descriptions of the suffering caused and of ways of alleviating it. Work is displayed. Students circulate to view the work of other groups.

Potential

This activity will elicit much discussion about what it means to suffer. By working from personal experiences of suffering, students' understanding of the concept is allowed to develop. This new understanding is then applied to animals with the greater likelihood that students will empathise with the situations presented on the cards. Suggesting ways of alleviating the suffering helps to avoid any sense of powerlessness.

Source

Jackie Harvey, after an idea in The National Association for the Advancement of Humane Education, *People and animals*, curriculum guide, 1981.

P

ANIMAL SUFFERING CARDS

A dog tied to a tree in a backyard all the time and left alone.

A chicken confined to a small wire cage in a battery farm, standing on a wire mesh floor and unable to stretch its wings.

A pig kept alone in the dark in a concrete fattening pen in which it can't turn round.

A horse left in its stable for long periods of time and not exercised or groomed properly.

A wild animal captured and confined to a small cage at a zoo.

A dog left in a car in full sunlight on a hot day.

A whale kept alone in a tank of water at an amusement park.

A calf separated from its mother, kept in the dark and fed on milk.

A parrot kept chained to a perch in a pet shop.

A large dog kept in a small flat and rarely taken for walks.

A poodle which wears a bow, is fed on chocolates and is never allowed to roll around in the dirt.

A wolf caught in a leg trap for three days hearing a human being approach.

IMAGES OF ANIMALS

Confusing messages about animals come at kids from books, television, and movies. Through animated, humanlike characters, children are presented with a bewildering array of 'good' animals and 'bad' animals'. Wolves, rats and crocodiles are usually portrayed as vicious and cruel. But the 'good' animals- lambs, deer, rabbits, and other smiling creatures don't bear much relation to real animals, either. It's hard for a child to understand, much less revere, the animal kingdom when exposed to these kind of hero and villain stereotypes. Children need to learn to respect all animals, whether predator or prey, whether wild animals who prefer to be left alone or domesticated animals who depend on our love, kindness, and care.
— The Animal Rights Handbook[4]

■ *ANIMAL ALPHABETS*

Suitable for

Primary

Time needed

Four sessions of 45 minutes each.

Resources

Twenty-six strips of paper — each with one of the letters of the alphabet written to the left of the strip — for each group of three students. A selection of pictures and posters of domestic and wild animals that are sometimes or often viewed negatively.

Procedure

The pictures are shown to the students one by one. As each picture is shown students are asked to brainstorm words describing the animal depicted. The words put forward are recorded. All contributions are accepted. The brainstorming complete, the class considers each word list and what it says about human attitudes to the animal in question. The process is then repeated but this time the class is encouraged to offer words that cast each animal in a favourable light. At the close of the brainstorming, students are encouraged to review their work and reflect on how the results make them feel. Groups of three are formed. Their task is to compose an *Animal Alphabet* by finding the name of an animal for each letter of the alphabet, linking it to an alliterative and positive descriptive word (e.g. beautiful baboon, happy hyena) and writing it on the appropriate strip of paper. If any letter finally proves impossible (e.g. X) the group is to feel free to find some humorous way around the problem! *Alphabets* are read out or displayed. Discussion follows.

Potential

A simple activity designed to encourage students to question, even shed, negative images and irrational fears of particular animals. In the concluding discussion students should be asked if the activity has led them to have second thoughts about particular animals. If so, why?

Extension

Groups choose one of the animals featured in their *Alphabet* and write, and illustrate, a poem promoting its positive qualities.

Source

Fiona Heads.

■ *ANIMAL AFFIRMATION*

Suitable for

Primary/secondary

Time needed

30 minutes

Resources

A sheet of plain paper for each student.

Procedure

The class brainstorms as many types of animal and insects as they can think of that they fear, dislike or find disgusting. All contributions are accepted. Groups of six to eight are then formed and each student writes the name of one of the creatures brainstormed at the *bottom* of their sheet of paper. The same creature must not be chosen by two people in the same group. Students pass their sheet to the person to their left who is asked to write a positive statement about the animal/insect in question at the top of the sheet beginning 'I like... because'. The statement is folded over so it cannot be read by anybody else. Sheets are then passed to the left for a further statement to be written by the next student. The process (which is conducted entirely in silence) continues until each sheet returns to its originator with one less positive statement than the number of people in the group. Sheets are unfurled and, one by one, read to the rest of the group. Group, then class, discussion follows.

Potential

A useful activity for helping students balance their negative emotional responses towards certain creatures with positive feelings. Discussion can focus on the sources and the validity of negative responses, differences in response to particular animals/insects amongst class members and reactions to the positive statements generated by the activity.

Extensions

1. Students are led in a guided visualisation to imagine what it might feel like to be one of the creatures highlighted by the activity.

2. Students create posters that make a positive statement, in words and images, about one of the creatures considered.

3. Groups research into the creatures thrown up by the activity using project collections and the school library.

Variation

The activity can be attempted with younger children by 'passing one animal or insect round at a time with positive feelings being shared orally. The teacher, or an adult leader, records contributions.

Source

Extensions 1 and 2: Amber Carroll.
Variation: Fiona Head.

■ *ANIMAL ADJECTIVES*

Suitable for
Primary/secondary

Time needed
25 minutes

Resources

A set of four half sheets of sugar paper for each group of six students. In the centre of each half sheet is a picture of an animal. Two pictures in any set should be chosen as likely to generate positive responses (e.g. cat, horse, koala bear); two as likely to elicit negative responses (e.g. spider, snake, bat). The group task is to take each sheet in turn and brainstorm adjectives describing the animal in the picture. These are written on the surrounding paper. [Instead of brainstorming, group members can move amongst the sheets and write in their own words.] The finished work is stuck to the classroom wall for inspection by members of other groups. Discussion follows.

> *The children enjoyed this although some of the groups took a long time to write down any responses — possibly linked with shyness about group work. Very suitable for this age group. Not everyone accepted all the adjectives written; this elicited a lot of discussion.*
>
> — Hertfordshire primary teacher (10-11 year olds)
>
> *So much can be made from what is, in principle, a simple, quick activity.*
>
> — Kent secondary teacher

Potential

A quick activity that will stimulate discussion about feelings towards certain animals and the degree of individual differences in attitude between class members. The class can be asked to compare the adjectives used for different animals and to think about what the choice of adjectives says about feelings of individuals and of the class as a whole towards particular animals. Why are a person's feelings for certain animals different from those for other animals? Why do certain animals attract a preponderance of positive adjectives and others negative images? Does everybody accept the adjectives chosen for particular animals? Are the words used in every case true and fair?

Variation

Students are given a sheet of lined paper. Down the left-hand side they write the names of insects, birds, reptiles and mammals brainstormed by the class. The list should include animals they like and animals they dislike. A series of columns are drawn down the sheet. Students use a column for each interview conducted with friends, class and family members. Interviewees are asked to assess each animal on a four-point scale (4 if they like the animal in question, 3 if they have no opinion, 2 if they dislike it and 1 if they fear it). Total numbers can be calculated (the highest figures representing the best-liked animals) and/or averages worked out. The class then engages in discussion around the findings. Did some individuals rate some animals high and some low? Why should that be? Did everyone agree on which animals they liked, disliked or feared? Why might some people fear a particular animal and others like it? Do the findings accord with the students' own attitudes?

Extension

Working in small groups, the class conducts a survey of the attitudes of particular interest groups in the community to some or all of the animals covered in the activity (others can be added as the students wish). Targets for interview might include veterinarians, farmers, pet shop owners, butchers, slaughterhouse workers, vegetarians, hunt members, naturalists, zoo workers, conservationists, anglers, members of humane societies. The interviews should concentrate on both attitudes to the animals and to human treatment of each animal. Having completed the interviews, students take turns role-playing one of the people they interviewed and answering questions from the class. Subsequent discussion can focus upon the degree of difference in attitude found amongst those interviewed and upon whether students agree or disagree with what the interviewees said.

■ *THE TEEMING ARK*

Suitable for

Primary/secondary

Time needed

1.   15 minutes

2.   40 minutes

Resources

Each student requires a *Teeming Ark* form such as the sample shown (*Fig. 5*); extra forms required if the group work approach (see 2 below) is used; a class chart (*Fig.6* or *7*).

Procedure

1.   Students are reminded of the story of Noah's Ark. They are asked to imagine a similar flood in which they find themselves in Noah's position but with space rapidly running out on board the boat. There are ten pairs of animals left on shore (a female and male of each species) and they are asked to decide which of the ten pairs they would want to make sure of space for first, which next, and so on. One or more pairs of animals may have to be left behind. Students are asked to read the form carefully and decide between the respective merits of the ten animals. They then make their decisions — without discussion — by putting 1 against the first pair of animals they would bring on board, a 2 against the second and so on. The pair of animals that are most likely to be left on land are numbered 10. The teacher then compiles a class chart (*Fig. 6*) so that everybody can see the priority given to each pair of animals by the class as a whole. Discussion follows.

OR

2.   Having filled in the form individually and without discussion, students form groups of three and discuss each other's decisions. After discussion, each group tries to negotiate a consensus list using an extra copy of the form. Groups then join with a second group and members of the groups so formed proceed to discuss their respective decisions before seeking to negotiate a

further consensus list. The class goes into plenary session. The enlarged groups report on their prioritisation and the teacher makes a record on a class chart (*Fig. 7*) before class discussion commences.

Potential

This activity will raise a number of questions about why we like some animals and dislike and fear others. Which animals did individuals/groups prefer? Why? What creates our positive or negative image of a particular animal? What characteristic(s), in each case, is the image built around? What helps perpetuate that image? Is it a fair or unfair image? What is the basis of our fear of certain animals? In what ways has our dislike or fear of such animals harmed their well-being and survival chances? Is it reasonable or realistic to single out certain animals as disagreeable given that all creatures are mutually-sustaining actors in the web of life?

Extensions

1. The class watches appropriate film material on one or more animals that tend to be negatively perceived (see box). Groups discuss whether, on the evidence of the film, the negative images are justified. Plenary discussion follows.

An excellent source of animal videos is Video Plus Direct, 1923 Manasty Road, Orton, Southgate, Peterborough, PEP 6UP from which source the following can purchased: **White Fang** (wolves, animated); **Blue Wilderness** (sharks); **Grizzly!** and **National Geographic — Grizzlies** (bears); **Realm of the Alligator; World of Discovery — the Realm of the Serpent** (snakes); **World of Discovery — The Crocodile's Revenge.**

---

2. Groups are each allotted an animal which currently has a 'bad' reputation (the ones used can be those listed on the *Teeming Ark* form plus, perhaps, bats, sharks and spiders). They are asked to imagine that they are a public relations group hired to improve the animal's image by producing a multimedia presentation, possibly including posters, leaflets, a song and dramatic performance. The finished production can be shared with the rest of the class, the school and the community.

Variations

1. With younger students, a boat outline with slits for ten (or less) animal pictures is provided for each group of three students. Students decide (and keep a record of) which animal is slotted in first, which next and so on. Class discussion follows. Groups then remove the pictures of all but the last animal put on board. Their task is to fill in the boat outline with drawings and pieces of writing pointing out the good things about the animal concerned.

2. The class divides into ten groups, each group speaking for a particular animal. Groups prepare, and present, the case for their animal going into the ark. In plenary session, the teacher takes the role of Noah, putting questions to each group following its presentation. If this variation is followed, it is preferable if the ten animals chosen are all ones that tend to elicit negative reactions (the animals brainstormed in *Animal Affirmation* could be used).

Source

Variation 2: Fiona Heads.

Fig. 5

☐	Tigers
☐	Deer
☐	Snakes
☐	Pandas
☐	Foxes
☐	Crocodiles
☐	Toads
☐	Chimpanzees
☐	Rats
☐	Camels

	1	2	3	4	5	6	7	8	9	10
Tigers										
Deer										
Snakes										
Pandas										
Foxes										
Crocodiles										
Toads										
Chimpanzees										
Rats										
Camels										

Fig. 6

	Tigers	Deer	Snakes	Pandas	Foxes	Crocodiles	Toads	Chimpanzees	Rats	Camels
Large Group 1										
Large Group 2										
Large Group 3										
Large Group 4										
Large Group 5										

Fig. 7

■ *BIG BAD WOLVES?*

Suitable for

Upper primary/secondary

Time needed

40 minutes

Resources

Sheet of sugar paper, two felt pens and a set of statements about wolves (see *Fig. 8*) for each group of three/four students.

Procedure

The teacher first leads a class brainstorming session (see p. xxx) of ideas, associations, idioms and sayings stimulated by the word 'wolf'. All suggestions are written up on the board or overhead projection transparency. Groups then form. Using the paper and pens provided, their first task is to divide the class responses into positive and negative images and to discuss and write down where they think the images of the wolf may have come from. A set of statements is then given to each group to promote further discussion. With which statements — or sentiments within statements — do they agree? With which do they disagree? Who do they think might have made such statements? Class discussion follows.

Potential

A useful activity for exploring stereotyping in attitudes towards a much-maligned animal.

Discussion is likely to focus upon why people tend to have a negative image of the wolf. What characteristics of wolves might generate fear and misunderstanding in humans? Which people might most feel their interests to be threatened by the wolf? Who might believe their interests to be best served by perpetuating fear and misunderstanding? How is the negative image of the wolf passed on to fresh generations? Is the image fair? Why do some people see the wolf in a very different way? What effect has the negative image of the wolf upon wolf populations?

1. The class watches a film exploring the reality of wolf behaviour and social interaction prior to further group and plenary discussion. Suitable films for primary use include: *Never Cry Wolf*, Disney Educational Productions, 1983, 30 mins.; *Where Timber Wolves Call*, Wombat 1977, 25 mins.; *Wolf Pack*, Canadian Wildlife Service, Ottawa, 1976, 20 mins.; *Wolves*, Owl TV Productions, no.37, Toronto, 1990; *Wolves*, Rainbow Educational Video, New York, 1990, 10 mins. Suitable films for secondary classroom include: *Death of a Legend*, National Film Board of Canada, 1971, 49 mins.; *The Wolf Saga*, BBC, 1990, 29 mins.; *Wolf*, ABC News Productions, New York, 1977, 22 mins.; *Wolves*, National Audobon Society, USA, 1988, 60 mins.; *Wolves and the Wolfman*, MGM, CA, 1971, 52 mins.

P

Fig. 8

Wolves are responsible for the cold blooded slaughter of huge numbers of defenceless sheep and other livestock. They are cruel and cunning animals. They are the criminal exploiters of nature; vermin deserving to be eradicated.

Wolves have been found to act as an important 'natural safety valve' on population of deer, moose, rabbits and other animals. They weed out the weaker members of the population, thus preventing overcrowding and allowing the stronger, fitter animals to flourish.

The Great Spirit is within the wolf as it is within all things. The wolf is the voice of the wilderness and it is part of the pattern of nature which connects us all. If we destroy the wolf, we destroy ourselves.

I wanted to give something of my past to my grandson. So I took him into the woods, to a quiet spot. Seated at my feet he listened as I told him of the powers that were given to each creature. He moved not a muscle as I explained how the woods had always provided us with food, homes, comfort, and religion. He was awed when I related to him how the wolf became our guardian, and when I told him that I would sing the sacred wolf song over him, he was overjoyed. When I had ended, it was as if the whole world listened with us to hear the wolf's reply. We waited a long time but none came. All of a sudden I realised why no wolves had heard my sacred song. There were none left! My heart filled with tears. I could no longer give my grandson faith in the past, our past.

THE MALIGNED WOLF

The forest was my home. I lived there and I cared about it. I tried to keep it neat and clean.

Then one sunny day, while I was cleaning up some garbage a camper had left behind, I heard footsteps. I leaped behind a tree and saw a rather plain little girl coming down the trail carrying a basket. I was suspicious of this little girl right away because she was dressed funny — all in red, and her head covered up so it seemed like she didn't want people to know who she was. Naturally, I stopped to check her out. I asked who she was, where she was going, where she had come from, and all that. She gave me a song and dance about going to her grandmother's house with a basket of lunch. She appeared to be a basically honest person, but she was in my forest and she certainly looked suspicious with that strange get-up of hers. So I decided to teach her just how serious it is to prance through the forest unannounced and dressed funny.

I let her go on her way, but I ran ahead to her grandmother's house. When I saw that nice old woman, I explained my problem, and she agreed that her granddaughter needed to learn a lesson, all right. The old woman agreed to stay out of sight until I called her. Actually, she hid under the bed.

When the girl arrived, I invited her into the bedroom where I was in bed, dressed like the grandmother. The girl came in all rosy-cheeked and said something nasty about my big ears. I've been insulted before so I made the best of it by suggesting that my big ears would help me to hear better. Now, what I meant was that I liked her and wanted to pay close attention to what she was saying. But she makes another insulting crack about my bulging eyes. Now you can see how I was beginning to feel about this girl who put on such a nice front, but was apparently a very nasty person. Still I've made it a policy to turn the other cheek, so I told her that my big eyes helped me to see her better.

Her next insult really got to me. I've got this problem with having big teeth. And that little girl made an insulting crack about them. I know that I should have had better control, but I leaped up from that bed and growled that my teeth would help me to eat her better.

Now, let's face it — no wolf would ever eat a little girl — everyone knows that — but that crazy girl started running around the house screaming — me chasing her to calm her down. I'd taken off the grandmother clothes, but that only seemed to make it worse. And all of a sudden the door came crashing open and a big lumberjack is standing there with his axe. I looked at him and it became clear that I was in trouble. There was an open window behind me and out I went.

I'd like to say that was the end of it. But that grandmother character never did tell my side of the story. Before long the word got around that I was a mean nasty guy. Everybody started avoiding me. I don't know about that little girl with the funny red outfit, but I didn't live happily ever after.

— by Leif Fearn, San Diego, California.

2. The negative images of wolves brainstormed by the class are apportioned between groups. Each group undertakes project collection/library research to find out if their selection of images are fair. Groups report back in plenary session.

3. Each group undertakes a co-operative rewriting of a children's story in which wolves feature — from the wolf's point of view. Stories might include *Little Red Riding Hood* (see *The Maligned Wolf* as an example), *The Three Little Pigs* and *The Wolf and the Seven Goats* (Grimm). Old and new versions of the stories are tried out on younger children and their respective effects assessed. The class goes on to read and reflect upon a selection of contemporary pro-wolf stories for children (see box).

4. Groups sift through collections of children's traditional fables, stories, songs and nursery rhymes for examples of creatures being portrayed as villains (e.g. *Little Miss Muffet*) or of animals being uncritically and complacently depicted as victims of cruelty and violence (e.g. *Three Blind Mice, Ding Dong Bell*). Examples are written up or summarised on sheets of sugar paper in felt pen of one colour and the students' general and specific criticisms of the text written in felt pen of a second colour. In addition, students can rewrite pro-animal versions of offending items. Group work is shared and the effect of negative and 'victim' depictions of animals on children's attitudes discussed. Letters of criticism with regard to newly-publishers anti-animal literature can be sent to the publishers concerned.

Some pro-wolf books for children:

❑ Jon Scieszka, *The True Story of the 3 Little Pigs!*, New York, Viking, 1989. Told from the wolf's point of view.

❑ Celia Godkin, *Wolf Island*, Markham, Ontario, Fitzhenry & Whiteside, 1993. Set on an island in Northern Ontario and based on an actual event. Chronicles what happens when the highest link in the food chain is removed.

❑ Farley Mowat, *Never Cry Wolf*, Toronto, Seal Books, McClelland-Bantam Inc., 1968. True story of life amongst the Arctic wolves.

■ *WHAT'S IN A NAME?*

Suitable for
Primary/secondary

Time needed
90 minutes

Resources
Books on the history of boats, cars, trains, civil and military aircraft, military equipment, space exploration; current car, farming machinery and sports/leisure clothing and equipment catalogues. Scissors, paste, felt pens and sugar paper.

Procedure
Each group of 3-4 students is allocated a particular topic (e.g. boats, cars, trains/railway engines, aircraft, rockets, military equipment, farm machinery, sports/leisure clothing and equipment) and asked to search the project collection for as many examples as possible of products being named after animals. The search complete, they put together a presentation on sugar paper laying out what they have found and offering explanations as to why manufacturers choose to associate their particular products with particular animals. Each group displays, and speaks to, their presentation prior to general class discussion.

Potential
An interesting way of approaching positive and negative perceptions of animals. Students are likely to conclude that animals are chosen as product names or trademarks because those animals carry certain desirable connotations which serve to enhance the product's attractiveness. Why is it that certain animals resonate with us and others do not? What human desires and longings are being particularly pandered to by the selection of particular animal names? What would be the response to a saloon car named the 'Donkey' or a sports shoe with the trademark 'Pig'? Do certain families or types of animal tend to be associated with certain types of product? What qualities of each animal selected are manufacturers homing in on? What qualities do they seem blind to? In what sense is the whole animal reduced by the image makers? Does the

naming of products after animals we view favourably help perpetuate negative images of other animals and tend to reinforce less than desirable qualities in ourselves? Why are animal names often used for vehicles, instruments and weapons of war? What is being glossed over by naming military paraphernalia after animals?

Extensions

1. The class visits the high street or shopping centre to search out and list products named after animals.

2. Students design/draw a product that is named after an unlikely choice of animal (e.g. a sports car called the 'Elephant') drawing upon its range of attractive characteristics.

USE/TREATMENT OF ANIMALS

Our task must be to free ourselves ... by widening our circle of compassion to embrace all living creatures and the whole of nature and its beauty.
— Albert Einstein.[5]

◼ *ANIMALS IN MY SHOPPING BAG*

Suitable for

Primary

Time needed

60-120 minutes

Resources

A bag of shopping (6-10 items), atlas and blank outline world map for each group; a *Shopping Chart* per student; a large world map on a pinboard; a supply of colour-headed pins; a chart or list identifying lesser known animal food products (see *Fig. 9*); display space and card/paper for labels for each group. A collection of information sheets or diet advice books explaining food additives and identifying the animal content of food.

Procedure

Students form groups of 4-6. Each group sits around a table and is handed a bag of shopping, containing tins and packets of food, all of which are priced. The items in the shopping bag are

ANIMAL PRODUCTS IN FOOD		
• MEAT	• FISH	
DAIRY PRODUCTS		
• MILK • CHEESE • YOGURT		• BUTTER • EGGS
• LARD	• GELATIN	• HONEY
ANIMAL FAT IN:	• BISCUITS • CRACKERS • CAKES • SOUPS • BREADS	
EGGS IN:	• CAKES/CAKE MIX • NOODLES • OTHER PASTA	

unpacked and examined. Groups are informed that their task is to look at the tin and packet labels to see which foods contain animal products, where they have come from and their cost. Group members are to keep a record of their findings on their own *Shopping Chart* (individuals can choose one food item to research, using the sheets and books, before sharing their findings with the rest of the group). Charts complete, they mark on their group map, the countries of origin of each food and, using colour-headed pins and small labels, they locate them on the large class map. Foods in their bag are laid out attractively on the group table, with labels showing any animal products and additives and the country of origin. When groups have completed their charts, maps and displays, students walk around to inspect the work of other groups, members taking turns to stay by their display to answer visitors' questions. The viewing complete, students return to their seats for plenary discussion.

Fig. 9

Potential

A co-operative activity which allows exploration of many food-related issues and raises awareness of the animal content of food. Plenary questions might include the following: Were you surprised that so many food items contained animal products? What other ingredients surprised you? What else did you discover of interest? Were you surprised at where the foods came from? Were there some foods which had 'hidden' animal products? Does cost seem in any way to relate to animal content or to the distance food has travelled? Do particular animal products come from particular parts of the world? Why? Were there many additives in the food? For what purpose? Do any of the information sheets or books referred to describe the additives as harmful?

Extension

1. Students design their own labels, showing all animal content clearly. Appropriate signs for foods suitable for vegetarians and vegans could also be developed.

2. The activity could be followed by a trip to a local supermarket to look for other foods containing animal products.

3. Products other than food could be examined. A collection could be made of items containing animal products.

4. The activity can be used as a platform for topic work on the treatment of animals in food production (see *Chapter 8*).

Source

SHOPPING CHART Adapted by Jackie Harvey from *The World in a Shopping Bag*, Oxfam Education.

■ *ANIMAL USES*

Suitable for

Primary/lower secondary

Time needed

60 minutes

Resources

A set of *Animal Uses* pictures cut up so that each student has one picture; a second set of all the pictures cut up and put in an envelope for each small group; sugar paper, paste and a felt tip pen for each group.

Procedure

Stage 1 Half the class is given pictures of animals and the other half is given pictures of animal uses. Students are asked to move around the room and find their partner.

Stage 2 Each pair then introduces themselves to the rest of the class and says how they are connected.

Stage 3 Two or three pairs join together to form a larger group. Each group is given a complete set of animal and animal uses pictures which they proceed to pair up. On sugar paper three

ITEM OF SHOPPING	ANIMAL CONTENT	MAIN OR SECONDARY INGREDIENT	ADDITIVES	COST	PLACE OF ORIGIN

columns are drawn, headed: 'Always Acceptable', 'Sometimes Acceptable' and 'Never Acceptable'. Students study their paired pictures and discuss which column they should be placed in. When the group has agreed on the placements, they stick the pictures in the appropriate column on the sugar paper. Reporting back and class discussion follows.

Potential

An activity designed to introduce students to how animals are used for economic gain. It can contribute to realising some of the goals of the cross-curricular theme of Education for Economic and Industrial Understanding (e.g. acquiring a sense of responsibility for the consequences of economic actions and sensitivity to the effects of economic choices on the environment). Which uses of animals did students feel happy about? Why? Which did they think were sometimes acceptable? Why only sometimes? Which did students feel unhappy about? Why? Which animal uses were the most difficult to assign to a column? Why?

Source

Pamela Pointon, Homerton College, Cambridge.

ANIMAL USES

I really like this activity. Highly visual. To help the children, I put a different border around animal and animal uses pictures and stress that any pair must have one of each border. — Cambridge infant teacher.

Extremely successful. The children were fully engaged throughout. They were taken aback at how much we use/abuse animals. We did not look at it from an economic gain perspective, but from an overall sense of right and wrong, fair and unfair. — Hertfordshire junior teacher.

Not too infantile for 16 year olds. They enjoyed it. Initial exercise of pairing regrouped the class. Generated lively discussion on several levels. — Cambridgeshire secondary teacher

P

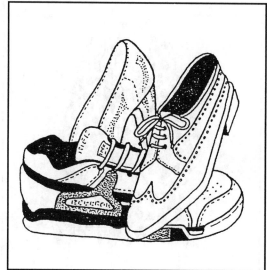

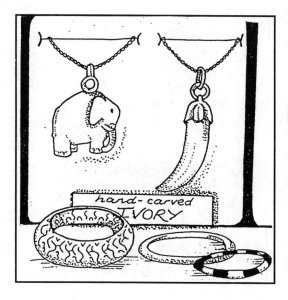

P

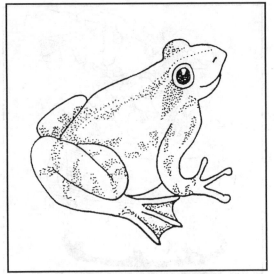

P

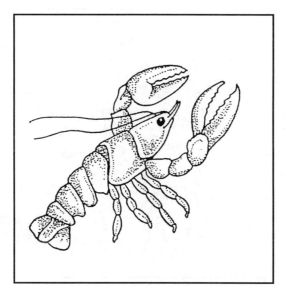

P

P

P

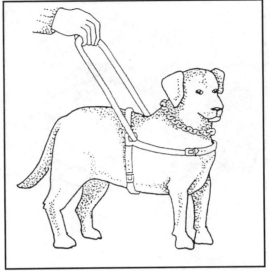

P

■ *TYPICAL MORNING*

Suitable for

Secondary

Time needed

15 minutes

Resources

A *Story Card* and a set of *Animal Abuse Detector Cards.* Two facilitators are required for this activity (two teachers or a teacher and a previously-primed student).

Procedure

One facilitator reads out the *Story Card* in role. When he has completed the last sentence, the other facilitator interrupts by suggesting that he has detected a number of instances of animal abuse in the story and, as his friend, would like to point these out. He asks for the story to be repeated. On the second reading the facilitator with the *Animal Abuse Detector Cards* interrupts abruptly, at the points indicated with an asterisk, by reading out the appropriate card.

The gender of the characters in the story can be changed with only minor amendments, e.g. 'After my husband, John, had finished shaving, I went to the bathroom to shower', and 'Returning to the bedroom, I dressed, choosing a silk blouse and cardigan, and then massaged cream into my face, sprayed on perfume and put on lipstick. As John hurried out of the bedroom, he grabbed his wallet'

Potential

An effective and time-economical way of raising student awareness of how our daily lives are predicated on the systematic abuse of animals. As such, it can be used as a stimulus to enquiry work of the type described in *Extensions* below. In discussion following the staged interaction, students can be asked to comment upon the degree to which they were surprised or shocked by the information conveyed. Had they been aware of the animal abuse underpinning many of the things we take for granted? Are Jane and John especially naïve or do they represent the current general level of awareness about humane issues? Are young people more aware than adults? How many class members regularly make buying and usage decisions based upon humane criteria? Can they give examples? Which 'abuses' touched upon in the interaction are regarded as exaggerated and/or inconsequential and which are rated as concerns for action? Are all the issues, for some class members, immaterial in that human well-being is far more important than that of animals? How should we respond to the meat and animal produce issues raised? By doing nothing, because current farming practices are economic and keep prices down? By insisting on having free-range farms in which all processes of meat, egg and dairy production are kept as humane as possible? By vegetarianism? By veganism? How should we respond to the animal experimentation issues raised? What repercussions, if any, will the story have on students' personal lives?

Story Card

Hello, my name is John Smith. I'd like to tell you about yesterday morning, a typical early morning in my life...

I raised my head from the pillow as the alarm bell rang and threw back the sheets and blankets*... my feet touched the soft pile of the bedroom carpet as I put on my slippers.*

I went to the bathroom and shaved and showered.*

Returning to the bedroom, I noticed my wife, Jane, massaging cream into her face, spraying on perfume and putting on lipstick* ... I finished dressing, choosing a light blue tie and jumper; as I hurried out of the bedroom, I grabbed my wallet.*

Jane was already eating her breakfast of tea, toast and bacon.*

Trying to cut down on eating meat I had scrambled eggs instead.*

Before leaving for work, I washed the breakfast pots and the wine glasses we had used the night before. I used fresh air spray to remove the bacon smell. *

Changing into my shoes and picking up my case, I left for work in the car.*

Variations

1. Greater class involvement in the staged interaction can be achieved by priming ten different students to interrupt the teacher with different *Detector Cards*.

2. Having outlined the typical morning and having been invited to repeat the story, the facilitator only reads enough to trigger the first *Detector Card*. The class briefly researches, then discusses, the issues raised by the card. At the beginning of the second lesson, the interaction is taken as far as the reading of the second *Detector Card* which provides the stimulus for more discussion and research. This process continues over ten lessons.

Extensions

1. Students keep a record of the things they do and use during part of a typical day at home or at school. In class they write their story; then, using the reference books available (see *Sources* below), they prepare a report assessing the degree of animal abuse woven into their story, and identifying alternative products they could use to make their story cruelty free.

2. Students survey the materials and products used at home and in school (especially laboratories, technology areas, gymnasium and kitchens) and ascertain the degree to which they are cruelty-free. Drawing upon the reference books available, they write reports to parents and relevant teachers recommending alternative materials and products for future purchase and use. Alternatively, they prepare, mount and person a 'Cruelty-free Home' exhibition in a local community or shopping centre and/or a 'Cruelty-free School' exhibition in the school foyer.

3. Students visit local supermarkets and the local shopping centre to assess the availability of cruelty-free alternatives. They have (pre-arranged) interviews with the supermarket managers to establish the degree of interest in cruelty-free products, whether that interest is growing and amongst which sections of the community. They also interview members of the public to ascertain whether humane considerations figure in their purchasing decisions. A report on their findings is prepared, including a section of recommendations. Copies go to the managers of the supermarkets and of each shop visited and to the editors of local newspapers.

4. Having researched into organic gardening (see *Sources* below), students visit the local garden centre to establish the degree to which environment and animal-friendly products are available. They interview the garden centre manager and, back in school, write a report on their findings.

Sources

The facts used in the *Animal Abuse Detector Cards* are drawn from Cruddas, H., *Why animal rights? An information booklet for schools*, Animal Aid Youth Group, 1989; Gold, M., *Living without cruelty*, Green Print, 1988; and Howlett, L., *Cruelty free shopper*, Bloomsbury, 1989. Another useful book, particularly for students wishing to survey the local garden centre, is Elkington, J., & Hailes, J., *The green consumer guide*, Gollancz, 1988, 66-106.

ANIMAL ABUSE DETECTOR CARDS

1. I raised my head from the pillow as the alarm bell rang and threw back the sheets and the blankets. Stop! Animal abuse already! Your pillow is full of soft down from the under-plumage of ducks and your blankets are 80% wool. All the feathers and much of the wool we use are not taken from live animals but are by-products of the meat industry. Wool shorn from live sheep comes from animals that have been selectively bred over the centuries to produce an amount of wool that is against their interests in that they endure misery during the hot summer months and frequently die of cold and shock after shearing.

2. My feet touched the soft pile of the bedroom carpet as I put on my slippers. Stop! Your feet have touched a 100% wool carpet taken from animals which, as lambs, had holes punched in their ears, had their tails tightly tied so they shrivelled and fell off and, if male, were castrated. All these operations were conducted without anaesthetic. Your feet have also settled into leather slippers made from the hides of cattle. Some 25-50% of slaughterhouse profits come from the sales of the hides of the four million cattle slaughtered annually in the United Kingdom.

3. I went to the bathroom and shaved and showered. Stop! There are animal products in the soaps and cosmetics you are using and most of them have been tested on animals. Your protein shampoo contains gelatine made by boiling the skin, tendons, ligaments, hooves and bones of animals killed in slaughterhouses. Your soap and shaving cream contain animals fats. Trial versions of your aftershave were tested on thousands of rabbits. Each rabbit was held in a clamp for up to seven days and had the aftershave dripped into its eyes to test whether either eye suffered. The rabbits were conscious throughout. Many developed swellings in their eyes, ulcers, bleeding and blindness. No pain relief was given. Trial versions of your shaving cream were tested on guinea pigs. The hair was shaved off their backs, their skin was torn and the cream applied to the broken skin. Often the skin became inflamed and blistered.

4. Returning to the bedroom, I noticed my wife, Jane, massaging cream into her face, spraying herself with perfume and putting on lipstick. Stop ! The face cream contains crushed snails added to give the cream its sheen. The perfume contains musk extracted from the anal gland of the civet cat of Central Africa. Tests were carried out on the lipstick Jane is using to find out if it contains materials that are poisonous for human beings by force-feeding the human equivalent of 1.8 kilograms of lipstick to different animals.

5. I finished dressing, choosing a light blue tie and jumper; as I hurried out of the bedroom, I grabbed my wallet. Stop! The tie is made of silk. The silk is obtained by boiling the cocoons of the silk moth with the live worm still inside. The wool jumper and leather wallet are yet further examples of our often unthinking reliance on the by-products of the slaughterhouse.

6. Jane was already eating her breakfast of tea, toast and bacon. Stop! The word 'bacon' nicely hides the fact that your wife is eating part of a pig. The pig's mother lived her life inside a factory farm, confined in a narrow (60 centimetres wide) stall unable to move more than one step forward and one step back and standing on a cold, uncomfortable concrete floor with no straw. The bacon on the plate comes from one of her first of many enforced litters. Metal bars prevented her from being close to her piglets and from ever becoming anything more than a source of milk. The piglets were taken away at three weeks, fattened in crowded dirty pens and slaughtered at seven months.

P

7. Trying to cut down on my meat eating, I had scrambled eggs instead. Stop! Sticking to scrambled eggs does not end your collusion in animal abuse either! The eggs are from battery hens which are packed into small wire cages, stand on sloping wire floors and can't even stretch their wings. Over 2 million battery hens die in their cages each year from injury and disease. The remainder spend up to two years in cages before their bodies are turned into chicken soup, tinned food and chicken stock cubes. The milk in your tea and scrambled eggs comes from cows made continually pregnant by artificial means, separated from their calves soon after birth and, after four to five pregnancies, ending up in a burger or tin of soup.

8. Before leaving for work, I washed the breakfast pots and the wine glasses we had used the night before. I put away the remaining slices of the cake with pink icing we had eaten. I used fresh air spray to remove the bacon smell. Stop! At it again? Was the air freshener tested on animals using the eye and skin tests described earlier? The washing-up liquid, like the lipsticks, may have been force-fed to groups of animals to find the dosage which would kill half of each group. This test is known as the LD (lethal dose) 50 test. The animals' reactions to the test can include vomiting, paralysis, convulsions and internal bleeding. No pain relief is given and animals can be left for up to 14 days in severe pain before they die. Incidentally, animal products such as gelatine, bone marrow, dried blood and fish oil were used in the production of the wine you drank last night. The pink in the cake icing comes from cochineal, a red food colouring, made from ground-up beetles.

9. Changing into my shoes and picking up my case, I left for work in the car. Stop! Leaving aside your shiny leather shoes and leather case, the chamois leather and the beeswax with which you clean the car, let's concentrate on the car itself. Driven at only moderate speed, it is a major assassin of birds and small mammals such as hedgehogs. It is a major polluter responsible for the build-up of poisons in animals and humans alike while the demand for ever more cars and lorries means the building of more and more new roads and motorways that destroy the habitat of many wild animals.

10. So, John, by just looking at an hour or so of one typical morning in your life, we have shown how our daily existence can so easily involve collusion in sustained and systematic cruelty towards animals, a collusion to which we are often blind. If we believe cruelty is wrong, it is time to think hard about the things we use and, if necessary, look for alternatives.

P

■ *WHERE DO WE DRAW THE LINE?*

Suitable for

Secondary (see *Variation 1* for suggestions for primary use)

Time needed

45 minutes

Resources

A set of twelve statements (see this page) and a long strip of paper for each student, each strip having a pencilled straight line along its length with a plus (+) sign at one end and a minus (-) sign at the other (see *Fig. 10a*). A pot of paste and a set of three thick felt pens for each four students (sets should contain the same three colours). An additional strip and set of statements for each group.

Procedure

Random groups of four are formed (for random grouping exercises, see p.64). Students are first asked to work individually, their task being to read and reflect upon the twelve statements and to decide which uses of animals they can personally accept and which they cannot. Using the strip of paper, the statement of use they can most readily accept is placed as close to the (+) sign as they feel appropriate, the statement they find it hardest to accept as close to the (-) sign as they deem fit. Other statements are placed in preferred order and with appropriate spacing between the two (see *Fig. 10b* by way of example). Following the colour code provided by the teacher, one felt pen is used to draw a thick double line at the point where the student would personally draw the line in terms of use of animals; i.e. uses to the (+) side of the line are the ones they condone, uses to the (-) side are ones they reject. The proportion of line to the (+) side of the double line is coloured in using the second felt pen; the proportion of line to the (-) side using the third felt pen. It is entirely possible for the student to put all the statements of use to one side of the double line. Having completed their individual task, students come together in their fours to explain and discuss their placings and where they each drew the line. After discussion,

Using animals for scientific experiments to test whether cosmetics and toiletries (perfumes, aftershaves, lipsticks, shampoos etc.) are safe for human use.
Hunting and trapping fur animals so their skins can be used to make fur coats and hats.
Keeping wild animals in zoos, aquaria and aviaries for purposes of amusement and education.
Using animals for military experiments to test the effects of new weapons of chemical, gas and biological warfare.
Intensive rearing of animals inside factory farms for eventual slaughter and consumption as food.
Using animals in scientific experiments to find cures for human diseases such as Aids and cancer.
Using animals as 'beasts of burden' for riding and pulling carts, carriages and ploughs.
Using specifically-bred and purpose-trained dogs to assist disabled people.
Hunting animals for pleasure — the thrill of the chase and catch.
Using specially-bred and freshly-killed animals for dissection purposes in school biology lessons.
Rearing of animals in free-range conditions (open yards, fields) for eventual slaughter and consumption as food.
Using animals in television commercials as a means of promoting products.

P

each group tries to negotiate a consensus using a new strip of paper and set of statements. If the students find this impossible, they should use the paper to prepare a presentation, laying out the differences of opinion which presented stumbling blocks to their completion of the task. Reporting back and plenary debriefing follows the group work.

Potential

This activity is likely to generate lively discussion and to reveal some strong differences of opinion around the use of animals. It will help students

One of the most powerful activities I have ever come across. It forces people to develop their ideas in way otherwise unlikely to happen. Students love this, once they get their teeth into it.
— Kent secondary teacher.

Activity was appreciated. Groups became very absorbed. **Very** *suitable for this age group. Raised question of our ability to* **do** *anything: the power of the individual/group/school/society. How does the school show its stance?*
— Cambridgeshire secondary teacher (15-16 year olds).

The activity was very successful. I think it's useful to follow up the discussion with a writing assignment. The class discussion revealed the contradictions in society's views towards animals and those in most people's views. I asked the students to write about any contradictions in their views and what they could do to eliminate them.
— Secondary teacher, Kingston, Ontario (16-17 year olds).

With a woman's group, I started with the **Animal Uses** *cartoons. They firstly put them into pairs. Then the whole group took it in turn to place the animal use on a long thin table from acceptable to unacceptable. Discussion went on for two hours and we never got anywhere near finishing the exercise.*
— Suffolk secondary/community teacher.

clarify their own thoughts, feelings and values whilst alerting them to a range of other opinions and perspectives. The debriefing will tend to revolve around the differing viewpoints as to where the line should be drawn and the various orderings of the statements. On what grounds did students find some uses of animals more/less acceptable than others? Where did they draw the double line and why? Was their decision made on moral, pragmatic or other grounds? Did their thinking change when they encountered the views of others? Were they able to achieve consensus? If so, on what basis? If not, why not? Might the line have been drawn differently depending on the specific circumstances surrounding each case? Does the decision depend upon the animal or type of animal in question? Might people of different age groups, cultures or countries have drawn the line elsewhere? Does gender appear to have been a significant factor in determining where students drew the line? It is also important to ask students to reflect upon whether their personal behaviours and patterns of consumption accord with the decisions they made as to where the line should be drawn and, if not, what they might do to achieve greater congruency. This challenge might best be confronted by first asking students to return to their groups for further reflection prior to a second debriefing period. *Where Do We Draw The Line?* can provide a springboard for research into the issues raised. Following research, the activity can usefully be repeated (sufficient time being set aside for what is likely to be an animated and challenging debriefing session).

Fig. 10

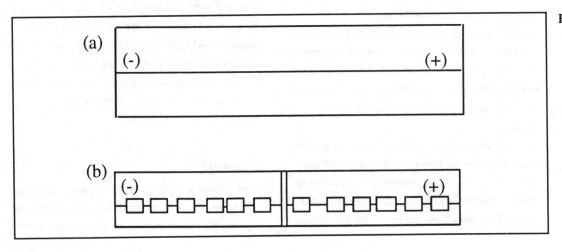

Variations

1. The activity can be attempted with primary students using duly simplified statements; alternatively, a set of statements on the treatment of pets and domestic animals can be used.

2. *Where Do We Draw The Line?* can be used as a vehicle for considering categories of action/protest against animal abuse (see p. 322).

■ *TACKLING A STATEMENT*

Suitable for

Upper primary/secondary

Time needed

20 minutes

Resources

Five trays of badges (twenty per tray for a class of thirty) indicating five positions on a continuum of opinion ranging from strong agreement to strong disagreement:

+ +	= **strongly agree**
+	= **agree**
?	= **can't decide or don't know**
—	= **disagree**
— —	= **strongly disagree**

Open space so that students can move freely about the classroom.

Procedure

A controversial statement (see below for examples) is written up on the board. The statement should be carefully designed to draw out a wide spectrum of responses.

> *Sample statement 3 chosen: 'it is more acceptable to kill a sheep than a whale'. Eight in the group felt it was wrong to kill any animals so had to choose a ' ? ' badge. The activity enabled many to talk at greater length than they often have. It would be useful to follow this with consideration of methods of whale hunting and sheep slaughter (with appropriate age groups); a number in this group found it difficult to consider the processes of slaughter, though we have previously discussed animal sacrifice when we have studied certain Old Testament passages.*
> *— West Yorkshire secondary teacher (religious education class, 12/13 year olds)*

❑ In defence of animals, I have the right to break the law.

❑ It is justifiable to use chimpanzees in Aids research.

❑ It is more acceptable to kill a sheep than a whale.

❑ Zoos, as we know them, should be abolished.

❑ Vegetarianism is the only cruelty-free way of feeding ourselves.

❑ It is wrong to bother about animal rights when there is so much human suffering in the world.

Students are asked to reflect on the statement for two minutes and then to choose and wear the badge which most faithfully represents their response to the statement. They next discuss the statement with a person wearing the same badge (three minutes). Students move on to discuss the statement with someone wearing a badge one position removed from their own badge (three minutes). They then enter discussion with someone wearing a badge two or more positions removed (three minutes). Finally, students are invited to return to the person with whom they originally talked, to review what they have heard and learnt. It is important to encourage students to engage in positive, constructive discussion and listening, rather than argument. Students can be invited to change badges between stages, should they wish.

Potential

This peer learning activity can be applied to a wide range of controversial statements and can be used with students of different age levels. It can also be used at many stages during the study of a topic. For instance:

❑ it can be employed as a starter exercise to alert students to the fact that there are perspectives on a topic other than their own;

❑ it can be used as a 'state of research' exercise during or at the end of a period of study enabling students to share what they have learned — and their new thinking — with others.

■ *ANIMAL AND HUMAN RIGHTS CONTINUUM*

Suitable for

Upper primary/secondary

Time needed

20-25 minutes (interaction 10-15, debriefing 5-10)

Resources

None save a clear space

Procedure

Students are asked to take up positions along a single line, stretching from one end of the room to the other, according to whether they agree or disagree with certain animal and human rights statements to be read out by the teacher (see box for examples). One end of the room should be clearly indicated for those who 'strongly agree'; the other for those who 'strongly disagree'. Students are at liberty to take up any position along the continuum. When they have found an initial position, participants are encouraged to share their thoughts on the statement under consideration with their immediate neighbours. They can alter their position, if necessary, in the light of their discussions. The teacher should allow a few minutes' discussion before asking students to consider the next rights statement.

Potential

A short, active exercise which asks students to clarify their own views and positions with regard to certain rights contentions. Some statements will achieve a good spread along the continuum; others will achieve less of a spread. In the latter eventuality, care should be taken that students in minority positions are listened to respectfully and that they are neither embarrassed nor victimised. Debriefing can focus on the spread of views revealed by — and the problems thrown up by the formulation of — each statement. Why were some of the statements more problematic or more controversial than others?

Suggested rights statements

- Dog owners have the right to hit their dogs if they misbehave
- Slugs have as much of a right to life as ladybirds
- People have the right to keep pet animals and birds in cages
- Chickens have the right to a free-range life
- People have the right to go fox-hunting
- Scientists have the right to test new human drugs and medicines on animals
- People have the right to use animals for sport and leisure
- Cats and dogs have the right not to be neutered
- Scientists have the right to genetically engineer new breeds of animal
- Animals have the right not to have pain inflicted upon them by human beings

Variations

When students are well spaced out along the continuum (i.e. there is a good spread of opinion), the teacher can promote further discussion in two ways:

1. By breaking the line at its mid-point and asking students in one half to slide along the other half. Discussion then takes place between pairs (or small groups) holding relatively different opinions.

    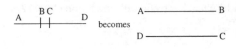

2. By breaking the line at its mid-point and asking a student at one of the two opposite ends to circle round so she faces the student at the other end (the rest of the half-line follows). The effect of this will be to promote discussion between opposing viewpoints at one end of the double line (but discussion with fairly like-minded classmates at the other end).

■ REACTIONS

Suitable for

Primary/secondary

Time needed

50 minutes plus film time (writing reactions 10, choosing 5, pairs/threes 10, groups 10, plenary 15).

Film Suggestions

- **Their Future in Your Hands** 13-minute VHS video available on free loan from Animal Aid, depicting human maltreatment of animals in a way that will not horrify students and offering constructive ideas for achieving a less cruel world. Suitable for secondary classes.

- **Through The Looking Glass** 13-minute VHS video available from British Union for the Abolition of Vivisection following Alice on a journey through the hidden world of suffering lurking behind many of the cosmetics and toiletries we use. Suitable for primary and secondary classes.

- **Britches** 20-minute VHS available from British Union for the Abolition of Vivisection. Features infant monkey rescued by direct action from a laboratory and now living in an animal sanctuary. Suitable for secondary age students.

- **What Price Beauty?** 20-minute VHS video from Beauty Without Cruelty covering the exploitation of whales, crocodiles, seal pups, karakul lambs, musk deer and civet; fur farming in the UK and cosmetics. Suitable for secondary classes.

- **There's a Pig in my Pasta!** 16-minute VHS video from Compassion in World Farming following Kate and Sam into Carlo's Italian Restaurant. The couple discover the extent to which the menu is based on animal exploitation. Suitable for secondary classes.

- **A Painful Luxury — the Cruelties of Foie Gras Production** 10-minute VHS video from EarthKind with footage of geese and ducks being force-fed for foie gras. Also live plucking of geese. Suitable for secondary classes.

See *Organisations* (pp.401-406 for details of the addresses and telephone numbers of the organisations listed above.

Resources

Four quarter A4 slips of paper per student; some extra slips of paper.

Procedure

After watching a film on a humane issue (see box for suggestions) or listening to a talk by a visiting speaker, students form groups of five or six. Group members work separately, writing four different reactions to the stimulus (one reaction per slip of paper). A reaction can be a short paragraph, a sentence or two, or one word. The reactions are collected in by one of the group, shuffled and dealt out as in a game of cards. Everyone looks at their 'hand', discarding into a central pool any reactions they wrote and any with which they are not prepared to identify. They continue to discard and pick up from the pool until they are satisfied with their hand. The aim is for every group member to end up with a final hand of up to three reactions which, to repeat, must be statements (a) they did not write themselves and (b) with which they are prepared to identify. Group members then break into twos or threes. They read their final hand to each other, explaining why they chose those particular reactions. They then prepare a composite reaction to the stimulus which may be a consensus statement, or an agreement to disagree. The whole group of five or six then joins together, the sub-groups sharing and explaining their composite reactions, before proceeding to write a final group reaction. Sharing of final statements and discussion in plenary session follows.

Potential

This activity is excellent for achieving a thoroughgoing sharing of reactions to whatever stimulus material on humane issues is offered. Participants are asked to reflect critically upon and accept or reject other ideas and perspectives, to negotiate a joint agreed position and, if this proves impossible, to at least clarify the nature of the disagreements that emerge and also their own perspectives/ values.

Source

Derived from Richardson, R., Flood, M. and Fisher, S., *Debate and decision: schools in a world of change*, World Studies Project, 1980.

■ *LIKE AN ANIMAL*

Suitable for

Upper primary/secondary

Time needed

90 minutes (in class)

Resources

Paper, Blutak

Procedure

Students are given a week-long task of browsing through newspapers, watching television, listening to radio, to their teachers and fellow students, and to out-of-school conversations, recording every occasion on which animal formulations are used to describe people's characters, habits and behaviours. As an attunement to the task, the class brainstorms usages that immediately come to mind. Contributions are recorded (for an example, see *Fig. 11*). At the end of the week students post their lists on the classroom wall (lists should indicate how many times they encountered each usage). The total number of different usages encountered is calculated (care being taken not to count any item twice) as is the total number of times that each usage was recorded. Groups of three are formed. Group tasks include:

❑ determining the overall percentage of positive, negative and neutral references to animals;

❑ identifying the most frequently employed references;

❑ compiling composite lists of animal references that are, overtly or indirectly, a) sexist, b) racist, c) classist, e) ageist (percentages of overall total under each heading to be calculated);

❑ compiling a list of pejorative references to animals arising out of conditions forced on them by human beings (e.g. 'their house is like a pigsty').

Groups report their findings (a record is kept on the board or overhead projection transparency) and class discussion follows.

> *There were no problems barring insensitivity in one case, i.e. a tubby young lady being described as a rhino by her 'macho' male partner.*
>
> — Two West Yorkshire secondary teachers who jointly field tested *Animal Adjectives* with a class of 15 year olds.

Potential

A thought-provoking activity that will pinpoint prejudice towards particular animals; it will demonstrate how those attitudes help sustain, and are themselves reinforced by, prejudice towards other humans on grounds of gender, race, class and age. As such, the activity can be a stimulus for exploring how one form of oppression tends to buttress other forms of oppression (see pp.17-22).

Fig. 11

■ *LINKING PICTURES*

Suitable for

Secondary (*Linking Pictures Set 1* is intended for lower secondary use; *Set 2* for senior secondary classes)

Time needed

30 minutes

Resources

A set of pictures for each group of eight to twelve students. Each set should be cut up into separate pictures and placed in an envelope.

Procedure

The groups form circles sitting on chairs or on the floor. Group members are handed one, or in some cases, two pictures. They are given two minutes to look at their pictures, permitting nobody else to see them and avoiding talking. At the end of the two minutes they hide their pictures away and, going around the circle, describe their pictures to each other (it is best to go around the circle twice so that those with two pictures do not describe both pictures one after the other). Then, still avoiding looking at the pictures, they discuss and negotiate an arrangement in which they think the pictures could be placed. As they move close to agreement, they can be asked to place the pictures face downwards on the table/floor. When this has been accomplished to the group's satisfaction, the group can turn the pictures over, reflect upon their chosen juxtaposition of pictures and then renegotiate the arrangement, if deemed necessary.

Potential

A powerful activity that may well engender some strong, perhaps conflicting, emotions within individuals and some strong disagreements between class members.

The *Set 1* pictures are likely to give rise to reflection on society's contradictory attitudes to animals. Chickens and rabbits provide us with powerful symbols of birth and renewal; a jolly piggy bank often provides a child with a focus for saving for something special. Yet we abuse and torture chickens, rabbits and pigs in a systematic way. The pictures also lay bare the background of cruelty behind comfortable home images. The three pictures suggesting alternatives to animal abuse and torture spur discussion on the likelihood, viability and importance of reducing/eliminating such maltreatment.

The *Set 2* pictures broach the complex and controversial issue of parallels between inhumane treatment of animals and oppressive treatment of people on the basis of gender and race (see pp.17-22). A general call for reactions to the activity, and the images presented, may well elicit responses ranging from absolute acceptance of the parallels being mooted to absolute rejection of any comparison as offensive. The teacher should encourage students to justify and examine the source and meaning of their personal responses. On what basis is acceptance or rejection of the parallel made? On the grounds that the *processes* or *dynamics* of the oppressions are similar/dissimilar? And/or, on the grounds that similar/different levels of *moral reprehensibility* are involved in the maltreatment of human beings and animals? In what specific ways are the processes dissimilar/different? On what basis is cruelty to and oppression of animals held to be equally/less contemptible? Are any relationships, direct or indirect, discernible between the oppression and abuse of animals and the oppression and abuse of people? Can either lead on to the other? Is it appropriate to use terms such as oppression, rights denial, debasement and objectification with respect to animals? Is the animal rights movement the latest link in the chain of liberation movements through the ages? In what ways is it a liberation movement with a difference?

Linking Pictures is an excellent activity for developing/ reinforcing a range of important skills such as memory, observation, oral description, listening, discussion, negotiation, lateral thinking, consensus-seeking, decision-making, perspective-sharing and reflection.

Extensions

1. Following discussion of the *Set 1* pictures, students are given the task of collecting as many examples as they can find of lack of

Linking Pictures Set 1

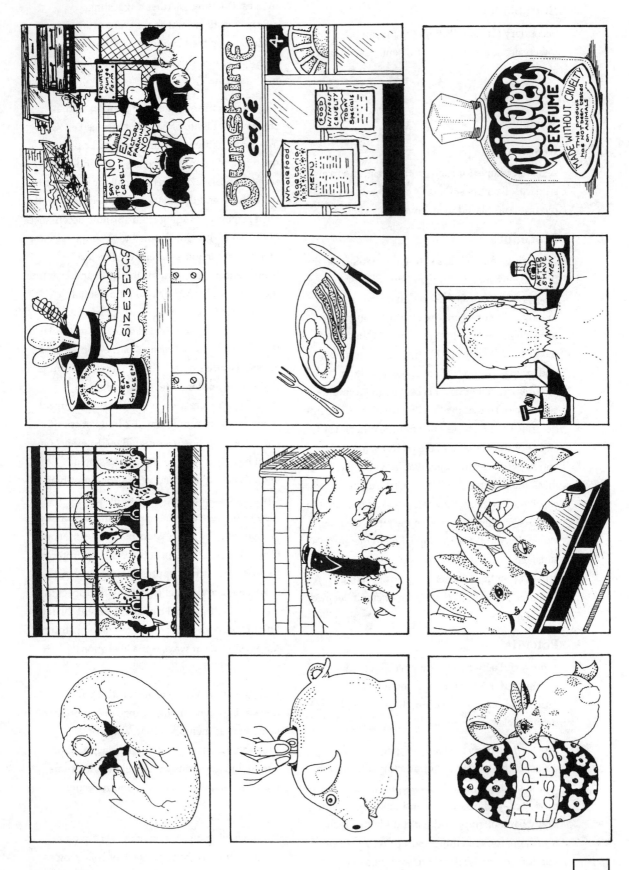

P

Linking Pictures Set 2

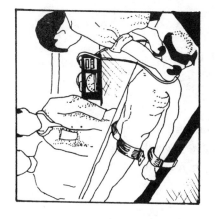

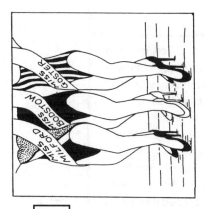

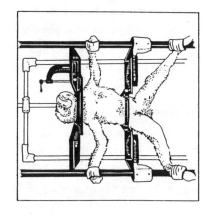

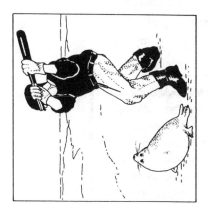

P

congruence within society's attitudes to, perceptions of, and behaviour towards animals. Collections can include newspaper cuttings, advertisements, anecdotes and observed behaviours. An *Incongruities Billboard* is built up in the classroom and, from time to time, used as the basis for discussion.

2. Following discussion of the *Set 2* pictures, groups of students seek out the opinions of community members (family members, friends, feminist and black groups, psychologists, abuse counsellors, psychotherapists, social workers, representatives of humane organisations) and, back in classroom, report on what they have learnt. Further class reflection and discussion follows.

Source

Developed from an idea in Fisher, S., and Hicks, D.W., *World studies 8-13. A teacher's handbook*, Oliver and Boyd, 1985, 142-5. Extension 1: Marg Buckholtz, Frontenac Secondary School, Ontario.

■ 'SILLY STUFF'

Suitable for

Upper secondary

Time needed

20 minutes

Resources

Copy of Mulroney/Yeltsin hunting photograph and of the Toronto *Globe and Mail* news clipping (see next page) for each group of four students; a role card (*Fig. 12*) for each student.

Procedure

Groups of four are formed and copies of the photograph and report handed out. The teacher first sketches in the background. On a trip to Russia in May 1993, the then Prime Minister of Canada, Brian Mulroney, took time off official duties to go wild boar hunting at the invitation of the President of Russia, Boris Yeltsin. Two wild boars were shot. A 'photo opportunity' gave newspaper photographers the chance to capture on film Mulroney and Yeltsin standing over the two dead boars. The photographs appeared in newspapers in Canada. Premier Mulroney subsequently dismissed criticisms voiced by Canadian animal rights activists as 'pretty silly stuff'.

Fig. 12

You are a Canadian citizen who holds that hunting and trapping have been very significant in the development of the Canadian economy and of Canada as a country. Native Canadian culture depended (and still, to some extent, depends) on them, and the search for furs was one important reason why Europeans ventured west. As the representative of Canada, it was, therefore, perfectly appropriate for Mulroney to go hunting.	You are a Canadian citizen who holds hunting to be a barbaric practice that should be outlawed. You feel that Mulroney should not have gone hunting, not least because the issue of hunting deeply divides the people of the country he was representing. The photographs gave inaccurate messages to the world about Canadian attitudes.
You are a Canadian citizen who believes that Mulroney was right to go hunting. Hunting is popular in Canada and Russia and the boar hunt was a good symbolic way of emphasising the mutual interests of the two countries. After all, if politicians representing their countries only did what would offend nobody, they would end up doing nothing!	You are a Canadian citizen who is very critical of the boar hunt. Why, you ask yourself, was the hunt chosen for the photo opportunity and not some other event? What sentiments and attitudes were advisers who set up the opportunity trying to appeal to (these things are *always* carefully staged)? In your view, the opportunity was aimed at the macho, strutting male attitudes still so prevalent in both societies. The event would not have happened if either the premier or the president had been a woman.

P

The Globe and Mail,
8 May 1993, A1

Boar brouhaha 'silly stuff,' PM says

Reuters News Agency

PARIS — Shooting wild boar is no shame, Prime Minister Brian Mulroney said yesterday, a week after drawing criticism from animal-rights groups.

Mr. Mulroney set some Canadian 'animal-rights' activists on edge last week when he was photographed with Russian President Boris Yeltsin over two dead boars they had hunted. The picture was printed in many Canadian newspapers.

Mr. Mulroney called the boar brouhaha 'pretty silly stuff'.

The Globe and Mail *15 May 1993, A14*

Potential

A role play activity that brings together issues concerning animal rights, hunting (see *Chapter 9*), animals as symbols in human rites and rituals, patriarchal values, and appropriate behaviours on the part of democratic or national representatives. An interesting topic for discussion is the cultural aspects of the case in question. Given the pervasiveness of hunting traditions in Canada and Russia, was it easier for Mulroney and Yeltsin to be photographed for public consumption with their 'bag' — and for Mulroney to dismiss objections as 'silly stuff' — than it would be for leaders of certain other countries?

Groups are asked to discuss the pros and cons of the affair. Before discussion begins, each group member is given a role card (see *Fig. 12*) and asked to read it carefully without showing or reading their card to anyone else. Students are urged to try to adhere to their role even if it runs counter to their convictions. Discussion in role should continue for about ten minutes. Coming out of role, group members are given a few minutes more to share their thoughts and vent their feelings before entering class discussion.

References

1. Van Matre, S., *Earth education: a new beginning,* cited in Sheehan, K., & Waidner, M., *Earthchild. Games, stories, activities, experiments & ideas about living lightly on planet Earth,* Tulsa, Council Oak Books, 1991, 264.

2. Fraser, L., et. al., *The animal rights handbook. Everyday ways to save animal lives,* Venice, California, Living Planet Press, 1990, 58.

3. Cited in Wilson, A., *The culture of nature. North American landscape from Disney to Exxon Valdez,* Toronto, Between the Lines, 1991, 117.

4. Fraser, L.,et. al.,op.cit., 58-9.

5. Cited in Fraser, L., *et. al., op. cit.,* iv.

Chapter 7

Pets

INTRODUCTION

For many people in Western societies pets are their first point of direct contact with the animal world and ownership of a pet the first opportunity a young person has to exercise responsibility for another living creature.

As discussed earlier (p.4-5), the twin objectives of promoting responsible pet care and, by extension, of promoting responsible, caring and compassionate attitudes to fellow human beings and other animals, domestic and wild, has long been at the core of humane education programs. Responsible pet care is perceived as going far beyond the provision of adequate nourishment and shelter for a pet. It includes research into the needs of the pet in question, prior to acquisition, and an honest evaluation of whether the intending owner can provide an appropriate home and environment; thinking through the implications, long- and short-term, of pet ownership, making a commitment to the animal for its lifetime and spending the time — and the money — required to keep the pet healthy and happy. It also encompasses a responsibility to ensure that the pet does not cause a nuisance in the neighbourhood and to prevent unwanted offspring (i.e. by neutering the pet or arranging good homes for the young prior to breeding).

Sadly, there is ample and often shocking evidence of high levels of irresponsible pet

purchase and care in the United Kingdom, a country somewhat stereotypically perceived as a nation of animal lovers. As the documents below indicate, hundreds of thousands of animals are abandoned each year by their owners and, in the absence of alternative homes, have to be destroyed.

The activities in this chapter are designed to help students think through the elements that go to make up responsible pet ownership and to understand the consequences that irresponsibility to pets can have particularly for the animals concerned but also for the community in which they live. A leitmotiv in the activities is the special bond that can exist between pets and their owners. A second is the overlapping nature of animal and human characteristics as evidenced in the behaviours, emotions and needs of pets. The activities here can, thus, be used alongside the collection of activities on animal/human similarities and dissimilarities in *Chapter 6* (pp.109-19).

One activity, *Animals are for Always*, raises the potentially thorny question of keeping pets in school. There are clearly sound *educational* reasons for this practice (for instance, educating children, especially those who do not have their own pets, in caring and responsible attitudes and behaviours towards animals, providing ready opportunities to observe and record animal behaviours, helping overcome phobias towards animals) but it is essential to ensure that those reasons are not allowed to in any way override considerations of *animal welfare*. The former Edinburgh headteacher's contribution to this chapter (p.162) describes the approach adopted in her own school. It is an approach which takes account of educational and welfare considerations and which tacitly recognises the psychological benefits accruing to disadvantaged and disturbed students, and students with low self-esteem, from having the opportunity to enjoy close contact with a pet and from being given responsibility for its care (p.37-9).

DOCUMENTS

1.

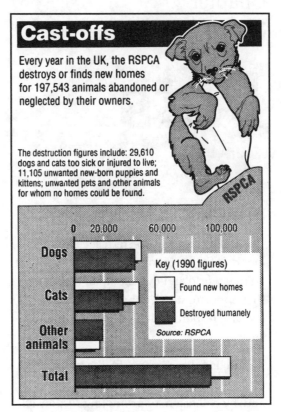

Cast-offs

Every year in the UK, the RSPCA destroys or finds new homes for 197,543 animals abandoned or neglected by their owners.

The destruction figures include: 29,610 dogs and cats too sick or injured to live; 11,105 unwanted new-born puppies and kittens; unwanted pets and other animals for whom no homes could be found.

Key (1990 figures)

☐ Found new homes

■ Destroyed humanely

Source: RSPCA

Dogs

Cats

Other animals

Total

— *Education Guardian*[1]

---

2. Last month the RSPCA asked 200 people for their views about giving animals as Christmas presents. Almost half of those surveyed thought that a puppy or a kitten would make a suitable gift for a lonely older person. More than one in ten believed these animals would be a good present for a child.

The RSPCA was disturbed by the survey's results. 'Some 15 per cent of those surveyed were perfectly happy to give a pet as a present,' a spokesperson said. 'They still believe that animals can be treated like consumer goods.'

Many people give pets as presents without realising how difficult and expensive they are to keep. For instance, it costs about £2,000 in food alone to look after a dog during its lifetime. On top of this there are vet's bills and kennel charges when the owners go on holiday.

Last year the RSPCA's Coventry home received about 100 unwanted puppies in the three months after Christmas. The puppies had been found dumped in rubbish chutes and dustbins or were roaming the streets. They included two 12 week-old puppies which had been abandoned during a blizzard. The RSPCA could find a new home for only 80 and had to destroy the rest.

— *Education Guardian*[2]

3.

4.

Big rise in number of stray cats

UNEMPLOYMENT, marriage break-ups and financial difficulties are just some of the reasons why Northamptonshire pet owners give up their cats, according to feline foster mother Sue Coppin.

Sue, who runs a cattery, said the number of stray and unwanted cats had increased dramatically over the past few months.

At the moment, she has 17 cats and kittens at her home in Puxley, near Deanshanger – and that is the maximum she can take.

"There does seem to be a big problem. I usually find July and August are the worst months, but over the past four or five weeks I have had so many brought in. Speaking to other people involved in animal welfare, it seems to be the same all round," said Sue.

"Sadly, I have had to turn away a number of cats in recent weeks because I don't have the space or time to look after any more in the correct manner."

Sue is the Northampton branch secretary of the RSPCA, the animal welfare charity which has a non-destructive policy with healthy animals.

"Unfortunately, we are faced with a problem. If we can't take them, what happens to them?

"Some people may well abandon them or have them put down, although most vets in Northampton now won't put healthy cats down without firm evidence that there's a good reason.

"One of the consequences of people abandoning cats is an increase in the problems with wild cats that are completely uncontrollable. A lot of people take sympathy with them and feed them, but it is vital that we get to know about them so we can get them neutered."

She said the belief that every cat must have one litter was an old wives' tale and it was vital to get a cat neutered as soon as possible.

— Northampton Chronicle and Echo[3]

Fears for 'latch-key' lost pets

DOG owners in the South are irresponsible about the welfare of their pets, claims an animal welfare group.

The region is the worst in the country for the number of stray dogs which are later reclaimed by their owners.

Nearly 70 per cent of strays picked up by dog wardens are collected by owners, according to a survey by the Canine Defence League.

The figures suggest people let their dogs roam the streets, said a league spokeswoman. 'This is highly irresponsible.

'People go out to work all day and let their dogs out before leaving home. Many are then picked up by dog wardens.'

She warned: 'With this kind of approach to dog ownership there is a danger that more animals will become so-called latch-key dogs.'

The survey shows the south destroys fewer strays than anywhere else in the country.

Just 1.72 per cent of strays are put down, compared with 63 per cent in Northern Ireland.

In the region, 18 per cent of strays are passed on to welfare organisations and nearly nine per cent re-housed by local authorities.

— Bournemouth Evening Echo[4]

---

5. This year the RSPCA will destroy in excess of 73,000 unwanted dogs and cats. For many, this untimely end will be the final chapter in a life of misery. With the incidence of mistreatment, cruelty and neglect so widespread, the solution does not lie in mopping up after society's indifference. The solution lies in the elimination of the circumstances which bring about the suffering. This can only be achieved by the dramatic reduction in the number of animals born.

Domestic animals are our creation. The majority of dogs exist in cities, in flats, in isolation. Basic instincts are suppressed, expression of natural behaviour chastised as dirty or bad — and these we consider the lucky ones. Cats evolved to hunt. Their physiology and nature made them expert predators, until humans, fascinated by their unfettered disposition, stepped in to tame and then denature them. For many cats and dogs, a short-lived entertainment becomes a hindrance and they are cast out onto the streets to run the gauntlet of abuse, starvation and injury. The Canine Defence League report that only one in three dogs will be homed in a reasonable environment.

The odds are stacked so heavily against dogs and cats living a reasonable life that the only solution lies in the rapid deceleration of the numbers needing homes. As an indication of the scale of the problem, over a five year period one unspayed bitch could be responsible for 4,400 offspring. Similarly, one unspayed cat could be responsible for 20,000 cats in the same period. *— Bev Cowley, National Neutering and Spaying Scheme*

— Turning Point[5]

ACTIVITIES

■ *PETCARE MESSAGEMATCH*

Suitable for

Primary/lower secondary.

Time needed

10 minutes

Resources

A piece of a message for each student; an open classroom space.

Procedure

When the message pieces have been distributed, students move around the room looking for people with whom they can join to complete a message. The total number of messages is given and it is explained that the class will only be successful when everybody is part of a message that makes sense. The task complete, each group reads out its message. If the class number is not a multiple of three, the teacher can join in or one student can be given two pieces from the same set.

A stimulating oral activity. Plenty of potential for writing, personal and practical.
— West Yorkshire secondary teacher
(11-12 year olds)

Actual messages were used to illustrate structure and function of language in a second lesson. This helped show one or two where they had gone wrong in matching up message parts.
— West Yorkshire secondary teacher
(12 year olds)

Cats and dogs need regular brushing / to remove loose hair / and keep their coats healthy and shiny.

It is cruel to leave / a pet in a parked car / on a hot summer's day.

Train your puppy to come when called / and to walk to heel / and not to jump up at people.

Before going on holiday / arrange for someone to look after your pet / until you return.

Cats and dogs need / a change of blankets and bedding each week / to protect their health.

Make sure your pet doesn't cause a nuisance / by barking or howling continually/or by fouling public property.

A healthy dog has clear eyes / a cool wet nose / and thick glossy fur.

Pets given as surprise Christmas presents / are often thrown out of the home / by New Year.

If your pet looks ill / take it to the vets / or animal welfare clinic as soon as you can.

Choose a pet to fit / the size of your home / and the money you can spend on food and care.

Make sure your pet has daily exercise / and is given food / and fresh water regularly.

Potential

A good fun activity that can stimulate a lively sharing of pet care experiences. What pets do students have? What do the various types of pet need if they are to stay healthy and contented? What responsibilities does this place on the pet owner? The messages can also be considered one by one with students pooling experiences and points of view.

A further avenue for discussion is the co-operative process engaged in during the activity. How did students set about finding out what the whole message might be? What made the task difficult? Easy? Did any group form only to have to disband again? Did students forget that success involved everybody being part of a message? Who was the easiest to find — the first or second person? Why? Did anybody refuse to join up with somebody else? How did the rejected person feel?

Extension

1. The *Messagematch* teams of three re-form and are asked to devise their own three-part petcare message, different from any of the messages used before and drawing upon ideas arising from the class discussion. The messages are preferably typed out, cut into three parts, pooled and jumbled and the activity repeated.

2. Points about responsible pet care raised in class discussion are recorded on the board or overhead projection transparency. The class uses the points listed to decide upon a chapter framework for a pet owner's manual or a section by section framework for a *Good Petkeeping* standing exhibition. Groups take responsibility for preparing different chapters/exhibition sections.

Source

After an idea devised by Graham Rowland, Feniton Primary School, Devon.

■ *PETS' NEEDS*

Suitable for

Primary/lower secondary

Time needed

30 minutes

Resources

Up to thirty sheets of sugar paper; thirty felt pens; Blu-tak.

Procedure

Students bring to school pictures (photographs or drawings) of their pets. The pictures, each stuck in the centre of a sheet of sugar paper, are hung on the classroom walls and/or laid on desks. The name of the pet and its age and gender are written below the picture. Class members move around the room drawing a picture or writing a description of things each pet needs so as to be content and well. They should draw/write only one need per picture, in each case trying to add something new rather than repeating a need somebody else has already identified. The activity continues until all students have contributed to as many sheets as they feel they can.

Potential

An effective means of stimulating thinking about, and care and concern for, the needs of animals that are part of many children's everyday experience. In discussing the activity, students can be asked to say whether some needs were listed which had not occurred to them before. They can also be asked to identify needs that are common to all pets and needs that are particular to certain types of pets (including those of a particular gender or at a particular stage in their life). Pet owners can be asked to comment on whether, as the person fully or partly responsible for the pet, they are meeting each of the pet's needs as identified during the activity (a more elaborate way of approaching this issue is offered under *Extensions* below).

Finally, the class can consider the degree of overlap and difference between their own needs and those of their pets.

Note: Students who are not pet owners can be encouraged to bring a picture of a pet belonging to a relative or neighbour or a picture of a domestic or wild animal of which they are fond. The latter option will provide for a comparison of the needs of humans, pets and other animals. Another way of avoiding any hurt to the feelings of non-pet owners is to ask every student to bring to class a drawing of a pet they would *like to have*.

Extensions

1. Students form groups to consider the needs of a particular pet animal. Using all the sheets for the animal in question, they compile a summary checklist of the pet's needs expressed in terms of human responsibilities; for instance, 'It is our responsibility to give a dog daily exercise'. The charts compiled are hung around the classroom and are used periodically to stimulate group reflection upon members' treatment of their own pets.

2. Working in small groups, students are asked to invent a new pet animal. In addition to drawing, painting and/or making a model of the animal and its habitat (sleeping quarters, food receptacles, play things and so on), they are asked to describe the creature's needs and things that make it happy/sad/angry and to draw up a pet care advice sheet.

■ *IF PETS COULD TALK*

Suitable for

Primary

Time needed

20 minutes

Resources

A selection of photographs of pets. Some of the photographs should illustrate positive aspects of pet ownership (e.g. dog playing ball with its owner, cat playing with ball of wool, some goldfish in a large garden pond); others should illustrate negative aspects (e.g. unhappy tethered dog, rabbit pressing its nose against the wire mesh of its hutch, solitary goldfish in a round, bare goldfish bowl).

Procedure

The photographs are laid on the floor. The class forms a circle around them and is asked to imagine that the animals in the photographs can talk. Going around the circle, students are invited to pick up a photograph, show it to the class and talk as though they were the animal depicted. At the end of the monologue, they replace the photograph. The next individual can pick it up and continue where the previous student left off or can choose a different photograph (the same photograph can, of course, be returned to later). It is at all times emphasised that students have the right to 'pass'.

Potential

A simple means of helping students empathise with pets. In the debriefing session, students can be asked to comment on what constitutes good pet care and what the owners of the 'unhappy' animals should do to make their pets' lives more enjoyable and fulfilling.

Extension

With a well-affirmed group, the activity can be extended to help students (and the teacher) become more aware of their own feelings about themselves through the use of projection. At midpoint in the time allotted, students can be asked to volunteer what the animal in the photograph would like to say to them as individuals, and to say what they have in common.

Source

After an idea in Canfield, J., & Wells, H,.C., *100 ways to enhance self-concept in the classroom*, Prentice Hall, 1976, 129.

■ *PET CHARADES*

Suitable for

Primary

Time needed

20 minutes

Resources

A selection of pet situations written on slips of paper (see box for examples) and placed in a container

---

- You are a dog and your owner gets out your leash for a walk.

- You are a pet rabbit and you are sitting in your owner's lap being stroked gently.

- You are a dog and have been left alone all day in the house.

- You are a dog and your owner accidentally stands on your paw.

- You are a dog left alone in the house and a stranger comes to the front door.

Procedure

Students take it in turns to take a situation slip out of the container and, using movements and sounds appropriate to the pet, they act out the situation. The class guesses what is being demonstrated.

Potential

In discussion following the activity, students can be asked to identify the emotions felt by the pet in each situation. The question can then be put as to whether human beings and animals share many of the same emotions. If so, what are the implications for responsible pet care?

Source

After an idea in Sheehan, K., & Waidner, M., *Earthchild. Games, stories, activities, experiments and ideas about living lightly on Planet Earth*, Tulsa, Council Oak Books, 1991.

■ *IT'S A DOG'S LIFE*

Suitable for

Primary

Time needed

40 minutes (making hand puppets); 40 minutes (circle time)

Resources

A selection of dog glove puppet templates; felt, scissors, needles, thread and pins; story slips in an envelope; cardboard bone.

Procedure

1. Students select a dog glove puppet template, pin it onto felt and cut out the shape. The edges are stitched.

2. Students sit in a chain story circle with their glove puppets on their hands. The teacher draws a story slip from the envelope and reads it aloud. The cardboard bone is passed around the circle. Any child wishing to continue the story talking through their dog puppet may do so once the bone is in their possession. The bone is then passed around until contributions dry up. Another story slip is chosen and the process repeated.

Potential

This sharing circle activity (see p. 67) encourages students to empathise with the feelings of dogs that are treated responsibly/irresponsibly by their owners. What are the consequences, in the short and long term, of irresponsible petcare?

Variation

Chain story circles can be used for stories told from a human point of view in which pets cause dangerous or bothersome situations as a result of their owner's irresponsibility. Story starters can include:

- ❏ The dog busily dug its way under the wire fence and into the chicken coop ...

- ❏ I was driving along when a big dog ran out right in front of my car ...

- ❏ I looked out of the window and saw the neighbour's dog knock my rubbish bin over. The wind blew the rubbish all over my garden ...

- ❏ The cat ran down my yard. It had killed another robin that had been feeding at the birdtable ...

It's a Dog's Life Story Slips

Yesterday my owners let me roam in the street without a leash ....

I spent a hot afternoon tied to a tree while my family played and had a picnic in the park ....

This evening I will be wearing a reflective badge on my collar when I go for a walk ....

Last week I was left alone all day in the house and didn't stop whining ....

I was so excited when my owner came home I couldn't stop barking and jumping up at him ....

I'm a big dog that needs lots of exercise and I'm not often taken for a good long walk ....

For a treat my owner bought me a new red bouncy ball ....

It was raining when we went for a walk and no one dried my feet when we got home ....

I got such a good brush my coat looked shiny and healthy ....

Source

Fiona Heads

■ *ANIMALS ARE FOR ALWAYS*

Suitable for

Primary/lower secondary

Time needed

Up to 4 hours for initial stages

Resources

Information books, leaflets, and, if available, video material about pets (see *Additional Resources*, p.168)

Procedure

Working in groups of four, students discuss their preferred choice of class pet, using the reference material available to identify pets' needs and to determine the appropriateness of various suggestions for pets made by group members. They reflect upon class members' ability to fulfil the needs of the various pets under discussion during term, weekend and vacation time. Each group reports on its choice of pet and the reasons for the choice (the inappropriateness of other choices considered can also be explained). A group is, of course, at liberty to make the case for no class pet. A shortlist of pets is drawn up from group recommendations (the shortlist to include any 'no pet' recommendations) and the shortlist put to the vote. If the vote is for a particular pet, the class discusses the caring attitudes and behaviours needed to ensure their pet would be contented and safe. A *Caring* checklist is drawn up, and signed by each student, to acknowledge that they subscribe to the guidelines it contains. The case for a pet is then put to the school authorities, to parents and to others deserving a say in the decision (e.g. a local veterinarian, the school caretakers), the students explaining the process of reflection and discussion in which they have been engaged and the contents of their *Caring* checklist. Should interested parties be in agreement, the classroom is made ready to greet the pet and a petcare schedule drawn up. From time to time, students are asked to review the checklist and to ask themselves whether it needs amending and whether they are abiding by its guidelines.

Potential

An activity encouraging students to think through the ramifications of responsible pet ownership. It is important that students be asked to confront squarely the question of the appropriateness of the chosen pet given that the classroom is primarily a place of work and study; also the question of having any pet at all given weekends and vacations and the fact that they will move on through the school during the expected lifetime of the pet. Will the classroom sometimes be too noisy for a pet? Are class members comfortable with the idea of keeping a pet in a cage? Should a pet be chosen that can often be allowed to roam the classroom? The rights of others to a say, in some cases an emphatic say, in any decision- making process surrounding pet acquisition by the class also need underlining. Any local education authority guidelines on keeping pets in schools should be brought to the students' attention as should the advice given in the RSPCA manuals, *Animals in Schools* and *Small Mammals in Schools* (see *Additional Resources*). A decision not to proceed with a pet does not negate from the value of the process of discussion, reflection and consultation and the higher level of sensitivity to pets' needs likely to result. In determining their position on the class pet proposal, school personnel and parents should be asked to place in the decisional balance our new understandings of the way responsibility for pets can enhance individual students' sense of self-worth (see pp.37-9).

Extension

An animal sanctuary worker is invited to class to explain and demonstrate how she looks after pets in her care.

Source

After an idea developed by Fiona Heads

■ *SUITABLE HOMES?*

Suitable for

Upper primary/secondary

Time needed

90 minutes

Resources

A copy of the *What Makes a Suitable Home for a Pet?*, *Further Guidelines* and *Suitable Homes? Suitable Owners? (1)* sheets for each group of three/four students. A print-form or overhead projection transparency copy of the *Suitable Homes? Suitable Owners? (2)* sheet.

Procedure

Students form into groups of three or four. Groups are asked to imagine that they are owners of an animal sanctuary who are keen to find homes for the animals in their care but are only prepared to let the animals be adopted if satisfied that the prospective owners and homes are suitable. Copies of the *What Makes a Suitable Home for a Pet?* and *Suitable Homes? Suitable Owners? (1)* sheets are distributed, one each per group. Students are asked to assess the suitability of prospective owners visiting the sanctuary as described in the latter, drawing upon their own knowledge and the guidelines laid down in the former. With each of the eleven requests from visitors to adopt an animal, groups make notes concerning the following:

❑ the circumstances, if any, under which they would allow the visitors to adopt the animal of their choice;

❑ the questions they would want to ask the visitors;

❑ what they would want to check out at the visitors' own homes;

❑ advice they would want to give the visitors.

As groups complete the task, they are handed a copy of the *What Makes a Suitable Home for a Pet? Further Guidelines* sheet and asked to evaluate their decisions and questions in the light of the information given. Have they overlooked important considerations in determining the suitability of owners and homes? Do the *Further Guidelines*, in their view, omit important factors?

KEEPING PETS IN SCHOOL
by a former primary school headteacher

'Our hamster escaped from his cage last night and set off the school burglar alarm' was the news item of the day for a Primary 2 pupil, when this incident occurred some years ago in our school. Such an incident might deter some teachers from keeping classroom pets, but I hope that I can suggest some positive reasons for keeping pets in schools, provided of course that the proper conditions and safeguards can be met.

Children are naturally attracted to animals especially the small warm furry variety, and they are keen to find out about animal lifestyles. However they do not usually appreciate the commitment required in caring for a pet, and schools can play a part in teaching children the importance of giving animals the correct care and attention.

Keeping a school or a class pet provides an ideal opportunity for children to learn first hand about an animal. Through observation and in discussion with their teacher, they are able to learn about the physical characteristics of the animal, its behaviour patterns, its needs — including diet, a place to sleep, careful handling — and something of its life cycle.

A mini-project on a class pet can create opportunities for work in many areas of the curriculum. The children's enthusiasm about a living creature usually generates interesting discussion, which leads in turn to exciting written language. There are obvious links with science as they learn about animal life cycles and reproduction, with mathematics as they engage in activities such as costing the amount of food required for a pet, perhaps measuring its daily intake of food, and also many opportunities for creative art and craft work. The study will enable children to develop the skills of observing, recording, classifying and predicting.

It is to be hoped that through their study children would not only know how to look after a particular pet, but that they would develop a concern for the welfare of all living creatures as that surely must be a prime objective.

Many children enjoy caring for a school pet because they are unable to have a pet of their own at home, and where children have no knowledge or experience of working with animals, a school pet can meet this need.

Keeping pets can give children great pleasure and looking after them can be a very worthwhile and rewarding experience, but considerable assistance from staff is also essential. Teachers need to know which pets are suitable for the classroom. They must ensure that the animals are properly cared for, and adequate provision made for them during holiday periods. Education authorities have policy statements regarding keeping living creatures in schools, and it is important to stress that these guidelines must be adhered to, in order to ensure the safety of both animal and pupil.

While children, under adult supervision, can be taught how to handle, feed and groom a pet, the more difficult tasks such as ensuring hygienic living conditions cannot be left solely to the children. With teacher direction children are usually enthusiastic about the daily tasks of feeding the pet and giving it regular care and attention. In some schools auxiliary helpers can be involved in supervising children as they carry out the necessary, but less attractive tasks such as cleaning a hutch.

Teachers also need to be knowledgeable about the animal they have chosen as some are clearly more suitable than others. A hamster makes an interesting pet, but since he is a nocturnal creature he may sleep for most of the day resulting in children seeing very little of his behaviour. Two hamsters are not a good idea because of their tendency to fight. This raises another important point, namely that some animals live happily on their own, while others are better living in pairs. Gerbils, guinea pigs, even goldfish or budgerigars are all possibilities for the classroom.

A rabbit makes an ideal pet but requires more space to exercise than a smaller animal. Keeping a rabbit confined to a hutch is not such a good idea, but if the school has an enclosed garden area where an outdoor run is possible, then a rabbit makes a very good pet as it can become very tame.

I know of a school which has kept rabbits for many years. It was fortunate to have an enclosed grassed courtyard, where the rabbits had the best of both worlds — a large hutch for shelter and freedom to run about in the courtyard. From time to time a doe was allowed to produce a litter of baby rabbits and this has been a most exciting and rewarding experience for the children.

Just as children are thrilled to see new born baby rabbits, so they must also learn to cope with the loss of a pet, and this is another learning experience for them as they realise that pets can have a relatively short lifespan.

The adults in school who are supervising the care of the pets need to be alert to signs of any deterioration in an animal and to seek advice from the veterinary surgeon.

Another factor to be considered in keeping pets is the cost. Most animals require a cage or a hutch. Food has to be purchased and the occasional vet's bill has to be paid. Where staff and children are enthusiastic these requirements can usually be worked out. Children can put odd amounts of money into a little rabbit bank and can also bring in greens from home as food.

Where children are introduced to caring for animals at an early stage in their lives, through looking after pets in school, it is to be hoped that this will result in them understanding the need to care for all living creatures.

The eleven cases are then discussed, one by one, in plenary session. At an appropriate point in the discussion of each case, the teacher reads out (or reveals on overhead projection transparency) the relevant section of *Suitable Homes? Suitable Owners? (2)*. It is pointed out these are not 'right answers' but the kind of response likely to be made to each case by an animal sanctuary or rescue centre applying a rigorous policy with respect to pet placement. The teacher should elicit reactions to these hypothetical responses. Are they fair? Do they take sufficient aspects of the case into account?

Potential

A lively means of sensitising students to the needs of pet animals and of alerting them to the risks attached to impulsive acquisition/purchase of pets for themselves and other people. The need to apply similar considerations in finding homes for pets they breed deserves emphasis towards the close of the session.

Extension

A representative of an animal sanctuary or rescue centre is invited to class to explain their work and pet placement policies and procedures.

Source

Phil Brooke

Homeless dogs caged in a sanctuary (Photo: Lee Tiller/ EarthKind)

What Makes a Suitable Home for a Pet?

Homes should be checked before a sanctuary allows someone to take a pet — the pet is likely to be there for a lifetime! This includes looking around the home, checking that facilities and equipment have been prepared and discussing the care of the animal with the new owners.

A home should be checked out however small the pet animal. It may be 'only a mouse' to some people, but the mouse might take a different view!

Important questions to consider include:

1. Will the pet be happy in the home?

2. Will the pet have companionship of its own kind (where appropriate)?

3. Will the pet get enough human attention?

4. Do the people know the costs of keeping this kind of pet and can they afford it?

5. How much do the people know about the care of this kind of pet? Have they any past experience? Have they read a lot about it?

6. Will they be able to look after the pet for the rest of its life? For example, do they have a job which might take them abroad or are they likely to move to accommodation where they couldn't keep pets?

7. How do the people intend to prevent the animal from breeding? (A lot of pets have to be put down, or given to unsuitable homes, because too many are born).

8. Pets of any kind should **NEVER** be given as presents to people without checking first that they are wanted and that the new owner will look after them properly.

P

SUITABLE HOMES? SUITABLE OWNERS? (1)

1. I want a companion when I come home from work now that I don't have a boyfriend. I've always loved animals and I'd like to help a homeless dog.

2. We have kept dogs since we were children and our last ones have just died. We would like a bitch so that we can breed from her. *When doing the home-check you find a large house and garden. The fence has fallen down in one place but is otherwise secure.*

3. I am at home all day; my husband is a serviceman and we have just returned from a posting abroad. We had a dog but had to have it put down before returning to England — we thought it cruel to put an eight-year old dog through quarantine. We would like to adopt an unwanted springer spaniel.

4. Do you have any terrapins or tortoises? We have always been fond of reptiles. We thought we'd try you before going to a pet shop. *You find you don't have either.*

5. We would like to adopt a pony for our daughter. We have a large garden with a three-quarter acre orchard in it with lots of lovely grass going to waste. We haven't kept horses before but are willing to learn.

6. We had two ponies but one contracted cancer and had to be put down. We would like to adopt a donkey to keep the other one company. We have a four-acre field with shelter and stabling.

7. We love cats and had four but three of them have been run over recently — they have just built a new by-pass near our house. We should like to adopt a homeless animal.

8. We would like to adopt a mother cat and one of its kittens. We would like a tabby if possible and we want to breed from her. We live out in the country and our last cat just died of old age.

9. We really wanted a dog, but since we both go out to work and go on holiday abroad three months a year we thought it would be fairer to adopt a more independent animal. We would like a cat, preferably a good mouser. We live near a farm so there will be plenty for the cat to eat when we are away.

10. We should like to adopt a pair of rabbits. We want to breed from them — we know a pet shop which says it may be able to sell the young for us. We don't have a garden, but we do have space for the hutch.

11. Can we adopt that rabbit? We have a guinea pig which is lonely and we want a companion for it. Our garden is fenced and we have a hutch with an outside run.

P

WHAT MAKES A SUITABLE HOME FOR A PET?
FURTHER GUIDELINES

DOGS

Dogs are pack animals which naturally would have companionship all day (and night!) long. If allowed out unsupervised or to escape they may foul pavements and attack other animals. They need frequent exercise, and access to a garden outside.

Further questions to ask of potential owners include:

- Will there be someone at home nearly all day?

- Is there a garden with a suitable fence around it?

- Will they be strong enough to manage the animal?

- If there are small children, will they be at any risk?

- How much exercise will they be able to give the dog?

- Will they groom the dog adequately?

- Will the dog be vaccinated and/or neutered?

- How tidy is the home? What effect will a dog have on it? How much damage could it do? Are the potential owners prepared for this?

CATS

Cats are more independent than dogs, but often still require a lot of companionship. Female cats do not usually stray far, but toms do. Cats rarely look before crossing roads and usually die young if a main road is within their territory. It is almost impossible to prevent an un-neutered female cat from becoming pregnant since they come on heat every two weeks.

Further questions to ask of potential owners include:

- Is the home near a main road?

- Can the cat get in and out easily?

- How often will they be in?

- Do they intend to have the cat vaccinated and/or neutered?

P

HORSES AND PONIES

Horses and ponies are *very* expensive to buy and *even more expensive to keep.* They need access to at least two acres of good grass *each*; they suffer if they do not have companionship of their own kind; they need supplementary feeding in winter; they also need it in summer if ridden a lot. They need stables and a shelter in the field — in winter from rain and wind and, even more important, from the sun in summer. Unless you have thousands of pounds to spend, you shouldn't consider keeping horses or ponies. Many suffer severely because their owners cannot afford to look after them properly.

RABBITS AND GUINEA PIGS

One major problem is their tendency to breed at a very rapid rate and the chances are that their owners will not always be able to find a good home for the young.

Where possible they need the company of their own kind, except that males cannot usually be kept together as they may kill each other. The ideal may be to keep a *neutered* male with a female or to keep one rabbit and one guinea pig, preferably of different sexes, together. Anyone who begrudges the cost of neutering because 'it is only a rabbit' is unlikely to be a suitable owner.

Both need access to grass outside for part of the day, but their run will need to be secure from both cats and dogs which often kill them.

Further questions to ask of potential owners include:

● Is the garden fenced?

● Is there space for a run?

● Do they have a hutch and run ready?

● How many do they intend to keep?

● Will the hutch be in a sheltered position? Guinea-pigs at least will need to be taken indoors in very cold weather, and both should have a cover over the wire mesh at night. Apart from anything else, this reduces the risk of being frightened by cats.

IMPORTED PETS

These include tortoises, terrapins, snakes, some kinds of frog and some tropical fish. They can be difficult to look after, some requiring expert handling.

Animal welfare organisations are STRONGLY OPPOSED to the importing of animals as pets. They are often captured from the wild and as many as 90% die before they reach this country. Some are becoming rare in the wild because of the pet trade and this is adversely affecting local ecological systems. This is why it is now illegal to import tortoises.

P

SUITABLE HOMES? SUITABLE OWNERS? (2)

1. Unsuitable. A dog needs someone at home nearly all the day and would probably suffer under these conditions, hard though it might seem on a lonely person.

2. They would have to wait for the dog until the fence was fixed since rehomed dogs are particularly likely to escape. The owners should be discouraged from breeding since there is a great over-population of dogs, not all of whom can be found homes. Otherwise likely to be a very suitable home.

3. Service personnel are not usually allowed to adopt dogs since they are likely to be posted to places where dogs can't be kept and animal homes often have to cope in consequence. If they adopt a dog it is quite likely it will have to be put down before it reaches old age.

4. They would be discouraged from buying one — for every exotic pet bought, several died on the way. In addition, terrapins and tortoises are difficult to keep alive — the climate doesn't suit them.

5. Three-quarters of an acre is NOT enough. The pony would probably kill the fruit trees unless they were protected. The intending owners would need to obtain access to at least two acres and be aware of the cost of keeping ponies in time and money before being allowed to adopt a pony. They would probably be discouraged.

6. This would be considered a happy arrangement subject to the usual checks.

7. It is best not to keep cats if living next to a main road. Any more adopted would probably be run over. Sadly, the offer would be refused.

8. Sounds like an excellent home, but breeding would be discouraged for reasons already mentioned. Some rescue centres neuter all animals for adoption.

9. Oh dear! Cats should NEVER be left to fend for themselves and are less independent than some people think. If they are away that much, pet keeping is not for them. Leaving a cat to fend for itself would be classed as abandonment — a criminal offence!

10. Rabbits ought to have a run for at least part of the day. This one would be a backyard prisoner.

11. Sounds good. Would the run be protected from cats?

P

ADDITIONAL RESOURCES

For the teacher ....

❑ RSPCA, *Animals in schools, a compendium for teachers*, 1986. Invaluable manual, pooling the experience of local education authorities and drawing on the advice of veterinary organisations, on keeping animals in schools.

❑ RSPCA, *Small mammals in schools. A compendium for teachers*, 1986. A companion to the above volume giving more specific advice on a range of small mammals suitable for keeping in school.

❑ Coggan, D.F., ed., *Visiting animal schemes. A guide to good practice for schools, local education authorities and VAS operators*, RSPCA/Council for Environmental Education, 1988. A manual designed to help teachers assess the educational and animal welfare pros and cons of the various visiting animal schemes now available to schools.

For the classroom ....

❑ Barnes, A., *A practical book of pet keeping*, Humane Education Centre/Crusade Against all Cruelty to Animals, 1972. Some outdated chapters (e.g. on tortoises) but helpful guidance on good care of a range of pet animals.

❑ *National Pet Week* (12 Belmont Road, Belfast, BT4 2AE, or P.O. Box 10, Hedge End, Southampton, S03 4ZL) provides an excellent opportunity to promote responsible pet ownership and to alert students to the professional services available to pets. Activities are usually organised in conjunction with the local veterinary practice.

❑ RSPCA, *If you were a guinea pig, If you were a gerbil, If you were a rabbit, If you were a hamster*, Collins, 1988. Four colourful books for 4-9 year olds helping them understand the needs of small pets kept at home or school by asking them to put themselves in the animals' place.

❑ St. Andrew Animal Fund, *Are you an animal lover?*, 1975. Pamphlet in cartoon form on the importance of neutering cats and dogs.

❑ The Cats Protection League has a *Teaching pack* for 5-9 year olds containing 30 work booklets and ideas for classroom activities and projects.

❑ The Scottish Society for the Prevention of Cruelty to Animals (SSPCA) publishes a series of *Petcare Booklets*; its VHS video, *Action for Animals*, 17 mins, includes sections on pets and is available on free loan.

❑ *Key humane organisations to contact (see* Organisations *list): Animal Concern, Cats Protection League, EarthKind, National Canine Defence League, National Petwatch, Royal Society for the Prevention of Cruelty to Animals, Scottish Society for the Prevention of Cruelty to Animals.*

References

1. *Education Guardian*, 10.12.1991, 1.
2. *Ibid.*, 3.
3. *Chronicle & Echo* (Northampton), 5.10.1993 (cutting supplied by EarthKind UK).
4. *Evening Echo* (Bournemouth), 2.10.1993 (cutting supplied by EarthKind UK).
5. Cowley, C., 'Spaying and neutering, *Turning Point*, July-Sept. 1992, 10. The National Neutering & Spaying Scheme is contactable via P.O. Box 170, Northampton, NN2 8AB.

Chapter 8

Down on the Farm

INTRODUCTION

Children's nursery rhymes, songs and stories convey an idyllic image of the farm: chickens scratching in the yard, cows lowing in the meadow, lambs frolicking, piglets scampering in an open field. The image is reinforced by dairy and meat product brand names, packaging and advertising. The reality is dramatically different. Most farm animals have their quality of life sacrificed to the financial imperatives of agribusiness (valued at about 10 billion per annum in the UK[1]). *Intensive* or *factory* farming allows the farmer to maximise efficiency and profits by encouraging animals to grow faster and produce more offspring in conditions which are the least labour intensive. As such, the cost of meat relative to average income has been slashed in the last thirty years in the case of animals that lend themselves to factory farming. In 1960 it took the industrial worker on average male earnings 34 minutes labour to earn a pound of chicken; in 1991 it took him 11 minutes. Cows and sheep do not respond well to intensive rearing and normally bear only one calf or lamb at a time with long intervals in between births. Accordingly, the cost of their meat has fallen much less in

proportion to earnings even though backed by heavy governmental subsidies (see *document 1*).[2]

In comparison to cows and sheep, sows produce up to fourteen piglets at each pregnancy. 60% of breeding sows in the UK are kept in individual, narrow stalls unable to move more than one step forwards or backwards and often tethered to the floor by chains with a strap around their middle or neck. When a sow is ready to give birth she is transferred to a *farrowing crate* where she cannot follow her instinct of building a nest of leaves and straw and caring for her offspring. Instead, she gives birth lying on a concrete floor and is then prevented by metal bars from any contact, beyond suckling, with her piglets. Her young are weaned at two to three weeks. After a week the sow will come on heat and be mated again. Three months, three weeks and three days later she will give birth and the process will begin again. On weaning, the piglets will be transferred to tiered and darkened cages, standing on uncomfortable wire mesh. Once strong enough they are removed to *fattening pens*, boxes with concrete walls and floors and a slatted area for drainage. The pigs are crowded together in near darkness with no bedding straw.

*Close confinement
(Photo: CIWF)*

They are slaughtered at about seven months.[3]

Poultry endure even more intensive methods that confound all or most of their basic behavioural needs (to peck in the earth for food, lay eggs in nests, live in flocks, make dustbaths, preen). *Battery hens*, i.e. egg-laying chickens subjected to factory farming conditions, are packed into small wire cages and spend their lives standing or crouching down on sloping wire floors. A typical cage for five hens measures 45 cm by 50 cm, a space per hen equivalent to the size of this page. They are unable to stretch their wings and also often suffer severe damage to their feet and claws. At the end of their productive lives, their bodies are used to make chicken soup, tinned chicken and chicken stock.[4] *Broiler chickens*, i.e. chickens raised for table, are reared in huge, dimly-lit indoor sheds that typically house 20,000 birds or more. They are bred and fed to reach slaughter weight when they are six or seven weeks' old. As they grow, they have less and less space in which to move and, lacking strength, their genetically-manipulated body weight causes them to slump onto the ammonia-ridden floor. As a result they go to slaughter with burns and ulcers on their legs and breasts and with chronic pain in joints unable to cope with their body weight.[5]

The most extreme form of factory farming is crated veal production. Within usually twenty-four hours of birth a calf is taken from its mother and placed in a slatted, darkened crate less than two feet wide. It remains there until about fourteen weeks' old and is denied all exercise. Throughout its time in the crate it is fed on an iron-deficient milk substitute gruel. This makes it anaemic and its meat unnaturally white. At three weeks the calf is too big to turn in the crate and can do nothing but stand. It soon becomes a cripple, spending the remainder of its life partially collapsed. Crated veal production was banned in the UK in 1990 but the export of veal calves was not, some 300,000 per year being sent, for instance, to the Netherlands where the law still permits veal crates.[6] Many of the exported calves return to the UK as carcasses to satisfy the gourmet 'white veal' trade.

Ducks, rabbits and turkeys are also reared in factory farms (turkeys spending between 12 and 24 weeks in conditions similar to those endured by broiler chickens). There is also

Chickens travelling to a processing plant. (Photo: Turning Point)

legislation to make factory farming more humane. They feel unable to implement unilaterally a voluntary code of practice, such as that put forward by the Farm Animal Welfare Council, because that would make them less competitive in the marketplace. For the same reason, they favour pan-European, as against specifically British, legislation (*document 4*). A few farmers have returned to (or never left) traditional or *free-range* farming in which animals and birds are kept outside in fields and pens where they can satisfy their behavioural needs. Their customers tend in the main to be found amongst higher socio-economic groups prepared to pay the extra cost for food.

Opponents of intensive farming argue that factory farm conditions are cruel, inhumane and a distortion of natural life that dehumanises both those directly involved (the producers) and those indirectly involved (the consumers). They argue, too, that factory-farmed meat can seriously endanger human health in that the antibiotics regularly administered to animals can cause antibiotic resistance which is then passed on to humans. Antibiotic treatments against human disease are, thus, rendered ineffectual. They also point out that factory-farmed animals cannot exercise and, hence, contain more fat which is transferred to the human population and is subsequently manifested in higher levels of heart disease. The suspected illegal use by some farmers of growth hormones, known to cause abnormalities in children, is a further cause for concern.[7] (For health issues, see *documents 5, 7*).

an increasing tendency for farmers to bring beef cattle indoors for fattening in concrete pens often devoid of bedding.

Farming interests tend to insist that there is no alternative to factory farming if the population's demand for cheap, plentiful meat is to be met; also, that animals are healthier and more contented in intensive conditions (see *documents 2, 3*). Some farmers favour the introduction of

Vegans (who avoid food and also other products derived from animals) and *total vegetarians* (who avoid meat, eggs and dairy products) not only oppose factory but also free-range farming, arguing that the latter, whilst more humane, necessarily involves some cruelty and, of course, loss of life. The transportation of animals between farm, market and slaughterhouse is, they argue, a distressing, even terrifying, experience. In overcrowded crates, piled high in the lorry, many poultry die from stress or suffocation. Cattle, sheep and pigs face both the bruising rigours of the journey and the noise and confusion of the livestock market. Exported animals face long journeys in cramped conditions, often with inadequate food and water. At the slaughterhouse birds are hung upside down on a conveyor line and rendered unconscious by an electric stunner. An automatic knife then cuts their throats. Given that the force of the electric shock shatters the birds' brittle bones, causing bone splinters in the meat, slaughterhouses often reduce the voltage of the stunner. This means that many birds meet the automatic knife fully conscious.[8] Cattle, sheep and pigs are, likewise, often insufficiently stunned to be rendered insensitive to pain.[9] Facts such as these, together with the intuitive panic that animals are likely to experience in an abattoir, lead those opposed to meat eating to say that there is no such thing as humane killing.

The dairy industry is also not cruelty-free, vegans and total vegetarians argue. Cows are forced to give birth every year to maintain their milk supply. After a few days, mother and calf are separated so that humans can drink the milk intended for the calf. Milked to capacity, the cow produces ten times as much milk as the calf would have needed had it been left to suckle. Worn out, she is slaughtered after two or three lactations at about five years of age when her natural lifespan would have been around twenty years.[10] *Lacto-vegetarians* (who include milk in their diet) may or may not rest easy with the facts of milk production whilst *lacto-ovo-vegetarians* (who eat dairy products and eggs) may or may not seek out free-range eggs. The activity, *Yum Yum*, p.185, offers a platform for consideration of vegetarian beliefs and practices.

Nobody tries to extend the romantic or traditional image of farming touched upon at the opening of this chapter to new kinds of farm that have sprung up in the United Kingdom in recent years. In the country's fifty-five mink farms, animals with a natural range of up to 6 kilometres spend their lives in cages as short as 61 centimetres in length. Solitary, roaming and territorial in the wild, they are often forced to share cages. Silver or Arctic fox are also reared on factory farms (some six in all), animals with a natural range of 2,000-15,000 acres being confined to cages often as small as 91 cm x 60 cm. Both mink and fox display stereotyped, abnormal behaviours. Self-mutilation and (in the case of the fox) cannibalism of the young by mothers are frequent. Fur farms in the United Kingdom produce some 250,000 skins annually.[11] Many would argue that, whilst humane farming of traditional farm animals is possible and financially viable, it is impossible to farm wild animals such as mink, fox and deer in ways that are both commercially sound and humane (*document 6*). Fur farms, and other latter-day kinds of farming development, are the object of strong criticism by the animal welfare and rights groups (*document 8*). Funny Farms, p.187, gives students the opportunity to explore these developments.

Farmed mink (Photo: BWCC)

DOCUMENTS

1.

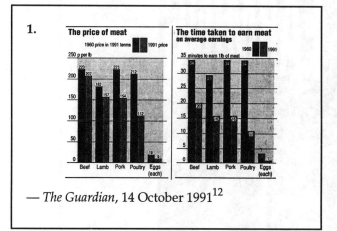

The price of meat

The time taken to earn meat on average earnings

— *The Guardian*, 14 October 1991[12]

2. Intensive modern pig units produce pork at reasonable cost, which is what today's customer wants, and there is nothing wrong with the system . A few farmers produce a superior and tastier free-range product at double the cost. But it is impractical to think this could be done on a sufficient scale to feed the nation.

— *Farmer Weekly*, 23 December 1988[13]

3. Intensive systems offer considerable benefits. Sows can be individually fed and inspected; controlled temperatures and ventilation help sows produce healthy and robust litters and enable pigs to gain weight easily; and pigs can be reared in clean and hygienic conditions, reducing the risk of disease.

— National Farmers Union, *Looking After Pigs*[14]

4. The meat factory

He spoke with quiet dignity but his words were a lament. 'It distresses me. I would prefer to be seen as a craftsman, not as a commercial exploiter of animals, but I feel I am being turned from one to the other.'

'When we started keeping broilers it took 84 days to rear them; now, thanks to genetic and nutritional 'progress' they reach the same weight in 42 days, exactly half the time.

'This means that a 42-day-old skeletal frame is being forced to carry an 84-day weight. Many birds, consequently suffer from leg, back, or heart failure.

'I am just a small cog in a big industry,' Mr Turton said. 'Today poultry management is dictated by the company accountant rather than the stockman, but the big companies are not so much villains, as victims of a system that dictates that only the economically ruthless shall survive.'

He also complains that the chicks supplied are 'soft'- genetically designed only to grow fast, but with weak hearts and soft skin that suffers 'burn' because their feet cannot stand the wet mix of dung and wood shavings in which they stand. Even the supermarkets can't disguise the brown discolouring which climbs to the knees of a third of birds sold.

As a result mortality, once 2 per cent, now exceeds 5 per cent. 'I used to walk through and just pick up the dead birds, but now I have to carry a container.' The prematurely dead are sold to the maggot angling bait industry.

On the 42nd day the company forklift comes to carry away the survivors, which by now present a nearly solid covering on the floor. The lights are dimmed. Chickens have poor eyesight and go dozy in the dark, and they can't see to run.

'A substantial number of dead birds are never found, and remain to rot under the carpet of living birds, detectable only by smell,' he said.

'So thick is the covering of birds that they are unable to move out of the path of the stockman as he shuffles slowly through them, accidentally treading on feet and causing physical damage as the birds struggle to release themselves.'

Only legislation can improve welfare, Mr Turton said, and it must be pan-European. He wants existing welfare codes to become law, backed by a rigorous inspection system. A legal age/weight limit would stop breeders from designing new super strains that grow even faster. 'It would be far better to breed back some of the natural hardiness of the original farm stock.'

— *The Guardian*, 15 October 1991[15]

5.

— Animal Aid leaflet[16]

6. The Council of Europe's Convention for the Protection of Animals Kept for Farming Purposes (1976) sets out the principle that farm animals should be kept in systems appropriate to their physiological and ethological needs. This principle was echoed by the Farm Animal Welfare Council in a press notice (1979) which laid down that ways of keeping farm animals should be appropriate [to the species] and allow the animals to exercise most normal patterns of behaviour. Clearly these constraints involve dramatic changes in the way in which some domesticated farm animals are reared — changes which are slowly being achieved.

For the 'farming' of the non-domesticated, wild, fur bearing animals, such as mink and foxes, the constraints are prohibitive and in the light of the many alternatives which exist, the ethical question must be posed as to whether fur farming should even be considered.

— Ruth Harrison[17]

7. Meat and Drugs

Drugs have become an indispensable part of modern livestock production If we look at pig production, for instance, we find that every stage of breeding and fattening involves some sort of pharmaceutical treatment, often to compensate for the unnatural pressure put upon animals in factory farms. Almost as soon as they are born, piglets reared for bacon, pork and ham are subject to their first treatment of antibiotics, as are their mothers, who are fed low levels throughout their continuous cycle of pregnancies. Sows may also be given drugs to induce birth at a convenient time for the stockman After the pigs have been weaned at an unnaturally early age, usually between 18 and 25 days, and thus deprived of the antibodies supplied by their mother's milk, they are particularly susceptible to disease. Consequently, 'antibacterial' is included in their high protein 'starter ration', both to promote growth and to control swine dysentery This continues until the pigs have grown sufficiently and are ready to move onto their 'grower ration' Once again low levels of antibiotics are included. And so it goes on until slaughter.

There is now mounting evidence to suggest that such automatic use of drugs may be responsible for health problems in humans because of what is known as transferable drug resistance. When animals are routinely fed antibiotics, the drugs do not simply destroy harmful bacteria in the gut; beneficial, protective bacteria are also killed. In turn, the gut may then be invaded by more hardy and dangerous strains, capable of developing resistance to a whole range of antibiotics. Such resistance may then eventually be passed on to humans when they consume meat, milk and eggs. When this pattern emerges it can render antibiotics in human medicine ineffective against an enormous range of infections.

Hormone treatment has been applied to cattle for the same profit-making reasons as antibiotics. It also creates similar dangers. After pressure from consumer organisations, EEC ministers felt that by the end of 1985 they could no longer legitimise the application of growth-promoting hormones and voted to ban their use completely. Despite British objections on the grounds that 'it flies in the face of scientific evidence', the UK became the first EEC nation to implement the ban, which officially came into effect in December 1986... The most damning evidence against hormones to date is in Puerto Rico, where premature sexual development in young children has been attributed to consumption of hormone-reared chicken Heart-breaking stories of girls aged five and a half reaching puberty, with some also developing ovarian cysts, have caused outrage and disquiet world-wide.

Although meat is often advertised as 'natural', it is, in fact, full of additives. An estimated 5% of the total colouring used in our food is found in meat products (though not in fresh meat). The most popular artificial flavouring added routinely to convenience meats is monosodium glutamate (MSG). MSG's health record is appalling, almost definitely causing side-effects ranging from dizziness and headaches to palpitations. As with all food additives, perhaps more disturbing is the fact that long-term effects on humans are unknown. MSG is often added to pâtés, pies and burgers.

This then is meat, the substance advertised as the most natural and healthy food for humans. It is difficult to imagine a more inaccurate description for a food that relies upon pharmaceuticals to ensure that animals reach the slaughterhouse alive; kills them in conditions where hygiene standards resemble a poorly maintained public lavatory, and then relies upon more chemicals to make the finished product look and taste edible.

— Mark Gold[18]

8. Ostrich Farming

A lucrative market for ostrich meat, skin, feathers and eggs has led to the birds being described as the farmer's best friend. But is the farmer any friend of the ostrich?

Ostriches certainly are good news for farmers hit by the agricultural slump. They're a bit like the proverbial goose that laid golden eggs. Practically every part of an ostrich can be used. Their low calorie, high protein meat has been hailed as the health food of the '90s. Ostriches produce more meat per year per acre than beef, which is another reason they are so attractive to farmers.

Ostrich hide, feathers and eggs also fetch high prices as decorative items. The best dressed urban cowboys in America are now strutting around in expensive boots made from ostrich leather, while executive types will pay up to £2,000 for a briefcase made from the same material.

As ostriches are prolific breeders — hens start laying eggs at the age of two or three years and will continue producing about 50 a year for the next 40 years — an initial outlay of a few thousand pounds per ostrich would be seen by a farmer as a good investment for the future.

Although generally docile, ostriches stand about six feet tall, can run at 40mph and have a kick powerful enough to kill lions in the wild. As they are easily frightened, ostriches can be difficult to handle. During the breeding season male ostriches become so protective and aggressive that farmers have to keep them locked up while they gather eggs.

Although Britain currently has only the one ostrich farm where a small number of birds are being kept in spacious enclosures, animal rights campaigners fear that if the farming becomes widespread the birds will suffer.

Philip Lymbery, CIWF campaigns officer, said, 'We feel that the ostrich is completely unsuitable for our agricultural system. When species that have been domesticated for thousands of years are treated so appallingly on farms, there's no justification for bringing a wild animal into the farming arena.'

CIWF is also worried about the future of the birds if ostrich farming takes off. 'At the moment they may be well looked after but that's easy to do if you've only got a handful of birds,' said Philip.

'If it becomes a large scale industry we may see them being treated in a similar commercial manner as other animals. In America, for instance, work is under way on artificial insemination for ostriches. We see that as one step down the road to intensive farming.

'I'm sure the people who began deer farming had the best intentions, yet ten years later we're seeing deer being subjected to some degree of intensive farming through the use of artificial insemination and growth promoting substances, and being transported long distances to slaughterhouses.

Whatever the outcome of ostrich farming in this country, one thing is sure — we can't bury our heads in the sand and hope the issue goes away.

— Tina Courtney[19]

ACTIVITIES

■ *CINQUAINS*

Suitable for

Primary/secondary

Time needed

45-75 minutes (depending on length of films)

Resources

Paper and pencil for each student. Examples of cinquains. A few short pieces of film showing farm animals moving.

Procedure

The pieces of film are shown, the students having been encouraged to pay careful attention to how the animals look, what they do, how they move and what sounds they make. After each film the class brainstorms words and phrases to describe the animal depicted. When the film viewing and brainstorming is complete, the nature of a cinquain is explained. A cinquain is a five-line poem with the following format: line 1 is a noun, stating the subject of the poem; line 2 is made up of two adjectives describing the subject; line 3 has three verbs or a verb phrase that relate to the subject; line 4 is a four-word phrase stating feelings about or interpretation of the subject; line 5 is one word, usually another noun, that restates the subject or a word that sums up the poem. Example:

> Spiders
> Tiny, busy
> Spinning, moving, floating
> Building fragile wispy webs
> Artists.

The students each choose a farm animal and create a cinquain to describe it and their impression of it. The poems can be illustrated and displayed around the room or collected in a book.

Potential

A simple, creative activity which builds upon the children's knowledge of language while increasing their understanding of, empathy with, and respect for particular farm animals.

Variation

A visit to a farm to watch real animals move would be another powerful stimulus for cinquain writing.

Extension

1. Dance and movement sessions could enhance this activity and develop the children's knowledge and empathy further.

2. The activity can, of course, focus upon animals in other situations and environments. 'Contrastive cinquains' can also be attempted, i.e. pairs of cinquains on, for instance, free range and factory farmed animals or animals in the wild and the same animals caged in zoos.

Source

Jackie Harvey

■ CARE POSTERS

Suitable for
Primary

Time needed
60 minutes

Resources
Sugar paper for each group of children; felt pens or paint for each group; books, pamphlets or information sheets from which students can research.

Procedure
Students identify five or six farm animals. The names of the animals are written on the board. The class divides into five or six groups and each group is assigned an animal. It is explained that the aim of the activity is to produce posters to highlight the care and conditions each animal requires and that this will first involve researching the behaviour and basic needs of the assigned animal. Groups should be encouraged to find out how much space the animal prefers, what it needs to eat to maintain its health, what sort of bedding and housing is best for it, whether it commonly lives in groups or alone, how it looks after its young and any particular habits it has. Having used the resource collection to research their animal, groups produce their posters which are then displayed under a collective heading such as 'Farm Animals Deserve Care'.

Potential
An activity that will reinforce student understanding of animals' basic needs and that allows for those needs to be presented in attractive and striking ways. Reflection and discussion on whether those needs are actively being met on most farms will almost certainly result.

Extension
The research aspect of this activity can be conducted through letter writing to animal welfare groups (see *Organisations* list pp.399-404); also by having a veterinarian speak to the class and/or by visiting farms or a farm centre.

Source
Jackie Harvey

■ YELLOW PAGES

Suitable for
Primary/secondary

Time needed
60 minutes

Resources
Copies of Yellow Pages and/or local newspapers and farming magazines. Paper and pencil for each student.

Procedure
Students work in small groups. They use the materials to generate a class list of sources of products or services upon which farmers rely for animal husbandry, e.g. feed stores, farm machinery manufacturers/supplier, veterinarians. Discussion follows on what each of the sources provides and whether the products/services are to the benefit or disbenefit of the animals themselves. Groups then each choose a different source and, perhaps (but not necessarily) following a period of research and enquiry, create an advertisement or poster describing the products/services provided and their positive or negative ramifications for the animals.

Potential
A way of actively involving students in identifying product sources and services available to the animal farmer that will promote their understanding of animal needs and reinforce their skimming and scanning skills. It also provides a springboard for the discussion of the impact upon animals of a consumerist society. To what extent do the products and services meet the real needs of animals? To what extent do they involve a denial of those needs? If the animals' needs are not being met or are being systematically denied, in whose interest is that happening?

Extensions
1. Students compile their own animal-friendly Yellow Pages or farming magazine inventing, if necessary, products and services that would truly meet the animals' needs.

2. Students investigate the products and services used at farms firmly committed to the welfare of their livestock and adhering to codes laid down by organisations such as Compassion in World Farming; for instance, the Real Meat Company (see *Additional Resources*).

Source

Jackie Harvey

■ *FACTORY LEARNING*

Suitable for

Primary/secondary

Time needed

20 minutes

Resources

An open space with a grid of taped squares (40 to 45 centimetre squares, or larger, depending on the size of the students) marked out on the floor, one square per student

OR

A row of desks, c. 65 x 135 cm, long side on, with a grid of six taped squares of equal size under each desk and with tables turned on their sides along one long side and the two short sides of the row.

Procedure

Students are told that the lesson is to be conducted under special circumstances. They are asked to stand in one of the taped squares (sit in a square under a table), taking with them a pen, pencil, some paper and a pad. From time to time reminded of the need to stay within their squares, the class is required to undertake a series of tasks (such as chanting their multiplication tables, writing notes as the teacher dictates/lectures, taking a spelling test, drawing a picture of a vase placed on a stand, working out a mathematical problem, composing a poem). The teacher should exercise vigilance and offer a way out of the activity for any student experiencing real discomfort. The programme of tasks completed, students are invited to stretch and exercise before the experience is debriefed. At no point before or during the experience should its purpose be explained.

Battery Egg Production

Of the 47 million egg-laying hens in Britain about 96% are kept in battery cages measuring 45 to 50 cm with four or five birds to a single cage. The floor of the cage is made of wire mesh to allow the droppings to fall through.

Dry Sow Stalls

During their sixteen and a half week pregnancy, sows are kept in narrow stalls with metal bars in which they cannot turn around. They are tethered around the neck or body and stand or lie on a bare concrete floor.

Potential

An experiential means of helping students understand the stress felt by animals in factory farms. The debriefing should begin by encouraging a sharing of emotions and reactions. How did students feel at the beginning? Did their feelings change later? How long was it before people began to feel uncomfortable? What were the reasons for their discomfort? Did students get on each others' nerves? How did the irritation manifest itself? Why did some students feel compelled to abandon the activity? The class can also be asked to imagine what it would be like if the activity were to continue for a longer period of time, or indefinitely, and to think of the physical and psychological effects even if food and water were provided. At an appropriate

---

I did this as part of our project on Survival — looking at psychological and physical needs for survival. It was extremely successful — the children felt a great deal of empathy with the chickens when it was explained to them. Tasks should be hard so the children feel more frustration which of course adds to their physical discomfort and unease. I afterwards discussed debeaking with them as extension to the discussion on aggression and frustration.
— Hertfordshire primary teacher (10-11 year olds).

Very powerfully effective and deeply thought-provoking. This is the best way to understand what is what regarding factory farming from the animal's view.
— Kent secondary teacher.

point in the discussion students are introduced to some basic facts about factory farming (see box) and are asked to pool their ideas as to the likely effect on the animals involved.

Variation

Immediately after the debriefing of the activity, students watch a film on factory farming such as *The Choice is Yours* from the Athene Trust (see *Additional Resources*), share reactions to the film and relate its scenes of intensive battery hen and pig farming to their own experience.

Extension

Students divide into groups of six. Each group chooses an animal subjected to factory farming. Two members research the natural behaviour of the animal concerned (i.e. its personal and social habits if permitted its freedom); two research the conditions the animals live in, and their behaviour, under intensive farming conditions; two research alternatives to factory farming. After the research period, the group comes together and prepares to present its findings as a wall display, talk or drama.

■ THE PRICE OF (SOME) FREEDOM

Suitable for

Upper primary/secondary

Time needed

One month (preparation); two hours (in class)

Resources

A copy of the chart below for each student. Leaflets (or information from the *Introduction* and *Documents* sections of this chapter) on factory farming for each group of students.

Above: Compassion in World Farming flyer.

Procedure

As an out-of-school activity, students complete the chart by enquiring at a local butcher's, grocer's and/or supermarket. They also monitor

COST OF	FACTORY-FARMED	FREE RANGE
4lb chicken		
10lb turkey		
15lb turkey		
6 eggs (small)		
6 eggs (standard)		
6 eggs (large)		

the egg consumption at home for a one-month period (numbers and size of eggs, whether factory-farmed or free range), and obtain figures for the number and poundage of factory-farmed and/or free-range chickens and turkeys eaten in a typical year. (Students belonging to vegetarian homes can ask meat and egg eating friends or neighbours to help them out and/or investigate the home rationale for, and economics of, vegetarian living). At the end of the month-long period, they form groups of three/four to discuss difficulties that became apparent during the information seeking (likely problems include different costs of fresh and frozen poultry, uncertainty in the home as to whether or not eggs and poultry are free range). They also address the following questions (working on the principle that an 'uncertain' response as to the origins of eggs/poultry should be taken to mean that it was factory-farmed):

❑ What would the per person per annum intake of eggs be in the homes surveyed?

❑ What would the per person per annum cost for eggs be?

❑ By what amount would the p.p.a. cost rise (fall) if the home went entirely over to free range (factory-farmed) eggs?

❑ How many pounds of chicken/turkey would be consumed per person per annum?

❑ What would the per person per annum cash cost of chicken/turkey consumption be?

❑ By what amount would the p.p.a. rise (fall) if the home went entirely over to free range (factory-farmed) poultry?

❑ How many eggs/birds would each person consume in their lifetime (70 adult years)?

❑ At present cost levels, what would the difference in cost be between a lifetime's free-range eating and a lifetime's eating of factory-farmed products?

Calculations are undertaken on the basis of equal appetites. The task complete, students are handed the information on factory farming and asked to discuss whether they would be prepared to pay the extra costs involved in more humane egg and poultry production, i.e. the price of (some) freedom. Class reporting back and discussion follows.

Potential

An activity offering practice in basic research and computational skills and alerting students to the economic and ethical considerations surrounding intensive farming. Did students opt to meet the costs involved in buying free range? What lay behind their decisions? Is 'ethical purchasing' a luxury only the well-to-do can afford? An interesting area for discussion will also be the degree to which students found an active consciousness of free-range alternatives in the home. Another will be to reflect on the perspectives and food choices in vegetarian homes surveyed.

Extensions

1. Students visit a factory farm. Back in school they share reflections and revisit the issues raised following the activity described above.

2. Based on the data collected, students construct and administer a short questionnaire to gauge public awareness of the issues involved and willingness to pay more for free-range eggs and poultry.

Source

Inspired by a 'Price of Freedom' activity developed by Phil Brooke.

■ *FACTORY FARMING SNAP GROUPS*

Suitable for

Secondary

Time needed

15 minutes per snap card

Resources

Copy of a 'snap' card per 4-5 students.

Procedure

At various points in a programme of work on animal farming, students move into 'snap groups' of 4-5 members. On each occasion a copy of the same 'snap' card is given to each group (see samples overleaf). Groups are given four minutes to discuss their 'snap' reactions to the card. Reactions, which should be noted down, can be in the form of feelings engendered, questions the statement seems to beg, challenges to the letter or spirit of the statement; issues needing further exploration or change/reform

SNAP CARDS

1. In 1991 Britain slaughtered 450 million chickens, 32 million turkeys, 19 million sheep, 13 million pigs, 8 million ducks, 3 million rabbits and 3 million cattle.

2. A pig's life expectancy is 15-20 years; the average slaughter age for a bacon pig is 5-7 months. A chicken's life expectancy is 7 years; the average slaughter age of a broiler chicken is 7 weeks.

3. In a lifetime, the average British meat eater eats 36 pigs, 36 sheep, 8 cattle and 550 poultry.

4. UK slaughterhouse regulations require that turkeys hang no longer than six minutes upside down and alive before they are slaughtered.

5. 'Shambles' is the old English word for a slaughterhouse. It also means state of total confusion. Animals die in agony because of poor slaughterhouse stunning methods and because slaughterers receive no formal training. It is in their interest to work quickly, not humanely, as they are paid by the number of animals slaughtered daily.

6. Pigs are held to be the most intelligent of animals raised for meat. Allowed to live naturally, they enjoy each others' company, are clean, and will agree on a common toilet area if given enough space.

7. Meat-eating contributes to world hunger. A plot of land that can feed approximately 10 people on a vegetarian diet, can feed only 1 person if the land is used to grow feed for animals that are subsequently eaten by humans.

8. One in 20 chickens reared on factory farms die before they reach slaughter weight in their seventh week, often as a result of a heart attack or disease/injury caused by overcrowding.

9. Dung and urine from factory-farmed animals drains into slurry pits, which leak and are the biggest source of water pollution in the UK.

10. Factory-farmed animals are a health-hazard for humans. Unable to exercise, they contain too much fat, contributing to heart disease. They are given antibiotics regularly and their resistance to antibiotics is passed to humans (meaning antibiotic cures sometimes don't work). Salmonella infects nearly 100% of poultry, meaning that live germs are left on kitchen surfaces and utensils and in undercooked meat.

11. Europe imports 14 million tonnes of the developing world's harvest each year to feed to its farmed animals.

12. The day will come when men such as I will look upon the murder of animals as we now look upon the murder of men. — Leonardo da Vinci

P

proposals. No response is ruled out. The teacher then calls upon each group to report back briefly and encourages class discussion of issues raised.

Potential

A simple means of focusing attention on what the meat-eating habit means for both animals and humans. The shared feelings, questions and challenges should provide a strong stimulus for further study, enquiry and personal reflection.

Source

Sources of snap cards are as follows: 1) Erlichman, J., 'Cruel cost of cheap pork and poultry', *The Guardian*, 14.10.91, 4; 2) Athene Trust, *Choices. The farm and you*, 1989, 28; 3) Cruddas, H., *Why animal rights?*, Animal Aid, 1991, 13; 4) Erlichman, J., 'Progress halves chickens' lifespan', *The Guardian*, 15.10.91, 4; 5) CIWF, *Shambles. The slaughter of animals. A modern holocaust*, flyer; 6) Erlichman, J., 'Pigs pay the price for market forces', *The Guardian*, 16.10.91, 5; 7) Animal Aid, *Make your next meal count*, flyer; 8) Erlichman, J., 'Progress halves chickens' lifespan', *The Guardian*, 15.10.91, 4; 9) Animal Aid, *op. cit.*; 10) CIWF, *Consumer alert!*, flyer; 11) CIWF, *Factory farming today*, flyer; 12) Cruddas, H., *op. cit.*, 13.

■ *DOWN ON THE FARM*

Suitable for

Upper primary/secondary

Time needed

30 minutes (Phase 1); 40 minutes plus film time (Phase 2).

Resources

A collection of advertisements, dairy/meat product packaging and illustrations and accompanying text from children's story-books, all depicting an idyllic image of farming; a paste stick, felt pen and two sheets of sugar paper sellotaped together for each group of three students; Blu-tak.

Procedure

Phase 1

Students paste one of the advertisements/packages/illustrations in the centre of the two sheets of sugar paper. Dividing the paper into four sections with the headings *Language, Visual Features, Content* and *Item as a Whole*, they discuss

---

Fig 1

Language

- What does the name of the product/story communicate?
- What is the tone of the text?
- What human needs, fears or desires are being appealed to?
- What claims are being made explicitly and/or implicitly?

Visual Features

- What is the general ambience or mood of the picture and how is it created?
- What colour scheme is used (words and picture) and how does it relate to the atmosphere of the picture?
- What is the relationship of the verbal and visual components?
- Are symbols used? If so, for what purposes?

Content

- What is happening in the picture? What are any people featured in it doing? What kind of people are they? How are they dressed?
- What does the setting communicate?

Item as a Whole

- What emotional 'hooks' are used to give the item its attraction?
- What are the values and outlook underpinning the item?
- What does the item suggest about us, our society and our relationship with animals and nature?
- What does the item fail to say?

and write in their responses to the questions listed in *Fig. 1* (the questions are appropriate for upper secondary use; they can be simplified for primary/lower secondary use or, alternatively, students can simply be asked to brainstorm — see p. x — their impressions of, and responses to, the piece in question). The task completed, each group attaches their chart to the classroom wall. One member of the group remains beside it as a 'guide'. Other members then look at the work of the other groups, asking the 'guide' for any necessary explanation or clarification (group members should take turns as 'guide' thus giving everybody an opportunity to circulate). Plenary discussion ensues.

Phase 2

Students watch a film on modern commercial farming such as *Kept in the Dark* suitable for primary use, *The Choice is Yours*, top primary/lower secondary, or *Hidden Suffering*, secondary (see *Additional Resources*), and discuss the images of farms considered earlier in the light of the new information. Groups re-form with the task of designing advertisements, packaging or story-book pages conveying a realistic impression of mainstream contemporary farming. Work produced is displayed on the classroom wall or in an open area of the school alongside the collection of materials with which the activity began.

Potential

A helpful activity for focusing student attention on the images of farming projected by commercial interests and by children's story-book writers. Why are idyllic images chosen? Are the story-book writer's reasons identical to those of the advertising manager? What emotional needs in ourselves are being targeted by the images and text presented? Is it fair for story-book writers to give children a utopian, but manifestly false, image of the modern farm? Why do they choose to do so? Why would writers and image makers fight shy of the kind of images prepared by the students in *Phase 2* of the activity? This activity can usefully be attempted alongside those described in *Chapter 12*.

Variation

Instead of print-form material, students work with television advertisements for dairy and meat products. In *Phase 2* they script, choose music, design graphics, programme and determine shots and camera angles for their own, realistic, advertisement. The advertisement is then video recorded, edited and presented to the class.

OLD MACDONALD HAD A FARM

Suitable for
Upper primary/secondary

Time needed
Four separate half-hour sessions (two for composition, one for practice, one for performing) with intervals of a day or more between each session.

Resources
None, save break-out practice areas for groups.

Procedure
Following project work on intensive farming involving, if possible, visits to one or more factory farms, students are asked to work co-operatively in groups of 4 to 6 on composing their own song about the conditions in which farm animals are reared (thereby offering an antidote to the impression of jollity and contentment conveyed by songs such as *Old Macdonald*). The song writing should not necessarily require advanced musical ability. Great things can result from putting new words to well-known tunes! After sufficient time for composition and practice, groups perform their songs in class.

Potential
Music provides a powerful way of conveying and sharing responses to a subject that is likely to have deeply troubled some students and offered a profound challenge to the assumptions and behaviours of many. It can have a healing effect for the individual, and for a group in which strong differences of opinion have been laid bare.

> *Excellent idea. 'Explicit' and 'Implicit' need explaining. The brainstorm is good for younger/less able students but a 'guide' of some sorts is a vital part of the activity, not to be missed out. The video variation is a 'must' for those so equipped.*
>
> — Kent secondary school teacher

■ *YUM YUM*

Suitable for

Upper primary/secondary (the activity can be made simpler or more involved, as required)

Time needed

Periods of time over several weeks

Resources

Pictures, or an actual selection, of vegetarian and vegan foods (see Procedure below for further guidance); a *Categories of Vegetarianism* chart (see box); a selection of vegetarian literature and cookbooks (see *Additional Resources* section); art materials; video camera and recording equipment (optional).

Procedure

1. Students are introduced to a variety of foods that are not made from the bodies of animals and do not contain animal products. The selection should go beyond actual fruits, nuts, root and other vegetables to include processed vegetarian products such as miso, tofu (bean curd), soy milk, tempeh, tofu burgers and soy cheese substitutes. It is explained that, taking the population of the world as a whole, there are almost as many vegetarians as meat eaters and that the number of vegetarians in the United Kingdom has grown rapidly in recent years, especially amongst the young.

2. The students are informed that they work for the Yum Yum Complete Meal Food Company, a company that promotes food lines made exclusively from non-animal products. The company's goal is to become a leading player in the food industry by the year 2010. Their task is to design a stage-by-stage strategy to realise this goal. The class divides into three company sections: *Market Research*, *Product Research* and *Public Relations*.

3. The task of the *Market Research* team is, firstly, to identify the various reasons why people are turning to vegetarian diets and, secondly, to research the strength and direction of trends in vegetarianism. These tasks they accomplish in part through a literature search but, more substantially, by designing and conducting an out-of-school questionnaire survey and by analysing the questionnaire returns. The questionnaire should seek to ascertain the percentage within different age groups up to age 80 which would fall into the six categories of vegetarianism and the percentage who are full-scale meat eaters. It should try to identify principal reasons for being/becoming vegetarian and ask meat eaters whether they have cut down their intake of meat in recent years, to what extent and why. Depending on the age level of the students, they can also seek information on gender, ethnic and socio-economic patterns in vegetarianism. Students belonging to the other two teams should be encouraged to participate in the survey to ensure sufficient completed returns. The *Market Research* team analyses the returns and extrapolates discerned trends forward to establish the likely market picture in 2000, 2005 and 2010. Meetings are held with both the *Product*

CATEGORIES OF VEGETARIANISM

Fructarian
— very strict vegetarians who only eat fruit and nuts and those parts of plants that can be collected without killing the plant.

Vegans
— strict vegetarians who only eat plant foods and who avoid using or wearing products from animals.

Lacto-Vegetarians
— vegetarians who also include milk and dairy products alongside their plant diet.

Lacto-Ovo-Vegetarians
— vegetarians who, in addition to milk and dairy products, eat eggs.

Pesco-Vegetarians
— principally vegetarian eaters who also eat fish (but no other meat).

Pollo-Vegetarians
— principally vegetarian eaters who also eat 'white meat' such as chicken, duck and turkey but no 'red' meat (i.e. beef, lamb, pork).

Research and *Public Relations* teams to explain the results and to jointly analyse the implications for their work.

4. The task of the *Product Research* team is to design potential best-selling complete meals for the years 2000, 2005 and 2010. This they do through a literature search on vegetarian cookery, by seeking advice from vegetarian organisations and, if possible, by interviewing vegetarian cooks. Their designs will necessarily be tentative until they have had the results of the *Market Research* team's survey. Subsequent to receipt of the survey results, they can ask the *Market Research* team to sample public responses to their revised designs. Joint meetings of the two teams can be held as often as necessary. The *Product Research* team also needs to keep its *Public Relations* colleagues advised of its plans and encourage feedback from them.

5. The task of the *Public Relations* team is to design posters, slogans, jingles and/or video commercials promoting Yum Yum products for the years 2000, 2005 and 2010. Whilst early planning and design is essential, final decisions will have to await analysis of the *Market Research* team's survey. It will be important to consult regularly *Market Research* colleagues in the decision-making process and, if deemed necessary, to ask them to test public response (by age group) to the various drafts of their posters, slogans, jingles and commercials.

6. The activity ends with a Yum Yum Company exhibition of its market research findings, and of proposed future product design and public relations campaigns.

Potential

An activity providing a platform for research and reflection around the subject of vegetarianism and, with its mini-enterprise format, meeting a range of objectives falling under the cross-curricular theme of education for economic and industrial understanding. In the post-activity debriefing, students can be asked to reflect and comment upon their learning. Were there any surprises? Have attitudes towards vegetarianism shifted to any extent? In what directions? Why is

vegetarianism on the increase? Are the reasons identified good ones? Is there a different emphasis in the motivation of people falling under the different categories of vegetarianism? What is the likelihood of the Yum Yum Food Company enjoying a big market by 2010? What are some of the economic, landscape, political and social implications of any wholesale shift to vegetarianism? How effective, in their judgement, was the work of the three sections of the Yum Yum Company? How effectively did the three teams interact and support each others' work? What further questions have been thrown up by the *Market Research* team's survey? What has been learnt about planning for possible/probable future market trends?

Extensions

1. Students compile a *Yum Yum Cookbook* and prepare some of the dishes.

2. Students divide into six groups. Each group takes one of the six categories of vegetarianism and undertakes either the *Humane Futures Wheel* or *Inventing a Humane Future (Backwards)* activities (p.297 and 298) around over half the UK population falling under the category by the year 2020. Alternatively, with a felt pen and sheet of sugar paper, students simply brainstorm all the economic, landscape, political and social implications of a majority of the population adopting their category of vegetarianism at some point in the near future.

I asked the children to design a series of posters for the company over the next 18 years. On the reverse side of each poster they identified the changes in choices and attitude in the wider community that would need targeting in order to promote consumer desire for a Yum Yum meal.

— Fiona Heads

Source

Inspired by an activity for 7-11 year olds developed by Fiona Heads (see box).

■ *FUNNY FARMS*

Suitable for

Primary/secondary

Time needed

60-70 minutes

Resources

Pictures of animals less familiar to students as farm animals, such as chinchilla, deer, earthworm, mink, musk ox, ostrich, oyster, rabbit, salmon, silkworm and trout; books and information sheets in which students can find information about each animal's life in its natural habitat; information on the farming of each animal (available from farming, fishing and humane organisations); sugar paper, felt pens, scissors and paste for each group of students.

Procedure

The class is asked to help the teacher compile a list of farm animals. The list will probably be restricted to more familiar ones such as cows, pigs and sheep. It is explained that many other animals are farmed to meet human needs or wants. The animals are introduced one by one and their pictures placed on display. Groups of three/four are given the task of researching one of the animals. Their first task is to find out about its life in the wild: how far it travels, how much territory it requires, what it eats, its characteristics and habits, whether it lives alone or in a community, how its young are bred and reared. The animal is then graded on a scale of 1-10 according to its suitability for farming (1 = absolutely unsuitable, 10 = entirely suitable). The group then moves onto its second task which is to find out about how the animal is farmed, what products come from it and the extent to which its natural behaviours and characteristics are curtailed/frustrated through the farming process. In the light of their research, groups review and, if necessary, amend their grading on the 1-10 scale. Finally, groups prepare displays reporting their findings in graphical and written form and conveying their personal opinion on the farming of the animal they have investigated. The *Circus* procedure, p.299 is followed, prior to a class plenary.

Potential

A useful introduction to new, and often little known, forms of farming. The plenary can begin with a sharing of reflections on what has been discovered. Were there any surprises? Were there animals that students had not realised were being farmed? What grading were animals given after

Goose being crammed on Hungarian foie gras farm — October 1992.
Foie gras is pâté made from the grossly swollen liver of ducks or geese force-fed and deprived of exercise until the liver swells painfully to more than seven times the normal size.
(Photo: EarthKind)

the first research round? Did the grading improve or worsen in the light of research into farming practices? Why? Is the farming being undertaken to meet human needs or human wants? Is it justifiable, especially if the animals are being used to satisfy people's desire for luxury or epicurean items?

Source

Jackie Harvey.

■ A FARM HERE?

Suitable for

Primary

Time needed

50- 75 minutes

Resources

An open space; one set of discussion cards.

Procedure

The teacher initiates a short class discussion on what happens as the human population grows and so needs more food. Where will it come from? Will we have to find more land for livestock and crops? What land could be chosen? Who will decide? Should/will others be given a say? It is explained that the class is going to think about one habitat, e.g. a wood, common grassland, an area of scrubland. That land has been earmarked to be ploughed up as farm land. The students are divided into groups of 4 or 5. Each group is to represent different parties interested in this land. They are going to be invited to a meeting where they have to put their case to the planning officer (teacher). Using their discussion card for guidance, they must plan a good case for or against the ploughing up of the land and elect one or two spokespeople to put their case. The students are then given time to work on their case. The teacher can circulate to encourage and help the development of good arguments. When the students are ready (15 - 20 minutes) the meeting is convened. The teacher acts as planning officer/chairperson and begins by explaining the guidelines for the conduct of the enquiry. Spokespeople for groups are to have no more than three minutes to present their case,

after which the chair will call for comments and questions. All interventions are to be through the chair and everyone is to listen carefully to others' arguments. After each group has had a fair hearing and responses to their case have been aired, there will be time for general discussion. The chair as planning officer then makes an interim decision (or allows the decision to arise naturally out of discussion).

Potential

A good way to explore all sides of an issue. The formality of the discussion encourages listening to all arguments and is a way of keeping emotions under control. It also gives the students some insight into the way such decisions are actually taken. The students could be asked, out of role, what they felt about the arguments. Were there any reasons for or against that they had not considered? Do they think the wild creatures living in the place will fare better if the farm opts for arable farming or animal husbandry? Would they have any concerns for the well-being of the livestock in the latter case? What do they think would be the best final solution? Students can write reports of the event as if they were newspaper reporters. Alternatively, they can return to role and write letters commenting on the interim decision to the planning officer. These are posted and can serve as stimulus for further discussion.

Source

Jackie Harvey after an idea in the National Association for the Advancement of Humane Education, *People and animals*, curriculum guide, 1981.

A FARM HERE? — DISCUSSION CARDS

FARMER
Think about reasons for the farmer wanting this land.
Is it good land for livestock or crops? Flat for machines? Close to her farm?
Is it better than any other land nearby?
Why does she want to expand her farm? More money? To meet the demand for food?
Any other reasons? Would there be a higher yield of food if the land was used for livestock or crops?

LARGER WILD CREATURES (e.g. fox, larger birds, badgers, weasels, stoats)
Think about the reasons the animals and birds might give for not wanting the land farmed.
You could speak for particular creatures or for all.
Is it their permanent home or one they return to each year in certain seasons? Why is it just right for them?
Is it the only land just right for them nearby?
Where would they go if the land was farmed? How would they get there? What dangers might they face?
Is there anywhere else they could get food? Is this place a specially good source of food?
Will the balance of nature be upset? Here? In the places they might move to?
What would life be like if they tried to stay?
Would pesticides and fertilisers affect them?

SMALLER WILD CREATURES (e.g. smaller birds, mice, voles, shrews, insects, spiders)
Think about reasons these creatures might give for not wanting this land disturbed and/or ploughed up.
You could speak for particular creatures or for all.
Is it their permanent home? Why is it just right for them?
Would the farmer want them around? If so, why? If not, why not? If not, how might she deal with them?
Will the balance of nature be upset? How? Here? In other places?

PLANTS AND TREES
Think about the reasons the various plants and trees might give for not wanting this land disturbed and/or ploughed up?
What would happen if the flowers disappear? Nettles and other 'weeds' too?
Would the farmer want wild plants and trees? If so, why? If not, why not? If not, what would she do?
How would that affect the animals and other creatures?
What would happen to all the living things in the trees and bushes?
What might happen to the soil?

LOCAL PEOPLE (expecting to benefit from the food and jobs produced)
Why do you want the land to be used to produce food?
How important is this food to you? How many jobs would result? What problems would you have if this land weren't used?
Do you think the animals will survive anyway? Or, if they don't, that there are plenty of animals around?
Or that survival of these particular ones doesn't matter? Are some of them nuisances?
Do you have gardens, meadows or other wild ground where many plants and animals are to be found?

LOCAL PEOPLE (who use the land for leisure and relaxation)
Why do you want to leave the land as it is? Would you miss your walks, bird-watching, fishing and other pursuits?
Is there anywhere else to go? Is this place especially beautiful?
Do you think your children, their children, and their children's children have a right to be able to use this land just as you do?
Are you worried about pollution? About noise? About what will happen to the animals and plants?
Are you worried that some day there may be no wild places left?
Would any jobs or local income depending on tourism, be lost if the land was farmed?

P

ADDITIONAL RESOURCES

For the teacher ....

- ❏ Carnell, P., *Alternatives to factory farming*, Earth Resources (258 Pentonville Road, London N1 9JX), 1983. Suggests that economic factors are not an insurmountable barrier to more humane farming practices.

- ❏ Cox, P., *Why you don't need meat*, Thorsons, 1986. Comprehensive statement on the effects of meat eating on health and on how to turn to a nutritionally-balanced and healthy non-meat diet.

- ❏ Druce, C., *Chicken and egg. Who pays the price?*, Green Print, 1989. In-depth treatment of the factory farming of chickens (battery egg production and the broiler chicken industry), opposition to intensive methods, and future possibilities and prospects.

- ❏ Gold, M., *Assault and battery*, Pluto Press, 1983. Facts and figures on factory farming.

- ❏ Gold, M., *Living without cruelty*, Green Print, 1988. Insightful coverage of the meat and dairy products industry; also very helpful chapters on cruelty-free living.

- ❏ Kay, L., *Living without cruelty*, Sidgwick & Jackson, London, 1990. A book to help people create their own lifestyle revolution by rejecting foods and other materials manufactured at the expense of animals.

- ❏ Lacey, R., *Unfit for human consumption*, Souvenir Press, London, 1991. Reveals the dangerous state of a food industry that puts profit before health and safety.

- ❏ Luba, A., *Nutritional guidelines for vegetarian catering in schools*, Animal Aid/The Athene Trust/The Vegetarian Society, 1988. A publication inspired by *Choice!*, the campaign for making available and improving vegetarian meals in schools (c/o Juliet Gellatley, Parkdale, Durham Road, Altrincham, Cheshire WA14 4QG).

- ❏ Lynx, *The case against fur factories*, 1991.

- ❏ Lynx, *The case against fur factories. Opinions*, 1991.

- ❏ Robbins, J., *Diet for a new America*, Walpole NH, Stillpoint, 1987. Beautifully written and intensely moving account of our dependence on animals for food, the inhumane conditions under which they are raised, and the physical, emotional and economic price we pay.

- ❏ Yates, G., *Food, need, greed and myopia*, Earthright Publications, 1986. The world food problem, population growth, food production, agriculture, land use and nutrition from a vegetarian perspective.

For the classroom ....

- ❏ *A painful luxury*, 9 min., VHS video, Earthkind. Disturbing video on foie gras production, including footage of goose and duck 'cramming'. Upper secondary only.

- ❏ Athene Trust, *Choices. The farm and you*, 1989. Very useful resource book for the classroom, full of ideas for projects and discussions.

- ❏ Compassion in World Farming, *All animals have rights*, undated. Teaching kit on factory farming, containing 15-slide set, slide notes, study sheets and work cards.

- ❏ Bird, M., *The scrumptious veggie cookbook for kids and others*, Green Print, 1991. An easy vegetarian/vegan cookbook for students aged six and upwards.

- ❏ *Farm animals — the inside story*, 15 min., VHS video, National Farmers' Union. Comprehensive presentation of the economies of production and increased efficiency. Perceived drawbacks of more relaxed farming approach (price rises, decline in supply, seasonal fluctuations) addressed.

- ❏ *Food without fear*, 20 min., VHS video, The Vegetarian Society, 1989. Explores the conditions in which animals are reared and the effect meat has on health, the environment and the developing world. Seeks to tackle myths surrounding vegetarianism.

- ❏ Grose, A., *The teenage vegetarian survival guide*, Red Fox/Vegetarian Society, 1992. The first half is theoretical, giving humane, health, economic and environmental reasons for vegetarianism; the second is practical, including advice on how the teenager can cope with family and friends on becoming vegetarian.

- ❏ *Hidden suffering*, 27 min., VHS video, Farm Animal Welfare Network (Fawn), 1993. Uncompromising and damning footage on factory farming of chickens, ducks and turkeys. Secondary.

❏ *Kept in the dark*, 20 min., VHS video, Athene Trust. Suitable for 7-10 year olds, it follows a group of 9-year olds on a school project investigating different types of farms.

❏ Scottish Society for the Prevention of Cruelty to Animals, *Animals or machines?*, 1990. Five resource packs, containing cassette tapes, transparencies, worksheets and notes for teachers. Very thorough treatment of modern farming methods. Secondary.

❏ *Screaming for change*, 9 min., VHS video, Compassion in World Farming. Examination of factory farming that gives footage to farmers who have changed to more humane methods. Official calls for reform are also considered.

❏ *The choice is yours — animal suffering or cruelty-free food?*, 15 min. VHS video, Athene Trust. Suitable for 10-14 year olds, it challenges them to consider the lives of farm animals in relation to the food they eat.

❏ The *Real Meat Company* (East Hill Farm, Heytesbury, Warminister, Wiltshire, BA12 OHR) can supply information on its animal welfare code, free-range and non-chemical policies.

❏ Vegetarian Society, *Vegetarian issues. A resource pack for secondary schools*, 1992. A four-part pack with sections entitled, 'Vegetarianism — animal welfare, ethics and religion', 'Vegetarian health and nutrition', 'Vegetarianism and the environment' and 'Vegetarianism and the developing world'. Photocopiable pages.

❏ For other sources of information on fur farming, see the *Additional Resources* section of chapter 9 (pp.225-6).

❏ *Key humane organisations to contact (see* Organisations *list): Animal Aid, Animal Concern (Scotland), Athene Trust, Compassion in World Farming, EarthKind, Farm and Food Society, Movement for Compassionate Living (The Vegan Way), Respect For Animals (on fur farming), Scottish Society for the Prevention of Cruelty to Animals, Vegan Society, Vegetarian Society.*

References

1. Erlichman, J., 'Cruel costs of cheap pork and poultry', *The Guardian*, 14.10.1991, 4.
2. *Ibid.*,.
3. Cruddas, H., *Why animal rights?*, Animal Aid, 1991, 10-11; Compassion in World Farming (CIWF), *Factory farm 1988* and *Factory farming today*, flyers.
4. Chicken's Lib, *Battery eggs. Can you face the facts?*, flyers.
5. Cruddas, H., *op. cit.*, 10; CIWF, *op. cit.*,.
6. 'Animal concentration camps', *Go for it*, Vegetarian Society flyer.
7. CIWF, *Factory farm 1988*, flyer.
8. Cruddas, H., *op. cit.*, 12, Chickens Lib, *op. cit.*,.
9. *Ibid.*,.
10. CIWF, *Milked for all she's worth*, flyer.
11. CIWF, *Born to be flayed* and *Only beasts wear fur*, flyers.
12. Erlichman, J., *op. cit.*, 4.
13. Cited in James, B., *Animal rights*, Wayland, 1990, 14.
14. Cited in *Ibid.*, 16.
15. Erlichman, J., 'Progress halves chickens' lifespan', *The Guardian*, 15.10.1991, 4.
16. Animal Aid, *Factory farming — it makes you sick*, flyer.
17. Cited in Lynx, *The case against fur factories. Opinions*, 1991, 6.
18. Gold, M., *Living without cruelty*, Green Print, 1988, 30-42.
19. Courtney, T., 'Feathers fly over the ostrich farm', *The Vegetarian*, February 1992, 24-5.

Chapter 9

Wild Animals in the Wild

INTRODUCTION

This chapter focuses upon the human treatment and exploitation of wild animals living in the wild, especially the highly charged topic of hunting and trapping; it also discusses the international trade in wild animals.

In the United Kingdom an estimated five and a half million people take part legally in 'blood sports' involving the hunting of animals. Of these, fishing is the most popular, then fox-hunting and bird-shooting. There is also a following for a number of illegal sports such as badger-baiting and dog-fighting. In the former, a badger is chained to a stake or confined to a pit and is set on by dogs; in the latter, dogs are bred for their fighting abilities and set against each other in a pit or boarded room. Hare-coursing, in which two dogs, usually greyhounds, compete in pursuit of a hare, remains legal; it has an estimated 1,000 followers.[1]

The bloodsport that has attracted the most consistent and vociferous opposition is fox-hunting. There are 194 registered fox hunts in England, Scotland and Wales.[2] To these can be added, four packs of staghounds (three in the southwest, and one in the south, of England) and some 150 packs of hounds that hunt hares and are followed on foot or horseback.[3]

The future of hunting looks even more precarious as the opposition to it grows in numbers and influence. The opposition is spearheaded by the League Against Cruel Sports (*document 1*) and the Hunt Saboteurs Association. Their case is that hunting is barbaric and cruel, a hangover from the days of bear-baiting and cock-fighting; that foxes are not detrimental to farming in that

Hounds rip apart a fox that has been hunted to exhaustion in the name of 'sport'. (Photo: League Against Cruel Sports)

their diet is principally composed of rabbits, rats and voles (themselves considered pests by farmers); and that fox predation on chickens and lambs is insignificant (modern forms of poultry farm are difficult to invade, they point out and, on farmers' own estimates, only one lamb in two hundred falls prey to a fox)[4]. Opposing groups also argue that the hunting of wild animals could be replaced by 'drag-hunting', in which a bag is dragged through the countryside laying a scent for the dogs to follow. There are 11 registered drag-hunts in the United Kingdom.[5]

The defence of hunting is principally conducted by the British Field Sports Society. It argues that only one in ten fox-hunts ends in a kill, that foxes need to be controlled as a threat to farm animals and nesting birds, that a hunt ban would cause environmental damage and would lead to the redundancy of full-time hunt staff.[6] Defenders also argue that a ban on hunting would be an affront to rural traditions; that hunt opponents are, at root, urbanites who do not understand country life, who wish to curtail others' freedoms to enjoy the sport of their choice and who are motivated by sentiments of class warfare.

On 14 January 1992 a Wild Animals (Protection) Bill was narrowly defeated in second reading in the House of Commons by 187 votes to 172 on a free vote. The Bill would have made it an offence 'to use a dog to kill, injure, pursue or attack a wild mammal'. *Document 2* offers a selection of contributions to the debate. The narrow defeat of the Bill, which enjoyed considerable cross-party support, and continuing opinion poll evidence that there is overwhelming support for an end to bloodsports (polls have recorded figures as high as 83% opposed) suggest the days of legal 'blood' hunting are numbered.

If the U.K. hunting fraternity has adopted very much of a siege mentality, the same cannot be said for those involved in the global trade in furs. The 1980s witnessed a dramatic decline in fur sales in the United Kingdom as a result of a spectacular 'mobilisation of disgust' spearheaded by the anti-fur campaigning organisation, Lynx (see *document 3*). Customs and Excise figures show that, in 1985, total fur imports were worth £62m; by 1990 the figure had fallen to £25m. Many well-known stores closed their fur departments and some specialist shops ceased trading. London, once the centre of fur auctions, gave way to centres in Russia and Scandinavia. Similar responses to the fur trade were evident in many parts of Europe and North America. In September 1990 the European Parliament voted for a ban on the import of fur from animals caught in leghold traps, to take effect from 1995. But, at the point when the fur trade seemed to be entering terminal decline, those whose interests were most threatened fought back with a campaigning platform matching the sophistication of (and outdistancing the investment in) the anti-fur campaign.

In May 1985 the Canadian Department of External Affairs, recognising that the decline of the fur industry would undermine a lucrative source of export income, prepared a discussion paper, *Defence of the Fur Trade*, in conjunction with a public relations agency. The paper identified several lines of defence that might be effectively employed 'to counter the anti-fur movement'. One was to suggest that opposition to the fur trade was tantamount to cultural genocide against the indigenous peoples of Canada. 'Defence of aboriginal cultures,' the paper said, 'could be a good counter-balance to anti-fur or anti-trapping campaigns.' Another was to promote the image of the fur trade as deeply woven into the Canadian heritage. A third was to portray the trapping of fur animals as congruent with the rhythms of nature. 'Trapping is a mechanism for augmenting or maintaining nature's balance. In the absence of trapping, animal populations would be controlled through starvation and disease... There is no humane death in nature.'[7]

North American marten fatally held in a steel jawed leg-hold trap. (Photo: Respect for Animals)

The arguments were further elaborated by a number of pro-fur organisations in Canada, notably the Fur Council of Canada and Indigenous Survival International (the indigenous pro-fur lobby). In Europe they were picked up by organisations such as the International Fur Trade Federation and the Fur Education Council (for addresses of organisations, see *Additional Resources*, pp.225-6). In addition, the pro-fur organisations characterised their opponents as urban-centric (and, hence, ignorant of the workings of nature), extremist in their espousal of animal rights at the expense of human rights and, in the final analysis, motivated by an anarchist or radical socialist political agenda (*document 7*). Thus, the pro-fur case coincides, in several respects, with the case mounted against hunting abolitionists by the UK pro-hunting lobby.

As part of the pro-fur campaigning strategy, spokespeople from North American indigenous pro-fur groups, especially Indigenous Survival International, were invited to Europe to undertake speaking tours. Some were funded by the Canadian government. The accusation that anti-fur

activists were 'threatening the traditional, subsistence life-styles of indigenous northern peoples' proved a powerful one, leading an organisation as intrepid as Greenpeace to draw back from a planned anti-fur campaign.[8] Many in the anti-fur lobby have, however, dismissed accusations of racism and cultural genocide as a cynical ploy on the part of a multi-million pound industry. Anti-fur spokespeople have pointed out that indigenous trapping is a very small slice (1-2%) of a North American trade that primarily takes place in the USA (where there are few native trappers) and which is dominated by non-indigenous trappers, seeking side income, and by fur farming; that imposed dependency on a trapping economy was actually responsible for eroding traditional indigenous culture; that native North Americans are the group at the lean end of the chain of primary and secondary actors that make up the fur trade and that their per capita income from trapping is extremely small (under £500 per annum).[9] Significantly, these same arguments are now being vociferously put forward by Native/Animal Brotherhood, an organisation of Canadian native peoples campaigning against the fur trade. A spokesperson for the Brotherhood has condemned the trade, and the Canadian government, for dragging 'token Indians all over Europe to get support for the white trapping and fashion fur industry'.[10]

The anti-fur movement, now spearheaded in the UK by Respect for Animals[11], continues to maintain that trapping is barbaric and cruel. Protestations from the fur trade that new 'humane' traps have removed cruelty from the taking of wild fur animals are rejected outright. The animals are often, it is argued, left to endure slow, lingering deaths in freezing temperatures, and the death of a parent animal can leave a family unprovided for and facing a similar fate. The movement also hotly disputes the impeccable environmental credentials claimed by the pro-fur lobby, arguing that trapping has led to the extinction of animals in many regions and that it inevitably operates indiscriminately against species, whether endangered or plentiful. The sentiment underpinning the pro-fur stance — that a cruel act forming part of a cultural tradition is morally permissible — is also roundly contested (*document 7*).

Respect for Animals points out that, although U.K. fur imports fell by a dramatic 71% between 1987 and 1991, there was an upsurge in imports in 1992 (*document 8*).

The less than comphrensive selection of documents on the fur trade set out in the next section (*nos. 3-7*) should be supplemented by a reading of the sixteen statements accompanying the activity, *Fur Flowcharts*, p.219. For a further activity on the fur trade, see *Fur Trade Images*, p.279. For information on the farmed fur industry in the UK, see *Chapter 8*, (pp.172 and 174).

The fur trade is governed by CITES, the Convention on International Trade in Endangered Species of Wild Fauna and Flora, as is the enormously profitable multi-million pound trade in live animals and in dead non-fur bearing animals. Set up in 1975, CITES bans international commercial trade in an agreed list of endangered species (the Appendix I list), and monitors and regulates trade in those species considered at risk of becoming endangered (the Appendix II list). Animals listed under Appendix II can only be traded if the country of origin certifies that their export will not be detrimental to the species' survival. Well over 100 countries have now adopted the Convention and meetings are held periodically to review whether animals on Appendix II should be promoted to Appendix I, and to add new names to Appendix II. The promotion of an animal to Appendix I is tantamount to officially ending legal trade in the dead parts of that animal. Hence, when the elephant was placed on Appendix I at the CITES meeting in October 1989 (to take effect January 1990) the international trade in ivory became, with some exceptions, illegal.[12] All countries

Illegal trade in endangered species causes terrible suffering. (Photo: EarthKind)

joining CITES are required to implement national laws enforcing its provisions. Some, such as the USA and EU member states, have introduced laws or regulations that are more stringent than CITES actually demands. Others, such as Argentina, Spain and Thailand, have become notorious for failing to implement the Convention.

Organisations working to prevent the trade in animals, have identified a number of ploys used by smugglers to circumvent CITES. These include faking captive births, mislabelling and concealment. CITES allows captive-born individuals of species on Appendix I to be traded as though they belonged to Appendix II. Thus, it is, possible to trade endangered animals captured in the wild by using forged certificates that certify that they were born at a circus or zoo. Mislabelling involves giving a false identity to the animal being smuggled (e.g. in 1987 three young gorillas were illegally exported from the Cameroons using documents describing them as 'monkeys'). It is frequently successful in that customs officials are often unable to identify even the better-known species. Tactics of concealment include hiding animal contraband about one's person (in September 1990 a Frenchman with a prominent abdomen was discovered by Bangkok airport security to be attempting to smuggle out three baby gibbons) and using secret compartments in crates of animals being legitimately exported.[13]

A tightening-up of CITES, and attendant national laws, is urgently needed. One important step would be to close the 'captive-born' loophole in the Convention and, thus, ban all trade in Appendix I species unless the animal concerned is listed in an international studbook. Another would be to enact stronger national laws (including so-called 'long-arm' laws by which national legislation can be used to control the illegal activities of nationals on a global scale) and to enforce them more stringently (fines on convicted smugglers tend to be paltry).[14] Another, strangely under-canvassed by animal protection groups, is aid-for-conservation arrangements so that governments in less developed countries, where much of the international trade in wild animals originates, have the wherewithal to implement CITES. Given the economic problems they face, many less developed countries find it impossible to implement the Convention — and their own laws — with any rigour (see *document 10*).

Live traded animals go to rich collectors, 'exotic' pet shops and the less reputable zoos. The feathers, pelts, shells, tusks, bones and heads of prized dead animals end up as upmarket fashion or home adornment items. The international trade in animals poses a threat to endangered species almost as great as that presented by habitat destruction. It involves a high degree of cruelty. Young animals are snatched from their parents and parents taken and the young left unprotected; also, given the illegality of the trade, live animals are transported in conditions that guarantee that many will die from overcrowding, malnutrition, starvation or asphyxiation.

Documents 9 to *11* give some insight into the animal trade. The activity, *On the Lists,* offers students the opportunity to have their say about the current workings and scope of CITES.

DOCUMENTS

1. Foxhounds are specially bred to run more slowly than the fox, but they can sustain a prolonged chase; accordingly the fox can outrun the hounds until it is exhausted and the bigger and stronger hounds are then able to catch it. The longer the fox can keep up its efforts, the more so-called 'sport' is obtained; therefore a weak, elderly or pregnant fox provides only a short hunt. A young, fit and strong fox can last up to two hours before it succumbs to fatigue, but the hounds can run for six or seven hours if necessary. If fast running dogs such as greyhounds or lurchers were used to hunt foxes, the whole thing would be over in seconds, but then there would be no 'sport'. Foxes are not a natural prey species and have never suffered predation as a governing factor on their population density. The distress suffered by a prey species must be considered when pursued by a predator, but the trauma must be far greater for a fox, not naturally adapted to endure long periods of pursuit. Even if the fox manages to find an unblocked earth or badger sett in which to hide, the 'sportsmen' will either 'evict' the terrified quarry with terriers so that it can be hunted again, or if it is too exhausted to 'bolt', the terriers keep it under attack until the hunt servants and terrier men can dig it out and kill it. The death itself, though violent and painful, may be relatively quick. However the real cruelty of foxhunting lies in the exhaustion, terror and trauma inflicted on the victim.

— League Against Cruel Sports[15]

2. Extracts from the Wild Mammals (Protection) Bill Debate, House of Commons, 14 January 1992

Opening the debate, Mr. McNamara, a Labour Northern Ireland spokesman and a vice-chair of the League Against Cruel Sports, said there was 'no domino theory' behind the Bill. It was not his intention to interfere with anglers, shooting or necessary pest control. 'JR Hartley may go to a second edition and Isaac Walton may rest safely in his grave. There is no need for him to toss and turn.'

He thought that few could object to the first clause which makes it an offence to cruelly ill-treat a wild mammal affording them the protection already granted to domestic animals.

He told how a gang of youths in Canterbury repeatedly shot a hedgehog with an air-rifle and then played football with it. 'They finally threw it, still alive, on to a bonfire. They admitted that the animal was alive and screaming after the game ended. The RSPCA attempted to prosecute but the case failed because the animal could not be defined as a domestic or captive animal.'

Turning to the most controversial part of the Bill, Mr. McNamara said that fox-hunting was never designed to be pest control. It was 'an entertainment'. The 12,000 to 13,000 foxes killed each year by hunts represented only about 2.5 per cent of the fox population.

Interrupting, Sir John Farr (C, Harborough) said that within a month of the clause becoming law 'up to one million horses will be put down, slaughtered because there will be no further practical use for them'.

Tony Benn (Lab, Chesterfield) said that Sir John's claim was like arguing for the continuation of crime because if crime were abolished the police would become redundant.

Mr. McNamara said that nothing in his Bill would make one horse, hound, or huntsman redundant. It would not prevent switching to drag hunting, already practised by a dozen packs in Britain and others overseas.

Citing a Gallup poll last November, which showed 79 per cent support for legislation to ban hunting, Mr. McNamara told the House: 'In common with the vast majority of people today, I believe that human entertainment is not sufficient justification for the hunting of an animal to exhaustion and death.'

Dame Janet Fookes (C, Plymouth Drake), an RSPCA council member, said that scientific evidence suggested the ill-fame of foxes was 'extremely nebulous'. In many cases when they were believed to have taken live lambs, the lambs were dead or dying. 'These matters can no longer be left to one side and must be tackled quickly,' she said.

Simon Hughes (Lib Dem, Southwark and Bermondsey) declared: 'Human beings have a duty the world over to be responsible and look after those creatures who have no votes.' He said the principle was different to boxing. 'Human beings have a choice whether to box or hunt, but the fox has no choice and that's the fundamental difference.'

Michael Jopling (C, Westmorland and Lonsdale), a farmer and former Minister of Agriculture, said that he was happy for hounds to hunt over his land. Sometimes farmers rang up and invited the local hunt on to their land because foxes were killing their lambs. 'Sheep farming in upland areas would become impossible, if there was not hunting by hounds.'

But Roger Gale (C, Thanet N) warned his colleagues: 'The time has come when we have to recognise the fact that fox-hunting and associated so-called pleasures must end.' Another Conservative supporter of the Bill, Sir Teddy Taylor (C, Southend E) said that he had received threatening letters telling him he was 'consorting with communists', 'supporting socialists and crackpots', and 'a repulsive creep'.

A non-hunter, John Townend (C, Bridlington), defended the sport on grounds of individual freedom and spoke of 'an organised campaign to victimise the rural community. In my view, our society and this House has had an unfortunate tendency in recent years to become too much of a busybody, looking into other people's lives.'

Mr. Townend blamed the Bill on 'old-fashioned, left-wing class prejudice' adding: 'If the hunting scene was part of the culture of some of our ethnic minorities, anybody who tried to stop it would be strongly attacked by Labour.'

Michael Colvin (C, Romsey and Waterside), chairman of the Council for Country Sports, claimed that the RSPCA was the victim of 'entryism' by people more interested in politics than animal welfare. He said that banning foxhunting would risk 16,500 jobs and £148m of trade.

But Andrew Bowden (Brighton Kemptown), Conservative vice-president of the League Against Cruel Sport, declared: 'The object of hunting with hounds is not conservation, not controlling numbers, not a quick chase and a swift kill, but to provide a cheap thrill for sadistic entertainment.'

— *The Independent*[16]

3. Many of the world's most beautiful fur-bearing animals are being systematically trapped and hunted in the wild for their skins. Within a few years they may no longer exist in the wild unless they are afforded international protection. The trade in wild animal furs has been responsible for the decline of many species over the past two centuries and has even brought about the extinction of the sea mink... Wolves and many of the world's foxes are also becoming scarcer as a consequence of large-scale hunting and trapping. The timber wolf was once common across the North American continent, but now is being forced back into a few isolated regions.

Trapping animals for their fur also involves a great deal of cruelty. The steel jawed trap is widely used throughout the U.S., USSR and Canada. When the powerful steel jaws of the trap snap shut on the paw of its victim, the animal may be left in agony for several days until the trapper arrives to inspect his catch. Britain banned the use of steel-jawed traps — or gin traps as we used to call them — thirty years ago, but in other countries they continue to be used quite legally... Some measure of the agony suffered by the trapped animal may be gauged from the fact that it will go to desperate lengths to free itself from the steel jaws, often attempting to gnaw off the trapped limb.

Trapping alarms wildlife experts and conservationists, too, because it is so widely destructive of a great range of wild animals other than those intended. Millions of other animals and birds — including swans, eagles, deer and domestic pets — are caught in traps each year and are discarded by the hunters as 'trash'. In one pilot study conducted in America, for example, it was discovered that a coyote trapping programme caught nearly ten times as many other animals and birds as it did coyotes. Bobcat, golden eagles and sheep were found among the victims. Clearly, this is a price the natural world cannot afford to pay, if our wild birds and animals are to survive.

— Lynx[17]

---

4. Seven Good Reasons Why You Should be Proud to Wear Fur: A Canadian Fur Trade Perspective.

1. The fur trade adheres strictly to national and international regulations and does not trap endangered or threatened species.

2.. Fur trappers do not harm the environment; rather they are on the front line in environmental protection. After all, if the fur-bearing animals and the environment in which they live were not conserved there would be no fur trade! Trappers live in the wilderness, maintain a close relationship with the land and have a deep respect for nature. Careful conservation policies are ensuring that animal populations are maintained.

3. Synthetic furs, which some say should replace natural fur garments, are the products of chemical processes that use non-renewable petroleum resources and release dangerous pollutants into the atmosphere. The wearing of natural fur is more environmentally-friendly, especially seeing that trappers are only controlling animal populations that would otherwise have to be checked in some other way.

4. The fur trade gives employment and some cash income to tens of thousands of people living in remote or marginal areas of Canada where little alternative employment is available.

5. It also enables indigenous or native peoples, who make up about half the trappers, to maintain their subsistence-oriented traditional cultures and lifestyles, within which the meat of fur-bearing animals is very important.

6. Canada has been very much to the fore in financing and promoting humane-trap research. The development and use of new devices such as quick-kill and soft-hold traps means that the fur industry is very humane. The fur trade is constantly seeking improvements in traps so that animals are treated as humanely as possible.

7. The majority of fur pelts come from fur farms where animals are treated as humanely as possible. Fur farmers know that the quality of an animal's fur depends on good food and living conditions.[18]

---

5. The Steel Jawed Leg-Hold Trap

The use of this trap troubled me for many years. I have been active in hunting and fishing all my life and my experience and observation of the use of the leg-hold trap, the cruelty and pain it inflicts has been a concern of mine for many years.

Unfortunately the people that use these traps do not feel as you and I do re: the cruelty of these traps and in fact a vast majority do not respect or obey the present laws governing trapping.

The law also states that traps must be tended within a 24 hours period, and this is rarely done if ever. I have had to kill dozens of skunks caught in leg-hold traps that have suffered for weeks where they had worn away all the bush within the trap chain radius.

I have found ducks, pheasant, rabbit, squirrels, woodchuck, dogs, cats caught in these leg-hold traps, and all of these have *no* open season. Some of the squirrels caught in these leg-hold traps had bitten off their leg to escape.

— Joe Sapper, ex-trapper[19]

6. The Leghold Leg Pull

In Canada — one of the major exporters of fur — figures supplied by the government and the fur industry indicate that there are some 80,000-105,000 trappers, about half of whom are native peoples. For many, trapping is a part-time job, supplementing income from other sources. In recent years, the trappers earned some C$45 million to C$85 million from the sale of raw pelts. Simple arithmetic suggests that the average earnings of a Canadian trapper currently range between $428.57 and $1,062.50 a year (approximately £200-£500)... It is estimated that the fur industry in Canada adds between $600 million and 1 billion annually to the gross national product. And Canada is just one of the participants in the multi-billion dollar international fur industry. In purely economic terms, it seems evident that the manufacturers of fur products, the fur exporters and the retailers have far more to lose than do native trappers if the anti-fur movement achieves its goals... A global ban on the use of the leghold trap (it has already been banned in the UK and in more than 60 countries around the world) would not prevent native peoples from living a traditional, subsistence life-style. Even if world fur markets collapse entirely, there would be nothing to stop aboriginal peoples from hunting and trapping to sustain a truly subsistence living — except for one thing: in recent years, the term subsistence has taken on a new meaning. For some native groups and for the Canadian government, subsistence now includes any activity that turns animals (so-called natural resources) into 'hard cash'. It is in this revised sense that trapping for the international fur trade is now considered part of a subsistence life-style.

To justify this view, some native groups and some anthropologists argue that aboriginal traditions must be redefined as their cultures evolve. They fail to see the irony that a rejection of fur by western society, if it comes to that, would also be a consequence of cultural evolution.

— David Lavigne[20]

---

7. Those who oppose hunting, trapping, or the killing of seals get represented as 'city slickers', indifferent to ancient cultural traditions and incapable of appreciating the deep understanding embodied in those traditions. Even the vocabulary used — animals are 'harvested', not killed, intimates a bucolic partnership with the natural world, beyond the urban ken. Huntsmen and trappers engage in their pursuits, it seems, less for fun or profit, than for the sake of protecting both cultural heritage and the ecological balance.

Before we are persuaded by this style of argument to accept the practices in question, we should satisfy ourselves on certain counts. First, are the practices really traditional? — or are they, rather, parodies and perversions of tradition? The helicopter-assisted mass slaughter of seals to fill the fur salons of Paris and New York has, I should think, as much relation to the trapping and bartering tradition of Canadian Indians as battery farming does to medieval husbandry.

Second, are the practices really an integral part of people's culture? To count as that, a practice must be more than an activity, like watching the News on TV, which the people happen to go in for. It must be one, the disappearance of which, would threaten people's sense of identity and the bonds which hold them together. It is hard to accept that fox-hunting — always the pursuit of the very few, and nowadays with many of its afficionados streaming out of the cities at weekends — has anything remotely akin to that status.

Third, even if a practice is a genuine part of cultural tradition, is it morally permissible? It would be as wrong in the area which concerns us as in any other, if such a tradition were regarded as 'off limits' for moral criticism. On that basis, no one should have challenged the institution of suttee in India or of slavery in the Deep South. No culture is beyond criticism.

—David Cooper[21]

---

8. U.K. Fur Imports

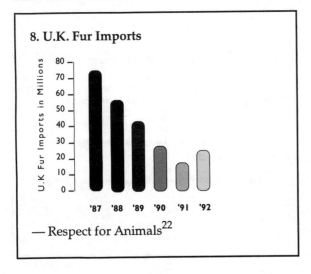

— Respect for Animals[22]

9. Rare parrots and other birds. with beaks and wings tightly taped, are slung inside bras, stuffed into girdles and crammed into the hollows of curlers. Hundreds of their eggs fit snugly into pockets of specially designed vests, allowing a smuggler to breeze easily through customs. Endangered snakes are rolled up in rugs and sewn into coatsleeves, while baby alligators lay hidden under false bottoms of suitcases, and angulated tortoises are rolled up inside socks. In an unending war, agents and inspectors face a constant barrage of endangered wildlife pouring into the country, while America's own native species are shipped out dead and alive, in a growing illegal and lucrative business that has skyrocketed in the past two decades.

In a shadowy world that feeds on what is rare, the enemy may be the local pet store selling endangered scarlet macaw or hyacinth parrots for $10,000 to $l5.000 a piece. The enemy is the large commercial dealer who supplies a voracious market of private collectors with everything from eagle feather head-dresses to live baby orangutans. The enemies are those who stock the Oriental medicinal market with gallbladders from slaughtered bears and antlers that have been hacked off the heads of elk in order to cure a plethora of ailments. The enemy is the illegal trophy hunter who craves that last rare Dall sheep's head to hang on the wall. The stories of what wildlife agents are up against seem endless.

— Jessica Speart [23]

10. The Bird Business

Each year, at least eight million wild birds are trapped, netted or stolen from the nest, in order to supply the demand of pet shops and zoos in America, Europe and Japan.

According to the International Council for Bird Preservation (ICBP), at least 41 species are threatened by international trade. Many more species may also be at risk but this is impossible to determine with any accuracy, as almost no studies have been carried out on the impact of the trade on wild populations. Barbaric methods of capture and transportation mean that widespread suffering is the routine for all birds destined for the pet trade, whether endangered species or not. The largest consumer of wild-caught birds in the world is Europe. Imports are estimated at between two and three million annually, whereas the legal US figure was only 500,000 in 1989. The most important European importing countries, the Netherlands and Belgium, only monitor imports relating to bird species listed under the Convention on International Trade in Endangered Species (CITES). Most imported wild-caught birds (in terms of numbers) are *not* listed under this Convention. During capture and transportation, wild caught birds die of shock, dehydration, starvation, change of diet, physical abuse, stress and disease. It is estimated that around 50% of all birds captured do not survive long enough to reach the airport in the exporting country.

In order to catch wild, free-flying birds, various methods are used. Live 'decoy birds' of the target species are placed near nets to lure other birds, tied by the foot to a peg in the ground with wing tips cut off to prevent any possibility of escape. 'Invisible' mist nets are set across fight paths or glue may be spread on perches set in favourite trees so birds are literally stuck to the branches. Attempts to escape, frequently result in broken wings and legs. Young are also removed from the nest and can die as a result, while the catchers who fell the trees to reach them destroy future nesting sites. After an overland journey to the airport, where long delays frequently occur, birds are shipped by air, often crammed in wooden crates with no room to stand upright and sometimes with insufficient food, water or ventilation to survive the journey. Once in the importing country, the remaining birds may not survive a two-five week period of quarantine and, again, in the pet shop it is not uncommon for mortalities to occur one or two days after arrival. Parrots are known to live for over fifty years in the wild whereas the average lifespan for a captive parrot is no more than five years

— Animals International [24]

11. Wildlife Trade in Egypt

Much of the live animal trade centres on Cairo's Sayyida Aisha market. Held every Friday and Sunday morning, the market is outwardly much like any other in the city — horribly congested and deafeningly noisy. The street is lined with stalls piled high with tiny wicker cages crammed with the usual array of budgerigars, wax-bills, doves and canaries, or with glass aquariums filled with goldfish and carp. Behind the stall-holders, other dealers haggle noisily for overlean alsatians and dogs of less determinate breed

Among these, the more exotic animals stand out. Diced water snakes are sold from writhing carrier bags for up to six Egyptian pounds (£1.13) Many of the aquariums are piled deep with Egyptian tortoises, sometimes topped with a layer of guinea pigs, a hedgehog or a hoopoe. Even more tortoises are spread on trestle tables or are heaped into metal cages. At eight Egyptian pounds (£1.50), they sell quickly and are replenished from hessian sacks behind the stalls. The opening up of the Egyptian frontier with Libya has flooded the market. Extremely rare in Egypt, the tortoises are now being brought across the border in their thousands to be sold at Sayyida Aisha, in the pet shops, or even from cardboard boxes in the street. The species is protected under the Convention on International Trade in Endangered Species (CITES) — to which Egypt is a signatory. It is also now protected under Egyptian law... The petshop in Sawart Street is probably the worst offender. Back in September, it had a green sea turtle for sale, kept in a plastic washing-up bowl full of *fresh* water. The species is ostensibly protected under CITES Appendix I and has just been added to the list of animals protected by Egyptian law. Other animals sold in the same shop over the past months have included crowned cranes, greater flamingos, short-eared and barn owls, spotted sandgrouse, and patas and velvet monkeys... There *are* laws to prevent the abuse of the country's wildlife. The problem is one of control. There are two agencies responsible for the internal monitoring of the trade in wildlife — the Egyptian Wildlife Service and the Egyptian Environmental Affairs Agency. These act under the Ministries of Agriculture and of Cabinet Affairs respectively. Responsibility for the implementation of CITES lies with the Wildlife Service, but the organisation is hopelessly understaffed and underfunded. It receives no money from the government, except for the salaries of its officers, which are so low that many leave for better-paid jobs.

In enforcing the law, the service gets little support from the police, who seem generally unaware of the laws and consider wildlife of precious little importance compared with other problems such as drugs and theft. Offenders are never prosecuted: any 'pets' are released and goods confiscated, and the vendor soon gets some more.

— Richard Hoath[25]

ACTIVITIES

■ *ENCOUNTERING WILDLIFE*

Suitable for

Primary/lower secondary (for upper secondary version see *Variation*).

Time needed

20 minutes

Resources

Set of *Encountering Wildlife* cards per pair of students; art materials, felt pens and two sheets of sugar paper for each group of four; paste sticks; Blu-tak.

Procedure

It is explained that humans choose to encounter wildlife and nature in many different ways. Some encounters are *destructive* in that they involve the loss of animal life and/or a serious threat to the well-being of animals; others are *non- destructive* in that they leave the animals unharmed and undisturbed. Working in pairs, students discuss each of their *Encountering Wildlife* cards, sorting them into *destructive* and *non-destructive* piles. Each pair then joins with another pair to explain their decisions and, if possible, reach consensus. The group then chooses a card from the *non-destructive* pile, sticking it in the centre of a sheet of sugar paper. Their task is to think of a range of examples of when the non-destructive encounter with wildlife could become destructive; e.g. bird-watchers approaching a nesting bird too closely and scaring it from the nest or a wildlife artist leaving behind poisonous waste materials. The examples are written up, and perhaps illustrated, on the sugar paper. A final task is to choose a card from the *destructive* pile and co-operatively prepare a poster warning of the harm to wildlife involved in the activity described on the card. Completed work is put on display for others to view prior to class discussion.

Potential

A simple activity alerting students to the threats to wildlife, actual and potential, presented by human leisure pursuits and sports. In plenary discussion, students' level of contentment with the placing of the cards and with definitions of the terms 'destructive' and 'non-destructive' should be elicited (there are likely to be strong feelings on the part of some as to whether fishing, fox-hunting and shooting are, in the wider scheme of things, 'destructive'). A second, important, focus for discussion should be how seemingly harmless pursuits can become destructive behaviours. Real or potential circumstances in which encounters deemed 'destructive' might be viewed in a new light should also be considered.

Variation

With upper secondary groups the terms *invasive* (i.e. tending to harm, exploit or adversely encroach upon the wildlife environment) and *non-invasive* are likely to trigger richer discussion and a more sophisticated comprehension that the differences between ways of encountering wildlife may, in the final analysis, be less stark than they seem on first impression and their acceptability ultimately a matter of perspective.

Extension

The class develops a *Wildlife Code* to guide their future behaviour.

Source

After an activity developed by Fiona Heads.

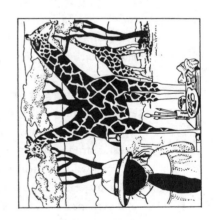

P

■ *FOXHUNT BRAINSTORM*

Suitable for

Upper primary/secondary

Time needed

40 minutes

Resources

8 sheets of sugar paper; felt pens.

Procedure

The class divides into four groups of equal size (A, B, C and D). Each group receives two sheets of sugar paper and a felt pen. They are informed that the activity will require them to brainstorm their thinking about foxhunting. *Brainstorming* involves listing ideas without discussion in immediate response to a given topic. The rules for brainstorming are:

❏ all ideas are accepted, everything is written down;

❏ no-one should comment, positively or negatively, on others' contributions;

❏ participants should feel free to offer any idea even if they feel unsure about it;

❏ 'piggybacking', i.e. taking somebody else's idea or contribution a stage further, is permitted.

Members of Group A are asked to brainstorm all the reasons they can think of as to why some people approve of foxhunting. Members of Group B are asked to brainstorm all the reasons they can think of as to why other people oppose, and seek the abolition of, foxhunting. Members of Group C are asked to brainstorm as many criteria as they can think of for judging whether foxhunting is a good or bad thing (to set them on their way the teacher illustrates the meaning of 'criterion', using examples). Members of Group D are asked to brainstorm images and feelings that come to mind when they think of foxhunting. Groups are to use only one of the sheets provided for this stage of the activity. When the flow of contributions slows to a trickle, the brainstorming is brought to a close. A second task is then set which, again, the groups tackle separately. Groups A and B are asked to review all the reasons put forward during their brainstorming and to form clusters of similar/overlapping reasons (a cluster can be one reason if it is especially distinctive). Each cluster should be given a summary title. The groups should present the clusters on their second sheet of sugar paper and should rank them on a continuum from most to least persuasive. Group C's new task is to rank the criteria brainstormed in order of descending importance. The ranking is written out on sugar paper. In undertaking the task, members of the group should try to achieve consensus but, if this proves impossible, should decide on the rank order by voting. Group D is asked to prepare a presentation on sugar paper analysing the range of images and feelings brainstormed. Plenary debriefing begins with group representatives speaking to their presentations.

Potential

A lively way of eliciting student thinking and feelings on a controversial topic much highlighted by the media in recent years. The facilitator can, perhaps, best engender discussion by seeking comment on links (positive and negative) between the four presentations. Did the images and feelings shared by Group D tend to reinforce the arguments for foxhunting reviewed by Group A or those against foxhunting as treated by Group B? Which images/feelings link especially strongly with which clusters in the A/B presentations? Do the criteria ranked by Group C lend succour to the case for or against foxhunting? How do the criteria relate to the images/feelings presented by Group D? Do the arguments ranked by Groups A and B cancel each other out or is one case the stronger?

Brainstorming can be used for a variety of purposes and at many points during a course (some teachers have the rules of brainstorming posted permanently in the classroom). It can be used to help students *think* creatively and laterally. Equally, it offers a means for focusing upon the *intuitive* and *feelings* dimensions of a topic or problem. At another level, it can be used as a warm-up activity. Again, it can be used to pool students' images of a topic prior to study/research (subsequent reference back to the brainstormed images thus providing a fertile way into consideration of stereotypes).

Brainstorming has many attractions as a learning technique in the humane classroom. It encourages everyone to take part since the rules protect the individual from criticism, laughter or ridicule. It is democratic in its emphasis upon everybody's right to speak and the value of their contribution. It is confidence building and encourages openness, open mindedness and a readiness to be imaginative and speculative. It promotes a lively, co-operative classroom climate. It can also bring to the surface a wide range of perspectives upon, and intellectual and emotional responses to, a particular problem.

Brainstorming lists can be used as the basis for class or group discussion, as raw material for ranking activities or for negotiating a course or study agenda. If the brainstorming has been written up on a chart, students can be given three coloured dots each to place against what they feel are the best suggestions. The results can be helpful in drawing up an agenda of topics for further exploration.

Sample Brainstorming Tasks

- brainstorm ways in which humans rely on animals

- brainstorm reasons for and against using animals in scientific experiments

- brainstorm ways in which the trade in 'exotic' animals from developing countries might be overcome

- brainstorm ideas on how the landscape would change if the vast majority of people became vegetarian

- brainstorm all the images that come to mind when you think of spiders

---

Variation

Brainstorming can also be carried out as a whole group activity.

■ *HUNTING OPINIONS*

Suitable for

Secondary

Time needed

90 minutes initially; 2-3 hours to collate and analyse returns and write report.

Resources

Overhead transparencies of *Gallup* and *NOP* data (*Figs. 1* and *2*).

Procedure

Working in groups of four, students review the opinion poll data on various forms of hunting to identify trends and significant/interesting returns (trends discerned in the *Gallup* data are extrapolated up to the present time). They discuss the reasons why certain blood sports are more frowned upon than others and why certain groups are likely to be more/less disapproving. They also note down things that the poll returns *do not* reveal about public opinion (e.g. whether there is an age or gender differential in attitudes towards hunting). Groups report back, the teacher listing the items upon which information is felt to be insufficient or missing. This is then used as a starting point for the design of a class questionnaire on hunting. Students have time out in the community to interview twenty people each (ensuring that their chosen interviewees are of varying age, gender, profession and ethnic group). Through an admixture of small and whole group work, the data is collated and analysed and a report written. The report is circulated to the local press and to interested organisations (eg. local political parties, local branches of farmers' associations, conservation groups and anti-hunt organisations).

Potential

This activity combines useful practice of important skills such as extrapolation, interviewing, report writing, questionnaire construction and analysis with an exploration of attitudes towards a controversial and emotive issue. Discussion arising out of the questionnaire returns should include comparison of the class results with the *Gallup* and *NOP* polls; also whether extrapolations from the *Gallup* returns

BLOODSPORTS: Gallup Data

Q. Would you approve or disapprove if
Parliament were to make laws forbidding:

%	Dec 1972	July 1975	Aug 1978	Nov 1980	July 1984	Feb 1986	Apr 1987
a) Foxhunting?							
Approve of ban	52	59	55	63	70	67	68
Disapprove	30	24	26	18	18	16	16
Don't Know	18	17	19	19	13	17	15
b) Staghunting?							
Approve of ban	58	67	59	68	75	72	73
Disapprove	26	18	22	15	13	13	12
Don't Know	16	16	19	17	12	14	14
c) Hare Coursing?							
Approve of ban	56	65	60	66	73	70	72
Disapprove	26	18	21	15	14	14	12
Don't Know	18	17	19	19	13	16	16

Fig.1

BLOODSPORTS: NOP DATA. 1983

%	Approve	Disapprove	Don't Know	Conservative Voters Disapproving	Labour Voters Disapproving	Liberal/SDP Voters Disapproving	Rural Dwellers Disapproving	Urban Dwellers Disapproving
Foxhunting	11	65	24	54	80	69	53	66
Staghunting [1]	14	81	5	76	88	84	79	81
Hare Coursing	4	80	16	78	86	84	77	80
Hare Hunting [2]	8	70	22	62	79	75	65	69

(1) - with dogs
(2) - with pack of beagles, basset hounds or harriers

Fig. 2

P

are borne out in their findings and the reasons why this is/is not the case.

Variation

Classes in two schools, one in a rural and one in an urban setting, use electronic mail to co-design a questionnaire which is then applied in their respective local communities. Data is shared, analysed, compared and contrasted. This approach is effective in pointing up rural-urban differences in opinion (see *NOP* data).

■ *BYLAND HUNT*

Suitable for

Upper secondary

Time needed

60-90 minutes (research); 60-90 minutes (public enquiry)

Resources

Sixteen *Key Witness (KW)* cards, three Enquiry Team (ET) cards; one Journalist (J) card; Resident (R) cards for remaining students. Sixteen red badges for the Key Witnesses; three white badges for the Enquiry Team; an orange badge for the Journalist, a green badge for each Resident. The badges should carry the title given on the cards (e.g. Farmer 2, Enquiry Team Member 3, Middleshire Resident) but should have space for students to write in their chosen forename and surname for the simulation. An *Enquiry Team To Consider Hunting Ban* press cutting for each student. A copy of the *Key Witness (KW)* cards and a gavel for the Enquiry Team Chairperson. An overhead projector, screen, blank transparencies and a selection of OHP pens for the Journalist. A collection of literature on fox hunting for students to consult (see *Reference Collection* box overleaf).

Procedure

Research Session(s)

The press cutting is distributed and the Byland Hunt controversy introduced. Students are informed that, in a subsequent session, the public enquiry is to be held with themselves in role. Their task, prior to that, is to research into fox hunting so that they can participate effectively in the enquiry. They are informed that their specific research task, as laid out on the cards to be distributed, might be an open-ended one or might involve them in taking a particular slant. Research briefs of the latter kind are to be adhered to, irrespective of personal opinions on fox hunting, as are any roles or viewpoints given. It is up to individuals to embellish their character in line with the letter and spirit of what is written on the card. Cards are in most cases distributed randomly (the teacher may wish to identify particular people for the enquiry team and

REFERENCE COLLECTION

Information on fox hunting can be obtained from:

- British Field Sports Society, 59 Kennington Road, London SE1 7PZ;

- The Countryside Foundation, 43/44 Berners Street, London WIP 3AA;

- Hunt Saboteurs Association, PO Box 1, Carlton, Nottingham NG4 2JY;

- League Against Cruel Sports, Sparling House, 83-7 Union Street, London SE1 1SJ

- RSPCA, Causeway, Horsham, West Sussex RH12 IHG.

In each case ask for multiple copies of the pamphlets and the newsletter/newspaper which the organisation publishes (including back numbers of the latter). The Reference Collection can also usefully include the following:

- *Bailey's Hunting Directory*, J.A. Allen, Nov. 1991;

- Huskisson, M., *Outfoxed*, Huskisson, 1983;

- McDonald, C., *Running with the Fox*, Guild Publishers, 1987;

- Thomas, R., *The Politics of Hunting*, Gower, Aldershot, 1983;

- Windeatt, P., *The Hunt and the Anti-hunt*, Prentice-Hall, 1982;

- League Against Cruel Sports, *Rural Vandals*, VHS video;

- British Field Sports society. *Hunting*, VHS video.

reporter roles). Students are asked to sit in particular combinations, i.e. the farmers, huntspeople, anti-hunt group, conservationists, enquiry team and residents (plus vicar and delivery van driver), in separate groups. The journalist is to sit at a table on her/his own. Students are given their respective badges to wear and are asked to choose a fictional first and second name and to write them in bold letters on their badge. They are advised that a journalist may wish to interview them and that they should watch out for further news and views on the proposed County Council ban from the *Byland Chronicle* (to appear from time to time on the overhead projection screen).

During the research session(s), students are encouraged to make good use of the Reference Collection and to spend some time exchanging ideas and opinions with members of their own and other groups (but always in role).

Public Enquiry Session

The room is laid out with rows of chairs facing a desk at the front around which the enquiry team sits. The chairperson controls the session, calls forward witnesses, calls upon her/his team colleagues to question witnesses and selects members of the public to respond to, and query, evidence and opinions put forward. Her/his chairpersonship should be very firm yet always fair. The enquiry continues until all witnesses have spoken or until the enquiry team deems that the issues have had a sufficient airing. As the enquiry unfolds, the journalist summarises key points on overhead projection transparency. After the chairperson has given the public an opportunity to air their views, the team retires to consider its recommendations and to prepare the text of a brief final statement. Returning to the enquiry room, the chairperson reads out the statement. At an early point in the de-briefing, the journalist projects a headline and accompanying story summarising the events and outcome of the enquiry.

NOTE: The teacher can shorten the public enquiry session by reducing the number of *Key Witness* cards.

Potential

This two-part research cum simulation activity can cause a build-up of excitement and generate intense feelings. The atmosphere at the enquiry may become very heated and it may prove difficult for some participants to break out of role at its conclusion. A *Mood Changer* activity (pp.60-4) may be needed before debriefing can begin. Participants can then be asked to reflect upon the experience in some or all of the following ways:

❑ How did you feel about the role you were asked to play? Does your own point of view on foxhunting tally with that you adopted in the simulation? If not, what problems or tensions did you experience?

❑ Has the research you undertook, or the opinions you heard during the enquiry, led you to reconsider your point of view in any way? What arguments coming from a point of view different to your own did you find the most worthy of serious attention?

❑ Did anybody's behaviour or contribution make you angry? If so, why?

❑ Which tactics at the enquiry did you find most effective? What can be learnt from them that might be useful in similar real-life situation?

❑ Do you think the recommendation made by the enquiry team faithfully reflected the quality of argument heard from both sides or, rather, their respective quality of performance? If the latter, is there cause for concern?

❑ How do the other members of the enquiry team feel about the Chairperson's use of the casting vote? How do participants feel about the performance of the enquiry team?

❑ How do participants feel about the contribution of the journalist? What impact did s/he have both during the research and enquiry sessions? What do you think about her/his concluding report?

❑ On what basis should an issue such as this be settled? On strictly ethical grounds?

From: The BYLAND CHRONICLE, Saturday 3 April 1994

ENQUIRY TEAM TO CONSIDER HUNTING BAN

Middleshire County Council has agreed to put on ice its proposal to ban fox hunting on Council-owned land. This move comes following outraged protests from members and supporters of the Byland Hunt and stormy scenes in the Council Chambers.

The Council is a substantial landowner in what is a very small county. The total land owned by the Council is in excess of 30,000 acres, much of which is situated in the area ridden by the Byland Hunt. The effect of the ban would be to put an end to the Hunt and its two hundred years' history.

The ban was proposed and passed at a Council session one month ago and was due to come into effect on 16 April. After the session, its proposer, Councillor Jane Sherwood, described the vote (25 in favour, 10 against) as 'an historic moment for Middleshire and humanity'.

Middleshire Council is a 'hung' council with a group of ten Independent Councillors holding the balance of power. Eight of the Independents originally voted for the foxhunting ban. In the light of the protests, the Independents have agreed to await the outcome of a public enquiry into the ban. 'If the enquiry recommends in favour of the ban, then it's to be implemented without delay,' said Independent Councillor Sue Hawkins. 'If it recommends against, then we'll have to think again.'

The public enquiry will open on Monday 3 May at the Grey Rooms, Shire Street, Byland. It is to be conducted by an enquiry team of three members. It is expected that leading farmers, huntspeople and conservationists will be called to give evidence as well as representatives of anti-hunt organisations. Local clergy will also be invited to give their views. Whilst there will obviously be a lot of interest in the enquiry amongst Middleshire's rural population, it will be interesting to see what people living in the small industrial town of Byland, with its multicultural, multifaith community, have to say about the ban.

P

Scientific grounds? On the basis of who has most power and influence? How, in reality, are they generally settled?

☐ To what extent were the arguments for and against the County Council ban premised upon animal welfare and/or animal rights considerations?

Variations

1. If deemed necessary, the teacher can take the role of the Enquiry Team Chairperson.

2. Students can be encouraged to interview farmers, huntspeople, conservationists, representatives of anti-hunt groups, clergy of various faiths, representatives of ethnic groups, and other local people as part of an (elongated) research stage.

3. A camcorder recording of the public enquiry can be used for analysis of effective and less effective public advocacy styles and strategies.

R Middleshire Resident

Your Profile

You live in the small County of Middleshire. It is up to you to decide whether you live in the rural part of the county where the Byland Hunt rides or in Byland itself. Byland is a small industrial town with a multicultural and multifaith population. It is also up to you to decide who you are and what job you do.

Your Task

To look into the arguments for and against fox hunting and to decide on your character's attitude to the proposed County Council ban (this may or may not coincide with the attitude you would really take to such a proposal). A time-effective way of doing this will be to go and ask witnesses (red badges) for their views on the ban as they prepare for the public enquiry. Be prepared to contribute to the public enquiry by giving evidence or by querying/making statements about what key witnesses say.

P

KW Farmer 1

Your Profile

You own a large sheep farm and are a long-standing member of the Byland Hunt. You enjoy the thrill of the chase and the regular opportunity the Hunt offers to socialise with important local people. You regard the fox as a pest that is a constant threat to lambs, chickens and other domestic fowl as well as wild nesting birds.

Your Task

To use the time before the public enquiry to research the best possible case against a County Council ban on fox hunting.

KW Farmer 2

Your Profile

You own a large sheep farm across which the Byland Hunt has passed on a number of occasions. On one such occasion the hounds ran amok among in-lamb ewes causing a stampede. One early lamb was mauled. Soon after, several ewes aborted. You have come to think that the hounds are a greater menace to lambs than foxes ever were. You intend to write to the Master of the Byland warning the Hunt to keep off your property or face legal action.

Your Task

To use the time before the public enquiry to research the best possible case in favour of a County Council ban on fox hunting.

KW Farmer 3

Your Profile

You own a large mixed farm. You do not hunt but have always enjoyed the sight and sound of riders and hounds and see them as a colourful feature of country life. Nonetheless, you are concerned about the cruelty involved in fox hunting and recognise that your image of the fox as the farmer's enemy is based on hearsay rather than fact. Somebody recently suggested to you that foxes are useful for keeping down rabbit and rodent numbers.

Your Task

To use the time before the public enquiry to find out more about hunting and, in the light of what you find, to decide whether or not to support the proposed County Council ban.

KW Huntsperson 1

Your Profile

You are the Master of the Byland Hunt, its figurehead, and lead the Hunt in the field. You are very aware that the Hunt has two hundred years' of history behind it and feel that it is your responsibility to uphold tradition. You regard the fox as a pest and believe that if hunting is curtailed or ended the farmers will turn to less humane ways of killing foxes such as gassing. You are worried that a County Council ban would lead to redundancies amongst the Hunt's paid employees. You are wealthy and give handsomely to local church funds.

Your Task

To use the time before the public enquiry to research the best possible case against a County Council ban on fox hunting.

KW Huntsperson 2

Your Profile

You are Huntsman of the Byland Hunt, a full-time paid employee of the Hunt who rides in front of the pack of hounds and sounds the hunting horn. You have worked with the Hunt for fifteen years. The job of Huntsman has been in your family for four generations. The day before a hunt you and the Whippers-in (three other full-time paid employees that follow behind the pack) go out to find where foxes are living. When the hunt begins you take the hounds to this area to pick up the scent of a fox. You are very worried that a County Council ban on foxhunting would lead to job losses amongst paid employees of the Hunt (the area is one of fairly high rural unemployment).

Your Task

To use the time before the public enquiry to research the best possible social and economic case against a County Council ban on fox hunting

KW Huntsperson 3

Your Profile

You are a member of the Byland Hunt and enjoy the exercise and good company that goes along with riding with the Hunt. You find the killing of the fox distasteful and do not go along with members of the Hunt who say that the fox does not suffer in that the hounds kill it instantly when it is caught. You are keen to look for ways in which the Hunt could continue without killing animals. You have heard that there are eleven registered 'drag hunts' in Britain in which the hounds follow a scent trail left by a bag dragged along a pre-arranged course.

Your Task

To use the time before the public enquiry to find out more about alternatives to fox hunting.

KW Huntsperson 4

Your Profile

You are a member of the Byland Hunt and particularly enjoy the pomp and ceremony that goes along with fox hunting. Born to a working class family in London, yet now well-to-do, you believe that hunting is no longer an upper class sport. Yes, the Byland includes many wealthy people but also some people from lower income groups. It is watched by a representative cross-section of people. You do not believe hunting is cruel. The horses and hounds are well looked after; the death of the fox a quick affair. You feel that hunt saboteurs — self-professed defenders of animals — are hypocritical in their concern for animal welfare in that their antics frequently frighten the horses.

Your Task

To use the time before the public enquiry to research the best possible case against a County Council ban on fox hunting.

KW Hunt Saboteur

Your Profile

You believe that fox hunting is cruel and inhumane. You became a hunt saboteur when you saw the Byland hounds tear a fox apart in front of your eyes while you were out walking in the countryside. You try to sabotage the Hunt by laying scent trails that lead the hounds off the scent of the fox. Some Hunt members behave very aggressively towards you, saying that you are spoiling a great British tradition. You cannot see how the cruel killing of a defenceless animal contributes to a rich cultural life.

Your Task

To use the time before the public enquiry to research the best possible case in favour of a County Council ban on fox hunting.

KW Member of the League Against Cruel Sports

Your Profile

You believe that fox hunting, like all blood sports, is a barbaric practice that should be abolished as were dog-fighting and badger-baiting in the past. You support any local or central government initiative to that end. The League estimates that one in three hunts ends in the death of a fox and that about 13,000 foxes are killed every year in Britain. You entirely dismiss claims by the hunting fraternity that they are animal lovers and that fox hunting is a humane way of keeping down the numbers of a troublesome pest.

Your Task

To use the time before the public enquiry to research the best possible case in favour of a County Council ban on fox hunting.

KW School Teacher

Your Profile

You have long been against fox hunting as a blatant example of the class-ridden nature of British society, in which a minority (the 'Establishment') enjoy special privilege. You believe it is profoundly unfair, for instance, that the 1991 Wildlife and Countryside Act makes it a criminal act for anyone to allow their dog to roam free in a field where there are sheep yet exempts owners of packs of hounds from the force of law. The pomp, ceremony and privileges of the Byland Hunt literally and metaphorically make you see red!

Your Task

To use the time before the public enquiry to research the best possible case in favour of a County Council ban on fox hunting.

KW Butcher

Your Profile

You had no strong opinions either way about fox hunting until the day when the hounds of the Byland Hunt chased a fox into your front garden, cornered it, and ripped it to pieces in front of your children. When the (previous) Master of the Hunt, now retired, arrived at your front gate, he seemed oblivious to the family's protests. You now believe that fox hunting should be abolished.

Your Task

To use the time before the public enquiry to research the best possible case in favour of a County Council ban on fox hunting.

KW Conservationist 1

Your Profile

You are in favour of fox hunting, believing that its popularity and influence through the ages has helped preserve hedges, woods, copses and other uncultivated areas where foxes live, that would otherwise have disappeared. You also hold that hunting in its traditional form has conserved the fox population which would otherwise have been subject to much more thorough and deadly forms of control such as shooting and gassing.

Your Task

To use the time before the public enquiry to research the best possible conservation case against a County Council ban on fox hunting.

P

KW Conservationist 2

Your Profile

You are unsure whether fox hunting is a good or bad thing in conservation terms. You are somewhat persuaded by arguments that the fox is a pest that has to be controlled so as to conserve the populations of other wild animals and of nesting birds. You are also keen to see traditional aspects of rural life preserved. On the other hand, you have read of recent research which says that if hunting were suspended the number of foxes would not rise dramatically. You are eager to learn more.

Your Task

To use the time before the public enquiry to find out whether or not fox hunting is a good thing from a conservation point of view and, in the light of what you discover, to decide on your position on the County Council ban.

KW Conservationist 3

Your Profile

You are opposed to fox hunting not only on cruelty grounds but also because it is unnecessary given facts about the breeding habits of the fox that have only come to light in the past twenty years. In family groups of foxes, only one dominant vixen givens birth, it appears, so reproduction is naturally controlled. Population control methods like hunting only serve to disrupt such natural social mechanisms of control.

Your Task

To use the time before the public enquiry to look for evidence on the natural history and breeding habits of the fox, and to prepare the best possible conservation case for a County Council ban on fox hunting.

KW Vicar

Your Profile

You are vicar of a group of churches situated in the area where the Byland Hunt meets. You go along with the Church Assembly's 1970 condemnation of fox hunting as cruel and as degrading to those involved, and are aware of moves within the Church of England to ban fox hunting on its land. On the other hand, you realise that leading figures in your congregation (who contribute handsomely to church funds) are members of the Byland Hunt and might be offended if you come out publicly against hunting. You know your opinion will be sought at the forthcoming public enquiry.

Your Task

To use the time before the public enquiry to decide on what you will say about the proposed County Council ban.

KW Delivery Van Driver

Your Profile

You are a long-standing and well-known supporter of the Byland Hunt, enjoying following the riders and hounds in your car. Some time ago, when you were driving your van through the area, some of the Byland hounds, seemingly unsupervised, poured across the road in front of you causing you to swerve into a young cyclist. The boy was knocked off his bike and needed fifteen stitches to head injuries. The incident has shaken your support for the Hunt and you are reviewing your position.

Your Task

To use the time before the public enquiry to decide what you will say about the proposed County Council ban.

ET Enquiry Team Chairperson

Your Role

You are to chair the public enquiry firmly and fairly, staying strictly neutral during the giving of evidence and public discussion and argument. Your role at the enquiry is to call forward witnesses to make brief statements (no longer than two minutes) on the proposed County Council ban before asking, firstly, one or more of your enquiry team colleagues and, secondly, members of the public to put questions to the witness. You have a set of biographical sketches of key witnesses but other residents can also be called upon to speak (they will be wearing green badges). You should intervene firmly if people become repetitive or long-winded or interrupt others. At the end of the hearing your role is to chair a brief meeting of the enquiry team to decide whether or not to recommend the County Council to ban fox hunting on its land (you have the casting vote). You then announce the decision and explain the thinking behind what has been decided.

Your Pre-Enquiry Task

1. To decide on an appropriate timetable and order for the enquiry. Find out the names of the key witnesses — they will be wearing red badges.
2. To familiarise yourself with the arguments for and against fox hunting.

ET Enquiry Team Member 2

Your Role

After each witness has given evidence, the chairperson will ask other members of the enquiry team to put questions to the witness. If the witness is *in favour* of the County Council ban, your role is to vigorously question her/him. Do not let the witness get away with anything ! You should avoid hostile questioning of witnesses who come out against the ban. At the end of the hearing you are to meet with the other two members of the enquiry team to decide whether or not to recommend the County Council to ban fox hunting on its land. The Chairperson has the casting vote.

Your Pre-Enquiry Task

To familiarise yourself with the arguments for and against fox hunting.

ET Enquiry Team member 3

Your Role

After each witness has given evidence, the Chairperson will ask other members of the enquiry team to put questions to the witness. If the witness is *against* the County Council ban, your role is to vigorously question her/him. Do not let the witness get away with anything! You should avoid hostile questioning of witnesses who come out *in favour of* the ban. At the end of the hearing you are to meet with the other two members of the enquiry team to decide whether or not to recommend the County Council to ban fox hunting on its land. The Chairperson has the casting vote.

Your Pre-Enquiry Task

To familiarise yourself with the arguments for and against fox hunting.

J Journalist

Your Role

You are a reporter with the *Byland Chronicle* given the task of covering the fox hunting controversy. As people prepare for the public enquiry, your task is to conduct brief interviews with likely key witnesses (red badges) and to quickly write up copy that will whip up interest in the issue and sharpen the controversy. Use overhead projection transparencies and project your news items on the screen at regular intervals. During the enquiry you are to summarise key points emerging on overhead projection transparency. After the enquiry you are to rapidly write up the *Chronicle's* coverage of the event so it can be read soon after the proceedings have finished.

R Middleshire Resident
Your Profile

You live in the small county of Middleshire. It is up to you to decide whether you live in the rural part of the county where the Byland Hunt rides or in Byland itself. Byland is a small industrial town with a multicultural and multifaith population. It is also up to you to decide who you are and what job you do.
Your Task

To look into the arguments for and against fox hunting and to decide on your character's attitude to the proposed County Council ban (this may or may not coincide with the attitude you would really take to such a proposal). A time-effective way of doing this will be to go and ask witnesses (red badges) for their views on the ban as they prepare for the public enquiry. Be prepared to contribute to the public enquiry by giving evidence or by querying/making statements about what key witnesses say.

R Middleshire Resident

Your Profile

You live in the small county of Middleshire. It is up to you to decide whether you live in the rural part of the county where the Byland Hunt rides or in Byland itself. Byland is a small industrial town with a multicultural and multifaith population. It is also up to you to decide who you are and what job you do.
Your Task

To look into the arguments for and against fox hunting and to decide on your character's attitude to the proposed County Council ban (this may or may not coincide with the attitude you would really take to such a proposal). A time-effective way of doing this will be to go and ask witnesses (red badges) for their views on the ban as they prepare for the public enquiry. Be prepared to contribute to the public enquiry by giving evidence or by querying/making statements about what key witnesses say.

R Middleshire Resident

Your Profile

You live in the small county of Middleshire. It is up to you to decide whether you live in the rural part of the county where the Byland Hunt rides or in Byland itself. Byland is a small industrial town with a multicultural and multifaith population. It is also up to you to decide who you are and what job you do.
Your Task

To look into the arguments for and against fox hunting and to decide on your character's attitude to the proposed County Council ban (this may or may not coincide with the attitude you would really take to such a proposal). A time-effective way of doing this will be to go and ask witnesses (red badges) for their views on the ban as they prepare for the public enquiry. Be prepared to contribute to the public enquiry by giving evidence or by querying/making statements about what key witnesses say.

P

■ *HOW MANY PELTS?*

Suitable for

Primary/secondary

Time needed

20 minutes

Resources

A *How Many Pelts?* sheet for each student. The activity is at its most effective if photographs of each animal listed are displayed on the classroom walls.

Procedure

Working individually, students complete the *How Many Pelts?* sheet, estimating how many animals are used to make a single fur coat. As they decide their estimates, they can tour the photographs on the walls. They then form into groups of four, discuss their estimates and amend their individual sheets if deemed necessary. The teacher then reads out the actual number (see box), explaining that a number range is given to take into account the varying size of animals and adult humans. Groups are asked to discuss their response to the actual figures before reporting back in plenary begins.

Potential

An effective means of introducing students to some basic facts concerning the fur trade, i.e. the animals used in making garments and the number of animals that go to make up that most well known of fur garments, the fur coat. In reporting back, groups should be encouraged to comment upon the accuracy of their estimates and to share their reactions to the actual figures.

Extensions

1. Students prepare a bar graph of the number of animals needed per coat for each species.

2. Students use the questionnaire (with or without photographs) for a community survey into levels of understanding of, and attitudes to, the fur industry. Did adults in the community estimate accurately? If not, how did they respond when given the real figures? Did they seem favourably disposed to, or hostile to, the fur industry?

3. Small groups each research a number of the animals on the list to identify their range, natural habitat, place in the ecosystem and scarcity. The information on each animal is presented on a piece of card and attached to the wall next to its photograph. On a large wall map of the world, the location and range of each animal is identified using colour-headed pins, cotton and a label. If pelts of an animal are imported into the United Kingdom cotton is attached to one of the pins and then to a central UK pin. If figures are available, a slip of paper giving the number of pelts imported in any recent year and the number of coats that would produce can be attached to the outer pin.

Source

After an idea in *Respect for Life*, Toronto Humane Society, 1988. The Toronto Humane Society figures have been amended following consultation with Carol McKenna of Respect for Animals (see *Organisations* list, p.401).

Bobcat	12-15	Muskrat	60-120
Beaver	16-20	*Ocelot	12-18
Blueback Seal	5-7	Otter	13-20
Chinchilla	130-200	Raccoon	20-30
Coypu	26-34	Sable	36-65
Ermine	180-240	Skunk	40-50
Fox	10-24	Squirrel	100-400
*Leopard	4-5	*Tiger	3-5
Lynx	12-15	*Whitecoat Seal	5-10
Mink	36-65	Wolf	3-5

*Protected from fur trading by the Convention on International Trade in Endangered Species (CITES)

HOW MANY PELTS?

How many animals are used to make a single fur coat for an adult? For each of the animals listed write in your estimate. Later you will be given the actual number used.

Type of Animal	Estimate	Actual Number
Bobcat		
Beaver		
Blueback Seal		
Chinchilla		
Coypu		
Ermine		
Fox		
Leopard		
Lynx		
Mink		
Muskrat		
Ocelot		
Otter		
Raccoon		
Sable		
Skunk		
Squirrel		
Tiger		
Whitecoat Seal		
Wolf		

P

The trapper approached, a five foot green birch club in hand. The coyote struggled frantically against the trap, pulling one leg loose and leaving the lifeless paw in the trap. The trapper poked at the coyote. The animal hissed and snapped at the club. Then, as the trapper slowly swished the club back and forth, the coyote became unusually calm. Mesmerised by steady motion, he crouched motionless, his eyes dutifully following the swishing club. Suddenly the club smashed across the coyote's nose and slammed him to the ground. But the blow was not delivered with precision. Almost instantly he was in a semi crouch: blood spurting from his nose. Eyes dazed, again the club fell. The trapper, in one practised motion, grabbed the stunned coyote by the hind legs, stretching the animal full length while planting his foot heavily on its neck.

The other foot delivered a series of thumping blows to the coyote's chest, expelling hollow gasps of air. Releasing the hind legs, the trapper rested one foot on the coyote's neck, the other on the chest. The coyote's eyes bulged. The mouth gaped, the tongue hung listlessly along the bloodstained jaw. Periodically stomping near the heart, the trapper maintained his position for 14 minutes. He indicated this was necessary to ensure that the animal was dead — 'once I had one leap up and bite me'. While focusing the camera, I thought how ridiculous it was for a 200 pound man to be stamping on an 18 pound coyote as if his very existence depended on the animal's elimination. The coyote, had he been given the opportunity, would not even have sought revenge. He would have tried to escape.

— Daniel Kelly

P

■ SPLITTING IMAGES

Suitable for

Top primary/secondary

Time needed

30 minutes

Resources

A photocopy of the photograph (see previous page), cut into two parts as indicated, and a sheet of sugar paper for each group of three students; 20 felt pens (10 each of two colours); 10 pencils, 10 sticks of paste.

Procedure

Students form groups of three and are given the small section of the picture. This they paste on their sheet of sugar paper (they are given no indication as to whether it is the top or bottom section). Their first task is to brainstorm feelings, responses and questions prompted by the part-picture, writing these in felt pen around the outside of the sugar paper adjacent to the image. Their second is to decide what the unseen part of the picture might contain. Their chosen content is drawn in in pencil as an extension of the part they have before them. Copies of the second part are then distributed and laid over the drawing. Groups then brainstorm feelings, responses and questions prompted by the complete picture, writing these on the sugar paper using a felt pen of a second colour.

Potential

The complete image will have a startling impact and will literally turn students' perspectives upside down in that most, if not all, will have assumed that the animal is at the top of the picture. There is likely to be intense discussion around human callousness and cruelty towards animals. What feelings and questions were prompted by the first part-picture? What type of animal did they think they were looking at and what did they think it was doing? What did they draw as the imagined second half of the picture? What were their reactions on being presented with the real picture? What did they think the person was doing? Did they assume it was a man? Why? At some stage the picture should be explained. What they are looking at is a practice used by fur trappers called 'suffocation'. Bullets are not used to kill trapped animals in that the fur is damaged. Instead trappers bludgeon the head of the animal and then 'suffocate' it by standing on the animal's vital organs until it expires. In the box on page 217, Daniel Kelly, the wildlife researcher who took the photograph, describes what he saw.

The sequence of photographs taken by Kelly are available from Respect for Animals (see *Organisations* list, p.401).

I read the story of the trapping to the class, gently and slowly and involved myself in their obvious pain and shock. They were deeply moved and this must be extremely sensitively handled with young children. Issues raised — could the photographer have intervened? What nationality was the trapper? Probably more effective with older children but I would do it again with this age group.
— Hertfordshire primary teacher, 10-11 year olds.

I feel that the image is too horrific for primary children and would not feel able to use it. The actual activity though, with another less graphic picture, I would use. Children will want to know how the cruelty depicted can be stopped.
— Cambridgeshire primary teacher.

It must be followed by something positive: A letter-writing session to a fur retailer, relating feelings or opinions generated, or to the picture source (Respect for Animals) expressing support for/disagreement with their work.
— Kent secondary teacher.

■ *FUR FLOWCHARTS*

Suitable for

Upper secondary

Time needed

60 minutes

Resources

For each group: a set of statements, each statement on a separate slip of paper; a large 'chart', made by sellotaping two or four sheets of sugar paper together; felt tip pens; a paste stick.

Procedure

Students work in groups of three or four. Each group is asked to read and discuss the sixteen statements and to arrange them in the pattern, cluster, sequence or flowchart formation of their choice (the formation may be the result of consensus within the group or expressive of members' disagreements). When a formation has been agreed, the slips are pasted to the sugar paper. Connecting two-way arrows between the slips can be drawn in (with, perhaps, one colour representing complementarities, and another representing tensions, between the statements). Cartoons, comments and small question marks (denoting questions raised by particular statements) can also be incorporated. Under large question marks, groups can note down questions, or clashes of opinion, that are not resolved by the set of statements taken as a whole. When groups have completed the task to their satisfaction, they come together as a class to explain their flowcharts, to report on main points of discussion, agreement and disagreement, and to pose issues which, in their opinion, have not been satisfactorily resolved by the collection of statements.

Potential

An effective means of introducing students to a range of perspectives on an extremely controversial topic. The flowchart formation can foster greater creativity in exploring both complementarities and tensions between statements whilst the use of large and small question marks can encourage a more critical examination of statements, taken individually and as a whole. The questions listed can provide the springboard for further research into the fur trade (see *Additional Resources*)

Sources of statements

Sources of statements are as follows: (1) *Born to be flayed*, Compassion in World Farming flyer; (3) Culled from statements in Lynx, *The steel jawed leg-hold trap. A summary of expert opinion*, 1989; (4) *Trapping and the environment*, Toronto Humane Society *Animal Talk*, 2; (5) Barber, J., 'The persecution of the fur trade', *Reader's Digest*, August 1991, 38; (6) *Ibid.*, 39-40; (7) *Trapping devices*, Toronto Humane Society *Animal Talk*, 1; (8) *Natives and the fur industry*, Guelph, Ontario, *Native/Animal Brotherhood*; (9) *No fur. No value. No life*, Fur Education Council pamphlet;
(11) *Fur trade fact sheet*, Lynx, 2; (12) *Natives and the fur industry*, Guelph, Ontario, Native / Animal Brotherhood; (13) Association for the Protection of Fur-Bearing Animals, *The fur bearers*, 1989, 6; (14) Woodcock, G., *A briefing on the fur trade and the aboriginal cultures*, Lynx reprint from *Skinned*, International Wildlife Coalition, 1989, 2. Statements 2, 10, 15 and 16 are written by the author and seek to faithfully reflect arguments put forward by the pro-fur Fur Institute of Canada and the International Fur Trade Federation. The two organisations jointly refused permission for verbatim extracts from their publications to be included with this activity and in the documents section of this chapter. For further details, see reference 18 at the end of the chapter.

1. TORTURE CHAMBER

The World is a vast torture chamber for fur-bearing animals. Animals die in agony in traps and go mad in tiny cages not because someone is hungry or ill, but for no other reason than luxury, vanity and adornment and to line the bloody pockets of furriers who get rich on the pain of tortured animals.
— *Richard Adams*

2. FUR IS ECO-FRIENDLY

Conservation is necessarily the cornerstone of the fur trade. The trade depends upon populations of fur-bearing animals being maintained. It needs to be vigilant and to act responsibly so that the natural environments in which the animals live are not harmed. The fur trade does not trap endangered species. It does not cause pollution. It promotes environmental protection. Fur is eco-frendly.

3. LEG-HOLD TRAPS

Animals caught in leg-hold traps suffer from terrible injuries to their jaws as well as to their limbs in their effort to escape... This barbaric device is still used to catch more than 12 million animals each year to supply the luxury fur trade. So-called padded, or rubber lined, traps often referred to by the fur industry are rarely, if ever, used by trappers and are merely a product of their fanciful public relations' advisers.
— *Lynx*

4. ENDANGERED SPECIES

World-wide, trapping is responsible for the extinction of three races of tigers, three races of bears, a dozen or more races of wolves and the Caribbean Monk Seal. Also extinct in certain regions in Canada is the black bear, the brown bear, the cougar, the lynx, the marten and the wolverine. The endangered species list has risen from 192 to 2 I I. Trappers cannot control what kind of animals fall into their traps. They may threaten the population of animals which are already on the endangered species list. In addition, trapping disrupts family and social structures. When a member of an animal family is killed, no consideration is given to the remaining members who may be dependent upon the stronger ones for their very existence.
— *Toronto Humane Society*

5. MISCONCEPTIONS

Ontario trapper Alcide Giroux fight(s) the misconceptions about trappers. 'When people say that trapping's cruel and inhumane,' he says, 'they don't have a clue what a trapper does.' Giroux was one of the first trappers in Canada to urge his colleagues to get serious about animal welfare. While the anti-fur campaign continues to focus dogmatically on the steel-jawed leg-hold trap, a device that can lead to lingering and painful death, Giroux points out that the propaganda bears no relationship to the trap's role in the fur trade today. About three quarters of all animals trapped in Canada die in quick-kill traps. And in the vast majority of cases in which the leg hold is still used for semi-aquatic animals such as beaver, it is set so the animal drowns within a few minutes. Giroux has helped government researchers field-test a new padded trap that could eliminate the use of conventional leg holds on wolves, coyotes, red foxes, bobcats and lynx. The traps promise to minimise pain and stress.
— *John Barber*

6. MORE THAN A LIVELIHOOD

For the tens of thousands of native families who rely on trapping, the anti-fur campaign threatens more than a livelihood. It threatens a way of life that has persisted for thousands of years. Stephen Kakfwi, former president of the Dene Nation, notes that the anti-fur campaign is 'potentially far more dangerous than the threat to our lands posed by resource developers'. In the eyes of virtually every native group in Canada, its goal — perhaps unintended but no less real — is simply cultural genocide. Says Thomas Coon, a James Bay Cree and executive of the native pro-fur lobby group, Indigenous Survival International: 'Those people who killed the seal market will eventually kill the fur trade. But for the people facing hardships, what are the alternatives? Do animal rights supersede human rights? What about us? What am I going to feed my little ones with?'
— *John Barber*

P

7. NO SUCH THING

There is no such thing as a humane trap. All trapped animals suffer whether it is from the excruciating pain of being squeezed to death by a body trap or from the stress and anxiety felt when trapped alive in the freezing cold. Trapped animals can never be protected. Trappers cannot ensure the humane treatment of animals. They lay traps which are not checked for days. Trappers cannot ensure that only target animals are being trapped. In many cases, non-target animals are caught. In 1987, 26% of animals trapped were accidental or non-target species.
— *Toronto Humane Society*

8. NOT THE NATIVE WAY

Native people are not the destroyers of the earth. We do not kill our animal brothers for joy or for money. Before fur traders arrived in Canada, we perceived animals as our brothers, as sharers of the earth. We talked to animals. We explained to them, if we had to kill them, why. We didn't kill animals for small amounts of fur. We didn't kill them for their pelts alone.

Fashion fur is not the Native way. Native tradition calls for the economical and respectful use of animals. No traditional Native would dream of killing 40 small animals to create a piece of clothing that one large animal would provide. Being forced to kill is an act distasteful to any of us and to kill for such a trivial reason as to make a fur coat is horrible indeed.
— *Native/Animal Brotherhood*

9. DOUBLE STANDARD

A moral objection to the use of fur can only be sustained by people who abstain from the use of ALL animals, whether for food or clothing or other products that make human life tolerable and interesting. Some religions fall into this category. The rest of us are all quite rightly animal users. The animal rights movement maintains that it is murder to use animals for their fur. Some activists question our right to kill animals for a wide range of human needs from food to vital medical research. If taken to its logical conclusion, this implies an objection also to the elimination of vermin that endanger human life through the spread of diseases or destruction of crops. Confronted with the double standard implicit in their argument — that it favours animals over human beings — the animal rightists change their tack and argue that fur is immoral because it is a luxury. Since when was luxury a crime? In a free society, and within the law, people must be able to spend their money as they see fit. Anything less diminishes their democratic rights.
— *Fur Education Council*

10. SOURCE OF CASH INCOME

What is a trapper? It's someone who, from late autumn until early spring, traps fur-bearing animals and prepares their pelts for market. Living in the remote Canadian north where employment opportunities are few, trapping offers a small but vital source of cash income to support an essentially subsistence way of life. Should that source fall away as a result of ill-considered opposition to the fur trade from urbanites and Europeans, long divorced from wilderness experience, the trapper may have to abandon his culture and way of life to find a job in a town or seek welfare assistance.

11. LESS THAN 1%

Most trapping by truly native people is carried out in the Yukon and North West Territories (N.W.T.) in Canada. During the 1982-83 trapping season, 200,000 animals were taken (by all categories of trapper) in these two provinces compared with the 4 million trapped in all Canada and 25 million in N. America as a whole. That is less that I % of North American trapped animals originate from native peoples. In other words, Native people are responsible for around a quarter of 1% of furs produced world-wide. In the N.W.T. trapping AND fishing represents 1% of the Territorial Gross Domestic Product as well as 1% of the labour force.
— *Lynx*

P

12. OUR SIDE OF THE STORY

Because of the deep sympathy Canadians and Europeans feel toward the plight of Native people, the Canadian government and the fur industry have chosen to use us to protect the entire billion-dollar fur industry. They have gone so far as to suggest that people opposed to commercial trade are advocates of cultural genocide. They continue to promote the myth that trapping is culturally and economically central to Canada's Natives. We believe that Native Canadians have become the victims of the federal government's policy to promote the fur industry. While claiming to help Native Canadians, in reality, it is the non-Native elements of the fur industry who most benefit. Meanwhile, the government too often fails to meet treaty obligations and resolve Native socio-economic concerns.
— *Native/Animal Brotherhood*

13. NOT A MAJOR SOURCE

The following information is from a government research paper compiled by the Northwest Territories Priorities and Planning Secretariat, March l5, 1984 (the population is basically native):
• The majority are part-time trappers who earn additional cash but not enough generally to cover equipment (snow-mobiles, traps, sleds) and operating costs.
• Trapping is not a major source of cash.
• Trapping interest declined in younger age groups (only l % expressed interest as a career).
• Average income (in the ten areas studied) was $938.
• 59% of native population is willing to migrate for employment.
• Students in grades 2-9 in Fort Simpson listed career aspirations which do not differ widely from those of southern Canada.
• Returns from trapping were generally much lower than other income sources, with less than 5% of trappers actually listing their occupation as trapper.
— *Association for the Protection of Fur-Bearing Animals*

14. UNFORGIVABLE

I find it unforgivable when the fur lobby so distorts history as to claim that their trade is part of aboriginal cultures, when in fact it was historically one of the principal factors in the disintegration of those cultures as they originally existed. The fur trade from the beginning involved a pattern of making the Indian and the Inuit dependent on an alien commercial world. Indeed, the very fact that nowadays variations in the fortune of the fur trade have an immediate adverse effect on the lives of native people is an indication of the endurance of that pattern of dependence which had done so much harm in the past.
— *George Woodcock*

15. SPARING THE ANIMALS

If furs can be made synthetically, some say, shouldn't we spare the animals? The point is that synthetics do not spare the animals. Synthetics are made from non-renewable (usually petroleum) resources. Their extraction, manufacture and disposal deplete and damage natural environments, releasing harmful pollutants into the atmosphere, onto the land and into surface and ground waters.

16. SHEER DELUSION

It's sheer delusion to believe that if fur-trapping ceases there will be less death and suffering in the world. Animal populations tend to grow. A point comes sooner or later when there are too many of a particular species for the habitat to support. Nature then checks the population growth through disease, starvation, predation or some other means. Can such checks really be held to be more 'humane' than the culling of the surplus population of fur-bearing animals by the trapper for the good of human beings?

P

■ ON THE LISTS

Suitable for

Primary/secondary

Time needed

Short periods of time over several weeks

Resources

A resource collection of books on wild animals, birds and reptiles around the world.

Procedure

The teacher explains the reasons for, and workings of, the Convention on International Trade in Endangered Species (see pp.196-7). Students write to organisations campaigning against the international trade in animals (see box) to obtain:

❑   information on the animals currently listed in CITES Appendices I and II;

❑   organisations' suggestions as to which animals listed in Appendix II should be promoted to Appendix I and their views as to which animals not currently protected under CITES should be listed;

❑   organisations' views as to current loopholes in the working of CITES.

Replies received, small groups review the suggestions made and, using the resource collection, agree upon an animal they wish to 'adopt' (groups should choose different animals). Details of the animal, its plight, and of its current status (or lack of status) under CITES form the subject of a wall display exhibit researched and developed by each group. Groups also write to relevant parties — their local MP, their MEP, the Department of the Environment (Tollgate House, Houlton Street, Bristol BS2 9DJ), the EC Environment Commission (200 Rue de la Loi, 1049, Brussels, Belgium), local and national newspapers — making the case for either the promotion of their chosen animal from Appendix II to Appendix I of the Convention or its inclusion under CITES. They comment upon any loopholes in CITES that concern them, offering any suggestions as to how to improve its effective operation, and, if appropriate, also write letters of concern to the embassies and/or leaders of countries that appear not to be affording proper protection to their 'adopted' animal. A section of the wall display is given over to a bulletin board of letters sent, replies received and newspaper cuttings resulting from the students' projects. The display can also be posted in the school entrance hall, community and shopping centres.

Potential

An action-oriented project that will both familiarise students with the trade in endangered species and international efforts to curtail that trade and give valuable practice in exercising their rights and responsibilities as citizens and in using the channels of influence open to all citizens within a democratic society. As such, it will help realise goals that are central to the cross-curricular themes of environmental education and education for citizenship.

Organisations Campaigning Against the International Trade in Animals

● Environmental Investigation Agency (EIA), 208-209 Upper Street, Islington, London NI IRL.

● International Primate Protection League, 116 Judd Street, London WCIH 9NS.

● Reptile Protection Trust, College Gates, 2 Deansway, Worcester WR1 2JD.

● Traffic International, 219 Huntingdon Road, Cambridge CB3 0DL

● World Society for the Protection of Animals (WSPA), Park Place, 10 Lawn Lane, London SW8 IUD.

● World Wide Fund for Nature (WWF), Panda House, Weyside Park, Catteshall Lane, Godalming, Surrey, GU7 1XR.

■ *ELEPHANT BAN ROLE PLAY*

Suitable for

Secondary

Time needed

40 minutes

Resources

Elephant Ban article for each group; sugar paper, paste stick, felt tip pens, approximately 10 small (1/4 A4) sheets of paper per group.

Procedure

Students form groups of five and are given a photocopy of the *Elephant Ban* article which they paste in the centre of the sheet of sugar paper. After reading and discussing the article, the group brainstorms actual and possible people who might have an interest, or be involved in the issue. Under each person identified notes should be made on how the person is involved, how they are affected by the ban and what their feelings and opinions might be. After notes have been completed, each student takes the role of at least one person and on the small sheet of paper writes out a more detailed role card. A few minutes can be spent before the role play actually begins for each person to think about their character and get into role. The role play is alowed to work itself through to a natural conclusion, or until the arguments have been exhausted.

CONSERVATION

Elephant ban

Zimbabwe says ivory trading should go on

On the face of it, the international ban on trade in ivory that came into effect in January is the best way to protect the elephant, which in parts of Africa is threatened with extinction. But five Southern African countries, led by Zimbabwe, oppose the ban, saying that they have more elephants than their environment can sustain. The argument raises basic questions about the relationship between people and wildlife.

Zimbabwe stands to lose some six million dollars a year from the closure of traditional ivory markets: at least 30 per cent of the 800 people employed in the industry face the immediate loss of their livelihood.

Rowan Martin, of the Department of Parks and Wildlife Management, believes that Zimbabwe has a successful wildlife conservation strategy. 'Unless natural resources have a very high value placed on them they tend to be displaced by other developments in the country,' he says. 'We've been very successful so far in extending that philosophy into all the rural areas of Zimbabwe, and our wildlife is continually increasing.'

Put simply, if wildlife has the same value for peasant farmers as their domestic livestock, they will look after it. When asked by a Western journalist if she had any qualms about wearing an ivory necklace, Zimbabwe's outspoken Minister of Tourism and Natural Resources, Victoria Chitepo, retorted: 'Do you have qualms about wearing shoes?'

Compared with East African countries, where animals have been fenced off and poached indiscriminately, Zimbabwe has 61,000 head of elephant — about twice the country's ideal carrying capacity. Now, with the ivory ban reducing the value of elephants, conservationists fear that more — not fewer — elephants are going to be killed. According to Rowan Martin, 'people are simply not prepared to have elephants on their property when it is a large, valueless animal that eats their crop.'

Martin says wildlife should not be considered an international resource. 'It belongs to the people who pay the cost of its upkeep, in the country where it lives. We regard our wildlife in much the same way as our domestic livestock. And no one thinks of cows and sheep as belonging to the world at large.'

Either way, the future of the African elephant in the wild is now in doubt.

Colleen Lowe Morna/Panos

— *New Internationalist*, April 1990[26]

P

Potential

Reporting back from each group could focus on the differing viewpoints expressed by people in role: what were the main issues; how did interests conflict; how did people feel at various points; were any conclusions reached? Should endangered species located in particular countries or regions be considered an international resource? Should wildlife be considered 'in much the same way as domestic livestock'? What issues of human rights are raised? What issues of animal rights are raised? This activity can usefully be followed by a showing and discussion of *The Elephant Harvest*, a 24-minutes VHS video available from Care for the Wild (see *Additional Resources*).

Source

Pamela Pointon, Homerton College, Cambridge and Graham Pike, International Institute for Global Education, University of Toronto.

ADDITIONAL RESOURCES

For the teacher ....

❑ Environmental Investigation Agency, *The trade in live wildlife*, 1990. A general review of the wild pet trade.

❑ Nelson, G., *The endangered species handbook*, Animal Welfare Institute (P.O. Box 3650, Washington DC 20007, U.S.A.), 1990. Covers the causes and consequences of endangerment and extinction, the trade in wild animals and international and national (US) regulations.

❑ Nichol, J., *The animal smugglers*, Christopher Helm, 1987. A discussion of the illegal trade in animals.

❑ Wenzel, G., *Animal rights, human rights. Ecology, economy and ideology in the Canadian Arctic*, University of Toronto Press, 1991. Essential background reading, setting out the cultural issues and conflicting perspectives on rights raised by the anti-sealing campaign.

For the classroom ....

❑ Aboriginal Trappers Federation of Canada, P.O. Box 579, Cornwall, Ontario, K6H 5T3, Canada (tel: 613-575-2377) and Indigenous Survival International, 55 Murray St., Third Floor, Ottawa, Ontario, KlN 5M3, Canada (tel: 613-562-3230) offer a pro-fur native North American perspective. Literature available.

❑ Animal Alliance of Canada (1640 Bayview Avenue, Suite 1916, Toronto, Ontario N4G 4E9, Canada) and International Wildlife Coalition (P.O. Box 461, Port Credit, Post Station, Mississauga, Ontario, L56 4M1, Canada) provide materials with an anti-fur perspective.

❑ *Animal talk*, Toronto Humane Society (11 River Street, Toronto, Ontario, M5A 4C2, Canada). Series of fact sheets on trapping devices, trapping and the environment, Canadian legislation on trapping and fur ranching.

❑ *BBC Wildlife*, monthly, regularly carries articles and updates on the working of CITES, as does *Animals International*, the quarterly journal of the World Society for the Protection of Animals.

- *Cry from the wild*, 15 mins., VHS video, World Society for the Protection of Animals. Examines the fur trade. Copy also available from Advocates for Animals (Scotland).

- *Dressed to kill?*, Beauty Without Cruelty Charity, 1992. An A3 poster for the classroom outlining the cruelties inflicted on more than 70 animals for fashion and beauty. Beauty without Cruelty Charity also has factsheets on the fur trade.

- *Fur. The bloody choice*, 10 mins., VHS video, 1993. Respect for Animals. Undercover footage of fur factories and traplines. Upper secondary use only. Respect will also forward pamphlets and information for classroom use.

- *Key facts about furs*, International Fur Trade Federation, Ecology Section (36 Vejlesoevej, DK 2840 Holte, Denmark), 1989. Pro-fur booklet, using question and answer format, seeking to project fur industry as occupying a welfarist position on animal issues.

- *Natives and the fur industry. Separating fact from fiction.* Pamphlet available from the anti-fur Native/Animal Brotherhood, 106-90 Carden Street, Guelph, Ontario, Canada, NlH 3A3. Tel: 519-821-8554.

- *No fur. No value. No life. Fur facts.* Pamphlet, available in multiple copies, from the Fur Education Council, P.O. Box lEW, London WlA lEW.

- *Pelts. Politics of the fur trade*, 56 mins., National Film Board of Canada, 1989. Looks at the emotional public relations war between the pro- and anti-fur lobbies and the arguments used by both sides. Secondary.

- *People, animals and the environment*, Fur Institute of Canada (10 Lower Spadina Avenue, no. 302, Toronto, Ontario, Canada M5V 2Z1). Simulation game for grades 8 to 12 in which various groups (animal rights 'activists', animal welfare 'advocates', environmental conservationists, fur farmers, the fur industry and fur trappers) put their arguments and perspectives to a Board of Enquiry.

- *Rural vandals*, League Against Cruel Sports, 1983. Four-part VHS video presentation on hare coursing, mink, stag and fox hunting. Teachers' pack also available.

- *The elephant harvest*, 24 mins., VHS video, 1993. Available from Care for the Wild, 1, Ashfolds, Horsham Rd., Rusper, West Sussex, RH12 4QX. Reviews the effects of the CITES ban on ivory sales. Are elephant populations increasing dramatically and destroying the Southern African ecosystem?

- *The fur bearers. Commentary on the native trapper situation in North America*, Association for the Protection of Fur-Bearing Animals (2235 Commercial Drive, Vancouver, British Columbia, VSN 4B6, Canada), 1989. Offers facts and figures on the extent of indigenous trapping in North America. Concludes that the limited amount of trapping by native North Americans is being used as an emotional cover to protect the $800 million luxury fur industry.

- *With respect to.* Folder of sheets on topics such as fur-bearing animals, fur trade history, trappers, trapper education, trap research and fur farming available from Fur Institute of Canada (address above).

- *Key UK-based humane organisations to contact (see* Organisations *list): Animal Aid, Beauty Without Cruelty Charity, Born Free Foundation, Campaign for the Abolition of Angling, Hunt Saboteurs Association, International Fund for Animal Welfare, League Against Cruel Sports, Respect for Animals, Royal Society for the Prevention of Cruelty to Animals, World Society for the Protection of Animals (see, also, boxes, pp.208 and 223).*

- *Other organisations: British Field Sports Society, 59 Kennington Road, London SEl 7PZ (defends and promotes field sports seeing them as playing a key role in countryside conservation; information packs for schools and VHS videos on* Hunting, Coursing, Falconry *and* The Shooting Year *available on loan); The Countryside Foundation, 43/44 Berners Street, London WlP 3AA.*

References

1. Information taken from 'Hue end cry', *Education Guardian*, 15 January 1991, 1-2.

2. *Ibid.*, 2.

3. Information taken from League Against Cruel Sports' pamphlets on *Deer and Staghunting* and *Harehunting and coursing*.

4. League Against Cruel Sports, *Foxes and foxhunting*, pamphlet

5. 'Uncertain future for the hunters', *Education Guardian*, 15 January 1991, 2.

6. *Ibid.*

7. Cited in Woodcock, G., *A briefing on the fur trade and the aboriginal cultures*, Lynx reprint from *Skinned*, International Wildlife Coalition, 1989, 1-2.

8. Lavigne, D., 'Canada's leghold leg-pull', *BBC Wildlife*, vol. 7, no. 3, March 1989, 133.

9. See, for instance, *The fur bearers*, Association for the Protection of Fur-Bearing Animals, 1989.

10. Mckenna (Respect for Animals) to Selby, 24 August 1993.

11. Respect for Animals (P.O. Box 500, Nottingham, NGl 3AS) was launched in February 1993, two months after Lynx went into liquidation following a successful libel action brought against it by a mink farm. Respect has a broader mandate than anti-fur campaigning and is, thus, more than a revamped Lynx.

12. 'Is the ivory trade extinct?', *Animals International* (WSPA), vol. XI, no. 39, Winter 1991, 12.

13. McGreal, S., 'Profiting from primates', *BBC Wildlife*, vol. 9, no. 4, April 1991, 258-9

14. *Ibid.*, 259.

15. League Against Cruel Sports, *Foxes and foxhunting*, flyer.

16. Goodwin, S., 'Fox-hunting lobby gets rough ride from Labour', *The Independent*, 15.2.1992, 5.

17. Lynx, *Introductory newsletter*, 4.

18. This document, written by the author, seeks to reflect faithfully the viewpoint of the Fur Institute of Canada and the International Fur Trade Federation (for addresses, see pp.226). The two organisations jointly refused permission to include verbatim extracts from their publications in this chapter. 'We feel that your material misrepresents the fur issue and the question of animal use in general,' writes Alison Beal, Executive Director of Fur Institute of Canada, 'reflecting an urban ideology that in no way recognises the profound respect and understanding that people in rural and remote communites must have in order to survive.' (Beal to Claire Weeks, EarthKind UK, 11.11.94).

19. Lynx, *The steel jawed leg-hold trap. A summary of expert opinion*, 1988,

20. Lavigne, D., *op. cit.*, 133.

21. Cooper D., 'Animals and cultural traditions', *Outrage* (Animal Aid), no. 76, October/November 1991, 12.

22. *Respect*, vol. 1, no. 1, Summer 1993, 2.

23. Speart, J., 'War within', *Buzzworm*, Boulder, Colorado, vol. V, no. 4, July/August 1993, 36.

24. 'The bird business', *Animals International* (WSPA), vol. XI, no. 38, Autumn 1991, 7.

25. Hoath, R., 'The bad bazaar', *BBC Wildlife*, vol. 8, no. 12, December 1990, 808- 10.

26. *New Internationalist*, no.206, April 1990, 27.

Chapter 10

Wild Animals in Captivity

INTRODUCTION

Zoos are the product of an industrial and imperial age. For recently urbanised populations with money to spare and leisure time to fill, they offered a means of overcoming their detachment from nature. For citizens of empires bent upon expansion, they showcased the exotic spoils

The Panther

In the Jardin des Plantes, Paris

His vision, from the constantly passing bars,
has grown so weary that it cannot hold
anything else. It seems to him there are
a thousand bars; and behind the bars, no world.

As he paces in cramped circles, over and over,
the movement of his powerful soft strides
is like a ritual dance around a centre
in which a mighty will stands paralysed.

Only at times, the curtain of the pupils
lifts, quietly. An image enters in,
rushes down through the tensed, arrested muscles,
plunges into the heart and is gone.

— Rainer Maria Rilke[1]

---

of colonialism. It is no coincidence that the first public zoo should be opened in Regent's Park, London, in 1847 amidst the then largest urban conurbation in the world and at the heart of the world's largest, and still expanding, empire.

Photo: EarthKind

229

When London Zoo's deep financial crisis broke media surface in 1991, the long-standing debate between supporters and opponents of zoos was rejoined with renewed intensity. Central to the case put by the former are the claims that zoos perform an essential role in conserving endangered species and that they fulfil an important educational function.

Zoo supporters point to a number of significant success stories in saving threatened species from extinction. The Arabian oryx, found in the deserts of Jordan and Saudi Arabia, had become extinct in the wild (a victim of hunting) by 1972. In 1962 oryx had been taken to Phoenix Zoo, Arizona, which orchestrated a captive breeding programme involving a number of other zoos. In 1982 oryx were released back into the wild in Jordan. Père David's deer, a deer found in China, was close to extinction by 1920 but as a result of successful zoo breeding of animals brought to Europe by French missionary, Father David, breeding couples have now been returned to the wild in China. The Hawaiian Goose, living on the sides of extinct volcanoes on the Hawaiian islands, was hunted to near extinction. In 1950 geese were brought to Britain and bred. Some 200 birds were since successfully released in the wilds of the Hawaiian island, Maui.[2]

Supporters also argue that zoos are educational; that millions of children visit them each year and enjoy a first-hand encounter with animals from around the world. A number of zoos, they point out, also have effective, professionally-staffed, education departments that enrich the young visitor's experience through film, lectures and resource packs. They, thus, play a significant part in promoting a concern for conservation amongst tomorrow's adults.

The conservation credentials of zoos are disputed by many environmentalists. Accepting that zoos have saved certain species from extinction, their work is seen as a drop in the ocean given the scale of the

A "GOOD DAY OUT" AT THE ZOO?

Photo taken from European Survey of Zoos

task. The 1986 list of endangered animal species totalled some 2,422 animals. The cost of saving the Arabian oryx was £25 million.[3] In no way, opponents argue, could that level of expenditure be maintained for each endangered animal. Expensive captive breeding programmes for a few species, critics continue, also siphon away money from where it should be spent, i.e. on protecting the habitats where endangered species live. 'With a global zoo 'budget' of around $500 million,' writes Will Travers, Director of Zoo Check, 'the question cannot be avoided. What could that sort of money do for the conservation of natural habitat, the conservation of plants and animals in that habitat and the support of local people who have, at the moment, no alternative but to exploit the environment to survive from day to day.'[4] In short, if the energy and money available are not spent on environmental protection, will there be a 'wild' to return animals to?[5] The conservation case for zoos is also undermined, in the eyes of their opponents, by the limited place endangered animals have in the array of species contained in zoo collections. Zoos world-wide contain nearly 3,000 species of which only 66 are part of endangered species' breeding programmes.[6]

A range of other disadvantages of zoo-based conservation are also highlighted by critics. In the first place, they question whether zoos, individually or collectively, have a sufficient pool of genetic diversity to prevent inbreeding. Second, they argue that zoo animals are not usually allowed to choose a mate but have one chosen for them by their human keepers, a process of 'unnatural' rather than 'natural' selection. Third, given that the animals which survive in captivity are the ones that can most easily adapt to the captive state, there are fears that zoos are breeding 'zoo animals different in many subtle ways from the wild counterpart'. Fourth, they point out that, when a species becomes extinct in an area, relationships within the ecosystem adapt to fill the vacated niche. The return of animals causes upheaval in the new balance thus created. Fifth, they point to evidence that reintroductions bring new diseases that can have a catastrophic effect on ethnic animal populations. The primate population of South America was only saved from a potentially deadly blood virus when golden lion tamarins bred at the US National Zoo and bound for Brazil were discovered to be carrying the virus. A suspected immuno-suppressant virus in pet tortoises released in California in the 1980s wiped out several populations of wild desert tortoises.[7] Sixth, they draw upon the experience of captive breeding programmes which tends to suggest that some animals do not reproduce well in captivity. The African elephant is often cited in this respect. Seventh, critics believe there to be a

fundamental difficulty in properly balancing the breeding and educational/entertainment aspects of a zoo's operation. 'Display and conservation,' says Travers, 'rarely go hand in hand.'[8]

The educational case for zoos is also roundly contested. Whilst opponents acknowledge that zoos were an understandable phenomenon in the days before modern communication systems, the experience of seeing caged live animals behaving in neurotic and abnormal ways as a result of the impoverished circumstances of their captivity and totally out of natural context is, they contend, hardly educational and certainly not a relevant education for the 1990s. 'Where's the pleasure,' asks Jonathon Porritt, 'in gawping at pale shadow-animals behind bars when you can thrill to the real things in its natural environmenta —albeit on the box?'[9] The promotion of a conservation ethic involves exposing people to the wonders of the natural world and helping them understand an animal's close and interdependent relationship with the fauna and flora and inorganic features of its habitat. This film and television can do in very vivid ways but zoos, as we have so far experienced them, cannot. Zoo educators could do their work as well, if not better, without imprisoned animals.

At the heart of the debate is the question of whether or not it is cruel to keep wild animals locked up. Zoo opponents compare the natural behaviours, range and habitat of animals with those of their captive counterparts and conclude that it would be virtually impossible to create zoos able to provide animals with the rich and diverse life they experience in nature. Zoo supporters, whilst acknowledging the mistakes of the past and admitting that conditions in many zoos around the world are indeed miserable, maintain that the better zoos have made significant advances in recent times in terms of providing animals with more challenging lives, more spacious and interesting environments and a more varied diet (*document 3*).[10] Safari parks, too, have allowed big animals to roam large areas and, thus, live a life approximating more closely to what they would experience in nature. Supporters also point out that any forced closure of zoos would be disastrous for their animal populations. As the National Federation of Zoos puts it: 'It does not take much imagination to realise that the closure of zoos would mean the deliberate destruction of wildlife on a scale never witnessed before.'[11] The scenario zoo supporters paint, of hundreds of thousands of animals having to be slaughtered in the wake of the closure of 'bad' zoos, is dismissed by the anti-zoo lobby as scare tactics. 'Winding down a zoo,' suggests Travers, 'is like closing a factory. Shut it tomorrow and there is immediate misery. But do it over two or three years and you can relocate some of the animals and natural wastage, if you stop breeding, will take care of much of the rest.'[12]

In the face of the identity crisis triggered by increasingly insistent calls for change, and the financial crisis caused by falling attendances, zoos have begun to rethink their role and direction. The Stanley Park Zoo in Vancouver, British Columbia, is changing both its name and its nature. To be renamed something like the 'Stanley Park Wildlife Biology Centre', it will 'switch its collections, dropping 'exotics' (non-native animals such as penguins and kangaroos) and specialising instead in the wildlife of British Columbia. While the reformed institution will continue to have exhibits, it will also treat sick or injured animals and hold creatures awaiting relocation back to the wild. 'We'll be both an animal hospital and an animal hostel'.[13] Critics of zoos will be watching closely to see whether the changes in train at a number of major zoos (including London) and the many current proposals for 'bioparks', 'theme parks', 'wildlife conservation parks' and 'conservation centres' turn out to offer substantive or merely cosmetic change.

The most exciting and innovative alternative to the traditional zoo so far put forward is that proposed by the Born Free Foundation. In December 1991 plans for projected WorldLife Centres were made public. Described in the promotional literature as a 'TechnEcoZoo' and 'the 21st Century's non-animal answer to the traditional zoo', WorldLife Centres will use state of the art communications and information technologies to provide visitors with a 'voyage of discovery through the natural world'. The focus will be on ecology, wildlife in the wild and conservation.'[14] 'Satellites will provide live links to the Amazon rainforests and the African plains, with computers offering schools the chance to tap into the centre's vast resources. Using technology including Virtual Reality ... visitors will be able to swap identities to find out what life is like as a lion, spider or lizard.'[15] (See *document 5*). It will be interesting to monitor the impact that the WorldLife Centre concept will have on the direction traditional zoos take in the next few years.

If zoos undergo a radical transformation so, it seems likely, will circuses. The traditional travelling circus, with its performing animals, has been condemned from many quarters as cruel and as having no place 'in an age characterised by more profound ecological awareness'. [16] Although circus owners deny that the animals in their care are treated cruelly, there appears to be an overwhelming case to answer. The routine of a travelling circus means that animals spend most of their time confined in 'beast wagons' of woefully inadequate dimensions, and often shackled. Their lives are characterised by monotony, lack of exercise and stimulus, and social deprivation. A recent (largely favourable) report on British circuses revealed that 'lions and tigers are confined to their beast wagons for 90 per cent of the time, each animal occupying a space of between 0.17 and 0.45 cubic metres; that elephants are shackled for 60 per cent of the time and are

Are the needs of this polar bear being met? (Photo: EarthKind)

only able to lie down with difficulty'.[17] For these reasons, 'circus animals often display distorted and unnatural behaviour; increased aggression, abnormal parental care, depression, apathy, self-mutilation and such stereotypical movements as weaving the head, rocking from side to side, biting the bars and pacing — classic signs of stress and deprivation.'[18] Bears, the pro-circus report mentioned above points out, spend more than a third of their time in such abnormal activity.[19] Training methods, whilst not universally cruel, as some opponents would suggest, necessarily involve a 'carrot and stick' approach in which soft words and tasty tit-bits of foods are combined with use of the whip, jabs to the body and other kinds of force to make the animal react to the trainer's signal and so perform unnatural acts on cue.[20] Pro-circus interests claim that animals enjoy performance. This claim, opponents argue, may contain some truth but any brief sense

of freedom experienced in the ring has to be set against a backdrop of an otherwise drab and uneventful existence. It also has to squared with evidence of animal resistance to performance. 40% of big cats, the report reveals, have to be forced into the ring 'by poking a broom handle into their wagon'. 'Animals that persistently show a dislike of entering the ring and do not act up to the audience applause, or cannot get used to the performance with the noise, lights etc., are culled.'[21]

Circus apologists make much of their (direct) educational and (indirect) conservation value. Circuses, the argument goes, give people a direct and dazzling experience of the beauty and intelligence of animals. They, thus, promote knowledge and appreciation of animal species and, by extension, a concern for their conservation in the wild. Such claims are refuted by circus opponents on a number of counts. It is miseducational, they argue, to see wild animals performing unnatural and undignified feats in an artificial environment. Second, the 'hidden agenda' of the circus performance is a message of human dominance over the animal world (the animal bending to the will of the trainer) and of animals having more value and deserving more consideration if they are able to perform sensational tricks that titillate and entertain. Such messages, it is insisted, are entirely inconsistent with an environmental ethic (see *document 6*). 'I find circuses deeply offensive,' declares Desmond Morris. 'We are just beginning to recognise animals as important in their own right. Circuses throw us back to the Middle Ages.'[22] 'In ten years,' predicts Canadian environmentalist, David Suzuki, 'people will look back at what we did with exotic animals in circuses with astonishment and revulsion... The use of animals in circuses and entertainment is an anachronistic practice that is no longer acceptable in a time of heightened concern about the

■ *continued on page 237*

DOCUMENTS

1. Today we know a great deal about the species that remain on earth, about their environmental needs, the food they naturally eat and what their social and spatial requirements are. Studies in the wild have led to documentary film which has opened a window on to the private lives of the spectacular and the not-so-spectacular life-forms around us. But unfortunately, zoos have failed to keep pace with this increase in knowledge.

Few humans have been to the Arctic and seen the Polar bear ranging over the vast icy wastes, digging snow caves in which to rear its cubs, stealthily hunting seals, swimming miles from ice-floe to ice-floe — yet, from television, we know that this is how it lives. Not on a few square metres of blue-rinsed concrete with a pond for a dip and an endless vision of sky and cement adorned by the heads of bored and listless humans trying to incorporate what they see with what they know to be true. Only a handful of people have been to the rain-drenched forests of Borneo to see 'The Old Man of The Forest', the Orang-utan, climbing slowly from tree to tree, searching for the tastiest shoots and fruit or resting in a small pool of sunlight that has broken through the thick canopy and reached the forest floor. Yet we now know enough to reject as unacceptable the iron bars, token ropes and plate glass that is so often this great ape's 'home' in the zoo.

— Will Travers[27]

2. In our increasingly urban environments we are becoming a more domestic species more detached from nature. Until recent times most people lived in direct and daily contact with the natural world. They understood that if you changed one thing it affected another. They learned and did not forget the limits of nature. They knew that everything is hitched to everything else.

We have lost that knowledge. Only the specialists comprehend the ecosystems that support our lifestyles, and at what price. We destroy forests on the hillsides not knowing that it causes the water table in the valleys to collapse. We pour away toxic wastes, not comprehending that they don't disappear when they go underground. We exterminate plants and animals we didn't even name, not realising what medicinal or food values they might have had.

If our zoos as places of natural history education, had been promoting knowledge of such things, would the widespread and casual destruction of nature be taking place? Would we have built factories over our most fertile valleys, turned the rivers into sewers, squandered the wetlands for shopping malls, wiped out or endangered hundreds of life forms?

Zoos may be one of the best vehicles we have for the conservation of nature. Millions of people visit them every year — more in fact than attend all professional sports activities combined. There is a vitally important need for institutions that can influence audiences on such a scale. It is urgent that we all develop a much better understanding of wildlife and a holistic view of nature.

But zoos in their present form cannot achieve this. The concept is outdated, not sufficient for the day. The public zoo is essentially a 19th century concept. The emergence of a middle class, the novelty of leisure time for family entertainment, a new belief in things edifying, the exploration of undiscovered wild places, the emergence of strange and unknown animals — all this combined to make London Zoo, which was the first such public facility to open, 165 years ago, a place of enormous popularity. The concept has remained virtually unchanged since.

The new demands on zoos mean that a great broadening of their scope is needed. They must find ways to demonstrate the connections and interdependence between all components of nature; they must create exhibits that explain the relationships between soils and flowers and frogs and snails and trees and elephants. And evolution. And extinction.

— David Hancocks,
© The Guardian[28]

3. Many of the most successful enrichment projects are aimed at providing food in a more interesting and challenging way. In the wild, chimpanzees use sticks to 'fish' termites out of termite mounds. Several zoos now provide artificial termite mounds which enable chimpanzees to use the same principle to obtain food. Studies at Edinburgh Zoo and London Zoo show that these enrichment devices are used by chimpanzees for quite long periods of time and significantly increase activity and time spent feeding. The fact that 'termite mounds' are used when other food is freely available and that they are prepared to eat foods not normally liked when presented in this way suggests that chimpanzees value the opportunity to engage in this activity. Orang-utans and gorillas will also use these 'termite mounds'.

At London Zoo we have successfully used simple, passive, live cricket and meal worm dispensers to enrich the environment of small carnivores. Observations show that these simple forms of enrichment can effectively increase activity and foraging behaviour at the expense of abnormal behaviours such as stereotypic pacing.

Sound is also part of the environment for most wild animals and can be used to enrich the environment for captive animals. At London Zoo a pair of gibbons are now able to hear the song of a neighbouring pair of gibbons (from a hidden loud-speaker on a time switch) as they would in the wild. They respond with spectacular brachiation and usually with a song of their own. Many other possibilities exist for enrichment using sound.

All these examples have one thing in common: they make the animals' environment more interesting in a way that allows them to interact with it, using behaviours evolved in their natural environment.

At the end of the day zoo animals are being kept captive in an artificial environment. However it is possible in many cases, using the techniques and philosophy of environmental enrichment, to provide a compromise environment that is satisfactory for the animal, the viewing public and the zoo's point of view.

— David Shepherdson[29]

4. Zoos — are they justified?

The adult male gorilla sits in the corner of a small, glass-fronted room and stares into space. One hand rests on a tyre hanging from the low ceiling, the other flicks at pieces of cardboard scattered across the bare floor.

Some people come laughing and joking into the ape house. 'Corr! Look at this one — big, isn't he?' 'Must be King Kong.' 'Look at him just sitting there, lazy old thing.' 'He's looking at you. Bet he'd like you for his dinner!' They move on to the chimps and tap on the glass.

One of the main justifications for zoos is meant to be the valuable contribution they make towards education. Zoos often claim that people need to see animals 'in the flesh' before taking an interest in their natural lives and the need to conserve them. But as the above typical situation shows, there are two ways in which the most traditional zoos are failing to carry out their claims about education.

The first way is to do with education in its narrowest sense:

... What does a zoo teach you about wild animals?
... What do you learn as you wander from cage to cage?

That gorillas live alone in small rooms and flick cardboard? Or that polar bears live in concrete pits and sway from side to side all day?
... Gorillas are very sociable, peaceful animals, living in well-ordered groups consisting of an adult male plus several females and their offspring. They live in the dense forests of Africa and feed on a variety of vegetation. They spend much of the time playing and grooming each other and have a complex system of communication — involving sounds, facial expressions and body language... Polar bears are often solitary, wandering across the ice and snow of the Arctic, feeding on seals, fish and birds. Bears are extremely inquisitive, intelligent animals.

The second way zoos are failing to live up to their claims about education lies in the broader sense of our *attitudes* towards wild animals:
... For many people zoos have always been here so they are the expected and accepted method of keeping exotic animals in captivity.
...Those people laughing at the gorilla have gone to the zoo for a good time, a day out. They keep cats and dogs and hate the thought of cruelty to animals. Indeed, every morning on her way to work one of the women in the group used to pass a garden where a dog was shut up in a small crate. It barked and barked. She found this situation totally unacceptable and reported it to the RSPCA. But she happily goes to the zoo and accepts conditions which are just as bad as those of the dog.

— Tess Lemmon[30]

5.

THE FANTASTIC JOURNEY
Beyond the 21st Century

"The bridge passes through a mysterious place, the air is heavy with sulphurous smells. Beneath a primeval soup bubbles and burns... there is no colour, hardly any light.... We are at the beginning of the world, crossing from the present to the early dawn of the planet."

John Sunderland, Designer of the WorldLife Centre, takes us on a conceptual journey around the centre

Our voyage begins in a large atrium leading to the **WorldLive News Earth Station** Using touchscreen graphics on the console, we can select areas on the enormous revolving globe which dominates the scene. Local, regional, national, international and global issues are all brought into focus in the 'eye' of the WorldLife Centre.

In the **Archive Vault - a Time Safari from Sunbeam to Satellite** - 'Jules Verne' Safari vehicles take us through the development of life, from emergent forms, to the earliest flora and fauna, following time and the evolution of **Worldlife**. We pass through genetic graveyards, a reminder that extinction is forever; while overhead displays count down the species believed to be on the brink of extinction.

Return to the Present We encounter the **Tree of Life**. The physical expression of current lifeforms, an electronic network of life with man clinging precariously to the uppermost branches; the pinnacle of creation - but for how long? We 'climb' its spreading limbs and sub-branches, reaching out to touch its electro-sensitive leaves, gathering information about the natural world. Three-dimensional representations of WorldLife forms live in the tree. With the help of our personal WorldLife Guide we are encouraged to find out more about each lifeform by keying in our personal visitor number.

In The Shadow of Man The Tree of Life is our first meeting with Man. In this 'human zoo' we can look at ourselves as we would other forms of life and examine our relationship with fellow animals. A Treetops hide becomes a special theatre. As we watch Man and the animals drinking at the waterhole beneath us, we explore our age-old relationship with wildlife.

State-of-the-art technology takes us deep into the natural world. **The Sensorium** lets us experience 'lifesense' through the bodies of other creatures. We explore the macro-environments of Arctic, tundra, temperate, sub-tropical, tropical and desert, exchanging places with a hawk, a gorilla, a bat,   a bee.......or a dolphin.

"Gathering speed, you manage to catch the swell and the sudden surge of water sends you rushing forward. Rising above the surface you open your lungs to the fresh air before re-entering the water to be caught up once again in the rush and exitement of bow-riding. Then, from the corner of your eye you suddenly glimpse a fearful shape - a shark. Playtime is over. You must defend your pod. You signal to the other dolphins "Danger". Time is running out, the shark moves closer. Turning swiftly you manage to avoid his attack, spinning round to face him you sum up all your strength to ram him in his side. He darts for cover. The danger has passed. You and your pod are safe"

Out of breath you step back - you have just experienced the Sensorium's Virtual Reality.

From the **Sensorium** we explore **Uncharted Worlds** using large scale environmental simulators and interactive computer modelling games to present possible future scenarios...... We are the decision makers, we control the rules and the results. The earth is our responsibility.

The **'World Live But Not Living'** uses satellite links to present up-to-the minute reports from around the globe.

The **Cutting Edge** combines the natural world with the world of big business. As products and production techniques increasingly take account of their environmental impact, the **Cutting Edge** offers a unique opportunity to showcase developments which will help us live a more sustainable, caring lifestyle.

Fantastic Classroom: the **WorldLife Centre** is an ear to the natural world, a place where we can tune in to the the planet's heartbeat and the individual pulses of a million different species. By using technology the Centre reaches out to people everywhere, 'talking' to schools, colleges and universities, factories and offices, even individuals in their homes. Through **WorldLife**, the world becomes a Fantastic Classroom to stimulate our wildest dreams".

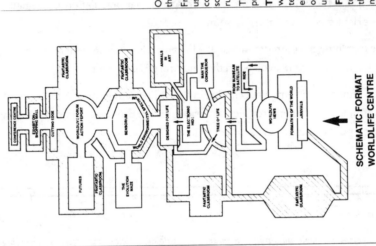

**SCHEMATIC FORMAT
WORLDLIFE CENTRE**

6. There is no educational value in watching animals performing totally unnatural tricks in an artificial environment. Even those manoeuvres that do represent extensions of natural behaviour are performed not for reasons of survival, but to show how ingenious and dominant the animal trainer is.

Circuses have never performed any useful conservation role. Historically, quite the contrary is true. Until fairly recently, circuses plundered wild populations in order to supplement their menageries. Now, at a time when excellent wildlife programmes on television are of inestimable value in presenting an educational and balanced view, the circus, by contrast, conveys the impression that animals are worthy of interest only insofar as they are capable of performing unnatural but amusing tricks — and the more unnatural the better. The circus strips animals of all dignity, respect and natural beauty, presenting them as freaks.

This distorted view of wildlife and its value is damaging to the whole philosophy of conservation, which holds that the health of the planet and, indeed, the long-term prospects for humanity, rely critically on our appreciation and maintenance of the delicate balance and diversity of the natural world. Crucial to this view is a respect for the value of wild animals in their natural habitats. As teachers, we have a responsibility not only to promote such a global perspective, but also to foster and encourage an animal welfare ethic which recognises that the gratuitous exploitation and abuse of animals is morally unacceptable.

This attitude is difficult to justify when a child can visit a circus and witness the general acceptance of the degradation of animals in the name of entertainment.

— Raymond Ings[32]

■ *continued from page 233*

natural world we share with all other life.'[23] At their 1981 conference, the National Association of Headteachers recommended that 'children should be discouraged from attending any exhibition or performance which involved animals in undignified displays or where they were housed in unsatisfactory conditions'.[24]

The circus equivalent of the WorldLife centre would be the animal-free 'Big Top'. The signs are of a growing public preference for the all-human circus. A unit of the Moscow State Circus enjoyed enormous success when it visited Britain in 1985 without animals whilst the animal-free Cirque du Soleil of Canada grew from an operating budget of $1.45 million in 1984 to a 1991 budget of $22 million.[25] 'New Circus,' writes Reg Bolton, 'tends to leave animals in peace and concentrate on the human endeavours of clowning and physical skills... All the traditional acts are there — acrobatics, wire-walking, juggling, trick cycling, trapeze, stilts and other displays of strength, balance and co-ordination... So circus is not dying, circus is alive and changing.'[26]

ACTIVITIES

■ *ANIMAL HOMES*

Suitable for

Primary

Time needed

1. 15-20 minutes

2. 30-50 minutes

Resources

1. Pictures of a range of habitats with which the class is familiar (the collection should include a picture of a zoo); pictures and/or models of a selection of wild animals that students can easily identify and which can be matched with the pictured habitats.

2. As above, plus a selection of materials with which students can make models of natural habitats, e.g. grass, fallen leaves, sand, soil, stones, twigs, water.

Procedure

1. The class is divided into groups of three or four. The habitat pictures are pinned up on the wall over empty tables. Each group is given a selection of pictures and/or models of wild animals. As a group, they must identify each animal's natural home and place the picture/model on the appropriate table. A class review of decisions follows. None of the animals should have been matched with the zoo picture. If any have,

then discussion and, if necessary, research should take place to identify its natural home. The animal is reassigned. Discussion around the following questions can then take place:

- ❑ If the zoo isn't a natural home for wild animals, why are they to be found in zoos?
- ❑ Are the reasons good reasons?
- ❑ What can be done to make zoo animals' captive homes more like their natural homes?

During discussion of the last question, the teacher can make a list of suggestions for making zoo environments more natural. Each student then draws a picture of an improved zoo environment for a chosen animal accompanied by an explanation of how the improvement helps the zoo facility approximate more closely to the animal's natural habitat.

2. Following the listing of suggestions, students go on to make a model of an improved zoo environment.

Potential

An activity that will widen and/or reinforce student's knowledge of wild animals' natural environments and confirm that, although zoos are no animal's real habitat, efforts can be made to make captive environments more natural and more humane. The class can assess the extent to which the drawn or modelled zoo facilities mirror each animal's natural habitat and the degree to which they still fall short of doing so. At some point in the discussion, the question of whether even improved zoos are necessary should be addressed.

Source

Adapted by Jackie Harvey from an activity in *People and animals. A humane education curriculum guide*, Washington, National Association for the Advancement of Humane Education,1981.

■ *AT ARMS' LENGTH?*

Suitable for
Primary/secondary

Time needed
1. 15 minutes
2. 10 minutes

Resources
1. White cards, identifying the topic of discussion, for half the class; coloured cards, giving the topic and stating a distance at which they are to stand from each discussion partner (e.g. 10cm, 20cm, 30cm, 40cm, at arms' length), for the other half of the class. There should be more coloured cards for the shorter distances. A pin per student. Slides

Sample white card and below sample coloured card

Discussion Topic: How I feel about keeping animals in zoos.

Instructions: 1. Each time the teacher asks you to pick a discussion partner, choose somebody with a red card.

2. Do not show or tell anybody what is written on this card.

Discussion Topic: How I feel about keeping animals in zoos.

Instructions: 1. Each time the teacher asks you to pick a discussion partner, choose somebody with a white card.

2. Face each partner and try to stand no more than 10 centimetres away from her/him; if s/he moves away, gently move up close again. Never draw attention to, or discuss, the fact that you are doing this. Never touch your partner.

3. Do not show or tell anybody what is written on this card.

---

or pictures of animals in overcrowded conditions (battery farms, broiler houses, at market, in farm lorries, in zoos) can usefully be shown during the debriefing.

2. A slide projector and screen; a school hall or gymnasium; a set of animal slides. A typical slide set might include pictures of a bear, a deer, an alsation off its lead, a rabbit, a venomous snake, a cheetah, a cow, a bull, a baby bear, a lion, a sheep, a kangaroo, an owl, a lion cub, an alsation on its lead, a baby owl, a poodle, a ram, a scorpion. For the debriefing session, slides or film footage of animals in zoos or safari parks would be useful

Procedure

1. Students are asked to choose a card and to read it carefully without revealing its contents to anybody else. They then pin their card on their chests back to front. The teacher explains that they are going to have the opportunity to discuss the chosen topic with a number of class members (the topic should be something like 'battery farms' or 'broiler houses' or 'zoos', involving animals being kept together in a confined space) Students then find a first discussion partner with whom they discuss the topic for the allotted two minutes. On a signal from the teacher, they move on to another partner. The teacher should allow up to six exchanges. Discussion follows.

> *An excellent PSE activity. Reference to tower blocks, crowded supermarkets and buses are inevitable, as are the classic rat studies with aberrant behaviour increasing with increased proximity. This should get discussion going even in the least discussion-oriented class!*
>
> — Kent secondary teacher

2. Students repair to the school hall. They watch slides of a range of animals projected on a screen set at one end of the hall. After each slide they walk the distance from the screen at which they would feel themselves comfortably far enough away from the animal in question (i.e. at less than that distance they would want bars, a screen or a car body between them and the animal). Discussion follows.

> *A couple of lions in a zoo have a less stressful life than three prides competing for territory in a safari park. Also, animals like tigers are solitary creatures, so placing ten in a park will cause problems.*
> — Bill Travers, Zoo Check

Potential

A sequence of activities that introduces students to the related concepts of *personal space*, i.e. the (partly territorial) desire not to have others of one's own kind encroach too close, and *flight distance*, i.e. the distance at which an animal feels comfortable and safe from another animal.

1. Class debriefing can begin with a sharing of the different viewpoints encountered in pair discussions. These can be listed on the board or overhead projector transparency in *pro* and *con* columns. At some stage it is likely that the question of peoples' behaviour during the activity will be raised, at which point the teacher can encourage individuals to report on their experiences. Did students with white cards feel uncomfortable with any of the partners they met? What feelings did they experience? What response did they make to having someone so close? Did the gender of the partner matter? Did some students with white cards feel comfortable with a partner? Why? How did the students with coloured cards feel about the behaviour they were instructed to adopt? At an appropriate point, the concept of *personal space* should be introduced. This can be related to student's individual experiences and to various contexts in which human beings experience overcrowding. Slides/pictures of animals in overcrowded conditions can be shown and students' views elicited.

2. In the debriefing, students can be asked to identify the various factors which determined their calculations as to how far to move away from the screen (these may well include 'uncertainty' if the animal is not known to them). They should also be asked to identify those animals likely to take flight before they do and to suggest at what distance that would occur. At an appropriate moment, it is explained that all animals have a biological *flight distance* and that, if forced to live too close to other animals, can suffer anxiety and stress. Finally, slides or film of animals in zoos and safari parks are shown and students asked to comment on whether the animals' flight distance needs are being violated.

Extension

Students choose a wild animal and research its natural behaviour to see what they can learn about its personal space and flight distance needs and how it reacts when they are violated. They then relate their learning to conditions in which the animals in question are kept in zoos and safari parks. Are their personal space and flight distance needs respected? If not, and they are too close to each other, to other animals and/or to the public, what are the effects in psychological and behavioural terms?

Source

1. After an idea in *People and animals. A humane education curriculum guide, level d*, Washington, National Association for the Advancement of Humane Education, 1981, 133.

2. Phil Brooke.

■ *ZOO EVALUATION*

Suitable for

Primary/secondary

Time needed

Periods of time over a few weeks.

Resources

A list of animals in the collection of a nearby zoo; a set of reference books on wild animals; video footage of animals in the zoo collection living their natural lives; pens, paper.

Procedure

Working in pairs, students choose an animal from the zoo list and research its natural behaviour and habitat, e.g. the area over which it moves, its hunting, hoarding and feeding habits, whether it is gregarious or generally prefers to be solitary (and, if the latter, how much distance it prefers between itself and the next member of the species), its forms of play, where it prefers to sleep, the temperature, seasons, landscape and terrain it would normally encounter. They also watch video film on the chosen animal, if available. They then draw up an agreed checklist of optimum natural conditions for the animal.

The class visits the zoo in question and pairs write notes evaluating the exhibit in which their animal is housed using the checklist they have devised. They also evaluate the exhibit in terms of the degree to which it is of educational value, i.e. whether or not the artificial habitat and interpretive material available convey a realistic impression of the animal's natural home. Back in school pairs write up a report and present it to the class. Discussion follows each presentation. A report collating and summarising the class' findings is drawn up and a copy sent to the zoo for reaction.

Potential

An activity that is likely to raise important questions concerning the standard and type of accommodation offered by zoos. Is it sufficient for a zoo to satisfy an animal's *physical* needs or is it equally important that its *behavioural* needs are met? Is it physically and economically feasible to satisfy the latter? Can a zoo strike a humane balance between the animal's needs and the interests of the visiting public? Do safari parks achieve that balance? Are zoos (and safari parks) better at meeting the needs of some animals than others? The activity also gives students field experience and the opportunity to arrive at their own conclusions regarding the humaneness of the local zoo and to put those conclusions to the zoo authorities. As such, it is a valuable exercise in active citizenship education.

Extensions

1. A representative of the zoo is invited into class to speak to the class' report and respond to students' questions and concerns.

2. The same activity is undertaken with respect to 'exotic' pets owned by students and/or on sale at pet shops in the locality. The process of investigating the conditions in which captive animals live, and setting findings against a checklist of optimal conditions can, of course, also be undertaken with factory-farmed animals.

The pet shop variation I have tried with GCSE Modular Science (Small Mammals) classes. The investigation at the pet shop may be set as a homework activity after the formulation work is complete.

— Kent secondary teacher

■ *ZOO DIAMOND RANKING*

Suitable for

Primary/secondary

Time needed

15 minutes in pairs, 20 minutes in sixes.

Resources

Nine statements representing a spread of opinions on zoos for each pair of students (see *Fig. 1* for a set of statements for top primary/lower secondary students and *Fig. 2* for a set for upper secondary use). Each set of statements should be cut up and stored in an envelope.

Procedure

Pairs are given an envelope containing the nine statements and are asked to rank them in diamond formation, i.e.

<pre>
          1

      2   2

  4   4   4

      7   7

          9
</pre>

A fairly loose criterion for ranking is given such as 'convincing', 'important', or 'thought provoking', the teacher resisting any requests for her to be more specific about the criterion. The most 'convincing', 'important' or 'thought provoking' statement is placed at the top of the diamond. The next two are placed in second equal position. The three across the centre are fourth equal. The next two are seventh equal. The statement placed at the foot of the diamond is the one considered by the pair to be the least 'convincing', 'important', or 'thought provoking'. When pairs have completed their task, they form into sixes. Each pair explains and seeks to justify its ranking to the other two pairs. The six then try to negotiate a consensus ranking for the group as a whole. Plenary reporting back and discussion follows.

Potential

This activity offers a means of familiarising students with most of the principal arguments surrounding the value of zoos. It also helps them clarify their own thoughts and feelings about the subject whilst alerting them to the opinions and perspectives of their classmates. Underpinning the activity is the unspoken assumption that everybody has something relevant and useful to bring to the discussion. The imprecise criterion is itself likely to give rise to debate. What meaning did pairs and sixes invest in the terms 'convincing', 'important' and 'thought provoking'? Did it become necessary to try and pin down what it meant more precisely? Skills used in this activity include discussion, negotiation, accommodation to other perspectives, and consensus seeking. In the plenary debriefing, a group reporting their inability to agree upon a ranking order is as important a focus for discussion as a group reporting that they have achieved consensus.

Extensions

Working in groups, students design and/or model the zoo of the future. As part of their work, they seek the views of organisations listed under *Additional Resources,* p.247 and 249, and/or in the *Organisations* list, p399-404.

Source

David Spratt of Life Support wrote a draft set of statements for the primary/lower secondary version of this activity (*Fig. 1*). Diamond ranking is based on an idea in Richardson, E., Flood, M., and Fisher, S., *Debate and decision*, World Studies Project, 1980.

Fig. 1

Best Place Zoos are the best place to learn about wild animals because most people cannot afford to go and see them where they live.	**Second Best** Zoos are a form of entertainment. They are there to attract visitors and make money. The health and happiness of the animals comes second best to that.
Best Way Television programmes like *Blue Peter* are the best way of learning about wild animals. You can watch them roaming free in their proper surroundings.	**Happy and Safe** Zoos are good because they keep animals happy and safe from the dangers and diseases of life in the wild. Keepers work in zoos because they love animals.
Prisoners Animals in zoos are like people put in prison for life. They have no freedom and are very unhappy. They often go a bit crazy, pacing up and down all day and twisting their head in a circle over and over again.	**Old Age** Most zoo animals don't die of old age. Many die earlier than they would in the wild because their cages stop them living a natural life. Many are killed to cut down on animal numbers. Some are used in science experiments that lead to their death.
Endangered Animals Zoos are important because they save animals that are in danger of dying out. They breed them and, when they have bred enough, they let them go in the wild again.	**Where They Live** Zoos have saved some animals that were in danger of dying out by helping them breed. But it is an expensive business. It would be better to use the money to protect the places where the animals live so they are safe and secure.
Nowhere to Go If they closed the zoos, thousands of animals that could not survive in the wild would have to be killed as there would be nowhere for them to go.	

P

Fig. 2

The Real Thing	Deliberate Destruction
Wildlife programmes such as *Survival* and *Trials of Life* have made the zoo, as we know it, redundant. Where's the pleasure is gawping at caged animals that are pale shadows of their wild cousins when we can learn about, and thrill to, the real thing in its natural environment on the box?	If zoos were forced to close, it would be disastrous for world conservation and for the animals in the zoos. Most zoo animals have been bred in captivity and few could survive in the wild. Zoo closure would thus involve the deliberate killing and destruction of wildlife on a scale never witnessed before.
An Illusion	**Only Solution**
It's an illusion that animals stay in zoos until they die peacefully of ripe old age. Their life expectancy is greatly reduced. Many zoos cull (kill) surplus stock. Some of the culled animals are used in experiments. In 1989 over twenty, six-month old, wallabies at London Zoo had their heads cut off in experiments to find out why human beings become depressed in winter and why we get jet lag from air travel.	Zoos have saved some animals from extinction but their contribution is tiny compared with the overall problem of at least 1,000 threatened species. It cost about 25 million to save the Arabian oryx. Could such an amount be found for every species in danger? Zoos are not the answer. A better, cheaper and surer approach would be to provide protected areas within the animals' natural environment, especially as some animals such as the African elephant do not reproduce well in captivity.
No Substitute	**New Zoo**
Zoos have an important role in educating children about animals and conservation. Millions of children visit them each year and have a real life experience for which television is no substitute	We need a new kind of zoo for the twenty-first century building on present best practice. The traditional zoo with its emphasis on public entertainment should give way to the 'conservation centre' specialising in a limited range of animals suited to captivity, and housing the animals in the best possible conditions. The emphasis should be on high quality multi-media educational provision highlighting particular natural environments, conservation work and specific environmental problems.
Simply Wrong	**In Decline**
It is simply wrong to keep animals in confined surroundings which fail to offer the life they would enjoy in the wild. Their frustration often turns into mental disorder which shows itself in behaviour like constant grooming and pacing up and down. When children visit zoos where animals are behaving in abnormal and neurotic ways, they are being mis-educated.	Zoos are in decline. 3 million people a year visited London Zoo in the 1950s. In 1990 it was visited by just over 1 million. A more environmentally-aware and cruelty-conscious public are voting with their feet. Zoos, however they are reformed, will always be an unhappy compromise between the need to entertain (and, hence, make money) and the best interests of the animals.
Captive Breeding	
The best zoos have developed captive breeding programmes designed to help preserve endangered species. Animals are bred in captivity and then reintroduced into their natural habitat to replenish numbers. The Arabian oryx, hunted almost to extinction by 1960, was the subject of such a programme. In 1982 a herd of oryx were released back into the wild. Zoos have an essential role in conservation.	

P

■ *LIFE OF CONFINEMENT*

Suitable for

Primary/secondary

Time needed

25 minutes

Resources

Overhead projector transparency and pen.

Procedure

Students form groups of six and then divide into pairs. One partner in nominated 'A', the other 'B'. The activity begins with a few minutes' silence in which everybody is asked to imagine what life would be like if they were to be confined to their bedroom for an indefinite period. For the sake of the activity, they are to imagine that their bedroom is adequately equipped so that food, water and hygienic needs will always be met. They are asked to think of things that give their life its quality and whether their needs would be satisfied if confined for a long time in such a minimal space. 'A' students are then asked to describe their imagined life of confinement — its positive and negative aspects — to their partner. 'B' listens actively, contributing only encouraging words and prompting questions if need be. After five minutes, 'B' recounts her imagined life of confinement whilst 'A' listens. The group of six then re-forms. The students are asked to take on the description offered by their partner and, in turn, to retell it to the group using the first person. When groups have completed the task, the teacher asks the class to brainstorm the emotions that came to mind as they imagined life long-term in their bedroom. The words brainstormed are recorded on the overhead projector.

Potential

A potentially powerful activity that can help students better appreciate the psychological effects of confinement and empathise with captive animals. Following the brainstorming students can be shown a film on animal confinement in zoos such as *Serving Time*, Canadian Broadcasting Corporation, 45 minutes. Alternatively, the reading on the next page can be circulated as it stands or in rewritten and

The children found this a good and worthwhile exercise and presented some valuable insights and comments, including several about cruelty to pets when they were young.
— Hertfordshire primary teacher (10-11 year olds)

It went well especially during the stage of pairs interacting. In the larger groups I detected a 'falling off' as I think they may have felt they were repeating points too much. Brainstorming produced a good range of emotions (fear of claustrophobia, frustration, depression, anger and fits of anger, loneliness, boredom, outrage, violence, self-destruction/suicide, envy/jealously of others).
— West Yorkshire secondary teacher (11-13 year olds)

Retelling is a powerful tool. Prison, mental hospitals, detention centres can be linked to this activity; life in refugee camps, frequently seen on TV, can be brought in too.
— Kent secondary teacher

abridged form to match the age and ability of the class. At an appropriate point in the ensuing discussion attention can be re-directed to the results of the brainstorming.

Variation

With a well-affirmed group the procedure described above can be employed to share accounts of, and individual's emotional responses to, ill-treatment of animals for which they were in part or wholly responsible and/or which they witnessed.

In a zoo the environment is rigid and monotonous. To some species this is not too much of a problem for they respond by spending more time resting and sleeping. To others ... it is extremely frustrating and they react in several ways which we have all seen at the zoo, even if we have not understood them.

The most obvious response is to perform rhythmic movements such as pacing up and down or walking in a circle or figure-of-eight path. Many develop other stereotype movements such as swaying, head bobbing or weaving. Some will spend so much time grooming and cleaning themselves that this may end in self-mutilation. This is particularly noticeable in monkeys and parrots.

Many try to relieve the boredom by reacting with the public or by playing with objects — even playing with their food. Some species pretend to stalk and 'kill' their food as they would do in the wild. Animals that normally prepare their food are not content to accept a ready-to-eat diet. Agoutis will conscientiously clean and peel their food and then eat the whole lot. Rodents will try, in vain, to bury their food in concrete.

More serious adaptations are an abnormal increase in the degree of reaction to normal stimuli, increase in sexual activity or aggression and repeated regurgitation and ingestion of food.

In the wild, an animal's time is predominantly taken up with avoiding enemies, seeking food and procreation. These occupational necessities disappear in captivity. So an artificial life-cycle must be created and it must be adequate to break the monotony of life under captive conditions. If the environment is restricted and impoverished, then one can expect abnormality of behaviour, and of brain development in those born in that environment. Examples of poor quality environment are lack of companions with which to interact and play; lack of complexity — no trees, no vegetation and no variation of the territory — and lack of the facilities necessary to fulfil basic instincts and desires, such as digging, climbing and hunting.

An animal's territory or home range in the wild is not determined by the animal's desire to control as big an area as possible. Several factors are involved. Availability of food is of prime importance and its ability to defend the area. Exercise is provided by the need to move about to gather food and to avoid danger. These factors also keep the animal busy and occupied. At other times they rest and sleep.

In the zoo where food is provided and danger removed, lack of exercise and boredom result. More important than size of enclosure is the quality and variety of the area, as well as the flight distance — the distance from danger at which the animal will turn and run away. Flight distance varies with each species and with each individual. Should the public be allowed within the individual's flight distance (i.e. too close) and the animal cannot hide away, it will be living in a state of tension.

- Bill Jordan[33]

■ *FUTURE ZOO*

Suitable for

Upper primary/secondary

Time needed

Several hours for group work; one to two hours for the presentation session.

Resources

Art paper and pens; a collection of literature on zoos (see *Additional Resources*).

Procedure

Working in groups of three or four, students are given the task of conceptualising and designing plans for the zoo of the future, according to the guidelines set out in *Fig. 3*. Given that the zoo is to be animal-free, students are asked to decide whether the title 'zoo' is still appropriate. If not they should think up an alternative name. Designs completed, groups present their ideas, and the thinking behind them, to the rest of the class. Questions and suggestions for improvement are encouraged after each presentation, the session ending with a reflection on the appropriateness of the several designs and names put forward and the general lessons that have been learnt. During the plenary, students can be invited to consider the Born Free Foundation's plans for wildlife centres (see p.232 and *document 5*), comparing and contrasting them with their own work.

Potential

A challenging design activity giving students the opportunity to work creatively around the question of how (better) to realise the entertainment and educational goals of zoos, whilst meeting mounting objections on humane grounds to the incarceration of animals in cages or confined spaces.

Fig. 3

Future Zoo: Guidelines

● The zoo is to contain no animals.

● The zoo should show animals in their natural habitat and also in their relationship to plants and other animals in that environment.

● The zoo should offer up-to-date information on what is happening to each animal, and its numbers, in the wild.

● The zoo should show the effect human beings are having on each animals' survival chances in the wild.

● The zoo should promote respect and concern for animals.

● Money is no object.

■ *GREATEST SHOW ON EARTH?*

Suitable for

Primary/secondary

Time needed

50 minutes

Resources

A copy of each of the seven circus photographs (overleaf); seven copies of the circus statements; sugar paper; paste sticks; felt pens.

Procedure

The class breaks into seven groups. Each group is given sugar paper, a photograph and a set of circus statements (it is pointed out that the statements rehearse claims often made on behalf of circuses). The photograph is stuck in the middle of the sheet of sugar paper and the paper divided into six sections. In each section, the group records members' responses to the photograph in the light of one of the statements (responses can take the form of questions, a brainstorming of emotional reactions, statements of principle, doubts, objections, etc.). Having considered their photograph from the perspective of each of the six statements, groups report back, plenary discussion following.

Circus Statements

1. Watching circus animals perform is good entertainment.

2. Watching circus animals perform increases your respect for their beauty and dignity.

3. Watching circus animals perform builds respect for their wild cousins and concern to preserve wildlife.

4. Watching circus animals perform is educational.

5. Watching circus animals perform human feats helps you understand the similarities between animals and humans.

6. There is no cruelty involved in training and keeping circus animals, and in having them perform.

Potential

An activity designed to elicit student responses to pro-circus arguments and to trigger interest in finding out more about the circus debate. In facilitating the debriefing, the teacher should draw out any tensions, inconsistencies and incongruities discerned between the seven photographs, and between any of the photographs and the different group responses. For instance, is it justifiable to tether elephants 'behind the scenes' even if their impact in the ring fosters positive attitudes towards elephants in the wild? Unresolved issues can be summarised in a 'questions we still need answering' list. The list can provide the springboard for further enquiry and/or project work.

ADDITIONAL RESOURCES

For the teacher ...

❑ Born Free Foundation, *Teachers' digest*, 1992, 30 pages of laminated information sheets in a ring folder, overviewing the organisation's goals, positions and projects.

❑ Bostock, S.S.C., *Zoos and animal rights: the ethics of keeping animals*, Routledge, 1993. Argues that animals have rights but that, at their best, zoos do not violate them.

❑ Johnson, W., *The rose-tinted menagerie*, Heretic Books, 1990. An outstanding account, verging on the encyclopaedic, of human exploitation of animals for performance purposes. An indictment, too, relentless in its detail, of the contemporary circus and dolphinarium.

❑ McKenna, V., Travers, W., Wray, J., eds., *Beyond the bars. The zoo dilemma*, Thorsons, 1987. A collection of essays on the morality of keeping animals in captivity and on the usefulness of zoos for educational purposes and for protecting endangered species.

❑ *Why zoos?*, UFAW courier, no. 24, July 1988. A collection of essays highlighting what the authors see as some of the positive aspects of zoos and explaining what is being done to overcome the problems and criticisms zoos face. Very useful on environmental enrichment.

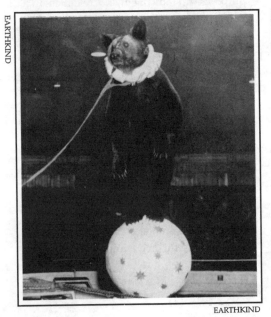

EARTHKIND

TURNING POINT

TURNING P

248

The misery of life behind bars (Photo: EarthKind)

❑ Born Free Foundation: *Zoo Check fact pack. Under 11's,* information on the disadvantages of conserving animals in zoos; *Circus fact pack,* sample letter by Foundation to councils requesting banning of circuses and extracts from RSPCA-commissioned report on circuses.

❑ *Why have zoos?,* Chester Zoo (The North of England Zoological Society, Zoological Gardens, Upton, Chester CH2 1LH), 1994. Two packs for English Key Stages 3 and 4.

❑ *Key humane organisations to contact (see* Organisations *list): Animal Aid, Born Free Foundation (includes Zoo Check project), Captive Animals' Protection Society, Animals' Defenders (National Anti-Vivisection Society), RSPCA, EarthKind.*

❑ *Other organisations to contact: Association of Circus Proprietors of Britain, P. O. Box 131, Blackburn, Lancashire, BBl 9DT; Dolphin Circle, 8 Dolby Road, London SW6 3NE.*

❑ *National Federation of Zoological Gardens of Great Britain and Ireland, Regents Park, London, NW1 4RY.*

For the classroom ...

❑ Born Free Foundation: *African elephant fact pack. Under 11's,* information on the biology of the African elephant, effects of the ivory trade, trade bans and effect of human population growth on elephant populations; *Asian elephant fact pack. Under 11's,* information on the biology of the Asian elephant, its domestication and threats to its survival; *Rhino fact pack,* information on problems facing the rhinoceros in the wild and steps taken to combat them.

References

1. Mitchell, S., ed., *The selected poetry of Rainer Maria Rilke*, New York, Random House, 1982, 25.

2. *Education Guardian*, 23.4.1991, 2-3.

3. Travers, W., 'A life of confinement', *World Magazine*, no. 8, Nov/Dec 1987, 59.

4. *Ibid.*, 60.

5. Zoo Check, *Some disadvantages to conservation in the zoo*, mimeo.

6. Travers, W., *op. cit.*, 59.

7. Zoo check, *op. cit.,*.

8. Travers, W., *op. cit.*, 59.

9. Porritt, J., 'Variations on a theme park', *The Guardian*, 28.6.1991, 31.

10. *Education Guardian*, 23.4.1991, 2-3.

11. *Ibid.*, 2.

12. Erlichman, J., 'Tales of booty and the beast', *The Guardian*, 28 June 1991, 31.

13. Strauss, S., 'Why zoos are dropping 'zoo' from their names', *The Globe and Mail* (Toronto), 5.2.1993, A13.

14. *World live*, promotional flyer of Worldlife Centres Ltd., Coldharbour, Dorking, Surrey, RH5 6HA.

15. *Leicester Mercury*, 11.12.1991, 1.

16. Johnson, W., *The rose-tinted menagerie*, Heretic Books, 1990, 324.

17. *Ibid.*, 320.

18. Laidlaw, R., 'The cruellest show on Earth', *The globe and mail* (Toronto), 5.2.1993, A24.

19. Johnson, W., *op. cit.*, 320.

20. RSPCA, *Animals in circuses*, undated, 5-8.

21. Johnson. W., *op. cit.*, 320.

22. *Ibid.*, 324.

23. Laidlaw, R., *op. cit.*, A24.

24. Cited in Sutcliffe, M., *The exhibition of animals in circuses should not be allowed*, Captive Animals' Protection Society, mimeo.

25. Johnson, W., *op. cit.*, 318; Laidlaw, R., op. cit., A24.

26. Johnson, W., *op. cit.*, 319.

27. Travers, W., from an article first published in *World Magazine* in November/December 1987. Permission for reproduction given by BBC Enterprises Ltd.

28. Hancocks, D., 'Endangered species', *The Guardian*, 27.9.1991, 21.

29. Adapted from Shepherdson, D., 'Environmental enrichment in the zoo' in *Why zoos?*, being *UFAW Courier*, no. 24, 1988, 50-1.

30. Lemmon, T., 'Zoos — are they justified?', *Greenscene*, no. 2, September 1988, 10.

31. *World live* (see reference 14).

32. Ings, R., 'Circuses with performing animals — a teacher's perspective', *RSPCA today*, Summer 1987, 23.

33. Jordan, B., in McKenna, V., *et. al.*, eds., *Beyond the bars. The zoo dilemma*, Thorsons, 1987, 50-2.

Chapter 11

Animal Experimentation

INTRODUCTION

Vivisection literally means the cutting up of live creatures but the term is now used to embrace all kinds of experiments on animals, whether or not dissection is involved. In 1991, according to the pro-experimentation Biomedical Research Education Trust, some 3,242,449 scientific procedures were performed on animals in the United Kingdom (the actual number of animals used was a slightly lower figure in that some animals were used more than once).[1] Animals are used in experiments for a variety of reasons:

❏ for studying the health and environmental safety of new products such as medicines, food additives, household and industrial chemicals, cosmetics and toiletries, fertilisers, herbicides and pesticides;

❏ for studying the health effects of legal but noxious substances such as tobacco and alcohol;

❏ for medical research into, amongst other things, the effects of disease, how hormones and parts of the body work, burning and scalding, the impact of injuries, new surgical techniques and new treatments and cures for diseases;

❏ for producing medical substances, such as antibodies, vaccines and hormones, in their blood or milk for extraction and use in diagnostic testing, basic research or medical treatment;

❏ for psychological research into, amongst other things, the separation of young from their mothers, food, water and light deprivation, solitary confinement, pain and drug addiction;

❏ for studying the physical and psychological effects of entry into hostile environments, e.g. deep sea diving and space travel;

❏ for weapons and combat zone surgery research.

Those who favour vivisection argue that the significant advances in medical knowledge and human health achieved in the last half-century would not have been possible without experimentation on live mammals (*documents 1 and 2*). Doctors and biomedical researchers needed to better understand the complex workings of the vertebrate body and to test and develop previously untried cures, treatments and surgical operations. They also needed live, intact bodies for testing the toxicity of products that would be applied to the human skin, added to human food and drink or administered within built or natural environments. For these purposes, animal experiments were, and continue to be, of central importance. In the first place, human beings are mammals and human biology is very similar to that of all other mammals. Secondly, and most importantly, experimentation on live human beings would be ethically unacceptable. Proponents of vivisection also point out that, in today's increasingly litigious society, animal experimentation of a thoroughgoing kind is required to protect the pharmaceutical and chemical industries. They argue, too, that experimentation has had important spin-offs for non-human animals through the incidental development of veterinary medicine and improved techniques in veterinary science and surgery. This last point notwithstanding, the essence of the vivisectionist position is that, in the final analysis, the human right to health takes precedence over any consideration of animal rights or welfare.

The essence of the anti-vivisectionist case is that it is wrong to kill animals or cause them pain or suffering even in the name of human progress. Biomedical procedures that have been particularly singled out for their cruelty and inhumanity have been the Draize eye test and the LD50 test. The former is used to measure the level of eye irritation caused by new cosmetic products such as hairsprays or shampoos; the latter is used to test the toxicity of new household cleaners, food additives and industrial or agricultural chemicals. The Draize test involves immobilising a rabbit for several days during which time the test substance, often in concentrated form, is dripped into its eye (*documents 3 and 4*). The LD50 test involves force-feeding the test substance to a group of animals to ascertain the dosage required to kill half of them, i.e. the Lethal Dose 50% or LD50. 'Reactions can include vomiting, paralysis, convulsions and internal bleeding. Sometimes the animals have to be fed so much of a substance that they die, not from poisoning, but from overloading and damaging the digestive system.'[2] Psychological (or behavioural)

experiments on animals are equally condemned as cruel and sadistic in that they often involve deprivation (of sleep, water, food, maternal protection) or the repeated administration of pain (e.g. electric shock treatment). Warfare experimentation involves the irradiation, gassing, poisoning, shooting and blowing up of animals to test the efficacy of new conventional, nuclear, chemical and biological weaponry (see pp.23-4).

If anti-vivisectionists see animal testing as *immoral*, they also regard it as *unnecessary*. Research on cosmetics and many household products is not, they say, for the good of humanity but to meet the profit motives of big business that need new products to maintain or boost sales levels and that are required by law to test all products designed for human use. We could easily make do with the cosmetics and products already on the market. Much research into new medical drugs is, likewise, research into new brand-named products with very similar ingredients to ones already marketed by rival companies. These 'me-too' or replica drugs raise the important question of 'how many remedies do we really need?'. 'The World Health Organisation estimates that only 200 drugs (approx.) are necessary to

Rabbit subjected to Draize eye test (Photo: BUAV)

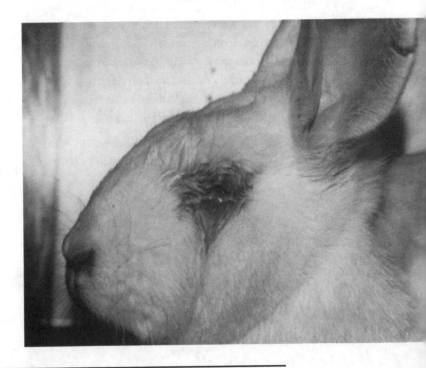

human health ... yet there an incredible 18,000 medicaments containing 3,000 active components on the British market alone.'[3]

The claims made by proponents of vivisection that animal experiments are of fundamental and continuing importance to advances in medicine and human health are also disputed. Whilst, admittedly, new drugs and treatments have been developed through animal experimentation, many health-care advances have been more the consequence of ameliorating social and environmental factors causing disease. For instance, the development of broad-spectrum antibiotics for curing infections in the 1940s is presented by vivisectionists as an animal-research success story that led to the containment or defeat of diseases such as scarlet fever, diphtheria,

Health with Humanity Campaign flyer

whooping cough and measles. Anti-vivisectionists point out that UK child deaths from such disease had dropped by about 90% in the preceding hundred years as a result of falls in poverty levels, improved nutrition, better living and working conditions, sanitation measures and clean water supplies.[4] A similar picture presents itself with regard to the decline in deaths from tuberculosis in the hundred or so years prior to the introduction of the B.C.G. vaccine (*document 5*). The search for a cure for cancer, anti-vivisectionists argue, points to a similar conclusion. Millions of animals have been used in cancer research but with, to date, little substantial progress in finding a cure. A primarily *preventative* approach, which recognised that most cancers are caused by factors such as smoking, bad diet, exposure to hazardous substances and (amendable) personality traits, would be both more humane and more successful.

Opponents of vivisection also argue that animal testing is *unreliable* in that animals are, in many ways, different to people not only in the way their bodies work, but also in their reaction to drugs and chemicals. Aspirin, which is beneficial for humans, kills cats and causes birth defeats in rats, mice and dogs. Penicillin, a lifesaver for humans, is a deadly poison for guinea pigs and hamsters. Chloroform, an anaesthetic for humans, kills dogs, whilst morphine, a sedative for humans, sends cats into a frenzy. Such differences make results from animal tests difficult, and sometimes dangerous, to extrapolate to humans and there is the ever-present danger that animal experimentation will lead to some valuable product being rejected, or a dangerous one accepted, for human use. Figures from Ciba Geigy, one of the world's largest pharmaceutical companies, suggest that 95% of drugs passed as safe and effective on the basis of animal tests fail when entered for clinical trials with healthy volunteers and patients. From time to time a drug that seemed hazard-free when tested on animals has slipped through the net with devastating effects for human beings. Thalidomide is a case in point. A sedative drug, it proved harmless to rats and mice, but caused approximately 10,000 birth defects (malformed limbs) in humans before its withdrawal from the market in 1961. Opren, an anti-athritic drug, was withdrawn in 1982 after causing more than sixty deaths in Britain and a further 3,500 cases involving serious side-effects to skin, eyes, circulation, liver and kidneys. Vaunted as slowing the progression of arthritis rather than simply alleviating its symptoms, Opren had proved effective and harmless in laboratory tests - on rats. Anti-vivisectionists also maintain that animal experimentation diverts attention and resources from the study of people which is a far more valid source of human health information (see *document 6*).[5]

Peter Singer has described the 'central dilemma' of the psychologist undertaking animal research thus: 'either the animal is not like us, in which case there is no reason for performing the experiment; or else the animal is like us, in which case we ought not to perform an experiment on the animal which would be considered outrageous if performed on one of us'.[6]

Alternatives to biomedical vivisection, opponents point out, are increasingly available. One of the most promising for screening new cosmetics and household products is known as *in vitro* (in glass) testing in which animal or human tissue (the latter being preferable to avoid problems of species difference) is kept alive in a culture dish or test tube and used to test for toxicity. Another is the use of 'lower order' organisms such as bacteria, algae, protozoa, fungi, insects and plants to give an early indication of genetic damage likely to arise from the application of a particular chemical. The problems here are that the ethical reservations concerning vivisection still apply and a hierarchical view of the world of living things (which underpinned the rationale for animal experimentation in

the first place) remains the guiding principle. Mathematical and computer modelling of biochemical and physiological processes is also now well advanced (reliant as modelling is upon information originally derived from animal experimentation) and has proved successful, for instance, in research into the effect of the herbicide paraquat on the human respiratory system. Epidemiology (the study of human populations) has enabled doctors to discover the social and environmental causes of certain diseases. The link between smoking and cancer was identified using epidemiological techniques (only for policy decisions to be held up when experiments forcing laboratory animals to inhale proved inconclusive). Clinical observation of actual human patients, together with autopsy reports, offers another way forward (again,

British Union for the Abolition of Vivisection poster

clinical investigations demonstrated the link between diabetes and a damaged pancreas, but the idea was not accepted for many years because experimenters found it difficult to reproduce the effects in laboratory animals).[7] The alternatives described above are, by no means, rejected by pro-vivisectionist opinion. Rather, they are seen as helpful auxiliary approaches which complement, but cannot replace, experimentation on complex, live organisms (see *document 7*).

It would be inaccurate to depict vivisectionists and anti-vivisectionists as occupying entirely irreconcilable positions on every particular of animal experimentation. On some issues there is a continuum rather than a gulf of opinion between the respective camps. Many vivisectionists regard themselves as under a moral obligation to spare animals unnecessary suffering; many have called publicly for a reduction in the number of animal experiments; some are on record as wishing for an end to frivolous or unnecessary experimentation, for instance, on new cosmetics or 'me-too' drugs. Whilst there is virtually complete consensus amongst anti-vivisectionists in opposition to cosmetic, product, 'me-too', psychological and warfare testing, there is some erosion of the consensus when it comes to leading-edge biomedical research that might lead to cures for life-threatening or debilitating human diseases (see *document 8*).

The animal experimentation debate is, in many aspects, replicated in the debate surrounding dissection in schools. Some biology teachers believe that it is essential for teaching about lifeforms; helping students to understand the internal structures of animals and gain 'hands-on' experience of them. Actively demonstrating the physiological complexities of the animals dissected promotes respect for life.

Opponents of dissection in school see it as undermining respect for living things. Its 'hidden agenda', they argue, is to reduce animals to mere commodities; disposable resources for our curiosity and convenience, possessing no value in their own right. Life is better understood and appreciated, they contend, by studying it alive. Alternative ways of studying the internal structures and workings of animals have recently become available, including computer simulations, video films and three-dimensional models that can be dismantled and put together again. Based on the latest technologies, these offer dynamic and life-affirming means of studying anatomy.

Dissection is no longer compulsory for school students wishing to take external examinations in biology so opting out of dissection at school level will not inhibit a student going on to take biology or medicine at university, in that dissection skills will be taught there. Opting out of dissection in some higher education courses is becoming increasingly possible. Both Animal Aid and the National Anti-Vivisection Society have energetic campaigns directed at eliminating dissection and animal exploitation from undergraduate science degrees (see *Additional Resources*).

The controversy over school dissection is both an animal rights and a students' rights question. Humane organisations attest to the increasing number of approaches by school students whose conscience is deeply troubled, and sensitivities outraged, by the classroom requirement that they participate in the dissection of animals (*document 9*). Dissection has become the focus of many school-based action projects (see *Chapter 15*). In consequence, examination boards and many teachers have made it optional. In 1991 Liverpool Council became the first council to ban dissection in its schools as a result of campaigning by local and national non-governmental organisations, supported by school students.[8] School dissection is being increasingly viewed as counter-productive and anti-educational (*document 10*).

DOCUMENTS

1.

Major advances in basic research that depended on animal experiments	
1600's	Discovery of blood circulation
	Discovery of the function of the lungs
1700's	Measurement of blood pressure
1800's	Vaccination to stimulate immunity
	Understanding of infectious diseases
1900's	Discovery of antibodies
	Understanding of hormone systems
1920's	Discovery of vitamins
1930's	Discovery of the mechanism of nerve impulses
	Discovery of tumour viruses
1940's	Understanding of embryonic development
1950's	Understanding of the control of muscle activity
	Understanding of energy metabolism
	Understanding the mechanism of hearing
1960's	Discovery of monoclonal antibodies
	Understanding the biochemical functions of the liver
1970's	Understanding of transplantation antigens
	Understanding the way the brain functions
	Discovery of prostaglandins
1980's	Development of transgenic animals
	Understanding the basis of memory

Major medical advances that depended on animal research	
1920's	Insulin for diabetes
1930's	Modern anaesthetics for surgery
	Diphtheria vaccine
1940's	Broad-spectrum antibiotics for infections
	Whooping cough vaccine
	Heart-lung machine for open-heart surgery
1950's	Kidney transplants
	Cardiac pacemakers and replacement heart valves
	Polio vaccine
	Drugs for high blood pressure
	Hip replacement surgery
1960's	
	Rubella vaccine
	Coronary bypass operations
	Heart transplants
	Drugs to treat mental illness
1970's	Drugs to treat ulcers
	Improved sutures and other surgical techniques
	Drugs to treat asthma
	Drugs to treat leukaemia
1980's	Immunosuppressant drugs for organ transplants
	CAT scanning for improved diagnosis
	Life-support systems for premature babies
	Drugs to treat viral disease

9

2. The discovery of insulin in the 1920s by Banting and Best in Canada is a good example of the contribution of animal research to medical progress. Their key finding was that injections of an extract of pancreatic cells, which contained the hormone insulin, relieved the symptoms of diabetes in dogs. Insulin was soon found to be highly effective in people and, as a result, many millions of diabetics are alive and well today. Diabetic dogs have also benefited from insulin treatment. Each decade since the discovery of insulin has seen the introduction of new kinds of treatments for many diseases. During the 1930s and '40s, sulphonamides and antibiotics were developed to treat bacterial infections, vaccines were introduced to control viral infections, and surgery advanced with modern anaesthetics and the heart-lung machine. Kidney transplants, hip replacement surgery, and drugs to control high blood pressure and mental illnesses followed in the '50s and afterwards. New treatments for leukaemia, asthma and ulcers appeared in the '60s and '70s. Drugs which delay the development of AIDS and other diseases caused by viruses, and improved drugs to prevent the rejection of transplants, were developed in the '80s and '90s. That each of these and the many other advances were critically dependent on animal experiments is a historical fact. Given continued research using animals, we can expect further advances in the treatment of diseases such as cancer, cystic fibrosis and crippling joint disease. It is very difficult to see how we could make such medical advances without animal research.

— *Biomedical Research Education Trust*[10]

3. The Draize Test, 1

Rabbits are the animals most often used. Concentrated solutions of the product to be tested are dripped into the rabbits' eyes, sometimes repeatedly over a period of several days. The damage is then measured according to the size of the area injured, the degree of swelling and redness, and other types of injury. One researcher employed by a large chemical company has described the highest level of reaction as follows:

Total loss of vision due to serious internal injury to cornea or internal structure.
Animal holds eye shut urgently. May squeal, claw at eye, jump and try to escape.

By shutting or clawing at the eye, however, the rabbit may succeed in dislodging the substance. To prevent this the animals are now usually immobilised in holding devices from which only their heads protrude. In addition their eyes may be held permanently open by the use of metal clips which keep the eyelids apart. Thus the animals can obtain no relief at all from the burning irritation of substances placed in their eyes.

— *Peter Singer*[11]

4. The Draize Test, 2

... the Draize test as generally used today involves testing products in diluted form and avoiding stressful features of the original Draize procedure. In most cases it is impossible to observe any signs of pain or discomfort in the animals.

— *Research Defence Society* from a pamphlet published in 1986 and no longer issued[12]

5. Respiratory tuberculosis chart[13]

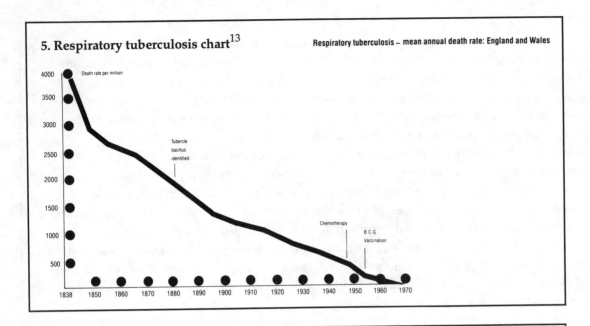

Respiratory tuberculosis – mean annual death rate: England and Wales

Death rate per million

Tubercle bacillus identified

Chemotherapy

B C G Vaccination

6. Dangers of animal experiments

The danger of relying on animal experiments is most dramatically illustrated by the increasing number of animal-tested drugs which are withdrawn from the market or restricted in their use after unexpected side-effects in patients. Examples include Eraldin, Opren, chloramphenicol, clioquinol, Flosint and Ibufenac. In the case of ICI's heart drug Eraldin, there were serious side-effects including damage to the eyes. Some patients went blind and there were 23 reported deaths. Yet animal experiments had given no warning and even after the disaster, the eye damage could not be reproduced in laboratory animals. Subsequently, ICI compensated more than 1,000 patients... The problem of unexpected side-effects is likely to be far worse than is generally appreciated because drug-induced disease is grossly under-reported: only around 1-10% of drug side-effects are reported by doctors and even fatal reactions are under-reported... Animal tests can also lead to the rejection of valuable medicines on the basis of side-effects which would never occur in people. If penicillin had been tested on guinea pigs during its development, we might never have had this useful antibiotic.

The evidence suggests that vivisection is an error not only because it often produces the wrong answers but because it diverts attention and resources from more reliable sources of information based on the study of people... Although the vital heart drug digitalis was discovered without animal experiments, its more widespread use was delayed because experiments on animals incorrectly predicted a dangerous rise in blood pressure. Animal experiments also hampered progress during the rapid developments in surgery following the discovery of anaesthetics. The great 19th Century surgeon Lawson Tait made a major contribution towards the advance of abdominal surgery yet, stated without hesitation that he had been led astray again and again by the published results of experiments on animals, so that eventually he had to discard them entirely.

— *British Union for the Abolition of Vivisection*[14]

7. Only by working with whole animals is it possible to study the complex interactions that occur between cells and organs in all living creatures. In living animals, no single function can be disturbed without a 'knock-on' effect on others. Many 'alternative' methods have been devised by scientists. These commonly use isolated cells, tissue cultures or organs taken from living animals. Such test-tube experiments are valuable for the detailed study of what happens in individual cells and tissues, and are very useful for quick identification of particular kinds of biological activity. However, they provide a different kind of information to that obtained in experiments on whole living animals and cannot be regarded as true alternatives; rather as complementary techniques... It is difficult even to imagine the range of test-tube techniques or the complexity of computer systems that would be necessary to mimic the amazing events that occur during the development and birth of a baby.

— *Biomedical Research Education Trust*[15]

8. Can alternatives always be used?

Many people believe that there are alternatives to all the animal experiments that are carried out at the moment. Unfortunately this is not true and more research is needed to develop more replacements for animals. In many cases, the only 'alternative' that avoids using animals is not to do the experiment. This always spares animals. Whether it matters or not to humans depends on the aim of the research, i.e. whether it is to develop a new household product or an AIDS vaccine...The RSPCA believes that much more time and money should be spent by the government and industry on looking for alternatives to animal experiments...The RSPCA also believes that much more time and money must be spent on finding ways to prevent pain and suffering in those animals that are still used. The actual need and justification for each individual experiment and each individual animal used must be looked at more closely... REPLACEMENT of animals in experiments and REFINEMENT of experiments to minimise suffering are priority issues.

— *Royal Society for the Prevention of Cruelty to Animals*[16]

9. Letters to Animal Aid

Last week it was our classes' turn to do dissection of bull's eyes; myself and 2 of my friends walked out of the lesson and the teacher set us some work to do out in the corridor. we could hear all our friends inside the lab laughing as they dissected the eyes; some of them came out of the lab with parts of eyes to let us see them. It was disgusting. my friend screamed when she saw it and the teacher told her off. We told the teacher that if we'd have wanted to see it, we would have joined in the lesson. She just told them to get inside, but they still kept coming out to us with peices of eye. It was really horrible. my form teacher (who just happens to be head of Biology) came down the corridor and asked us what we were doing out there. when we told him he said "oh you are stupid and silly. you don't know what you're missing — it's good fun." I got really mad and got into a blasing row with him.

- From Claire Haddon, Coventry, 14 February 1992

I brought one of your badges with 'I refuse to dissect' on it, and so did some of my other friends. Our science teacher said that we were going to dissect a fish the next day and he said everyone had to do it.

The next day I wore my badge, and so did some of my other friends when our teacher saw the badges he said we had to do it anyway but I said 'you can't force me to and I won't' then he said 'well you can do written work instead' and I said 'I'd rather do that'.

So me and my friends ended up doing written work; but I didn't care, as long as I wasn't cutting up a helpless little fish. The reason I didn't dissect was not because I don't have the stomach for seeing blood and guts etc. but because I think dissecting is so cruel and unfair. we could learn from diagrams instead.

- From Caroline Adams, Ickenham, Middlesex, 9 May 1992[17]

17

10. A lesson to be avoided

A crucial rite of passage in biology class is the dissection, in which students explore the innards of a rat, frog, or some other small animals. True, biologists are supposed to approach the task with curiosity, to learn how living things function. However, the reality is rather different.

We have the good fortune to live in a community which invests heavily in its schools, so students encounter their first dissection at 12. My elder daughter found the whole matter rather repulsive, but endured it. However, my younger daughter is fighting it as a budding advocate of animal rights. She became a vegetarian a few months ago, and now threatens to picket stores selling fur coats. She refuses on ethical grounds to dissect any animal, even one already dead, and even at the cost of a lower grade in science.

Their reactions have made me ponder the unintended lessons students might learn from dissection. As a student, I found it distasteful enough that I avoided college biology. My daughters' friends also seem to find dissection distasteful at best, a feeling far from unique in students. If you saw the film E.T., you must surely remember the scene where children, under E.T.'s influence, release frogs intended for the dissection knife. Do biology teachers really want to leave many of their students with the feeling that science is, to borrow a word from my daughters' generation, 'gross'? Or, worse, to show them that scientists do things they consider morally objectionable?

I do not know when dissection entered the classroom, but I do know that times have changed. Our popular culture humanises animals. Most children today know animals as pets rather than as agricultural products destined for the dinner table. We know intellectually that meat comes from animals, but emotionally we deny the connection, and many people prefer food packaged so its origins are not evident. Students who think of animals primarily as friendly pets are not likely to be enthusiastic about dissecting them. They may wonder about the motives of people who apparently do enjoy cutting up living creatures. Indeed, they may confuse would-be scientists with sadists who enjoy torturing animals — a misconception that I suspect is far more common than scientists would like to think.

How could schools teach animal physiology without dissection? Probably much better than you might think, and perhaps even better than by basing their lessons on dissection. Good colour graphics can illustrate body parts very effectively, especially with transparent overlays. Models can show the shapes, positions and relationships of organs. Computer simulations are another possibility. All have their limitations, of course, and lack the realism of a true dissection — but the 'blood and guts' aspects of realism can get in the way of learning. Models and illustrations can avoid conveying the impression that biomedical science is disgusting and/or sadistic.

Biomedical professionals may need dissections as part of their training, but that belongs in advanced courses, not at the introductory level. I wonder how many members of the Animal Liberation Front got their first push in that direction as sensitive children forced into the dissection laboratory. How many would-be naturalists are turned off the entire matter of science by well-intentioned efforts to teach them the internal organs of a frog?

— Jeff Hecht, *New Scientist*[18]

WHERE DO I STAND?			
Statement	Agree	Undecided/ Don't Know	Disagree
Animals, like humans, feel pain, fear and distress			
Preventing human suffering justifies the use of animals in scientific experiments to test new medicines.			
Given the choice, I would buy a 'cruelty-free' shampoo to one tested on animals if it was double the cost.			
Testing substances on animals is unreliable because they often respond differently to human beings.			
Animal experimentation to ensure the safety of products that make us look, smell or feel nicer is absolutely unjustified.			
With diseases such as cancer, Aids and multiple sclerosis to conquer, animals will have an important part to play in medical research for the foreseeable future.			
The major killers in wealthy societies (heart disease, cancer and road accidents) can best be prevented by changes in life-style, not animal tests.			
Animals should not be subjected to painful and often lethal tests just to satisfy the business world's incessant demand for new products to maintain or improve profit levels.			
We need to conduct experiments on animals to cure diseases in the so-called 'Third World'.			
There are good alternatives (e.g. computer simulations, tissue culture and testing outside the body) which, with the right financial investment to refine procedures, could replace all animal tests.			
Most 'Third World' deaths result from poverty so action to ensure enough food, clean water and better living conditions would do most to stamp out disease.			
Animal research is wrong on two counts: it is wrong to kill and it is wrong to cause pain and suffering.			
Animal experiments have played an essential part in medical progress.			
Firms advertising 'cruelty-free' cosmetics are deceiving the public in that they are using ingredients previously screened on animals and, hence, not requiring re-testing.			

P

ACTIVITIES

■ *WHERE DO I STAND?*

Suitable for

Upper secondary

Time needed

40 minutes

Resources

A *Where do I Stand?* sheet for each participant. (page 261). Additional copies for each pair of students and for each group of six.

Procedure

Having completed the *Where do I Stand?* sheet individually and without discussion, students form into pairs to explain and discuss their respective decisions and the thinking behind them. Using an additional copy of the sheet, they try to achieve consensus around each statement. Pairs then join to form sixes and repeat the process of explanation, discussion and consensus-seeking. Plenary reporting back and discussion follows.

Potential

A useful activity for stimulating debate on the question of animal experimentation prior to the class engaging in topic/research work around the issue. The statements on the sheet are designed to give students a sense of the range of issues and perspectives at play around what is a very controversial issue, to stimulate them to find out more by making them aware of gaps in their present level of knowledge of the subject, and to help them begin to identify their own values position. The activity can usefully be repeated at the close of the research period when an important additional dimension to the discussion will be a comparison of pre- and post-research sheets.

■ *TESTING TIMES*

Suitable for

Upper primary/secondary

Time needed

70 minutes

Resources

For 35 students: 5 each of the 7 *Background Cards*; 5 each of the following badges: Dr. U.B. Well Medical Research Team, Fashion People with Allergies, Green Earth Cosmetics, Humane Society, National Diabetic Association, Beautiful People Cosmetics, Animal Rights League. 60-80 small animal models spread out on the floor in the centre of a large open space. A whistle or bell. Floodlights for television panel (optional).

Procedure

1. Students group themselves around the open area where the model animals are set out. The teacher gives a brief overview of the controversy surrounding animal testing. Each student is given an information card and a badge indicating the name of the group or company which s/he represents. Students pin their badges on and join others belonging to the same group. Groups read their information cards and discuss the purpose, beliefs and goals of the group. (10 minutes)

2. It is emphasised that the role individuals are assuming does not necessarily represent their real opinions but, to maximise learning outcomes, should be adhered to until the debriefing stage. Groups choose a spokesperson who, in plenary session, introduces their group giving a brief summary of the group's belief and purpose. After all the groups have been introduced, they are asked to begin to strike up connections with other groups. They can lobby, coalesce, or to try to influence individuals or groups with opposing views. (10 minutes)

3. A whistle is blown or bell rung. It is explained that, as the groups continue interacting, the whistle/bell will be sounded every four minutes. On hearing the signal,

groups endorsing animal testing may remove one animal per person from the centre of the area. (20 minutes)

4. (Optional) The teacher announces a 'taking stock' period (of 5 to 10 minutes) when no inter-group interactions or animal removal can take place. Participants discuss in their groups what has happened and what they have learnt, and further develop their case for a television panel discussion that is to take place.

5. The final stage of the activity consists of setting up a television talk show with the teacher in role as the host. Each group chooses one of their members to serve on the TV panel. The rest of the class serves as the audience. As the discussion develops each speaker on the panel has the opportunity to express the point of view of their group (one minute each). Later, members of the audience can direct their questions to the various speakers and become involved in the discussion. (20 minutes).

Potential

This simulation can generate impassioned feelings and action including the protection by some groups of the remaining animals by obstruction and, sometimes, brute force. This can trigger equally fervent attempts by opposing groups seeking to remove them. A *Mood Changer* activity (pp.60-4) may be in order before debriefing begins.

The activity allows students to explore the wide range of issues involved in the use of animals for testing and to reflect critically upon their own and various other positions, opinions and perspectives. The unfolding of the simulation can give valuable insights into a range of action strategies for influencing opinion and effecting change, e.g. lobbying, negotiating, media presentations, non-violent protest and protest involving force. Participants can be asked to reflect upon the experience in the following ways:

❑ How did you feel about the role you were asked to play?

❑ Why did you think of the arguments employed by allied and opposing groups?

❑ Which opposing arguments did you find most persuasive? Why? How effective were you in rebutting those arguments?

❑ How effective were the various strategies employed by the anti-testing groups in their efforts to save the animals?

❑ What, on reflection, has been learnt about ways of influencing people and effecting change?

The simulation can be employed as the culmination of a program of work on animal experimentation. Alternatively, it can stand on its own. In the latter case, it is advisable to build in research and reading time, with literature on the issue available, between stages 1 and 2.

Source

Devised by Carol Adamthwaite and Marie Lardino, Lord Lansdowne Junior & Senior Public Schools, Toronto, Ontario. Simulation framework taken from 'Timber!' in Pike, G., & Selby, D., *Global teacher, global learner*, Hodder & Stoughton, 1988.

BACKGROUND CARDS

Dr. U.B. Well and Medical Research Team

You are medical researchers under the leadership of Dr. U.B. Well who use animals to test new drugs and medical procedures. You believe that animals are treated humanely and seldom suffer pain in laboratories. 20 million animals are abandoned annually and people regularly kill animals for food. Of the 1.5 million animals used for research in 1984 one-half were fish used to determine levels of pollutants in our drinking water.

Without experimentation people would have been denied the knowledge of how to treat many diseases, as well as great advances in treatment techniques such as biofeedback. Animal experiments were involved in the control of diabetes and in the development of all the new surgical techniques for heart disease, brain disease, cancer and organ transplants, and in understanding multiple sclerosis and muscular dystrophy.

The ultimate choice is using animals or humans. You feel animal testing is justified.

Fashion People with Allergies

You belong to a group of people working in the world of fashion. Your appearance really matters. You suffer severe allergies often caused by certain chemicals used in eye shadows, foundation, lipsticks, creams and eyeliners. This means that you have to be extremely cautious about the type of make-up you buy because certain products will cause your eyes to become red, swollen, puffy or itchy. Your skin is easily affected too. You are concerned about finding the most suitable cosmetic line for your type of skin and colouring. The fact that scientists are testing cosmetics on animals' eyes and skin, cannot be our first priority or concern. Your appearance is directly related to your job and your allergies take precedence. Looking good and feeling good must remain your top priorities.

Green Earth Cosmetics

You represent a successful cosmetic company that does NOT test your products on animals. Your company uses alternatives to animal testing such as computer simulations and tissue sample tests. Your company is not overly concerned about lawsuits as they have pretested all products for allergic reactions and carry liability Insurance.

You believe that consumers are more aware of how these products have been tested than in the past and that they will choose to buy products that have not been developed using processes that are cruel to animals. You maintain that this is one of the reasons why your company has had greatly increased profits in each of the past five years and why it is now busily opening outlets in several foreign countries.

Humane Society

You see yourself as representing animals that are unable to speak for themselves. You feel that the use of animals for testing is inhumane, cruel and unnecessary. Between 2 and 10 million animals in North America are subjected to painful procedures and killed each year in order to test new and improved products for consumers. You maintain that old-fashioned, environmentally-friendly cleaning products such as vinegar and baking soda are both effective and inexpensive.

According to U.S. government records the use of animals has increased over the last 6 years. Technicians force feed toxic chemicals to unanesthetized animals and apply caustic chemicals to animals' eyes and raw shaved skin. In some experiments monkeys die of head injuries or are paralysed. Sometimes this research is carried out with no practical medical application in view. Often these animals are unclaimed and homeless pets from municipal and humane society animal shelters.

You believe that testing using animals should be stopped.

P

BACKGROUND CARDS

National Diabetic Association

You have the disease called diabetes mellitus (Type 1). This means that you have abnormally high levels of sugar in both your blood and urine. Your disease occurs when the body does not produce enough of the hormone insulin, or when the body cannot use the insulin available.

If your disease goes untreated, a life-threatening condition called ketoacidosis develops rapidly. First symptoms include excessive thirst, appetite loss and vomiting. If not treated quickly, coma and death can follow.

To stay alive, you require insulin injections daily. In discovering the treatment for your disease researchers experimented with animals. Now your disease is under control but a cure is still needed. Your life is important to you and, if it is necessary to use animals to find a cure, you support testing. You are much less convinced about the need for animal testing of cosmetics or household products.

Beautiful People Cosmetics

Your represent an industry that does pounds worth of business every year in the UK. Your company employs 3000 people in your manufacturing and sales divisions.

The success of your company depends on providing safe cosmetic products for the consumer. If the health of a consumer is damaged or if they have an allergic reaction to one of your products your company could be sued. This could reduce the profits to your shareholders and could bankrupt the company.

You feel you must test your new products on animals to protect the company from lawsuits.

Animal Rights League

As animal rights activists you believe that animals should not be used for any kind of research, or for economic gain, regardless of whether they are wild animals, pets or laboratory animals especially bred for the purpose.

You feel that all research involves needless pain, torture and death to animals. Repeating the same experiments with different species of animals is unnecessary and should not be allowed. Manufacturers do not have the right to test the safety of new products on animals. Alternatives to animal testing such as computer simulations and tissue samples tests should be used instead.

The effectiveness of testing, using animals, is doubtful. Animals do not respond the same way as humans. Thalidomide was tested extensively on animals but resulted in severe deformities in humans.

You are angry with society's treatment of animals and feel that animals must have equal rights.

P

■ *DISSECTING DISSECTION*

Suitable for

Upper secondary

Time needed

45 minutes

Resources

A set of Dissection Statements, cut up and placed in an envelope, for each pair of students. Two blank slips of paper per envelope.

Procedure

Students form into pairs. Each pair is handed a set of statements and is asked to sort the statements into two piles: those with which they agree and those with which they disagree. Pairs can use the two blank slips provided to write up points for or against dissection in school which they feel are not adequately covered by the other statements. These are placed on either of the two piles. Pairs are also asked to place the 'agree' statements in rank order with the statements with which they most strongly agree at the top. Having completed their task, pairs form sixes. Each pair explains and seeks to justify their sifting and ranking to the other two pairs. The six then try to reach consensus as to which statements should be included in the 'agree' pile and about the ranking of those statements. Plenary reporting back and discussion follow.

Potential

This activity enables students to clarify their thoughts and feelings about a topic that continues to give rise to controversy. It also serves to alert them to a wide range of opinions and perspectives on the topic. It is, perhaps, best debriefed by asking each group in turn to report on one or two key points or disagreements emerging from their discussions (there is every likelihood that consensus proved impossible to achieve) and by eliciting reactions to each report. The facilitator can play devil's advocate if she finds that certain statements have been overlooked and/or their implications missed.

Extension

Students conduct a survey into the prevalence of, and attitudes to, dissection in their own school and other local schools. This can be conducted by interview and/or questionnaire. Useful focuses of investigation might include: differences in attitude between students in different age groups and between male and female students; the degree of correlation between attitudes to dissection and religious affiliation; the number and species of animals used annually and with which year groups; whether the animals are obtained from a supplier or reared in school and the conditions in which they are kept; whether the animals are killed at school and, if so, how it is done and who monitors the operation to ensure it is done swiftly, effectively and humanely; the degree to which the inclusion of dissection in the curriculum deters students from choosing biology/science options; the availability of GCSE and A-level courses in which dissection has been dropped or made optional.

Source

Developed from an activity devised by Stuart Twiss, Dorset Science Team Leader. The statements are based upon views expressed in documents published by the Association for Science Education, the British Union for the Abolition of Vivisection, the Institute of Biology, the Royal Society for the Prevention of Cruelty to Animals and the Universities Federation for Animal Welfare; also in, Cochrane, W., & Docherty, W., 'The role of dissection in schools', *The biologist*, vol. 31, no. 5, 250-5; O'Donoghue, P.N., *Hume Memorial Lecture*, (29 November 1990), Universities Federation for Animal Welfare, 1990.

> *Excellent for the purpose of allowing individuals to examine closely views that they may have held without much challenge beforehand.*
>
> — Cambridgeshire secondary teacher

DISSECTION STATEMENTS

Off-putting Dissection puts students off taking biology courses and off taking up careers in biology.	**Entity** Dissection allows students to appreciate the organism as a whole rather than as a collection of separately studied organ systems.
Active Involvement (1) Dissection improves student learning through active involvement and decision making. It gives them the chance to make decisions, individually and jointly, about the sequence of their work.	**Lose Respect** Some students see dissection as distasteful, sickening and cruel and lose respect for the teacher as a result.
Desensitising An aim of school biology is to teach respect for living creatures. Dissection cheapens and devalues life and desensitises students to the taking of animal life.	**Necessary Preparation** Dissection in school is a necessary preparation for certain careers and some university courses.
Knowledge and Understanding Dissection allows students to gain knowledge and understanding of internal structures and of variation between individual organisms of the same species.	**Morally Wrong** Dissection involves the taking of life. It is morally wrong to breed, rear and kill healthy animals to be used as 'tools' in the teaching of basic biological facts.
Minority Groups Consideration needs to be given to the cultural and religious sensitivities of students and parents belonging to ethnic minority groups who find it offensive to dissect or handle certain animals	**Alternatives** Dissection in school is unnecessary. Alternatives include models, films, videos and computer simulations of the inside of an animal's body. These alternatives are more humane, long lasting and re-usable. Unlike dissection, they allow for repetition and correction of mistakes.
Fascination with Gore Dissection may unintentionally kindle a fascination with gore in some students; the teacher may unconsciously encourage childish cruelties and inspire further unsupervised experiments.	**No Sense** It makes no sense to be against dissection in schools while still eating meat and wearing leather shoes.
Voluntary Dissection should be entirely voluntary. No student should be forced to carry out or witness a dissection against their will. No student conscientiously objecting should be victimised, lose marks or be singled out.	**Ecological Observation** Simple ecological observations of live animals is the most effective way of learning about variation between individuals of the same species.

P

DISSECTION STATEMENTS

Young People
The views of the growing number of young people who are vegetarian or vegan, or who support animal rights more generally, need to be taken into account by teachers who include dissection in their programmes.

Fragility and Strength
Dissection allows students to gain personal experience of both the fragility and strength of fresh tissue

Live Animals
Purchasing and/or rearing of live animals for dissection is often preferred as preserved specimens differ greatly from the freshly killed. Live animals suffer in that they may well live in overcrowded cages, be denied access to sufficient food and water and be inexpertly killed.

Dissection Skills
Many school science students will never use their dissection skills after taking their examinations; those who need to use them will be taught them again.

Active Involvement (2)
Active involvement is dependent upon the teaching approach used and not the material used. Following a step by step dissection plan as faithfully as possible is not active involvement.

Preserved Specimens
The tissues of preserved specimens do not resemble fresh tissues and thus the animal dies needlessly because little relevant learning takes place.

Female Students
Female students disapprove of dissection and the use of animals in science experiments much more strongly than male students.

Rights
Animals have rights. Not all the rights we typically claim as humans but at least the right to life and the right not to be caused suffering. On both these counts, dissection is wrong.

Breeds Callousness
Having animals in cages in the school laboratory when everyone knows they are to be killed for dissection breeds callousness; it's the school equivalent of the trout tank at the restaurant.

Parts
It is wrong to kill whole animals for dissection but fine to cut up parts (hearts, kidneys, eyes) obtained from a butcher.

P

■ *WHICH ANIMALS HAVE RIGHTS?*

Suitable for

Upper secondary

Time needed

45 minutes

Resources

A copy of the *Animals in Science Lessons* sheet (p.270) for each student; an overhead projector transparency of the sheet and an overhead projector pen.

Procedure

Working individually and avoiding discussion, students are asked to complete the *Animals in Science Lessons* sheet, indicating the degree to which they are prepared to countenance the use of each animal for the purposes listed. All the purposes, they are told, are ones that animals might be put to in a science lesson and all the animals are ones that could feature in a school laboratory. In completing the sheet, they use the following code:

5 = **Totally acceptable**
4 = **Moderately acceptable**
3 = **Undecided**
2 = **Somewhat unacceptable**
1 = **Totally unacceptable**

The task completed, students tot up their totals before joining groups of three or four to discuss their decisions and the reasons behind them. They are also asked to make a tally of their combined totals and to feed the figures to the teacher so she can collate them and prepare a class record on the overhead projector transparency.

Potential

Plenary debriefing can begin with a consideration of the class record. Where are the high scores? The low scores? How might these be explained? Once ideas have been pooled and, perhaps, recorded on a flip chart, groups are asked to report back in turn on their discussions, relating areas of agreement/disagreement, identifying points of particular controversy and seeking to explain the nature and basis of differences of opinion. After each report, members of other groups should be encouraged to comment on what they have heard, to play devil's advocate, and to put questions to individuals or the group as a whole. As the process unfolds, it is likely that a number of key areas for discussion will emerge.

❑ **Animal rights** — did individuals base their decisions partly or wholly on a belief in animal rights; if so, what rights did they have in mind; on what grounds and in what sense do they consider animals possess rights; which of the six purposes listed did they reject as violating animal rights; are each of the fifteen animals listed in equal possession of rights; do they have the characteristics that entitle them to the same rights; is it justifiable and congruent to use some of the animals, but not others, for the purposes listed?

❑ **Animal welfare** — did individuals base their decisions on animal welfare considerations; if so, why do they consider animal welfare important; do their grounds for embracing animal welfare fall short of allowing them to accept that animals have rights; if so, why; does their concern for animal welfare apply equally to all animals in the list; if not, why not?

❑ **Positive/negative images of animals** — to what extent did the appeal of particular animals, and a distaste for others, influence student decisions; from whence arises that appeal or lack of appeal; should our liking for some animals and not others influence our level of concern about their welfare, especially if we hold that the animals in question can all suffer fear and pain?

❑ **Gender** — to what extent was gender a significant factor in the choices individuals made; if so, why might that be the case?

Source

Developed from an activity devised by Stuart Twiss, Dorset Science Team Leader.

Excellent for years 11 and 12; ideal for a new class starting A-level work. I like the extent of analytical work possible here, with the numerical scores.

— Kent secondary teacher

By 'animal' I refer to all animal life but more particularly to those species which are biologically nearest to ourselves. There is no need to apologise for anthropocentrism — what else could, or in nature should, anthropoids be? So chimpanzees, cats, cuckoos, crocodiles, cod, crickets and cestodes are included but in that increasingly remote order.

— Philip O'Donoghue, 1990[19]

ANIMALS IN SCIENCE LESSONS USES / Animals	Dissection of organisms, bred for dissection, killed and preserved elsewhere.	Kept alive in the laboratory, killed by the lab technician and used fresh for dissection.	Dissection of remains of an animal that died of natural causes.	Kept alive and administered small doses of toxic substance to demonstrate its effects over a period of time.	Kept captive in the laboratory for observation of behaviour.	Brought in temporarily from home or the wild for observation purposes.	TOTALS
Dog							
Cat							
Rat							
Guinea Pig							
Budgerigar							
Blackbird							
Frog							
Goldfish							
Eel							
Crab							
Stick Insect							
House Spider							
Millipede							
Slug							
Earthworm							
TOTALS							

P

ADDITIONAL RESOURCES

For the teacher ...

❑ Close, B.S., Dolins, F., & Mason, G., *Animal use in education*. Proceedings of the Second International Conference of the European Network of Individuals and Campaigns for Humane Education, Edinburgh, 2-5 April 1989. EURONICHE assists students who are against the compulsory use of animals in undergraduate teaching in colleges and universities across Europe. Address: Lankforst 30-13, 6538 JE Nijmegen, The Netherlands (tel: 080-4489-86; fax: 080-44-86-71). This collection was published by the Humane Education Centre (see *Organisations* list, entry for EarthKind).

❑ Langley, G., ed., *Animal experimentation. The consensus changes*, Macmillan, 1989. Series of essays addressing the philosophical, practical, policy and political questions surrounding animal experimentation.

❑ Lock, R., and Millett, K., *The Animals and Science Education Project, 1990-1991. Project report*, University of Birmingham School of Education, August 1991. Investigation of students' understanding of, and attitudes to, dissection, vivisection, intensive farming and medical experiments involving animals.

❑ National Association for the Advancement of Humane Education, *The living science: a humane approach to the study of animals in elementary and secondary school biology*, undated. A pamphlet offering detailed advice to teachers on acceptable and unacceptable procedures for a humane classroom. The companion pamphlet for students is 'Does the idea of dissecting or experimenting on animals in biology class disturb you?' Both available from NAHEE at Box 362, East Haddam, CT 06423, USA.

❑ Sharpe, R., *The cruel deception. The use of animals in medical research*, Thorsons, 1988. Detailed and thoroughly researched and referenced critique of animal experimentation, seeking to expose both its waste and invalidity.

❑ Universities Federation for Animal Welfare, *Animals in science teaching. A directory of audio visual alternatives*, UFAW in conjunction with British Universities Film and Video Council, 1988. Aimed at tertiary institutions, this guide will be of use to sixth-form teachers.

For the classroom ...

❑ Animal Aid, *The ethical scientist*, 1991. Students and scientists opposed to animal-based research state their case. Contributions by Gill Langley and Robert Sharpe. This is the campaign magazine for Animal Aid's Campaign for Ethical Science aimed at informing first-year undergraduates of the case against animal experiments and of their right to refuse to carry out practicals (details available on request). The Campaign has also published an excellent four-page essay, *A degree of compassion*, by Robert Sharpe.

❑ Animal Legal Defense Fund, *Objecting to dissection. A student handbook*, undated. Helpful pamphlet advising students on the steps to take if they wish to opt out, and protest against, dissection in the classroom. Available from ALDS, 1363 Lincoln Avenue, San Rafael, California, CA 94901, USA (tel: 415-459-0885).

❑ British Union for Abolition of Vivisection (BUAV), *An introduction to animal experimentation*, 1990. Useful six-page factsheet. Other BUAV factsheets include: *Dissection in schools* and *Campaigning for a ban on dissection in schools*.

❑ BUAV, *Health with Humanity*, undated. Excellently presented and commendably lucid exposition of the anti-vivisectionist case. Suitable for secondary use.

❑ BUAV, *What is vivisection?*, undated. Excellent wallchart providing a powerful stimulus for groupwork and group/class discussions.

❑ Cruddas, H., *Why animal rights?*, Animal Aid, 1991. An information booklet for secondary use with six excellent pages of material on animal experimentation.

❑ Fund for the Replacement of Animals in Medical Experiments, *Alternatives to animal experiments*, 1985. Factsheet surveying alternatives to biomedical research using animals. Drawbacks presented.

❑ Humane Research Trust, *Humane research education pack*, undated. Contains two booklets, *How are animals used?* and *Alternatives to animals*, ten attractively presented study cards, a reading list and teachers' notes. Suitable for top primary and secondary use. Available from HRT at Brook House, 29 Bramhall Lane South, Bramhall, Cheshire SK7 2DN (tel: 0161-4398041 /3869).

❏ Lord Dowding Fund for Humane Research, *Progress without pain*, undated leaflet. Useful brief overview of alternatives to animal-based research. The fund can be contacted via the National Anti-Vivisection Society.

❏ National Anti-Vivisection Society, *The good science guide. Science education without animal exploitation. A student's prospectus for progressive science teaching in higher and further education*, 1991. A survey of tertiary science courses available that do not involve animal exploitation. The publication is a product of NAVS' 'Violence-Free Science' national campaign (details available on request).

❏ *Key humane organisations to contact (see* Organisations *list): Advocates for Animals, Animal Aid, Animal Concern, Beauty Without Cruelty Charity, British Union for the Abolition of Vivisection, Disabled Against Animal Research and Exploitation, Dr. Hadwen Trust for Humane Research, Fund for the Replacement of Animals in Medical Experiments, Humane Research Trust, National Anti-Vivisection Society, Plan 2000, Royal Society for the Prevention of Cruelty to Animals, Universities Federation for Animal Welfare. Information is also available from Doctors in Britain Against Animal Experiments, P.O. Box 302, London N8 9HD (tel: 0181-340-9813; fax: 0181-342-9878).*

❏ *Other organisations to contact. Research Defence Society/Biomedical Research Education Trust, 58 Great Malborough St., London W1V IDD (tel: 0171-287-2818; fax: 0171-287-2627). RDS argues the necessity for 'humane, controlled medical research that uses laboratory animals'. Its VHS videos for schools include* What about people?, *1989, 15 mins., suitable for 12-16 year olds, arguing in favour of animal research and* Animals and the human kidney, *1989, 15 mins., suitable for 16+. The Biomedical Research Education Trust publishes a range of pamphlets that are suitable for the secondary classroom including* Information about animal research, Why are animal experiments necessary? *and* Myth versus reality.

References

1. Biomedical Research Education Trust, *Information about animal research*, undated pamphlet, 3.
2. Cruddas, H., *Why animal rights?*, Animal Aid, 1991, 5.
3. *Ibid.*, 6
4. *Ibid.*, 7; British Union for the Abolition of Vivisection (BUAV), *Health with humanity*, undated, 6.
5. BUAV, *op. cit.*, 8-9, Campaign to End Fraudulent Medical Research, *Human victims of fraudulent research*, undated pamphlet; Cruddas, H., *op. cit.*, 6-7.
6. Singer, P., *Animal liberation. Towards an end to man's inhumanity to animals*, Thorsons/Random House, 1983, 49.
7. Fund for the Replacement of Animals in Medical Experiments (FRAME), *Alternatives to animal experiments*, 1985 information sheet; BUAV, *op. cit.*, 11-12.
8. Information on school dissection provided by Animal Aid and the National Anti-Vivisection Society.
9. Biomedical Research Trust, *op. cit.*, 4.
10. Biomedical Research Trust, *Myth versus reality*, undated pamphlet.
11. Singer, P., *op. cit.*, 50-1.
12. Research Defence Society, *Are animal experiments necessary for cosmetic products?*, cited in James, B., *Animal rights*, Wayland 1990, 25.
13. BUAV, *op. cit.*, 7.
14. *Ibid.*, 8-9.
15. Biomedical Research Trust, *Myth versus reality*, undated pamphlet.
16. RSPCA, *Alternatives to animal experiments*, pamphlet, 1993.
17. Letters kindly supplied by Ann Harriman, Education Officer, Animal Aid.
18. Hecht, J., 'A lesson to be avoided', *New Scientist*, 19 May 1990, 70.
19. O'Donoghue, P.N., *Hume memorial lecture*, 29 November 1990, Universities Federation for Animal Welfare, 1990.

Chapter 12

Animals in the Media

INTRODUCTION

In the modern age, increasing numbers of human beings have lost daily contact with animals and with the natural world. Our reliance on media images of nature has grown commensurately with the ever-present danger that those images will be uncritically assimilated. One function of humane education programmes is to foster a critical discernment with regard to media treatment and depiction of animals. At this point humane education and media literacy education overlap. 'The media-literate student should be able to make conscious critical assessments of the media, to maintain a critical distance on popular culture, and to resist manipulation.'[1] The specific goals of media literacy include:

❑ helping students understand that media are carefully crafted constructions of reality, not reality itself, and helping them develop the knowledge, skills and attitudes required to interpret the ways in which the media construct reality;

❑ developing awareness of the cultural, social, economic and political implications of media constructions; of how media reflect and, at the same time, legitimise and reinforce cultural, social, economic and political trends;

❑ developing in students the ability to decode/deconstruct media in order to identify the cultural practices, ideas, ideological and values messages they contain;

❑ helping students recognise that those who construct media are subject to many motivations, controls and constraints (economic, political, organisational, technical, social and cultural) many of which actively affirm dominant ideologies and the existing social system.[2]

Although animals are frequently depicted in cartoons and commercials and although nature and animal-related programmes are a regular and ever-popular feature of our radio and television diet, the field of media literacy education has paid but scant attention to animals in the media.[3]

This chapter offers a collection of activities designed to help students engage critically with media depictions of animals. The activities cover print-form cartoons (*Animal Cartoons*), print-form posters and advertisements (*Animal Posters, Fur Trade Images, Teeshirts and Sweatshirts*) and television/film (*Grand National, Deconstructing Animal Commercials, Shooting Animals*). The latter title is chosen advisedly.

'The metaphors we use to talk about photography are strangely revealing: we take pictures, we capture or even shoot something on film. These are the metaphors of the hunt.'[4] The group of activities on positive and negative images of animals (*Chapter 6*) can be used alongside the activities described here, as can *Down on the Farm* (p.183) and *Splitting Images* (p.218).

ACTIVITIES

■ *ANIMAL CARTOONS*

Suitable for

Primary/secondary

Time needed

60 minutes.

Resources

A lettered set of up to nine photocopied cartoons on human/animal relationships, animal rights and welfare issues (see pp. 276-7) for each group of three or four students. Sets should contain the same cartoons.

Procedure

The cartoons are spread out on the floor or table and individuals are asked to rank them for their immediate impact. Discussion is avoided at this stage, individuals jotting down their rank order. They also write down their own explanations of what each cartoon is trying to say. Group members then share and discuss their rankings and explanations (the aim being to achieve understanding of each others' thinking rather than consensus). The teacher then lists one or more specific criteria for ranking (such as 'clever', 'disagreeable', 'disturbing', 'funny', 'perceptive', 'puzzling', 'thought-provoking') and groups are asked to try and agree upon a ranking of the cartoons for each criterion given. Reporting back and discussion follows.

Potential

Cartoons convey ideas and perspectives on an issue in a direct, humorous and telling way. As such, they provide a pleasurable springboard for considering animal rights and welfare issues and particular media perceptions and judgements on those issues. In plenary discussion students should be encouraged to share and discuss explanations of the point of a particular cartoon before proceeding to discuss it according to the criteria listed by the teacher. They should also be invited to suggest other criteria which the class might profitably use for ranking purposes. Students can be asked to comment upon how each cartoon achieves its effect and to suggest particular groups of people who might react negatively to, or feel threatened by, its message. Some of the activities listed under *Extensions* below can be woven into the plenary session, with students returning to their groups for short periods of time.

Variation

Groups are given a small set of cartoons and a set of cards purporting to explain each cartoon's message. Their task is to agree upon which explanation card they find most plausible in each case

Extensions

1. Students write alternative captions for the cartoons.

2. Pairs are given an outline verbal description of a particular cartoon and are told what the caption is. They sketch it for themselves then compare their own version with the original.

3. Students recreate a cartoon as a brief dramatic sketch using puppets.

4. Groups imagine themselves as historians in 2050 who come across a collection of cartoons from the late twentieth century. They prepare a commentary on them linking them to the historical trends of the period and saying why the cartoons and messages they contain now look rather passé.

5. Students draw their own cartoons on human/animal relations, animal rights and welfare issues. These are used in a rerun of the group activity described under *Procedure* above.

6. Students analyse cartoons featuring animals, but not on animal issues, to pinpoint the reasons why animals have been included by the cartoonist and to explore the image(s) of the animal(s) conveyed.

7. Students search magazines and newspapers for further animal cartoons over a period of weeks. The cartoons are displayed on a cartoon billboard and are used, from time to time, as a focus for class discussion or for one of the activities described above.

Source

Built upon suggestions in Richardson, R., *Learning for change in world society. Reflections, activities and resources*, World Studies Project, 1976, 51.

Cartoon References

A, *The Independent magazine*, 23.11.1991, 12; B, *Daily Mail*, 12.6.1990, 2; C, *Daily Mail*; D, *Financial Times*; E, *Arkangel*, Winter 1989, no. 1, 30; E, *Private Eye*; F, *Arkangel*, Winter 1989, no. 1, 52; G, *New Internationalist*, May 1991, 2; H, Hewison, W., ed., *Creature comforts. Punch in the animal kingdom*, Grafton, 1989, unpaginated; J-M, *Ibid*.

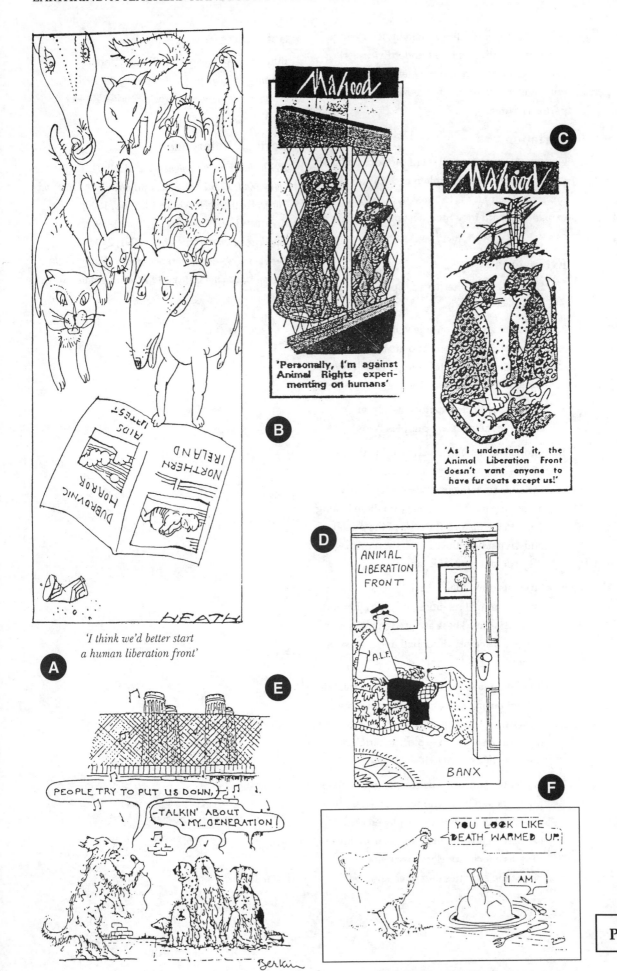

G

H

I

J

K

L

P

M

■ *ANIMAL POSTERS*

Suitable for

Primary/secondary.

Time needed

40 minutes.

Resources

A selection of twenty posters from a range of animal rights and welfare organisations hung at various points around the classroom walls (see *Organisations* list for organisations to approach). The selection should include posters conveying ideas and images of a more compassionate world and posters focusing upon present-day abuse and ill-treatment of animals. A blank sheet of paper and felt pen for each student. Blu-tak.

Procedure

Students are asked to walk around the classroom and carefully examine all the posters. Avoiding discussion, they are to choose two posters that they feel convey the most positive impression (representing, perhaps, something to aspire to, to strive for) and the two posters leaving the most negative impression (representing, perhaps, a barrier to a gentler, kinder and more compassionate world). Having made their individual choices, they team up with a partner. Pairs explain and discuss their initial individual choices before revisiting the posters and negotiating a consensus on the two most positive and two most negative posters. Pairs form into fours and the process is repeated. Students then break away from their group and briefly summarise what they have gained from the activity, using no more than three sentences, each beginning 'I learned'. Their completed sheet is stuck next to the poster they feel to be the most appropriate. The activity ends with students circulating to read each others' statements.

Potential

A lively way of introducing students to a range of pro-animal viewpoints and values and, through eliciting their response to them, of helping students clarify their own values. In the debriefing session, individuals can be asked to explain their initial choices and any conflicts and dilemmas that arose as they worked in pairs and fours. How deep-rooted were those conflicts and dilemmas? Were they to do with conflicting interpretations or conflicting values? Did

My friend talked me into going to the Bobcaygeon Wildlife Art Show a couple of summers ago, and I came away quite disturbed by what I saw as a real sentimentalization of nature by artists who were creating the kind of images of animals that people obviously wanted to own. The problem is not so much with any one image, many of which are admirable studies of particular animals, but with what tends to get represented, and the fact that, as in other media, what is not presented is as revealing as what is. For example, we often see predators depicted, but rarely doing what they do with their prey. (Is there any market for a wolf with its snout in the guts of a caribou calf?) Images tend to be of perfect specimens—perfectly successful animals. Has no one ever seen a bedraggled and starving hawk? The often clichéd construction of nature which these images create for us (through selection, pose, action, etc.) says a great deal more about us and what we want nature to be than, I think, about nature itself. I think there is also a kind of human hierarchy of animals that operates here too: predators are highly valued and admired, big animals are magnificent, males especially, small animals are cute, especially if they have soft fur, herd animals are boring, scavengers have very low status, warm blood is better than cold, although fish are okay if they are big. — *Rick Shepherd, media educator, Toronto*

consensus prove impossible? Did students opt for posters with a rights or welfarist slant? To what extent did people's views of the posters shift as a result of the process? What reflections do students have on the 'I learned' statements? Is the final juxtaposition of statement to poster in each case easily explainable?

The activity also offers rich possibilities for practice in media analysis. The class can be asked to comment upon: the relative impact of the posters; the appropriateness and effectiveness of linking particular combinations of words to particular images; the audience at which each poster is targeted; the response different groups are likely to have to its message (do the posters seek to disarm or provoke possible objections, to polarise opinion, to sway a majority of opinion and leave a rump isolated?).

Extension

Working in small groups, students design their own animal rights/welfare posters. These are displayed prominently in a public area of the school.

Variation

Nine posters are used for a diamond ranking exercise (see p. 241).

Source

Based upon an activity in Richardson, R., *Learning for change in world society. Reflections, activities and resources*, World Studies Project, 1976, 53.

■ FUR TRADE IMAGES

Suitable for

Upper secondary

Time needed

40 minutes (20 in separate groups, 20 for groups to meet together).

Resources

Four posters advertising fur coats (available via the Fur Education Council, P.O. Box IEW, London WlA lEW, or from a local furrier), and four anti-fur posters. Respect for Animals (see *Organisations* list) is an excellent source for the latter. Alternatively, enlarged photocopies of the well-known Lynx posters (see below) can be used. Eight sheets of sugar paper and eight felt pens.

Procedure

Students form into eight groups. Groups are asked to divide their sheet of sugar paper into four sections and write in the headings as in *Fig. 1*. Working clockwise around the sections, they analyse the values and assumptions of the poster, decide who benefits and who loses by the poster's message and note down any problems they have with the poster. Having completed their task, groups with posters advertising fur coats each join a group with a poster opposing the fur trade to share and discuss their respective work. Plenary debriefing follows.

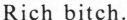

Rich bitch.   Poor bitch.

If you don't want millions of animals tortured and killed in leg-hold traps don't buy a fur coat. **LYNX**

It takes up to 40 dumb animals to make a fur coat.

But only one to wear it.

LYNX

If you don't want animals gassed, electrocuted, trapped or strangled, don't buy a fur coat. P O Box 509 Dunmow, Essex Tel: 0371 872016

Fighting the fur trade

P

		Fig. 1
1. WHAT VALUES DO YOU THINK THE PEOPLE HAVE WHO PREPARED THIS POSTER?	2. WHO BENEFITS FROM THE POSTER'S MESSAGE?	
4. WHAT PROBLEMS ARE RAISED FOR YOU BY THE POSTER?	3. WHO LOSES BY THE POSTER'S MESSAGE?	

Potential

An image analysis activity likely to open up a number of controversial questions surrounding the fur trade and the publicity strategies used by both its proponents and opponents. To whom is fur trade advertising being directed and what view of the 'good life' is being promoted? What image of women is conveyed by the pro-fur posters? Would the posters have the same effect if they showed men rather than women? What image of women is conveyed by the Lynx (or similar) posters? Why are women used in the posters rather than men? How do students respond to the words in the posters? Is the image of women conveyed by the Lynx posters justifiable in terms of the cause that is being promoted? Would the pro- and anti-fur posters have the same effect if they showed Inuit women wearing furs as they traditionally have? Do the responses to the 'who benefits?' and 'who loses?' sections tend to support the case for the continuation or discontinuation of the fur trade?

Variations

There are a number of possible variations using the Lynx posters. For instance, the 'Rich bitch. Poor bitch' poster can be cut in half so that pairs within each group of four describe their piece to each other before the images are revealed, joined together and discussed. Both posters can be discussed with their captions, firstly hidden and, then, revealed. Alternatively, the word 'bitch' can be hidden in the 'Rich bitch. Poor bitch' poster and only revealed some way into the discussion. Another approach would be to hide the captions and ask groups to invent their own, prior to learning what the actual captions are. Captions can also be invented for the fur trade posters from a pro-fur and anti-fur stance.

Extension

Class research into the case for and against the fur trade (see case study material, pp.199-200 and 220-2).

Source

Variations suggested by Stuart Twiss, Dorset Science Team Leader.

I rate this very highly; an excellent PSE activity raising a wide range of moral issues concerning human and animal rights and welfare. The principal behind this activity — comparison of standpoints as expressed through images — can be extended to areas such as factory farming, meat eating and animal experiments. In every case, the potential for a powerful, deep study is there, using this technique.

— Kent secondary teacher

I like the balance here between various agendas...You might find an interesting split between the responses of urban and rural or northern kids in Canada; you could ask kids to speculate or role play the reactions of members of the other group.

— Toronto secondary teacher

■ *TEESHIRTS AND SWEATSHIRTS*

Suitable for
Primary/secondary

Time needed
Several hours

Resources
A numbered set of six to ten pictures of teeshirts and sweatshirts marketed by animal welfare and rights organisations for each four students (pictures are usually included in product catalogues). The pictures should show only the front of the garment. Alternatively, a numbered set of actual teeshirts/ sweatshirts arranged around the classroom (only the front should be on display). *A Teeshirt and Sweatshirt* worksheet (see *Fig.* 2) for each student. Art paper, crayons, paints and brushes. Plain white teeshirt per student; fabric printing dyes.

Procedure
Working individually, students complete the worksheet for each teeshirt/sweatshirt, additionally circling the number of the shirt which they feel is most effective in conveying an animal rights/welfare message. Forming groups of four, students exchange reflections on the shirts and try to reach consensus on which is the most effective and which most in need of redesign and rewording. Using the art materials available, they collaborate in the following tasks:

❑ the redesign of the shirt which they consider to be most in need of reworking;

❑ the design of the reverse of the teeshirt/sweatshirt which they consider the most effective;

❑ the design of the front and reverse of a brand new teeshirt/sweatshirt on a specific animal rights/welfare issue.

Once groups have completed their new teeshirt design to all members' satisfaction, students transfer the designs onto plain white teeshirts using the fabric print dyes.

Work is displayed in the classroom and/or in a public area of the school. Photographs of redesigns, and of new designs, can be forwarded to relevant animal welfare and rights organisations for comment and feedback.

Potential
An exciting design appreciation and creative activity that draws upon student interest in a perennially fashionable article of clothing to raise awareness of animal welfare/rights issues.

Groups can be asked to present their work, and the thinking behind it, to the class. If actual teeshirts/sweatshirts have been used or if pictures of the reverse side of shirts are available (some catalogues carry these), the students' work can be compared with the actual product. In reviewing pictures of people wearing shirts and their own creations, students can be encouraged to speculate on what message wearers of specific shirts might feel they are giving about themselves.

Extension
As part of the school's education for economic and industrial understanding programme, students market their teeshirts in both school and community as a mini-enterprise project.

Fig. 2

No.	What I like about the teeshirt/sweatshirt	What I don't like about the teeshirt/sweatshirt	What changes I would make to the design/words

■ GRAND NATIONAL

Suitable for

Primary/secondary.

Time needed

90 minutes

Resources

A video recording of a three-minute section of the Grand National or other steeplechase; audio cassette recorders; a blank audio cassette for each group of three or four students.

Procedure

The class watches the video recording twice; on the first occasion to obtain a general impression of the race, on the second for class members to identify particular racehorses from the perspective of which they will prepare an alternative commentary on the race. Groups of three or four focus on one racehorse. Watching the video again (with sound off and slow motion repeats as necessary), they write detailed notes on their horse's experience of the race and brainstorm ideas on what the race might be like from the horse's perspective, as it is forced to negotiate ditches, hedges, and fences amidst falling horses and noise and with a rider on its back with spurs and whip. Each group then drafts a script and records it on audio cassette using the video recording to help them synchronise their commentary with the action. Group presentations follow.

Potential

A creative way of encouraging students to think about a popular sport — often regarded as amongst the most humane of sports involving animals — from the vantage point of the animal.

Variation

Film of a bullfight, rodeo or fox/stag hunt or a television programme on angling is used as a basis for the activity.

> *Excellent, thought-provoking. Scripts can be written down to record, one group at a time, onto one cassette recorder. The rodeo version is especially good. What is done to the bullock can be mentioned afterwards to heighten the sense of injustice and unfair play.*
> — Kent secondary teacher.

■ DECONSTRUCTING ANIMAL COMMERCIALS

Suitable for

Secondary

Time needed

Three to four hours

Resources

One or more video cassette recorders (with counters) and monitors; a recorded selection of television commercials featuring animals; an *Animals in Commercials* hand-out, p.284, for each student.

Procedure

To introduce the topic, the teacher initiates a general discussion about television commercials. Students are asked to give their views on commercials, to identify commercials they like and dislike and explain why. During the discussion the class is made aware of the size of the advertising industry and of the costs of producing commercials for national television networking (often higher than for a half hour television programme). The discussion should also touch on people's reasons for watching (or avoiding watching) commercials. In closing the discussion, the teacher should point out that animals are regularly featured in television commercials and that this and subsequent lessons will be used for a detailed examination of the images of animals presented. The class watches the first recorded commercial two or three times over. Before further showings, the hand-out is distributed and read through (the term 'jolts' is explained: i.e. moments of excitement generated by laughter; high emotion; sudden, unexpected, acts; movement of people or objects; noise or rapid cutting — to sustain audience attention). The video is then re-shown several times so that students can jot down answers to the questions in the hand-out. The tape can be frozen as often as necessary to allow students to examine in detail the content of different frames. The commercial can be shown in slow motion and audio and video tracks examined separately. The counting of shots is particularly important (see box, opposite) and

Shot counting is an extremely useful exercise for students who are unfamiliar with the deconstruction of film or video material. Students simply count the number of shots in a commercial. The actual number of shots is not particularly important, except as a measure of the pace of the advertisement; however, the activity forces students to see the commercial as a construction of many separate parts and, by extension, the result of many separate decisions. Visual material is normally processed more or less unconsciously by the right side of the brain; the activity of counting forces the left side of the brain, with its more linear critical faculties, to remain involved. Television and film tend to be perceived by students as seamless extensions of reality; this exercise makes the seams visible.

— Ontario Ministry of Education, *Media literacy resource guide*, 1989, 184.

might best be attempted by the class as a whole. The class then deconstructs the commercial by sharing responses to the questions in the hand-out, the video being re-shown when disagreements arise or as otherwise deemed necessary. Groups of three or four are then formed with the task for each of deconstructing one of several animal commercials now shown to the class. Having worked through the hand-out, groups prepare an oral presentation of their findings. Each group presentation is followed by class discussion. The presentations completed, key learnings from the exercise are identified.

Potential

Commercials are amongst the most carefully produced material on television. Designed to persuade, to manipulate peoples' sense of what is important and to play upon an audience's needs, fears and desires, they are rich in imagery, allusion and suggestiveness. They are also brief. As such, they make ideal material for helping students develop a sensitivity to visual media and attendant analytical and observational skills. The close study of commercials can provide an effective jumping off point for work on deconstructing television programmes and series featuring animals (see *Extensions* and *Shooting Animals* p.285).

This particular activity raises questions surrounding the reasons for, and morality of, using animals to sell products. Important areas for discussion include: the human emotions, needs, fears and desires being appealed to through the use of animals; the values underpinning the commercial as a whole and the use of the animal in particular; the desirability of using animals in commercials; the negative/positive effects on people's conception and image of the animal and (not to be underestimated) the links between the animal image and human sexuality.

Extensions

1. Students simulate the role of a creative team of an advertising agency. They are each given a product description and asked to prepare a storyboard for a television commercial (including plot, dialogue, types of shot, music, 'jolts', etc.) in which one or more animals will figure. The teams come together and each presents and defends its proposed commercial which is appraised by the other teams.

2. Working in groups, students devise a hand-out for deconstructing television films or dramas in which animals figure centrally. Draft hand-outs are shared, discussed and critiqued in plenary and a collective second draft negotiated. The hand-out is applied to a previously unseen animal film following which the film is deconstructed and the hand-out reassessed and redrafted.

3. Working in groups, students devise guidelines covering the humane use of animals in television commercials.

Source

This activity draws on ideas in the Ontario Ministry of Education's *Media literacy resource guide*, 1989, 181-5.

ANIMALS IN COMMERCIALS

1. General
- How long is the commercial?
- What product is being advertised?
- What animal is featured?
- For how many seconds does the animal appear?
- Has the animal any direct connection with the product?
- Does the commercial tell a story? If so, what is the animal's role in the story? Does the commercial convey a particular desired lifestyle?
- If so, how is the animal used to reinforce that lifestyle message?
- Does the commercial seek to make the product attractive in another way? How is the animal used to achieve that aim?
- What location is used? What relationship, if any, is there between the animal and the location?
- Is any lack of any clear animal-location relationship significant?

2. Target Audience
- Is the commercial local or national?
- What is the probable age, sex and economic level of its target audience?
- What part does the animal have in 'hooking' the target audience?
- What connection is there between the animal and the target audience?

3. Animal
- Is the animal employed young or old; female or male?
- What image or impression of the animal does the commercial convey?
- Is it a realistic or unrealistic image/impression?
- What human needs, fears, hopes and desires are being appealed to through the animal?
- What kinds of human beings, or human groups, are pictured with the animal? Why?
- What does the commercial fail to say about the animal?
- Is it likely that the animal suffered in the making of the commercial?
- Did any animal suffer in the making of the product? Will any suffer in the use of the product? If animal suffering is involved at any point, what does that suggest about the advertiser's use of animals in the commercial?

4. Visual Component
- How many shots are there in the commercial (the more shots the greater its *pace*)?
- Are short and long shots mixed and to what effect?
- In what kind of shots does the animal appear?
- What types of shots (e.g. close-ups, long shots, low camera angles, high angles) are used for the animal and to what effect?
- Is the animal portrayed in sharp or soft focus and/or using special lighting or colour effects? Why?
- How many 'jolts' are there in the commercial and how is the animal used to create 'jolts'?

5. Audio Component
- What kind of music and/or sound effects are used in different shots to project the desired image of the animal and product?
- What are the tone and pace of the voice in different shots and how do they help convey the desired image of the animal and product?
- Is the voice-over male or female, young or old?
- Why has a person of that gender and age been chosen for the voice-over?

P

■ *SHOOTING ANIMALS*

Suitable for

Senior secondary

Time

Several lessons

Resources

A videotape of one or more animal-related natural history television films. A video cassette recorder (with counter) and monitor. A *Shooting Animals* checklist, (p.286), per student.

Procedure

The teacher numbers off the students as '1', '2', '3' or '4' and groups of 4-6 of each number are formed. The film is introduced and the relevant checklist section (1, 2, 3 or 4) read through by the group and discussed. Where necessary, explanation is sought from the teacher. Students are asked to apply the questions in their section to the film as it is shown, taking notes as they see fit. Following the viewing, group members share their responses to the questions (they are encouraged to raise other questions they regard as appropriate to their section theme, but not included in the checklist). Second, they prepare a presentation for the class, incorporating video clips in support of the points they wish to make. Group presentations follow, with opportunities for questioning and discussion after each presentation. The activity can be repeated around further films with groups taking on different checklist sections (the class being invited to suggest amendments and refinements to the checklist during time allocated to pre-viewing discussion).

Potential

An activity designed to develop students' sensitivity to, and understanding of, the messages, overt and covert, of natural history films. In discussion sessions, a number of key issues may emerge:

❑ **Anthropomorphism** Is anthropomorphism undesirable in its projection of human perceptions onto the animal world (e.g. with regard to dominance and submission, rank and order)? Are animals, their behaviours and relationships, misconstrued as a result? Is anthropomorphism defensible, even desirable, in that it provides one means of breaching the species-barrier between

---

The early Disney movies came with their own constricting logic. The animal stories they trafficked in were among other things transparent allegories of progress, paeans to the official cult of exploration, industrial development, and an ever rising standard of living. Those blooming flowers in 'living colour' — a signature of Disney's film work — legitimized our metaphors about economic growth. The flowers were typically shown only to the point of 'perfection.' Rarely did we see them fading, decaying, consumed by micro-organisms that returned them to the earth — part of some other economy, a larger collective cycle of life and death of which we humans are also a part. Like nineteenth-century accounts of the 'winning' of the American West, these post-war nature stories were told over and again. They were fictions of victory for the new Century of Progress.

Humans have always invented ways to form an interactive relationship with the Earth, often by endowing that Earth with the qualities of the only subjects we know — ourselves. Nature and wildlife movies (and particularly the early work of Walt Disney) are thus one expression of a long human tradition of investing the natural world with meaning. Those meanings are as often as not, laden with sexism, colonialism, and species hierarchy. *Bear Country and Beaver Valley* are good examples of Disney's early work in the genre. Made in the early 1950s, they are stories of human families living like bears and beavers in a North American Arcadia. Here, we're told, 'Nature is the dramatist.' Mother bear looks after the youngsters while papa bear hunts for food. The cubs are taught to be obedient — to stay out of trouble or they'll get sent to the den to bed. Meanwhile, when he's out fishing papa bear greets lordly moose, timid deer, and Mrs. Wren opening her family's summer cottage. Over in Beaver Valley life is much the same, only in that society beavers seem to be mired in wage labour while otters practise primitive communism. Beavers are solid (Canadian) citizens who build solid houses. And not only houses, but dams, canals, bridges, and other engineering works. They're helped in this by crayfish bulldozers. Well-mannered and unassuming, the beavers disapprove of the carefree otters — vagabonds who sleep anywhere and have no respect for honest work. All of the animals in the valley are heterosexual, of course, and observe marriage — with celebrations and proper honeymoon protocol.

— *Alexander Wilson*[5]

SHOOTING ANIMALS: A CHECKLIST FOR EXPLORING NATURE FILMS

1. ANTHROPOMORPHISM (i.e. attributing human behaviours, characteristics and motivations to animals)
- Are individual animals focused upon as 'leading characters'? Are they given names?
- Are the lives of animals portrayed in narrative form; as an adventure story?
- Are explanations for animal behaviour offered that draw upon observed human behaviour?
- Are animal behaviours depicted as comic or cute? How are baby animals described?
- Are criteria for understanding social relations in human society applied to social relationships between animals?
- In sequences showing animal movement, is the movement described in terms borrowed from human dance or sport?

2. DEPICTION OF THE NATURAL WORLD
- Is the natural environment in which the animals live depicted as an unspoilt paradise? As a refuge to which humans can turn for emotional and spiritual refreshment? As a commodity to be consumed by humans in terms of sightseeing or tourism? As under threat?
- Is the animal world portrayed as being about the survival of the fittest? A constant struggle for dominance? A world divided into predator and prey? Or is it portrayed as one in which there is co-existence and mutual reliance?
- Is the environment depicted as isolated from and, hence, unaffected and uncontaminated by the rest of the world?
- Do humans, and the impact of human activity, feature in the portrayal of the animal's environment?

3. WHAT WORLDVIEW DOES THE FILM EMBRACE?
- Does the film opt for the portrayal of individual animals? Or is there careful exploration of animals within their community/ecosystem?
- Are humans depicted as destroyers or saviours of nature (i.e. as developers, poachers, careless campers or as protectors of endangered species, environmental campaigners) or as both?
- Is the portrayal of nature used to showcase the wonders of technology (i.e. photographic technology or the technology of animal research/species protection)?
- Does the film state or imply that human encroachment on wilderness is inevitable and that the best we can hope for are effective conservation programmes?
- Does the film offer an environmental ethic critical of human attitudes and behaviours towards the natural world?

4. WHERE DOES THE SHOOT STOP?
- Does it stop with the animals and leave the viewer with the message that all is right with their world?
- Or, does it depict the animals' environment as under threat or in crisis without really exploring the roots of the threat/crisis?
- Or, does it focus on, and critique, economic and political causes behind species loss and the destruction of the natural world?
- And, does it address the ethical (and spiritual) implications of loss and destruction?

P

humans and non-human animals and, as such, helps foster humane attitudes?

❑ **Ideologies** What are the range of ideological stances evident in nature films? Is the ideology *accommodationist/conformist* in that the principle of economic growth is left unchallenged and it is explicitly or implicitly suggested that further development/ resource depletion is inevitable, indeed desirable? Is careful conservation management held to be a sufficient strategy to protect nature? Is it *reformist* in that the factors behind environmental destruction are identified but the solution strategies offered, nonetheless, fall short of demanding a halt to consumerism and economic growth? Is it *transformative* in that the social, political and personal implications of turning away from a growth-driven economy are considered?

❑ **Conventions** To what extent are conventional wisdom or long-standing shibboleths — about the survival of the fittest, child rearing, gender roles, the innateness of competitive drives — embraced unreservedly in nature films and applied uncritically to the animal world?

❑ **The medium of film** Is it possible to engage in effective environmental advocacy through the medium of film? Or is the advocacy enervated by the medium (just as a contribution to a Sunday colour supplement condemning consumerism is enfeebled by the consumerist thrust of the organ in which it appears)?

Extension

As a longer media studies project, this activity can be undertaken several times using representative animal-related natural history television films from each decade since the 1950s. An understanding of how nature films have evolved in terms of style, content and focus can, thus, be built up. Environmentally-oriented movies also provide good stimulus material for the activity; for instance, *The Emerald Forest* (1988) or *The Bear* (1988).

Source

This activity has been inspired by Alexander Wilson's reflections on natural history television programmes and movies in *The culture of nature. North American landscape from Disney to the Exxon Valdez*, Toronto, Between the Lines, 1991.

References

1. Ontario Ministry of Education, *Media literacy resource guide*, 1989, 7.
2. *Ibid.*, 7-10.
3. Len Masterman to David Selby, 30.1.1992. The most thoroughgoing study of animals in the media is to be found in Alexander Wilson's, *The culture of nature. North American landscape from Disney to the Exxon Valdez*, Toronto, Between the Lines, 1991. Chapter 4 is entitled 'Looking at the nonhuman. Nature movies and TV'.
4. Wilson, A., *op. cit.*, 121.
5. *Ibid.*, 118-19, 129.

Chapter 13

Humane Futures

INTRODUCTION

The term *alternative futures* is used to signify the wide range of futures, at all levels, personal to global, open to us at any point in time. Alternative futures are commonly divided up into *possible, probable* and *preferred* futures. *Possible futures* include all future scenarios that *might conceivably come about.* The broadest category of all, they include futures in the short, medium and long term, scenarios emanating from multiple and diverse perspectives and scenarios that are not hidebound by dominant paradigms and seemingly inexorable contemporary trends. In educational terms, the category of possible futures offers the greatest scope for developing and honing lateral and divergent thinking skills and the creative use of the imagination. *Probable futures* encompass all future scenarios that are *likely to come about.* They are the firmest category in that they, for the most part, involve the short-term projection and interplay of current cultural, economic, political and social trends. *Preferred futures* are futures *we would like to come about* given our values and priorities. Exploration of preferred futures offers excellent scope for values clarification work in the classroom.

The interplay of the three categories within the educational process (*Fig. 1*) is important. Our choice of preferred futures is likely to be based upon a narrow range of options unless study programmes encourage exploration of the wealth of possible futures. In the final analysis, there can be no freedom of choice unless 'one understands the full range of options available *and* the

Fig. 1

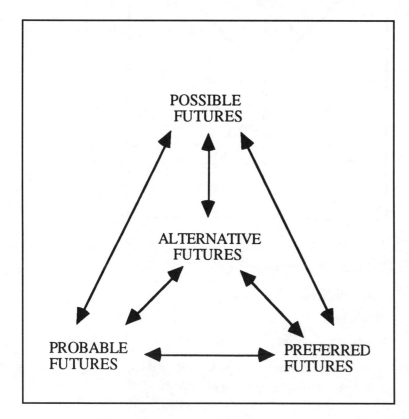

POSSIBLE
FUTURES

ALTERNATIVE
FUTURES

PROBABLE
FUTURES

PREFERRED
FUTURES

possible consequences of each option'[1]. Likewise, our exploration of probable futures is likely to lead us into embracing a 'business as usual' view of the future unless we are actively encouraged to think about how we might translate the possible and preferred into the probable.

Possible and probable future scenarios can embrace both the *optimistic* and *pessimistic*. Preferred futures are mostly optimistic but may involve 'better of two evils' choices amongst those with a pessimistic view of the future. Other useful ways of exploring alternative futures is to consider them from the point of view of *desirability* and *plausibility*.

Futures-oriented education is only in a limited sense about *prediction* of what is going to happen. It is rather about the future as a *'zone of potentiality'*, about knowledge of what is possible rather than knowledge of certainties.[2] It is also about helping students recognise that human choices and actions (including their own choices and actions) flow into, and help shape, the future.

Newly prominent concepts within futures thinking that relate directly to the values of humane education are those of *intergenerational justice* and *sustainability*. The former suggests that those alive today have a responsibility to subsequent generations as much as to their own. 'Treat the earth well. It was not given to you by your parents. It was loaned to you by your children'. The concept of *intergenerational rights*, and its implications for our present-day behaviours and decisions, provides a powerful focus for the humane classroom (see the activity, *Our Inheritance, Their Inheritance*). *Sustainability* likewise asks that we review, and radically readjust, our expectations out of respect for the Earth and so as to ensure a future for humans, animals and the environment.

The EarthKind classroom is, by definition, futures-oriented. Humane educators seek to promote kindness, caring, compassion,

respect for all living things, human and non-human, and a commitment to justice, as a means of creating a better tomorrow. They advocate an educational process predicated upon those values and having as a principal outcome the emergence of 'practical visionaries', i.e. people with both a clear vision of a preferred future and the commitment, confidence and practical skills to go about realising that vision.

The EarthKind classroom provides a springboard for practising being a practical visionary'. Having identified their individually and collectively preferred futures, students can be encouraged to take steps to realise those futures through school-based social, political and environmental action projects (see *Chapter 15*). This is what Alvin Toffler has called the process of 'anticipatory democracy'.

ACTIVITIES

■ *FUTURE TIME LINES*

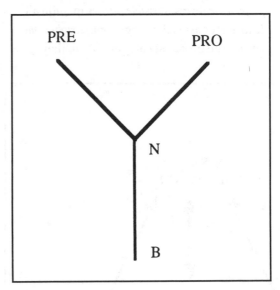

Fig. 2

Suitable for
Upper primary/secondary

Time needed
30 minutes

Resources
A large sheet of sugar paper and four felt tip pens of different colours for each pair of students.

Procedure

1. Students, working in pairs, prepare time lines (see *Fig. 2*). Between point B (birth) and N (now), they fill in key events that have happened so far during their lives which they think will influence the future. It is up to pairs to decide whether they focus upon personal, local, national or global events or whether they operate at more than one level. From N to PRO (probable futures), they fill in events they consider *are likely to happen* in their lifetimes. From N to PRE (preferred futures), they fill in events that they *would like to see happen* during their lifetimes. It is for pairs to decide how far apart the PRO and PRE stems should be. If what they consider probable is also their preference, then the two stems can merge into one. If their visions of the probable and preferred are far apart, then that can be represented by two highly divergent lines. Different coloured felt pens can be used to indicate events particular to an individual and/or a failure to achieve consensus around probable and preferred futures. Pairs join together to share their work prior to plenary debriefing.

2. Students, working in pairs, prepare timelines specifically on human treatment of animals. Between B and N, they log events, developments and trends during their lifetimes that mark either a more or a less humane treatment of animals. From N to PRO, they record developments and trends likely to occur in the future. From N to PRE, they fill in events they would prefer to see happen. Pairs come together to share and discuss their probable and preferred future scenarios.

Potential

The activity provides a framework for reviewing significant events, developments and trends during students' lifetimes before asking them to project forward. The focus on preferred futures offers scope for values clarification, whilst the likely gap between preferred and probable futures highlights the nature and scale of efforts required to achieve more humane, environmentally-friendly and sustainable

societies. During the debriefing of the activity, students can be asked to brainstorm (see p.205) things they could do to help towards the realisation of a preferred future shared in common. This might, in turn, lead to the kind of action projects described in *Chapter 15*.

Source

After an exercise described by Cathie Holden in *World Studies Journal*, vol. 6, no. l.

The future of the past is in the present
The future of the present is in the past
The future of the future is in the present.

— John McHale

■ *TIME CHAIRS*

Suitable for

Secondary (see note at end of *Procedure* for primary use)

Time needed

50 minutes

Resources

An open classroom space; three chairs for each pair of students; a tape recorder or compact disc player with a recording of electronic or New Age music; a chart or overhead projector transparency of the sets of questions (see samples, *Fig. 3*).

Procedure

The class forms into pairs. Each pair sets up their three chairs in a line facing in the same direction. One partner sits in the centre chair. The standing partner is told that she has the role of interviewer. The seated partner chooses the set of questions upon which she wishes to be interviewed and the interview begins (follow-up questions are permitted). Some five minutes are allowed for interviews to run their course. Seated students are then told that, when the music begins, they will move from the centre (present) chair ten years back in time to the rear (past) chair. As they move back, they should try to express physically how they looked, and moved, ten years back. When the music stops, the interviewer is to repeat the interview (same set of questions) and the questions are to be answered as if in the past. After five minutes, the music moves the interviewee past the present chair and ten years into the future (the front chair). As before, she should try to express how she thinks she will look, and move, in ten years' time. The interview is repeated. Time is given for a short feedback session (so that impressions are secured as part of the collective memory) before the interviewer and interviewee change roles and the entire procedure is repeated. The new interviewee has the right to opt for the set of questions of her choice. When the second round of interviews is concluded, a thorough class debriefing follows.

[*Note:* the number of years into the past and future should, of course, be reduced for younger students; the activity can, indeed, be attempted using a span of several months rather than several years.]

Potential

An activity in which students are likely to become absorbed in freshly-recalled memories and future imaginings; so much so that it may prove impossible to restrict interviews to five minutes ! The debriefing can usefully begin with a sharing of feelings engendered. The sharing can lead directly into discussion of a number of interesting areas. Was it more difficult to be interviewed about past, present or future? Why?

Which set of questions proved most daunting, especially during the 'past' and 'future' interviews? Why? Did interviewees find it easy or difficult to recall their past attitudes and hopes? Were they thinking about animal welfare or globally, ten (or chosen number of) years back? Were their views of the future optimistic or pessimistic? Did they feel they could affect the future? What thoughts has the interview experience raised, about the speed and effects of change at all levels, personal to global? In what ways, if any, has it highlighted the interlocking of past, present and future?

Follow-up

A stimulating follow-up activity is to ask students to design sets of questions for other groups.

Variation

The three chairs can be set facing forward in a triangle. The rear chair represents the present; the two front chairs the probable and preferred future, respectively. Seated students are interviewed on their chosen set of questions, answering in the present, and from the vantage point of their envisaged probable and preferred futures.

Source

Michal Pasternak, International School of Geneva.

Fig. 3

Personal
1. How old are you?
2. What is your home situation?
3. Describe an ordinary day in your life.
4. What do you consider the most important thing you have learned over the last ten years?
5. What is your greatest personal wish?

Animal-related
1. How old are you?
2. Which animals are you closest to at this time?
3. What things most concern you about the treatment of animals at this time?
4. What positive changes in the treatment of animals have taken place in the last ten years?
5. What are your hopes for change in the way we treat animals in the next ten years?

Global
1. How old are you?
2. What three things please you about the state of the planet?
3. What three things concern you about the state of the planet?
4. What do you think has been the greatest tragedy for humankind in the last ten years?
5. What positive changes for humankind have you seen over the last ten years?

■ *FUTURE CIRCLE*

Suitable for

Primary/secondary

Time needed

5 minutes

Resources

None, save an open space

Procedure

Students form a circle. They turn so they are each facing a neighbour (the facilitator should join in, if necessary, so that everybody is paired). They are then asked to reflect for a while on the one human quality they would most like to take into the future, so the future is a better place to be. At a signal from the facilitator, they share the quality with the person they are facing, avoiding explanation or discussion. As they pass each other, they take on the other person's chosen quality as their own and offer it to the next person they face. The process continues until they again face their original partner.

Potential

A brisk and lively way of focusing upon those human characteristics that appear to most lend themselves to realising preferred futures. In the debriefing students can be asked to reflect upon the degree of commonality/overlap in the qualities chosen. To what extent are they the most prized qualities in today's society? What would happen if individuals, groups and institutions sought to adjust their attitudes, behaviours and relationships (to humans and to non-human animals) to more accord with the cluster of qualities pooled? The qualities can be written up in chart form and subsequently used as a focus for reflection on whether the class, individually and collectively, is 'walking their talk'. The activity can be used, without debriefing, as a good closing energiser to a session on humane futures. As an end-of-year staff development exercise, it can be used to share and record qualities that colleagues most wish to take into the next school year. The list is referred back to at staff meetings during the year.

■ *ACRONYM*

Suitable for

Upper primary/secondary

Time needed

40 minutes

Resources

Sheet of paper and felt pen for each student; a selection of felt pens of different colours; seven half sheets of sugar paper.

Procedure

The term, acronym, is explained and examples given, e.g. UNESCO, PLO, PTO, SWALK. Class members are also asked to volunteer acronyms with which they are familiar. Working individually, students are then set the task of devising a snappy, attractive-sounding acronym of four to ten letters that reflects their favoured vision of the world of the future, e.g. ROBE (Respecting Our Beautiful Earth), WOMB (Women Overturn Macho Behaviour), PRIDE (People Respecting Individual Differences Everywhere), CAKE (Caring and Kindness Everywhere), HUMANE (Hopeful, Understanding, Multiracial, Aware, Non-violent, Ecological). The acronym should reflect the sense of what it stands for if at all possible. Sufficient time having elapsed, students form groups of four or five. One by one, they read their acronyms to each other and explain the thinking behind their choice. The group's next task is to devise a new acronym reflecting the shared aspects of their vision of the world of the future. Using felt pens, the acronym is written on the sugar paper provided along with appropriate decoration and embellishment. Other possibilities at this stage include the design and drawing of logos or symbols reflecting the acronym, badge production, and the preparation and presentation of short dramatic sketches pointing up the message of the acronym. Groups display their work and share their thinking with the rest of the class. Discussion follows.

Potential

An activity that encourages students to reflect upon and share their values, and that is likely to involve some challenge to those values. How easy was it for individuals to express their favoured vision of the world of the future given the constraints of the acronym? To what extent did their difficulty mirror the problem of living to one's values in the real world? Were acronyms broad-focused, covering a range of issues, or narrow-focused? If the latter, what issues in particular were focused upon? Did acronyms concentrate on personal, local, national or global futures? When groups formed, what degree of overlap was there between the acronyms? How easy was it to achieve a consensus view of a preferred future and an acronym sufficiently reflecting that view? Was the final acronym a bold visionary statement or a watered-down version of individual acronyms? A useful activity for exercising lateral thinking, consensus-seeking and negotiation skills.

■ OUR INHERITANCE, THEIR INHERITANCE

Suitable for

Primary/secondary

Time needed

60 minutes

Resources

Two copies of the *Inheritance* chart (*Fig. 4*) and a blank sheet of paper for each group of 3/4 students.

Procedure

Students are introduced to the idea that what one generation does can in some respects improve, and, in others, lead to a deterioration in, life quality for subsequent generations. A few examples are given of how life today has been beneficially and adversely affected by the actions of past generations. Groups are first asked to make their own lists of the positive and negative inheritance from previous generations on the first *Inheritance* chart. Lists are shared and discussed as a class.

In completing the second chart, groups imagine themselves as young people in two generations' time and list ways in which the past few generations have a) enhanced and b) undermined their quality of life. They then compose a 'To

INHERITANCE	
POSITIVE	**NEGATIVE**

Fig. 4

Whomsoever it May Concern' letter to somebody living in the 1990s pointing out what was and what was not being done then to ensure that future generations enjoyed equal life benefits and opportunities. Lists are shared and letters read out.

Potential

A simple, but effective, way of helping students understand the concept of intergenerational justice. A comparison of the two sets of lists can be very instructive. Are we storing up a more negative inheritance for future generations than our predecessors left us? Is there a shift of emphasis in the positive and negative aspects of our own inheritance and of the likely inheritance of future generations? What are the main problems we are leaving people in the future? Are they problems that are easily overcome or are they intractable in nature? How should we set about leaving a better inheritance?

The Iroquois tribal council began each meeting with this invocation: 'Let us remember in our deliberations the effect our decisions may have on the next seven generations'. Any vote taken was not only for those present, but also for those who would live two hundred years in the future.

—*Kathryn Sheehan and Mary Waidner*[3]

■ *NEW YEAR RESOLUTIONS*

Suitable for

Upper secondary

Time needed

50 minutes

Resources

A copy of *Story of a Year*; a metronome; a sheet of sugar paper and felt pen for each pair of students.

Procedure

With the metronome ticking, the teacher reads *Story of a Year*. At the close of the reading, students are asked to form pairs and are given five minutes to decide what the next two sentences in the story might be. Sentences are shared with the class. Pairs are then asked to agree upon ten new year resolutions. The resolutions are written, in prioritised order, on sugar paper. Pairs then form sixes to share and discuss their lists and to negotiate an agreed list of ten resolutions. Reporting back and class discussion follows.

Potential

A provocative fable, designed to put the enormous impact of human beings on the planet into a proper time perspective, *Story of a Year* can elicit strong reactions. Some students are likely to easily identify with its thrust; others are likely to object to the heavy responsibility it places on the 'rich North' for the present state of the planet. [The differences aired and particular points of contention identified can provide a stimulus for subsequent individual and group research.] Some students may respond to the challenge of the story with positive and innovative ideas for personal and social change; some may be daunted by the range and scale of the problems we face. The resolutions can be discussed in terms of their relevance for our present global condition, whether they are realistic, their acceptability and their likely impact should they be embraced. Resolutions most commonly occurring should be identified and the reason(s) for their prevalence discussed. Would groups of students in other countries, cultures or sections of

---

STORY OF A YEAR

And then, as the bells chimed the beginning of the new year, the people had the world to themselves. For many months, so far as we know, they were very quiet. From 1 January until the end of September, they just wandered around in a small groups — hunting animals with spears and arrows; sheltering in caves, dressing themselves in animal skins. On about 1 October they began to learn about seeds and manure and so on, and about how to herd and milk animals. By about 23 October some of them were living in biggish cities. This was mainly in Egypt and North India, and in the countries between.

Moses came and went on about 11 November. Buddha in India, Socrates in Greece, Confucius in China, all came and went together, though they didn't know each other, on about 3 December. Christ appeared on 8 December, as also, give or take a few hours, did the great wall of China and Julius Caesar; Mahomet on 15 December.

On about 23 December there began to be biggish cities in northern Europe. On about 27 December and into the next day people went out from these cities and they began stealing from the rest of the world. They stole the Americas, both North and South, they stole India, and during the last hour of 29 December they stole Africa. Just before midday on 30 December they had a big war amongst themselves, and then had another big war late in the afternoon.

In the last thirty hours of the year these people from northern Europe were pushed back out of India and Africa, and also back out of many other countries, though not out of North America and parts of Oceania, where they had become very settled indeed. Also, as the closing hours of the year fled away, these people invented nuclear weapons, they landed on the moon and were responsible for helping to double the world's population. Their beguiling materialist culture caused more oil and more metal to be used up than had been used in the previous three hundred and sixty-four days put together. It was also responsible for the enslavement of domestic animals in factory forms, an unprecedented rate of destruction of natural and wilderness environments, and a phenomenal escalation in pollution of land, sea and air.

The bells were chiming again. It was the start of a new year ...

society have come up with similar reactions to the story and similar lists and prioritizations? At some point, the teacher should remind the class that most resolutions made on New Year's Eve are broken on New Year's Day. What is likely to happen if we fail to make, or adhere to, our resolutions for the future?

Source

The story is based upon (but much changed from) *History of a Day* in Richardson, R., *Learning for change in world society: reflections, activities and resources*, World Studies Project, 1979, 59.

> *The old hen stood up and squinted at the new arrivals. 'Listen, sisters, as this is the first day of your new life, I will tell the short, sad story of the battery hen. For the next year you will live a cramped life of egg-laying misery. You will squabble and fight and become like me. If you are a good layer you may be allowed to live a little longer. But in the end, it's the chicken-soup lorry for all of us, as sure as eggs is eggs.' Attila stared at her. 'But they can't do that'.*
> © Paddy Mounter 1991.
> Extracted from *Attila the Hen*, published by Corgi Books. All rights reserved.

■ *THE GREAT EGGSCAPE*

Suitable for

Primary

Time needed

Blocks of time over several days

Resources

A copy of Paddy Mounter's, *Attila the Hen* (Corgi Books, 1991); paper, pens and felt pens for each groups of three students.

Procedure

Attila the Hen is read in sections to the class. At decisive points in the story (for example, after Attila's dream of the soup monster and before the great Eggscape), groups are asked to predict the continuation of the story, to write what happens next in their own words and to draw pictures illustrating their agreed version. The stories are read out and drawings shared. The class discusses the alternative versions, and opinions are shared as to which might be closest to the story itself (it should be emphasised that this is not a discussion of the quality of the alternatives, and that excellent stories could veer far away from the original). The next section of *Attila* is then read out and the class discusses how close they came to predicting what happened. The process is repeated three or four times during the reading of the story.

Potential

An excellent technique for exploring the problems surrounding prediction. How accurately were students able to predict what happened next? Were they able to extrapolate from clues, obvious or not so obvious, in the story so far? Or, were there just too many variables at play to make prediction easy? What lessons can be drawn about making predictions in real life? *Attila the Hen* will also provide fruitful opportunities for discussing the practice and ethics of factory farming. Activities from *Chapter 8*, for example, *Factory Learning* (p.179), can be linked to this activity.

The same technique can, of course, be used with other stories and with plays and film dramas.

■ *HUMANE FUTURES WHEEL*

Suitable for

Upper primary/secondary

Time needed

45 minutes

Resources

Large sheet of paper and felt tip pen per three/four students.

Procedure

An event, idea or trend, likely to lead to a more humane future, is drawn and circled in the centre of each group's sheet. Groups are then asked to consider possible consequences of that event, idea or trend. Single lines are drawn outwards and the consequences written in and circled. Groups go on to consider the range of possible repercussions emanating from the first-order consequences, this time drawing double lines outwards and writing in and circling second-order consequences. The process is continued for third, fourth and, possibly, fifth-order consequences.

Potential

Groups should be given the opportunity to carefully examine each other's work. Discussion can usefully focus upon differences in group presentations, the problematic nature of forecasting, given the unknowns and variables involved, and possible interrelationships between the various second, third, fourth and fifth-order consequences. Future wheels offer a linear model of causality, and it is not only important to consider the relationship between items not directly linked together on the wheel — an additional exercise can be for students to discuss and draw in links — but also to reflect upon whether any of the outward-moving causal links might thus be reversed.

Variation

A newspaper article describing a likely future humane development or trend can be used for the centre of the wheel. Students proceed to examine first, second, third, fourth and fifth-order consequences.

Source

From an idea in Fitch, R.M. and Svengalis, C.M., *Futures unlimited*, Washington DC, National Council for the Social Studies, 1979.

Fig. 5 Humane Futures Wheel

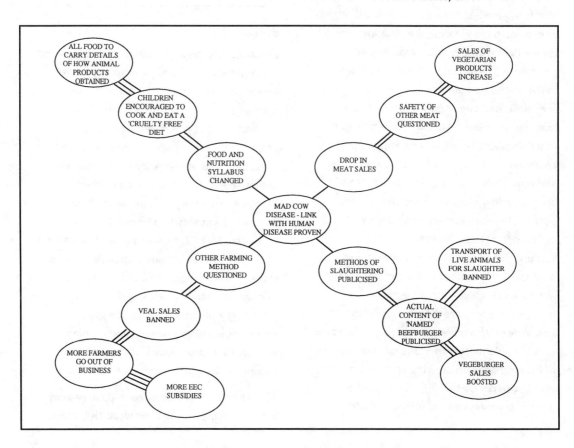

■ *INVENTING A HUMANE FUTURE (BACKWARDS)*

Suitable for

Secondary (primary in simplified form — see box under *Procedure*).

Time needed

This activity is best attempted in stages over a period of several weeks.

Resources

Six large sheets of paper, felt-tip pens, pens and pencils for each group of students.

Procedure

Students form groups of four. Each group is asked to decide upon a major breakthrough towards the realisation of a more humane world that they think could happen in the mid-term future (i.e. 2000–2050) or more distant future (2050+); for example, the end of factory farming, the promulgation of a U.N. Declaration of Species' Rights in 2048 on the centenary of the U.N. Declaration of Human Rights, comprehensive legislation banning all cruel sports, the withdrawal of all meat dishes from school meal menus. In choosing an event, students are asked to give some initial thoughts as to how, in broad terms, the situation evolved from where we are now to what they are envisaging as happening. Groups then move on to the central part of the activity, which is to prepare a front page newspaper story and headline covering the event in question, plus *five* other stories and headlines covering important landmarks in the chain of events between then and now. Each front page is to be dated and to show clearly the linkages, negative and/or positive, between successive landmarks. In filling out each front page, groups are asked to take into account, and examine, the possible ecological, economic, political, social and technological impact and implications of the particular development they are describing, and to speculate on repercussions that might then arise, which would in turn affect the rate and direction of future change. In drawing up their front pages, groups can decide to follow the style of a particular newspaper or, alternatively, try to

reflect the changing face of newspapers through future years as they imagine them. As they work on their front page stories, groups may well wish to explore library or project collections on their chosen topic and/or to consult people in the community with a special knowledge or interest in the topic. Their task is complete when they have prepared six front pages that, together, present a comprehensive picture of how their envisaged future breakthrough towards a more humane world actually came about.

> *Really good for primary children. It's best to give them the end headline and then brainstorm what may lead to that event. In groups of four, ask them to draw the lead-up events with the newspaper headline only. To make it sound more exciting, tell them that they are the photographer and ask them to draw what they would photograph. Give them the dates for each sixth, as many would be unable to break the years into equal lengths. I think that even younger children, i.e. 7, could cope with this activity. For more able children, ask them to write the newspaper's opening paragraph. Children could use their pictures as a stimulus for drama, by recreating their images as a series of stills.*
>
> — Cambridgeshire primary teacher

Potential

This is a powerful and multi-faceted approach to exploring alternative, more humane, futures. It allows free rein to the imagination whilst requiring that students think through the implications and repercussions of their future projections. It also gives students the opportunity to examine and, if necessary, adjust their values as they speculate about future possibilities and the impact of those possibilities on various stakeholders in society. The process of writing history backwards, draws upon and helps refine, divergent, convergent and reflective thinking skills, creative writing skills, research and information retrieval skills, and forecasting skills. The activity places a premium on group consensus-seeking, planning and problem solving. Facilitators may wish to encourage groups to allot particular roles to members.

The activity can be debriefed in plenary with each group presenting their work and taking questions. Alternatively, the *Circus* procedure can be adopted. Each group sticks their six front pages up on the classroom wall and leaves one member of the group beside the pages as a 'guide'. Other members go to examine the work of other groups, asking the 'guide' in question for any necessary explanation or clarification. Group members take turns as 'guide' so giving everybody a chance to circulate. Plenary discussion follows the *Circus*.

Variations

1. An alternative, resources allowing, is to ask groups to prepare a tape-slide or video presentation based around their future scenario. This could be done by drawing from slide collections, by collecting pictures that can be made into slides or filmed, or by taking new slide photographs. The students write and tape an accompanying narrative, adding appropriate background music.

2. Groups compose their six front pages on computer.

3. The students can be given the option of choosing positive or negative future scenarios. If a group chooses a less humane future, a crucial part of the debriefing will be to challenge the group in particular and the class in general to confront the question of what they, and others, could do to avert such a future.

4. *Short activity.* A breakthrough at a fixed date is chosen. Groups prepare the front page of a newspaper that includes an article explaining developments since our actual present.

■ *FUTURESCAPES*

Suitable for

Secondary

Time needed

50 minutes

Resources

A *Futurescapes* chart (see *Fig. 6*) for each student; a sheet of sugar paper and felt pen for each group of six.

Procedure

Working individually, students complete the *Futurescapes* chart, indicating whether each of the future scenarios described is, in their view, *possible* (i.e. a future that *might just* come about), *probable* (i.e. a future that is *likely* to come about) or *impossible* (i.e. a future that could *never* happen); also whether it is *desired* or *not desired* (i.e. a future they would or would not like to happen). A tick should be placed in one of the first three columns, a second tick in one of the last two columns. Students then form into pairs to share, explain and discuss their individual decisions. If, as a result of the interchange, a pair or individual change their mind about the placing of a tick this should be indicated by circling the tick with a different coloured pen and drawing an arrow to the column now preferred. Pairs now form into groups of six and repeat the process of sharing, explaining, reviewing and amending their decisions. In addition, they choose one scenario which all group members have identified as a desired future and, using the sugar paper provided, brainstorm ideas as to what they could do individually and collectively, to help realise that future. Should there be no common desired scenario, the group can break into two to brainstorm ideas around two different scenarios. Plenary discussion follows.

Potential

An activity requiring students to confront a range of perspectives and value positions on animal and environmental issues; also to explore in some detail the social, economic and ethical implications of different future scenarios. The final brainstorming section provides students with an opportunity to consider and evaluate

Fig. 6: FUTURESCAPES					
DURING MY LIFETIME:	**POSSIBLE**	**PROBABLE**	**IMPOSSIBLE**	**DESIRED**	**UNDESIRED**
1. There will be laws forbidding blood sports such as fox and deer hunting. Hunting will be looked back upon as a feature of a less civilised age.					
2. There will be major breakthroughs in genetic engineering so that we will have farm animals, looking quite different to those we now know, which will produce a higher yield of meat for less food intake in a shorter space of time.					
3. Experiments on animals will be drastically reduced as all animal testing of soaps and cosmetics is outlawed and as animal experiments to test new medicines and new surgical techniques are, for the most part, replaced by computer simulations and tests on willing human beings.					
4. Rural communities and the rural landscape will be radically transforned with the decline of animal farming and its replacement by vast forest tracts, windmill parks for energy production and the growing of new crops, to meet the dietary protein needs of vegetarians and for fuel purposes. Many communities will disappear altogether.					
5. There will be an end to factory farming as people show they are prepared to pay more for free range meat and animal products, to avoid cruelty to animals.					
6. Zoos will enjoy a new lease of life as a means of helping urban dwellers, especially children, learn about the natural world, and of conserving endangered species. People will go to see the animals but also to watch multi-media presentations on conservation and ecology.					
7. A binding international agreement will be reached to protect all remaining wilderness areas — the remaining rainforests, Antarctica, the Canadian North and others — from exploitation by humans.					
8. For health reasons and to avoid cruelty to animals, vegetarianism (eating no meat), veganism (eating neither meat nor animal produce), become so widespread that meat eaters are reduced to a small minority.					

P

strategies for change. The debriefing can begin by asking one group to report their discussions around a scenario that provoked controversy and disagreement. The issues raised can then be thrown open to the whole class. At appropriate moments, other groups can be asked to share responses to other scenarios as a stimulus to further class discussion. Consideration of action plans is best left until responses to the eight scenarios have been aired.

Extension

The activity is undertaken simultaneously in rural and urban schools and the results (and a report on the plenary discussion) shared by mail or computer link-up. Comments on respective results and reports are subsequently exchanged and the dialogue continued until it has run its course.

Variations

Students are given a skeleton chart and asked to write in one scenario each prior to forming into pairs. Each student writes in their partner's scenario and ticks the columns best reflecting their reaction to that scenario. Pair discussion follows. Groups of six or eight are then formed and scenarios written in and columns ticked prior to discussion.

The teacher can also replace some or all of the scenarios. With due simplification, *Futurescapes* can be attempted with top primary students.

■ *FUTURE SCENARIOS*

Suitable for

Upper secondary

Time needed

40 minutes

Resources

A *Future Scenarios* and *Five Future Scenarios* sheet for each three students.

Procedure

Students are first familiarised with James Robertson's five future scenarios (see p.302); in particular, the three scenarios offering recipes for avoiding global disaster and creating a sustainable future (Authoritarian Control, Hyper-Expansion and Sane, Humane, Ecological). Groups of three are formed and the sheets handed out. A challenge facing humankind is written at the top of the *Future Scenarios* sheet; for example, global warming, the rapid spread of AIDS, the destruction of the tropical rain forests, the trade in rare animal species. The group's task is to decide how those working within the framework of each scenario would seek to address the challenge in question. Groups can work on the same challenge or different ones. The final section of the *Future Scenarios* sheet gives students the opportunity to go beyond the Robertson framework and invent and work with an additional scenario. Reporting back and debriefing follows.

Potential

An activity that challenges students to work through the practical and real-life implications of contrasting prescriptions for a workable, sustainable future. In the debriefing, the class can be asked to evaluate critically, yet constructively, the work of each group and to comment upon the acceptability, feasibility and relevance of the five scenarios presented by Robertson. Groups should be invited to introduce and elaborate upon scenarios they invent. To what extent do students see the scenarios as mutually exclusive and to what extent can they be combined? Robertson says that the acronyms of the Hyper-Expansion future (HE) and the Sane, Humane, Ecological

FIVE FUTURE SCENARIOS

❑ **Business as usual.**
The future will not be radically different from the present. Change, problems and conflicts there will be, but no fundamental rethink of the methods by which we handle them and our outlook and attitudes, is necessary or possible.

❑ **Disaster.**
The future will see an intensification and conflation of the crises the world now faces, such as hunger and starvation, environmental degradation, social breakdown and inter-ethnic strife, leading at some point to global breakdown.

❑ **Authoritarian Control.**
Future disaster will be averted by strong authoritarian government that will enforce law and order; that will use coercive powers to distribute dwindling resources (as it sees fit) and protect the environment.

❑ **Hyper-Expansion.**
Present problems will be overcome by accelerating the development , and more effective use, of science and technology. Progress and increasing technical sophistication are synonymous. Economic, scientific and technological expansion can continue indefinitely.

❑ **Sane, Humane, Ecological.**
The future will require a radical change of direction involving decentralisation, heightened ecological sensitivity and concern, a shift away from elitist and hierarchical power structures and towards sustainable lifestyles and more humane and convivial relationships.[4]

future (SHE) usefully reflect the fact that adherents of the former are predominantly male whilst exponents of the latter see current world crises as the outcome of masculinist values. How do students react to this insight?

P

FUTURE SCENARIOS

THE CHALLENGE

THE AUTHORITARIAN CONTROL RESPONSE

THE HYPER-EXPANSIONIST RESPONSE

THE SANE, HUMANE, ECOLOGICAL RESPONSE

THE...RESPONSE

P

■ *WEIGHTING STATEMENTS ABOUT THE FUTURE*

Suitable for

Upper primary and secondary

Time needed

40 minutes (*Paired Weighting*);
50 minutes (*Shared Weighting*)

Resources

A *Paired Weighting or Shared Weighting* chart (see *Fig. 7*) and statements about the future for each pair of students. A set of statements for use with secondary students is given in *Fig. 8*.

Procedure

1. **Paired Weighting.** Pairs read the statements carefully and then begin to weigh the statements against each other in terms of the degree to which they reflect their view of the future. First, statement one is weighed against statement two; then statement one against statement three, and so on, until every statement has been weighed against every other statement (with six statements there are fifteen decisions to make). In each case, the statement which is agreed to reflect best a pair's view is circled, e.g. 5/6. If a pair cannot reach agreement numbers are left uncircled. Pairs should jot down brief notes on the reasons behind all their decisions. Having weighed all statements against each other, each pair calculates the number of occasions on which each statement has been circled. This will give an overall ranking.

2. **Shared Weighting.** The same procedure is followed but in this case pairs try to agree on an appropriate distribution of percentage points in weighing statements against each other, e.g. 40/60, 70/30, 10/90. This allows for a more subtle assessment of the degree to which the two statements reflect their view of the future. Having weighed all statements against each other, total percentage points, and the average percentage for each statement, obtained by dividing by one less than the number of statements, are inserted in columns 1 and 2 respectively.

3. When pairs have completed their **Paired Weighting** or **Shared Weighting** chart, they form into sixes. Each six explores and reviews the decisions its members have made. Plenary reporting back and discussion follows.

Potential

This activity helps students to recognise their own assumptions about the future through a decision-making process which brings them face to face with other opinions, perspectives and value positions. Skills used include discussion, listening, consensus-seeking and negotiation. In plenary, a pair reporting their inability to weigh some (or even all) statements may be as productive a discussion point as a pair reporting they have achieved consensus. A critical question to ask all students is: 'What are the implications of the decisions you have made for the way you live your life, and the degree of control you have over your own future?'.

Extension

The activity can lead to strong, often very personal, feelings being expressed about freedom of choice or its lack. It is a good idea to give students the chance to reflect their feeling through drawing or painting during or after the debriefing.

Variations

The number of statements can be reduced or increased. The complexity of the statements and the criteria for weighing them can, of course, also be varied. This activity will work equally well with statements on any topic around which there are likely to be a range of perspectives and value positions, e.g. the environment, sustainable development, human and animal rights, race and gender.

Source

Statements 1, 4, 5 and 6 in the sample are drawn from Kaufman, D., *Teaching the future*, Palm Springs (CA), ETC Publications, 1976.

Paired Weighting Chart

1.	$\frac{1}{2}$	$\frac{1}{3}$	$\frac{1}{4}$	$\frac{1}{5}$	$\frac{1}{6}$	Circled Ones =
2.		$\frac{2}{3}$	$\frac{2}{4}$	$\frac{2}{5}$	$\frac{2}{6}$	Circled Twos =
3.			$\frac{3}{4}$	$\frac{3}{5}$	$\frac{3}{6}$	Circled Threes =
4.				$\frac{4}{5}$	$\frac{4}{6}$	Circled Fours =
5.					$\frac{5}{6}$	Circled Fives =
						Circled Sixes =

Shared Weighting Chart

							1. Total for statement	2. Average % for statement	
1.	/	$\frac{1}{2}$▭	$\frac{1}{3}$▭	$\frac{1}{4}$▭	$\frac{1}{5}$▭	$\frac{1}{6}$▭			1
2.	/	/	$\frac{2}{3}$▭	$\frac{2}{4}$▭	$\frac{2}{5}$▭	$\frac{2}{6}$▭			2
3.	/	/	/	$\frac{3}{4}$▭	$\frac{3}{5}$▭	$\frac{3}{6}$▭			3
4.	/	/	/	/	$\frac{4}{5}$▭	$\frac{4}{6}$▭			4
5.	/	/	/	/	/	$\frac{5}{6}$▭			5
6.	/	/	/	/	/	/			6

Fig. 7

P

■ *FUTURES BAG*

Suitable for
Upper secondary

Time needed
15 minutes

Resources
A bag of objects (one per class member).
Examples: rubber band, ball of wool, plasticine, unused exercise book, dice, piece of model railway track, toy ship, rubber ball, pack of cards, toy arrow, calculator, Christmas cracker, whistle, paper dart, bagatelle game, balsa wood, kaleidoscope, binoculars.

Procedure
Each student picks an object from the bag (no rummaging!) and thinks about it as a metaphor for the future. At a signal from the teacher, class members circulate and share metaphors.

Potential
A lively, interesting, and often humorous way of promoting reflection on the relationship between present and future and on human control over the process and direction of change. Did the metaphors promoted by the objects suggest that the future is predetermined, open to human influence or a lottery? Did students find that others were able to suggest alternative metaphors for the object they had picked from the bag? How did they respond to the suggestions offered? To what extent does their chosen metaphor actually reflect their view of the future and of the degree of human control over the future? Is it possible to create a typology of views of the future from the metaphors shared? Which metaphors are students unwilling to embrace? Why?

Source
After an idea suggested by Eleanor Ralph, Frontenac Secondary School, Kingston, Ontario, and Lois Kuebler, Moira Secondary School, Belleville, Ontario.

References
1. Kauffman, D.L., Futurism and future studies, National Education Association of the United States, 1976, 11.
2. *Ibid.,*.
3. Sheehan, K., & Waidner, M., *Earthchild. Games, stories, activities, experiments & ideas about living lightly on planet Earth*, Tulsa, Council Oak Books, 1991, 5.
4. Robertson, J., *The sane alternative. A choice of futures*, James Robertson (Spring Cottage, 9 New Road, Ironbridge, Shropshire, TF8 7AU), 1983, 14-23.

Sample Statements

1. The future is like a great roller coaster on a moonless night. It exists, twisting ahead of us in the dark, although we can only see each part as we come to it. We are locked in our seats, and nothing we may know or do will change the course that is laid out for us.

2. The future is like a blank sheet of paper. It is there for us all to fill in by our actions and decisions in the present. If we choose the future we want and consciously and purposefully set about trying to make it happen in our daily lives, it might well materialise. If we leave the powers-that-be to decide upon and plan the future, we will get a certain kind of future — one dominated by the powerful.

3. The future is like a railway track between two great cities. The direction is set but we may be able to switch points now and then and ride along parallel or divergent tracks to the same destination. We also have some choices about what to do in our carriage as the train rattles along.

4. The future is entirely random, a colossal dice game. A bullet is deflected by twig and kills one person instead of another. A scientist checks a spoiled culture and throws it away, or looks more closely at it and discovers penicillin. Since everything is chance, all we can do is play the game, pray to the gods of fortune, and enjoy what good luck comes our way.

5. The future is like a great ocean — there are many possible destinations at all levels, personal to global, and many different routes to each destination. We can choose whatever future we want, if we work with a purpose for it. There will always be currents, storms and reefs to be dealt with but we can sail our ship to where we want it to go. In short, human actions and decisions shape the future.

6. The future is a mighty river and we are in a boat on the river. With great force the river flows steadily on; there are definite banks and a strong current. We have to follow the river, but we can look ahead and avoid the whirlpools and sandbars and pick the best path through the rapids. We have some, limited, control over where we go.

Fig. 8

P

Chapter 14
___

Codes, Charters, Conventions and Declarations

INTRODUCTION

Over the last two hundred years, codes, charters, conventions and declarations have played an important part in creating and helping sustain juster, more democratic, more humane and more rights-respectful societies. From the French Declaration of the Rights of Man of August 1789 up to the United Nations Convention on the Rights of the Child of November 1989, such documents have embodied the aspirations and ideals of those who value freedom, justice and human dignity. They have also been instrumental in helping embed those aspirations and ideals in popular consciousness. Codes, charters, conventions and declarations have been seen by their originators as an effective means of summarising first principles and of helping us recall our rights and obligations. They have also served the purpose of laying down benchmarks against which the actions and behaviours of individuals, groups and governments can be judged.

In this chapter, activities giving students the opportunity to devise their own codes, charters, conventions and declarations are described. They involve brainstorming, drafting, debate, consensus seeking, co-operative decision making, negotiating and voting; in short, processes that are central to the humane classroom. They also present opportunities for students to enter dialogue with community, environmental, humane, political and religious organisations around the documents produced (as such, they can be usefully linked with *Children's Hearings*, p.322).

The landmark codes, charters, conventions and declarations of the past two hundred years have been human-centric documents. Underpinning the activities presented here is the strong suggestion that, as we approach the twenty-first century, it is time to devise statements of values and intent predicated upon a biocentric ethic and seeking the well-being of the entire biotic community.

ACTIVITIES

■ *IN THE NEWS*

Suitable for

Primary/lower secondary

Time needed

1. 60 minutes; 2. 40 minutes; 3. to be judged by the teacher.

Resources

A selection of pictures of animals being treated well and treated badly from humane organisations' newspapers and newsletters.

Procedure

1. Students are asked to collect pictures from newspapers and magazines showing people and animals being treated in different ways. Groups of three or four are formed and group members' cuttings mixed together in one pile. A small selection of pictures provided by the teacher are added to each pile. Groups are asked to examine the pictures, one by one, and place them in two piles; one of pictures of people and animals being treated well, the other of people and animals being treated badly. They then look through each pile and make lists of types of kind treatment and types of ill-treatment as evidenced in the pictures. Plenary debriefing begins with groups reading out their two lists. The teacher records the lists on the board or overhead projection transparency. Discussion follows. Do people and animals seem to be treated equally well/badly? Were the types of ill-treatment similar/different? Were class members upset as much by evidence of animal ill-treatment as by that of ill-treatment of people? Is ill-treatment of animals and people equally unacceptable or is one more blameworthy than the other? Do animals deserve equal consideration? What can we do to ensure that animals and people are treated kindly? What could we do if we witnessed an animal or person being badly treated?

2. At an appropriate point in the discussion, the teacher suggests that the class draw up a

Kindness Code for our treatment of animals and each other. Groups re-form and are asked to translate their lists into a number of short statements beginning 'Kindness to people and animals means ...'. In plenary session, groups, one by one volunteer one of their statements. After others have had the chance to seek any clarification felt necessary, the statement is voted upon. Statements receiving the vote of more than half the students are written on a large sheet of paper and are adopted as the class' *Kindness Code*. The *Code* is displayed prominently in the classroom.

3. Students are encouraged to continue to bring such pictures to school. At appropriate moments, they introduce their pictures, perhaps using *Circle Time* (p.67), and the class discusses which items in the *Kindness Code* are being upheld/flouted. If the picture is one of ill-treatment, they consider what could be done to ensure more compassionate behaviours. If it becomes apparent that the *Code* is insufficiently all-embracing, new statements can be proposed and voted upon. From time to time, the class can also consider whether they are living up to the letter and spirit of their own *Code*.

Potential

An activity helping students to clarify what kind and compassionate attitudes mean in practical terms and providing for an exploration of the concept of equality of consideration.

Extension

Students role-play scenarios of people and animals being treated inappropriately and attempts at mediation/intervention. The class assesses the effectiveness of the role and style adopted by the student who mediates/intervenes.

Source

Developed from an activity devised by Fiona Heads.

■ *A CHARTER FOR ANIMALS*
Suitable for
Upper primary/secondary

Time needed
50 minutes

Resources
Twelve sheets of sugar paper, six felt pens, thirty copies of the abridged version of the Plymouth City Council *Welfare of Animals Charter* (it will require further abridgement and simplification for primary use).[1]

Procedure

The teacher introduces the idea of a municipal charter for animals, explaining that some forward-thinking towns and cities in Europe and North America have issued statements to protect the rights and welfare of animals in the municipality. Students form groups of five or six and are asked to brainstorm as many ideas as possible as to what such a charter might include (examples can be given as a stimulus to groups). A brainstorming of a minimum of fifteen items per group should be the target.

It is then explained that the Plymouth City Council issued a *Welfare of Animals Charter* in 1992. Groups are asked to get together with another group to negotiate and write down on sugar paper a joint twenty-clause charter using their respective brainstormings as a starting point. This process may involve omitting some ideas entirely, collapsing ideas together under a more all-embracing heading or simply editing two closely approximating ideas so they can stand as one clause. Groups are requested to devote the first clause of the charter to a preamble explaining the thinking behind the charter. The other nineteen clauses are to contain more specific guidelines or cautions concerning the treatment of animals.

Their charter completed, the combined groups are given multiple copies of the abridged version of the Plymouth *Charter*. They are asked to compare and contrast it with their own work. Are there any important areas of animal welfare that, on reflection, they as a group overlooked? Are

Plymouth City Council Welfare of Animals Charter (Abridged)

In as much as there is ample evidence that many animal species are capable of feeling, we condemn totally the infliction of unnecessary suffering upon our fellow creatures and the unreasonable curtailment of their behavioural and other needs.

We do not accept that a difference in species alone can justify wanton exploitation or oppression in the name of science or sport, or for the use as food, for commercial profit or for other human gain.

We believe that as moral agents humans have a responsibility for the welfare of all captive and domestic animals and all wild animals in so far that human activities impinge upon them.

We therefore call for the establishment of highest welfare standards for all those animals used by humans and for the protection of every animal against unnecessary suffering.

Companion Animals

To help control and protect dogs, Council will publicise the Dog Warden Service; Council supports the introduction of a National Dog Registration Scheme; Council supports the reduction of numbers of feral cats through neutering, and a policy of rehoming unwanted, mistreated and abandoned animals.

Pet Shops

[Council will continue to licence pet shops under the Pet Animals Act 1951; the Environmental Health Officer will interview intending pet shop owners to ensure they are fit and proper people to run a pet shop.]

The licence holder of a pet shop should not stock or sell wild caught animals banned from trade.

Council will consider ways in which it can assist the animal welfare organisations in publicising healthy rescued animals seeking new homes.

Exotic Animals

Council will continue to enforce rigorously the Dangerous Wild Animals Act 1976 and will do all it can to discourage the keeping and sale of exotic animals.

Animals as Prizes

Council supports the animal welfare organisations in opposing the giving of animals as prizes.

Control of Animal Boarding and Breeding Establishments

[Council will rigorously enforce the Animal Boarding Establishments Act 1963, the Riding Establishment Acts 1964 and 1970, and the Breeding of Dogs Acts 1973 and 1991.

Performing Animals

Council will not allow circuses or travelling menageries which include performing animals on any Council-owned land and will use its statutory powers to prevent performing animal acts in theatres wherever possible.

Council will not allow rodeos on any Council-owned or managed land.

Council will ensure that minimum standards are maintained at donkey derbies held on all Council-owned land.

Council will not allow the following practices at showjumping and eventing held on Council-owned or managed land.

a. Striking with the whip, so as to cause distress or suffering.

b. Competition where obstacles are unreasonably difficult.

c. The use of training methods which cause distress or suffering.

d. The use of drugs to alter the performance of the horse or to enable it to compete.

Animals in Films

Council will oppose the public showing of any film where its production has involved the infliction of pain or terror on any animal, or the cruel goading of an animal to fury.

Wild Life

Council will support measures aimed at the conservation of wild life through the establishment of local wildlife parks, nature reserves, trails and conservation areas within the urban area.

P

Hunting with Dogs

Council is opposed to hunting fox, deer or hare with dogs and will not allow hunting with dogs on land owned or administered by the Council.

Agrochemicals and Pesticides

Council opposes the unnecessary use of poisons, will not allow its employees to use strychnine to control animal populations, and will use human labour or environmentally harmless chemicals to control weeds.

Council opposes the indiscriminate destruction of animal habitats caused as a direct result of unnecessary drainage of wetlands, the felling of trees, the removal of hedgerows and the filling in of ponds.

Snares

Council is opposed to the use of snares and other traps which cause suffering to animals.

Animal Products

Council supports the sale and use of cruelty-free products and non-violent campaigns seeking a ban on the sale of goods which involve the use of wild animal skins.

Council supports the rigorous enforcement of regulations applying the Convention on the International Trade in Endangered Species (CITES).

Angling

[Council puts forward a nine-point Code of Practice which it will encourage anglers to adopt. Its provisions include use of barbless hooks, careful handling of fish to minimise damage to skin and mucus covering the scales, avoidance of prolonged 'playing' of fish, humane despatch of fish which are not to be returned to the water.]

Education

Council calls upon the local education authority to use videos and computer simulations for teaching anatomy and physiology, and to include wildlife and conservation as part of the curriculum in both primary and secondary schools.

Transport of Food Animals

[Council calls upon the Ministry of Agriculture, Food and Fisheries to enforce strongly its animal transport regulations; it supports a ban on the transport of live equines to continental Europe for slaughter; it supports the European campaign for a maximum journey time from farm to slaughterhouse of eight hours.]

Meals

In Council-run facilities, or where it has an influence, at least one vegetarian meal will appear on all menus and vegan food will be made available on request.

Animal Experimentation

[Council will do all it can to ensure that the spirit and provisions of the Animals (Scientific Procedures) Act, 1986, and the relevant European Community directive is followed.]

Slaughtering of Food Animals

[Council will ensure that laws governing humane slaughter of food animals are strictly enforced, including the Slaughterhouses Act 1974, the Slaughter of Animals (Humane Conditions) Regulations 1990, and the Welfare of Animals at Slaughter Act 1991]

Tethering of Horses and Ponies

[Council will not allow the tethering of horses and ponies over long periods on land it owns or manages.]

P

there areas which the Plymouth *Charter* fails to include? Groups are invited to amend their charter, in the light of what they have read. Plenary debriefing follows.

Potential

A sequence of group tasks that can promote a very high level of involvement and engagement especially if attempted after students have had some opportunity to confront animal rights and welfare issues. The plenary debriefing can begin with each group presenting their charter, speaking to the extent to which it is different from/similar to the Plymouth *Charter* and taking questions from the rest of the class. Students can then be asked to share their views as to the usefulness of such documents. What also might have to happen to ensure they are not simply 'window dressing' or 'put on the shelf' ? Which groups in the community are likely to react adversely to an animal charter? How might their objections best be pre-empted or dealt with? Senior secondary students can be asked to pay special attention to the terminology used in their charter's title and preamble during the charter-writing stage of the activity, and to decide whether the orientation is to be towards animal *welfare* or animal *rights*. Decisions made can be a principal focus of the debriefing session. To what extent is the Plymouth *Charter*, in reality, a welfare document; to what extent a rights document? The *Charter*, with its several references to laws to protect animals, can also provide a springboard for enquiry into the current state of animal welfare legislation in the UK.

Extensions

1. Further rounds of discussion and negotiation take place until a class charter is agreed. A copy of the charter is sent to the leaders or environmental spokespeople of groups represented on the municipal or county council, asking for responses to the document and calling for an animal charter to be promulgated by the council.

2. Students write descriptions of and/or draw pictures of a town or city of the future in which their charter is fully implemented and observed.

■ *DECLARATION OF INTERDEPENDENCE*

Suitable for
Upper secondary

Time needed
3 hours

Resources
Sugar paper, felt pens and Blu-tak.

Procedure

1. Towards the close of a course or programme of study that has explored interdependencies within ecosystems, human-animal relationships, the interrelationship between human societies and the natural world and/or the interdependence of lands and peoples globally, students are given the challenge of devising a *Declaration of Interdependence*. Historical examples of national and international declarations are introduced (see next two pages) and their style, format, nature and purposes discussed. It is important to point out that most declarations are, in effect, three documents in one: a catalogue of problems or grievances to be confronted, a general statement of values or first principles, and a listing of particular rights and obligations that follow from the values/first principles enunciated.

2. Dividing into groups of seven or eight members, students brainstorm:

❑ the *various forms of interdependency* which they think should be taken account of in the *Declaration* (e.g. interdependencies at various levels of human society, local to global, between species, between the organic and inorganic);

❑ the *problems, distortions, inequities and threats to planetary health* that presently mark the workings of the interdependencies identified (e.g. the inequalities between the developed and developing worlds, between different groups within societies, the exploitation of animals, the destruction of species and ecosystems);

❑ the *values* that should be embraced if interdependent relationships are to be

We hold these truths to be self-evident: That all men are created equal; that they are endowed by their Creator with certain unalienable rights; that among these are life, liberty and the pursuit of happiness; that, to secure these rights, governments are instituted among men, deriving their just powers from the consent of the governed; that whenever any form of government becomes destructive of these ends, it is the right of the people to alter or to abolish it, and to institute new government, laying the foundation on such principles, and organising the powers in such form, as to them shall seem most likely to effect their safety and happiness.

— *Declaration of Independence of the American People*, 4 July 1776.

The representatives of the French people, organised in National Assembly, considering that ignorance, forgetfulness, or contempt of the rights of man are the sole causes of public misfortunes and of the corruption of governments, have resolved to set forth in a solemn declaration the natural, inalienable and sacred rights of man, in order that such declaration, continually before all members of the social body, may be a perpetual reminder of their rights and duties... Accordingly, the National Assembly recognises and proclaims the following rights of man and citizen.

1.   Men are born and remain free and equal in rights; social distinctions may be based only upon general usefulness.

4.   Liberty consists of the power to do whatever is not injurious to others (etc.).

— *Declaration of the Rights of Man and of the Citizen*, France, 27 August 1789.

Whereas recognition of the inherent dignity and of the equal and inalienable rights of all members of the human family is the foundation of freedom, justice and peace in the world,

Whereas disregard and contempt for human rights have resulted in barbarous acts which have outraged the conscience of mankind, and the advent of a world in which human beings shall enjoy freedom of speech and belief and freedom from fear and want has been proclaimed as the highest aspiration of the common people,

Now, therefore, the General Assembly proclaims this Universal Declaration of Human Rights as a common standard of achievement for all peoples and all nations, to the end that every individual and every organ of society, keeping this Declaration constantly in mind, shall strive by teaching and education to promote respect for these rights and freedoms and by progressive measures, national and international, to secure their universal and effective recognition and observance, both among the peoples of Member States themselves and among the peoples of territories under their jurisdiction.

Article 1
All human beings are born free and equal in dignity and rights. They are endowed with reason and conscience and should act towards one another in a spirit of brotherhood.

Article 2
Everyone is entitled to all the rights and freedoms set forth in this Declaration, without distinction of any kind, such as race, colour, sex, language, religion, political or other opinion, national or social origin, property, birth or other status.

Article 3
Everyone has the right to life, liberty and security of person.

Article 4
No one shall be held in slavery or servitude; slavery and the slave trade shall be prohibited in all their forms.

Article 5
No one shall be subjected to torture or to cruel, inhuman or degrading treatment or punishment.

United National Declaration of Human Rights, 10 December 1948.

P

Earth Covenant: A Citizens' Treaty for Common Ecological Security

Preamble

We, the peoples of the Earth, rejoice in the beauty and wonder of the lands, skies, waters, and life in all its diversity. Earth is our home. We share it with all other living beings.

Yet we are rendering the Earth uninhabitable for the human community and for many species of life. Lands are becoming barren, skies fouled, waters poisoned. The cry of people whose land, livelihood and health are being destroyed is heard around the world. The Earth itself is calling us to awaken.

We and all living beings depend upon the Earth and upon one another for our common existence, well-being, and development. Our common future depends upon a re-examination of our most basic assumptions about humankind's relationship to the Earth. We must develop common principles and systems to shape this future in harmony with the Earth.

Governments alone cannot secure the environment. As citizens of the world, we accept responsibility in our personal, occupational and community lives, to protect the integrity of the Earth.

Principles and Commitments

In covenant with each other and on behalf of the whole Earth community, we commit ourselves to the following principles and actions:

❏ *Relationship with the Earth*: All Life forms are sacred. Each human being is unique and integral part of the Earth's community of life and has a special responsibility to care for life in all its diverse forms.

Therefore, we will act and live in a way that preserves the natural life processes of the Earth and respects all species and their habitats. We will work to prevent ecological degradation.

❏ *Relationship with Each Other*: Each human being has the right to a healthful environment and to access to the fruits of the Earth. Each also has a continual duty to work for the realisation of these rights for present and future generations.

Therefore — concerned that every person have food, shelter, pure air, potable water, education, employment, and all that is necessary to enjoy the full measure of human rights — we will work for more equitable access to the Earth's resources.

❏ *Relationship Between Economic and Ecological Security*: Since human life is rooted in the natural processes of the Earth, economic development, to be sustainable, must preserve the life-support systems of the Earth.

Therefore, we will use environmentally protective technologies and promote their availability to people in all parts of the Earth. When doubtful about the consequences of economic goals and technologies on the environment, we will allow an extra margin of protection for nature.

❏ *Governance and Ecological Security*: The protection and enhancement of life on Earth demand adequate legislative, administrative and judicial systems at appropriate local, national, regional, and international levels. In order to be effective, these systems must be empowering, participatory, and based on openness of information.

Therefore, we will work for the enactment of laws that protect the environment and promote their observance through educational, political and legal action. We shall advance policies of prevention rather than only reacting to ecological harm.

Declaring our partnership with one another and with our Earth, we give our word of honour to be faithful to the above commitments.

(Signature)

The Earth Covenant was drafted by a team of economists, educators, environmentalists, lawyers and religious leaders from Canada, Netherlands, India, Philippines, the USA and the then USSR. Promoted by Global Education Associates[2], the *Covenant* was signed by individuals around the world and kept for 'reflection and commitment'. Those signing could also forward their names and addresses for entry in the *Register of Signatories to the Earth Covenant*. The Register was presented at the World Conference on the Environment, Rio de Janeiro, 1992.

P

played out in the future in ways that promote the interests and well-being of all people and all species;

❏ the *rights* that all people and all species should enjoy and, consequently, the *obligations* upon human beings within an interdependent global system.

3. Four brief rounds of reporting back follow, the teacher collating ideas presented by groups under each of the four brainstormed headings. The class then discusses differences of opinion and emphasis that have emerged prior to determining a framework and structure for the *Declaration*. Groups are then assigned the task of drafting one or more sections of the *Declaration*, drawing upon the lists of ideas and taking into account the issues raised in plenary session. To the agreed order, draft sections are presented, discussed and amended (should an impasse occur, students can be asked to return to their groups to draft alternatives to the disputed text before reconvening to consider each others' drafts). The resulting *Declaration* is examined for ambiguities and inconsistencies, first in groups then in plenary session, before its final approval by the class.

Potential

A demanding but rewarding co-operative process that will help students identify the shifts in values, priorities and behaviours necessary if juster and more equitable relationships are to be achieved within and between human societies, and if human beings are to live more lightly on the Earth. Copies of the *Declaration* can be sent to community, environmental and humane organisations, to political and religious groups, and to politicians, for feedback and comment.

References

1. *The welfare of animals* charter is available from the Head of Environmental Services, Plymouth City Council, Civic Centre, Plymouth, PL1 2EW.

2. *World Goodwill Newsletter,* 1990, no. 3, 7 (World Goodwill, 3 Whitehall Court, Suite 54, London, SW1A 2EF). The address of Global Education Associates is 475 Riverside Drive, Suite 456, New York, N.Y. 10115, U.S.A.

Chapter 15

Action

INTRODUCTION

We must encourage and assist our students in identifying their own value and action priorities in the light of their concern about particular global issues. We must help them discover their own strengths and learn how they can be most effective. We must help each person find his or her entry point for action.
— David Shirman and David Conrad[1]

The humane classroom is open, democratic, co-operative and participatory; it is characterised by horizontal dialogue and multi-directional flows of ideas, information and opinion. It places a premium upon building self-esteem and creating and sustaining affirmative relationships within the learning community. So it is practically inevitable that, as students become more deeply aware of the dissonances, injustices, inequities and cruelties to be found in our relationships to each other, to other living creatures and to the environment, some will begin to ask what they can do, individually and collectively, to help bring about a better world.

An essential quality of the humane teacher is the ability to give life and scope to students' potential and their readiness to help effect change; to recognise and respond to the 'subtle indicators of energy and compassion' in young people.[2] Opportunities to practice involvement from the safe and secure base of the classroom are essential if young people are to develop the confidence and competence to be active

citizens. 'It is unrealistic to expect them to become responsible, participating adult citizens at the age of 16, 18 or 21 without prior exposure to the skills and responsibilities involved.'[3] What is needed are well-conceived and well-structured programmes to promote 'involvement literacy' throughout the formal years of schooling so that students are able to make ever more mature and informed choices about the level, direction and form of their involvement in social causes. 'Involvement literacy' is not simply a question of helping students develop and hone their social action skills, important as that is. It encompasses the exploration and evaluation of the range of avenues and strategies open to those who wish to effect change. It calls for mature reflection upon the effectiveness, ethics, limitations, pitfalls and ramifications of different types of action and upon the rights and responsibilities of both the change agent and those who will be caught up in the change process. It requires that students leave school with a knowledge of the multiple possibilities for involvement around contemporary social concerns, and with an appreciation that change is a complex affair, requiring sustained application, and that obsessive preoccupation with 'putting the world to rights' at the expense of physical and inner well-being is likely to lead to burn-out.[4] Much that is embraced by the concept can be addressed within the classroom, through participatory learning and through surrogate real-life experiences such as role-play and simulation, but reflective involvement in school and community action projects offers the surest apprenticeship for the responsible active citizen.

Roger Hart offers a 'beginning typology' for thinking about young people's involvement in social action projects. Underpinning his eight-rung 'Ladder of Participation' (*Fig. 1*) is the conviction that ownership of a project is essential if involvement is to be a real learning experience; also that the best kinds of project are those that, at some stage, involve consultation or, better still, shared action and decision-making between children and adults.

The first three rungs of the ladder Hart describes as non-participation posing as participation. They are:

1. **Manipulation.** Forms of action in which adults involve young people without giving them any understanding of the issues and, hence, of the reasons for, or likely consequences of, their actions. The adults maintain a pretence that the action is child-inspired. An example would be where pre-school students are asked to carry placards about complex child-related issues. Another would be where a 'children's design' playground is developed by architects based upon children's drawings of their ideal playground but with no attempt at ongoing dialogue with the children.

2. **Decoration.** Forms of action in which young people fulfil a merely decorative function; for instance, by singing or dancing at an event, the purposes of which they do not understand and in the organisation of which they have had no say. Hart sees this as one rung up from manipulation in that the adults do not pretend that the cause is inspired by children.

3. **Tokenism.** Forms of action in which young people are apparently given a voice but have little or no say in the choice of subject or style of communication, and little or no opportunity to formulate their own opinions or to consult peer opinion so they can genuinely represent that opinion. The presence of charming, articulate but ill-prepared children on conference panels falls within this category.[5]

Hart's five categories of genuine child participation are as follows:

4. **Assigned but Informed.** Forms of action which, although not child-initiated, conform to the following criteria: the children understand the intentions of the project; they know who made the decisions concerning their involvement and why; they have a meaningful (as against decorative) role; they volunteer for the project *after* the project is explained.

5. **Consulted and Informed.** Forms of action determined, frameworked and run by adults but in which children understand the process and their opinions are treated seriously. An example would be a television company which designs a new programme in consultation with children and which asks the children to critique succeeding trial versions of the programme.

6. **Adult-Initiated, Shared Decisions with Children.** Hart sees this category as the first rung of 'true participation': although projects are initiated by adults, young people are involved in the decision-making from the outset. An example would be a community project which is conceived by adults but gives children the opportunity on an ongoing basis to shape its goals, scope and direction.

7. **Child-Initiated and Directed.** Forms of action in which the project is conceived

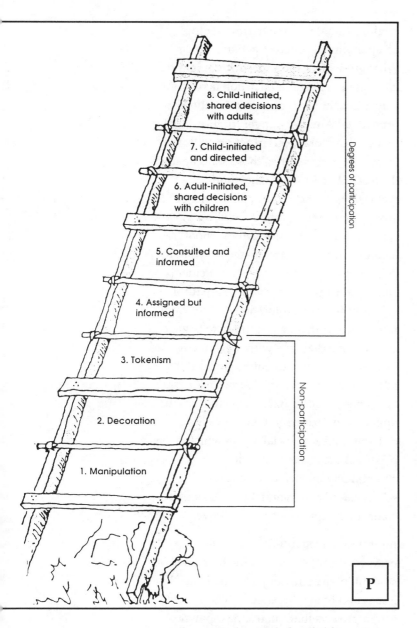

8. Child-initiated,
shared decisions
with adults

7. Child-initiated
and directed

6. Adult-initiated,
shared decisions
with children

5. Consulted and
informed

4. Assigned but
informed

3. Tokenism

2. Decoration

1. Manipulation

Degrees of participation

Non-participation

P

g. 1 Ladder of
rticipation.
urce: Roger Hart, A.
ildren's Participation:
om Tokenism to
tizenship, UNICEF
nocent: Essay no. 4,
92, p.9.

and executed entirely by children. An example might be mural painting at a school or community centre. Hart points out that child-initiated community projects are few and far between. 'A primary reason for this,' he suggests, 'is that adults are not usually good at responding to young people's own initiatives.'

8. **Child-Initiated, Shared Decisions with Adults.** Forms of action in which the project is conceived, and then executed in its initial stages, by young people before involving adults in further stages of decision-making (and action) . An example would be a student-inspired

petition drive calling for changes in certain school practices, which leads to meetings involving the school leadership and staff and the decision to implement the changes agreed collectively. Such projects, on the 'highest rung of the ladder of participation', Hart describes as 'all too rare', a fact he attributes to 'the absence of caring adults attuned to the particular interests of young people'.[6]

Hart's ladder offers a provisional but helpful means of assessing the quality of student involvement in social and community action projects (see *Ladder of Participation*, p.379, for a staff development activity asking teachers to reflect on the quality of student involvement in their schools using Hart's ladder and also to critique the validity of Hart's typology). Another is to place examples of involvement on a continuum that, at one end, embraces forms of conformative (status quo non-critical) and, at the other, forms of transformative (status quo critical) action.

In 1989 the Speaker's Commission on Citizenship commissioned a survey of citizenship education in maintained secondary schools in England and Wales. One focus of the survey, published in 1990, was student involvement in community activity (students aged 12-13 and 15-16 were surveyed). The survey team found that the most regularly undertaken form of social and community involvement amongst the younger group was organising and taking part in fund raising (86% of schools reported at least some 12-13 year old involvement). 'Environmental projects' (22%) and visiting the elderly in their homes (15%) ranked second and third. The most regularly undertaken forms of involvement amongst the older age group were visiting the elderly in their homes (40%), visiting the elderly in hospitals/hostels (40%), fund raising (26%) and visiting children in nursery or primary schools (24%).[7] Conspicuous by their virtual absence in the survey are references to learning processes in which students develop a critical analysis of society and subsequently become involved in forms of transformative action.[8]

The National Curriculum Council's, *Curriculum Guidance 8. Education for Citizenship* (1990), identifies 'democracy in action' as one of eight essential components of citizenship education. Whilst the goals laid down under the heading look promising ('To participate fully as citizens, pupils need to know about political systems and processes, have a positive attitude towards exercising their responsibilities and rights in a democratic society, and acquire the skills needed to participate effectively'), the examples of activities offered for Key Stages 1-4, such as collecting and assessing local planning proposals (KS3) and observing local elections at all their stages (KS4), will do little to embolden teachers who conceive of schools as both arenas for democratic participation and springboards for socially-critical action.[9] This should not unduly surprise us. 'As the primary socialising instrument of the state,' writes Hart, 'schools are concerned with guaranteeing stability.' With some notable exceptions, 'the practice of democratic principles is typically limited to the election of class representatives to sit on school councils, serving only in an advisory or consulting capacity'.[10]

The potential hazards for the teacher and school in giving scope for socially critical and transformative action need to be recognised. What if a 'Cruelty-Free Science' group, opposed to animal experimentation, chooses to demonstrate against a visit to school by a careers representative of a pharmaceutical firm involved in such research? What if the same group trains its sights on a local branch of the firm where many parents are employed? What if a group of students, fired by concern for the environment, take some form of action against council plans to pipe and thus destroy life in a local stream? What criteria

might a school use in determining the acceptability of different action projects? What guidelines and procedures might be laid down to ensure that action taken by students adheres to basic democratic principles? Another danger for the school is that students practiced in action skills may from time to time direct those skills against the institution in which they find themselves.[11] The 'Cruelty-Free Science' group, for instance, might well lead a campaign against dissection in school biology. Is the school prepared to 'walk the democratic talk' of its mission statement and stand firmly by the core procedural values of freedom, toleration, fairness and respect for truth and reasoning; to engage in constructive dialogue with the students and to allow the issue a full airing in both the school and community? *Where Do We Draw the (Action) Line?*, p.322, gives students the opportunity to clarify their views on different forms of social action whilst *Action*, p.378, asks teachers to decide upon the acceptability of various examples of school-based action and, by extension, to confront the questions raised above.

Information from humane organisations bears powerful witness to the high level of student interest in animal welfare and rights issues and the wide range of school-based action projects that interest has spawned. Projects include:

❑ Arranging an Animal Welfare week at school, with poster displays, daily assemblies on animal rights topics, and extra vegetarian meals supplied by the school caterers.

❑ Campaigning and petitioning to stop dissection in school.

❑ Campaigning to replace battery eggs used in school meals with free-range eggs.

❑ Compiling, publishing and selling an animal welfare/vegetarian guide to the city in which the school is situated.

❏ Holding frog and toad watches from February to April to protect amphibians from death on the roads as they head *en masse* for their breeding ponds.

❏ Establishing an Earth and Animal Protection Club in school.

❏ Holding a Veggie Pledge week to alert school and community to the benefits (for animals and humans) of vegetarianism and to encourage people to give up eating meat.

❏ Mounting a campaign to stop a circus with performing animals from performing in the locality by means of poster displays and leaflets in school; persuading friends and family not to attend; holding group sessions for writing letters of protest to the local council, local newspapers and radio; inviting representatives of animal welfare groups to speak in school assembly; petitioning the local council not to allow the circus to return; asking shopkeepers not to display circus posters and explaining why.

❏ Senior secondary students mounting a weekly vigil outside the psychology school of a well-known university to protest against psychological experiments on cats.

❏ Writing to congratulate politicians, companies and other organisations for taking positive steps to prevent cruelty to animals and environmental destruction.

❏ Organising a poster protest against using animals to test cosmetics (and attracting local press coverage).

❏ Organising a publicity campaign to persuade the local mayor to remove the fur from his ceremonial robes.

❏ Participating in local radio phone-ins on animal-related issues, either as panel members or callers.

❏ Sending an open letter to local newspapers at Christmastide exposing the cruelties involved in the season of 'peace and goodwill' and recommending 'cruelty-free' alternatives.

❏ Setting up a school library display on alternatives to cruelty, accompanied by a lunchtime 'veggie' buffet; setting up a display on animal abuse at the local library.

❏ Undertaking activities to show the benefits of having pets, to promote responsible pet ownership and to increase awareness of professional services available to pets (usually in conjunction with a local veterinary practice) during National Pet Week (see p.168).

❏ Undertaking work experience or voluntary work at a local kennels, animal rescue centre or veterinarians.

❏ Wearing black armbands and organising a minute's silence on World Day for Laboratory Animals.

❏ Writing letters of protest to cosmetics firms still testing their products on animals; visiting local cosmetics shops to explain the cruelty of cosmetics tests to the managers and asking them to adopt a 'cruelty-free' policy.

❏ Writing to local newspapers and petitioning the Spanish Embassy about bullfighting; also urging boycotts of Spanish holidays and goods, especially those directly associated with bullfighting (e.g. certain brands of sherry).

❏ Writing to MPs and MEPs in support of the CITES 1989 ban on the ivory trade (see p.196) at a time when six African nations were calling for the ban to be lifted (Spring 1992).[12]

ACTIVITIES

■ WHERE DO WE DRAW THE (ACTION) LINE?

Working individually and then in groups, students follow the procedure described on pages 141-2, using the set of statements opposite. The activity, and subsequent plenary discussion, will help clarify individual attitudes towards different forms of social action whilst at the same time alerting students to a range of conflicting viewpoints and perspectives. The statements cover a wide spectrum of possibilities, from illegal direct action involving violence to property, through non-violent direct action of varying levels of risk and intensity, to action using well-established channels of persuasion existing in democratic society. A range of important issues are there to be aired in plenary session. Which action strategies are felt to be most effective? What is meant by 'effective' ? For what reasons do individuals rule out certain forms of action? Does everybody agree? If not, why not? To what extent does the choice of form of action depend on the severity of the injustice/oppression perceived? To what extent is it reasonable to resort to forms of action that might be considered more 'extreme' upon the transparent failure of other channels of persuasion to halt the injustice/oppression? Is direct action in defence of animals involving a threat to person or property ever justifiable? Is it congruent with the values that led those undertaking such action to oppose the abuse of animals in the first place? What would students say to the people described in the twelve statements if they could be present in class?

A powerful alternative to the above is to have half the groups organise the statements on an acceptable-unacceptable continuum and the other half organise them on an effective-ineffective continuum. Groups that have undertaken the activity using the different criteria are then brought together to discuss, compare and contrast the results.

An activity for senior secondary students.

■ CHILDREN'S HEARINGS

Suitable for
Secondary

Time needed
Occasional periods over several weeks.

Resources
Postcards and sheets of paper.

Procedure
In an assembly or an orchestrated series of individual lessons, students are introduced to the Norwegian-inspired *Voice of the Children International Campaign* and the concept of *Children's Hearings*. Following the meeting of the World Commission on Environment and Development in Bergen, Norway, in May 1990, ten Norwegian children were given the opportunity to put their hopes, fears, demands and visions for the world's future to their country's leaders at a Children's Hearing. The Hearing, which received widespread media coverage in Norway, was the culmination of a process which had started with letters to schools inviting students to send postcards conveying their thoughts and feelings about the state of the world's environment and world development. Some 6,000 postcards were received. An editing group clustered the cards under a number of headings and drew up a *Children's Appeal* reflecting the children's opinions and using their own words. At the Hearing, the ten children selected put questions to a panel that included the Norwegian prime minister, Gro Harlem Bruntland, and other national figures. The Norwegian Children's Ombudsman chaired the Hearing and ensured that questions were answered without evasion. After the Hearing, the *Appeal* was presented to the media, non-governmental organisations and schools. Looking back on the event, Gro Harlem Bruntland wrote:

> I believe this was an important event — for the children who were invited to take part in the political process at a very high level, for the political leadership who had to face the challenges from the children taking part, and for the children and grown-ups in the audience who became part of the process.

Sit-down Protest Opponents of factory farming mount a peaceful sit-down protest at the entrance to a battery farm.	**Lobby** A representative group from organisations concerned about the international trade in animals visit Parliament to meet MPs and press for further restrictions on the trade.
Letters A network of people opposed to entertainment involving performing animals write letters of protest to the local MP, councillors, and local radio and newspapers objecting to the circus coming to town.	**Break-in** Opponents of scientific research involving animals break into a laboratory and release beagles intended for use in experiments.
Saboteurs Hunt saboteurs use non-violent methods to thwart a hunt, such as scent-dullers (to prevent hounds from finding the scent of a fox) and placing themselves in the fox earth (to stop the fox being dug out).	**Personal Change** An individual contributes to a more humane world by making lifestyle and purchasing decisions that avoid cruelty to animals.
Slogans Opponents of the slaughter of animals for food spray a meat factory with slogans and put glue in the locks.	**Petition Drive** Members of local animal welfare groups combine to obtain signatures for a petition calling upon the local council to revoke the licence of the town's zoo.
Clean-up An animal rights group campaigns to make a local lake safer for wildlife by collecting discarded fishing tackle, ensuring their efforts receive ample media coverage.	**Bomb Hoax** A person opposed to the fur trade phones a bomb hoax to a department store selling furs, causing the store to close for two hours.
Picketing Anti-fur trade protesters mount a regular picket outside a fur shop, leafleting people, requesting them not to enter and engaging them in discussion about the fur industry.	**Demonstration** Opponents of vivisection join an organised demonstration and march to protest against the continued use of animals in medical and other scientific experiments.

P

We need engaged, informed, active young people. We need young people who believe they can be part of the process, who have enough faith and enough self confidence to fight for their future and the future of the world.

The Voice of the Children International Campaign is now promoting Children's Hearings at school, local, regional, national and global levels (a global children's hearing was held in Rio de Janeiro during the Earth Summit in June 1992).

Through assemblies or lessons, students are also alerted to the fact that Article 12 of the United Nations Convention on the Rights of the Child lays down that each child has the right to be heard in all matters affecting her. It is emphasised that it is important for children to be heard, and that it is just as important for adults to be told in the children's own words what they are concerned about: their hopes, fears, visions and demands for the future.

Students are encouraged to take part in a Children's Hearing process in school so as to establish open channels of communication between themselves and adult society and representative decision makers. To begin the process they are asked to do two things: firstly, to prepare a postcard (or letter, poster, drawing or poem) expressing their ideas, concerns, questions and demands about vital issues such as the state of the environment, human rights, world peace, the treatment of animals, world development, unemployment, poverty and hunger; secondly, to elect a student committee to organise the Hearing (a male and female representative from each year would produce a committee of reasonable size). The committee would have the right to co-opt teachers to serve in an advisory and supportive capacity.

The committee's initial task is to encourage students to send in postcards etc., and to collect and synthesise the views expressed therein, the aim being to produce a concise, frank, document — a *Children's Appeal* — of one or two sides of paper summarising students' concerns. During this process, the interest of the whole student body can be maintained by regularly producing a newsheet and by committee members occasionally reporting back to class or year groups.

The *Children's Appeal* should provide the basis for the school-based Children's Hearing. The student committee sets a date and invites parents, local politicians, local clergy, trade union and media representatives and other decision/opinion makers to join a panel (of 6-8 members) to respond to children's views and questions. The committee also invites applications from students who would like to represent the views of the student body and actually address the panel (applicants should explain which major world issues they are particularly concerned about and why they would be a good choice for the children's panel). The committee's task is to choose about 10-12 students for the lead role in the Hearing (those chosen should be representative of the student body in terms of age, gender and ethnicity and should have shown themselves, through their postcards and their overall contribution to school and local life, to be genuinely concerned about environment, development, human rights and peace issues). The student panel should be decided in time for the chosen students to brief themselves and plan the content and sequencing of their questions/statements carefully (using the *Children's Appeal* as their framework).

An invitation to the Hearing, plus a copy of the *Children's Appeal*, should be sent to all students and their parents and the event should be widely publicised in the community. The media (local radio, press and television) should be invited. An exhibition of students' postcards etc., should be displayed in the hall where the Hearing is to take place.

A sympathetic, well-qualified mediator or ombudsperson should be invited to the Hearing to chair the event firmly and ensure that the questions/concerns raised by the students are directly addressed to by the grown-ups without evasion (the person chosen should have time to talk to the students in advance). In addition, a few experts on global issues can be asked along to clarify factual matters as and when called upon (they should be briefed about the questions to be put beforehand). It is a good idea to include

CHILDREN'S APPEAL TO WORLD LEADERS, RIO DE JANEIRO, JUNE 1992

WE WANT TO INHERIT A CLEAN EARTH. We would like everybody to understand that the Earth is like a beautiful garden in which no one has the right to destroy anything. We would like our grandchildren to know: What is a tree, a fish, a dog. Leave us trees to climb in.

ECOLOGY IS NOT JUST TREES, ANIMALS AND RIVERS, IT IS ALSO HUNGER AND THE HOMELESS. We should all help our brothers and sisters who have been abandoned on the streets. Eliminate poverty. We want you to understand that all excessive consumption affects developing countries most.

WE WANT CHILDREN'S RIGHTS TO BE RESPECTED ALL OVER THE WORLD. No child should be imprisoned or beaten, no child should die of hunger or from diseases that could easily be prevented. All children have a right to have parents.

WE WANT EVERY GIRL AND BOY IN THE WORLD TO GET AN EDUCATION FOR A BETTER START IN LIFE. WE WANT TO SEE ILLITERACY WIPED OUT. It is our future and we want to have a say in it. We want to be educated in such a way that we get the courage to speak our minds. We want a world without discrimination.

WE WANT VERY STRICT LAWS AGAINST DESTROYING NATURE. Anybody polluting the environment should have to pay large fines. Stop producing materials that harm the ozone layer or it will be broken and the sun's rays will burn us. Stop global warming, reduce CO_2 emissions. Cut the use of fossil fuels, use sun and wind power. Instead of drilling for more oil, use energy less wastefully.

WE WANT YOU TO STOP USING NUCLEAR POWER. End nuclear testing in our oceans and seas. We demand the removal of all nuclear power stations.

WE DON'T WANT OUR CITES TO BE RUINED BY CARS. We don't want to be sick from exhaust fumes. We want you to make cars that don't pollute. Public transportation should be better, cheaper and more efficient than private cars. Make it easier for us all to use our bicycles.

WE DON'T WANT OUR WORLD TO DROWN IN RUBBISH. NOBODY SHOULD BE ALLOWED TO DUMP THEIR RUBBISH IN OTHER COUNTRIES. Stop littering, make less waste. We don't need all the packaging materials.

WE WOULD LIKE ALL THINGS TO BE RECYCLED. Make it easier for people to recycle their rubbish. Stop producing disposables.

PLEASE, LEADERS OF THE WORLD, GIVE US CLEAN DRINKING WATER. Without water there is no life. Too many children are drinking clayish water from shallow wells, pipe borne water is still a luxury. Too many children spend hours walking a long way to find water.

WE FEAR THAT WHEN WE GROW UP THERE WILL BE NO FISH IN THE OCEAN. We want you to stop oil spills in the oceans, to stop factories from releasing their sewage and waste into rivers and lakes. The sea cannot absorb poison without being harmed.

ANIMALS HAVE AS MUCH RIGHT TO LIVE ON THIS EARTH AS WE DO. Protect endangered animals, stop buying products made from rare animals. People should be able to do without real fur coats, crocodile leather or jewellery from ivory. Ban animal testing for cosmetics, ban killing animals for sport.

WE WANT MORE DONE TO SAVE WHAT IS LEFT OF THE NATIVE FORESTS. The rainforests are home to many people and animals. We want indigenous peoples to be able to live by their own rules. Don't cut down all the native trees, because the birds need homes, just like all the children in the world.

WE ARE AFRAID OF BEING SWEPT OFF THE FACE OF OUR COUNTRY BY THE APPROACHING DESERT. Stop bush-burning and over-grazing that is killing our trees and hurting our grassland vegetation. We want canals to be built alongside the main rivers to prevent flooding. Stop building large dams against people's wishes.

ALL HAVE A RIGHT TO LIVE IN PEACE. The money spent on military armaments should be spent on saving the planet. Instead of making bombs, improve the standard of living in the world.

THE EARTH IS A SINGLE COUNTRY, AND ALL PEOPLE ARE ITS CITIZENS. We have to share this planet, so don't be selfish. We want food to be shared so that everyone has enough. We want clean water and a home for all people. We are worried about pollution, war and children starving, while others don't appreciate the food they get. We are afraid that the world will soon belong only to the rich.

THIS EARTH IS MORE VALUABLE THAN ALL THE MONEY IN THE WORLD.

WE WANT ALL COUNTRIES TO WORK TOGETHER TO PROTECT IT.

in the programme some student-initiated musical or dramatic entertainment relevant to the event.

At appropriate moments during the Hearing the mediator should encourage contributions from children in the audience (but not from adults as their role, on this occasion, is to listen). It is a good idea to end the Hearing by having one or several children read the *Children's Appeal* to the audience.

Encouragement should be given to the media to interview members of the students' committee and participating students and to take photographs of the exhibition.

Potential

A demanding yet potentially hugely effective process that offers students the opportunity to speak their minds to the adult world, to decision makers and opinion formers. Involvement in such a process, even if it leads to no immediate solid changes, can build in students a conviction that their collective actions can help create a better world. This feeling of empowerment is the most important objective in organising a school-based Children's Hearing. Hence, the more the process is controlled by students the better. The event should be made known to the Secretariat of the Voice of the Children International Campaign (attn. Kristin Eskeland, c/o Norwegian People's Aid, P.O. Box 8844, Youngstorget, N-0028 Oslo 1, Norway), sending documentation (eg. a copy of the *Children's Appeal* and newspaper cuttings). Students could then be sure that their views would also be noted in international fora.

It is recommended that the Hearing should become an annual school event, providing students with the opportunity to put their views to local leaders and to hold them to account for promises made at previous Hearings that remain unfulfilled.

Source

Voice of the Children International Campaign.

The process itself is the real goal: to give children the opportunity to act, and to speak their minds to the grown-up world. Whether their concerns are poverty, hunger, lack of housing or clean water, or worries about depletion of the ozone layer and the destruction of the rainforests, **the aim is to establish channels of communication between children and adult society, between children and the decision makers.** Even if the grown-ups are unwilling or unable to take the children's views into account, the process, the involvement and activities of the children, have a value in itself. No one can guarantee that politicians and other decision makers will take the children's view points really seriously or that they are willing or able to take their opinions into account when final decisions are made. But children's voices should be heard as well as the voices of other sectors of society.

Children today are worried, often angry. They blame the adults for the problems, and rightly so. They get a lot of depressing information about the state of the world; they realize that their own future is at stake. A continued flow of information about environmental degradation, about poverty, hunger, war; coupled with a feeling that there is nothing they can do about it, no one is interested in their ideas, might lead to new generations of youngsters with no hope. They might turn into an aggressive group who would use any means to produce a change, or — much worse, a gang of frustrated, lethargic youngsters with no direction. As adults they are likely to have very little faith in their own ability to play an active role in the democratic process.

The Campaign Voice of the Children wants to prevent this from happening by giving active, knowledgeable kids a chance to speak their minds to the people in charge, by speaking TRUTH TO POWER.

Voice of the Children International Campaign

ADDITIONAL RESOURCES

❑ Environment Canada, *What we can do for our environment. Hundreds of things to do now*, 1991. A compilation of good ideas for more environmentally-friendly lifestyles and action projects. Available free from Inquiry Centre, Environment Canada, 351 St. Joseph Boulevard, Hull, Quebec, KlA OH3, Canada.

❑ *HSUS student action guide*, Humane Society of the United States (Youth Education Division, 67 Salem Road, East Haddam, CT 06423-0320), 1991. Excellent eight-page newspaper-format guide, full of ideas for school-based animal and environmental protection projects.

❑ James, B., *The young person's action guide to animal rights*, Virago, 1992. An A to Z of animal rights and welfare issues. At the end of every topic are answers to the important question: What can you do? Highly recommended.

❑ Levinson, R., *Spring clean your planet*, Beaver, 1987. A book of easy-to-follow scientific experiments about pollution, designed to enable students to make informed decisions about what action to take to help clean up the planet.

❑ Lewis, B., *The kid's guide to social action*, Minneapolis, Free Spirit Publishing, 1991. Subtitled, *How to solve the social problems you choose — and turn creative thinking into positive action*, this is an indispensable guide to young people's social action that should be in every school library, its US orientation notwithstanding.

❑ Newkirk, I., *Save the animals! 101 easy things you can do*, Angus and Robertson, 1991. Practical advice for campaigners and consumers.

❑ Silver, D., and Vallely, B., *The young person's guide to saving the planet*, Virago, 1990. Over one hundred environmental issues presented in an A to Z format. Each topic ends with a 'What can you do?' section.

❑ Key humane education organisations to contact (see *Organisations* list): Animal Aid, Animal Concern, Beauty Without Cruelty Charity, British Union for the Abolition of Vivisection, EarthKind, National Anti-Vivisection Society.

References

1. Shirman, D., and Conrad, D., 'Awareness, understanding and action: a global conscience in the classroom', *The New Era*, vol. 58, no. 6, December 1977, 163-7.

2. Hart, R.A., *Children's participation. From tokenism to citizenship*, Florence, Italy, UNICEF International Child Development Centre Innocenti Essay no. 4, 1992, 17.

3. *Ibid.*, 5.

4. Selby, D., 'Europe and the wider world: a Brighton conference report', *World Studies Journal*, vol. 4, no. 3, 38-41.

5. Hart, R.A., *op, cit.*, 8, 10.

6. *Ibid.*, 12-17.

7. Fogelman, K., *Citizenship in secondary schools: a national survey*, School of Education, University of Leicester, 2-3.

8. Davies, I., *Are you an active citizen?*, Citizenship Papers, Department of Educational Studies, University of York, 3.

9. National Curriculum Council, *Curriculum guidance 8. Education for citizenship*, 1990, 7, 21, 23, 25, 27.

10. Hart, R.A., *op. cit.*, 43.

11. Lister, I., *Issues in teaching and learning about human rights*, University of York Political Education Research Unit, document no. 32, 1981, 6.

12. Information for the summary list of projects is taken from information sheets, journals, newsletters and copies of students' letters provided by Animal Aid, The Animals' Defenders, Compassion in World Farming, the World Society for the Protection of Animals, the British Union for the Abolition of Vivisection, the Fund for the Replacement of Animals in Medical Experiments and Beauty Without Cruelty Charity.

THE EARTHKIND CURRICULUM

Chapter 16

Humane Education and the National Curriculum

Subject-based Approaches to Humane Education

The purpose here is to offer some suggestions as to what humane education across the curriculum might involve. It is not the intention to identify each and every opportunity afforded by the core and foundation subjects of the National Curriculum for consideration of humane issues. Teachers seeking information on how the activities described in this book relate to the National Curriculum attainment targets and cross-curricular elements should refer to the annually updated *EarthKind and the National Curriculum* supplement published by EarthKind UK.[1] Nor is it the intention to rehearse again what has been said about aims and objectives, teaching and learning styles and classroom climate and relationships. These are of equal importance for all teachers, irrespective of subject specialism. Rather, the object is to paint a broad-brush picture of how humane education can be infused into different subjects. At best, such an infusion is a mutually beneficial process, vivifying the content of each subject whilst reinforcing the concerns of humane education across the entire school programme.

1. The Core Subjects

English

❑ stories, novels, plays, poems and fables from around the world on animal-related themes and issues;

❑ comprehension, creative writing and discussion on animal-related topics to develop analytical, communication, language, literary discernment and reflective skills;

❑ drama and role-play to elucidate attitudes and perspectives on animal rights and welfare issues;

❑ media studies programmes around the depiction of animals in advertising, newspapers and magazines, radio, television and film;

❑ the study of animal imagery, similes and metaphors in different forms of spoken and written English; of how animal movement, shape and sound have coloured the language;

❑ the study of speciesist language and terminology; of anthropomorphism and pejorative reference to animals in spoken and written English.

Mathematics

❑ interpreting statistics on human exploitation of animals (for instance, fur trade imports and sales, annual figures for animals used in scientific experiments); drawing pie charts, scattergrams, bar or line graphs based on the statistics; summarising the data, and the ethical/social issues it raises, in written form;

❑ using statistics as a basis for extrapolative work and future projection (for instance, using a base figure of original tropical rainforest area and per annum figures for rainforest loss to calculate when the forests will be gone if clearance continues unabated);

❑ calculation of costs of pet ownership over the life time of the animal;

❑ work on fractions, decimal fractions, percentage, ratio and proportion around, for instance, calorific value, protein, fat, carbohydrate and vitamin content of sample carnivorous, vegan, lacto-, lacto-ovo, pesco- and pollo-vegetarian diets;

❑ understanding geometric progression through calculating, generation by generation, the offspring of unneutered or unspayed pets;

❑ weaving basic measurement and computational skills into animal-related themes; for instance, measuring out the legal minimum size for battery cages or pig pens, calculating their size in square centimetres/metres, measuring the size of mature chickens/pigs and determining whether the legal minimum is humane;

❑ expression of the natural range of wild animals and the space they are allowed in zoos and wildlife parks as a proportion or ratio.

Science

❑ comparative study of the human species and non-human animals in terms of physiology and needs;

❑ food chains and webs, biodiversity, ecosystems and the impact on ecosystems of, for instance, inorganic fertilisers, pesticides, global warming, hedge removal, the international trade in animals, deforestation;

❑ discussion of the issues surrounding dissection in biology lessons;

❑ inquiry into the arguments for and against the use of animals in scientific/ medical research; exploration of alternatives to vivisection;

❑ exploring the scientific aspects of animal husbandry and the impact on soil and atmosphere of a partial/complete shift to crop agriculture;

- ❏ the place of animals in the science and cosmography of indigenous and non-European peoples;
- ❏ scientific exploration of the relative merits/demerits of vegan, vegetarian and omnivorous diets.

2. Foundation Subjects

Art
- ❏ interpreting an animal-related theme or issue through drawing, painting, graffiti or three-dimensional work;
- ❏ sensitising students to the beauty of the environment or animal world through creative work or art appreciation sessions;
- ❏ the study and interpretation of the fine art of different historical periods to elucidate what it has to say about contemporary perceptions of wild and domestic animals and about human-animal relationships; conventions used by artists of different periods to depict animals;
- ❏ the depiction of the environment/animals in folk, ethnic, indigenous and community art;
- ❏ envisioning a more humane future through a medium of the student's choice.

Geography
- ❏ developing a critical appreciation of the concepts of sustainability, sustainable development, sustainable growth, stewardship of the Earth, conservation;
- ❏ investigating the geography of animal use and abuse locally;
- ❏ using issues-oriented atlases, such as *The Gaia Atlas of Planet Management*[2], to research environmental and animal-related themes;
- ❏ applying humane criteria to forms of animal farming studied;
- ❏ studying the geography of the international trade in endangered species (trading routes, key exporting and importing countries, key 'laundering' countries); assessing the impact of CITES since its inception in 1975;
- ❏ exploring interdependencies between living things in the areas and regions studied, also the interconnections between the organic and inorganic; exploring animal-human relationships and human use and abuse of animals in the societies studied;
- ❏ considering the environmental impact of current development trends.

History
- ❏ oral history projects recording older peoples' reflections on past treatment of animals, and mapping changes in attitudes, values and behaviours over the years;
- ❏ studying the history of animal rights and welfare philosophies, of humane organisations, of animal legislation; identifying historical links between human and animal liberation movements; exploring the lives of historical figures who have championed the cause of animals, e.g. Henry Salt, Mary Wollstonecroft;
- ❏ examining the history of the fur trade; the trade as a manifestation of colonialism; the creation of cultures and economies of dependency amongst indigenous peoples; the role of fur in North America's economic development;
- ❏ studying the impact on farm animals of the agricultural revolutions of the eighteenth and twentieth centuries;
- ❏ exploring the links between Western imperialism and the emergence of zoos (showcasing the spoils of imperial triumph) as a popular entertainment form;
- ❏ the human impact on the environment through the ages (habitat destruction,

species decline and loss, environmental degradation, pollution)[3];

❑ reappraisal of local, national and international events, developments and trends using animal rights and welfare criteria.

Modern Foreign Languages

❑ using affirmation and co-operative activities (see *Chapter 4*) to promote the self-confidence and preparedness to take risks that is essential to successful language acquisition;

❑ using materials on animal themes and issues, especially authentic materials from countries where the language is spoken (campaign leaflets, advertisements, articles, cartoons, posters, newsheets and factsheets from humane societies), to practice and develop written and spoken language skills;

❑ simple, structured conversations around photographs depicting, for instance, wilderness and ravaged natural environments, animal behaviours, animal exploitation;

❑ using pair and group discussion, role play and drama around animal-related issues to promote communicative competence (many of the activities in this book can be easily adapted for the language classroom);

❑ studying the significance of oral communication in animals and what it has to tell us about human communication;

❑ exploring perspectives, especially youth perspectives, on animal rights and welfare in the countries where the language is spoken;

❑ using activities on probable and preferred futures (see *Chapter 13*) to practise the future and future conditional tenses;

❑ writing letters to magazines, politicians and/or humane societies/preparing a radio item or video/making a poster or mounting an exhibition on animal exploitation, using the language being studied;

❑ undertaking a project on an animal-related issue as part of an exchange or study visit.

Music

❑ composing and performing song using stimulus material on animal rights and welfare issues;

❑ interpreting music from different countries and cultures on animal and environmental themes, e.g. Schubert's *Trout Quintet*, Prokofiev's *Peter and the Wolf*;

❑ weaving music into experiential learning forms, such as guided fantasy journeys and guided visualisations;

❑ listening to, or making, animal sound recordings and incorporating them within musical compositions[4];

❑ using songs on past and current manifestations of injustice, oppression, inhumanity and environmental despoliation to promote discussion and reflection on social, political, economic and environmental issues.

Physical Education/Games

❑ co-operative games and sports;

❑ the ethics of sport involving animals such as dog racing, horse riding, eventing, show jumping, steeple-chasing;

❑ discussion of whether 'blood sports', such as fox hunting and hare coursing, fall within accepted, and acceptable, definitions of 'sports';

❑ movement sessions based upon the movements, stances and mannerisms of chosen animals;

❑ appreciating the environment through outdoor activities such as walking, jogging, orienteering, canoeing, cross-country ski-ing.

Technology

- ❏ designing and developing environmentally-sustainable, equity-promoting and animal-friendly technologies;

- ❏ investigating traditional and new intermediate/appropriate technologies that involve animals and assessing their humaneness;

- ❏ selecting, retrieving and using data from an animal/environmental database;

- ❏ using information technologies to present data on animals and the environment in innovative ways;

- ❏ exploring the environmental and humane implications of current technological trends and the research, design, development and marketing processes upon which technology depends;

- ❏ employing various media (e.g. fabrics, glass, metal, wood) to depict an animal-related theme or issue.

3. Other Subjects

Economics

- ❏ the economic implications of resource depletion, pollution, environmental degradation and habitat destruction;

- ❏ the economics of battery and other forms of intensive farming contrasted with the economics of free-range farming;

- ❏ the economics of the fur trade and other forms of trading in (non-food) animal products;

- ❏ the links between animal exploitation and economic maldevelopment;

- ❏ constructing future economic scenarios arising from a marked take-up of vegetarianism and/or other animal-friendly life-styles;

- ❏ researching a business concern based upon environmental- or animal-friendly policies, e.g. The Body Shop;

- ❏ investigating the economic and business impact of a decision, real or hypothetical, by a cosmetics firm to phase out products tested on animals.

Home Economics

- ❏ identifying the animal origins of food and non-food products found in the home;

- ❏ exploring environmental- and animal-friendly shopping and home styles;

- ❏ assessing the cost (direct and indirect), time and health implications of omnivorous, vegetarian and vegan diets;

- ❏ vegetarian cookery in different countries and cultures;

- ❏ pet care and pet hygiene;

- ❏ the role of animal toys and pets in child development; the role of companion animals within the home or family group.

Religious Education

- ❏ the place of animals within the narrative, cosmology, imagery, symbolism, belief systems, and rituals of different world religions;

- ❏ the teachings of world religions on humanity's relationship to, and behaviour towards, non-human animals; religious perspectives on the concept of animal rights;

- ❏ exploring green spirituality; indigenous beliefs and cosmologies;

- ❏ considering personal responsibility towards all living things, and for the well-being of the planet;

- ❏ the ethics of ritual sacrifice; the role of animals within religious ceremonies and festivals;

- ❏ discussion of the ethical dimensions of human treatment of animals;

- ❏ study of key religious figures who have epitomised, and sought to foster, compassion for animals, e.g. St. Francis of Assisi, Albert Schweitzer.

Social Studies/Sociology

❑ study of animal rights and welfare organisations; their origins, goals, structure and styles as campaigning/pressure groups; identifying and evaluating different types of animal rights/welfare activism;

❑ comparing and contrasting cultural perspectives on animals; studying taboos surrounding animals in different cultures;

❑ exploring the arguments for and against the concept of animal rights; examining the overlaps and tensions between animal and human rights theories;

❑ sociological interpretations of human-animal relationships; e.g. the prevalence of companion animals in western societies, the role of animals within a class society;

❑ study of animal societies (hierarchies, pecking orders, dominance and submissiveness, altruistic behaviours, co-operation, friendship and rivalries, courtship).[5]

Cross-curricular Opportunities for Humane Education

Section 1 of the 1988 Education Reform Act (ERA) placed on schools in England and Wales the statutory responsibility to promote students' 'spiritual, moral, cultural, mental and physical development' and to prepare them for 'the opportunities, responsibilities and experiences of adult life'. As details of the National Curriculum emerged through successive pronouncements and publications in 1989 and 1990, it became increasingly apparent that the 'basic curriculum as prescribed by law' (i.e. the 'core' and 'other foundation' subjects plus religious education) could not address all that Section 1 required.[6] The concept of the 'whole curriculum' thus emerged; something going 'far beyond the formal timetable' and involving 'a range of policies and practices to promote the

personal and social development of pupils, to accommodate different teaching and learning styles, to develop positive attitudes and values, and to forge an effective partnership with parents and the local community'.[7] Most fully discussed in the National Curriculum Council's *Curriculum guidance 3. The whole curriculum*, the concept came to be understood as a fusion of four elements: the 'basic' curriculum; cross-curricular dimensions, skills and themes; extra-curricular activities and 'contributory factors' (see *Fig. 1*).[8]

The earlier part of this chapter has outlined opportunities for humane education within the 'basic' curriculum, and additional subjects, whilst earlier chapters have explored teaching/learning styles from a humane perspective (*Chapter 3*) and the rich seam of possibilities for animal-related extra-curricular activities (see, especially, *Chapter 15*). The object here is to identify opportunities for humane education within the cross-curricular elements and, particularly, the five cross-curricular *themes*.

First, a word on cross-curricular *dimensions*. The former are depicted as indispensable, omnipresent features within both the curriculum and school life in general, fostering personal and social development. They include equal opportunities and education for life in a multicultural society and require 'the development of positive attitudes in all staff and pupils towards cultural diversity, gender equality and people with disabilities'.[9] It has been suggested that consideration of speciesism cannot be excluded from our confrontation of sexism and racism (p.17-22); that all forms of prejudice and discrimination are antipathetic to a humane ethic; that self-esteem building, an essential thrust within humane education, is crucial for fostering altruistic attitudes and behaviours to other people and other life forms (pp.36-40). In these ways, the humane educator has a distinctive contribution to make to the

Fig. 1 The Whole Curriculum		
1. THE 'BASIC' CURRICULUM		
Core Subjects	**Other Foundation Subjects**	**Religious Education**
English	Art	
Mathematics	Geography	
Science	History	
	Modern Foreign Language	
	Music	
	Physical Education	
	Technology	
2. CROSS-CURRICULAR ELEMENTS		
Dimensions	**Skills**	**Themes**
Education for a Multicultural Society	Communication	Careers Education and Guidance
Equal Opportunities	Information Technology	Economic and Industrial Understanding
Special Needs	Numeracy	Education for Citizenship
	Personal and Social	Environmental Education
	Problem Solving	Health Education
	Study	
3. EXTRA-CURRICULAR ACTIVITIES		
4. CONTRIBUTORY FACTORS		
The 'Hidden Curriculum' or 'Intangibles'	Teaching and Learning Style Diversity	Effective Curriculum/School Management

realisation of the cross-curricular dimensions.

Cross-curricular themes are perceived of as 'more structured and less pervasive' than other forms of cross-curricular provision, and are likely to be taught at a range of identifiable points within the curriculum, including discrete courses in personal and social education.[10] Five themes have so far been identified: economic and industrial understanding, careers education and guidance, environmental education, health education and citizenship. Each theme was elaborated in a document in the National Curriculum Council's *Curriculum Guidance* series during 1990.

Curriculum guidance 4. Education for economic and industrial understanding offers considerable scope for schools to work on animal-related themes and issues. A school-wide programme on education for economic and industrial understanding, the document points out, will involve dealing

with 'controversial issues, such as the impact of economic activity on the environment'. Students 'should be encouraged to explore values and beliefs, both their own and those of others'.[11] Amongst the knowledge and understanding goals laid down, are 'how business enterprise creates wealth' and 'how consumer decisions are made and the implications of these decisions', focuses that allow for study of both ethical business and ethical consumerism. The attitudinal goals include: 'concern for the use of scarce resources', 'a sense of responsibility for the consequences of (one's own) economic actions', 'respect for alternative economic viewpoints and a willingness to reflect critically on (one's own) economic views and values', 'sensitivity to the effects of economic choices on the environment' and 'concern for human rights, as these are affected by economic decisions'.[12] *Curriculum guidance 4* also lays down that students at all key stages should 'visit and investigate industries and other places of work' and, over the age of 15, should take up work experience placements; also, that they should take part in small-scale business and community enterprise projects.[13] Interestingly, two of the five photographs in the document depicting visits concern animal-related places of work (the captions are 'Service industries: pupils find out about the work of a local vet' and 'Middle school pupils visit a dairy farm to find out about milk production'[14]) whilst the mini-enterprise depicted is a school farm ('Business enterprise: pupils rear and assess cattle for market'[15]). It would, thus, be absolutely in accordance with both the letter and spirit of *Curriculum guidance 4* to design a school programme for economic and industrial understanding that, *inter alia*, incorporated projects on cruelty-free consumerism, study of ethical aspects of factory farming, zoos and business-led vivisection, visits to places of animal-related work, during which the treatment of animals was one important focus of study, and work placements with, say, a humane society.

Curriculum guidance 5. Health education, likewise, provides innumerable starting points for the creative teacher to introduce humane themes and issues. 'Food and nutrition', one of the nine health education strands to be addressed across key stages 1-4, includes consideration of the relationship between diet and health, the nutritional quality of different foods, food safety and healthy food choices. As such it provides a platform for exploring the relative merits of vegan, vegetarian and meat (factory farmed and free range) diets; also non-meat diets in different cultures, current food labelling systems and the health risks of meat additives. 'Family life education' and 'psychological aspects of health education' both give scope for consideration of the role of pets in family or home group life, their contribution to emotional well-being and stress reduction, and the self-esteem building aspects of

personal responsibility for an animal (see pp.37-9). A further strand offering fertile ground for animal-related topics is 'Environmental aspects of health education', covering environmental attitudes, values and beliefs and responsibility for environmental care.[16]

The aims laid out in *Curriculum guidance 6. Careers education and guidance*, require that students 'consider controversial issues related to work' (key stage 3), thus providing scope for study and discussion of work situations which are exploitative of animals and/or the environment. The several aims for key stage 4 directing students to contemplate career choice also allow for ongoing personal and group reflection on ethical work, training and research.[17]

Not unexpectedly, *Curriculum guidance 7. Environmental education*, is the richest in potential from a humane education viewpoint. Citing the Chair of the World Commission on Environment and Development, Gro Harlem Bruntland ('The global environment has deteriorated to such an extent that the great life supporting systems of the planet's biosphere are being threatened ...We must therefore redouble our commitment to sustainable development'), it asks that students should develop knowledge and understanding of, *inter alia*, natural processes in the environment, the impact of human activities on the environment, environmental issues and the conflicts surrounding them, and environment legislation and protection. Amongst the attitudinal goals laid down is 'appreciation of, and care and concern for the environment and for other living things', whilst specific mention is made of endangered species and conservation, exploitation of wild animals and destruction of natural habitats as issues for study. One of the case studies offered in the document is of a class of 9-10 year olds involved in a research/action project on the gassing of badgers (see *Fig. 2*). Given the

---

Fig. 2 The Gassing of Badgers

The Activity

A class of 9- to 10-year olds carried out an investigation into the gassing of badgers to prevent the spread of bovine tuberculosis among dairy cattle and infection of humans. Pupils themselves raised the issue during class discussion and planned all aspects of the enquiry. The project enabled them to clarify their own views on the issue, to find out about other points of view and to suggest possible plans of action.

Method

In a class discussion, pupils expressed their concerns about the gassing of badgers in the Southwest of England and decided to investigate the issue.

They collected information on different aspects of the issue from books and newspapers. Through the local newspaper they invited people to tell them about badgers' setts in the area. With the help of an expert, they investigated badger signs, tracks and holes in the school woods.

Letters were sent to various organisations (Ministry of Agriculture, conservation societies, television programmes and the police) to express their concerns and to get more information about badgers.

A questionnaire was designed and sent to different local schools to hear other children's perceptions of the issue. The results were presented in the form of pie and bar charts.

Pupils identified the arguments for and against the gassing of badgers. A vote was taken, and a majority was found to disagree with the practice. Recommendations were then made concerning the prevention of bovine tuberculosis.

Note

This example illustrates how controversial issues relating to the environment can be introduced to young children to encourage in them an awareness and motivation for action. The use of an action-based approach may stimulate them to form their own judgement in the light of evidence.

— NCC, *Curriculum Guidance 7. Environmental Education*, 1990, 25.

---

knowledge/understanding, skills and attitudinal goals laid down and given that the theme is clearly held to embrace study of both natural and human-made environments, it is hard to think of a humane education topic that could not with good justification be dealt with under the National Curriculum.[18]

Curriculum guidance 8. Education for citizenship is in some respects, the most speciesist of the documents elaborating the cross-curricular themes. The description of the 'Community' component omits any reference to biotic community; bioregionalism is disregarded as a source of identity and focus of allegiance; discussion of rights is restricted throughout to human

rights, and discussion of the responsibilities of the citizen stops short of responsibilities to non-human animals. The document by no means, however, shuts the door decisively on consideration of human-animal relationships in that, as with the other cross-curricular themes, it is left for teachers to determine the precise content falling under each of the eight components. The 'Pluralist Society' component can incorporate multicultural and multifaith perspectives on animals; the suggested study of pressure groups under the 'Democracy in Action' component can be directed to animal rights and welfare organisations; research into animal protection legislation could fall under the umbrella of 'The Citizen and the Law'; the pros and cons of hunting could, with justification, be studied as a 'costs and consequences' of leisure topic, under the 'Work, Employment and Leisure' component.[19] The emphasis on encouraging in students 'a desire to participate in events happening in the world about them' provides legitimisation for the kind of action projects suggested in *Chapter 15*.[20] An innovative citizenship course, weaving in humane education activities to positive effect, is described in *Chapter 17* (pp.353-7).

The humane educator should also recall that the 'whole curriculum' concept, as principally developed by the National Curriculum Council, is not regarded as final; it is seen as provisional (for instance, 'The National Curriculum Council has identified five themes which, although by no means a conclusive list, seem to most people to be pre-eminent'[21]). The inclusion of humane education as a cross-curricular dimension or theme in its own right, or as a more conspicuous and self-evident strand within existing cross-curricular elements, is an advocacy task for the next several years.

References

1. Selby, D., ed., *EarthKind in the National Curriculum*, EarthKind UK, 1995 (but annually updated). Available from EarthKind, Humane Education Centre, Bounds Green Road. London N22 4EU.

2. Myers, N., ed., *The Gaia atlas of planet management*, Pan, 1985.

3. Excellent source books are Ponting, C., *A green history of the world*, Penguin, 1991; Simmons, I.G., *Changing the face of the Earth: culture, environment, history*, Basil Blackwell, 1989; Worster, D., ed., *The ends of the Earth: perspectives on modern environmental history*, CUP, 1988.

4. An inspirational melding of animal and natural sound with human music has been achieved by Paul Winter and Don Gibson. The former's *Whales Alive*, Living Music, 1987, and the latter's *Harmony*, 1989, are excellent examples of their work. For a catalogue of Don Gibson's recorded work, write to Don Gibson Production Ltd., P.O. Box 1200, Stn. Z, Toronto, Ontario, MSN 2Z7.

5. An excellent introduction to this area is offered in Attenborough, D., *The trials of life. A natural history of animal behaviour*, Collins/BBC, 1990.

6. National Curriculum Council, *Circular no. 6. The National Curriculum and whole curriculum planning: preliminary guidance*, October 1989, paras. 1-4.

7. *Ibid.*

8. See National Curriculum Council, *Curriculum guidance 3. The whole curriculum*, March 1990, 1.

9. National Curriculum Council, *Circular no. 6. The National Curriculum and whole curriculum planning: preliminary guidance*, October 1989, paras. 9-11.

10. *Ibid.*, paras. 15-17.

11. National Curriculum Council, *Curriculum guidance 4. Education for economic and industrial understanding*, April 1990, 3.

12. *Ibid.*, 4-5.

13. *Ibid.*. 5-6.

14. *Ibid.*, 5 and 22.

15. *Ibid.*, 45.

16. National Curriculum *Council, Curriculum guidance 5. Health education*, June 1990, 4-5, 11-20.

17. National Curriculum Council, *Curriculum guidance 6. Careers education and guidance*, June 1990, 31, 35-43.

18. National Curriculum Council, *Curriculum guidance 7. Environmental education*, September 1990, 4, 6, 10, 25.

19. National Curriculum Council, *Curriculum guidance 8. Education for citizenship*, November 1990, 3-9.

20. *Ibid.*, 10.

21. National Curriculum *Council, Curriculum guidance 3. The whole curriculum*, March 1990, 4.

Chapter 17

Sample Primary and Secondary Topics

INTRODUCTION

In this chapter three teachers, one primary, two secondary, offer snapshots of the EarthKind curriculum in practice. Topics for Years 1, 3 and 4 are described by Jackie Harvey. Pam Gill writes about a Year 9 science course. Sandra Bush sets in context and outlines a successful humane education course for Year 11 students which both enriched and vivified the global education thrust already strongly in evidence within the school's Personal and Social Education programme. The warning bell sounded towards the end of her report is an important reminder of how curriculum predicated upon humane, democratic and egalitarian values can easily be undermined by insensitive and inappropriate means of testing.

Each primary topic description is accompanied by a *Topic Web*, a *Topic Chart* and a *Balanced Curriculum Grid*. The *Topic Chart* indicates the National Curriculum attainment targets and cross-curricular themes dealt with by the topic unit; also the humane education knowledge, skills and attitudinal objectives (see p.50-6) to which the units relate. The *Balanced Curriculum Grid* analyses the topic using the nine curriculum areas identified in the Department of Education and Science's *Curriculum 5 to 16* document.[1]

■ *TOPIC FOR YEAR 1: WILD ANIMALS by Jackie Harvey*

Introduction

This topic has been designed to last about half a term (six weeks). It can stand in its own right or be incorporated into other topics; for example, as a contrast to a topic on pet animals or to complement a study of plants. It is intended as a springboard for fieldwork in the local environment and so could also incorporate work on ecology, conservation and/or pollution. There are opportunities to weight the topic towards science and geography. With this age group the need is perhaps to go from the familiar to the less familiar and to use the immediate surroundings, as much as possible, before considering more physically remote situations. Children are usually fascinated to find 'wild' animals in their own vicinity and this fascination can be used to develop in them a greater respect for all environments. It should be possible to adapt the topic to most localities, with work on as many habitats as suits the students and the teacher. The whole thing is open-ended enough to cater for a wide range of abilities.

Topic outline

Aims:

❑ To develop in students the concept of a 'habitat';

❑ To develop an appreciation of interdependence within the natural world;

❑ To consider human responsibilities to the natural world.

The first part of the topic sets out to teach the concept of a 'habitat'. Perhaps the best way to begin is by visiting a variety of habitats close to the school, one or more of which could be subsequently studied in greater detail; for example, the sea-shore, a rockpool, a cave, a pond, an area of the school grounds, a field, an area of waste land, a wood. The children should observe, list, draw and, if possible, take photographs of, animals living in their community. In the classroom, discussion can take in animals found, any unusual places they were

found in and other animals that were not observed but which might also share the area (were any clues to the presence of other animals found?). A class book or display, *Animals That Share Our Community,* could be developed, containing pictures of, and sentences about, the animals.

Further work could be undertaken on one or more habitats. Provided that breeding times are avoided and caring for the animals is greatly emphasised, one or two specimens might be collected for careful observation and drawing. The children will need to know where to return any animal and will have to take great care not to destroy its habitat. In class they could also construct models of the habitats (for example, ponds or rock-pools made from cardboard boxes, showing both above and below water habitats, and including models of plants and creatures they have observed). Accurate modelling will demand careful observation of form, texture and colour. In this way they will develop an understanding of the variety of life in even a small area, and will come to know the chosen habitat(s) especially well. Movement sessions can be used to foster greater appreciation of animal movement (a variation of *Pet Charades*, p.159, could be used here). Sentences can be written describing animals and their movements. Activities like *Animal Symphony*, p.61, and *What's Your Smell?*, p.76, could be introduced to further encourage empathy with animals. Later, discussion might centre around how the school environment could be improved to entice more wildlife. The children could design, even make, a conservation or wild area for the whole school.

The next part of the topic concentrates on the concept of interdependence in nature. Many activities in the initial section of the topic can be carried out through co-operative and collaborative work which will help reinforce the idea of interdependence. The activity, *Woolly Web*, p.89, is a good introduction to this concept, providing a tangible and visual form of the idea of a food web. Animals with which the children have become familiar could be included. *Frogs And Flies*, p.93, will further illustrate the dynamic system of checks and balances within the natural world. Students can then be encouraged to think about the habitats they have encountered and about what could happen to disturb them. A class list of possibilities can be drawn up. Next, the class can think of what they could do to protect these areas and to make sure that animals continue to live there. They can design posters for individual animals, containing the name of the animal, a brief description of its habitat, and one way in which the habitat could be protected or improved (a variation of *Care Posters*, p.178, could be used).

The third part of the topic goes on to develop the idea of human responsibilities. The teacher needs to draw out the integral parts of a habitat (e.g. air, shelter, protection from enemies, the availability of food and water). This can be done by reference to a human habitat, identifying its component parts (e.g. house, family, food, beds, clothing, furnishings). The students can then relate their learning to the habitat of a familiar native wild animal (perhaps one they have encountered during the project). Alternatively, one or more of the activities comparing animal and human needs, pp.113-19, could be employed. A model of a human habitat could be constructed, with labels to point out similarities to the chosen animal's habitat. Discussion can follow on the importance of maintaining habitats in good condition and the responsibility humans have to their own kind and to animals. Litter can be chosen as one way humans do not look after the environment. Students can be asked to think of potential dangers posed by excessive litter for both themselves and animals. This could be followed by a litter pick-up in the school or neighbourhood, or in one of the habitats explored. Looking at the type of rubbish collected can lead to further discussion of how it might affect humans and animals. The children can devise a code or set of guidelines to alert others to the dangers. In drama sessions they can act out situations where litter has caused particular problems for humans or animals. An anti-litter campaign can be launched and regular collections made and weighed to see if the problem is decreasing. The class can look into recycling too.

The fourth part of the topic looks at habitats more remote from the children and goes on to develop the concept of extinction. Given the popularity of *Jurassic Park*, children will probably know quite a lot about dinosaurs. Discussion can focus on what the earth was like then and why dinosaurs became extinct. Another extinct animal can be introduced, e.g. the passenger pigeon, and the reasons for its demise explored. This time the story will involve interference by humans. One by one, pictures of different endangered species can be revealed, the teacher explaining how these animals are threatened as a consequence of human action (for example, through habitat destruction, over-hunting and pollution). The children can draw an animal, extinct or endangered, and pin their drawing in the appropriate part of a board divided into two sections; one headed 'It Happened To Them', the other 'It's Happening Again'.

This idea can be reinforced through a circle activity (see p.67). The students suggest animals that they would always want to have around. They each choose a picture of an animal from a selection provided by the teacher and scattered, face upwards, on the floor (not only animals threatened by extinction). The students form a circle, hold up their picture and take turns to talk about one good characteristic of the animal portrayed. On finishing they put their picture face down on the floor. Other students can then say how they would feel if that particular animal no longer existed. A summation to the work can involve the production of a class booklet on endangered animals. Each student would produce one page on a different animal. Each page could include a drawing of the animal and, possibly, its habitat, its name and one or two positive words describing it. Possible, preferred and likely futures for the animal could also be summarised.

The topic could end here or it would be possible to extend the work to zoos and the keeping of wild animals in captivity. The aim would be to make students aware of some of the agencies which keep wild animals in captivity and their reasons for doing so. The students would also have the opportunity to explore the responsibility

TOPIC WEB (YEAR ONE)

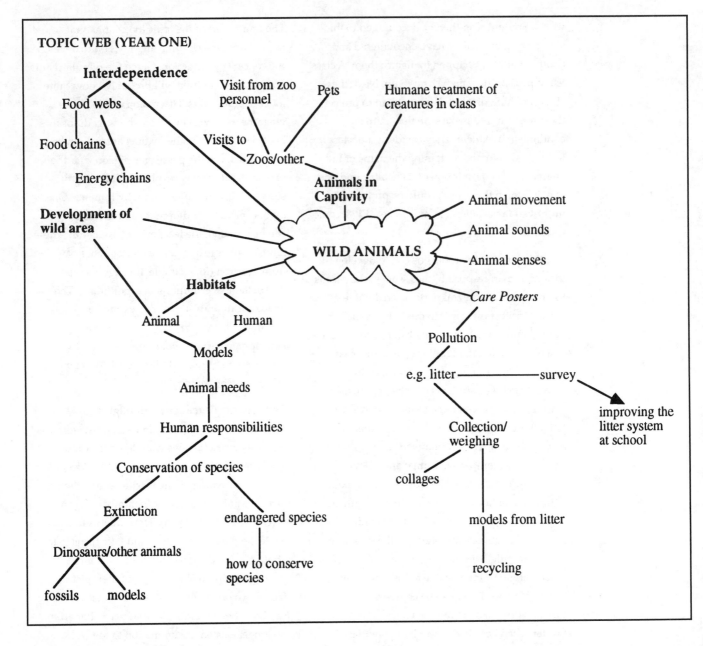

humans have to allow wild animals in captivity to live as naturally as possible. Initially a list of all the agencies and individuals which keep wild animals in captivity could be made (zoos, aquaria, circuses, fur farms, research laboratories, trainers of animals who work in TV and films, pet owners). The children could each choose a wild animal and draw it in its natural habitat and in captivity. The homes could be compared and contrasted. In which will the animal feel happiest? Could the captive home be made more like the natural? An activity like *Animal Homes*, p.237, would reinforce this work. A visit to a zoo might be organised and/or a visit to a school by a zoo-worker. Films showing different types of zoo as well as animals in their natural habitat would be helpful and promote discussion. The activity, *The Teeming Ark*, p.122, adapted to this age group as suggested in the variation, would be a good way to end the topic.

TOPIC CHART (YEAR ONE)

TOPIC CHART (YEAR ONE)	ATTAINMENT TARGETS	CROSS-CURRICULAR THEMES	OBJECTIVES OF HUMANE EDUCATION (see Chapter 3)
Visits to habitat	Science AT 2 English AT 1,2, 3, 4, 5 Geog AT 1, 2	Environment	K 2a, 5a S 1a, 1b A 2a, 2b, 2c, 3a, 3b
Class display	Science AT 2 English AT 2, 3, 4, 5 Art AT 1	Environment	K 2a, 3b, 5a S 1a, 1b, 3c, 4g A 2a, 2b, 2c, 3a, 3b, 7a
Model of a habitat	Techology AT 2, 3 Art AT 1 Science AT 2 English AT 3, 4, 5 Geog AT 1, 2	Environment	K 2a, 3b, 5a S 1a, 1b, 3c, 4g A 2a, 2b, 2c, 3a, 3b, 7a
Animal movement	Science AT 2 Dance/PE		S 1a, 1b A 2a, 2b, 3a, 3b
ANIMAL SYMPHONY	Science AT 2		S 1a, 3c; A 2b, 7a
WHAT'S YOUR SMELL?	Science AT 2		S 1a, 3c; A 2b, 7a
Design & production of 'wild' area	Technology AT 1, 2, 3, 4 Science AT 2 Geog AT 1, 3 English AT 1, 2, 3, 4, 5	Environment Citizenship	K 2a, 3b, 5a, 5c S 1a, 1b, 3c, 3d, 5b, 5f, 6a A 2a, 2b, 2c, 3b, 3c
WOOLLY WEB	Science AT 2	Environment	K 2a, 3a, 3b; S 1a, 1b, 3c, 5c; A 2a, 7a
FROGS & FLIES	Science AT 2	Environment	K 2a, 3a, 3b; S 1a, 1b, 3c, 5c; A 2a, 7a
Posters	Technology AT 2 Art AT 1 Science AT 2	Environment	K 2a, 5a, 5b, 5c S 1a, 1b, 3c A 2a, 2c, 3a, 3b, 3c, 7a
Human habitat	Science AT 2	Environment Health	K 3a, 3b, 4a, 5a; S 1a, 1b, 1c, 3c, 5c; A 2c, 4c
Litter collections	Maths AT 2	Health Citizenship Environment	K 4b, 6g S 3c, 6b A 7a, 7c
Extinct and endangered animals	History AT 1, 3 Science AT 2	Environment Citizenship	K 4b, 5b; S 1a, 1b; A 2a, 2b, 3a, 3b, 3c, 4c, 7b
CIRCLE activity on above	Science AT 2 English AT 1, 3, 4, 5	Environment Citizenship	K 4b, 5b; S 1a; A 2a, 2b, 3a, 3b, 3c, 4c, 7b
Animals in captivity	Science AT 2 English AT 1, 2, 3, 4, 5	Citizenship Economic/Industrial	K 5a, 5b, 5c, 5d, 6d; S 1a, 1b, 3e, 4c, 5e; A 3a, 3b, 3c, 4c
ANIMAL HOMES	Science AT 2 English AT 1, 2, 3, 4, 5	Environment Citizenship	K 4a, 5a, 5b, 5d, 6d; S 3c, 4b, 4c; A 3a, 3b, 3c, 4c
THE TEEMING ARK	Science AT 2 English AT 1		K 2a, 3b, 5e; S 3a, 3c, 3d, 4a; A 3a, 3b, 4c

BALANCED CURRICULUM GRID (YEAR ONE)

Topic: Wild Animals

	Aesthetic & Creative (Art, Dance/Drama, Music & Design)	Human & Social (History, Geography, Current Affairs, Social Skills)	Linguistic & Literary (English-Reading, Writing, Speaking & Listening)	Mathematical (Any mathematical activity)	Moral (May have spiritual content but not necessarily so)	Spiritual (That which has religious content)	Physical (PE, Games, Swimming, Dance/Drama)	Scientific (Science)	Technological (CDT)
Visit to habitat		•	•		•			•	
Animals in community	•	•	•					•	
Model of habitat	•	•	•	•				•	•
Animal movement	•	•	•				•	•	
Animal Symphony	•	•	•					•	
What's Your Smell?	•	•	•					•	
Design/create wildlife area	•	•	•	•	•			•	•
Woolly Web		•	•		•			•	
Frogs and Flies		•	•	•			•	•	
Animal protection posters	•	•	•		•			•	•
Human habitats	•	•	•	•				•	•
Comparing habitats		•	•		•			•	
Litter survey & collections	•	•	•	•	•			•	•
Recycling		•	•		•			•	•
Extinct animals		•	•		•			•	
Extinction circle		•	•		•			•	
Endangered animals book	•	•	•		•			•	
Animals in captivity		•	•		•			•	
Animal Homes		•	•		•			•	
Zoo visit/visit from zoo-worker		•			•				
The Teeming Ark		•	•		•			•	

■ *TOPIC FOR YEAR 3 OR 4: FARMING by Jackie Harvey*

Introduction

This topic could be incorporated into the curriculum in many ways. It could be extended to act as the basis of a term's work (twelve weeks) which would include investigation of both crop and livestock farming. It could be a shorter element in a larger topic on food, animals or industry and commerce. It could be an extension to a historically-based study of farming, which might look at the past, its contribution to the present state of farming, and then at farming in the future. There are obvious opportunities to tilt the emphasis towards history, geography or social studies; also to draw on a wide range of examples. It should not be too difficult to tailor the outline, or specific activities, to the needs of individual classes. The whole thing is open-ended enough to cater for a wide range of abilities.

Topic Outline

❑   To develop understanding of forms of farming;

❑   To explore the reasons for farming;

❑   To explore the effects of farming on livestock and countryside.

The first part of the topic seeks to answer the question 'what is a farm?' A visit from a local farmer, or to a farm, could be a starting point.[2] Students, working in groups, can then research various types of farming (subsistence, profit-making, sheep, cattle, dairy, mixed, hill and so on). The choice should reflect the locality, the varied cultures in the school and the learning resources available. Once research has been completed the children can then do one of several things. They can present their findings to the rest of the class through a talk and display. They can paint pictures to illustrate their findings and write a report to accompany them for display on a class frieze (this information can then be shared in discussion or through presentations). They can produce a taped 'radio' or 'television' programme on different types of farming.

The class can go on to look at their local area, using maps and aerial photographs,[3] and locate and identify different types of farms. This knowledge could be transferred to a map of the U.K. with other sorts of farming added for other areas. The class can discuss why farms are located as they are and how the choice of location relates to the geography, topography and climate of the area. By now the students should have acquired enough background to look at one aspect of farming in more detail.

The second part of the topic aims to look specifically at animal farming and to answer the question 'why do we farm animals?' The activity, *Animal Uses*, p.129., could provide the springboard, exploring as it does the uses to which we put animals. This could be followed by looking at animals as a source of food through *Animals In My Shopping Bag*, p.128. The students might make cardboard looms and weave with wool, to develop their understanding of the farming of sheep for their wool. It might also be possible for a visiting craftsperson to demonstrate carding, spinning and weaving on a larger loom.[4] Pattern could be explored by weaving with different coloured paper strips. Finally, to help them think beyond the familiar, the students can undertake an activity such as *Funny Farms*, p.187. This should widen their understanding of the reasons why animals are farmed, and provoke them to think further about the appropriateness of the treatment of animals on farms.

The third part of the topic still concentrates on animal farming but looks at the needs of the animals, confronting the questions 'what needs do animals have?' and 'to what extent are these met or denied by farms?' A visit from a local veterinarian or to a vet's surgery might be useful. But it might be better, with this age group, to look at their own needs first. This could be done through brainstorming, discussion and elimination until the group has come up with five or six important needs. Activities from the *Similarities and Differences* section of *Chapter 6*, pp.109-19 would help students to think about animal needs. Empathy with, and understanding of animals could also be developed through

TOPIC WEB (YEARS 3/4)

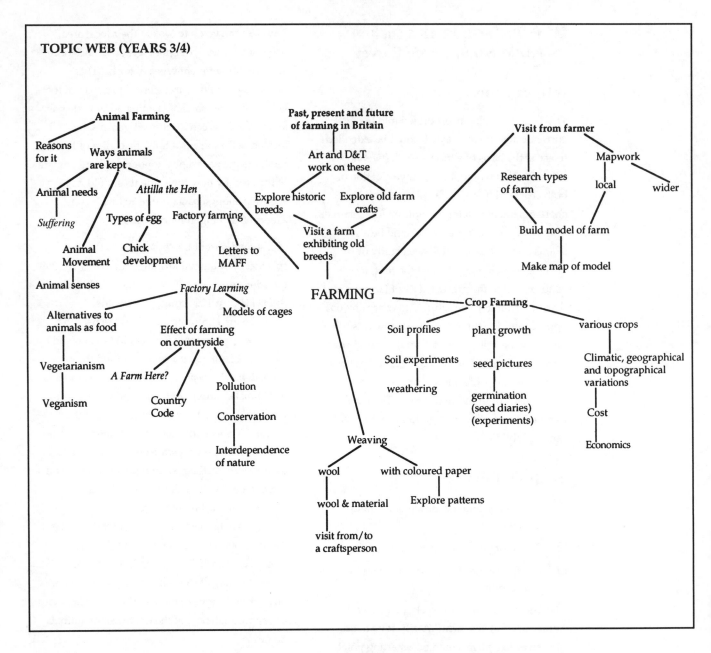

movement and language activities. The children could watch films showing animals to find out how they move and what sounds they make. In a movement session they could explore moving and sounding like different farm animals. *Menagerie*, p. 62, or *Animal Symphony*, p.61, could reinforce this work. The class could go on to *Cinquains* and *Care Posters.*, pp.177-8. They could also explore services available to the farmer through the activity, *Yellow Pages*, p.178.

The fourth part of the topic looks at the effect on animals if their needs are not met. It tries to address the question 'what is it like to be an animal on a farm?'. It could begin with a discussion about what it means to suffer. Is it always physical hurt? Can you suffer because your feelings are hurt? Because you are bored? Lonely? Frightened? *Suffering*, p.118, is a language- based activity which helps children to think about how animals might suffer and how that suffering might be alleviated. *At Arm's Length?*, p.238, and *Factory Learning*, p.179, are experiential activities which try to help the children understand 'suffering' as something more than just lack of attention to physical needs. The book, *Attilla the Hen*, by Paddy Mounter[5] is an amusing account of how one hen in a battery farm leads a revolt. It provides good stimulus material for drama, play-writing, and a variety of artwork. A futures-oriented approach to the book

TOPIC CHART (YEARS 3/4)

TOPIC CHART (YEARS 3/4)	ATTAINMENT TARGETS	CROSS-CURRICULAR THEMES	OBJECTIVES OF HUMANE EDUCATION (see Chapter 3)
Visit, research and presentation	English AT 1, 2, 3, 4, 5; Art AT 1, 2	Economic/Industrial	K 4a; S 1a, 1b, 4g; A 3c
Map work	Geog AT 1, 2, 5	Environment	S 1a, 1b, 1c
ANIMAL USES	English AT 1; Science 2, 3	Economic/Industrial	K 5b, 5c, 5d; S 3a, 3c, 3d, 3e, 4a, 4c; A 1b, 3c, 4c
ANIMALS IN MY SHOPPING BAG	Geog AT 1; English AT 1, 2, 3, 4, 5	Environment; Economic/Industrial	K 3a, 3b, 5b, 5c, 5d; S 1a, 1b, 3c, 4a, 4c; A 1b, 3c, 4c
Weaving	Art AT 1, 2; Maths AT 3		S 2a
FUNNY FARMS	English AT 1, 2, 3, 4, 5		K 5b, 5c, 5d; 4a, 4c; A 3a, 3b, 3c, 4c
Brainstorm needs	English AT 1	PSE	K 5a, 5b, 5c; S 3a, 3c; A 3a, 3b, 3c
NEEDS ACTIVITIES	Science AT 2; English AT 1, 3	PSE; Health	K 5a, 5b, 5c; S 3a, 3c; A 3a, 3b, 3c
Animal movement	Science AT 2; PE/Dance		S 1a, 1b; A 2a, 2b, 3a, 3b
MENAGERIE	Science AT 2		S 1a, 3c; A 2b; 7a
ANIMAL SYMPHONY	Science AT 2		S 1a, 3c; A 2b; 7a
CINQUAINS	English AT 3, 4, 5		K 2a; S 1a, 1b; A 2a, 2b, 3b
CARE POSTERS	English AT 1, 2, 3, 4, 5; Technology AT 2; Art AT		K 2a, 5a, 5b, 5c; S 1a, 1b, 1c, 4g; A 2a, 2b, 3a, 3b, 3c, 4c
YELLOW PAGES	English AT 2, 3, 4, 5	Citizenship	K 5b, 5c, 5d; S 1a, 1b, 1c; A 3a, 3b, 3c
SUFFERING	English AT 1, 2, 3, 4, 5	Citizenship; Health	K 5b, 5c, 5d; S 4a, 4c; A 3a, 3b, 3c, 4a, 4c
AT ARM'S LENGTH?	Science AT 2; English AT 1	Health	K 5a, 5b, 5c, 5d; S 1a; A 3a, 3b, 3c, 3e, 4a, 4c
FACTORY LEARNING	English AT 1	Health; Economic/Industrial	K 5a, 5b, 5c, 5d; S 1a, 1b; A 3a, 3b, 3c, 3e, 4a, 4c
ATTILLA THE HEN/THE GREAT EGGSCAPE	All areas	Economic/Industrial	K 5b, 5c, 5d, 6h; S 1a, 1b; A 3a, 3b, 3c, 4a, 4c, 5f
Cage models	Technology AT 2, 3; Art AT; Maths AT 1, 2	Health; Economic/Industrial	K 5b, 5c, 5d; S 1a, 1b, 3c, 4a, 4c; A 3a, 3b, 3c
Letters	English AT 3, 4, 5		K 6g; S 6a, 6b, 6g; A 7c
WOOLLY WEB	Science AT 2	Environment	K 2a, 3a, 3b; S 1a, 1b, 3c, 5c; A 2a, 7a
A FARM HERE?	English AT 1; Science AT 2	Environment	K 2a, 3a, 3b, 4a, 4b, 5a, 5b, 5c, 6g; S 1a, 1b, 3a, 3c, 3d; A 2b, 2c, 3b, 3c, 7a, 7c
FOOD CHAIN	Science AT 2; Maths AT 2	Economic/Industrial; Citizenship	K 3a, 3c, 4b; S 3c; A 2a, 2e, 3b
YUM YUM	English AT 1, 2, 3; Technology AT 2; Art AT 1	Health; Economic/Industrial; Environment	K 3c, 5h; S 1a, 1b, 1c, 3c, 5a, 5b, 5f, 6a; A 3b, 3c, 4c

BALANCED CURRICULUM GRID (YEAR 3/4)

Topic: Farming

ACTIVITIES	Aesthetic & Creative (Art, Dance/Drama, Music & Design)	Human & Social (History, Geog, Current Affairs, Social Skills)	Linguistic & Literary (English-Reading, Writing, Speaking & Listening)	Mathematical (Any mathematical activity)	Moral (May have spiritual content but not necessarily so)	Spiritual (That which has religious content)	Physical (PE, Games, Swimming, Dance/Drama)	Scientific (Science)	Technological (CDT)
Visit to a farm/from a farmer		•	•					•	
Research into types of farming		•	•					•	
Present/report on above	•	•	•					•	•
Local area - mapwork		•	•	•					
Animal Uses		•	•					•	
Animals in My Shopping Bag	•	•	•		•				•
Weaving	•			•					•
Funny Farms		•	•		•				
Vet (visit from)		•	•		•			•	
Brainstorm needs		•	•		•			•	
Needs Activities		•	•		•				
Animal movement	•						•	•	
Menagerie	•						•		
Animal Symphony	•								
Cinquains	•				•			•	
Care Posters	•	•	•		•			•	•
Yellow Pages	•	•	•	•					
Suffering	•	•	•		•				
At Arm's Length?	•	•	•		•		•	•	•
Factory Learning		•	•		•		•		
Attila the Hen/The Great Eggscape	•	•	•		•				
Letters to MAFF		•	•		•				
Models of cages	•			•					•
Woolly Web			•		•			•	
A Farm Here?	•	•	•		•		•	•	
Food Chain	•	•	•	•	•			•	
Yum Yum	•	•	•		•	•			•

is provided by the activity, *The Great Eggscape*, p.296, Models of the cages, using actual measures, can be made. The children could write letters to the Ministry of Agriculture, Food and Fisheries (MAFF)[6] to ask for details of legal requirements for hens or sows, for example. They could also investigate the health and safety requirements for school-children by way of comparison. They could write to MAFF to express their opinions on the conditions in which some animals are kept. They could research the meanings of various types of egg available in supermarkets — free range, perchery and so on. *Which?*, the magazine of the Consumer Association, and the Association itself are good sources of information.[7]

The fifth and final part of the topic looks at the interdependence of nature and how using land for farms might affect the countryside. *Woolly Web*, p.89, demonstrates interdependence and balance within nature. Following this with a drama-simulation like *A Farm Here?*, p.188, should provide immediate and powerful ways of exploring some of the issues involved in the destruction of wild areas for farming. The teacher could end the topic with a look at alternatives to using animals for food. An activity such as *Food Chain*, p.92, will help students understand how energy available decreases along a food chain and how meat eating is an inefficient use of land. A simplified version of *Yum Yum*, p.185, will raise a range of issues surrounding meat eating and vegetarianism. The topic might end with a vegetarian feast prepared by the students themselves.

■ *A YEAR 9 SCIENCE COURSE by Pam Gill*

I decided to attempt a unit on the use of animals with my two grade 9 advanced science classes (14-15 years old). I began by asking them to fill out a questionnaire on uses of animals (see *Fig.1*). I asked the students to complete the task fairly quickly and go with initial reactions. The completed questionnaires were kept until the end of the unit.

Next I used *Which Animals Have Rights?*, p.269. With the second class I cut down the number of creatures and I think this helped. Some of the small animals listed, e.g. millipede, are unfamiliar to the students and this was rather distracting. I put the final totals on the board and we had a class discussion around the reasons for the totals. It was a good starting discussion with a lot of gut reactions which I tried to focus on, asking reasons for their feelings.

We did *Where Do I Stand?*, p.262, in the next session and this was a big hit, lasting for a complete 70-minute period. It led to a very heated discussion especially around tests on animals for medical and cosmetic purposes. Many students found they had originally given conflicting answers on the sheet and had to analyse their views later. For feedback I asked for an analysis of the activity, comments on the organisation of the discussion and suggestions for topics we should explore further.

Typical comments were:

❑   I think we should have more activities like this. I never really thought about the issue much but it really got me thinking when we got those sheets. (Hemraj Beersa).

Fig. 1

	OK to use all animals?	Any exceptions?	Reasons?
Food			
Clothing			
Sport			
Dissection			
Medical Testing			
Product Testing			

❑ In the beginning I thought everybody would have the same views but as we went on people expressed their views differently and got really serious (Debbie da Cunha).

❑ I enjoyed it because I had a chance to speak out and let people hear what I had to say. (Haida Gebru).

We later had two days' library research and presentations on the topics they found most interesting. In the main, these were alternatives to animal testing.

I had arranged to visit a medical laboratory to follow this up but it fell through on account of illness there. I had a speaker in from the Body Shop. This was interesting on testing methods and alternatives and the organisation's general philosophy. Lots of questions were also asked about running a business and training. *Futurescapes*, p.299, was the next lesson's activity. This was less successful with this age group. I should have simplified its content. The form was completed individually then discussed in groups of four. It did, however, trigger a discussion on vegetarianism: the class' next research topic.

First, I gave out copies of articles from the *Opposing Viewpoints* series: 'The case for vegetarianism' and 'The case for eating meat'.[8] Each is 3-4 sides long and interesting in that both use some of the same data in an attempt to prove opposing points! I drew attention to the way they are written, especially the use of emotive words.

The students first had to make summaries of each article to help them focus on the main points. For the next day they were asked to bring in two articles or other pieces of literature on the topic. I also provided a book collection. Students worked in small groups to research and develop their own viewpoint.

We also had a class discussion and they asked me to join in. It was very interesting and some usually quiet students volunteered very firm, well-expressed views. They also asked me a lot of questions. Much of the discussion focused on how circumstances can alter our stand on issues; for instance, would vegetarians think differently if marooned in the bush? The discussion was heated and, I gather, raged through lunch in the cafeteria! Feedback from students told me that rather than disliking those with different views the exchanges increased their respect for each other.

We next attempted *Splitting Images*, p.218. A very powerful activity. Many students thought the initial part-picture was of an angry duck and were very startled later on. After doing the activity and exchanging ideas and opinions between groups, I read the description from the photographer. It led to a discussion on trapping and furs. I nudged it towards shades of grey around leather and feathers too. Discussion also veered onto the topic of 'natural vs. synthetic'. Next day I showed the National Film Board of Canada film, *Pelts. Politics of the Fur Trade*, which airs a wide range of, often very conflicting, views.[9] Students were informed that, after the film, they would be asked to write a critical analysis of the positions and arguments of the pro- and anti-fur spokespeople represented. They were so engrossed that they wouldn't let me pause the video, so we reviewed it a second time the next day to obtain the names of people and organisations. In addition to analysing viewpoints expressed, students were asked to write their own views on the fur trade, fur farming and the use of fur. We had some class discussion to see if the film had changed anyone's mind. There was less enthusiasm for fur farms than before the film — but not 100% opposition. I was impressed with the quality of the discussion. Students recognised how complex the issues were. They considered the type of animal used, whether it was wild or farmed, the method of killing, the number of pelts used for one coat, and who was using the fur and why.

For wrap up, I asked the class once again to complete the questionnaire with which the unit began. I then returned their original version. Working individually, then in groups, students were asked to review the extent to which attitudes had changed or remained the same and why that might be. The main changes commented upon were about food and clothing. Two students decided to try vegetarianism and several commented that they had modified their views on fur coats (one student no longer wished to wear one; others did not want to wear pelts from wild animals). One student said he now felt furs were acceptable as they were comparable with leather. There was a good summary comment from Karen Naraine: 'The discussions have taught me a lot about other people's opinions. Some of my opinions have changed. I've become more realistic towards the issue of animal rights. I think we shall always be killing animals but we have to learn to respect them more.' My sense was that shifts in attitude did occur even when students said they had not really changed their views.

The unit ended with an evaluation session and an invitation to suggest ways in which the program might be improved. Feedback was *very* positive:

❑ This was enjoyable because I like to talk and argue about something I believe in. (Abil Blackman)

❑ Personally I think there is no absolutely right or wrong answer. (Vish Gagie)

❑ I really did enjoy the debate. (Vietnhan)

❑ It was great. (Debbie da Cunha)

❑ It felt like the real thing was happening in the class. Instead of talking I was an observer sometimes, because I had to think about what others said. (Dionne Levy)

❑ This really got my mind going. (Peter Sipsis)

For me some of the most positive aspects of the unit were:

❑ practising debating and discussion skills;

❑ hearing others' views;

❑ analysing and reflecting on others' arguments;

❑ thinking about issues not touched on previously in science class;

❑ the recognition by many students that issues often do not have easy 'yes' or 'no' answers and that perspective often depends on circumstances.

■ *MATCHING MEDIUM AND MESSAGE: GLOBAL AND HUMANE EDUCATION THROUGH PSE AT DEACON'S SCHOOL, PETERBOROUGH* by Sandra Bush

1. Overview

In the two years since the completion of my global education advanced diploma with the Centre for Global Education, University of York, much has changed nationally and in the situation within my own school.

My diploma report speaks in optimistic terms of the 'whole curriculum', 'education for all', mixed ability classes, opportunities for in-service training and of growing interest in and commitment to the aims of global education. The report, entitled *Gender Masks,* focused on a course I created with a team of tutors in order to tackle gender education with our cohort of 130 Year 11 students within an extensive Personal and Social Education programme. Taking our lead from NCC documents on *The Whole Curriculum*[10] and on the five cross-curricular themes, we had evolved a rich and stimulating set of interwoven courses underpinned with clear aims and objectives, not to mention an explicit framework for negotiation, feedback, monitoring and evaluation.

As leader of the initiative I was able to inform the process of designing units and modules, setting objectives and writing materials inspired by my studies in global education. I was helped by both the willingness of senior management in the school to support the initiative, and the co-operation of the tutor team in going about things with a particular aim in mind. In other words, we were not just putting together a range of topics and sub-topics suggested by the *Curriculum Guidance* booklets which happened to cover the cross-curricular themes, but we were engaged in an activity which reflected the aims of the school, its ethos and supposed purpose. The PSE programme had to make sense as a whole to students and tutors. If tutors designed an individual course, it had to meet the aims and objectives of the whole programme, as well as provide for a variety of teaching and learning strategies and attendant activities that engaged the students in dialogue with each other and their tutor. Targets needed to be set with regard to knowledge, skills and attitudes. Methods of assessing whether those targets were achieved had to be included.

In line with the philosophy of global education, the area of study was wide: standard PSE reference books were often inappropriate for our school with its 38% population of ethnic minority (mainly Pakistani Muslim) students. In any case, design and ownership of our own material was important. It was often useful to encounter an activity described in books such as *Global Teacher, Global Learner*[11], but activities were there to be adapted to fit our schemes not simply to he 'lifted'.

The match between theory and practice became an important precept. In the four-week core courses which became the mainstay of the programme we would often create 'mirror' courses. For example, in Year 10 PSE, there were two environment courses: one looked at the 'big' issues of rainforests, acid rain, global warming and the like, in the form of project work resulting in displays, student presentations and charity fund raising; the other course used the leadership of a council play co-ordinator to consider, plan and undertake the transformation of various areas of the school environment. I should emphasise that the team of ten tutors (with two others in support) had to be used flexibly and creatively in a somewhat complicated timetable to achieve the programme; and that senior management had to commit two fifty-minute periods a week to the enterprise.

Some schools have opted for infusing the cross-curricular model through the subjects, with the occasional 'collapsed timetable' day to see a topic through. My own experience indicates that a mixture of locations for cross-curricular themes is more appropriate. Discrete PSE time is necessary in these times of changing and narrowing syllabuses in subject areas and the growing importance of SATS. However, experience shows that co-ordination of the cross-curricular themes is important to ensure continuity of purpose through the phases and stages.

The traditional fodder of PSE courses — the 'drugs, sex and rock-and-roll' syndrome — may well have failed to engage young peoples' interest. In the same way that Religious Education in the 1970s became a diluted moral issues course, so PSE can become 'talking about anything' — without purpose and without value in the students' (and many teachers') eyes.

How different that is from the reaction of our Year 11 students when faced with a humane education course. Those very students who found human rights issues quite puzzling and difficult at times were absorbed in the concepts of humane education, specifically animal rights. They argued, they debated, they acquired knowledge about animals and animal rights issues throughout the world, and the link between that debate and human rights began to make sense to them and engender a related interest and momentum. We put humane education under the auspices of Citizenship but it could well have been placed elsewhere if given a different emphasis; for example, Environmental Education, Health Education or Economic and Industrial Understanding.

I began with an intimation that the optimistic tone of my global education report of two years ago might not be repeated now. That is not entirely the case: my own school has enshrined the beliefs of global education in its aims, its school development plan, its support for the whole curriculum and its appointment of cross-curricular co-ordinators. What has changed is that our commitment to 'education for all' has been dislodged by changes in the National Curriculum provision for testing and GCSE syllabuses. We are approaching the time when only in PSE and PE will students be able to be in mixed ability groups, neither streamed nor setted. Subjects which rely on a particular grasp of a particular type of English inevitably produce setting in a multicultural school with a bilingual bias.

The message which that gives is not the message of global education but of differentiation on racial grounds. The PSE programme I oversee is a good, well balanced one incorporating the principles of global education and cross-curricular themes. The context in which it now operates is not a fertile one for those principles. There is a mismatch.

2. Year 11 PSE Humane Education Unit

Time Available:
4 lessons of 50 minutes

Aim:
To introduce students to the concept of humane education with a view to an exploration of rights issues: human and animal.

Objectives:
1. **Knowledge** — to gather information on animal experimentation and the justifications put forward by those who support vivisection.

2. **Attitudinal** — to analyse the attitudes of others on the issues; to explore how attitudes might be changed; to listen to others' opinions respectfully and reflectively.

3. **Skills** — Communication, particularly discussion, of controversial issues using factual information as a tool of debate.

Lesson 1: Do Animals Have Rights?
1. Introduction by the teacher. Aims/objectives briefly explained.

2. **Activity One: Find A Partner**

Six statements posted:

☐ Would wear a fur coat.

☐ Could be vegetarian.

☐ Would dissect an animal.

☐ Would kill an animal for food.

☐ Would not eat a dog.

☐ Would like to own more than one pet.

Students asked to choose the statement best describing them and then to find someone else who chose the same statement. Discussion in pairs (spilling into larger groups). Class discussion of the six statements. Link ideas: 1. Britain's spending on pet food. 2. The way we kill animals for food.

3. **Activity Two: Where Do I Stand?** (see p.262)

Sheet handed out. Completed by individuals. Attempts to achieve consensus. Plenary discussion.

Another useful activity allowing students to work in groups and seek consensus. Time permitting, it works most successfully if students begin the exercise on their own, move to a small group, and then to larger groups to generate discussion. In the plenary discussion, we ended up with four large groups communicating their views through a spokesperson, and we focused our attention on points which stirred most debate within each group. On the first occasion on which we ran this activity, it proved to be quite difficult for students on account of the higher language levels involved (the group was mixed ability with some bilingual students), so for the second run-through, I cut down the sections and simplified or at least clarified the language.

4. **Activity Three: Which Animals Have Rights?** (see p. 269)

Students loved this activity. It really made them think because, initially, they often see themselves as 'protectors of animal life' in a rather romanticised way, redolent of Walt Disney cartoons or perhaps, more appropriately, a film such as *Homeward Bound: The Incredible Journey II* (Walt Disney Enterprises, 1994) in which the old cliché 'cuddly is best' pertains. In other words, the stereotypes of good animals and bad animals are perpetuated and clearly some creatures do not count as animals at all! Therefore, to think in terms of whether a worm should be experimented upon at first bemuses and confuses and then elicits strong feelings and healthy debate.

5. Preparation for next lesson: students asked to bring to class a picture of a good/bad use of an animal.

Lesson 2: Animal Uses

Aims:

❑ To explore which animals have rights. Is there a hierarchy of animals?

❑ To discuss the ways animals are used by humans. Knowledge gathering. Decision making.

1. Recapitulation. Brief discussion of pictures brought to class.

   We reminded ourselves of the aims of, and views expressed during, the previous lesson. Students were able to 'revisit' their answer sheets but with my second 'trial' group I was more ambitious, had videotaped the previous lesson and asked our technician to edit it into a five-minute montage. That was very appealing to the class and put them in exactly the frame of mind required for this lesson.

   Most remembered to bring pictures of animals. Some (surprisingly for 16 year olds?) brought photos of pets, but most brought news or magazine cuttings which tended to polarise neatly into horror stories of animal cruelty and glossy posed pictures of adorable kittens (one photo was a still of the television advertisement featuring dog, cat and mouse sitting happily together in front of 'real' fire!). My intention of keeping the discussion brief was thwarted. This activity could be a lesson in itself, possibly along the lines of a very effective RE lesson we do in which we place a vase of fresh, beautiful flowers in the centre of the class. Students express their feelings about the flowers in poetry or prose. Then the flowers are replaced by dead or rotting ones and the class express their new feelings. Contrasting images of animals could engender similar work.

2. **Which Animals Have Rights?** (continued). Recapitulation. Discussion. Analysis of scores.

   It was important to return to the *Which Animals Have Rights?* activity and to analyse the scores: exploring differences between groups and whether they had been thinking

about the issues in the intervening week (which they invariably had). The previous picture activity added depth to the discussion.

3. Follow up: **Top Ten Animals.** This activity can be undertaken in a variety of ways. Students working individually can compile their list of ten favourite animals and then pair up and/or move into larger groups to compile a combined or consensus list of favourite animals. The teacher can compile a class list recording individual, pair or group votes on the board or flip chart (a Eurovision Song Contest scoring system is good fun). This can be a very fast or more reflective activity, possibly illustrating changing attitudes to 'favourite' animals half way through the course (worms did receive several votes!).

4. **Activity Four: Animal Uses** (see p. 129). Matching pictures. Groups (two pairs together) discuss acceptability of animal uses shown in complete set of pictures.

   I have employed *Animal Uses* in many different contexts and it is always a successful, co-operative exercise. It immediately promotes discussion in groups, initially around deciding which are the correct pairs of pictures and then around which sets are acceptable and which are not. Group findings can be compared in plenary session or one person from each group can visit the next group to report and hence stimulate further discussion. Although aimed at the primary or lower secondary classroom, *Animal Uses* is appropriate for upper secondary groups and even adults, as was shown at a Deacon's School in-service day.

5. Larger groups repeat **Animal Uses** activity using pictures brought to class. Plenary follows.

6. Preparation for next lesson: students asked to locate newspaper and magazine stories and pictures concerning animal and human rights issues and to bring them to class.

Lesson 3:
Animal and Human Rights Issues

Aims:
- To link human and animal rights issues more closely.
- To establish parallels in the treatment of humans and animals.

1. **Activity Five: People Search** (see p. 106)

   After two lessons, it was important to re-form groups to encourage maximum sharing of perspectives and to ensure that everyone had a chance to talk to everybody else. *People Search* encourages a wide interchange of ideas and perspectives. Plenary discussion followed.

2. Group analysis of stories and pictures brought to class. In effect, the pictures and stories were from the school's Information Technology network. On this are CDs of *The Times* and *The Sunday Times* over a two-year period. It is easy to locate stories and pictures linked to specific words or ideas and we found 200+ possible extracts. We selected twenty relating to animals and twenty to humans. Students also brought in favourite books with human and animal characters.

   With different classes, we used the resource in different ways. A suitable amount of reading and browsing time is necessary. Following that, an individual might select and introduce a cutting, and the class stand in approve/neutral/disapprove lines; a few students being asked to explain their reasons for standing where they did. Alternatively, students might arrange the cuttings on sugar paper or on a pin board linking them with key words and phrases, or grouped according to preferences or certain criteria.

   Discussion tended to centre initially on the animal stories but gradually gravitated towards questions such as:

- Is animal suffering comparable with human suffering?
- Can humans cope with pain and suffering better than animals?

- What are the cultural differences in the ways people treat humans and animals?
- How have people's views about animal rights and welfare been changed? By whom? By what?

  At this point, additional time would have been helpful and one group was keen to compile a class magazine on the issues raised.

Lesson 4: Summary/Evaluation
Final lesson in which class summarised and evaluated what had been learnt.

Activity Six:
1. **Where Do We Draw The Line?** (see p.141). A good closing activity; challenging but simple. 30 minutes approximately.

   As with the *Animal Uses, Where Do We Draw The Line?* can be used in modified form with groups of all ages and abilities. The process of deciding upon the acceptability or unacceptability of actions engaged attention wonderfully but the act of deciding where to draw the line promoted such serious discussion that the students were totally absorbed.

2. A brief evaluation followed linked to how these four weeks could be extended into other subject areas and assemblies or even translated into action within the school. A measure of the students' enjoyment of the course was that they were largely in favour of more animal-related topics being taught ('particularly to the younger ones' said one!).

Conclusion

The success of this course with the year 11 students was gratifying but I worry about where we can go from here. We are fortunate with our provision for PSE in years 10 and 11, but more demands are being made on that time by careers guidance and national record of achievement work. Whereas we might have created space in certain subject areas previously, new syllabus demands make that less likely although science, drama, religious education and art teachers were sympathetic to suggestions made as to how they might become involved in humane education.

Nevertheless, when I completed the first run of the course, two other tutors volunteered to teach it the following year. I am, at the time of writing, designing a similar course for sixth formers.

References

1. Department of Education and Science, *The curriculum from 5 to 16*, Curriculum matters 2, HMSO, 16-36.

2. For farms prepared to host school visits approach the National Farmers' Union Regional Information Officer or contact the Chief Regional Information Officer at NFU, Agriculture House, Knightsbridge, London SW1X 7NJ.

3. Information on Ordinance Survey Maps, aerial photographs and historical maps available from Ordinance Survey, Romsey Road, Maybush, Southampton, S09 4DH (tel: 0703-792000).

4. Contacts available via International Wool Secretariat, 6 Carlton Gardens, London SW1 Y5AE (tel: 0171-930-7300).

5. Mounter, P., *Attila the hen*, Yearling Books, 1991.

6. MAFF (Headquarters), Whitehall Place, London, SW1A 2HH (tel: 0171-270-3000)

7. *Which?*, The Consumer Association, 2 Marylebone Rd., London NW1 4DX.

8. Rohr, J., *Animal rights*, Greenhaven Press Opposing Viewpoints series, 1989, 121 *et seq.* and 127 *et seq.*

9. *Pelts. Politics of the fur trade*, 56 minutes, National Film Board of Canada, 1989.

10. See, especially, National Curriculum Council, *Curriculum guidance three: the whole curriculum*, 1990.

11. Pike, G., & Selby, D., *Global teacher, global learner*, Hodder & Stoughton, 1988.

THE EARTHKIND TEACHER

Chapter 18

The Humane Teacher: A Profile

I have come to a frightening conclusion. I am the decisive element in the classroom. It is my personal approach that creates the climate. It is my daily mood that makes the weather. As a teacher I possess tremendous power to make a child's life miserable or joyous. I can be a tool of torture or an instrument of inspiration. I can humiliate, hurt or heal. In all situations, it is my response that decides whether a crisis will be escalated or de-escalated, and a child humanised or dehumanised. — Haim Ginot[1]

❑ **The humane teacher is biophilic and biocentric.** She seeks to cultivate caring, compassionate and concerned attitudes and behaviours towards human beings and non-human animals. She nurtures respect for the intrinsic value of natural environments and all living beings and fosters a critical awareness of the anthropocentricity underpinning and woven through the dominant worldview. Questions of prejudice, discrimination, cruelty, exploitation, injustice, oppression, and environmental degradation are dealt with thoroughly and comprehensively in the classroom. Her curriculum is, accordingly, issues-oriented and designed to highlight the arguments, perspectives, controversies and value positions surrounding the issues studied. She helps her students see that learning mirrors life; that is an exciting, vital progress; an unending flow.

❑ **The humane teacher is future-oriented.** Her commitment to educational programmes and processes that foster, *inter alia*, the values of caring, compassion, co-operation, eco-friendliness, equity and justice, arises out of concern for a humane and sustainable future. She holds it to be vitally important that students are given the opportunity to study and reflect upon possible, probable and preferred futures. It is equally crucial, she believes, for students to come to see the future as a zone of potential that they can individually and collectively strive to influence. From that empowering premise, they can learn, and practise, the skills necessary for effective participation in projects and movements for social change.

❑ **The humane teacher builds classrooms of affirmation.** She sees self-esteem as an essential pre-requisite for successful learning and for building altruistic, compassionate and humane attitudes to other people and to animals. She also recognises the links between level of self-esteem and preparedness for involvement in democratic change processes. She is aware of the therapeutic and esteem-building effect that close and regular contact with classroom pets can have. Her goal is to nurture self-esteem within a warm, relaxed and friendly classroom built on caring, sharing and trusting relationships. In pursuance of her goal, she recognises the importance of establishing genuine, self-disclosing relations with her class, of responsiveness to students' feelings and ideas, of giving praise. She tries very hard to view the world through each student's eyes. She realises that staffrooms of affirmation are also vitally important if her co-teachers are to have the confidence to try new forms of teaching and learning and a readiness to nurture student self-esteem.

❑ **The humane teacher has a profound belief in human potential.** She recognises the intrinsic value of each and every learner and honours and builds upon the insights, experiences, perspectives, skills and qualities that each student brings to the classroom. She has a positive conception of the learner and believes that, offered a challenging mix of learning approaches within a positive classroom climate, students will be motivated, eager to learn, discover and solve problems, and capable of exercising individual and collective self-discipline.

❑ **The humane teacher creates an ecology of teaching and learning approaches in the classroom.** She accepts as a basic premise of her art that there are diverse and complementary dimensions to human learning including the abstract, the concrete, the analytical, the synthesising, the rational, the intuitive and the emotional. She recognises, furthermore, that most schools and classrooms fail to achieve a balance between the several dimensions. To rectify that imbalance, her students are offered a varied diet of teaching and learning approaches including self-esteem and group bonding activities, small and large group discussion work, co-operative group projects, experiential units, simulation games, drama, action research, individual study and teacher input. Her skill as an educator lies, to a considerable extent, in the synergistic juxtaposition of these approaches within the learning process.

❑ **The humane teacher is especially concerned to foster relational modes of knowing and learning.** She is at pains to help students understand the interconnections and interdependencies that exist within and between people, other lifeforms, human-made environments, natural environments, places, events and issues. She values, and often employs, co-operative learning approaches, not least as a means of helping students acquire a lived understanding of the concept of interdependence. She employs a range of learning approaches — including guided fantasy and visualisation, movement and dance, drama and role play, meditation and relaxation — that attune students to their inner voice, that nurture sensitivity and responsiveness to the needs and feelings of others (including non-human animals), and that cultivate a sense of connectedness to life and existence as a whole.

❑ **The humane teacher devolves power within the classroom.** As students acquire self-confidence, a sense of their worth and individual and collective self-discipline, she gradually devolves power to the group. Her goal is the autonomy and empowerment of the individual within an affirmed, democratic, humane and participatory learning community. One important means of achieving that goal is by establishing mechanisms and opportunities for student evaluation of the learning programme.

❑ **The humane teacher opens her class to the outside world.** She recognises the importance for her students of structured personal involvement in the local community and natural world if their understanding of environments and of environmental and animal-related issues is to come alive. She knows, too, that immersion in the natural world is one of the best ways of helping students appreciate the beauty of the planet. She sees the community as the context for undertaking animal-related action projects arising out of what has been studied in the classroom and of, thus, helping students practise and hone their skills of change agency and advocacy.

❑ **The humane teacher prizes congruence.** She uses gentle and non-threatening ways of helping students recognise inconsistencies within their professed attitudes to animals and their actual behaviours and patterns of consumption. She is ever alert to the dangers of structural hypocrisy in both classroom and school; of a mismatch between the medium (the reality) and the mission statement (the rhetoric). She is concerned, too, to avoid dissonance between her professional and personal life (for instance, emphasising the importance of kindness to pets and keeping a dog locked up at home all day). She is human and humane enough to recognise that total congruence between our professed goals and values and our actual actions and behaviours is rarely, if ever, achieved.

❑ **The humane teacher has a vision of the humane school.** She is clear about the values underpinning humane education and, in her mind's eye, applies those values to the school as an institution; to its management, administration, climate, relationships, decision-making processes, practices and to its exchanges with the community in which it is set. She seeks to foment change in the direction of her vision, recognising the importance of working with change strategies that are themselves congruent with the values of humane education, i.e. open, consensus-building, co-operative, democratic, non-hierarchical.

Reference

1. Cited in Finch, P., 'Learning from the past' in Paterson, D., & Palmer, M., eds., *The status of animals. Ethics, education and welfare*, Humane Education Foundation/C.A.B. International, 1989, 71.

Chapter 19

Teacher Education

In the pages that follow, a range of teacher education activities are described and five sample staff development programmes outlined.

ACTIVITIES

■ INTRODUCTIONS AND EXPECTATIONS

Time needed
20 minutes

Resources
An open space with chairs; a large sheet of sugar paper and felt tip pen for each group of four/six.

Procedure
Participants find a partner. For four to five minutes one member of each pair talks to the other about 'who am I and what are my fears and expectations of this course'. The other partner listens carefully without interrupting. The process is then reversed. Pairs then join with one or two other pairs to form groups of four or six. Each member of the newly-formed group introduces their original partner to the others. Another member acts as secretary recording all the hopes, fears and expectations expressed. The various sheets are put on the wall to serve as a focus for evaluation and reflection during the remainder of the course.

Potential
A useful confidence-building technique which helps small groups of participants to get to know each other and which alerts the facilitators to participants' expectations. It is important that participants work with as wide a range of course members as possible. The groups formed by this activity should not, therefore, be kept together for too long before fresh groups are formed, perhaps using random grouping exercises (see p.64).

Source
Various

■ *LINE OF LEAST ACQUAINTANCE*

Time needed
25 minutes

Resources
None, save a clear space.

Procedure
Stage 1: The aim of the initial stage of the activity is to end up with participants in standing or sitting circles of five to six people. The facilitator divides the total number in the group by five or six to determine how many 'starters' are needed; for example, with a group of forty people, eight 'starters' will be required to create groups of five. Each 'starter' chosen approaches someone they do not know at all or know very little. When the 'starter' has picked one person, that person goes on to choose someone of least acquaintance and invites her to join the group, the process continuing until groups of five or six have been formed.

Stage 2: Standing or sitting in a circle, group members speak on the following topics for one minute each:

❑ the professional me

❑ the personal me

❑ the most important thing to know about me right now.

The first topic goes clockwise around the circle (the person to the left acting as timekeeper). The group moves onto the second topic and, after each member has spoken, moves onto the third.

Potential
A useful device for introducing participants and helping build a cohesive group spirit especially when the group contains a mixture of some who know each other and some who do not. The topics can, of course, be varied to suit the purposes and confidence level of the group.

Source
From an activity idea in *Making a world of difference: creative activities for global learning*, New York, Friendship Press, 1990.

■ *COMMON TREE*

Time needed
15 minutes

Resources
An outline of a tree drawn on a large sheet of paper hung on the wall; a collection of felt pens or crayons (to include a number in green shades).

Procedure
Participants form pairs to identify an interest, need, concern, hope or other characteristic they share in common. They draw a leaf, flower or fruit on the tree and write in their forenames together with the shared characteristic. New pairs are formed, the process continuing until the winter skeleton of the tree takes on its summer mantle.

Potential
A pleasurable, non-obtrusive and non-threatening way for participants to get to know each other and to discover what they have in common.

Variation
Participants cut out a leaf, flower or fruit shape from coloured paper and, having written on their names and shared characteristic, hang it from a bare branch brought into the workshop room.

Extension
The tree is left on the wall. As the workshop unfolds, and more commonalities become apparent, these are added to the tree.

Source
Deri, A., *et. al.*, *Environmental education. An active approach. A report of workshops in Kecskemét, Tamási and Pécs*, Hungary, 1991, 14-15.

■ *DEMOGRAPHICS*

Time needed
5-10 minutes

Resources
None, save a clear space

Procedure
The group is asked to sit on the floor. Questions and statements are put one by one and participants asked to respond in lively manner to what is required of them (the requirements can be of a straightforward 'stand up if' or, more entertainingly, can be varied by the facilitator so that the group is involved in taking up a variety of physical positions, e.g. 'hands above your head if', 'stand if you agree, lie flat on the floor if you disagree, kneel if you're not sure'). The examples in the box are illustrative and can be varied according to the nature of the event, group and locale. At a certain point the facilitator can turn the process over to the participants so that individuals can elicit a response to things they would like to know about the group.

Potential
A useful exercise for helping participants and the facilitator build a profile of the group and for injecting some movement and humour at the beginning of an event.

Variation
Participants stand in the centre of the room. The facilitator calls out a statement and indicates two positions at opposite ends of the room — one for those who strongly agree with the statement, the other for those who strongly disagree.
Participants can take up any position on the line between the two corners indicated. When in position they discuss the statement with their nearest neighbour. Statements, as in the box, should be a mix of the lighthearted and serious.

Source
After an idea in *Making a world of difference: creative activities for global learning*, New York, Friendship Press, 1990.

(Stand up) if you:

- ❑ own a pet dog
- ❑ have lived outside (name of country)
- ❑ have travelled outside (name of country)
- ❑ read the paper daily
- ❑ believe all the news you read
- ❑ feel compelled to dent empty drink cans
- ❑ hang toilet paper so it unrolls on the outside/inside
- ❑ have worked in animal-related employment
- ❑ squeeze your toothpaste tube from the top/roll it carefully from the bottom
- ❑ believe that animals have rights
- ❑ are optimistic/pessimistic about the future
- ❑ would rather be back in the classroom

■ ART GALLERY

Time needed
30 minutes (15 to prepare presentations, 15 to view 'art gallery')

Resources
A sheet of sugar paper and one or more felt pens for each participant. Blu-tak.

Procedure
Participants are asked to fold their sheet of paper into quarters, reopen it and draw in lines and a central circle as in *Fig. 1*. In the upper left quarter participants write in some personal and professional details; in the upper right quarter, they describe any current involvement in humane issues and humane education; in the lower right quarter, they list their special talents, skills, abilities and interests; in the lower left quarter, they register their hopes and concerns for the conference/workshop and identify what they hope to learn from the event; in the central circle, they draw a logo that tries to capture the essence of themselves and their view of the world. When the sheets are completed, participants stick them on the wall. The group is then invited to take a walk around the 'art gallery' to learn about others. They are encouraged to browse the 'exhibits' and note any person with whom they particularly want to share ideas and experiences. The activity can end at that point or, alternatively, participants can be invited to stand by their sheets and take turns to introduce themselves and briefly speak on two items they have included on their sheet. The 'art gallery' can usefully be left for further browsing during the remainder of the event.

Potential
An excellent activity for building a sense of community within the group and for revealing the wealth of talent and experience amongst the members. Whilst also alerting the facilitators to participants' expectations, it has the additional advantage of immediately building a sense of group ownership of the room in that, at an early stage, the walls are bedecked with participants' work. The topics for each quarter can, of course, be varied. For example:

❑ How I became involved in humane issues/humane education;

❑ The animal welfare/rights issue that concerns me most;

❑ A success story in promoting animal welfare/rights in which I was involved;

❑ Two books/people/events that have particularly influenced the way I see the world.

Source
After an idea in *Making a world of difference: creative activities for global learning*, New York, Friendship Press, 1990.

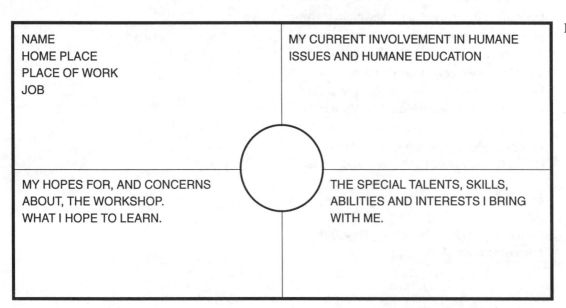

Fig. 1

■ *TANGENTIAL QUESTIONING*

Time needed
30-40 minutes

Resources
An open space; a pencil and paper for each participant.

Procedure
As teachers register for a course or workshop, they are asked to volunteer one surprising or little known fact about themselves which they do not mind other participants eventually learning about. The facts thus collected are written up on a chart which is displayed in the workshop area. Participants are asked to identify which fact fits which participant but to avoid asking direct questions which would immediately reveal the answer. Hence, if one of the facts was; 'I once rode across the Sahara on a camel', participants should not be asked such obvious questions as 'Have you visited the Sahara?' or 'Have you ridden on a camel?' The facilitator later takes the group through each of the listed facts asking for indicators that a particular participant might be the person concerned. Participants only own to their fact at the end of this process.

Potential
A lively and often very humorous activity enabling participants to learn more about each other and helping to bond a group together. An analysis of the strategies and skills employed in seeking to identify the owners of the listed facts can be instructive.

■ *DRAWING OUT ATTITUDES*

Time needed
15 minutes close to the beginning of a humane education in-service course of one or more days' duration and 30 minutes towards its end.

Resources
Two sheets of drawing paper per participant, a generous supply of crayons of different colours.

Procedure
1. Participants are asked to reflect on their feeling about themselves, the theme, the group and their personal involvement in the event as the course gets underway and to represent how they feel by drawing a picture of the animal of their choice. They are asked not to discuss or show each other their drawing. The pictures should be signed, folded and filed away.

2. In the closing stages, participants are again asked to reflect on their feelings and to draw a second animal picture (without looking at the first). They then form groups of four to six to share their first and second drawings and explore what the drawings reveal about initial and subsequent feelings towards humane education, the group and their membership of the group.

Potential
Drawing often brings out unconscious feelings in a way that no amount of verbalisation can. A thorough and detailed scrutiny and discussion of the pictures within each group may well help individuals to recognise things about themselves, their attitude to humane education and to the group which would otherwise not have surfaced just as a comparison of each participant's two drawings may tease out features signalling a shift in attitude. Group members should be encouraged by the facilitator to scrutinise every aspect of each picture; size, colours used, style, type and look of the animal, atmosphere, what the animal is doing, context/environment in which the animal finds itself, area drawn upon, empty spaces and so on.

■ *ANIMAL RIGHTS DIAMOND RANKING*

Participants, following the sequence of steps described on page 241, rank nine statements on animals and rights. Possible criteria for ranking include 'significance', 'level of acceptability', 'degree of contentiousness' and 'usefulness for developing a humane ethic for the twenty-first century'.

In most cases, statements are taken from (but, for purposes of brevity, do not exactly follow) extracts in published works. The exceptions are statements 2, 5 and 7 which are drawn up by the author. Sources of quotations are: (1) Singer, P., *Animal liberation*, Thorsons, 1983, 9; (3) Benney, N., 'All of one flesh', in Caldecott, L., & Leland, S., eds., *Reclaim the Earth*, Womens Press, 1983, 141-2; (4) Baxter, W.F., *'People or penguins'* in Van De Veer, D., & Pierce, C., *People, penguins, and plastic trees*, Wadsworth, CA., 1986, 215; (6) Fiddes, N., 'Dying animal passions — are meat eaters an endangered species?', *Weekend Guardian*, 14-15 September 1991, 16; (8) Bentham, J., *Principles of morals and legislation*, cited in Wynne-Tyson, J., *The extended circle*, Cardinal, 1990, 24; (9) RSPCA, *Declaration of animal rights*, 1984.

P

1. Identical Pattern

The racist violates the principle of equality by giving greater weight to the interests of members of his own race. The sexist violates the principle of equality by favouring the interests of his own sex. The speciesist allows the interests of his own species to override the greater interests of members of other species. The pattern is identical in each case.

2. Which Animals?

Let's accept, for the sake of argument, that animals do have rights. Which animals are we talking about? Probably first on the list would be those most like us — apes, monkeys and the like — and next most other mammals. But where do we stand on rats, mosquitoes, wasps and slugs and the bacteria inside of us? And what about plants which, some say, possess feelings too?

3. Pecking Order

We should not participate in the victimisation of those worse off than ourselves in the patriarchal pecking order. Liberty is an holistic concept. It is neither fair nor just to claim freedom for ourselves, without at the same time claiming freedom for the creatures which share the planet, which are cruelly oppressed by patriarchal attitudes and systems, and which do not have women's power to organise themselves.

4. People Not Penguins

Damage to penguins, or sugar pines, or geological marvels is, without more, simply irrelevant. Penguins are important only because people enjoy seeing them walk about rocks. I have no interest in preserving penguins for their own sake.

5. Human Rights

Human beings are precious. They have rights because they possess characteristics unique in the animal world. They are capable, for instance, of conceptual thinking, sophisticated language, planning, deliberating, evaluating, accepting responsibility for their actions. Other animals are capable of none of these things. I cannot concern myself with the well-being of animals when there is still so much human suffering in the world.

6. Supreme Power

The reason we eat so much meat is that we love the feeling of supreme power we get from devouring portions of once living, breathing creatures. Our apparent obsession derives from a desire to dominate the beast whose carcasses we consume. Since time immemorial, we have needed to conquer nature and reassure each other of our place at the pinnacle of creation. How better than by consuming the flesh of lesser animals, prey?

7. Animal Welfare

We would be well advised to couch our concern for animals in terms of welfare rather than rights. Animal rights are contentious and problematic but most people will accept that we should, as much as possible, ensure the welfare and well-being of animals during their lives even if their final intention is to use them for human ends.

8. Can They Suffer?

The day may come when the rest of the animal creation may acquire those rights which never could have been withheld from them but by the hand of tyranny. A full-grown horse or dog is beyond comparison a more rational animal than an infant of a day, or a week or even a month old. But suppose the case were otherwise, what would it avail? The question is not, can they reason? Nor, can they talk? But **can they suffer?**

9. Moral Kinship

We do not accept that a difference in species alone (any more than a difference in race) can justify wanton exploitation or oppression in the name of science or sport, or for use as food, for commercial profit or for other human gain. We believe in the evolutionary and moral kinship of all animals and declare our belief that all sentient and feeling creatures have rights to life, liberty and natural enjoyment.

■ *PUZZLING OUT HUMANE EDUCATION*

Time needed
40 minutes

Resources
The twelve quotations (p.372) in enlarged bold type and pasted onto card so that each straddles two jigsaw pieces (as in *Fig. 2*). The entire jigsaw should measure about 50cm x 1 20cm. A jigsaw template of the same size on the classroom wall. A flipchart and felt pen.

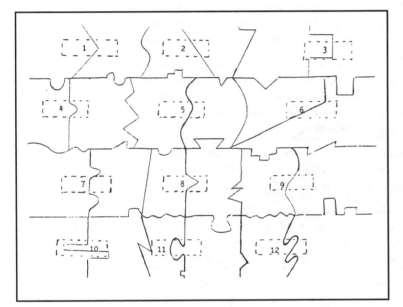

Fig. 2

Procedure
Participants choose a piece of jigsaw and seek out the person whose puzzle piece, combined with their own, makes a complete quotation. Pairs discuss the content of the quotation and what it tells them about the possible nature, goals and scope of humane education. They also share any concerns or reservations they may have about the quotation. Pairs then seek out another pair whose combined jigsaw pieces dovetail with their own. Reflections on respective quotations are shared and discussed as are any links or tensions discerned between the two quotations. Each group of four then joins with a second group of four having jigsaw pieces that fit together with their own. The four quotations thus brought together are discussed. Finally, the three groups of eight present their quotations, and their reflections upon them, in plenary session. As the presentations unfold, the facilitator builds up a 'picture' of the nature, goals, scope and problems of humane education on the flipchart. As groups present, their pieces are stuck on the template. Whole group discussion follows each presentation. The completed template is left on the wall as a stimulus to further, informal, discussion

The jigsaw is designed for twenty-four participants. Should the number of participants be above twenty-four, pairs can be initially assigned to as many of the individual jigsaw pieces as is necessary. Should the number fall below twenty-four, some participants can be given two pieces making up a full quotation (in the first round of discussion they would be involved with one, or two, participants in considering two quotations).

Potential
A time effective and lively way of introducing participants to the field of humane education and to some of the dilemmas and questions raised by the field. To what extent is there tension or conflict between the goals of humane education? Are some goals more realisable in the school situation than others? From what quarters is resistance to humane education likely to spring? With what other fields does humane education seem to overlap? Is humane education more likely to achieve acceptance as a discrete field or as one of a cluster of fields concerned with social, political and moral education? The 'picture' of humane education built up on the flipchart can be returned to at one or more points in the workshop and can be refined, extended and reassembled.

Source
Sources of quotations are as follows: (1) Isaacs, S., *Intellectual growth in young children*, Routledge and Kegan Paul, 1930, 160; (2) Palmer, M., *Believing in the environment*, Council for Environmental Education, cited in James, B., *Animal rights*, Wayland, 1990, 6; (3) Ormerod, E., 'Humane education', *Journal of Society for Companion Animal Studies*, 1990, 2, 2, 9-10; (4) Cooper, D., 'Animals and schools: education or indoctrination?', *Humane Education Newsletter*,

1. *What children make of our injunctions to be 'kind', and our horror at any impulse of cruelty on their part, in the face of our own deeds, and the everyday facts of animal death for our uses and pleasures, would be hard to say. There is probably no moral field in which the child sees so many puzzling inconsistencies, as here.* — Susan Isaacs, 1930

2. *What is a fox? At one level a fox is a reddish brown animal. To the agro-business farmer, the fox is ample justification for keeping the hens cooped up inside impregnable huts. To the romantic city poet, the fox is a symbol of beauty and wildness of the countryside. To the hunt saboteur, the fox is the innocent victim of cruelty. To many Hindus or Buddhists, the fox is a reincarnated soul possibly even of a dead relative. To many Chinese and Japanese the fox is one of the most fearful harbingers of evil and demonic powers taking over the physical body and mind of human beings.* — Martin Palmer, 1988

3. *Some professionals have introduced programmes for people with special needs such as: children with disabilities, children at risk, senior citizens, juvenile offenders and prisoners. In these programmes individuals are placed in contact with animals and taught how to care for them. Respect and empathy for animals is developed and negative attitudes overcome. This improves self-esteem and, in offenders, results in improved behaviour, with a greater sense of responsibility and reduced rate of recidivism.* — Elizabeth Ormerod, 1990

4. *It is no longer possible to keep animal matters outside the school. To begin with, animals are already there. Most schools keep classroom pets, and many of them have laboratories and even miniature farms. Dissection is still practised in many biology lessons. It is surely incumbent on teachers to promote consideration and discussion of such practices. Second, animal issues are also already there in the classroom. Health education, for example, can hardly omit discussion of experimentation in medical progress or the risks to health posed by intensive farming.* — David Cooper, 1991

5. *If Humane Education encompasses humans as well as non-human animals, as it surely does, how does one deal with the element of conflict between human and non-human interests which is central to the debate? On what basis does one recognise and accord value to the interests of other species? Do animals have intrinsic rights or should we more properly be concerned with our responsibilities than rights which animals themselves have little realistic opportunity to exercise?* — Cindy Milburn, 1989

6. *Humane education is teaching in the schools and colleges of the nations the principles of justice, goodwill, and humanity toward all life. The cultivation of the spirit of kindness to animals is but the starting point toward that larger humanity that includes one's fellow of every race and clime. A generation of people trained in these principles will solve their international difficulties as neighbours and not as enemies.* — National PTA Congress, 1933

7. *A child's world is fresh and new and beautiful, full of wonder and excitement. It is our misfortune that for most of us that clear-eyed vision, that true instinct for what is beautiful and awe-inspiring is dimmed and even lost before we reach adulthood. (A) gift to each child in the world (would) be a sense of wonder so indestructible that it would last throughout life.* —Rachel Carson, 1956

8. *Few members of a class presented with literature and a lecture on the cruelty of battery hen farming will act to change battery hen farming, although they may express a negative attitude toward the practice. Consider, however, a group which visits such a facility, examines alternative egg-producing arrangements, and is required to stop eating battery eggs for a week as part of a project. Their knowledge is less likely to remain inert, and will be accessed and applied to relevant situations outside the classroom.* — Alan Bowd, 1989

9. *The humane education movement is a broad one, reaching from humane treatment of animals on the one hand to peace with all nations on the other. It implies a step beyond animal rights. It implies character building. Society first said that needless suffering should be prevented. Society now says that children must not be permitted to cause pain because of the effect on the children themselves.* —Sarah Eddy, 1897

10. *Humane education involves far more than the teaching of simple animal-related content. It is a process through which we (1) assist children in developing compassion, a sense of justice, and a respect for the value of all living creatures; (2) provide the knowledge and understanding necessary for children to behave according to those principles; and (3) foster a sense of responsibility on the part of children to affirm and act upon their personal beliefs.*
— US National Association for the Advancement of Humane Education, 1981

11. *I think the future lies in whole education approaches. A whole education approach, I would argue, would be some form of education for citizenship — for democracy. This would take on board all the issues; global education, development education, human rights, environmental education, humane education. We are moving towards an exciting synthesis. If we could achieve that, we would see major advances in the way we treat each other and other living beings on the planet..* — Julian Agyeman, 1992

12. *We need to remind environmental educators, who are often predisposed to the humane ethic, that without humane education, environmental education reaches the mountains, but not the trapped coyote; the oceans, but not the aquarium-bound whale; the Arctic, but not the clubbed seal; the cities but not the stray dog; the open ranges, but not the cinched rodeo horse; the farm-lands, but not the crated veal calf; the endangered species, but not the abused animals.* — Patty Finch, 1989

P

1991, 2, 1, 3; (5) Milburn, C., 'Humane education — a personal overview', in *Animal use in education*, Proceedings of the Second International Conference of the European Network of Individuals and Campaigns for Humane Education (EURONICHE), 2-5 April 1989, Humane Education Centre, 1989, 182; (6) National Association for Humane and Environmental Education, *KIND workshop leader's guide*, NAHEE, 1991, 3; (7) Carson, R., *A sense of wonder*, Harper & Row, 1956, 42-3; (8) Bowd, A., 'The educational dilemma' in Paterson, D., & Palmer, M., *The status of animals. Ethics, education and welfare*, Humane Education Foundation/C.A.B. International, 1989, 56; (9) NAHEE, *op. cit.*, 2; (10) National Association for the Advancement of Humane Education, *People and animals. A humane education curriculum guide*, NAAHE, 1981, iii; (11) Agyeman, J., 'Environmental education and global politics', *Humane Education Newsletter,* 1991, 3, 1, 5; (12) Finch, P., 'Learning from the past', in Paterson, D., & Palmer, M., *op. cit.*, 69.

Objectives Flowchart

Using the flowchart formula outlined on page 219, participants in groups of four prepare a graphical presentation of a range of humane objectives. A specimen set of objectives is given on the following pages. Participants are at liberty to reject any objectives and to write new ones (blank slips should be provided). Flowchart production can take up to 45 minutes. It can be followed by a plenary session involving group presentations and debriefing or by the use of the *Circus* technique (see p.299).

SYSTEMS An objective is to help students perceive life as a dynamic, multi-layered web of interconnected factors and actors and to see the world as a system linking the local to the global, the personal to the planetary.	**SENSE OF WORTH** An objective is to foster a personal sense of worth by giving students the opportunity to relate to, care and be responsible for, an animal that will give unconditional affection in return.
LEGISLATION An objective is to create a critical awareness of current legislation regarding the treatment of, and cruelty towards, animals.	**REVERENCE** An objective is to foster an appreciation of and reverence for living things and the natural environment.
CONGRUENCE An objective is to make students aware of, and help them work upon, any inconsistencies within and between their professed attitudes and actual behaviours towards animals.	**GENUINENESS** An objective is to help students to be open and genuine in identifying, owning and sharing their thoughts and feelings about ethical issues.
CRITICAL SKILLS An objective is to hone students' skills of critical analysis and to help them identify anthropocentrism (seeing human beings as a central fact in the universe) and anthropomorphism (attributing human personality to animals) wherever they occur.	**EXPLOITATION** An objective is to develop a critical awareness of the institutionalised exploitation of animals in sport, entertainment, medical and scientific experimentation, product testing and food production.
SELF-ESTEEM An objective is to build each student's self-esteem as both an end in itself and as effective means of fostering altruistic, sharing and caring attitudes to other people and animals.	**INHERENT VALUE** An objective is to develop understanding of and respect for the inherent value of all living things.
BIODIVERSITY An objective is to help students understand the importance of preserving the rich diversity of life forms on Earth and the threat presented to many of those life forms by human activity.	**VEGETARIAN DIET** An objective is to help students explore the effects of meat eating on human and planetary well-being and to assess the economic, environmental and health benefits and disbenefits of vegetarian and vegan diets.

P

HUMAN RIGHTS
An objective is to develop in students a sense of justice and a commitment to human rights and responsibilities.

STEREOTYPES
An objective is to help students shed stereotypes, negative images and irrational fears of particular animals and of people of a different race, culture, gender or sexual orientation.

RELATIONSHIPS
An objective is to help students develop attitudes, insights and skills necessary for enriching their personal relationships and for working co-operatively with others.

KINDNESS
An objective is to cultivate caring and compassionate attitudes to other people and to animals, especially the distressed, oppressed, exploited, disadvantaged and downtrodden.

PET OWNERSHIP
An objective is to develop a responsible attitude to pet ownership and the purchase of pets.

FUTURES
An objective is to help students envision and reflect upon possible, probable and preferred futures, personal to global, and to give them the skills needed to go about realising the future of their choice.

ANIMAL RIGHTS
An objective is to help students understand the grounds upon which the claim is made that animals have rights, and to explore their personal responses to that claim and to criticisms of the species exclusivity of the concept of human rights.

EQUALITY OF CONSIDERATION
An objective is to help students explore attitudinal and institutionalised racism, sexism and speciesism and to promote the basic principle of equality of consideration regardless of race, sex or species.

PARTICIPATION
An objective is to help students develop and practise the skills necessary for democratic participation and effective non-violent change agency at school, local, national and global levels.

SUSTAINABILITY
An objective is to help students appreciate that there should be equitable access to the Earth's resources for all human beings and that those resources should be drawn upon in ways that do not detract from the inheritance of future generations.

DIFFERENT CULTURES
An objective is to help students understand that people in different cultures perceive and treat animals in different ways and appreciate the reasons for those differences.

NEEDS
An objective is to help students understand that human and non-human animals share many of the same basic needs.

P

■ *BREAKING THE CYCLE OF ABUSE*

Time needed

60 minutes

Resources

A *Cycle of Abuse* sheet and set of slips of paper, marked '1', '2' and '3', for each participant. A *Key Concepts* chart *(Fig.3)* and *What Can We Do?* sheet for each participant.

Procedure

Participants are introduced to the key concepts and informed that they are drawn from up-to-date research (see pp.25-6). *Cycle of Abuse* sheets and slips of paper are distributed. Participants read the first extract silently and decide which of concepts 1, 2 and 3 are illustrated by the extract. In accordance with their decision, they hold up cards 1, 2 and/or 3. Discussion follows. The process is repeated for each subsequent extract. Groups of 4-6 are then formed to discuss the implications of what has been learnt that is of significance for the school in general and for their work as teachers. Towards the end of the group discussion period, *What Can We Do?* sheets are distributed. Plenary reporting back and discussion follows.

Potential

A useful way of introducing current thinking on the relationship between child and animal abuse and of exploring implications for both classroom and school. In the concluding plenary teachers should also be given the opportunity to air any reservations they have about the research, key concepts or lessons to be drawn from the extracts.

Source

NAHEE, *KIND workshop leader's guide,* National Association for Humane and Environmental Education, 1991. The *What Can We Do?* sheet is taken from a NAHEE pamphlet, *Breaking the cycle of abuse,* 1989. Reproduced with permission of the NAHEE, publishers of *KIND News*, PO Box 362, East Haddam, CT 06423-0362, USA.

P

CYCLE OF ABUSE

A. Anthropologist Margaret Mead once observed, 'One of the most dangerous things that can happen to a child is to kill or torture an animal and get away with it'.

B. In a 1984 study, Alan Felthous and Stephen Kellert surveyed 152 prisoners in Kansas and Connecticut penal institutions. They interviewed prison guards to identify prisoners as 'aggressive' toward people or 'non-aggressive'. The researchers found that twenty-five percent of 'aggressive' prisoners reported having repeatedly abused animals as children. Only six percent of 'non-aggressive' prisoners reported having repeatedly abused animals as children.

C. In the final hours before his execution, serial killer Theodore Bundy said that his early years were spent at home with a grandfather who tormented animals.

D. One group of violent adults studied by Alan Felthous was made up of psychiatric patients who had repeatedly tortured dogs and cats. The patients shared a common history characterised by brutal punishment inflicted on them by parents and all showed high levels of aggression toward people.

E. Sixteen-year-old Brenda Spencer killed two children and wounded eight at a San Diego elementary school in 1979. Earlier, she had abused dogs and cats by setting their tails on fire.

F. A 1982 study of child-abusing families conducted by Elizabeth Deviney and Jeffrey Dickert showed that among the New Jersey families referred to Youth and Family Services for physical child abuse, eighty-eight percent of the households included a member who had physically abused animals. In most cases an abusive parent had killed or injured pets as a way of disciplining the children.

G. Convicted of the murder in 1979 of two sixteen-year-old boys, Robert Alton Harris had had a previous conviction. Four years earlier, he had killed a neighbour by dousing him with lighter fluid and tossing matches at him. Harris' initial run-in with police, at age ten, was for killing neighbourhood cats.

H. In 1984 a National Center for the Analysis of Violent Crime was established at the FBI Academy in Quantico, Virginia. Here, computerised histories of known criminals enable the FBI to profile the serial criminal-at-large. The FBI has found that a history of cruelty to animals is one of the traits that regularly appears in its computer records of serial rapists as well as murderers.

I. James Hutton reviewed the animal cruelty reports for one community in England. Of the twenty-three families with a history of animal abuse, 83 percent had been identified by social service agencies as having children at risk of abuse or neglect.

Fig. 3

P

KEY CONCEPTS

1. Animal abuse in the home, whether perpetrated by parents or child, often means that child abuse is taking place as well.
2. A child who is abusing animals has taken the first step on the path of violence towards other people, a step that should be taken seriously.
3. Animal abuse is a gender issue.

WHAT WE CAN DO?

As educators and other guardians of youth, we must affirm that any child who abuses animals is in need of immediate help. We must further recognise that if animal abuse is occurring in a family, child abuse may be happening also. Most importantly, we must intervene to break the cycle of abuse.

BE AWARE

Do not ignore even minor acts of cruelty. Correct the child and express your concerns to his or her parents. Urge your school district, judicial system and child welfare service agency to take acts of animal cruelty seriously.

Take seriously children's reports of animal abuse in the home. Animal abuse, by a parent or child, is one indicator that a child may be at risk of abuse. Early intervention can sometimes prevent the abuse from ever occurring. Some children who will not talk about their own abuse will tell about what is happening to their pet. If a child describes animal abuse in the home, the school counsellor and psychologist should be immediately notified, as well as the local animal welfare agency which can check up on the care of any animals in the home.

Be on the look-out for other indicators of child abuse and neglect.

REPORT IT

If you suspect child abuse or neglect, do not hesitate to report it. All states require this of teachers. Some states require teachers to immediately report even suspicions of abuse or neglect. Others expect cases to be fairly well documented. Know the guidelines for your state and school district. All states provide reporting teachers with immunity.

If you believe an animal is being mistreated, contact your local animal welfare agency (or the police, if there is no such agency). As a rule, failure to provide adequate food, water and shelter or the use of physical force sufficient to leave a mark or otherwise cause injury constitutes cruelty to animals according to most state laws. Your actions may not only help the animal, but may also identify a person in need of help. Intervention can prevent escalation of abuse.

Don't assume someone else would know if something was wrong.

Be ready and willing to testify against abuse and neglect. Document conversations and evidence.

MOBILISE, ORGANISE

Make others aware of the link between abuse and other violent crimes, including child abuse. Speak to your local PTA, child welfare service agency, animal welfare organisation, clergy, school counsellor and psychologist, veterinarians, juvenile judges, police, and others. Urge agencies to share information with each other

Establish a task force in your school to work on breaking the cycle of abuse. Procedures can be established concerning what to do if a student abuses an animal on the school grounds or while waiting for the bus. Teachers can be informed about the warning signs that indicate a family is in need of help. Guidelines for contacting social services can be distributed, as well as suggestions on communications with suspected abusive parents. Teachers need to know, for instance, what to do if the parent of a suspected abused child demands that the child be removed from the reporting teachers' class.

— *US National Association for Humane and Environmental Education, 1989*

P

■ *ACTION*

Time needed
20 minutes

Resources
A set of *Action Cards,* sheet of sugar paper and paste stick for each three participants. Some blank slips per group.

Procedure
Participants form groups of three. On the sheet of paper, they draw two large overlapping circles, marked as follows:

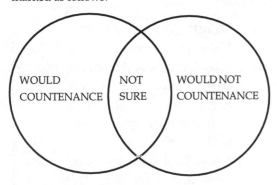

WOULD COUNTENANCE | NOT SURE | WOULD NOT COUNTENANCE

Each action statement is discussed with a view to determining the group's position on whether they would, or would not, countenance the student action described taking place in/from their school. It is then pasted in the appropriate segment. Statements over which the group is divided, or requires more information before coming to a decision, are placed in the 'Not Sure' segment. Their final task is to try to re-write the 'Not Sure' statements on the blank slips provided so that they can be stuck in the 'Would Countenance' segment.

Potential
An activity that will help participants confront many of the often very sensitive issues surrounding student involvement and the many factors that have to be taken into account in determining the acceptability of different forms of action (see pp.317-21). A useful extension is to ask groups to write a set of guidelines against which the acceptability of proposed student action projects can be judged.

Students follow a national election in all its stages, interviewing voters in the local constituency and attending local election meetings to raise their animal-related concerns with candidates of all political parties.

Following a course on the pros and cons of vivisection, students mount a sit-down protest at the school gates to stop an exhibitor from a large pharmaceutical firm, known to use animals in product tests, from participating in the school careers convention.

Students form an Amnesty International Urgent Action Appeal group to write letters to heads of state, political leaders and other influential people on behalf of prisoners of conscience or people facing the death penalty because of their beliefs and opinions.

Students conduct a protest campaign against a factory dumping toxic waste into a local river, writing letters to the press, politicians and the factory manager and picketing the factory after school.

Primary students engage in letter-writing campaigns to the advertising manager of a well-known toy firm asking him to change the exclusively male orientation of the constructional toys catalogue.

Students organise a day of sponsored stunts and competitions to raise money to provide emergency food aid for a developing country.

Students campaign against the exploitative wages offered by a multinational company in its Western African branch. The multinational's local branch is a major employer of parents in the community.

Following a learning programme on animal rights, students mount a sit-down protest at a local zoo to draw attention to the conditions in which the animals are kept, phoning the press to attend.

Students prepare a wildlife garden in the school grounds as part of their environmental awareness programme.

Elementary students undertake a playground use survey and, working in conjunction with architects and planners, they re-design the playground. Later, they are involved in implementing the plans.

Students mount a campaign to alert the community to the cruelties of factory farming by distributing leaflets they have designed and produced to local homes.

Students undertake street theatre on safe sex at the local shopping centre to advise young people of the threat of Aids.

P

■ *LADDER OF PARTICIPATION*

Time needed
25 minutes

Resources
A copy of the *Ladder of Participation*, p.319, per participant.

Procedure
The hand-out is distributed and the facilitator explains Roger Hart's *Ladder of Participation* (see pp.318-9). In groups of three or four, participants judge on which rung of the ladder different action projects that have taken place in their school(s) would fit. Each decision made is written in alongside the relevant rung. Groups are also asked to use their experience of student involvement to critique the validity of the ranking proposed by Hart.

Potential
A thought-provoking activity that will encourage participants to reflect on whether a climate of democracy and participation actually obtains in their schools, whether such a climate is possible and how it could be achieved. A cautionary note is likely to be struck as to whether the *Ladder* is equally relevant to every context and every age group. If the workshop membership is composed of clusters of teachers from different local schools, then single-school groups are a good idea for this activity in that it will then be possible to compare the level of democracy seeming to obtain in different institutions.

■ *CREATING A CURRICULAR PROGRAMME*

Time needed
60-90 minutes

Resources
A short (5-15 minutes) film or video tape; 10 sheets of sugar paper; assorted felt tip pens; Blutak.

Procedure
Participants are told that the aim of the activity is to create a two-hour curriculum programme, using the film or video as stimulus material at some point in the programme. Participants can decide for themselves for what age range and ability levels the programme is intended, and how the two-hour period is to be used (i.e. either as a single block, or divided into separate lessons). They are asked, however, to be sensitive to the range of preferred learning styles likely to be found amongst any group of students in drawing up their programme. Participants then watch the film/video, taking notes if they wish. Some tried and tested films and videos for this activity are:

❏ *The Choice is Yours*, a video challenging young people to think about the origins of the animal products they eat and the place of farm animals in our society (available from the Athene Trust);

❏ *Through the Looking Glass*, a video which follows Alice's journey through the hidden world of suffering that lurks behind the testing of cosmetics and toiletries on animals (available from the British Union for the Abolition of Vivisection).

Working, if feasible, in mixed primary and secondary groups of five or six, participants have 45-60 minutes to discuss and devise the content and methodology of the two-hour programme, giving details and timings of each activity or stage. The final negotiated programme is written up on the sheets of sugar paper and stuck on the wall. Participants then look at each other's programmes using the *Circus* technique (see p.299).

Potential

Coming, as it should, towards the end of a course which has explored and demonstrated humane education theory and practice, this activity provides a much-needed outlet for the creative potential of individuals and groups. The mix of primary and secondary teachers in each group, although initially providing some difficulties over the choice of target age range, encourages the cross-fertilisation of ideas and experiences from the two levels of schooling. Through this activity participants are asked to establish a definite context and framework in which to place some of the ideas and activities introduced on the course, thereby exploring their practical potential and seeing their appropriateness in terms of the overall form and rhythm of the two-hour programme. The resulting programmes are often innovative and of high quality, giving participants a well-deserved sense of achievement. They can be typed up and copies distributed to all workshop participants.

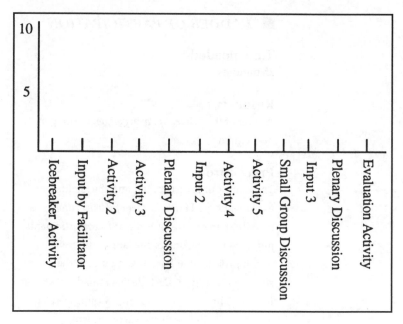

Track 2: Starting with small groups. Participants, working in groups of 4 to 6, make a copy of a centrally displayed *Chuff Chart* on the sugar paper provided. They discuss each element in the programme and try to achieve a consensus ranking of it, on the 1-10 scale. Plenary reporting back by each group (allowing space for dissentient voices within the group to make themselves heard) follows.

Fig. 4

■ *CHUFF CHARTS*

Time needed
30 minutes

Resources
A *Chuff Chart* sheet per participant (*Track 1*) **or** a felt pen and sheet of sugar paper for each 4-6 participants and one large and prominently displayed *Chuff Chart* (*Track 2*).

Procedure
Track 1: Starting with individuals. Participants, working on their own, complete the *Chuff Chart* sheet (see *Fig. 4* for example), indicating their level of satisfaction with each element in the workshop programme. A rough and ready scale of 10 (extremely 'chuffed') down to 1 (extremely 'dischuffed') is employed. Having completed their sheet, participants form into small groups of 4 to 6 to share and discuss their reactions to the workshop. Reporting back and discussion in plenary session follows.

Potential
A helpful way of alerting both faciliator and participants to the range of reactions to the whole workshop and to its constituent parts.

Source
Adapted from Deri, A. *et al. Environmental education. An active approach. A report of workshops in Kecskemét, Tamási and Pécs, Hungary,* 1991, 27.

■ *MOOD MESSAGES*

Time needed
2-5 minutes

Resources
None

Procedure
Standing or sitting in a circle, participants take turns to convey how they are feeling by reference to a theme such as the weather, seasons, animals, birds and plants. For example:

❏ There have been a lot of dark clouds around in the last day or two, but the sun is starting to break through

❏ I feel like a hedgehog, slow and rather prickly

❏ When I came in, I was a sparrow, small and unnoticed, but now I feel like a kingfisher.

Potential
This activity, in which the facilitator should participate, can be used at the beginning or end of a course, or after a particular exercise has been completed. It provides an outlet for everyone to express their mood and sensitises the facilitator and the group as a whole to how individuals are feeling. Each message should be accepted without question or comment.

■ *REACTIONS AND REFLECTIONS*

Time needed
A few minutes at the end of each workshop session.

Resources
A half-A4 *Reactions and Reflections* sheet (see *Fig. 5*) for each session for each participant.

Procedure
At the close of each session or course unit, participants are asked to complete a *Reactions and Reflections* sheet in which they comment on what they have experienced, express concerns, identify points or issues they would like to have had addressed and engage in self-reflection/self-evaluation. It is up to the participant as to whether or not the sheet is signed. The sheets can be 'posted' in a box by the exit door.

Fig 5

Reactions and Reflections   *Session 3*

■ *TESTING THE WATER*

Time needed

20 minutes

Resources

An open space with a large circle marked out by tape.

Procedure

Participants stand outside the circle. They are asked to imagine that they are standing at the edge of a pool. Shallow waters lap at their feet but there is very deep water in the middle of the pool. How much have they been involved in the workshop? Have they just been getting their toes wet? Have they been up to their necks? Out of their depth? Did they test the water and then step back? Have they stayed on the bank throughout? Participants are asked to place themselves at an appropriate point inside or outside the pool and then discuss the nature and level of their involvement in the workshop with the person(s) standing closest to them. The activity can then be repeated but, on this occasion, participants form groups of 4-6 and discuss where each other should be placed.

Potential

A useful and symbolic way for participants to reflect upon their involvement in the workshop and the factors lying behind the relative shallowness or depth of that involvement. Facilitators should recognise the potentially threatening nature of the activity. The second stage, in particular, should only be attempted with a fairly well affirmed group.

Variation

Testing the Water can also be used to effect at the end of an activity that has engendered high levels of emotion or deep disagreement.

Source

After an activity in Deri, A., *et. al.*, *Environmental education. An active approach. A report on workshops in Kecskemét, Tamási and Pécs*, Hungary, 1991, 26.

■ *WHERE NOW?*

Time needed

25-30 minutes (groups of 15-20, plenary/circus 10).

Resources

A sugar paper chart (see *Fig. 6*) and three different coloured felt pens for each group of three or four participants.

SHORT TERM	MEDIUM TERM	LONG TERM

Procedure

Towards the close of the in-service event, participants are divided into groups of three or four to decide and write down what action they intend to take at school in the light of what has been discussed and learnt. Decisions can be short term (i.e. things they will do in the next few weeks), medium term (i.e. things they will do over the next few months) and long term (i.e. things they will do over the next few years). A different coloured pen is used for writing down decisions in the three columns of the chart provided. The activity can end with reporting back and discussion in plenary session or by means of the *Circus* technique (see p.299).

Fig. 5

Potential

This activity represents a simple but effective way of translating what has been learnt into practical plans for the future. According to context, it can be useful for schools to organise the activity around faculty, departmental or pastoral team groups and for the work of all groups to be collated, typed up and circulated to all staff. The momentum of change can often be reinforced by holding meetings to review what has been achieved after, say, two months, six months, one year and two years. At such meetings, staff can evaluate why they have been successful in achieving certain aims and not others as well as updating, revising and extending, their action plans. This process can become an integral part of the curriculum audit process (see *NCC Curriculum Guidance 3. The Whole Curriculum*, 1990).

■ *STRENGTHS THAT OTHERS SEE IN ME*

Time needed
25 minutes

Resources
An envelope, containing four to six library cards, for each participant.

Procedure
Groups of five to seven members are formed using one of the random group formation activities described elsewhere (see p.64). Group members sit in a circle. Each person is given an envelope containing one card less than the number of people in the group. Everyone writes their name on their envelope before passing it to the person to their left. That person takes out a card and jots down the strengths, as they see them, of the person whose envelope they are holding. They also note down the interesting ideas and other positive contributions that the person has made to the workshop. The card is returned to the envelope, passed to the left and the process repeated. When the envelopes have gone full circle, they are returned to their owners who, one by one, share with the rest of the group what has been recorded on the cards. During the sharing process, the owner can tell the others what they feel about the strengths listed. The authors of particular comments can be invited to elaborate if it is felt that elaboration would be helpful.

Potential
A useful activity for ending a workshop on a positive note. The good feelings generated enhance the likelihood of future networking and purposeful action by group members.

Source
Kinghorn, J.R., and Shaw, W.P., *Handbook for global education. A working manual*, Dayton, Ohio, Charles F. Kettering Foundation, 1977.

PROGRAMMES

There follow five sample staff development programmes in humane education. Two are all-day programmes. Two are two-hour 'twilight' session programmes. One is a weekend workshop programme. All are equally suitable for primary and secondary school teachers.

The first day programme offers a relatively low-risk introductory agenda which asks participants to reflect upon the scope, aims and objectives of humane education. They are then introduced to humane education as a component of National Curriculum cross-curricular provision and the 'whole curriculum' concept. The last session gives teachers the opportunity to apply what they have learnt by devising a two-hour programme that they can take back to the classroom. Such a session can be of crucial importance as a practical demonstration of the benefits of team planning and of how easy and enlivening it can be to weave humane education themes and activities into the curriculum.

The second day programme is better suited to a group of teachers who have already given some consideration to humane issues and humane education. The programme gives participants the opportunity to clarify their own responses, priorities and values with regard to human/animal relationships and the treatment of animals. It then explores appropriate teaching/learning approaches for the humane classroom and the links between self-esteem building, co-operative learning and the development of altruistic attitudes to animals and other people. In the last part of the programme, teachers are encouraged to explore the concept of the humane school and to make decisions about what goals they would like to set for themselves and their school in the short, medium and long term. The results can be woven into a school's whole curriculum development plan.

The first 'twilight' session is designed to introduce a teaching staff to humane education and the place of humane education in the National Curriculum in a very time-effective way. Central to the programme is the time given to groups of teachers to reflect upon how humane education can be realised through, and can complement, their subject(s) and the school's pastoral provision.

The second 'twilight' session is designed for a group of teachers already sharing some understanding of humane education. It asks them to assess how humane their school is; to identify short, medium and long-term goals and to map out detailed strategies for realising some of those goals.

The weekend programme is intended for teachers with some level of understanding of, and commitment to, humane education and related fields. The assumption is that most participants have not met before. The Friday evening session is given over to becoming acquainted, establishing a group sense and outlining the scope and nature of humane education. On Saturday participants are asked to explore individual and group responses to the question of animal rights before going on to explore the aims and objectives of humane education, the interface between humane education and other 'educations', the place of humane education within the National Curriculum and the learning styles implications of humane education. A long day ends with a lively simulation session. Consideration of appropriate learning approaches continues on the Sunday morning, before participants are challenged to work together to devise learning programmes to take back to the classroom.

Finally, a note on facilitation. It is important that the facilitator gives clear guidelines for each activity (it is always a good idea to repeat guidelines a second time); also that she gives participants a clear idea of how much time she is intending to allow for the activity. While an activity is underway, the facilitator should move around to obtain a sense of what is being achieved and what issues/tensions are coming to the surface. The facilitator's skill in debriefing each activity is of paramount importance. She should ask for individual/group feedback that is brief and to the point; she should summarise what has been said and, especially, if it is in any way controversial, ask for reactions; she should avoid getting into a direct confrontation with any

group or individual; she should not allow discussion to be monopolised by any particular group or individual; she must avoid letting the discussion 'dig itself into a hole' and she should be prepared to apply a guillotine at what she holds to be an appropriate moment. The facilitator should try to adhere more or less to the session plan but should not allow it to become a strait-jacket. As participants' needs become evident, it may become necessary to rejig or even jettison a particular section of the programme. It is essential to finish on time or, at least, to negotiate a new end-time with the group well in advance.

It should be noted that many of the activities described in this chapter can, with due amendment, be used in the classroom. The evaluation activities (pp.380-2), for instance, can play an essential part in encouraging the open, democratic classroom climate that, this book argues, is of critical importance to the successful implementation of humane education. A useful question to put to participants in debriefing any in-service activity is: 'could it be used in the classroom and, if so, how?' .

STAFF DEVELOPMENT DAY PROGRAMME: SAMPLE 1		
Session 1: What is Humane Education?		
9.15	**Special Animals** (see p.108)	Whole Group
9.30	**Puzzling out Humane Education** (see p.371)	Small Groups/Whole Group
10.10	Input: Humane Education, Scope and Goals (based on information in *Chapters 1, 2* and *3*)	Facilitator
10.25	**Tackling a Statement** (see p.143)	Whole Group
10.45	Coffee	
Session 2: A Place for Humane Education?		
11.15	**What's Your Smell?** (see p.76)	Whole Group
11.30	**Objectives Flowchart** (see p.373)	Small Groups/Whole Group
12.15	Input: Humane Education and the National Curriculum (based on information in *Chapter 14*)	Facilitator
12.30	Feedback and Discussion	Whole Group
12.45	Lunch	
Session 3: Humane Education and the Whole Curriculum		
13.30	**Animal Uses**, Stages 1 and 3 (see p.129)	Small Groups/Whole Group
13.55	**Web of Life** (see p.96)	Whole Group
14.15	Input: the place of Humane Education within the National Curriculum 'whole curriculum' concept (based on information in *Chapter 14*)	Facilitator
14.30	Tea	
Session 4: Putting it all Together		
14.45	**Creating a Curriculum Programme** (see p.379)	Small Groups
15.45	**Reactions and Reflections** sheet on the day (see p.381)	Individuals
15.55	**Rainstorm** (see p.63)	Whole Group
16.00	Close	

STAFF DEVELOPMENT DAY PROGRAMME: SAMPLE 2		
Session 1: Personal Responses to Humane Issues		
9.00	**People Search** (see p.106)	Whole Group
9.15	**Animal Rights Diamond Ranking** (see p.370)	Pairs/Small Groups/Whole Group
10.00	Film	Whole Group
10.20	**Reactions** (see p.145)	Whole Group
11.00	Coffee	Small Groups/Whole Group
Session 2: The Caring, Convivial Classroom		
11.20	**Petcare Messagematch** (see p.156)	Whole Group
11.30	Input: Humane Education and the Learning Process (based on information in *Chapter 2*, pp.33-47)	Facilitator
11.45	**Where Do We Draw the Line?** (see p.141)	Small Group/Whole Group
12.25	**Breaking the Cycle of Abuse**, shortened version restricted to holding up cards and discussion (see p.376)	Whole Group
12.45	Input: Self-esteem, Co-operation and Compassion (based on information in *Chapter 2*, pp.36-42)	Facilitator
13.00	Lunch	
Session 3: Towards the EarthKind Classroom and School		
14.00	**Animal and Human Rights Continuum** (see p.144)	Whole Group
14.15	**Futurescapes** (see p.299)	Pairs/Small Groups/Whole Group
15.00	Input: The EarthKind School (based on information in *Chapter 18*)	Facilitator
15.15	**Where Now?** (see p.382)	Small Groups/Whole Group
15.45	**Reactions and Reflections** sheet on the day (see p.381)	Individuals
15.50	**Animal Symphony** (see p.61)	Whole Group
16.00	Close	

TWILIGHT SESSION: SAMPLE 1		
Topic: Humane Education and the National Curriculum		
16.00	**Special Animals** (see p.108)	Whole Group
16.15	**Objectives Flowchart** (see p.373)	Small Groups/Whole Group
17.00	Input: Humane Education and the National Curriculum (based on information in *Chapter 14*)	Facilitator
17.20	Discussion on implementing humane education objectives across the curriculum	Small subject or interdisciplinary Groups
17.40	Feedback and discussion	Whole Group
17.55	**Rainstorm** (see p.63)	Whole Group
18.00	Close	
Evaluation: brief **Mood Messages** (see p.381) half way through and at the end of the programme.		

TWILIGHT SESSION: SAMPLE 2		
Topic: The EarthKind School		
16.00	**What's Your Smell?** (see p.76)	Whole Group
16.15	**How Humane is Our School?** Using the **EarthKind School Checklist** (see p.394) as a checklist, pairs (10 minutes) and then fours (10 minutes) assess their own school environment. Plenary discussion follows.	Pairs/Fours/Whole Group
16.50	**Animal and Human Rights Continuum** (see p.144)	Whole Group
17.05	**Where Now?** (see p.382).	Small Groups
17.25	**Futures Wheel** activity (see p.297) in same groups and based upon an issue identified by each group in the medium or long-term columns of the **Where Now?** activity	Small Groups
17.45	Reporting back and discussion	Whole Group
18.00	Close	
Evaluation: **Reactions and Reflections** sheet (see p.381) on the workshop as a whole		

SAMPLE WEEKEND WORKSHOP PROGRAMME		
Friday: Session 1: Getting Acquainted/Raising Some Issues		
19.30	**Line of Least Acquaintance** (see p.366)	Small Groups
19.55	**Common Tree** (see p.366)	Pairs
20.10	**Art Gallery** (see p.368)	Individuals/Whole Group
20.40	**Puzzling out Humane Education** (see p.371)	Pairs/Small Groups/Whole Group
21.20	**Pru-ee** (see p.61)	Whole Group
21.30	Close	
Saturday: Session 2: Animals and Rights		
9.15	**People Search** (see p.106)	Whole Group
9.30	**Animal and Human Characteristics 1** (see p.113). Note: Shortened version, involving writing of slips and sharing of examples only	Pairs/Whole Group
10.00	**Animal Rights Diamond Ranking** (see p.370)	Pairs/Small Groups/Whole Group
10.45	Coffee	
Session 3: Humane Education, Scope and Goals		
11.15	**Typical Morning,** (see p.137)	Facilitators
11.30	**Objectives Flowchart** (see p.373)	Small Groups
12.15	Input: Humane Education, Scope and Goals (based on information in *Chapter 1*, pp.3-5)	Facilitator
12.30	Feedback and Discussion	Whole Group
12.50	**What's Your Smell?** (see p.76)	Whole Group
13.00	Lunch	
Session 4: Humane Education and Other 'Educations'		
14.00	**Tackling a Statement** (see p.143)	Whole Group
14.20	Input: Humane Education and Human Rights Education (based on information in *Chapter 1*, pp.6-16)	Facilitator
14.35	**Animal Affirmation (**see p.120)	Whole Group/Small Groups
14.55	Input: Humane Education, Peace and Development Education (based on information in *Chapter 1*, pp.22-8)	Facilitator
15.10	**Web of Life** (see p.96)	Whole Group
15.35	Input: Humane Education and Environmental Education (based on information in *Chapter 1*, pp.6-16)	Facilitator
15.45	Tea	

Session 5: Humane Education, Other Educations and the National Curriculum		
16.05	**Linking Pictures** (see p.147)	Whole Group
16.35	Input: Extending the Circle of Compassion — Humane Education and Education for Race and Gender Equity (based on information in *Chapter 1*, pp.17-22)	Facilitator
16.50	**Animal Uses** (se p.129) In the debriefing, the facilitator should point out the relevance of the activity to the National Curriculum cross-curricular theme of Economic and Industrial Understanding	Pairs/Small Groups/Whole Group
17.25	Discussion of the potential for Humane Education within the National Curriculum 'whole curriculum' concept. The facilitators should be ready to feed in ideas from *Chapter 14* and should recall the emphasis within National Curriculum documents on teaching and learning style diversity, in readiness for the next two sessions.	Whole Group
17.50	**Menagerie** (see p.62)	Whole Group
18.00	Break/Dinner	
Session 6: Humane Education and the Learning Process (1)		
19.30	(Half Group) **Splitting Images** (see p.218) (Half Group) **Fur Trade Images** (see p.279) Reporting back and discussion of both activities	Small Groups Small Groups Whole Group
20.15	Brainstorming of thoughts and reflections on the implications of the day's work on Humane Education for the learning process (for brainstorming, see p.205)	Small Groups
20.25	**Circus** — for sharing of thoughts and reflections (see p.299)	Whole Group
20.35	**Byland Hunt** (see p.207) Note: Shortened version covering Public Enquiry Session only	Whole Group
21.30	Close	
Session 7: Humane Education and the Learning Process (2)		
9.00	**Special Animals** (see p.108)	Whole Group
9.10	Input: Humane Education and the Learning Process (based on information in *Chapter 2*, pp.34-6, 42-7)	Facilitator
9.30	**Where Do We Draw the Line?** (see p.141)	Small Groups/Whole Group
10.10	Input: The Convivial Classroom — the place of self-esteem building and co-operative learning in Humane Education programmes (based on information in *Chapter 2*, pp.36-42)	Facilitator
10.25	**The Teeming Ark** (see p.122)	Small Groups/Whole Group
10.50	Input: Humane Education within Global Education — an overview (based on information in *Chapter 1 and 3.*)	Facilitator
11.00	Coffee	

Session 8: Creating a Curriculum Programme/Review		
11.20	Short film on humane issues	Whole Group
11.35	**Creating a Curriculum Programme** (see p.379)	Small Group
12.20	**Circus** (see p.299)	Whole Group
12.35	Discussion of the weekend and of future intentions following completion of individual **Where Now?** sheets (see p.382)	Individuals
13.00	**Animal Symphony** (see p.61)	Whole Group
13.10	Lunch	
Note: Participants complete a **Reactions and Reflections** sheet (see p.381) after each of the eight sessions.		

Below are a selection of responses to a weekend workshop similar to the one outlined above, as recorded on *Reactions and Reflections* sheets:

'Getting to know you' activities effective—what a diverse group! This should make for an interesting weekend.

The jigsaw (*Puzzling out Humane Education*) activity was provocatively thought provoking but it did reveal the depth of feelings we all held about animals and it stimulated a lively discussion and revealed to me a wide range of attitudes.

The whole evening has focused my awareness of two issues. Humane education is necessary for (1) letting children love without anguish and (2) helping create a generation of peaceful people.

We could not define humane education from the (objectives) statements, but we were aware that we had many questions to raise amongst ourselves before the notion of humane education could be internalised and used in our own situations.

Very useful for me. I realise I have a strong bias towards information rather than activity sessions although I appreciate the value of the activities.

A rattling good discussion. The polarisation of views was permitted to good effect

Found the 'spectrum of views' (*Tackling a Statement*) discussion spellbinding.

The discussion which followed, trying to bring together some of the issues about where humane education fitted in with global and environmental education—showing people's perspectives on extreme ends of the continuum—was the most useful of all.

I hadn't realised there would be such congruence between the needs and characteristics of people and animals.

(The) presentation seemed to be logical and sequential but I felt that maybe there could be another line of argument that would lead one to different 'conclusions'. Or maybe because I don't feel comfortable with the end of the (presenter's) line, I am looking for 'out'.

Linking Pictures comparison of forms of oppression thought provoking, powerful and upsetting. Shocking pictures. A profound effect; clarifying the issues.

The video. How can we raise issues with children without scaring them to death? Horrific. Can it be like that? Can it continue? Really awful. My own ignorance staggered me.

Useful to go into the learning process—highlights the need for all teachers to receive structured training in co-operative learning.

The poster session (*Fur Trade Images*) raised all sorts of underlying issues around the central theme. The power behind the posters is not to be underestimated

A very important session for me—I am still wrestling with my own position. My biggest fear in the classroom is ensuring students also wrestle with the issue. It is all too easy to take the 'soft' option—this is barbaric, cruel, etc. What about the underlying questions concerning cultural and class differences?

<u>The right on rights</u> questionaire

Are you ready for Humane education?

You see a man beating a dog with a stick do you:

   a) get a stick and join in

   b) get a stick and beat the man

   c) protect the dog

 d) stop the man and explain with reference to Descartes, logical positivism and any <u>named</u> theologian of standing from the last century that animals have rights.

e) help the man by developing his self esteem

- Reactions and Reflections sheet

<u>Ants at home.</u>

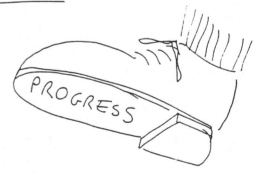

- Reactions and Reflections sheet

THE EARTHKIND SCHOOL

Chapter 20

_____

The Humane School: A Checklist

Woven though the pages of this book —
sometimes quite explicitly, sometimes fairly
implicitly — have been indications about
the characteristics of the humane school.
The threads are now drawn together in the
form of a checklist which can be used for
staff development and school assessment
purposes.

	Comments	Action Needed
ENTITLEMENT CURRICULUM 1. Do your mission or policy statements (and prospectus) clearly indicate your commitment to, and aims and objectives for, humane education?		
2. Do you have effective co-ordination and monitoring of humane education as a cross-curricular theme?		
3. Have the overlaps and connections between humane education and other cross-curricular elements been thoroughly explored and exploited?		
4. Are you taking every opportunity to introduce humane education into all subjects?		
5. Are you ensuring appropriate progression and continuity for humane education through the grade levels?		
6. As a staff, are you actively engaged in collective evaluation of your humane education provision?		
EQUAL CONSIDERATION 7. Is the prevailing ethos of the school and the curriculum, including the specific humane education provision, sensitive to issues of gender equity?		
8. Does the prevailing ethos of the school and the curriculum, including the specific humane education provision, adequately prepare students for life in a multicultural society?		
9. Are the special needs of the individual people and animals making up the school population properly considered and actively catered for?		
10. Are the learning approaches employed rich and varied enough to effectively foster altruistic and empathetic attitudes to people and animals, and to meet the diverse learning needs of the student population?		

P

	Comments	Action Needed
11. Have all staff, regardless of specialism, been engaged in professional development so that they can more effectively realise the aims and objectives of humane education in their classrooms?		
12. Does your school have clearly laid-down policies and strategies for following up reported cases of animal abuse (often linked to child abuse)?		
ANIMAL FRIENDLINESS 13. Is respect for the intrinsic value of all living things a central tenet of the school as an institution and of each and every classroom?		
14. Does your curriculum, in a sustained and structured way, directly address questions surrounding human-animal commonalities and relationships, cruelty to and exploitation of animals, and animal rights and welfare?		
15. Is guidance on responsible pet purchase and care part of the curriculum?		
16. Does the treatment of animals kept in school accord with any local education authority guidelines and with the best advice offered by humane organisations?[1]		
17. Are attractive vegetarian options offered daily in your school cafeteria?		
18. Are all students, through pets in school, field visits or other means, given the opportunity to develop comfort and security in direct interaction with animals?		
19. Is dissection and the display of stuffed animals banned in your school's science laboratories?		
20. Does your school offer guidance to students on careers that avoid explotation of animals and on tertiary science courses not involving dissection and animal explotiation?[2]		

P

	Comments	Action Needed
ECO-FRIENDLINESS 21. Does your curriculum continuously build respect for the Earth, its myriad lifeforms and environments?		
22. Does your school purchase and use resources with a view to minimising harm to the environment and avoiding cruelty to animals?		
23. Does your school use recycled materials whenever possible and have an active and thoroughgoing recycling policy?		
24. Does your school actively promote and practise energy efficiency?		
25. Do your school grounds provide a pleasing natural environment for students and staff to enjoy and an hospitable environment for wild animals to live and breed?		
EMPOWERING ETHOS 26. Does your school place a premium on fostering humane personal relationships grounded in the enhancement of self-esteem and mutual regard?		
27. Are staff and student rights respected and are all given the opportunity to contribute to decision-making processes?		
28. Are students given the opportunities, confidence and skills to participate constructively in animal-related and environmental community action projects?		
29. Does your school play an active role in effecting change in the community, and do community members actively effect change in the school?		
30. Does the prevailing ethos of the school demonstrate that people matter and that everyone has a contribution to make to social and environmental improvement?		

P

References
1. See p. 168 for good examples of guidance available from humane organisations on keeping animals in schools.
2. See pp.271-2 for literature on tertiary science courses that avoid dissection/animal experimentation.

Sources, Resources and References

Animal Rights and Welfare Organisations Offering Services to Schools

Key:
C— catalogue available;
LIF— leaflets, information and factsheets available;
MN— publishes magazine and/or newsletter;
P— posters available;
PL— publications list available;
SP— speakers can be arranged;
TS— teeshirts and sweatshirts for purchase;
TSI— illustrations or photographs of teeshirt/sweatshirt design available.

ADVOCATES FOR ANIMALS

10 Queensferry Street, Edinburgh, EH2 4PG. Tel: 0131 -225-6039. Fax: 0131-220-6377. Works to prevent the infliction of suffering on animals and for the abolition of vivisection. VHS videos available on free loan (service run in conjunction with St. Andrew Animal Fund). Video catalogue. Schools information pack covering range of animal protection/welfare issues. **Pictorial review** published annually. LIF, MN (**Advocates for Animals Newsletter**, six per year), P, SP. Contact: Campaign/Information Officer.

ANIMAL AID

The Old Chapel, Bradford Street, Tonbridge, Kent, TN9 lAW. Tel: 01732-364546. Fax: 01732-366533. Campaigns against all forms of animal abuse but particularly factory farming and vivisection and seeks to raise public awareness of animal exploitation and to promote compassionate attitudes and cruelty-free lifestyles. Membership of Animal Aid Youth Group for students under 18. School group network. List of local groups available. **Why Animal Rights?**, an information booklet for secondary students. VHS video, **Their Future in your Hands**, looks at the way we can change our lives to help animals, humans and the environment, 1992, 13 mins. List of films, videos and visual aids on animal abuse. Sheet of suggestions for school project work. Publishes brief guide to campaigning locally against dissection in schools. Schools leaflet package containing 300 leaflets (on subjects

such as dissection in schools, animal experiments, cosmetic testing and factory farming) available free. **Chickens' Lib**, the well-known organisation opposing battery cage and other forms of poultry abuse, is now part of Animal Aid. LIF, MN (**Outrage**, bi-monthly), P, SP, TS, TSI Contact: Schools/Educational Officer.

ANIMAL CONCERN

62 Old Dumbarton Road, Glasgow, G3 8RE. Tel: 0141-334-6014. Fax: 0141-445-6470. Campaigns against all forms of animal exploitation including animal circuses, bloodsports, factory farms, fish farms, the fur trade, live transport of animals, misuse of air weapons, pet trade, pet neutering, puppy farming, scientific procedures on living animals, seal killing and zoos. Book and video library on animal issues. LIF, MN (**Animal Concern News**, quarterly). Contact: Office Administrator.

ATHENE TRUST

(see Compassion in World Farming Trust).

BEAUTY WITHOUT CRUELTY CHARITY

57 King Henry's Walk, London, N1 4NH. Tel: 0171-254-2929. Fax: 0171-923-4702. Poster for schools, **Dressed To Kill?**, outlines cruelties inflicted on animals for fashion and beauty. VHS videos include **Down With Cruelty**, 8 mins., on the live-plucking of geese, and **Trash!**, 20 mins, a role reversal drama in which animals become traders in human skin (accompanying script for live performances). LIF, MN (*Compassion*, twice per year), P, PL, SP, TS, TSI. Contact: Executive Director.

BORN FREE FOUNDATION

Coldharbour, Dorking, Surrey, RH5 6HA. Tel: 01306-712091/713320/713431. Fax: 01306-713350. Works for a future in which animals are no longer restrained in captivity and live in their natural habitats with minimum interference from humans. Runs projects such as **Elefriends, Zoo Check, The Great Ape Escape, Into the**

Blue and **Operation Wolf. Teachers' Digest**, an 80-page folder, reviews the organisation's goals, positions and activities. **African Elephant Fact Pack** and **Zoo-Check Fact Pack** for under-11s. Offers theatre-in-education opportunities. LIF, MN (**Trumpet** for under-14s, **Wildlife Times** for over-14s, both three times per year), P, SP, TS, TSI. Contact: Director, Education Services.

BRITISH UNION FOR THE ABOLITION OF VIVISECTION
16A Crane Grove, Islington, London, N7 8LB. Tel: 0171-700-4888. Fax: 0171-700-0252. Campaigns to end experiments on animals. Factsheets on dissection in schools. **Suggested Reading** and **Things To Do at School** sheets available. Booklet, **Health with Humanity**, on animal experimentation and alternatives, suitable for secondary use. **Schools Project Booklet,** 18 pages on animal experimentation, is suitable for 14-18 year olds. VHS videos for hire include **The Animals Film**, 1982, 2 hours, examining society's mass exploitation of animals— in factory farms, on the streets, in the wild and in the research laboratory; **Health with Humanity**, 1988, 27 mins, arguing that animal experiments are irrelevant to human health needs; **Through the Looking Glass**, 1987, 13 mins., targeted at young people and following Alice on a journey through the world of suffering caused by the testing of cosmetics and toiletries on animals. Video hire list available. LIF, MN (quarterly), P, PL, SP, TS, TSI. Contact: Information Officer.

BRITISH VETERINARY ASSOCIATION ANIMAL WELFARE FOUNDATION
7 Mansfield Street, London, W1M 0AT. Tel: 0171-636-6541. Fax: 0171-436-2970. Mobilises veterinary expertise to identify, and find solutions to, animal welfare problems. LIF, MN (**Animal Welfare News**, annually), P, PL, TS. Contact: Secretary.

CAMPAIGN FOR THE ABOLITION OF ANGLING
P.O. Box 90, Bristol, BS99 1ND. Tel: 01179-441175. Seeks to raise awareness of the suffering, pain and stress inflicted on fish by angling and the damage to wildlife caused by lost or discarded tackle. VHS video, **Angling. The Neglected Bloodsport**, 18 mins., 1992, suitable for secondary use. **Schools' Project Sheet** and **Schools' Fact Sheet** available for both 7-11 and 12-18 age

ranges. Youth membership scheme. LIF, MIV (**Pisces**, quarterly; youth newsletter, quarterly), P, PL, SP, TS, TSI. Contact: Schools Officer.

CAPTIVE ANIMALS' PROTECTION SOCIETY,
163 Marsden Road, Blackpool, Lancashire, FY4 3DT. Tel: 01253-765072. Campaigns to prevent the use of captive performing animals, especially in circuses. LIF, MN (**Annual Report**). Contact: Assistant Secretary.

CATS PROTECTION LEAGUE
17 Kings Road, Horsham, West Sussex, RH13 5PN. Tel: 01403-261947. Fax: 01403-218414. Rescues stray and unwanted cats and seeks to rehome them; encourages the neutering of all cats not required for breeding; seeks to inform the public on cat care. Free teaching pack, containing 30 work booklets and ideas for classroom activities and projects, for 5-11 age group. Termly **Junior News** for same age group, an 8-page newsletter with project ideas, educational puzzles, stories, photos, poems and an A3 colour poster. Free to primary pupils and teachers. VHS video, **The Cats Protection League**, 20 mins., 1990, on CPL's work and cat care. School visits to local CPL shelters arranged. LIF, MN (**The Cat**, bi-monthly), P, TS, junior membership available. Educational contact: CPL Junior Education Department.

COMPASSION IN WORLD FARMING TRUST
Charles House, 5A Charles Street, Petersfield, Hants, GU32, 3EH. Tel: 01730-268070. Fax: 01730-260791. Promotes animal welfare through schools and public education. VHS video, **There's a Pig In My Pasta!**, 16 mins., 1993, looks at cruelty in food production through a birthday visit to an Italian restaurant (suitable for 12+, teachers' notes included). Video loan scheme. Slide set, **Work of CIWF**, 1993, contains 40 slides (accompanying teachers' notes). LIF, MN (**Farmwatch**, termly, for 8-14 year olds), P, PL, SP, TS, TSI. Note: resource items attributed to Athene Trust are available from CIWF. Contact: Education Officer.

DISABLED AGAINST ANIMAL RESEARCH AND EXPLOITATION

P.O. Box 8, Daventry, Northants, NN1 4RQ. Tel: 01327-71568. Campaigns for the total abolition of animal experiments, seeing vivisection as both unscientific and unethical. Information pack available (sae). DAARE booklet puts forward arguments as to why the disabled should oppose vivisection. LIF, MN (**DAARE to Liberate!**, three times per year), P, TS, TSI. Contact: Co-ordinator.

DR. HADWEN TRUST FOR HUMANE RESEARCH

22 Bancroft, Hitchin, Herts., SG5 lJW. Tel: 01462-436819. Funds medical and scientific research to replace animal experiments. Humane alternatives seen as more relevant to human health needs. C, LIF, MN (**Alternative News**, quarterly), P, TS, TSI. Contact: Information Officer.

EARTHKIND, HUMANE EDUCATION CENTRE

Avenue Lodge, Bounds Green Road, London N22 4EU. Tel: 0181-889 1595. Fax: 0181-881 7662. All-embracing philosophy based on the 'interdependence' of life on earth— animals and people need to live in harmony with the living earth for the benefit of all life. President is James Lovelock, instigator of the famous Gaia theory which views the earth as a living, self-regulating organism. EarthKind works for the well-being of *all* animals— farm, domestic, captive, wildlife, marine, irrespective of species or sentimental appeal. Latest initiative in ongoing humane education programme— this handbook for teachers! **EarthKind Ocean Defender**, launched 1994, an ex-whaling ship refitted as a rescue vessel and Britain's first 'lifeboat' for sea mammals and birds, is also used for conservation projects and as an educational centre for schools and the public to visit. On-board lecture facilities and information for schools on the marine environment. Ocean Defender tours Britain— please check with theEarthKind office to find out if she will be visiting near your school. **Earthlings** youth group encourages the EarthKind way of life through information and action ideas in a lively, fact-filled magazine (special school membership available). VHS video **A**

Painful Luxury, 9 mins, exposes the cruelty of foie gras production. **Think Dog!**—audio-visual materials for younger children on being safe with dogs. Range of educational materials is constantly being updated— please write for more information on what is available. C, LIF, MN (**The Living World**, three times per year, **All Living Things**, three times per year, **EarthKind Ocean Defender News Log**, three times a year), P, TS, TSI. Contact: Education Officer or Publications Officer.

ENVIRONMENT COUNCIL

80 York Way, London, N1 9AG. Tel: 0171-278- 4736. Fax: 0171-837-9688. A forum for individuals and organisations seeking solutions to environmental problems. The Council has two supporting programmes: the Business and Environment Programme, and the Information Programme (providing directories and guides on environmental organisations, films and other resources). LIF, MN (**Habitat**, 10 times a year). Contact: Information Programme.

FARM AND FOOD SOCIETY

4 Willifield Way, London, NW11 7XT. Tel: 0181-455-0634. Concerned with ethics in agriculture and humane, wholesome and fair farming. Seeks to combine the best traditional methods with wise use of technology and to promote a movement away from industrialised agriculture to forms of farming in harmony with the environment. Publications, suitable for upper secondary use, include **Responsible Husbandry as a Basic Educational Principle**, 1984, and **The Long Way Ahead: New Concepts of Agriculture**, 1985. MN (**Farm and Food News**, three per year). Contact: Hon. Secretary.

FARM ANIMAL WELFARE NETWORK

P.O. Box 40, Holmfirth, Huddersfield, HD7 1 QY. Tel: 01484-688650. Fax: 01484-689408. FAWN seeks to expose cruelties within intensive animal farming (especially poultry) and further humane education. VHS video, **Hidden Suffering**, 27 mins., 1992, explores battery and broiler farming and makes the comparison between slavery, child labour and animal exploitation (suitable for 11+, there is an accompanying booklet, and French and Spanish language video versions). LIF (three-monthly factsheets). Contact: National Organiser.

FUND FOR THE REPLACEMENT OF ANIMALS IN MEDICAL EXPERIMENTS

Eastgate House, 34 Stoney Street, Nottingham, NG1 lNB. Tel: 01159-584740. Fax: 01159-503570. Promotes alternatives to the use of live animals in research and toxicity testing; FRAME research groups are working on the development and validation of methods for use by industry to identify potentially hazardous chemicals and products that do not involve animals. Factsheets on animal experimentation, cosmetic testing and the use of animals in education. Two A-level booklets, **Issues: Animal Experiments** and **Biology Now! Alternatives to Animal Experimentation**, FRAME/Hobsons, 1992. LIF, MN (**FRAME News**, 3 times per year), P, SP, TS. Contact: Scientific Liaison Officer.

HUMANE RESEARCH TRUST

Brook House, 29 Bramhall Lane South, Bramhall, Cheshire, SK7 2DN. Tel: 0161-439-8041/3869. Fax: 0161-439-3713. Supports research in which the use of living animals is replaced by other methods. VHS video, **The Right To Life**, offers a simple introduction to the issues surrounding the use of animals in medical research and explains alternatives. Education pack. **Animate** is the Trust's branch for under-18s. LlF, MN (**Annual Report; Newsletter** published twice yearly), P, SP, TS, TSI. Contact: Trust Secretary

HUNT SABOTEURS ASSOCIATION

P.O. Box 1, Nottingham, NG4 2JY. Tel: 01159-590357. Campaigns, and takes non-violent direct action, against all bloodsports. Video footage of successful sabotaging of events available. Pack for schools includes introductory booklet, map of fox and hare hunting counties of England, Wales and Scotland and sample magazine. Youth section, Fox Cubs, for 8-13 year olds, focuses on hunting wildlife and other forms of animal abuse. C, LIF, MN (**Howl**, quarterly, for HSA members), P, SP, TS, TSI. Contact: Schools Officer.

INTERNATIONAL FUND FOR ANIMAL WELFARE

Tubwell House, New Road, Crowborough, East Sussex, TN6 2QH. Tel: 01892-663374/663819. Fax: 01892-665460. VHS video, **Peace on Ice**, on founder, Brian Davies' campaigning work to end the Canadian baby seal cull. LIF, MN (monthly to members), P, SP (within day reach), TS. Contact: Executive Director.

LEAGUE AGAINST CRUEL SPORTS

Sparling House, 83-7 Union Street, London, SEl 1SG. Tel: 0171-403-6155. Fax: 0171-403-4532. Campaigns for legislation banning the hunting of wildlife with hounds and for the protection of wildlife from unnecessary suffering. VHS videos available on free loan include **Rural Vandals**, a four-part presentation covering hare coursing, mink hunting, stag hunting and fox hunting. Teachers' pack available. Information to school students on request (sae). LIF, MN (**Wildlife Guardian**, quarterly), P, TS, TSI. Contact: Information Officer.

MOVEMENT FOR COMPASSIONATE LIVING, THE VEGAN WAY

47 Highlands Road, Leatherhead, Surrey, KT22 8NQ. Tel: 01372-372389. Promotes a way of life that would allow an even increased global human population to live within the planet's resources and without exploitation of people or animals. 10-sheet educational display, **Food for Everyone**, explores the value of plants for solving global food and environmental problems. VHS videos on health and environmental aspects of veganism: **A Better Future for All Life**, 30 mins., 1976; **Food for a Future**, 30 mins., 1984. LIF, MN (**New Leaves**, quarterly), PL, SP (expenses only). Contact: Co-ordinator.

NATIONAL ANTI-VIVISECTION SOCIETY

261 Goldhawk Road, London, W12 9PE. Tel: 0181-846-9777. Fax: 0181-846-9712. Campaigns for changes in the law governing animal experimentation. **The Good Science Guide**, 1993, offers advice to school students wishing to undertake tertiary level study in the sciences and wishing to avoid vivisection. Violence-free science pack containing advice sheets about dissection in schools and universities. Range of videos on animal experimentation

available (free loan, returnable deposit). Number of computer simulations, including **Respiratory Pharmacology**, replacing the use of live guinea pigs and **Muscle Physiology**, replacing the use of frogs (suitable for A-level students). Youth group, **Animals' Defenders**, for information sheets plus action on the above and other issues. Animals' Defenders VHS video, **Circus Madness,** 15 mins., accompanying pack, 1993, features undercover footage depicting daily suffering of circus animals, contrasted with life in the wild (suitable for all ages). LIF, MN (**The Campaigner,** quarterly for NAVS members; **The Animals' Defender**, quarterly for AD members), P, SP, TS, TSI. Contact: Public Relations Officer.

NATIONAL CANINE DEFENCE LEAGUE
1 Pratt Mews, London, NWl OAD. Tel: 0171-388-0137. Fax: 0171-383-5474. Rescues and rehouses stray and abandoned dogs via 15 rescue centres across the UK. Schools invited to visit rescue centres which can also provide visiting speakers. LIF, MN (**NCDL News,** twice per year), P, SP, TS, TSI. Contact: Public Relations Department.

NATIONAL PETWATCH
P.O. Box 16, Brighouse, West Yorkshire, HD6 lD5. Tel: 01484-722411. Fax: 01484-400104. An investigative organisation, NPW monitors the loss and theft of family pets; its research has revealed the systematic theft of pets for the fur trade, animal experimentation, breeding and use in blood sports such as coursing. Information pack for teachers. Project materials for students. LIF, MN (**The Petwatcher,** three times per year), P, SP (50 miles radius from office or further if travel expenses paid). Contact: Director.

PLAN 2000
P.O. Box 54, Bristol, Avon, BS99 lPH. Tel/Fax: 011791-553230. Aims to stop animal experimentation by the year 2000. VHS video, **Target Debate**, 30 mins., features MPs discussing the question of ending animal experimentation. Phone line for campaign updates. LIF, MN (quarterly), P, SP, TS, TSI. Contact: Information/Press Officer.

RESPECT FOR ANIMALS
P.O. Box, Nottingham, NG1 3AS. Tel: 01159-525440. Fax: 01159-799159. Seeks to destroy the consumer market for products of animal cruelty through public education, advertising campaigns and parliamentary lobbying. VHS video, **Fur. The Bloody Choice,** 10 mins., 1993, explores the reality of animal suffering behind the glamorous image of fur projected by the fur trade. C, LIF, MN (**Respect for Animals,** quarterly), P, SP, TS, TSI. Contact: Information Officer.

ROYAL SOCIETY FOR THE PREVENTION OF CRUELTY TO ANIMALS
Causeway, Horsham, West Sussex, RHl2 lHG. Tel: 01403-264181. Fax: 01403- 241048. Established in 1824, the RSPCA aims to promote kindness, and prevent cruelty, to animals. Extensive array of print-form and audio-visual resources for school. Slide sets (with accompanying teachers' notes include: **Companion Animals**, 1990; **Food for Thought**, on animal welfare issues surrounding intensive farming, 1991; **Wildlife Concerns**, on the treatment of wild animals in the wild and captivity (each set was created for secondary use but, with judicious selection, is suitable for the primary classroom). **Animal Wise**, 1993, is a teachers' resource pack on pets for science, maths and English at Key Stage 2. **Partners in Animal Welfare** is RSPCA's teachers' club (members receive a newsletter, binder and updates). The RSPCA Education Department and its ten regional officers (address list available) offer in service training and guidance on introducing animal welfare issues into the National Curriculum. C (print-form and audio-visual), LIF, MN (**Animal World**, junior readership; **Animal Focus,** teacher readership; **Animal Life**, adult lay readership; each published six times per year), P, PL, SP, TS. Contact: Education Department.

SCOTTISH SOCIETY FOR THE PREVENTION OF CRUELTY TO ANIMALS
19 Melville Street, Edinburgh, EH3 7PL. Tel: 0131-225-6418. Fax: 0131- 220-4675. Works to prevent cruelty to animals and to promote kindness and humanity in their treatment. **SSPCA teacher's pack,** 1989, a

general animal welfare pack for 8-12 year olds and their teachers, covering companion animals, farm animals and wildlife. **Animals or Machines?**, 1990, series of five resource packs linked to Scottish Standard Grade courses in history, geography, economics, CSS and modern studies. Infant colouring sheets on pets and animals. VHS videos: **Action for Animals**, 1988, 17 mins., for 8-12 year olds, showing problems SSPCA Inspectors have to deal with and suggesting ways in which children can help; **A Caring Society**, 1986, 45 mins., for secondary students and adults, detailing the work of the Inspectorate. Annual schools competitions for primary and secondary students. Educational units within animal welfare centres available for school visits. Brochures outlining SSPCA services to primary and secondary schools. Junior membership for students up to 16. LIF, MN (**SSPCA News**, quarterly; **Animal Express**, junior magazine, quarterly), P, SP (illustrated talks). Contact: Senior Education Officer.

UNIVERSITIES FEDERATION FOR ANIMAL WELFARE

8 Hamilton Close, South Mimms, Potters Bar, Herts., EN6 3Q9. Tel: 0170-58202. Fax: 0170-49279. A technical and scientific organisation promoting animal welfare at tertiary level. Some UFAW publications— and the organisation's VHS video, **Environmental Enrichment: Advancing Animal Care**, 1990, 35 mins., describing the behavioural needs of animals and offering practical suggestions for improving their lives— are suitable for sixth-form use. Publishes pamphlet, **The Place of Animals in Education**, 1986, in conjunction with Institute of Biology, and **Animals in Science Teaching. A Directory of Audio-visual Alternatives**, 1988, 60pp., in conjunction with British Universities Film and Video Council. AR, LIF, MN, PL. Contact: Information Office.

VEGAN SOCIETY

7 Battle Road, St. Leonards-on-Sea, East Sussex, TN37 7AA. Tel/Fax: 01424-427393. Promotes a way of life entirely free of animal products as beneficial to humans, animals and the environment. Teachers' information pack. LIF, MN (**The Vegan**, quarterly, with a 'Young Vegans' section), PL, SP. Contact: Office Manager.

VEGETARIAN SOCIETY

Parkdale, Dunham Road, Altrincham, Cheshire, WA14 4QG. Tel: 0161-928-0793. Fax: 0161-926-9182. Aims to promote awareness of the benefits of a vegetarian diet in terms of ecology, animal cruelty/ ethics, health and famine reduction. VHS video, **Food Without Fear,** 20 mins., explores the conditions in factory farms and looks at the effect meat-eating has on human health, the environment and the 'Third World'. **Vegetarian Issues**, 90-page resource pack for secondary schools. **SCREAM!!** (School Campaign for Reaction Against Meat) relaunched September 1993. C, LIF, MN (**Greenscene**, quarterly, only magazine for young vegetarians; **Vegetarian Quarterly**), P, PL, SP, TS, TSI. Contact: Youth Education Manager.

WORLD SOCIETY FOR THE PROTECTION OF ANIMALS

2 Langley Lane, London, SW8 lTJ. Tel: 0171-793-0540. Fax: 0171-793-0208. An umbrella society working through a network of international animal welfare organisations to protect domestic and wild animals. Publishes campaign packs (e.g. on bullfighting, the fur trade, the threat to bears globally). LIF, MN (**Animals International**, quarterly, describing field projects and providing updates on animal-related issues), P, TS, TSI. Contact: Communications Officer.

NOTE: A regularly-updated and comprehensive directory of UK animal rights and welfare organisations and groups, **The Animals' Contact List**, is available from Veggies Catering Campaign, The Rainbow Centre, 180 Mansfield Road, Nottingham, NGl 3HW. Tel: 01159-585666.

Select Bibliography

General Reading

Fraser, L., Zawistowski, S., Horwitz, J., and Tukel, S., *The animal rights handbook: Everyday ways to save animal lives*, Venice, California, Living Planet Press, 1990. A step by step practical guide to understanding animal rights issues and compassionate living.

Gaard, G., ed., *Ecofeminism. Women, animals, nature*, Philadelphia, Temple University Press, 1993. Outstanding collection of essays rejecting the nature/culture dualism of patriarchal thought and locating humans within nature. An important antidote to Regan and Singer (see below).

James, B., *The young person's action guide to animal rights*, Virago, 1992. Explores animal issues using a simple A-Z format. Rich in facts, figures and statistics with, as the title suggests, a strong practical orientation.

James, R., *Animal rights*, Wayland, 1990. Excellent, easy-to-understand and richly illustrated overview of animal rights issues. Ideal for the secondary classroom.

Paterson, D., and Palmer, M., *The status of animals. Ethics, education and welfare*, Humane Education Foundation/C.A.B. International, 1989. In addition to sections on ethics, farming, experimentation, human/animal interactions, the role of the veterinarian and animals in the media, there is a very useful education section with essays by Alan Bowd, David Paterson, Patty Finch and Cindy Milburn.

Regan, T., *The case for animal rights*, Routledge, 1988. Rigorous and painstaking presentation of the case for animal rights. Should be read alongside Singer's *Animal liberation* (see below).

Salt, H.S., *Animals' rights considered in relation to social progress*, Centuar, 1980. A reprint of Salt's outstanding animal rights thesis of 1892. 'Defenders of animals, myself included,' writes Peter Singer in his preface (viii), 'have been able to add relatively little to the essential case Salt outlined in 1892.'

Singer, P., *Animal liberation. Towards an end to man's inhumanity to man*, Thorsons, 1983. The classic that first spelt out the philosophy of the modern animal liberation movement.

Singer, P., ed., *In defence of animals*, Basil Blackwell, 1985. Excellent collection of essays exploring animal rights philosophies, areas of abuse, and the activists and their various strategies.

Wynne-Tyson, J., *The extended circle. An anthology of humane thought*, Cardinal, 1990. An A to Z compendium of writings calling for compassion and environmental responsibility.

Humane education and related fields

Borba, M., and C., *Self-esteem: a classroom affair*, Minneapolis, Winston Press, 1978. A treasure trove of ideas and activities for enhancing self-esteem. Particularly appropriate for the primary classroom.

Borba, M., and C., *Self-esteem. A classroom affair. Volume 2.*, Minneapolis, Winston Press, 1982. A second highly imaginative collection of esteem-building activities.

Canfield, J., and Wells, H.C., *100 ways to enhance self-concept in the classroom*, New Jersey, Prentice-Hall, 1976. Excellent ideas for self-esteem building in a beautifully presented book.

Cedoline, A.J., *The effect of affect*, San Rafael, California, Academic Therapy Publications, 1977. More than 100 classroom activities to promote self-esteem and good relationships and to develop decision-making skills.

Church, A., Edwards, L., and Romain, E., *Co-operation in the classroom*, Global Co-operation for a Better World, 1988. A useful collection of co-operative activities, a number being based upon an accompanying photopack.

Dunphy, S., Holden, P., and Ings, R., *Animal wise: A teachers' resource pack for science*,

English and maths at key stage 2, RSPCA, 1993. Lively, imaginative and well-presented material on pets with photocopiable material included.

Fisher, S., and Hicks, D.W., *World studies 8-13: A teacher's handbook*, Oliver and Boyd, 1985. Attractively presented and deservedly popular handbook for top junior and lower secondary students. Contains a teacher education section.

Greig, S., Pike, G., and Selby, D., *Earthrights. Education as if the planet really mattered*, Kogan Page/World Wildlife Fund UK, 1987. Offers an overview of current global problems and trends and explores the implications of the person/planet relationship for schools.

Hicks, D.W., *Educating for the future. A practical classroom guide*, World Wide Fund for Nature UK, 1994. Offers a good range of activities for teachers wishing to give their classroom a more explicit futures orientation.

Hicks, D.W., and Steiner, M., eds., *Making global connections. A world studies workbook*, Oliver and Boyd, 1989. Case studies of issues of global concern with activities, resource ideas and guidance for teaching the issues.

Judson, S., ed., *A manual on non-violence and children*, Philadelphia Yearly Meeting of the Religious Society of Friends-Peace Committee/New Society Publishers, 1984. Excellent handbook of co-operative approaches and activities for the classroom, interspersed with the theory of non-violent action and case study examples.

Pike, G., and Selby, D., *Global teacher, global learner*, Hodder and Stoughton, 1988. Reconceptualises the term global education, examines appropriate teaching and learning approaches and offers a range of primary and secondary classroom activities.

Pike, G., and Selby, D., *Greening the staffroom. A staff development file in environmental education*, World Wide Fund for Nature UK/Centre for Global Education/BBC, 1990. A comprehensive range of activities for staff development in environmental education at primary and secondary level. Sample programmes suggested. VHS video comes with the file.

Pike, G., and Selby, D., *Reconnecting. From national to global curriculum*, World Wide Fund for Nature UK, 1995. Activities for infusing global education across the secondary school curriculum.

Prutzman, P., Burger, M.L., Bodenhammer, G., and Stern, L., *The friendly classroom for a small planet*, New Jersey, Avery, 1978. A classic handbook for the co-operative classroom, full of imaginative ideas and activities. Underlying philosophy fully explained.

Sheehan, K., and Waidner, M., *Earthchild. Games, stories, activities, experiments and ideas about living lightly on Planet Earth*, Tulsa, Council Oak Books, 1991. Excellent collection of environmental and animal-related activities. A goldmine of resource suggestions.

Stanish, B., *Connecting rainbows*, Carthage, Illinois, Good Apple, 1982. An excellent, often innovative, collection of activities designed to encourage students to think better about themselves, to co-operate and to value others.

Wade, R.C., *Joining hands. From personal to planetary friendship in the primary classroom*, Tucson, Zephyr Press, 1991. Ideas for developing a caring classroom community.

Walters, J.L., and Hamilton, L., *Integrating environmental education into the curriculum painlessly*, Bloomington, National Educational Service, 1992. Cross-curricular and subject-specific projects on environmental and animal-related items (primary and intermediate).

Activities Index

(Entries in **bold** denote genres of activities; numbers in **bold** denote references to the activities other than in the activity descriptions)

About EarthKind

EarthKind brings a new perspective to the 'green' scene by uniting environmental and animal welfare issues and striving to promote international recognition of the crucial interdependence of humankind with the rest of the living world. This holistic philosophy is based on a commitment to a dynamic compassion for *all* living creatures — not just those with a popular or 'cuddly' image — and respect for the Earth herself, for the benefit of all. Actively campaigning on behalf of pets, farm animals, wildlife and animals in captivity and to prevent destruction of the environment, EarthKind's methods are responsible, rational and non-violent. It works through humane education and, where appropriate, by promoting new legislation. EarthKind encourages people to *be* EarthKind through a twelve-point pledge to follow a cruelty-free and environmentally-friendly lifestyle. EarthKind's philosophy and activities are linked globally through EarthKind international.

About the Author

David Selby is Professor of Education and Co-Director of the International Institute for Global Education at the University of Toronto, Ontario, Canada. He was previously (1982-92) Director of the Centre for Global Education at the University of York, England. He has written extensively on global education and other educational issues, his publications including *Human Rights* (Cambridge University Press, 1987), *Earthrights. Education as if the Planet Really Mattered*, with Sue Greig and Graham Pike, (World Wildlife Fund/Kogan Page, 1987), *Global Teacher, Global Learner*, with Graham Pike, (Hodder & Stoughton, 1988), *Greenprints for Changing Schools*, with Sue Greig and Graham Pike, (World Wide Fund for Nature/Kogan Page, 1989), *Greening the Staffroom*, with Graham Pike, (BBC/WWF/ Centre for Global Education, 1990), *Reconnecting. From National to Global Curriculum*, with Graham Pike, (World Wide Fund for Nature, 1994) and *Perspectives on Childhood*, with Bob Hill and Graham Pike, (Cassell, 1995).